MOTIVATION

BIOSOCIAL APPROACHES

McGraw-Hill Series in Psychology <u> </u> CONSULTING EDITOR
Norman Garmezy

Adams: Human Memory
Berlyne: Conflict, Arousal, and Curiosity
Bernstein and Nietzel: Introduction to Clinical Psychology
Blum: Psychoanalytic Theories of Personality
Bock: Multivariate Statistical Methods in Behavioral Research
Brown: The Motivation of Behavior
Campbell, Dunnette, Lawler, and Weick: Managerial Behavior, Performance, and Effectiveness
Crites: Vocational Psychology
D'Amato: Experimental Psychology: Methodology, Psychophysics, and Learning
Dollard and Miller: Personality and Psychotherapy
Ferguson: Statistical Analysis in Psychology and Education
Fodor, Bever, and Garrett: The Psychology of Language: An Introduction to Psycholinguistics and Generative Grammar
Forgus and Melamed: Perception: A Cognitive-Stage Approach
Franks: Behavior Therapy: Appraisal and Status
Gilmer and Deci: Industrial and Organizational Psychology
Guilford: Psychometric Methods
Guilford: The Nature of Human Intelligence
Guilford and Fruchter: Fundamental Statistics in Psychology and Education
Guion: Personnel Testing
Hetherington and Parke: Child Psychology: A Contemporary Viewpoint
Hirsh: The Measurement of Hearing
Hjelle and Ziegler: Personality Theories: Basic Assumptions, Research, and Applications
Horowitz: Elements of Statistics for Psychology and Education
Hulse, Egeth, and Deese: The Psychology of Learning
Hurlock: Adolescent Development
Hurlock: Child Development
Hurlock: Developmental Psychology: A Life-Span Approach
Klein: Motivation: Biosocial Approaches
Krech, Crutchfield, and Ballachey: Individual in Society
Lakin: Interpersonal Encounter: Theory and Practice in Sensitivity Training
Lawler: Pay and Organizational Effectiveness: A Psychological View

Lazarus, A.: Behavior Therapy and Beyond
Lazarus, R.: Patterns of Adjustment
Lewin: A Dynamic Theory of Personality
Maher: Principles of Psychopathology
Marascuilo: Statistical Methods for Behavioral Science Research
Marx and Hillix: Systems and Theories in Psychology
Morgan: Physiological Psychology
Novick and Jackson: Statistical Methods for Educational and Psychological Research
Nunnally: Introduction to Statistics for Psychology and Education
Nunnally: Psychometric Theory
Overall and Klett: Applied Multivariate Analysis
Porter, Lawler, and Hackman: Behavior in Organizations
Robinson and Robinson: The Mentally Retarded Child
Ross: Psychological Disorders of Children: A Behavioral Approach to Theory, Research, and Therapy
Shaw: Group Dynamics: The Psychology of Small Group Behavior
Shaw and Costanzo: Theories of Social Psychology
Shaw and Wright: Scales for the Measurement of Attitudes
Sidowski: Experimental Methods and Instrumentation in Psychology
Siegel: Nonparametric Statistics for the Behavioral Sciences
Steers and Porter: Motivation and Work Behavior
Vinacke: The Psychology of Thinking
Winer: Statistical Principles in Experimental Design

MOTIVATION
BIOSOCIAL APPROACHES

STEPHEN B. KLEIN
Associate Professor of Psychology
Old Dominion University

McGRAW-HILL BOOK COMPANY
New York St. Louis San Francisco Auckland Bogotá Hamburg
Johannesburg London Madrid Mexico Montreal New Delhi
Panama Paris São Paulo Singapore Sydney Tokyo Toronto

Weatherford, Oklahoma

To my wife, Jan,
and my children, Dora, David, and Jason,
for their encouragement, understanding,
and love

MOTIVATION
BIOSOCIAL APPROACHES

1234567890DODO898765432

ISBN 0-07-035051-5

This book was set in Goudy Old Style by Black Dot, Inc. (ECU).
The editors were Patricia S. Nave and Susan Gamer;
the designer was Anne Canevari Green;
the production supervisor was Dominick Petrellese.
The drawings were done by VIP Graphics.
R. R. Donnelley & Sons Company was printer and binder.

Library of Congress Cataloging in Publication Data

Klein, Stephen B.
 Motivation: biosocial approaches.

 (McGraw-Hill series in psychology)
 Bibliography: p.
 Includes indexes.
 1. Motivation (Psychology) I. Title. II. Series.
BF503.K53 153.8 81-11741
ISBN 0-07-035051-5 AACR2

CONTENTS

vii

CHAPTER 9

CHAPTER 10

CHAPTER 11

CHAPTER 12

$\mathcal{P}$REFACE _____

My children recently asked me why I wanted to write this book. After I described several reasons which I believe motivated me, they seemed convinced of my insanity. Their question is not atypical; people frequently want to know the reason for their behavior or the behavior of others. The aim of this textbook is to describe discoveries which have been made during the past hundred years about the motivational determinants of behavior.

The chapters fall into three sections, or groups. The first section, Chapter 1, describes the history of motivational thought. You'll see the changes which have occurred in the psychological view of motivation during the past century and how contemporary motivational thinking has been shaped by the ideas developed during the past.

The second group of chapters (Chapters 2, 3, and 4) focuses on the three major processes governing motivated behavior. Chapter 2 details the concept of drive, a theory which assumes that impulse automatically motivates behavior. Chapter 3 looks at the cognitive approach, a view which theorizes that behavior is flexible and is guided by the expectation of gaining a desired reward or avoiding an unpleasant event. Chapter 4 presents biological systems which have an important influence on all motivated behavior. Some biological systems affect all motivated actions; others influence only specific behaviors. The internal processes which control all behaviors are described in Chapter 4. The biological systems which govern specific motivated responses are detailed in the third group of chapters.

Whereas Chapters 2 through 4 describe the general processes which motivate all behaviors, Chapters 5 through 13—the third group of chapters—detail the motivational basis of nine separate behaviors. To illustrate the influence of the basic processes which guide motivated behavior, a wide range of behaviors are presented: Chapter 5 discusses the motivational basis of eating behavior; Chapter 6 describes the processes which motivate sexual behavior; Chapter 7 presents the determinants of aggressive actions; Chapter 8 details the causes of depression; Chapter 9 discusses the motivational basis of affiliative behavior; Chapter 10 describes the processes which motivate achievement behavior; Chapter 11 presents the factors which enable us to behave consistently; Chapter 12 details the processes which motivate people to adhere to social norms of acceptable behavior; Chapter 13 discusses the motivational basis of cooperation and helping behavior. The wide range of behaviors presented in this third group of chapters will give the instructor enough flexibility to structure a course to suit his or her specific goals and allow the student to see how the basic principles detailed in Chapters 2, 3, and 4 apply to specific motivated behaviors.

This text presents the important contributions of both animal and human research since both are crucial to our understanding of the motivational basis of behavior. In many instances, animal experimentation and human experimentation have yielded identical results, indicating the generality of the processes governing a specific motivated behavior. In some situations, only animal research can be ethically conducted; in others, only human research can identify the motivational basis of activity which is unique to people. This text describes the research necessary to illustrate the motivational basis of particular behaviors.

Several features have been incorporated into this textbook to increase the relevance of the abstract concepts which govern motivated behavior. At the beginning of each chapter is a vignette intended to give you a preview of the material to be presented in that chapter as well as to stimulate your interest. Many real-world examples of motivational concepts provided throughout the text will, it is hoped, allow you to see how the abstract concepts detailed in the text actually determine motivated behavior. Applications of the basic concepts described in the textbook are included to demonstrate that the basic motivational principles have been successfully used to alter behavior. My students have appreciated the balanced approach between a description of basic motivational processes and a presentation of how these basic principles produce a specific behavior. I hope that you, too, will like this approach.

This textbook has had input from many people. I thank the students in my motivation classes who read drafts of the chapters and pointed out which sections they liked, which they disliked, and which were unclear. Not only was their feedback very helpful to me, but I'm certain that it contributed to the readability and the quality of the text. Two of my students, Sue Rosenberg and Margaret Zimmerman, read most of the chapters and made extensive suggestions; their help is greatly appreciated.

I also thank my colleagues who reviewed chapters of this text. I am especially grateful to Dr. Janusz Grezak, University of Warsaw, Poland; Dr. Leonard Hamilton, Rutgers— The State University; Dr. Robert Hicks, San Jose State University; Dr. Phyllis Hornbuckle, Virginia Commonwealth University; Dr. Milton Trapold, Memphis State University; Dr. Robert Wilson, West Virginia College of Graduate Studies, and Dr. Barbara Winstead, Old Dominion University, for their special contribution to the text.

The staff at McGraw-Hill played an important role in the creation of this text. The psychology editors, Nelson Black and Pat Nave, guided the development of the text from its inception to this final product. Susan Gamer, the editing supervisor, ensured that the text was not only easy to read but also esthetically appealing.

The contribution of my wife, Jan, is difficult to put into words. She deciphered the first draft of every chapter, made useful comments, and typed—and retyped—the manuscript. Without her great effort, patience, and support, this book could not have been written. I apologize to my children, Dora, David, and Jason, for the time they spent alone while their parents worked on this text and appreciate their understanding during the two-year period of preparation. I only hope that they will feel their sacrifice was worthwhile.

Stephen B. Klein

HISTORICAL VIEWS OF MOTIVATION

CHAPTER 1

The joy of discovery

Laura entered college 3 years ago to become an anthropologist. Her interest in primitive cultures had been stimulated by Margaret Mead's writings. However, during the past year, several psychology courses have proved more exciting and challenging than her anthropology classes, and she now wants to obtain a degree in clinical psychology. Laura's interest in psychology has also been spurred by her younger brother Jonathan's addiction to heroin. Jonathan, an outstanding student before his addiction, became dependent upon drugs, quit school, and finally ran away from home. Laura has become determined to understand the factors which motivate addictive behavior and to learn how to contribute to the development of an effective therapy for drug addiction.

Dr. Bellamy, Laura's advisor, suggested that she enroll in a course in motivation to meet the psychology department's degree requirements. Studying rats and countless experimental results did not appeal to Laura;

in fact, she dreaded taking this course. She was interested only in people and wondered how the course could benefit her. But she was afraid that not taking the class would influence Dr. Bellamy's evaluation of her for graduate school, and so she enrolled.

Laura soon discovered that her preconceived idea of the motivation course was wrong. She found that human and animal research complement each other in revealing the nature of the processes which motivate behavior. The experiments, far from being boring, made the motivational principles described in class seem realistic. Laura learned that many factors determine (or motivate) a person's behavior; some of these factors increase, while others decrease, the likelihood of certain behaviors. The class taught her how basic research has stimulated the development of techniques for modifying behavior and how an understanding of the principles of motivation benefits even the most ardent student of clinical psychology.

Another important idea which Laura

1

gained from the course was an appreciation of the fact that although psychology has changed dramatically during the past two decades, contemporary thought about motivation represents a synthesis of theories proposed by previous generations of psychologists. She had expected to find early psychologists and their ideas irrelevant; instead, she came to see that these ideas have shaped modern psychology. Laura discovered that although psychologists in the past attempted to use a single approach to describe the motivational process, contemporary psychology recognizes that

several processes motivate our behavior. She learned that both biological and psychological factors motivate behavior and that the motivational process is governed by complex, yet lawful, principles. Laura now feels that the knowledge gained from the class will undoubtedly help her develop an effective treatment for addictive behavior.

You will discover from this text what Laura learned about motivation in her course. I hope that your experience will be as positive as hers. The discussion begins by tracing the history of motivational thought.

EARLY PHILOSOPHICAL THOUGHT

Last year, my 8-year-old son participated on a local recreation league flag football team. When asked why he wanted to play, he responded, "To get a trophy." His older brother had earned several trophies playing ball; he too wanted one. My son's response suggests that he was aware of the reason why he wanted to play football, and he freely chose to participate in accordance with his motivation. His behavior illustrates the manner in which early philosophers such as Aristotle and Plato portrayed human nature. They believed that people have *free will* and that behavior is governed by intellect and reason. Thus, if we behave in a socially inappropriate manner, we have freely chosen that behavior and are, therefore, accountable for our actions. Although many contemporary psychologists no longer accept this view of human nature, the "free will" view of human behavior still dominates our social and legal system. Our society generally views those who commit crimes as doing so willfully. Being accountable, criminals are expected to pay for their freely chosen, but unacceptable, behavior by fine or imprisonment.

In the late seventeenth century, René Descartes described his dualistic view of animal and human behavior. He believed that different processes motivate animal and human action. Descartes proposed that animals are similar to machines in that their behavior is mechanistic and determined by their internal processes—instincts and reflexes. Unlike human beings, they have neither reasoning abilities nor free will. Having no "mind," lower animals cannot be held accountable for their behavior. Human beings, on the other hand, are capable of determining their own fate; the mind controls their action, while the body determines the behavior of lower animals. According to the eighteenth-century philosopher Immanuel Kant, our knowledge and rationality should control our passions and our body. In 1859, Charles Darwin's *On the Origin of Species* challenged this idealized view of human beings as a unique and essentially cerebral species; his theory acknowledged the animal nature in all of us.

DARWIN'S INFLUENCE

The idea that the process which motivates the behavior of humans is distinctively different from that of lower animals came under attack during the 1860s; the controversy concerning the nature of human behavior still rages today. Charles Darwin proposed that the differences between humans and lower animals are quantitative rather than qualitative, that the major force motivating all animals, including humans, is survival. Humans may be more adept at survival, but the same general process determines the nature of both humans and lower animals. According to Darwin, survival requires that animals and people possess specific characteristics—both behavioral and physical—which are *adaptive* to their environment. If an animal, either human or nonhuman, has these characteristics, it will survive. For example, a deer that can run faster than its predator will survive. In contrast, animals or humans that do not possess the adaptive characteristics will perish; the sluggish deer becomes the cougar's meal. Darwin's phrase *survival of the fittest* reflects his observation that in an environment with limited resources, only the able creatures will live to reproduce. An important—and obviously controversial—aspect of Darwin's theory is the assumption that humans are not unique but are motivated by the same factors that influence the behavior of other animals.

Theory of Evolution

As revolutionary as Darwin's evolutionary theory was, much of the alarm expressed by theologians and philosophers probably resulted from its misinterpretation rather than any inherent antireligious content. In fact, Darwin presented only a statement of the structure of our environment; his theory did not suggest a lack of guidance for this system. Darwin asserted that each successful species possesses characteristics enabling it to survive in a particular environment. When an environment changes, the species must either respond to that change or become extinct. If the environmental change is a slow one, some members of the species may adapt through adventitious genetic mutations, and others may possess characteristics adaptive to their new environment; they alone will live to reproduce, passing along to their offspring their adaptive characteristics. Thus, a species changes as a result of selective loss of some group members. For example, if an environment becomes colder, only those bears with a very thick coat will survive, and future generations of bears will have thicker coats than the average in the preceding generations. If the environment should continue to change, a different species of animal will evolve, a species adapted to the new environment. Unfortunately, too rapid a change in the environment typically results in extinction of a species. *Evolution* represents the changes of the behavioral and physical characteristics that a species undergoes in order to survive in a new environment. Knowledge of the evolutionary process is not limited to biologists. Cattle breeders have known for generations that a fatter or healthier breed of cattle can result from selective breeding. During "natural" evolution, the environment itself selectively breeds the members of a species, "choosing" which ones will survive and reproduce.

Darwin's theory shocked society and presented it with a controversy. The prevailing philosophical view suggested that humans—motivated by reason and knowledge—were unlike other animals. In contrast, Darwinian thought presented humans as motivated by the same biological pressures influencing lower animals. From this viewpoint, the forces motivating our behavior are beyond our control. The conflict between these two views of human nature—the *mentalism* of the early philosophers versus the *mechanistic* view of Darwin—has occupied the attention of many psychologists since the late nineteenth century. We turn now to psychology's response to this conflict.

Functionalism

To a great extent, *functionalism* developed to incorporate evolutionary theory into the earlier philosophical view of human nature. The functionalists expressed varied ideas concerning the mechanisms motivating human behavior; in fact, the only common element among the functionalists was their belief in the adaptive function of behavior. According to John Dewey (1886), the mechanistic survival behaviors of the lower animals have been replaced in the human being by the mind, which has evolved as the primary mechanism for human survival. The function of the brain is to enable the individual to adapt to the environment. Thus, while Dewey's functionalism stressed the importance of survival and environmental adaptation—characteristics of Darwin's evolutionary theory—it retained the *dualism* evident in early philosophical thought by asserting that the manner of human survival is different from that of lower animals.

In contrast to Dewey's dualism, William James, a nineteenth-century psychologist, argued that the major difference between humans and lower animals is the character of their respective inborn or instinctive motives. According to James, human beings possess a larger number of instincts which guide behavior (for example, rivalry, sympathy, fear, sociability, cleanliness, modesty, and love) than lower animals do. These human social instincts directly enhance (or reduce) our successful interaction with our environment, and thus our survival. William James (1890) also concluded that all instincts have a mentalistic quality possessing both purpose and direction, attributes previously accorded only to humans. His is essentially a continuity theory, which—unlike Dewey's dualism— did not demand a distinctive break between humans and nonhuman animals. William McDougall expanded James's ideas into a major instinct theory of motivation.

McDougall's Hormic Theory

McDougall (1908) proposed that instincts are the most important determinants of human behavior. In his view, there are ten major instincts: flight, repulsion, curiosity, pugnacity, self-abasement, self-assertion, reproduction, gregariousness, acquisition, and construction. The first seven instincts operate by producing a distinctive emotional state which directly motivates behavior. For example, our flight instinct produces an internal fear, and the emotion of fear motivates avoidance of a dangerous event. Thus, instincts do not directly motivate behavior: the emotion accompanying the instinct produces behavior. According to McDougall, the last three major instincts do not produce distinctive emotions. The complexity of human behavior, in McDougall's view, is due to the combination of instincts and their distinctive emotions.

McDougall thought that an instinct represents an innate predisposition to perceive the presence of a particular object and to react emotionally to that object. This emotional reaction produces an impulse which causes us to respond in a specific manner to that object. McDougall named his approach *hormic psychology* (from the Greek *hormē*, "impulse") in order to convey the impulsive character of an instinct. As an example of his approach, consider sexual behavior: the presence of a sexual object stimulates the reproductive instinct. The tender emotion produced by this instinct creates the urge for sexual behavior.

There were several controversial aspects of McDougall's approach to motivation. *First, he did not envision an instinct as a reflexive response to an object; rather, he thought that an animal or human decides whether or not to behave.* This concept of self-determination, *vitalism,* was central to McDougall's theory. It implied that both animals and humans actively participate in the decision-making process. *Second, McDougall felt that an animal or human possesses knowledge of the purpose and direction of its behavior.* This awareness of the goal-orientation of behavior is called *teleology.* Many questioned McDougall's vitalistic and teleological approach to motivation; the idea that the supposedly human qualities of awareness and free will applied to animal behavior was difficult to accept. *Finally, McDougall believed that though learning could modify the behavioral response to an instinct and the type of situation arousing the instinct, learning could not alter the underlying instinct or the emotional response produced by the instinct.* Those who believed that learning played the central role in motivation strongly opposed McDougall's emphasis on instinct.

The attack on McDougall's instinct theory came from two directions: (1) an approach developed within functionalism, *mechanistic biology*, which disagreed with McDougall's mentalistic view of instinct; (2) a new approach, *behaviorism*, which stressed the role of learning in motivating behavior. Let us now look at the mechanistic biologists' approach to instinct. Later this chapter examines the learning approach to motivation which replaced instinct theory and the reasons for the behaviorists' rejection of the importance of instincts in motivated behavior.

Mechanistic Biology

Many psychologists disagreed with McDougall's mentalistic concept of instinct (see Troland, 1928); they argued that internal biochemical forces motivate behavior in all species. This school of thought retained the similarity between humans and lower animals but substituted a mechanistic view for McDougall's mentalism.

The concepts of energy which were developed in physics and chemistry during the second half of the nineteenth century provided a framework for the mechanistic approach to motivation. Ernst Brücke stated in 1874 that "the living organism is a dynamic system in which the laws of chemistry and physics apply," a view which led to great advances in physiology. The functionalists used this physiochemical approach to explain the motivation for human and animal behavior.

Some conflicts were present in the mechanistic approach to instinct. Jacques Leob's view stressed the influence of external stimulation on behavior. Thinking that animal and human behavior was inflexible and comparable to a plant's tropism to light, he labeled his concept the *tropistic school.* Internal forces, according to Leob, play only a minor role in motivation. In contrast, H. S. Jennings did not believe that an animal's physiological (internal) state which produced behavior was inflexible; instead, he argued that learning could alter internal systems and thereby influence motivated behavior. A mechanistic view of motivation has appealed to many psychologists during this century. Their attempts to utilize both Leob's and Jennings's approaches are discussed in the remainder of this chapter.

This chapter has indicated already that several divergent instinct views of motivation were expressed during the early part of this century. In response to these views, two approaches to motivation developed: psychoanalytic theory and behaviorism. Freud's psychoanalytic approach represented an attempt to develop a unified instinct concept of motivation. In contrast, behaviorism rejected the emphasis on instinct and focused on the learning mechanisms responsible for motivated behavior. We will first examine Freud's view and then examine behaviorism.

FREUD'S PSYCHOANALYTIC THEORY

Darwin's theory not only challenged the philosophical view that human beings are qualitatively different from lower animals; it also presented psychology with a question: How could the need to survive motivate our behavior when we perceive that other motives determine our actions? Sigmund Freud's *psychoanalytic theory* presented a simple, yet obvious, answer (Freud, 1915a). Freud, accepting the Darwinian concept of survival, proposed that the conscious explanations for our behavior do not reflect the actual motivational basis of our acts. Instead, human behavior is motivated to satisfy biological needs which are crucial for survival; the process of satisfying these biological needs operates at an unconscious level. Thus, from the psychoanalytic viewpoint, the process which motivates our behavior is beyond our awareness, in our *unconscious*.

Freud developed a unique instinct theory of motivation. He did not expand any of the narrow, conflicting early-twentieth-century views of motivation but instead incorporated some aspects of each approach into a coherent picture of human nature. Freud adopted the instinct orientation of purpose and direction present in the views of James and McDougall, but rejected the concepts of vitalism and teleology. Freud felt that internal biological forces motivate behavior—an approach advocated by the mechanistic biology movement, but inconsistent with McDougall's self-determination (vitalism). In addition, the concept of unconscious control of motivated behavior argues against the teleological view of awareness of purpose and direction. Furthermore, Freud agreed with McDougall in suggesting that learning could alter behavior but could not change the underlying instinctive basis of motivation. Let us briefly consider Freud's motivational approach. Contemporary psychologists have adopted many of Freud's concepts; we will see his influence on psychology throughout this text.

Instinct Theory

Freud's *Instincts and Their Vicissitudes* (1915b) outlined his instinct theory of motivation. This theory maintains that instincts, the cause of all human behavior, exist to satisfy bodily needs.

Two basic instincts.   Freud proposed two main classes of instincts: (1) the *life instinct*, or *Eros*, and (2) the *death instinct*, or *Thanatos*. The functions of the life instinct are reproduction and maintenance of life. In Freud's view, sexual instincts serve our reproductive needs, while instincts such as hunger and thirst act to maintain life. Several factors caused Freud to propose the existence of a death instinct. First, the devastation which Freud observed during World War I convinced him of humankind's inherent brutality. Second, Freud adopted the *biogenetic principle*: since nonlife preceded life, then nonlife must be the ultimate goal. According to Freud, our self-destructive behavior is motivated by this death instinct, with aggression reflecting this self-destruction turned outward.

The conflict between the life and death instincts, according to Freud, is a fundamental aspect of human nature, and a manifestation of this conflict is apparent in all situations. For example, Freud asserted that the painful aspects of sexual arousal and intercourse reflect this antagonism. The destructive facets of eating—chewing and biting—are another example of the interaction of life and death instincts. Freud's view of an interplay of motives which determine behavior represents an important contribution to understanding human motivation. We frequently encounter the importance of conflict in discussions of motivation.

Characteristics of an instinct.   How does a person satisfy his or her needs? According to Freud, the four characteristics of an instinct—*source, impetus, aim,* and *object*—describe the process of obtaining satisfaction. *First, changes in internal processes create a biological need which serves as the source of each motivated behavior. Second, this instinctive biological need creates tension within a person.* This tension, labeled *psychic energy* by Freud, is the impetus which motivates behavior. Freud used the term *psychic energy* for a significant reason. Impressed with the idea of conservation and exchange of energy described by Ernst Brücke in 1874, Freud suggested that a fixed amount of energy exists within each of us and that internal chemical and physical energies can be transformed into psychic energy. The level of psychic energy depends on the intensity of biological need: the greater the need, the stronger the force which motivates behavior. Freud thought that psychic energy differed for each class of instincts and that this caused the motivation of behavior appropriate to a specific instinct. For example, Freud's labeling of sexual energy as *libido* acted to distinguish sexual energy from maintenance energy. *Third, the aim of each instinct is to eliminate internal tension.* For example, we eat to reduce the hunger pangs produced by the instinctive biological need for nourishment. However, we cannot always reduce this tension immediately. Under adverse conditions, an intermediate aim exists which eventually enables the satisfaction of biological needs. Thus, a hungry person seeks food (an intermediate aim), and attaining food eventually reduces tension. *Fourth, a distinctive environmental object exists to satisfy an instinct.* The aim of this instinct is to reach an object in order to reduce tension. Although Freud thought that instincts are inherited, he believed that there is no innate connection between an instinct and an object: an object which satisfies us will frequently change during our lifetime. This statement points to Freud's belief in the potential flexibility of human behavior.

Three personality systems. Freud proposed that satisfaction of the life and death instincts is associated with obtaining pleasure. This is first accomplished through the *id*—an instinctive behavioral system present at birth which is capable of producing pleasure and reducing tension. The id can obtain pleasure in two ways—through *reflex action* and through the *primary process.* Reflex actions are instinctive reactions which can produce immediate reduction of tension. Frequently, as a person matures, these instinctive reactions no longer represent an acceptable way of obtaining pleasure. For example, to satisfy hunger, infants reflexively suck on the mother's breast. When the mother tires of breast-feeding her infant, the child must obtain satisfaction in other ways. The primary process—the other id process—then attempts to reduce tension indirectly by forming an image of the desired object. For example, a hungry person imagines food, but this mental image, called *wish fulfillment,* cannot by itself reduce tension.

The failure of the id to obtain complete pleasure causes the development of a second personality system which Freud labeled the *ego.* The ego operates according to the *reality principle,* which satisfies the instincts through the *secondary process.* The secondary process enables a person to match the mental image with an object in the real world, thus reducing the person's biological need. Once the desired object is identified, the secondary process motivates persons to postpone their demands for satisfaction while they search for an acceptable real-world object. Thus, rather than focusing on the mental image of food, a hungry person acts to locate food in the environment. The function of the ego is, therefore, to channel the instinctive demands of the id to productive manipulations of the environment.

The final personality system to develop is the *superego,* the internal representation of society's values which motivates a person to seek perfection rather than mere pleasure. According to Freud, the superego develops partially in response to parental reward and punishment, and serves to control instinctive id impulses. Freud called this component of the superego our *conscience.* He proposed that a second element of the superego contains an idealized mode of action. Freud thought that this element, which he labeled the *ego ideal,* develops through identification with our parents and represents our striving to imitate our parents' behavior.

Under normal conditions, the three aspects of an individual's personality act together, under the direction of the ego, to interact effectively with the environment. The ego functions to satisfy the conflicting demands of the id, the superego, and the environment. There are times when persons have difficulty in coordinating the needs of the different aspects of their personality. This conflict produces additional tension; if the strain becomes so severe that people cannot resolve their conflict, behavioral disorders

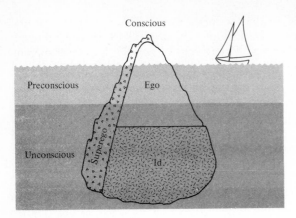

Figure 1.1
Freud's proposed relationship between our level of awareness and his personality systems. In the Freudian system, only a portion of superego and ego functioning is conscious; all of the id and most of the superego and ego operate on an unconscious level. We are not currently aware of preconscious thought, but these ideas can enter consciousness when needed. (Adapted from Houston, J. P., Bee, H., Hatfield, E., & Rimm, D. C. Invitation to psychology. *New York: Academic Press, 1979.)*

can result. The relationship between the Freudian personality systems and our awareness is presented in Figure 1.1.

Freud identified two processes—*identification* and *displacement*—which are necessary to develop effective control of the id by the ego and superego. The inhibition of children's id impulses creates stress; thus they must discover appropriate means of satisfying their biological motives. This is accomplished through observing the behavior of their parents or others nearby and incorporating the characteristics of adult personalities which appear to reduce tension. Children's personalities change as they discover characteristics which serve to fulfill their own needs. Thus, Freud proposed that our adult personality contains the synthesis of our identification with the significant people whom we encounter. Through identification, people are capable of developing socially appropriate behavior.

One question still remains: How do these behaviors satisfy our biological motives? Freud offered the concept of *displacement* as an explanation. He believed that we can displace one object of our motivation with another object in the process of attempting to achieve gratification. Although some reduction of tension does occur when we obtain this substitute object (for example, rather than sucking on a bottle, we might smoke a cigarette in order to obtain oral satisfaction), the substitute object rarely is as satisfying as the original object. Freud hypothesized that the failure to obtain complete satisfaction causes some tension to remain within us. As this undischarged tension accumulates, we are constantly searching for new and better ways to reduce it.

Psychosexual stages. The particular instinctive id motives which are activated depend upon a person's maturational state. Various id needs mature, according to Freud, during five *psychosexual stages* of development.

The only receptors mature enough to release energy in the newborn are the oral receptors. During the *oral stage*, an infant obtains pleasure from sucking on a bottle or the mother's breast. As the infant matures, the environment, usually the mother, requires that the child inhibit id impulses and search for other acceptable forms of oral stimulation. The infant, motivated to obtain pleasure, learns to drink from a cup, and this successful incorporation of more sophisticated behavior results in ego development. A permissive mother, failing to require alternative forms of oral satisfaction when the child is ready, creates an imbalance between the id and ego; the result is an immature personality. Also, too-strict parental control can inhibit ego development.

The second biological motivation appears during the latter part of the child's first year. As the child's anal receptors develop, pleasure can be experienced through defecation. Immediate gratification during this *anal stage* is short-lived, as toilet training by the parents (incorporated as superego strictures) causes the ego to inhibit the child's id impulses until an appropriate time and place is secured. Again, the failure of parents to institute control of the child's anal impulses prevents the ego's maturation and leaves the id impulses unchecked.

During the *phallic stage* children experience pleasure by stimulating their genitals; masturbation is a normally observed behavior in young children. Freud suggested that in addition to the direct satisfaction of sexual drive, the child experiences both sexual and aggressive fantasies during the phallic stage: the 3- to 5-year-old child wants to displace the same-sexed parent and to possess the opposite-sexed parent. This conflict—the *Oedipus complex* in the male and the *Electra complex* in the female—causes great stress within the young child. Its resolution leads to the development of socially appropriate sex roles and parental attachments. (We will examine this resolution process further in Chapters 6 and 9.) Additionally, Freud assumed that the successful resolution of phallic experiences serves to strengthen the ego and leads to the development of the superego.

No new biological motives develop during the *latency stage*; but in the *genital stage*, adult sources of pleasure mature. The adolescent and the adult experience satisfaction not only through self-love but also from social activities. The pleasure experienced by interacting with other people does not mean that oral, anal, and phallic motives are eliminated, but rather that multiple objects satisfy our biological drives.

Defense mechanisms. Circumstances unfortunately do exist which place too much pressure on people, rendering them unable to resolve their conflicts. Freud contended that anxiety reflects the inability of the ego to control effectively either the id impulses, the superego demands, or the environmental pressures. When extreme anxiety exists, the ego adopts measures, which Freud termed *defense mechanisms,* in order to reduce it. These defense mechanisms, operating at the unconscious level, serve to lower anxiety to tolerable levels by either denying or distorting reality. A description of some of these defense mechanisms is presented in Table 1.1. The motivation for each defense mechanism is the reduction of excessive anxiety. Although a defense mechanism may be temporarily effective, it does not enable a person to eliminate or resolve the source of the anxiety; therefore, the defense mechanism ultimately fails and the anxiety reappears. This recurrence of anxiety forces a person to rely even more heavily on defense mechanisms which, by interfering with the effective solution to conflict, are ultimately self-defeating. From the psychoanalytic standpoint, excessive reliance on defense mechanisms reflects the first stage in the development of behavior pathology. If a disturbed person's defense mechanisms continue to fail to reduce tension, he or she resorts to even more extreme pathological forms (for example, extreme withdrawal) to deal with the anxiety.

Freud's psychoanalytic theory has had an enormous impact on psychological thought. His theory stresses the importance of the dynamic interplay between instinctive motives and environmental events. Persons are portrayed as attempting to deal with conflict and anxiety in ways that are often effective, yet sometimes ineffective. Although frequently criticized as too vague and incapable of predicting the direction of psychological developments, Freud's motivational concepts have been discussed and investigated by many psychologists for more than 50 years. These concepts are encountered throughout this text.

Table 1.1
Some Freudian Defense Mechanisms

Mechanism	One Possible Manifestation
Repression Keeping painful or dangerous thoughts in the unconscious; this is thought to be the most basic of defense mechanisms.	A soldier comes very close to death, but remembers no details of the event.
Rationalization Attempting to prove that one's behavior is "rational" and justifiable.	A grown man who loves his mother too dearly treats her with extreme consideration, kindness, and devotion but convinces himself that he is motivated by duty and not by love.
Compensation Covering up weakness by emphasizing another trait.	A person unsure of sexuality becomes a bookworm.
Fantasy Gratifying frustrated desires in imaginary achievements.	A baseball player dreams of hitting the winning home run.
Reaction formation Behavior is the opposite of what the individual would like it to be.	A woman loves an unobtainable man and behaves as though she dislikes him.
Projection Persons come to believe that their own undesirable feelings or inclinations are more descriptive of others than of themselves.	A claustrophobic person who unconsciously avoids closed spaces is amazed at the number of persons who suffer from claustrophobia.

Adapted from: *Psychology* by Guy R. Lefrancois. © 1980 by Wadsworth, Inc. Reprinted by permission of Wadsworth Publishing Company, Belmont, California 94002.

Criticisms of Instinct Theory

Many psychologists strongly criticized the concept of instinct which the functionalists had initially proposed and which was later used in Freudian psychoanalytic theory. Several factors led to this criticism: *(1) Anthropologists pointed to a variety of values, beliefs, and behaviors among different cultures, a view inconsistent with the idea of universal human instincts. (2) Watson and Morgan's observations (1917) of human infants led them to conclude that only three innate emotional responses—fear, rage, and love—existed and that these could be elicited by only a small number of stimuli. (3) The widespread and uncritical use of the concept of instinct did not advance our understanding of the nature of human conduct.* Bernard's analysis (1924) of this concept is a good example of the criticism prominent during the 1920s. Bernard identified several thousand, often conflicting, instincts which the functionalists had proposed. One example which Bernard found was the idea that "with a glance of the eye we can estimate *instinctively* the age of a passerby." It is not surprising that many psychologists reacted so negatively to the concept.

In the 1930s American psychology stopped using instinct to explain human motivation and replaced it with an emphasis on the learning process. The instinct concept reappeared in American psychology when the writings of the European animal behaviorists, called *ethologists*, surfaced during the 1950s. The ethological view of instinct was not readily accepted, even though it did not coincide with the earlier functionalist view. American psychology has only recently accepted the importance of instinctive processes in motivation. At this point, let us look at the behaviorism which replaced the functionalism in American psychology. Later in this chapter the use of instinct in the ethological approach is described.

BEHAVIORISM

According to behaviorists, we possess instinctive motives, but the important determinants of our behavior are learned ones. Acquired drives typically motivate us; our behavior that responds to these motives is also learned through a process of interaction with the environment. For example, a behaviorist assumes that your motivation to attend school is a learned one and that your behaviors while attending school are also learned. One main goal of the behaviorist is to uncover the laws governing learning—a concern which has dominated academic psychology since the 1920s. However, the origins of behaviorism began with the Greek philosopher Aristotle and his concept of association of ideas.

Associationism

A friend approaches you outside of your classroom and remarks that your party last week was terrific. This remark causes you to recall the very attractive person whom you met at your party, which, in turn, reminds you to ask this person for a date. This whole thought process reflects the concept of association of ideas: two events can become associated with each other; thus, when you think of one event you automatically recall the other. Aristotle proposed that in order for an association to develop the two events must be *contiguous* (temporally paired), similar, or opposite from each other.

During the seventeenth century British empiricists described the association process in greater detail. David Hume added another factor—causal events—which he hypothesized could become associated. For example, if you overslept and missed your class, your learned association might be that oversleeping causes you to miss class. As discussed later in this chapter, contemporary views of motivation assume that our thoughts on why we behave in a particular way have an important influence on how we subsequently behave.

The relative influence of inherited and learned characteristics has been an issue of special interest to psychologists during this century. This issue was of foremost importance to the empiricist John Locke. He attacked Descartes's idea of innate ideas, or *nativism,* and argued that we develop all of our ideas through experience. Locke's theory maintains that an infant is born with no ideas at all; his concept of *tabula rasa* suggests that an infant's mind is like a blank slate upon which ideas are subsequently imprinted.

The concept of acquired associations is the foundation of behaviorism. The task of the behaviorists is to explain what associations develop through experience; behaviorists have yet to agree on this issue. The role of the associative process in motivation is detailed in the following sections.

Thorndike

The work of Edward Thorndike marked a turning point in the history of psychology. Less than a century ago it was generally assumed that animal behavior is inflexible. However, Thorndike's publication of his studies in 1898 established that animal behavior could change as a consequence of experience. His ideas on learning and motivation developed from his research with his famous puzzle box (see Figure 1.2). In these studies, he placed a hungry cat in a locked box with food outside. The cat could escape from the box and then

Figure 1.2
Thorndike's famous puzzle box. The cat can escape by exhibiting one of several potential escape responses and thereby obtain food. (Adapted from Theories of learning: Traditional perspectives/contemporary developments *by Leland C. Swenson. © 1980 by Wadsworth, Inc. Reprinted by permission of Wadsworth Publishing Company, Belmont, California 94002.)*

obtain food by exhibiting one of a number of possible behaviors; two effective behaviors were pulling on a string and pressing a pedal. Not only did the cat escape, but also, with each successive trial, the time needed to escape decreased. It appears that the cat's escape from the box progressed from a chance act to a learned behavior.

The law of effect.   Thorndike proposed that the cat formed an association between the stimulus situation (the box) and the correct response. Learning, according to Thorndike, reflects the development of a stimulus-response (S-R) association; thus, the occurrence of the stimulus elicits an appropriate response. Thorndike asserted that the animal is not conscious of this association, but is instead exhibiting a mechanistic habit in response to a particular stimulus. The S-R association developed because the cat was *rewarded:* when the cat was hungry, the appropriate response was followed by the presentation of food, which produced a satisfying state and strengthened the S-R bond. Thorndike labeled this strengthening of an association produced by pleasant events the *law of effect.*

Thorndike did not think that the law of effect is representative only of animal behavior; he believed that it also reflects the human learning process. Thorndike (1932) presented his human subjects with a concept to be learned. He found that knowledge of success (reward) was essential to his subjects' learning the concept; those subjects who did not know whether or not they had responded correctly did not acquire the concept. Although Thorndike initially proposed that unpleasant events weakened the S-R bond, his later studies (1932) indicated that there was no change in his human subjects' behavior when told that they were wrong or not given any feedback about the correctness of their response. On the other hand, contemporary researchers have demonstrated that aversive events can often modify both animal and human behavior. We will examine the influence of unpleasant experiences on motivated behavior throughout this text.

The law of readiness. Thorndike's views concerning the nature of the learning process are quite specific, although his ideas on the motivational process which determines behavior seem vague. According to Thorndike, if a particular event is satisfying, it serves as a reward; however, this pattern of behavior occurs only if the animal or human is "ready." Thorndike's *law of readiness* reflects his assumption that the animal or human must be motivated in order either to develop an association or to exhibit a previously established habit. Thorndike did not hypothesize concerning the nature of the motivation mechanism, leaving such endeavors to future psychologists. Indeed, the motivational basis of behavior became of critical concern to later generations of behaviorists.

How did the cat initially choose the correct response in Thorndike's puzzle-box studies? Thorndike explained that the process was one of trial and error; the cat simply switched behaviors until it discovered the correct one. Reward then functioned to strengthen that correct response. However, the research of Ivan Pavlov (1927) portrayed the learning process as anything but trial and error. According to Pavlov, definite preset rules determine which behavior occurs in the learning situation.

Pavlov

Few people contribute as much enlightenment to a discipline as the Russian physiologist Ivan Pavlov did to psychology. His description of the conditioning process excited the psychological community even before his work was translated into English in 1927. Interestingly, Pavlov's initial interest was to uncover the laws governing digestion. Pavlov discovered that animals exhibit numerous innate reflexive responses when food is placed in their mouth (for example, salivation and gastric secretion). The function of these responses is to aid in the digestion process. He also developed a unique method for determining the relative quantity of a dog's gastric secretion in relation to the amount of food placed in its stomach. To determine this, he brought a slice of the stomach tissue out of the body. The relative volume of gastric secretion which occurred in response to the food could be measured from this tissue. He discovered that the amount and type of food fed to the dog determined the amount of gastric secretion. Next, Pavlov cut the dog's esophagus and brought it out of the neck; this procedure allowed the dog to chew and swallow food, but the food then fell onto the ground rather than traveling to the stomach. The amount of gastric secretion was the same if the food was in the dog's mouth or in its stomach; he concluded that food in the mouth produced the gastric secretion in the stomach.

The conditioned reflex. Pavlov then made another important discovery: his dogs began to secrete stomach juices when they saw food or when it was placed in their food dish. He concluded that the dogs had learned a new behavior, since he had not observed this response to the sight of food during their first exposure to it. To explain his observation, he suggested that both animals and humans possess instinctive or *unconditioned reflexes*. An unconditioned reflex consists of two components: an *unconditioned stimulus* (UCS; for example, food) which involuntarily elicits the second component, the *unconditioned response* (UCR; for example, saliva or gastric juice). A new or *conditioned reflex* develops when environmental events (for example, sight of food) occur with the unconditioned stimulus. As conditioning progresses, the *conditioned stimulus* (CS; sight of food) becomes able to elicit the learned or *conditioned response* (CR; saliva or gastric secretion). The conditioned response is strengthened by increasing the number of pairings of the conditioned stimulus with the unconditioned stimulus. Pavlov assumed a mechanistic view of behavior; stimuli either innately have the capacity or acquire the ability to elicit behavior.

Pavlov's demonstration of a learned reflex in animals stands as an important discovery, showing not only an animal's ability to learn but also the mechanism responsible for the learned behavior. According to Pavlov, any neutral stimulus paired with the unconditioned stimulus could, through conditioning, develop the capacity to elicit a CR. In his classic demonstration of the conditioning process, he first implanted a tube, called a *fistula*, in a dog's salivary glands in order to collect saliva (see Figure 1.3). He then presented the conditioned stimulus, the sound of a metronome, and shortly thereafter placed the unconditioned stimulus, meat powder, in the dog's mouth. On the first presentation, only the meat powder produced saliva (UCR). However, with repeated pairings of the tone with food, the tone (CS) began to elicit saliva (CR). The strength of the conditioned response increased with increased pairings of the conditioned and unconditioned stimuli. Figure 1.4 presents a diagram of Pavlov's classical conditioning process.

Conditioning principles.   Pavlov conducted an extensive investigation of the conditioning process by identifying many procedures which influence an animal's learned behaviors; many of his ideas continue to be accepted today. Pavlov showed that if, after conditioning, the conditioned stimulus is presented without the unconditioned stimulus, the strength of the conditioned response diminishes. Pavlov named this process of eliminating an established conditioned response *extinction*. Animals also *generalize* their conditioned response to similar stimuli. Pavlov found that his dogs salivated not only in response to the presentation of the conditioned stimulus but also in response to stimuli which were similar to the conditioned stimulus. For example, Pavlov's dogs salivated in

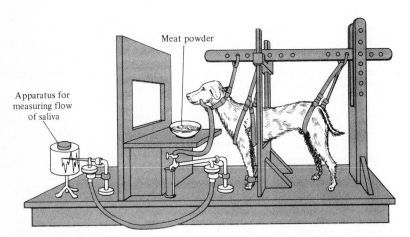

Figure 1.3
Pavlov's salivary conditioning apparatus. The experimenter can measure saliva output when either a conditioned stimulus (for example, a bell) or an unconditioned stimulus (meat powder) is presented to the dog. The dog is placed in a harness to minimize movement; this ensures an accurate measure of the salivary response. (Adapted from Yerkes, R. M., & Margulis, S. The method of Pavlov in animal psychology. Psychological Bulletin, 1909, 6, 257–273. Copyright 1909 by the American Psychological Association. Reprinted by permission.)

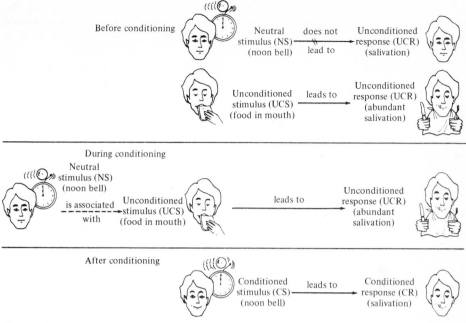

Figure 1.4
Schematic illustration of Pavlovian conditioning of salivation to a tone. Before conditioning, the presentation of the tone elicits no response when presented alone. During conditioning, the tone is followed by the unconditioned stimulus, meat powder, which can produce the physiological response of salivation (the UCR). After conditioning, the presentation of the tone elicits the conditioned salivation response. [From Davidoff, L. L. Introduction to psychology (2nd ed.). New York: McGraw-Hill, 1980.]

response to tones which were either louder or softer than the conditioned stimulus. He also discovered that dogs could learn not to generalize to similar stimuli, a process which Pavlov labeled *discrimination*. When a stimulus similar to that of the conditioned stimulus is presented in the absence of the unconditioned stimulus, the conditioned response will be elicited by the conditioned stimulus (called the CS +) but not by the similar stimulus (called the CS −).

Several additional processes deserve our attention. Pavlov proposed that stimuli could inhibit as well as elicit responses. For example, a novel stimulus presented during conditioning reduces the strength of the conditioned response. If the novel stimulus is not presented on the next trial, the strength of the conditioned response will return to its prior level. This process is called *external inhibition*. The presentation of a novel stimulus during extinction also causes disruption; however, in this case the novel stimulus causes an increase in the strength of the conditioned response, suggesting that it is the process of learning *not* to respond which is interrupted. The extinction process will proceed normally on the next trial if the novel stimulus is not presented. Pavlov labeled this process *disinhibition*. The disruption by a novel stimulus occurs only during the acquisition and extinction of a conditioned response; well-learned behaviors or completely extinguished behaviors are not influenced by novel stimuli. The inhibition of a behavior can also become permanent: If a stimulus (CS −) similar to the conditioned stimulus (CS +) is presented in the absence of the unconditioned stimulus, it will act to inhibit a CR to the CS + This process of developing a permanent inhibitor is known as *conditioned inhibition.* Finally, Pavlov found that a stimulus could produce a conditioned response without ever having been directly paired with the unconditioned stimulus, a process called *higher-order conditioning.* Following the direct pairing of a conditioned stimulus (for example, a tone) with the UCS (for example, food), the conditioned stimulus is then paired with another stimulus (for example, a light) without the presence of the unconditioned stimulus. After several tone-light pairings, the animal will salivate when presented with the light, even though the light was never paired directly with the UCS.

Pavlov's observations have profoundly influenced psychology. His conditioning process, often called *Pavlovian conditioning,* has been demonstrated in various animals, including humans. Conditioned responses also have been established to many different unconditioned stimuli, and psychologists have shown that most environmental stimuli can become conditioned ones.

Pavlov and Thorndike described two different learning processes: Pavlovian conditioning and instrumental conditioning. In the past, especially during the two decades following the publication of Pavlov's work, the Pavlovian or classical conditioning process has been emphasized. Later, during the 1940s and 1950s, researchers focused on the instrumental or operant conditioning process initially described by Thorndike. A resurgence of interest in Pavlovian conditioning has occurred since the 1970s.

Watson

Pavlov and Thorndike described the learning process, but it was John B. Watson who demonstrated its importance in human behavior. Watson, the chief spokesman of his day for American behaviorism, rejected the concept of mental ideas and instead emphasized that all behaviors represent either unconditioned or acquired habits. According to Watson, our thoughts are merely feedback from our muscular responses to environmental stimuli.

Watson, arguing that the important adult behaviors are learned ones, stressed the importance of the learning process. Although Pavlov's research excited Watson, the work of another Russian, Bechterev, played a central role in his thinking. Bechterev and Pavlov conducted their research simultaneously, and the American publication of Bechterev's experimentation, in 1913, preceded that of Pavlov's. Whereas Pavlov used positive or pleasant UCS, Bechterev employed aversive or unpleasant ones (for example, shock) in order to study the conditioning process. Bechterev found that a conditioned response (for example, withdrawal of the finger) could be established by pairing a neutral stimulus with the shock. In his duplication of Bechterev's studies, Watson showed that after several pairings, a previously neutral stimulus elicited not only a physical response (withdrawal of the leg) but also emotional arousal (revealed by increased heart rate) as the conditioned response. Although Watson was not the first to demonstrate the conditioning, or acquired learning, of emotional responses, this evidence was important to his concepts of human behavior and emotionality.

Watson assumed that abnormal, as well as normal, behavior is learned. He was particularly concerned with demonstrating that human fears are acquired through Pavlovian conditioning. To illustrate this point, Watson and Raynor (1920) presented Albert, a healthy infant attending a day-care center, with a white rat. As the child reached for the rat, he heard a loud sound (UCS) produced by Watson's hitting a heavy iron rail with a hammer (see Figure 1.5). After three CS-UCS pairings, Watson and Raynor observed that presentation of the rat (CS) alone produced a fear response in the child. The rat elicited strong emotional arousal, demonstrated by the child's attempts to escape from it, after six CS-UCS pairings. The authors observed a strong generalization to similar objects: the child also showed fear of a white rabbit and a white fur coat.

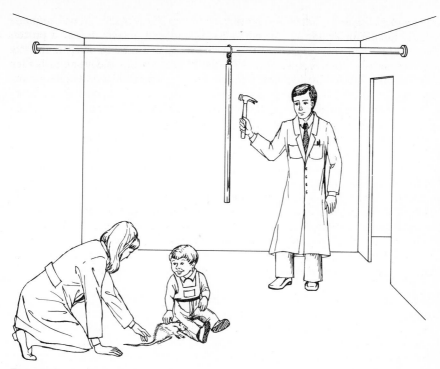

Figure 1.5
While "little Albert" was playing with a white rat, Watson struck a suspended steel bar with a hammer. The loud sound disturbed the child, causing him to develop a conditioned fear of the white rat. Rosalie Raynor, Watson's assistant, distracted "little Albert" while Watson approached the bar. (Adapted from Theories of learning: Traditional perspectives/contemporary developments by Leland C. Swenson. © 1980 by Wadsworth, Inc. Reprinted by permission of Wadsworth Publishing Company, Belmont, California 94002.)

Watson enjoyed poking fun at psychoanalysis. He suggested that a psychoanalyst might attribute Albert's strange fear to an unresolved Oedipus complex. It is obvious to us—just as it was obvious to Watson—that conditioning was responsible for Albert's fear. Unfortunately, little Albert retained his fear; Albert's mother withdrew him from the day-care center before Watson and Raynor could extinguish his fear.

Mary Cover Jones, a student working with Watson, developed an effective technique in 1924 for eliminating conditioned fears, using a young child as the subject. Jones paired a white rabbit with a loud noise often enough for the rabbit to elicit a fear response on its own. Once the fear was well established, she brought the rabbit into the same room with the child while the child was eating, being careful to keep the distance between the rabbit and child great enough that the child was not alarmed. She then moved the rabbit closer and closer to the eating child, allowing him to grow accustomed to it in gradual steps. Eventually the child was able to touch and hold the formerly fear-inducing animal. According to Jones, the child had eliminated fear by developing a response to the rabbit which inhibited the fear. The acquisition of such a fear-inhibiting response is called *counterconditioning*. Approximately 30 years later, her study played an important role in the development of an effective treatment of human phobic behavior.

Many different views of human nature developed during the early part of the twentieth century. Some of these views stressed the mentalistic aspect of our behavior; others presented human beings as automatically responding to events in the environment. The role of instincts was central to some theories of behavior; learning as the determinant of human action was the core of others. However, psychology was still in its infancy and all these views remained essentially untested. Fortunately, our understanding of the motivational basis of our behavior expanded during the 1930s and 1940s. Let us now see what psychologists discovered about behavior during this period.

THE MIDDLE YEARS (THE 1930s AND 1940s)

Mechanistic Approaches

The mechanistic approach was the dominant view of motivation during the 1930s and 1940s. There were actually several different mechanistic views. One theory, the Freudian psychoanalytic theory described earlier, portrayed internal tension (psychic energy) as the factor which motivates human behavior to reduce this tension by obtaining pleasure. Freud's approach became quite influential, especially in clinical areas of psychology, and contributed to the current popularity of psychology.

Neo-Freudian approaches. However, many psychologists who studied with Freud modified the traditional psychoanalytic approach to motivation. They objected to Freud's gloomy view of human nature, a view that we are motivated by blind, pleasure-seeking animal instincts which too often control the intellectual and cultural aspects of personality. These psychologists, the *neo-Freudians*, retained Freud's concept of dynamic personality—the complex interplay of the id, ego, and superego—but rejected the emphasis which Freud placed on sexual and aggressive motives. We will briefly examine the views of four neo-Freudians—Jung, Adler, Fromm, and Sullivan. Their contribution to our understanding of human behavior will be evident in the rest of this text.

Jung's theory. Carl Jung (1938) proposed that humans possess not only a *personal unconscious*—memories, sensory impressions, and repressed wishes developed during childhood—but also a *collective unconscious.* This collective unconscious represents instincts, called *archetypes,* inherited from our ancestors. For example, the way in which we respond to others is partly determined by inherited systems of action which have been effective for past generations.

Adler's view. In contrast to Jung's concepts of both a collective and a personal unconscious, Alfred Adler (1927) minimized the influence of instinctive biological motives and instead stressed the importance of innate cognitive and social motivation. According to Adler, humans have an instinctive drive to become both competent and perfect. The *creative self* develops to fulfill these drives.

According to Adler, during our development we often feel that people nearby us are more competent than ourselves; these feelings can create an *inferiority complex* within us. Our feelings of inferiority then are overcome by excelling in a certain area. For example, if we perceive ourselves as physically weak, we might be motivated to excel in school in order to compensate for our feelings of inferiority. One other effective method of reducing a sense of inferiority is through social interaction. Adler believed that humans possess inherited social motives, innate desires to cooperate with others in order to create a better society. His theory asserted that we are aware of our motives and, therefore, can control our own destinies. Adler's optimistic view of human nature contrasts sharply with Freud's pessimistic outlook.

Fromm's approach. Erich Fromm (1941) suggested that humans have five basic innate social needs: relatedness, transcendence, rootedness, identity, and frame of orientation. According to Fromm, we will feel lonely and isolated if we have not satisfied each of these social needs. Our social behavior, asserts Fromm, is motivated to resolve these innate social needs. Fromm felt that although social needs are innate, the form of social behavior which people use to satisfy these needs varies from culture to culture: society can allow its members to obtain satisfaction through cooperation with others or by submitting to the authority of others.

Sullivan's theory. In contrast to Adler's and Fromm's innate social need approach, Harry Stack Sullivan (1947) proposed that social behavior is performed in order to resolve one of two innate needs: satisfaction and security. According to Sullivan, tension occurs either when biological needs are not met or when helplessness causes insecurity. An individual's behavior is motivated to reduce this internal tension.

Each of these neo-Freudian views retains the central aspects of Freud's traditional view: (1) *Instinctive needs motivate behavior.* (2) *The failure to resolve these needs produces tension.* (3) *The aim of an individual's motivated behavior is to reduce this tension.* However, these views do differ: Each has its own theory as to which instincts motivate our behavior. In contrast to the psychoanalytic instinct views, many psychologists developed mechanistic views which stressed the learned aspects of motivation.

The drive view. In 1918, Robert S. Woodworth introduced the concept of *drive* to psychology. He defined drive as an intense internal force which motivates behavior. The drive concept retains the impulse or urge characteristic of McDougall's instinct approach, but does not contain the idea of purpose. Although drive theorists (see Miller & Dollard, 1941) recognized that some drives were innate, they believed that acquired drives motivated most human behavior. Let us now turn to Clark Hull's drive approach (1943), which is the most influential drive theory.

Hull's drive theory. Hull proposed that an animal or human becomes more active when a biological need is created within it. This higher level of activity then increases the likelihood that the animal will choose the correct response necessary to eliminate the biological need and thus solve the biological problem. The reduction in need acts as a reinforcer and thereby strengthens the connection between stimuli (S) which are present and the response (R) which reduces the need.

According to Hull, a biological need initiates an intense internal arousal or drive (D). Hull assumed that drive is nonspecific: a common internal arousal state is activated by each need. He further stated that drive energizes behaviors, or habits. The strength of a specific S-R bond is determined by the innate strength of a specific response to a stimulus ($_sU_R$) and the learned strength ($_sH_R$) which develops with reinforcement. Thus, drive motivates behavior, but environmental stimuli determine which habit will be elicited when the animal or person is motivated.

In Hull's theory, biological needs are not the only source of drive. Intense internal and external events are also capable of inducing drive. In addition, environmental stimuli can acquire the capacity for producing drive through association with an internal drive state. Hunger at lunchtime and fear of tests are two examples of acquired drives.

Let's look at one final example to illustrate Hull's view of drive. You arrive home from school and eat a snack from the refrigerator. Hull would maintain that you were "driven" to the refrigerator in order to reduce your internal hunger and that the reduction of hunger, in turn, strengthened the bond between the sight of the refrigerator and the act of opening it and taking food. Furthermore, if you have previously associated the sight of the refrigerator with hunger, the refrigerator can motivate eating even though you are not biologically hungry.

Dollard-Miller reconciliation.   Psychologists have recognized frequent intense antagonism between behaviorism and psychoanalytic theory. This led to an assumption that the two views must represent two opposing approaches to human nature. However, John Dollard and Neal Miller's elegant theory (1950) demonstrated the underlying similarity of these two theories by integrating the fundamental concepts of Freudian psychoanalytic theory with those of Hullian drive theory. According to their approach, Freud's psychic energy represented the same motivational quality found in Hull's drive state. In addition, Freud's id is similar to Hull's innate habit strength while the ego consists of acquired habits. The superego represents motives acquired through the classical conditioning process in Hull's view.

Many psychologists found Freud's terminology difficult. Moreover, Freud's ideas are not readily amenable to empirical testing. Thus, Dollard and Miller's restatement of the psychoanalytic view into behavioral language made it more acceptable to many psychologists. This approach stimulated much research investigating the dynamic interplay of animals or humans with their environment. These studies have enhanced our understanding of the motivational process, and their results appear frequently in this text.

We must note, however, that the psychoanalytic and Hullian approaches are not identical: *(1) The Freudian view assumes that several types of energy exist; Hull's theory assumes that there is a single drive state. (2) According to Freud, a person's behavior is goal-oriented; according to Hull, behavior does not possess purpose and direction.* Yet, Freud does not believe either that we are aware of this purpose or that we can control our behavior; therefore, his view is closer to Hull's drive approach than to McDougall's instinct theory. This text will classify an approach as a drive theory if it assumes that tension automatically motivates behavior. On the basis of this orientation, both the psychoanalytic approach and Hull's view will be considered drive theories of motivation.

Two additional approaches—Tolman's expectancy model and Skinner's reinforcement view—were proposed during this period. These views became extremely important in the 1970s, though they lacked impact when first formulated. This chapter considers next Tolman's and Skinner's ideas as presented during the 1930s and 1940s, and then examines the importance of these approaches in contemporary psychology.

Tolman's Mentalism

Edward Tolman proposed a mentalistic view of motivation, an approach entirely outside the mainstream of American psychology during the 1930s and 1940s. Tolman rejected Hull's mechanistic S-R approach and argued instead that our behavior is capable of flexibility and is not an involuntary response to a stimulus. Tolman insisted that our behavior is goal-directed. For example, both hungry rats and hungry humans direct their behavior to obtaining food. Tolman (1932) coined the term *purposive behavior* to describe the action occurring when animals or humans behave *as if* they have a purpose. However, his theory does not imply the awareness assumed to exist in earlier functionalistic views.

How does an animal or human know that a particular behavior is responsible for achieving a goal? Tolman proposed a new type of association in order to answer this question. Rather than using the S-R association which had been the centerpiece of behaviorism, Tolman suggested that we form S-R-S associations. In this view, the events occurring when a reward is presented become associated, and the animal or human learns that a particular behavior will produce reward. To describe the animal's or human's behavior Tolman introduced the concept of *expectancy:* the animal or human expects that during instances in which they are in the presence of a particular stimulus, a specific behavior leads to a certain reward. For example, hungry children, arriving home from school, want food; yet they expect to receive it only if they perform some action such as raiding the refrigerator. In contrast to this cognitive view, the Hullian view assumes that you are "driven" to the refrigerator by hunger.

Tolman theorized that it is motivation which determines whether or not an animal or human behaves. If animals or humans are not sufficiently motivated, they will not display any behavior in order to obtain a reward or goal. Tolman suggested that two types of processes are responsible for motivating behavior. First, behavior can be motivated by deprivation; the longer the time which has elapsed since an animal or human has received a reward, the more motivated it will be to obtain its goal. Second, animals and people, according to Tolman, are motivated to obtain a specific reward. For example, a person expecting a steak would not be satisfied by the arrival of a TV dinner. Tolman referred to the motivation produced by the expectation of a specific goal as *incentive motivation.*

Skinner's Radical Behaviorism

B. F. Skinner proposed a radical new behaviorism: psychologists should not speculate upon the internal determinants of behavior, but rather should focus their attention on determining the conditions under which behavior occurs. For example, the idea of an S-R bond is merely an inference from a correlation between the presence of a particular stimulus and a specific response. According to Skinner, the description of the circumstances which produce a specific behavior is sufficient; to theorize about why we act in the way we do serves only to prevent psychology from uncovering the laws governing behavior.

Methodology.   Skinner was an extremely imaginative person. He needed only a simply structured environment in order to study behavior, and so he invented his own. This apparatus, not surprisingly called a *Skinner box,* creates an enclosed environment with a small bar on the inside wall. There is a dispenser for presenting either food or liquid reinforcement when a subject presses the bar. (A more elaborate version has the capacity to present tones or lights in order to study generalization and discrimination.) The Skinner box has been modified to accommodate many different animal species. Figure 1.6 presents a basic Skinner box for use with pigeons in which a pecking key replaces the bar-press used for some species. In addition to his well-known box and many other ingenious inventions, he developed his own methodology for studying behavior. More interested in observing the rate of a behavior than the intensity of a specific response, he developed the cumulative recorder (refer to Figure 1.6) to measure this rate. The pen attached to the recorder moves at a specific rate across the page; at the same time, each bar-press or key response produces an upward movement on the pen, thus enabling the experimenter to determine the rate of behavior.

Types of learning.   In 1938, Skinner identified two types of learning: *respondent* and *operant conditioning.* Respondent conditioning refers to the learning situation investigated by Pavlov; the conditioned and unconditioned stimuli are paired, and the conditioned stimulus subsequently elicits the conditioned response. In this type of learning, the animal or person responds passively to an environmental stimulus. Respondent behaviors are primarily internal responses in the form of emotional and glandular reactions to

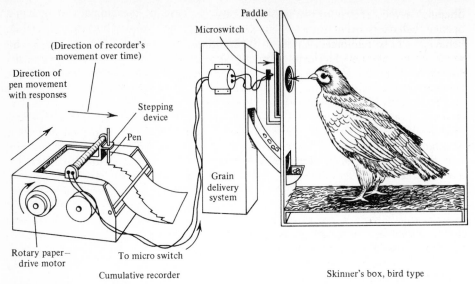

Figure 1.6
Skinner box designed for pigeons. When the pigeon pecks the key, reinforcement (a pellet) is delivered. Each peck produces an upward deflection on the cumulative recorder, providing a permanent record of the pigeon's behavior. (Adapted from Theories of learning: Traditional perspectives/contempory developments *by Leland C. Swenson. © 1980 by Wadsworth, Inc. Reprinted by permission of Wadsworth Publishing Company, Belmont, California 94002.)*

stimuli. However, Skinner was most interested in operant conditioning, the type of learning situation investigated by Thorndike. Skinner asserted that, in operant conditioning, an animal or person actively interacts with the environment to obtain reward. Operant behavior is not elicited by a stimulus; rather, in anticipation of the consequences of the behavior, an animal or person voluntarily emits a specific behavior when that behavior produces reinforcement. Skinner named this relationship between behavior and reinforcer a *contingency*. The environment determines contingencies, and the animal or human must learn to emit an appropriate behavior to obtain a desired reward.

The reinforcement process.   Skinner did not specify the underlying mechanism of reinforcement; he felt that it was sufficient to show the effect of reinforcement on behavior. According to Skinner, a *reinforcer* is an event which increases the frequency of the behavior preceding it. One cannot predict whether or not an event will be a reinforcer: the influence of the event on behavior determines if it is a reinforcement. For example, a piece of candy may be an effective reinforcer for some children, but not for others. Only by observing the influence which candy has on a particular child's behavior can its reinforcing value be determined.

Skinner identified two types of reinforcers: primary and secondary. *Primary reinforcers* have innate reinforcing properties; *secondary reinforcers* develop their reinforcing properties through their association with primary reinforcers. For example, food is a primary reinforcer, while money is a secondary one. In addition, the occurrence of a desirable event is not the only type of reinforcer. Termination of an aversive event can also be reinforcing. Skinner observed that an animal can learn to press a bar not only to produce food, but also to turn off shock.

Shaping. Another important observation of Skinner's is his *shaping* methodology. Many operant behaviors occur infrequently or not at all, and so it is unlikely that these behaviors will be reinforced. Under such conditions, no change in the rate of behaving would occur. Skinner developed shaping—also known as the *successive approximation procedure*—to ensure that the operant behavior would be learned. During shaping, a behavior with a higher baseline rate of responding than the desired behavior is selected and reinforced. When this behavior increases in frequency, the contingency is then changed and behavior which is a closer approximation to the desired final behavior is reinforced. The contingency is slowly changed until the only way in which an animal can obtain reward is to perform the appropriate behavior. Many scientists have demonstrated that this method of employing reinforcement modifies behavior both effectively and quickly. Let us consider one example of shaping behavior. Suppose that you want your children to use their forks when eating. Should you choose to reinforce only this final desired behavior, there is little likelihood it will ever develop. Using Skinner's shaping technique, however, you would begin by reinforcing any small behavior which even slightly resembles that of eating with a fork. For example, you might begin by reinforcing the child for holding the fork. By successively reinforcing behaviors which more closely resemble the ultimately desired behavior, you would eventually have the children eating properly with their forks. Other applications of shaping are discussed in Chapters 5, 6, 7, and 8.

Response elimination. Skinner also discovered several methods of eliminating an inappropriate previously reinforced behavior. One method, obviously, is stopping the reinforcement of the behavior. Skinner felt that *extinction*—the process of eliminating reinforcement—was the most effective method to employ in order to suppress behavior. *Punishment* is another method; an aversive event occurs following an inappropriate behavior. However, Estes and Skinner (1941) observed that an aversive event only temporarily suppresses the inappropriate behavior; therefore, unless an alternative behavior is reinforced, the animal or human will soon emit the punished behavior again in order to obtain reward. Contemporary research indicates that intense punishment can permanently suppress a behavior. Finally, an inappropriate behavior can be eliminated if an interval of time follows the occurrence of the behavior in which no reward is available regardless of the individual's behavior. Skinner called this response-prevention technique a *time-out period from reinforcement.*

CONTEMPORARY VIEWS

Since the early 1950s, attempts to develop general views of behavior have been abandoned. Research has focused instead on the motivational basis of specific behaviors. General approaches continue to be used, but the dominant influence of drive theory no longer exists. It is now recognized that a number of processes can motivate behavior. Contemporary psychologists have introduced new approaches to motivation and have tested the applicability of existing views to specific behaviors. The importance of these approaches will be apparent throughout the remainder of the text. A brief overview of these contemporary approaches follows.

Drive Approaches

Psychoanalytic view. The emphasis in psychoanalytic thinking has shifted from the id to the ego. Freud felt that the id was the most important structure of personality and that the function of the ego was to control instinctive energy and maintain one's unity. Contemporary psychoanalytic thinking (for example, Hartmann, 1958) suggests that there is an instinctive ego structure which develops independently of the id. The primary inborn ego structure contains capacities—perception, learning, and memory—which facilitate adaptation to the environment. As we mature, we acquire abilities such as habits and defenses which enhance this adaptation process. According to Hartmann, the ego is motivated by energy which is independent of the instinctive needs. An autonomous ego explains the existence of culturally divergent social behavior patterns: ego development is controlled by the specific social environment. This *ego psychology* movement has brought psychoanalytic theory and Hullian drive theory closer together which, in turn, has led to further testing of many traditional psychoanalytic concepts (for example, defense mechanisms and aggression). The results of this evaluation are described later.

Ethological approach.   Interest in the importance of innate determinants of behavior has increased in recent decades. Konrad Lorenz (1950) and Niko Tinbergen (1951) were the chief proponents of the *ethological view* which proposes that instincts play a critical role in motivating behavior. The ethologists research began during the 1930s and 1940s, but American psychology did not discover their work until the 1950s.

The motivational system developed by Lorenz and Tinbergen assumes that a separate *action-specific energy* exists for each major instinct. When a sufficient level of energy exists, the stored energy motivates *appetitive behavior*. The appetitive response continues until an animal or person locates a *sign stimulus*. The sign stimulus activates an *innate releasing mechanism (IRM)*. The IRM unlocks the block which has been preventing the release of the stored energy. When the block is removed, the action-specific energy is released which causes the exhibition of the *fixed action pattern*.

Consider the following example of the ethological approach. Several hours have passed since your last meal. Accumulated energy (hunger) motivates you to seek food (appetitive behavior). When you find food (a sign stimulus), your inhibited eating response (fixed action pattern) is released and your hunger declines.

The function of this instinctive motivational system is to enhance adaptation. In some cases, a single fixed action provides sufficient adaptation. Yet, in most situations, a chain of behaviors is produced during an animal's or person's attempt to survive. Although the motivation system is often inflexible, there are many occasions when an invariant instinctive system would hinder adaptability. In these circumstances, the genetic programming provides the flexibility needed to survive. The flexibility needed to adapt may be built into the existing releasing mechanisms, or instinctive behavior, or both. Otherwise, new releasing stimuli or behaviors are conditioned as the consequence of successful or nonsuccessful experiences.

The anti-instinct sentiment of the 1920s reappeared with the introduction of the ethological approach into American psychology (see Beach, 1955). However, an acceptance of a role for innate factors in motivation has developed since the 1960s, although no direct evidence exists for the energy model. Chapter 2 presents a more detailed description of the ethological approach, along with some criticisms and supporting evidence. The role which instincts play in influencing specific motives is described throughout the text.

Hull's drive approach.   The drive view of motivation proposed by Hull (1943) has since undergone considerable change. Hull's original view was that reward value influenced learning but not motivation; however, in 1952 he described a second motivational system. In addition to drive, Hull suggested that the incentive value of reward also motivates behavior. According to Hull, incentive motivation develops through classical conditioning. He proposed that the environmental cues present during prior reward develop the ability to motivate behavior.

The importance of drive in contemporary motivational thinking has varied considerably over the last 30 years or so. In the 1950s and early 1960s, the drive view continued to be dominant. While Hull developed a general theory of learning and motivation, other psychologists used drive to explain the causes of many different behaviors. For example, Taylor (1956) utilized a drive approach to explain human anxiety, while Miller's research (1959) described the establishment and resolution of conflict within a drive framework. Drive models were also developed to explain fear, avoidance behàvior, aggression, and social behavior. All these models paved the way for developing effective treatments for a number of behavioral disorders.

However, more recently the influence of the drive approach has diminished, as more and more evidence has accumulated indicating its inability to explain completely the occurrence of a number of motivated behaviors. Other approaches have emerged to fill the void. These alternative views are discussed in the next sections of this chapter. Yet, you should not think that the drive concept is invalid; drive still represents an important aspect of the motivational process.

Cognitive Approaches

Expectancy-value theory. As was noted above, the concept of drive dominated American psychology in the 1950s and early 1960s. Now the pendulum has swung to the position of the *expectancy-value approach* to motivation which gained substantial momentum in the 1960s and 1970s. Evidence for this view sprang from both animal and human research. Julian Rotter's *social-learning theory* (Rotter, 1954) proposed that a person's expectation of attaining a goal and the value he or she places on it determines the likelihood that a specific behavior will occur. The nature of a person's expectation is determined by the past history of obtaining reward or avoiding punishment. The term *locus of control,* coined by Rotter (1966), conveys his impression that our past experiences influence our expectation of whether or not we can control the outcome of our behavior; if we believe that our behavior influences the occurrence of an event, then we are motivated to obtain that event. Rotter calls this an *internal expectation of control.* On the other hand, if we think that we do not control events, we are thus not motivated to behave. This process reflects what Rotter calls an *external expectation of control.* His expectancy theory led to a renewed interest in the role of expectation in human motivation.

Psychologists have implicated expectancy in the motivation of many animal and human behaviors. For example, Bandura's research (Bandura, Ross, & Ross, 1963) suggested that the expectation of reward and punishment influenced the likelihood of aggression, while the expectation of an absence of control of events has been related to depression (Seligman, 1975). Moreover, expectancy theory has been applied to explaining avoidance behavior, achievement motivation, and social behavior.

Effective clinical treatments for various behavior disorders have been developed by utilizing the expectancy-value approach to motivation. Bandura's modeling therapy (for example, Bandura, Grusec, & Menlove, 1967) reduces phobic behavior by modifying the individual's expectation of the consequences of failing to avoid a phobic object: for example, a claustrophobic person failing to avoid an enclosed place. Individuals undergoing this therapy learn not to expect an aversive consequence to occur when they remain in the previously aversive situation. Bandura's participant modeling (Bandura,

Blanchard, & Ritter, 1969) is perhaps the most effective treatment of phobic behavior, presumably because it not only modifies phobic persons' expectation of the consequences of not avoiding, but it also changes their expectation of being in control of the situation; previously phobic individuals learn to believe that they actually voluntarily encounter a phobic object. *Self-efficacy* is the term Bandura (1977) used for this development of an expectation of control. Self-efficacy appears to play an important role in the effective treatment of phobic behavior. A more detailed description of the expectancy-value approach is presented in Chapter 3.

Attribution theory.   One problem with the expectancy-value approach is the absence of a system for understanding how expectations develop. Both animals and humans expect that a particular behavior leads to reinforcement, but what process enables them to form this expectation? A second cognitive motivational approach—attribution theory—answers this question. Fritz Heider (1958) described the process through which expectations are formed. According to Heider, the actual causes of our behavior may be very different from the causes as we perceive them. And it is the perceived causes, or *attributions*, which produce our expectations of future events and motivate our behavior.

Heider proposed that two types of attributions exist. We can attribute the outcome of our behavior either to *personal* (internal) forces or to *environmental* (external) forces. The personal forces can be categorized as either power or motivation. Power refers to our perceived ability; motivation, to our perceived intention or effort. The likelihood that a person will behave is determined by attributions of past success or failure. For example, if we attribute failure to our own lack of effort, we are more motivated to succeed in the future. However, if we ascribe our failure to environmental forces, we may stop trying to succeed.

This attributional approach has enhanced our understanding of the mechanisms responsible for the development of our expectations of future events. Researchers have studied the attribution process in numerous situations, including those involving achievement motivation, social behavior, and the labeling of emotional states. In addition, many think that self-attributions maintain deviant behavior and that attributional changes can alter behavioral problems. Chapter 3 describes in greater detail the influence of attributions on motivated behavior.

Biological Approach

Many of the motivational theories discussed so far propose that some internal mechanism is responsible for causing environmental events to trigger behavior. For example, Pavlov thought that the strong activation of the cortex which is produced by the unconditioned stimulus in turn radiates a field of neural activity. Presenting the conditioned stimulus activates yet another area of the cortex which itself activates adjacent neural tissue. If these two fields of neural activity overlap, Pavlov suggested, the conditioned stimulus will become capable of activating the same neural activity as the unconditioned stimulus; therefore, the conditioned stimulus will elicit the unconditioned response, now known as the conditioned response. Most contemporary psychologists have not taken Pavlov's brain theory very seriously; and, indeed, recent research has shown it to be incorrect. This research has demonstrated that the conditioned response is not identical to the unconditioned response (fear is different from pain). In some cases the conditioned response is actually opposite to the unconditioned response. For example, Siegel (1977) demonstrated that although the unconditioned response to morphine (a UCS) is lowered responsivity to pain, the conditioned response is heightened sensitivity to pain. The mechanism responsible for Siegel's results is explained in Chapter 4. The biological theories of other psychologists have met with a fate similar to that of Pavlov's theory.

These early biological views were incorrect because they were based on an inaccurate understanding of brain functioning. However, recent developments in physiology and anatomy have permitted a more accurate view of the biological mechanisms motivating behavior. The emergence of physiological psychology during the 1950s has led to an enormously increased understanding of the biological systems influencing behavior. Research has focused on the brain areas motivating specific behaviors as well as on neural and physiological mechanisms through which the brain translates motives into behavior. The effect of the disruption of brain functioning on motivated behavior has also been explored. For example, contemporary research has identified (1) the biological systems controlling our sensitivity to reward and punishment, (2) the internal systems aroused during stress and their effect on behavior, and (3) the biological systems motivating addictive behavior. Also, contemporary psychologists have explored the neural and physiological systems controlling a number of specific motives—thirst, sleep, hunger, sex, and aggression.

Reinforcement Approach

Since about 1960, Skinner's behaviorism has shifted from establishing the laws of learning to applying them. A behavioral technology has emerged which applies operant conditioning techniques to solving problems in applied settings. The application of Skinner's behavioral technology in order to modify human motivational problems is explored in Chapters 5, 6, 7, 8, and 9.

The Humanistic Approach

A final approach to motivation stands apart from the views that have been discussed so far. The humanistic approach, originally proposed by Carl Rogers (1959) and Abraham Maslow (1970), does not see human behavior as motivated solely by drives or expectations. In contrast to other approaches, the humanistic view simply assumes that humans are motivated to grow and mature. According to Rogers, the need for fulfillment is innate and human nature is motivated toward positive change.

Rogers's theory. Rogers says that *self-concept* is the foundation of personality: it represents our thoughts and the way we perceive ourselves. He believes that we are motivated to develop a positive self-image. We also strive to realize our inherent potential, a process Rogers called *self-actualization.*

Rogers proposed that one cause of mental illness is concern with the loss of affection and ways to avoid the loss rather than with acting to fulfill needs for growth. According to Rogers, we develop a negative self-image if we receive *conditional love*—love which is dependent upon acceptable behavior. In this type of situation, any unacceptable act produces a withdrawal of our loved one's affection. As a result we develop *conditions of worth;* that is, unrealistic and unattainable goals which we believe we must achieve in order to think well of ourselves. Such an impossible task leads to a negative self-concept. For example, if our parents rejected us when we were children because we stole candy bars from the corner grocery or were messy with our toys or failed to get top marks in school, we might have felt that we were "bad" rather than that our behavior was inappropriate.

On the other hand, we establish a positive self-image when love is unconditional. With *unconditional love,* we feel that our behavior does not influence whether or not we are loved. As children, we felt loved, regardless of our behavior. Although our parents punished us for wrongdoing, they did not challenge our inherent "goodness." A positive self-concept enables us to overcome conflict and develop a more mature personality.

According to Rogers, anxiety is an emotion which interferes with the self-realization process. He suggested that anxiety occurs when we behave in a manner contrary to our self-concept. When we were children, all of us undoubtedly at some time lied to our parents—saying, for instance, that we had completed our homework when in fact we had not. Had we responded positively when our lies were discovered, we would have accepted the fact that we lied and yet would not hate ourselves for lying. Such recognition of faults is a characteristic of the mature person. However, a child caught in a lie may deny it—may say, for example, that homework has been lost when in fact it simply has been left undone. The more the child denies inappropriate actions, the more likely it is that anxiety will be experienced. Rogers proposed that people will stop denying their faults and move toward self-fulfillment if others provide them with unconditional love. When the overly anxious person receives genuine unconditional love, faults can be accepted, virtues recognized, and positive relationships established with other people. Each of us has the potential to grow; we simply need to feel secure when expressing ourselves in order to realize this potential.

Maslow's approach.   Although Maslow's theory shares some common ground with Rogers's approach, it expanded the humanistic approach to clarify the conditions necessary to express our inherent need for self-actualization. Both Maslow and Rogers felt that even though humans are basically good and possess an innate tendency toward growth and self-fulfillment, these motives could easily be inhibited by social pressures. Maslow's view differed from Rogers's in that Maslow distinguished *deficiency motivation* from *growth motivation*. In his view, persons seeking to restore physical or psychological deficiencies cannot act to satisfy their needs for growth. Only when their deficiencies are taken care of can these persons develop their potential. Maslow suggested that our innate motives are organized in a hierarchy (see Figure 1.7). If we fulfill our needs on one level, we can then focus on satisfying the needs on the next higher level. Thus, after we satisfy our physiological needs (for example, hunger, thirst, and sex), then safety or security needs on the second level become important to us. Our need for love and "belonging-ness" is on the third level of the hierarchy; esteem and success represent fourth-level needs. The top level is our need for self-actualization. Thus, according to Maslow, we can self-actualize only after we have resolved our other innate needs. Although few of us ever achieve complete self-actualization, it does represent a goal which we all strive to attain.

Maslow studied the lives of many people whom he considered to be self-actualized (for example, Jane Addams, Albert Einstein, William James, Eleanor Roosevelt, and Albert Schweitzer) and identified 15 characteristics of self-actualized people, including these abilities: (1) to *perceive reality accurately*, (2) to *tolerate uncertainty*, (3) to *accept oneself without guilt or anxiety*, (4) to *solve problems effectively*, (5) to *possess a strong social awareness*, (6) to *develop meaningful interpersonal relationships*, and (7) to *be relatively independent of environment and culture*. According to Maslow, behaviors which initially satisfy a basic need can later serve the self-actualization process. For example, an individual may initially satisfy the basic need for security in an interpersonal relationship; later this same relationship may allow this individual to grow and mature.

It is far more pleasant for us to believe in the inherent goodness of human beings than to think that we are "driven" by primitive needs or "manipulated" by the expectation of reward or punishment. Yet humanism has not been universally accepted as a theory of motivation. There are several major problems with the humanistic approach. First, the concepts are fuzzy and are not clearly defined. Second, the theory is stated only in general

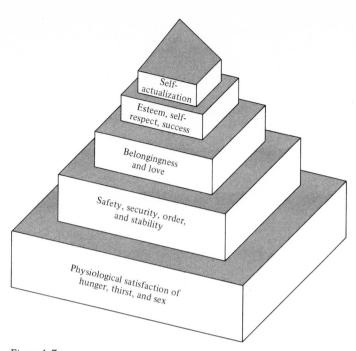

Figure 1.7
Maslow's hierarchy of needs. When we satisfy a need at one level, we can move up and attempt to obtain satisfaction of the need at the next level.

terms, so that it is difficult to test in an experimental setting. Finally, humanistic theory deemphasizes the environmental determinants of behavior and focuses mainly on the individual. Despite the appeal of the humanistic approach, evidence suggests that environmental forces play far too great a role in human motivation to be ignored. Even with its weaknesses, the humanistic approach has enhanced our understanding of the motivational process. The nature of that influence is described in Chapters 4 and 10.

SUMMARY

The causes of human behavior are of great interest to both psychologists and lay people. Our increased understanding of the motivational base of behavior has improved our ability both to prevent and to correct behavioral problems. This increased understanding is reflected in the major changes which psychology has undergone since the late nineteenth century. Motivational thought initially presented a simplistic view of human nature. Contemporary views suggest that a complex interaction of motivational processes underlies human behavior.

Opposing viewpoints have characterized the history of motivational thought. The early mentalism of the Greek philosophers contrasts sharply with that of the biological psychoanalytic view. Are we aware of our motives, and can we choose how, when, and if to satisfy them? Or is our behavior motivated by forces beyond our control? These two theories of motivation obviously portray human nature in completely different ways.

Psychologists have also disagreed about the relative importance of innate versus acquired motives; the "nature-nurture" controversy has played an important role in psychological history. The view of human beings moved by tension or drive also sharply differs from the view of goal-directed human behavior. Some theorists have stressed the biological aspect of human motivation, while others feel that social motives dominate. Although divergent views continue in contemporary psychology, evidence points to an interaction of factors contributing to motivated behavior. For some behaviors, one process may be more important than others, but each factor plays some role in motivating each behavior. One aim of this book is to demonstrate that many processes motivate behavior and to indicate the relative importance of each factor in influencing the behaviors described in the text.

The remainder of the chapters fall into two groups. In Chapters 2, 3, and 4, three major contemporary views of motivation (drive, cognitive, and biological) are presented. We will explore the evidence supporting each view as well as the applications of these motivational theories in solving human behavioral problems. The role of these processes in motivating behavior will be evident throughout the text.

Specific motivated behaviors are studied in Chapters 5 through 13 (for example, the causes of eating and overeating in Chapter 5). Although an integrated view of each motivated behavior is presented, one important point for you to keep in mind as you read the material is that motivation is a complex process and that each view makes a unique contribution to our understanding of each behavior. I hope that you appreciate not only the complexity but also the lawfulness of the motivational influence on our behavior. Real-world examples are presented throughout the text, both to illustrate the process being discussed and to help you relate the material to your own experiences.

THE CONCEPT OF DRIVE

CHAPTER 2

Terror of a spider

John dreads bedtime; he insists that his mother spray his room with a bug killer every night. In fact, a daily ritual precedes his sleep: he carefully inspects sheets and blankets, as well as the area around his bed. Feeling relieved after this inspection, he sleeps.

John's disturbed behavior began approximately 1 year ago, when he was bitten by a spider before he went to sleep. His hand was swollen and painful for several days. After this aversive experience, John began to search his bedroom each night for spiders. When he found one, he summoned his mother or father to kill it. The fear of spiders slowly declined when several weeks passed in which he found few spiders. Then John was again bitten before falling asleep. This second bite reinstated and aggravated the problem: now John refuses to go to bed until his mother sprays the bedroom and he inspects it.

John's father, upset over the spiders and his son's behavior, searched for openings through which the spiders might be entering the room. Upon discovering that they were coming in through the space between the floor and wall, he carefully caulked around the bedroom floor and assured his son that there would be no more spiders. However, his father's assurance that there would be no more spiders in his room has not diminished John's fear of them. His compulsion to have his mother spray the room and then to search for spiders before he will get into his bed continues. Although John's fear of spiders concerns his parents, they have been unable to eradicate it.

This chapter discusses the factors which led to John's strong fear of spiders as well as the process which would enable him to cope with his fear. Several techniques that could help John overcome his fear of spiders are described.

DRIVE—THE FORCE MOTIVATING US

People often use the concept of drive to explain their behavior. They suggest that they are "driven" to behave in a particular way. Such persons assume that they have no control over their behavior; they are acting in response to internal pressure. Here is an example of the drive approach to motivation. Suppose that you are walking to class and pass an ice cream machine. At that moment you have an intense urge for an ice cream sandwich. In response to your impulse, you put a quarter into the vending machine and quickly consume the treat. Although you are on a diet, the thought of the ice cream sandwich was so appealing that you could not resist the temptation to buy one.

This mechanistic approach to motivation has played a central role in modern psychological thought. Although the early philosophical view limited internal factors as a source of motivation to lower animals, many twentieth-century psychologists have assumed that drive motivates human behavior. Three major drive theories were proposed. Although the theories differed, each stressed that internal tension motivates behavior and that the act of behaving reduces this tension. As a result of this dissipation of the internal tension, the animal or human is unlikely to respond until the tension reappears. Freud's psychoanalytic view was described in Chapter 1. This chapter examines the ethological and Hullian drive theories.

Before the ethological and Hullian drive theories are described in detail, let us look at some of their similarities and differences. These two views of motivation assume that internal tension motivates behavior; however, there are two major differences between them. *First, although both approaches acknowledge the importance of both instinctive and learned determinants of our behavior, the ethological view stresses the instinctive factors while the Hullian view focuses on the learning factors. Second, the ethological approach assumes that a specific drive motivates each major class of behaviors; for example, the drive motivating reproductive behaviors differs from that motivating predatory or feeding behaviors. In contrast, the Hullian theory suggests that a general drive state motivates all behavior.* The distinction between a specific versus a general concept of drive is important: by asserting that specific drives exist for various behaviors, ethologists assume that internal processes determine which response occurs. The Hullian view that a single drive motivates all behavior suggests that the environment governs the particular action exhibited by a motivated animal or person. Evidence presented in this chapter and throughout the text supports both views: specific internal systems motivate some behaviors; yet, other biological systems also govern all motivated behavior. This chapter considers the general concepts central to both views as well as evidence supporting or refuting them. The significance of each approach to a specific motivated behavior (for example, eating) is presented throughout the remainder of the text. The ethological approach is discussed first, and a description of Hull's drive view follows.

THE ETHOLOGICAL APPROACH

A renewed interest in an unlearned, instinctive basis of behavior has taken place since the 1960s. Many animal behaviorists' research and writings have contributed to the emergence of *ethology* as a major part of psychology. Contemporary psychology recognizes the significance of instinctive processes governing motivated behavior in animals and humans. These inherited systems play a critical role in enabling both lower animals and people to adapt to their environment. Let us consider the ethological view of this adaptation process.

The Adaptation Process

Our ability to function effectively.   Konrad Lorenz (1969) suggested that instinctive systems enhance an animal's or human's ability to adapt to the environment. Adaptation sometimes involves internal energy (or tension) motivating a predetermined sequence of behaviors which a specific environmental stimulus (or stimuli) elicits. In these cases experience affects neither the eliciting stimuli nor the behavior; in other cases, however, experience can alter the eliciting environmental stimulus (or stimuli), the instinctive action (or actions) motivated by internal tension, or both.

According to Lorenz, the ability to learn from experience and respond differentially to varied environmental circumstances is programmed into the genetic structure of a species and provides the flexibility needed to adapt to changing conditions. Sometimes experience merely alters the effectiveness of environmental events in eliciting behavior, the specific instinctive behavior elicited by a particular stimulus, or both. Under other conditions, learning provides the new eliciting stimuli, the new behaviors, or both, which enhance survival. Lorenz contends that although learning aids in an animal's or person's adaptation to the environment, the ability to learn is innate.

The search for energy and knowledge.   The evolutionary process is central to an animal's or person's capacity to adapt (see Lorenz, 1969). In Lorenz's view, two factors enhance adaptability. First, energy motivates behavior; the incorporation of the ability to generate additional energy into a particular species' genetic structure through natural selection increases that species' behavioral potential. Thus, the more energy that a species evolves to motivate behavior, the better this species will be able to adapt to its environment. Second, an environment contains much information, and *knowledge* of this information provides an animal or person with adaptive capacity. Lorenz asserts that knowledge represents an increased sensitivity to particular aspects of the environment. A species' ability to adapt increases as, through natural selection, it incorporates knowledge about its environment into its genetic programming. According to Lorenz, evolution occurs when a species incorporates into its genetic structure, the capacity to generate additional energy, to absorb additional environmental knowledge, or both.

Human tradition.   The development of our enormous capability to adapt has occurred not only through increased knowledge of our physical environment but also through the establishment of culture. Lorenz suggests that social tradition provides an effective means of transmitting environmental knowledge and that the evolution of this social tradition has enhanced our ability to adapt. He further theorizes that our social systems facilitate the acquisition of new knowledge which, in turn, increases adaptability. The evolution of culture, according to Lorenz, does not reflect the incorporation of the contents of a specific culture into our genetic structure but rather represents the development of an innate receptivity to social information. Once responsivity to social knowledge evolved, human cultures changed quickly to detect new environmental information. Lorenz argues that *psychosocial evolution*, in contrast to the slow process of genetic evolution, has been rapid and is responsible for our great ability to adapt to varied environments.

The following example illustrates Lorenz's view of the role of instinctive processes in human behavior. A genetically programmed disturbance in cultural responsivity occurs at puberty which causes adolescents to reject traditional childhood norms and search for new ones. By the end of puberty, adolescents have adopted adult norms. Lorenz sees human adolescence as part of an evolutionary process which enables children to become adults. According to Lorenz, this programmed turmoil of adolescence can be compared to the experience of crustaceans after shedding their old shell but before growing a new one. This period between shells is dangerous for crustaceans but necessary in order to develop a new exoskeleton which can accommodate the animals' larger size. Lorenz assumes that from the end of childhood until adulthood, adolescents experience conflict which enables them to establish more adaptive characteristics than children have.

A consequence of evolution.   Evolution typically enhances behavioral effectiveness. However, behavior pathology follows evolution if essential knowledge is unavailable to a particular species or members of that species. For example, in a zoo environment an absence of the events which naturally motivate adaptive behavior causes animals to regress to more primitive behaviors. This regression produces the abnormal behaviors seen in captive animals. Lorenz argues that the loss of social information also causes the increased behavioral disturbances seen in our modern society. According to Lorenz, lack of contact with parents and other sources of cultural knowledge deprives children of the stimulation necessary for normal development and reduces their ability to adapt to our complex environment.

Consider the genetically programmed turmoil of puberty. The adolescent requires cultural knowledge to establish adaptive adult norms. But today many adolescents are isolated from adults and therefore do not have the social contact to acquire the cultural information necessary for the transition into adulthood. In Lorenz's view, modern technology has isolated many of us from the social environment essential for our adaptability, thus causing the behavior pathology seen too often in our culture. Lorenz is not optimistic about our future, but feels that we can alter the trend by reestablishing the cultural tradition which fostered human adaptiveness.

This discussion has pointed to the importance of instinctive processes for an animal's or person's adaptation to a specific environment. Let us now examine Lorenz and Tinbergen's detailed theory of the instinctive mechanism which translated motives into behavior.

The Motivation Process

Lorenz and Tinbergen developed their motivational system from years of observing animal behavior. To illustrate their model, one of Lorenz and Tinbergen's classic observations is presented; this is followed by their analysis of the motivational system controlling this observed behavior. In 1938, Lorenz and Tinbergen reported their observations of the egg-rolling behavior of the greylag goose. This species builds a shallow nest on the ground to incubate its eggs. When an egg rolls to the side of the nest, the goose reacts by stretching toward the egg and bending its neck, so that its bill is brought toward its breast. This action causes the egg to roll to the center of the nest. If during transit the egg begins to veer to one side, the goose adjusts the position of its bill to reverse the egg's direction. Although the behavior of the greylag goose appears to be a single action, the goose's stretching and bending movements and the adjustment to the roll of the egg are two separate behaviors. The stretching movement and adjustment reaction are both appetitive behaviors, while the bending movement is a fixed action pattern. The difference between appetitive behavior and fixed action pattern can be clearly seen if the egg rolls beyond the goose's reach. In this situation, the bird ceases adjusting to changes in the direction of the egg but continues to exhibit the bend-

ing movement until the process is completed. On the basis of the greylag goose's behavior and similar observations, Lorenz and Tinbergen developed their motivational
system.

Energy model.   According to Lorenz (1950), *action-specific energy* constantly accumulates (see Figure 2.1). This accumulation of energy resembles the concept of filling a
reservoir with water: the more liquid in the reservoir, the greater the internal pressure for
its release. In behavioral terms, the relationship is that the greater the pressure, the more
motivated the animal is to behave. This internal pressure motivates *appetitive behavior*
which enables an animal to reach an environment containing a distinctive event, a *sign*

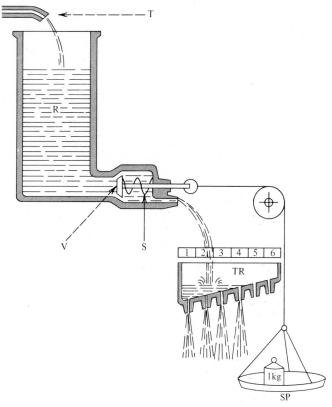

Figure 2.1
*Diagram of Lorenz's energy system. The energy flows constantly from the tap T into the reservoir R. The
cone valve V represents the releasing mechanism which is open when the sign stimulus exerts pressure on the
scale pan SP. The weight on the pan corresponds to the intensity of stimulation. The spring S represents
inhibition from higher centers. Energy released from the reservoir R flows into the reservoirs for lower
instinctive levels TR. The diagram shows the interaction of internal pressure which occurs from the
accumulation of action-specific energy and the external stimulation of the sign stimulation; both act to
release the stored energy. [Adapted from Lorenz, K. The comparative method of studying innate behavior
patterns. In Danelli, J. F., & Brown, R. Symposia of the Society for Experimental Biology (No. 4),
Physiological mechanisms in animal behavior. New York: Academic Press, 1950.]*

stimulus. The presence of the sign stimulus releases the accumulated energy. Thus, assuming that the greylag goose's previous retrieval behavior has dissipated the energy reserve, the bird will allow the egg to remain at the side of the nest until sufficient action-specific energy has accumulated to motivate the bird to return the egg to the middle of the nest.

Appetitive behavior can be either an instinctive or a learned orientation to a specific goal. The bird's stretching movement is an example of an instinctive appetitive behavior, while a human being's movement toward a refrigerator represents a learned appetitive behavior. In the absence of any specific guiding stimuli, the animal or human exhibits random activity: it continues to explore until it reaches the appropriate sign stimuli.

The goose does not exhibit the retrieving behavior until it has reached the egg. The retrieving behavior is one example of a *fixed action pattern,* an instinctive behavior which is released by the presence of a specific environmental cue, the sign stimulus. An internal block exists for each fixed action pattern, preventing the occurrence of the behavior until the appropriate time. The animal's appetitive behavior, stimulated by the buildup of action-specific energy, produces the appropriate releasing stimulus. Thus, the goose's orientation and movement toward the egg places the bird in a position so that the egg (the sign stimulus) releases the retrieving response. According to Lorenz and Tinbergen, the sign stimulus acts to remove the block by stimulating an internal *innate releasing mechanism* (IRM). The IRM removes the block, thereby releasing the fixed action pattern. The sight of the egg stimulates the appropriate IRM, which releases the retrieving response in the goose. An IRM can be envisioned as a key which unlocks the block to a specific behavior. Once a behavior is released, it no longer depends upon external stimulation and is then automatically exhibited by the animal.

In some situations, a chain of fixed action patterns occurs (see Figure 2.1). In this case there is a block existing for each specific fixed action pattern in the sequence, and the appropriate releasing mechanism must be activated for each behavior. For example, a male Siamese fighting fish exhibits a ritualistic aggressive display when he sees another male or even when he sees a reflection of himself in a mirror. However, no actual physical aggressive behavior occurs until one male intrudes on the other's territory. The second fixed action pattern is blocked until the two males come into close proximity. Although a sequence of behaviors may give the impression of a single behavior, a number of sign stimuli and releasing mechanisms are involved in the sequence. Additionally, after the fixed action pattern is released, energy begins to accumulate at the next stage in the sequence and appetitive behavior occurs which enables the animal to reach the next sign stimulus in the chain. Thus, if neither fish retreats after the ritualistic display, the fish then approach each other (an appetitive act) and fighting behavior is released. This second fixed action pattern does not happen if one of the fish is able to retreat.

Hierarchial system. Lorenz proposed that action-specific energy exists for each fixed action pattern. It is now clear, however, that the motivational basis of functionally equivalent behaviors depends upon a common source. Tinbergen (1951) suggested that a central instinctive system (for example, the reproductive instinct of stickleback fish) controls the occurrence of a number of potential behaviors (refer to Figure 2.2). Energy accumulates in a specific brain center for each major instinct. Numerous systems can contribute energy for each instinct. Internal, or intrinsic, motivational impulses can develop from the release of energy from a higher center following the occurrence of a fixed action pattern, or from energy buildup at the level on which the animal is presently operating, or from both. Hormones or other internal stimuli as well as external motivational forces can also generate energy. All of these influence the level of accumulated energy and the likelihood of additional behavior.

Once an effective sign stimulus releases energy, this energy flows to lower brain centers. The next fixed action pattern (or patterns) occurring in the chain depends upon the prevailing environmental conditions. There may be several fixed action patterns which could be released, but the sign stimulus which is present determines the specific fixed action pattern which is exhibited.

Let's consider the reproductive instinct of the male stickleback fish to illustrate Tinbergen's hierarchical system (see Figure 2.2). If sufficient space exists, the reproductive instinct will be activated when a mature male is placed in an aquarium. The stimulation of the reproductive instinct causes the male to establish a territory and releases energy to lower brain systems which control specific instinctive behaviors. The presence of specific environmental events determines which of the lower center's IRMs will be activated and, therefore, which specific fixed action pattern (or patterns) will occur. Thus, the male stickleback will defend his territory only if another male stickleback invades it; the presence of another male stickleback fish is necessary to release fighting. Also, this fish will dig a 2-inch pit in the sand at the bottom of his territory and use threadlike weeds to build a nest. However, the nest-building instinct is not activated

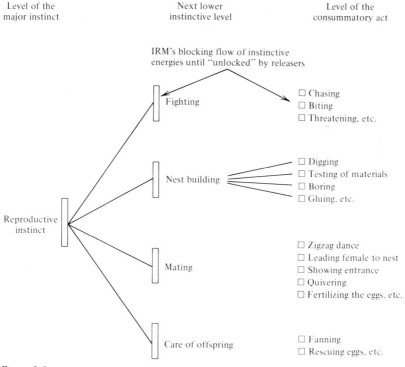

Figure 2.2
Reproductive instinct of the male stickleback fish. The diagram shows the fixed action patterns which can be released by the appropriate sign stimuli at each level of the hierarchy. (Adapted from Tinbergen, N. The study of instinct. *Oxford: Clarendon, 1951.)*

if there is no sand or weeds in the territory. Similarly, the mating and care-of-offspring instincts also depend upon the presence of appropriate releasing stimuli. If a female swollen with eggs approaches the male's territory, the male displays a ritualistic courtship pattern. First, the fish exhibits a zigzag dance and then leads the female to his nest. The male's quivering behavior causes the female to lay her eggs in his nest, and then the male fertilizes them. The presence of the eggs activates the care-of-offspring instinct and motivates the male to fan the eggs, which enables them to hatch. Thus, the presence of appropriate releasing sign stimuli determine which of the instinctive behaviors controlled by the reproductive instinct occur.

Von Holst and Von St. Paul in 1962 found support for Tinbergen's hierarchical theory in their study of the manner in which chickens go to sleep. A chicken exhibits a ritualistic behavior pattern before sleeping—standing on one leg and putting its head under one wing. Von Holst and Von St. Paul discovered that electrical stimulation of one brain site elicited the whole behavioral sequence; however, stimulation of other locations elicited only specific behavioral components such as the bird's presleeping ritual. These results indicate that different brain systems mediate the central instinctive motive and specific fixed action patterns controlled by this motive.

Environmental release.   In some cases, the sign stimulus for a particular fixed action pattern is a simple environmental stimulus. For example, Tinbergen (1951) observed that the red belly of the male stickleback is the sign stimulus which releases fighting behavior between two male sticklebacks. Evidence supporting this conclusion is the demonstration that an experimental dummy stickleback, which resembles the stickleback only in color, releases aggressive behavior in a real male stickleback. For other fixed action patterns, the releasing sign stimulus can be quite complex; the sexual pursuit of the male grayling butterfly (see Tinbergen, 1951) is an example. Tinbergen found that a female grayling flying past a male was pursued by the male. Although the color and shape of a model grayling did not influence the male's flight behavior, influencing factors were the darkness of the females, the distance from the male, and the pattern of movement that simulated the male's forward and backward flight. Tinbergen noticed that the absence of one female characteristic could be compensated for by an increased value of another component. For instance, if the model did not pass near the male, no flight reaction was elicited. However, with the presentation of a darker model at the same distance, male pursuit occurred.

The likelihood of eliciting a fixed action pattern depends upon both the accumulated level of action-specific energy and the intensity of the sign stimulus: the greater the level of energy, the weaker the sign stimulus which can still release a particular fixed action pattern. Baerends, Brouwer, and Waterbolk (1955) demonstrated the interaction between the intensity of the sign stimulus and the time since an animal last exhibited the fixed action pattern by investigating the eliciting power of different female models on the courtship behavior of male guppies. The external markings of male guppies are related to their readiness for courtship; each male's markings change since the previous courtship. Thus, the changes in the male's marking serve as an indication of the level of accumulated action-specific energy. Baerends, Brouwer, and Waterbolk presented guppies with female models of different sizes and observed the courtship behavior of the males. They saw that both the size of the female and the male's level of readiness determined the intensity of courtship behavior. A large female model released courtship behavior even in a male that was typically unresponsive (as indicated by body markings).

Both Lorenz and Tinbergen suggested an explanation of why an animal's or human's reliance on external stimulation for the release of a fixed action pattern decreases as the time increases since the animal or person last responded. Lorenz (1950) envisioned an IRM as a gate blocking the release of stored energy. The gate is opened either by pulling from external stimulation or by pushing from within. As the pressure within the reservoir increases, the amount of external pull needed to open the gate and release the behavior decreases. Another view, proposed by Tinbergen (1951), suggested that an animal's sensitivity to the sign stimulus changes as a function of time since the occurrence of the specific behavior. According to Tinbergen, the innate releasing mechanism's sensitivity to the sign stimulus increases when there has been no recent fixed action pattern. Thus, a weak sign stimulus releases this fixed action pattern because the IRM is relatively more sensitive to the sign stimulus.

There are also circumstances when an animal or human exhibits a specific fixed action pattern in the absence of the releasing sign stimulus. Behavior occurring in the absence of a releaser is called *vacuum behavior*. Let us examine several instances of vacuum behavior. For example, a caged jackdaw, a crowlike bird, intermittently exhibits a complex sequence of hunting, killing, and eating an imaginary prey; the bird releases this sequence of fixed action patterns because these behaviors have not occurred recently. Likewise, a captured female jackdaw may attempt to build a nest from her own feathers. Again, this bird's behavior takes place in the absence of a sign stimulus and therefore is vacuum behavior. One final example of vacuum behavior might be a male child pretending to fight a foe; his aggressive behavior is released without the foe because the boy has not recently behaved aggressively.

Lorenz and Tinbergen also proposed an explanation of vaccum behavior. Lorenz thought that vacuum behavior happened in the absence of an external releaser when the internal pressure became sufficient to free the stored energy. On the other hand, Tinbergen thought that the fixed action pattern was released, without the appropriate sign stimulus, when the stimulus threshold reached zero; following the fixed action pattern, the stimulus threshold returns to normal. Although the actual internal mechanism responsible for vaccum behavior remains unresolved, it is still an important and frequently occurring behavior.

Conflicting motives.   An often observed phenomenon takes place when an animal or human experiences two incompatible sign stimuli; the animal's or human's response is different from the fixed action patterns typically released by either sign stimuli acting alone. According to Tinbergen (1951), when an animal or human is experiencing conflict due to the presence of two antagonistic sign stimuli, energy overflows into another motivational instinct system and releases a behavior from this other system. The process of activating a third instinct system, which is different from the two involved in the conflict, is called *displacement*.

Naturalistic settings are ideal for observing displacement behaviors. Tinbergen and Van Iersel (1947) reported that the stickleback between its own territory and the territory of another stickleback often displays nest-building behavior. This "out-of-context" nest building is presumably due to the fish's conflict between attacking the neighbor's territory and escaping into its own territory. A person who whistles nervously before a date may be reflecting displaced activity resulting from the conflict between anticipation of dating an attractive person and fear of acting inappropriately. Other displaced behaviors resulting from this nervousness could be increased eating and drinking.

You might have the impression that an animal's or human's instinctive response is inflexible or that the releasing sign stimulus cannot be altered. Although this view is often an accurate concept of the instinctive processes, there are some circumstances in which experience can modify the instinctive response, the releasing stimulus, or both.

We saw earlier in this chapter that flexibility is sometimes programmed into the genetic structure of an animal or human. Learning can also aid adaptability by establishing new releasing stimuli or behavior. We now turn our attention to evidence that instinctive processes can be altered by experience.

The Role of Experience

Built-in flexibility.   Lorenz (1969) described many situations in which experience alters the sign stimulus or instinctive behavior. The following three examples demonstrate that adaptive modification produced by experience is often part of a species' genetic programming.

Motor facilitation by exercise.   Automobiles once required several hundred miles of use before they could be operated at full effectiveness. Likewise, many response systems become more efficient with experience. For example, Wells (1962) discovered that practice improves a young squid's ability to catch prey. Although a young squid's prey-catching form does not differ from that of an adult squid, its response is slower and less certain than the adult's. Also, Hess (1956) observed that the aim of young chickens' food-pecking response improves with experience. To demonstrate that success did not cause the improvement, Hess put goggles on the chicks which caused the food to appear to be where it was not. Wearing the goggles, the chicks always missed the food; however, the more they pecked, the closer they came to where they thought the food was located. In this case the improvement in pecking behavior was unrelated to the chickens' success in obtaining food.

Imprinting.   Imprinting is the development of a strong attachment to an object or person; it occurs only during a sensitive developmental period. For example, Lorenz (1952) found that a newly hatched bird approaches, follows, and forms a social attachment to the first moving object which it encounters. Although typically the first object that the young bird sees is its mother, birds have imprinted to many different and sometimes peculiar objects. In a classic demonstration of imprinting, newly hatched goslings imprinted on Konrad Lorenz and thereafter followed him everywhere. Birds have imprinted to colored boxes and other inanimate objects, as well as to animals of different species. After imprinting, the young bird prefers the imprinted object to its real mother; this indicates the strength of imprinting.

There appears to be a *sensitive period* when imprinting occurs; after this period, the attachment will not form. A young duck will not imprint on moving objects after it is 24 hours old (see Hess, 1962). The critical period for maternal attachment in nonhuman primates is 3 to 6 months of age, although they seem to become attached only to soft objects. An analogous phenomenon appears to happen in humans from 6 to 12 months of age (see Chapter 9). This imprinting phenomenon serves two valuable functions: (1) it ensures that a dependent offspring remains near the protective mother, and (2) it allows the young (animal or human) to feel secure in a threatening environment.

A young animal's or person's attachment to "mother" is not the only form of imprinting. The sexual preference of many birds is established during a sensitive phase and appears to be another example of this phenomenon (see Lorenz, 1969). The birds' sexual preference does not have to be for their own species, although in the absence of the preferred, imprinted species, sexual behavior will occur with their own kind. However, the sexual preference of these birds does not depend upon reinforcement, since it occurs at a time when copulation is not possible. Also, the imprinted bird's sexual fixation is not modified even after sexual experience with another bird species. This sexual imprinting could be a cause of the development and persistence of human sexual preferences.

This discussion has indicated that there is no instinctive releasing stimulus for imprinted behavior. The effective releasing stimulus for imprinted behavior develops through experience during a sensitive period of receptivity. Imprinting represents another illustration of the flexibility which genetic programming provides. This section has discussed adaptive modification which is produced by experience but which does not depend on the success or failure of that experience. However, in conditioning the success or failure of an experience does affect the ability to adapt (see Chapter 1 for a description of conditioning). Let us consider Lorenz's view of the conditioning process.

The conditioning process. Lorenz (1969) suggested that the instinctive systems of lower animals and human beings are programmed to change as the result of both successful and failed experiences. These experiences, referred to as *learning,* or *conditioning,* provide additional knowledge about the environment; this enhances adaptability. According to Lorenz, a conditioning experience can alter instinctive behavior, the releasing mechanism for instinctive behavior, or both. Only the *consummatory response* at the end of the behavior chain, according to Lorenz, is resistant to modification. Conditioning can alter the effectiveness of existing appetitive behavior or change the releasing mechanism's sensitivity to the sign stimulus. Depending upon the nature of the conditioning experience, this change can be either increased or decreased sensitivity. In addition, new behaviors or releasing stimuli can be developed through conditioning. All of these modifications increase an animal's or person's ability to adapt to the environment.

Howard Liddell's experiment (reported by Lorenz, 1969) illustrates Lorenz's view. Working in Pavlov's laboratory, Liddell observed that Pavlov's dogs, conditioned to salivate when a metronome was presented, ran to the machine when they were released from their harness. The dogs then wagged their tails, barked, and jumped on the machine. What caused this behavior? According to Lorenz, these dogs behaved as they would if begging another dog for food. Apparently, as the result of conditioning, the machine developed the capacity to release in dogs the same instinctive actions as those which might have been produced by their seeing another dog with food. When hungry, my family dog behaves in a manner similar to Pavlov's dogs. She approaches the bag containing her food and paws it until she is fed.

Lorenz also observed the learning process in natural settings. He discovered that the jackdaw does not instinctively know the best type of twigs to use as nesting material. This bird displays an instinctive nest-building response—stuffing twigs into a foundation—but must try different twigs until it finds one that lodges firmly and does not break. Having discovered a successful type of twig, the bird then selects only that type. According to Lorenz, the twig gained the ability to release instinctive behavior as the result of the bird's success.

An Overview

It is important to distinguish the ethological approach and the hypothetical energy system. Our understanding of the motivational factors which govern a wide range of behaviors has benefited from the ethological approach. However, recent physiological research has raised questions concerning certain aspects of Lorenz and Tinbergen's theory. Although scientists have identified brain systems responsible for the release of both appetitive behavior and fixed action patterns, there is no physiological system which operates according to the structure of the energy model. Energy does not appear to accumulate in any identified brain systems (or center), nor does it appear to flow from one system to another. Brain structures do communicate and interact, but not in accordance with Lorenz and Tingergen's energy model.

Lorenz and Tinbergen's theorizing, which infers physiological processes from behavioral observations, is not unique to ethologists. A similar situation appeared in Chapter 1, in the discussion of Pavlov's ideas of the internal systems involved in the classical conditioning process. Pavlov's invalid physiological thinking did not reduce the influence of his description of the conditioning process. The same is true of the ethological approach: the fact that the internal process does not operate as Lorenz or Tinbergen envisioned should not detract from their important observations on the influence of instinctive processes on motivated behavior. Contemporary ethology continues the investigation of the motivational process governing instinctive behavior. The results of these studies frequently appear in this text's discussions of specific motivated behaviors.

Lorenz assumed that conditioning enhanced a species' adaptation to its environment and that the ability to learn is programmed into each species' genetic structure. However, Lorenz did not detail the mechanism responsible for translation of learning into motivated behavior. In addition, the factors determining the effectiveness of conditioning on motivated behavior were not investigated by the ethologists. Clark Hull's theory does describe the role of learning in motivating behavior; let us examine it now.

HULLIAN DRIVE THEORY

Clark Hull's drive theory of motivation prevailed for much of this century. From the 1930s until the middle of the 1960s, most psychologists assumed that an intense internal arousal, called *drive*, motivates animal and human behavior. Hull's theory, which he outlined in detail in 1943, contained five main propositions: (1) *Specific antecedent conditions are responsible for the activation of the internal drive state.* Both internal and external events are capable of inducing drive. (2) *Environmental events become learned or acquired drives through the classical conditioning process.* Thus, the events present when we experience the internal drive state develop the capability to energize or motivate behavior. Our subsequent encountering of these environmental cues creates an internal drive state, even in the absence of the natural antecedent conditions which previously induced drive and motivated behavior. (3) *The effect of the drive state is to energize or induce an animal's or human's behavioral action.* An animal or human continues to behave until the drive state is eliminated. (4) *Reduction of drive is reinforcing for animals and humans; the influence of this reduction is to intensify habit strength—that is, the strength of the bond between the stimulus conditions which were present during reinforcement and the specific behavior which preceded drive reduction.* Thus, according to Hull's drive view, environmental events develop the ability to direct, or elicit, our behavior as the result of drive reduction. (5) *Behavioral inhibition develops when a specific response does not reduce drive.* Initially, this inhibition temporarily suppresses all behavior, but the continued failure of a habit to reduce drive leads to the permanent inhibition of the unsuccessful habit. In 1952, Hull added a sixth major component to his view of drive: *Environmental stimuli can develop the ability to motivate behavior through association with reward as well as with primary drive stimuli.* According to Hull, incentive motivation, like acquired drive, is established through classical conditioning. The strength of incentive motivation depends on the value of the reinforcer: the greater the value of the reward, the stronger the incentive motivation produced by the environmental events present during reinforcement. The following sections will briefly discuss the mechanisms responsible for establishing each component of Hull's drive theory.

Antecedent Conditions

Imagine the "butterflies" that you experience before taking a test. The scheduled examination creates this arousal, or nervousness; the prior scheduling of the exam is the antecedent condition producing the internal drive state. Your nervousness motivates the behavior which in the past reduced drive; that behavior ought to include learning what will be covered on the examination, finding out what kind of examination it will be, and studying for it. Let us begin our discussion by examining the antecedent conditions inducing drive and motivating behavior.

Deprivation-induced drive. Hull (1943) proposed that events threatening the survival of the animal or human (for example, failure to obtain food) create the internal drive state. In order for animals or people to survive, their internal biological systems must operate effectively. A deficiency existing in these internal systems threatens the animal's or human's survival and represents, according to Hull, the antecedent conditions which motivate them to restore these biological systems to normal. In some cases, the animal or human may restore normal functioning through an internal adjustment. For instance, in the absence of food, an individual will use stored energy to maintain normal functioning. However, if the deficiency persists, behavior will be activated to resolve the deficiency. Thus, animals or humans using too much stored energy are forced to obtain food and to restore the essential energy reserves necessary for survival. The animal's or human's natural response (either biological or behavioral) which restores efficient physiological functioning is called *homeostasis*. Hull asserted that a disruption of this effective physiological functioning causes an internal need which represents the antecedent condition motivating behavior.

Empirical evidence indicates that deprivation represents an important antecedent condition for motivated behavior. Although the number of hours of deprivation is frequently used as an index of motivation in psychological research, it is not an ideal measure (see Bolles, 1975). Two animals which have not eaten for the same length of time may not be equally deprived: a specific number of hours of food deprivation affects a lighter animal more than a heavier one. Proportion of weight loss to body weight appears to be a better estimate of actual food or water deprivation than does the length of deprivation. To illustrate the effect of deprivation on motivation, Stolurow (1951) varied the percentage of weight loss resulting from food deprivation and observed that a rat's level of instrumental behavior increased with its level of weight loss. This observation shows that the level of deprivation determines the intensity of an animal's motivation to terminate deprivation; the greater the deprivation, the more intense the motivated behavior will be to eliminate the deprivation.

Other sources of drive. Hull's theory (1952) acknowledged that events which do not threaten an animal's or human's survival can also motivate behavior. Several types of studies forced Hull to acknowledge that an internal drive state can appear even in the absence of deprivation. First, animals show a strong preference for saccharin, consuming large quantities even when they are not hungry. Although saccharin has no caloric value, deprived animals eat it in preference to a less desirable but nutritionally valuable food. Also, hungry rats can learn an instrumental behavior in order to secure saccharin (Sheffield & Roby, 1950). Thus, motivated behavior can obviously occur in the absence of a biologically induced deficiency. Let us study several classes of nondeprivation events which induce drive and thereby motivate behavior.

Hull assumed that intense environmental events motivate behavior by activating the internal drive state. Electric shock is one external stimulus that can induce internal arousal. The shock may be aversive, but does not threaten the animal's or human's survival. Yet, the presentation of electrical shock is one antecedent condition motivating defensive behavior.

Internal biological systems unrelated to a condition of deprivation can also motivate behavior. For example, the heightened estrogen level during the middle of a female cat's estrus cycle motivates increased sexual responsivity. The female cat without a high estrogen level will not exhibit sexual behavior with a male cat. Thus, sexual behavior seems to be independent of deprivation; rather, it occurs when both the appropriate external cue (male cat) and the appropriate internal cue (estrogen) are present for the female cat.

This discussion indicates that internal events—both deprivation and nondeprivation—and external cues produce the internal drive state which motivates behavior. The ability of these events to produce drive and motivate behavior is instinctive. However, many stimuli in our environment acquire the capacity to induce the internal drive state. We will now turn our attention to the development of acquired drives.

Acquired Drives

Hull (1943) suggested that environmental stimuli can acquire the ability to produce internal drive through classical conditioning. In this view, the association of environmental cues with the antecedent conditions which produce an unconditioned drive state causes the development of a conditioned drive state. Once this conditioned drive state has developed, these cues can induce internal arousal and thus can motivate behavior on subsequent occasions even in the absence of the unconditioned drive-inducing stimuli.

Consider the following example to illustrate Hull's acquired-drive concept. Suppose that a construction worker visits a bar every day after work and drinks several glasses of beer before departing. Since he rarely consumes alcohol at other times, the drinking appears to be motivated by a specific environmental circumstance—the end of work.

How did this stimulus develop the capacity to motivate this construction worker to walk several blocks to the bar in order to obtain a few glasses of beer? One possibility is that the internal need state of thirst motivated the initial trip to the bar; this need was created after a very hot day of working outdoors. Thus, thirst motivated the first trip to the bar, and the beer reduced the thirst. Because of this experience, the stimulus of leaving work became associated through classical conditioning with the worker's internal drive state: the end of work was now a stimulus which by itself could produce some internal drive. With each successive trip to the bar on a hot day, the stimulus of work's end developed stronger drive capacities. This man now visits the bar every day after work, even if the weather is not hot and no biologically induced thirst exists. Thus, the ability of the end of work to motivate behavior in the absence of an unconditioned drive state indicates that the end of the day has acquired drive properties.

Hull described two classes of acquired drives: *conditioned appetitive* and *conditioned aversive drives*. Acquired appetitive drives develop through association with deprivation states, such as hunger and thirst. In contrast, stimuli develop aversive properties through association with unpleasant events such as shock or loud noise. This discussion of acquired drives continues by describing evidence for the existence of Hull's acquired appetitive drives. A presentation of the empirical support for acquired aversive drives follows.

Acquired appetitive drives. Evidence of conditioned appetitive drives is mixed; some studies have reported evidence that environmental cues associated with food or water deprivation develop drive properties, while other studies have not. For example, Calvin, Bicknell, and Sperling (1953) found that animals ate more food in an environment associated with 22-hour food deprivation than other animals did in an environment associated with 1-hour deprivation. However, other researchers (for instance, Scarborough & Goodson, 1957) have been unable to obtain a conditioned hunger effect. A similar problem exists with conditioned thirst. On the one hand, Weissman (1972) discovered that a discriminative cue (previously paired with thirst) increased bar-press responding for water in satiated rats; on the other hand, Novin and Miller (1962) reported failure of an environmental cue associated with thirst to affect instrumental responding for water.

It seems logical to conclude from the literature just presented that the effect of the conditioned appetitive drive is small and difficult to obtain. This observation may not be startling: deprivation influences the tendency to eat but not the amount consumed (see Chapter 5). Once they have begun to eat, both deprived and satiated animals eat equal amounts (Miller, 1965). The explanation of these results is that as an animal starts to eat, the incentive-motivating influence of food controls eating. Since the amount consumed depends upon the incentive value of the food or liquid and not upon the deprivation state, it would be surprising to find that stimuli associated with deprivation could influence the level of consummatory behavior.

Acquired aversive drives. Attempts to produce a conditioned aversive drive state have yielded more promising results. Watson (1916) reported that rats exhibited increased emotionality (as indicated by a faster heart rate) to a buzzer which was previously paired with an electric shock. Later experiments demonstrated that this acquired fear had motivational properties. In a classic study in 1948, Neal Miller observed that rats learned behaviors allowing them to escape from a fearful situation. To demonstrate the motivational properties of fear, Miller first conditioned fear in rats by presenting electric shock in a white compartment of a shuttle-box apparatus (see Figure 2.3). Upon administering shock, Miller allowed the rats to escape into the black compartment. Following the initial pairing of the white compartment with shock, he confined the animals in the white compartment without any additional shock. However, each rat could escape the white chamber by turning a wheel to open the door to the black compartment. Miller found that about half of the rats learned to turn the wheel to escape the aversive white chamber; the other half "froze" and did not learn the required response. These results indicated that an environmental cue associated with an unconditioned aversive event acquired motivational properties.

The development of an acquired aversive drive can be seen in the phobia described at the beginning of the chapter: John's strong fear of spiders reflects the acquisition of a fear response. He associates spiders with being bitten (an aversive drive–inducing event) and thus exhibits a strong emotional response to them. It is also likely that John equates bedtime with being bitten. This fear motivates John to take extreme precautions before sleeping to ensure that no spiders are in his room.

Energizing Effect

The last two sections presented many antecedent conditions that motivate behavior. According to Hull, these antecedent events indirectly influence our behavior. Each antecedent condition produces an intense internal arousal or drive (D). This drive state is nonspecific: each antecedent condition activates a single drive state in Hull's view. The

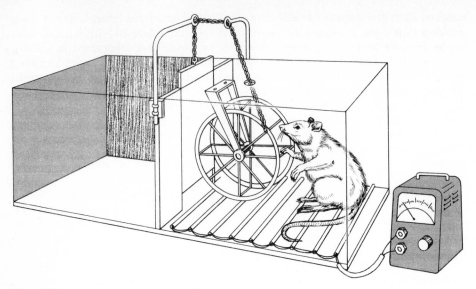

Figure 2.3
Apparatus similar to that employed by Miller (1948) to investigate acquisition of a fear response. The rat's emotional response to the white chamber, previously paired with shock, motivates the rat to learn to turn the wheel which raises the gate and allows it to escape. (Adapted from Theories of learning: Traditional perspectives/contemporary developments *by Leland C. Swenson. © 1980 by Wadsworth, Inc. Reprinted by permission of Wadsworth Publishing Company, Belmont, California, 94002.)*

effect of drive is to energize or activate behavior. However, the specific behavior produced is not dependent on drive; drive is the motivational force behind all behavior. In Hull's theory, behavior is directed by the prevailing cues—both external and internal—present when an animal is aroused. Thus, specific behavior (for example, eating) relies upon both internal drive and an appropriate eliciting stimulus.

Studies evaluating the influence of deprivation on the latency (or speed) of consummatory behavior represent the most convincing evidence for an energizing effect of drive. These studies indicate that an animal responds more readily to a specific environmental stimulus if its deprivation—and therefore its drive—increases. This is apparent in several types of deprivation. Bolles (1965) observed that a rat's response latency to eat decreased linearly with increased weight loss. As the rat's need for food increased, the internal drive state became stronger and enhanced the rapidity with which the rat approached food. Similarly reduced response latency has been observed with thirst (Bolles, 1962), sleep deprivation (Webb, 1957), and sexual deprivation (Beach & Jordon, 1956).

Unfortunately, the role of deprivation on behavioral measures other than response latency cannot be assessed independently from other sources of drive. You learned in the preceding section that only the initial response to food or water depends upon the animal's deprivation state; the amount of food or water consumed seems to be unaffected by deprivation. Moreover, the stimulus conditions associated with the consummatory behavior also influence the amount of consummatory behavior, thereby making it difficult to evaluate the effects of deprivation on well-learned behavior. Kessen, Kimble, and Hillman's study (1960) exemplifies this process. These authors gave their rats water at the same time each day for 5 weeks and then tested them during various periods of deprivation up to 47 hours, as well as during their regular drinking time. Results showed maximal water consumption after 24 hours of deprivation and higher intake at the regular drinking time than at other times, even with equivalent levels of deprivation. These results indicate that the motivational effects of deprivation diminished as the cues associated with drinking gained control over the animal's behavior. In all likelihood, both the animals' internal state and the environmental cues present during the regular drinking session possessed motivational properties.

Drive energizes instrumental as well as consummatory behavior. Using rats, Kimble (1951) assessed the influence of varying periods of food deprivation on the tendency to emit a previously acquired bar-press response and observed that response latency decreased with increased food deprivation. This relationship was true only 30 minutes to 1 hour after these rats ate; each animal responded very slowly for a short time after eating. It seems that for about 1 hour after the consummatory behavior, an animal is not motivated to emit behavior capable of producing food.

One interesting aspect of Hull's theory is his view that the motivation of a specific behavior can be enhanced by deprivation states or other drive-inducing conditions unrelated to the response. He thought that the intensity of motivated behavior is determined by the total level of drive produced by the summation of all antecedent conditions. For example, hunger and thirst should increase sexual behavior as a result of their drive-inducing effects. Support for this view is mixed; some studies show that deprivation states can be combined to determine behavior, while other studies indicate that an irrelevant motive either has no motivational influence or reduces motivated behavior. Most of the research combined hunger deprivation and thirst deprivation. Several studies (for example, Teel, 1952) demonstrated that a hungry animal that learned a specific behavior to obtain food also exhibited the behavior when shifted from food deprivation to water deprivation. However, these results have lost their impact because it is now clear that a thirsty animal is also hungry (Verplanck & Hayes, 1953): water deprivation causes animal to reduce its intake of dry food.

The situation is also confusing when other drive interactions are used. For example, Dinsmoor (1958) observed equivalent escape behavior in hungry and satiated rats. In contrast, Franchina (1966) found that hunger enhanced escape behavior, and Leander (1973) demonstrated a decrement in escape latency in hungry rats compared with satiated rats. A similar contradiction existed when investigators looked at the influence of sexual motivation on eating behavior. Ball reported in 1926 that a female rat's food-seeking behavior in a maze was not enhanced during the time of estrus-induced sexual responsivity, but Moss (1968) found that the rate of bar pressing did increase during estrus. However, Harris and Heistad (1970) observed less bar pressing for food in estrus than nonestrus females.

The reason for the contradictory results may be the inherent problem of producing an irrelevant drive free of distinctive stimuli associated with that drive. In Hull's view, stimuli direct an animal's behavior; the ability of these cues to produce a specific behavior depends upon both inherited and experiential factors. Thus, if the introduction of an irrelevant drive creates stimuli associated with that drive, the animal will behave according to these stimuli. We can in all probability conclude that if food-related cues are present, an animal or human will be motivated to obtain food and may not respond to the drive state which the experimenter is investigating.

The foregoing discussion suggests that motivation is enhanced by an irrelevant drive only when the source of the irrelevant drive is not apparent. In support of this view, Amsel and Maltzman (1950) discovered that shocked rats removed to a different environment from the one where the shock occurred ate more than animals that had not been shocked, even though neither the shocked nor the nonshocked rats were deprived of food. The authors thought that the emotional arousal produced by shock lasted for about 1 hour. Their animals were no longer afraid, since they had been removed from the environment in which they were shocked; therefore, the source of their arousal was not apparent. Under these specific conditions, emotional arousal produced by shock intensified eating. However, shocked rats which remained in the shock compartment following this aversive experience (see Amsel & Cole, 1953) ate less than nonshocked animals. In this situation, the environmental cues produced fear which then motivated an escape response and prevented eating; escaping the aversive location was apparently more important than eating.

Reinforcing Functions

In the Hullian view, drive motivates behavior, but each specific reflexive behavior depends upon the environment—that is, environmental events direct behavior. But which behaviors does a specific stimulus elicit? Hull thought that when an animal or human is motivated (when drive exists), the environmental cue that is present automatically elicits a response; the response with the strongest innate habit strength ($_sU_R$) to that stimulus will occur. If that stimulus reduces drive, the bond between the stimulus and response is strengthened; thus, habit strength is the result of drive reduction. The habit strength increases with each successful occasion on which the behavior produces a reduction of drive. According to Hull, the strength of an S-R association depends upon both the innate habit strength ($_sU_R$) and the acquired habit strength ($_sH_R$).

Unsuccessful behavior causes drive to persist in the animal or human. If this happens, all behavior is temporarily inhibited, a process referred to as *reactive inhibition*. If the drive state persists, this habitual behavior will occur again when the reactive inhibition declines. However, continued failure of a habit to reduce drive leads to a permanent or *conditioned inhibition*. Conditioned inhibition is specific to a particular response and acts to reduce the excitatory strength of the dominant response. The continued failure of this behavior to reduce drive causes the second-strongest response in the *habit hierarchy* to become the dominant habit. If this behavior is successful (that is, if it reduces drive), the habit strength of the response increases and the response is again elicited when the animal is motivated. The conditioned inhibition process will be repeated if the second habit in the hierarchy is ineffective; thus the animal will continue down the habit hierarchy until a successful response occurs.

In addition to the inhibition of the dominant habit, there is a second way in which the habit hierarchy can be rearranged. If the strongest habit cannot occur, the next response in the hierarchy will be elicited. According to Hull, the habit strength of this second response will be increased if it reduces drive. The continued success of this habit will cause it to become the dominant habit in the hierarchy.

Let us examine how the Hullian view of reinforcement would explain the construction worker's daily trip to the bar. His primary drive initially motivated him to reduce his thirst. Suppose that the strongest habit in this situation was a trip to the water fountain, but the water in the fountain was lukewarm, and his drive persisted. Next, he tried a nearby vending machine only to find that it was empty. Finally, he walked to the bar several blocks from the construction site and ordered a beer. Hull would assert that the drive reduction strengthened the bond between the end of work and going to the bar for beer. Each subsequent trip strengthened the bond until the behavior became habitual.

There are two major assumptions to this portion of Hull's theory: (1) *drive reduction strengthens behavior* and (2) *the stimuli present during drive reduction direct specific behavior.* Let us briefly examine attempts to validate these two ideas.

Drive-reduction effect. Let us first consider the drive-reduction hypothesis. Although Hull (1943) proposed that reinforcement occurs when an animal's need is reduced, a study by Sheffield and Roby (1950) presented strong evidence to the contrary. They observed that hungry rats learned an instrumental response to obtain saccharin even though saccharin could not reduce the animal's need. Neal Miller (1951) suggested that any intense stimulation can induce drive and that behavior is strengthened when drive is reduced. Since an animal learns an instrumental behavior for saccharin, the ingestion of saccharin must reduce drive. Miller (1957), in support of his view, observed that food-deprived rats drank less immediately after they consumed saccharin. In addition, these rats were less willing to press a bar for saccharin than animals not receiving saccharin.

However, two types of evidence challenge the traditional drive-reduction view of reinforcement. First, numerous experiments—the initial observation by Olds and Milner (1954) is still classic—demonstrate that direct stimulation of the brain is reinforcing. Olds and Milner (1954) placed a small wire, an electrode, into a rat's brain and passed an electric current through the electrode. They noted that their rats learned to press a bar to obtain this brain stimulation. Other studies have reported that rats will learn the correct path in a maze for this reinforcement (see Mendelson & Chorover, 1965). The reinforcing property of brain stimulation argues against a drive-reduction interpretation of reinforcement.

Sheffield (1966) argued that drive induction rather than reduction strengthens instrumental behavior. In addition, according to Sheffield, reinforcers produce excitement or arousal which motivates subsequent behavior. For example, it is the excitement produced by the presentation of food that reinforces the instrumental behavior; the food subsequently motivates eating. This interpretation of reinforcement explains one characteristic of secondary or learned reinforcers which was an enigma in the Hullian view. (Secondary reinforcers acquire the ability to reinforce behavior through association with primary reinforcers.) A secondary reinforcer not only reinforces behavior but also motivates future behavior. For example, consider money: not only does money reinforce work, but many people are intensely motivated to spend it as they obtain it. The drive-induction interpretation also appears to explain the observation that sensory-deprived animals are motivated to obtain stimulation. For example, Butler and Harlow (1954) discovered that monkeys would learn an instrumental response so that they could view a normal laboratory environment from their isolation chamber.

Directional influence. Possibly the aspect of Hull's theory receiving most support is his idea that stimuli present during reinforcement develop the capacity to direct the specific behavior which preceded reinforcement. Newman's study (1955) provides an excellent example of the importance of stimulus context on instrumental behavior. Newman trained food-deprived rats to run toward a circle for food. He tested some rats under the same stimulus conditions as were used during training; with others, he altered the diameter of the circle. Newman found that instrumental performance (indicated by running speed) decreased as the similarity between the stimulus context of the training and test phases diminished. Psychologists have observed for 50 years or more that environmental cues (both internal and external) control instrumental behavior in many different tasks and in a wide range of species, including humans.

Incentive Motivation

To suggest that the construction worker would continue to visit the bar if it no longer stocked beer is in all probability inaccurate; his behavior does reflect to some degree his desire to drink beer. Hull's theory of 1943 assumed that the value of reward influences only the strength of the S-R bond; a more valuable reward reduces drive more and therefore produces a stronger habit. Once established, an animal's or human's motivation depends, Hull asserted, on the level of drive but not on the value of the reward. However, various studies (for example, Crespi, 1942) showed that the value of the reinforcer has an important influence on the level of motivation. Crespi (1942) found that shifts in the magnitude of the reward produced a rapid change in rats' runway performance for food. When he increased the reward from 1 to 16 pellets on trial 20, performance after just 2 to 3 trials was equal to that of animals which had always received the higher reward. If magnitude influenced only learning level, as Hull had suggested, the animals' change in running speed should have been gradual. The rapidity with which the rats' behavior shifted indicates that the magnitude of the reward influenced their motivation; the use of a higher magnitude increased motivation. A similar rapid change in behavior occurred when the reward was lowered from 256 to 16 pellets. The rats receiving it quickly decreased their running speed to a level equal to that of rats receiving the lower reward on each trial. Figure 2.4 presents the results of Crespi's study.

Anticipatory goal mechanism.   To explain how the value of reward influences motivated behavior, Hull (1952) introduced the concept of incentive motivation (K). Although Hull indicated that an animal or human would be more motivated after receiving a large reward than after receiving a small one, Kenneth Spence (1956), Hull's student, detailed the transformation of K into behavior. His view explains why an animal or human is more motivated by a large than a small reward. Let us use the behavior of the construction worker to describe Spence's view (refer to Figure 2.5). In this example, the worker starts at the construction site (A) and walks three blocks to arrive at his goal (the bar, F).

Spence suggested that when a reward (beer) is obtained in a goal environment, this reward elicits a goal response (R_G). For example, when the thirsty construction worker

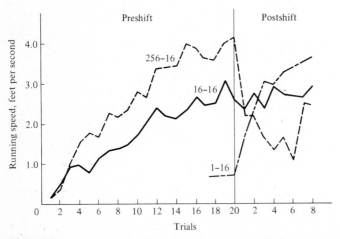

Figure 2.4
Speed in the runway as a function of magnitude of reinforcement. The rats received either 1, 16, or 256 pellets of food (the acquisition data for the 1-pellet group are not presented). Sixteen pellets were given to each rat after trial 20. (Adapted from Crespi, L. P. Qualitative variations of incentive and performance in the white rat. American Journal of Psychology, 1942, 55, 467–517.)

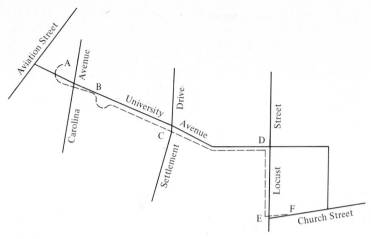

Figure 2.5
Route that the construction worker must take from the construction site (A) to the bar (F).

sees and tastes the beer, the beer initiates an internal response. This internal response (for example, salivation or gastric secretion) produces an internal stimulus state (S_G) which motivates the worker to drink the beer. The characteristics of S_G resemble those of Hull's drive state (D): they represent an internal arousal which motivates behavior. The internal response is intensified as the worker drinks. Until drinking is inhibited, the beer will continue to elicit the internal goal response. Thus, the intensity of the worker's goal response is determined by the value of the reward; the greater the magnitude of the reward, the stronger the goal response.

Spence thought that during the first few experiences, the environmental cues (for example, the bar) are associated with reward and subsequently produce a conditioned or anticipatory goal response (r_G). This conditioned goal response then causes internal stimulus changes (s_G) which motivate behavior. After the establishment of the r_G to the bar, the sight of the bar from the intersection of Church and Locust Streets (point E) will elicit the r_G-s_G complex which then motivates the worker to approach the bar more readily than on earlier experiences. As the strength of the r_G-s_G mechanism increases on every reinforced trip to the bar, the construction worker more rapidly approaches the bar. Upon entering the bar, the worker orders a beer and begins drinking. Since he saw the bar from the Church and Locust intersection (point E), the stimulus characteristics of point E also become able to produce the r_G-s_G mechanism through higher-order conditioning (see Chapter 1). After the establishment of the r_G to point E, the anticipatory response will occur when the worker sees point E upon reaching the intersection of University Avenue and Locust Street (point D). The sight of E motivates him to approach point E. Now at the intersection of Church and Locust Streets, the worker can see the bar; this causes him to approach it and have another reinforcing experience. Because the worker saw the conditioned stimulus (point E) from point D, the higher-order conditioning process causes the r_G-s_G mechanism to be conditioned to the stimulus characteristics of the corner of Locust Street and University Avenue. The higher-order conditioning process will continue until each landmark becomes capable of producing the r_G-s_G mechanism which will motivate the worker to approach the next landmark. When conditioning is completed, the worker will begin walking from the construction site toward the bar. The ability of each landmark (points A, B, C, D, E, and

F) to motivate approach behavior increases with each subsequent reinforcing trip to the bar. The effect of this increased incentive motivation makes the worker walk faster on successive reinforced experiences; the walking speed increases until a maximum is reached.

The magnitude of reward used during conditioning determines the maximum level of responding. Since a large reward creates a more intense R_G than a smaller reward, Spence assumed that the environmental cues associated with the large reward produce a stronger r_G than they would if paired with a small reward. This idea conforms to basic classical conditioning principles: the strength of a CR is dependent upon UCS intensity; the stronger the UCS, the greater the CR. Spence's concept of incentive motivation is supported by observations (for example, Crespi, 1942) that performance level improves with greater reward. As noted above, Crespi (1942) found that rats ran down an alley more quickly for a large reward than for a smaller one.

Hull recognized the need for the r_G-s_G mechanism as early as 1931. Since the classical conditioning process operates according to a contiguity principle (the greater the delay between CS and UCS, the weaker the CR), and since the reinforcement in the bar is not likely to be temporally paired with the cues present at the construction site, a mechanism must exist to enable the worker to associate the construction site with walking toward the bar. Thus, the higher-order conditioning of the r_G-s_G mechanism to the construction site and to intervening points proposed by Spence enables the worker to remain motivated until he reaches the bar and beer.

Nature of anticipatory goal response.   Rescorla and Solomon (1967) pointed to a serious problem with the r_G-s_G mechanism proposed by Kenneth Spence. Although incentive value does influence an animal's motivational level, there are no peripheral physiological changes (for example, salivation) which are always related to an animal's motivated behavior. Psychologists (for example, Lewis, 1959; Kintsch & Witte, 1962) who attempted to observe r_G directly and evaluate its influence on behavior have found that salivation might precede instrumental behavior, or occur after it, while at other times an animal might salivate without responding or respond without salivating. Apparently, salivation is not the r_G in Spence's incentive motivational view. Rescorla and Solomon suggested that r_G is a central, rather than peripheral, event. This central process is classically conditioned and has its strength determined by the magnitude of reward; its effect is to motivate behavior. As we will see later in the chapter, Rescorla and Solomon (1967) also suggested that fear is a central rather than a peripheral event.

Hull's Mathematical Theory

Clark Hull (1952) believed that the combined influence of several factors determines the intensity of instrumental behavior. The relationship is represented as behavioral potential ($_sE_R$)=drive (D) × incentive (K)× habit strength (H) − inhibition (I). The factors which influence each aspect of Hull's theory are presented in Figure 2.6. According to Hull, accurate prediction of animal or human behavior is possible only when each factor in the mathematical relationship is known. Let us briefly examine the research investigating Hull's mathematical formula.

The interaction of drive and habit strength.   Research evaluating the D × H aspect of Hull's view has been positive. A study by Perin (1942) is one of many that support Hull's formula. Perin trained rats that had been deprived of food for 23 hours to press a bar for food. He varied the habit strength of the instrumental behavior by providing from 5 to 90

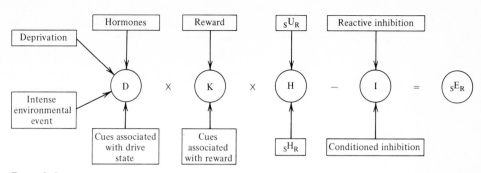

Figure 2.6

Diagram of Hull's theory. Drive (D) times incentive (K) times habit strength (H) minus inhibition (I) determines the likelihood of behavior ($_sE_R$). The arrows show the factors which influence each major process.

reinforced trials. Following the establishment of varying habit strengths, an animal's bar-press response was extinguished under either a high (22-hour) or a low (1-hour) deprivation level. Perin found, in accordance with Hull's formula, that habit strength and drive (deprivation) level jointly determined extinction rate. The divergence of performance in the high- and low-deprivation groups as habit strength increased (with greater reinforced trials) indicates that an interactive relationship exists.

Human studies have also reported an interaction of drive and habit strength. For example, Kenneth Spence and Janet Taylor (1951) studied the influence of anxiety (drive) on the acquisition of a conditioned eyelid response. A tone (CS) paired with a puff of air (UCS) to the eye became capable of producing an eye blink (CR). Spence and Taylor classified their subjects as having either high or low anxiety (drive). They obtained an anxiety score from Taylor's Manifest Anxiety Scale, a scale of 50 items used to measure anxiety from the Minnesota Multiphasic Personality Inventory. Spence and Taylor reported that "high anxiety" subjects learned the response more readily than "low anxiety" subjects. Furthermore, the difference between the "high anxiety" and "low anxiety" subjects became greater with increased conditioning trials. These results, just as Hull predicted, indicate an interactive relationship between drive and habit strength.

The influence of incentive.   Although there is empirical support for Hull's theory of drive and habit strength, the mathematical impact of incentive (K) is unclear. Several studies (for example, Collier & Myers, 1961; Kintsch, 1962) support Hull's D × K interactive relationship. However, other experiments (for example, Ellis, 1968; Reynolds & Pavlik, 1960) indicate that the D + K additive relationship proposed by Kenneth Spence in 1956 accurately describes the influence of incentive on motivated behavior.

The relationship between D and K is important for two reasons. First, the influence of incentive when drive level is zero is different in Hull's and Spence's views. Hull predicts no motivated behavior when no drive exists. (Multiply zero by any number to see why Hull's D × K model makes that prediction.) In constrast, Spence's hypothesis assumes that incentive operates independent of drive. (Add zero to any number to see why Spence's D + K model predicts an independence of drive and incentive.) Second, the combined influence of incentive and drive is much greater in Hull's D × K model than in Spence's D + K model. Although it is clear that both drive and incentive motivate behavior, the exact relationship between drive and incentive unfortunately remains unsettled. Apparently, the motivational process is more complex than either

Hull or Spence predicted; other factors (for example, previous experience) probably affect the way that incentive and drive influence behavior (see Bolles, 1975, for a review of this literature).

The influence of inhibition.   Inhibition, produced when a habit fails to reduce drive, can suppress behavior; however, nonreward also can intensify responding. In the next section, we will discover the conditions during which inhibition suppresses motivated behavior and the circumstances in which nonreward enhances motivated behavior.

Clark Hull's theory stressed the influence of instinctive sources of drive and drive reduction (reinforcement) on behavior. In contrast, drive theories which developed during the 1950s and 1960s focused on the conditioning mechanisms responsible for the development of acquired drives. These views explained motivation by using the conditioned emotional-response system initially described by Spence. The majority of research in this area concerned aversive motivated behavior. Since aversive motives influence each of the specific behaviors described in this text, the present chapter briefly examines the drive theorists' view concerning the processes that govern behavior directed toward avoiding unpleasant events. Throughout the text, we will look frequently at the effects of aversive motives on behavior.

ACQUIRED-DRIVE APPROACHES

The validity of Hull's drive theory was tested using several aversive situations; two of them are discussed in this section. The first test situation involves an investigation of nonreward in a context in which reward was previously experienced. According to the drive view, nonreward produces an intense internal emotional state called *frustration*. Frustration is thought to have a strong motivational influence on both animal and human behavior. As early as the 1930s, Miller and Dollard (see Dollard, Doob, Miller, Mowrer, & Sears, 1939) suggested that frustration produces aggression. Although Miller in 1941 modified this earlier view by proposing that aggressive behavior is only one possible outcome of frustration, the Miller-Dollard frustration-aggression hypothesis generated considerable interest and represented an important attempt to explain the motivational basis of aggressive behavior. During the next 25 years, evidence accumulated supporting the idea that frustration motivates behavior. Additionally, two theories (Brown & Farber, 1951; Amsel, 1958) were developed to explain the mechanism responsible for translating frustration into behavior.

The other test of Hull's drive theory deals with an animal's or person's attempt to cope with painful experiences. Remember the case history at the beginning of the chapter: John's excessive fear of spiders developed after he was bitten twice. John refused to sleep until he and his mother performed nightly rituals to assure him that his room was free of spiders. In 1956, O. H. Mowrer proposed a Hullian-based view of avoidance learning. According to Mowrer, John's fear would be a response to spiders developed through the classical conditioning process: the spider's bite elicits pain, and intense fear is established when John is bitten. John is motivated to reduce his fear once it has been established and accomplishes this by asking his mother to spray his room and remove any spiders. Mowrer would say that John's bedtime rituals are motivated by fear and developed because they were successful in reducing his fear. According to Mowrer, John's bedtime ritual is not behavior to prevent him from being bitten by spiders (a cognitive view), but rather an instrumental escape response to his fear—a response which has been reinforced in the past by drive reduction.

Although Mowrer's view received initial support, several researchers (see Bolles, 1975) have cast doubt on its validity. Recent theorists (for example, D'Amato in 1970) successfully restructured Mowrer's view into a contemporary drive theory of avoidance behavior. In addition, other psychologists (for example, Wolpe, 1958) used the drive model to explain human phobias. (However, others believe that cognitive and biological processes are also involved in motivating phobic behavior. We will address their roles in Chapters 3 and 4.) According to the drive view, human phobic behavior reflects a situation in which a fear that was once appropriate (because an aversive event did occur) is no longer realistic. For example, John's father assures him—after caulking the holes in John's room—that there will be no more spiders. Yet, John's phobic behavior does not diminish; his intense fear renders him unable to comprehend that he will not be bitten again. In many situations, the original aversive event may not be readily apparent. The individual may have forgotten the unpleasant event, or the phobic response may have developed through higher-order conditioning. The phobic response is due perhaps to stimulus generalization; for example, a child attacked by a peer generalized this fear to all children. Evidence supporting the contemporary drive view of phobic behavior, as well as several phobic behavior treatments based on this view, is presented in this section. The discussion begins by describing the effects of nonreward on motivated behavior and then considers the contemporary drive views of avoidance behavior.

Influence of Nonreward

Hull's view. According to Hull, nonreward inhibits ongoing behavior. Hull proposed that two types of inhibition of a specific behavior are produced by nonreward: (1) *reactive inhibition* (I_R) *is the temporary inhibition produced when behavior does not produce reward and the animal becomes fatigued, and* (2) *conditioned inhibition* ($_sI_R$) *represents the process of permanent behavioral inhibition produced when environmental events are associated with the inhibitory nonreward state.* These cues subsequently reduce the likelihood that a particular behavior will occur. Hull thought that drive, incentive motivation, and habit strength facilitate the occurrence of a specific response and that inhibition (both reactive and conditioned) reduces the tendency to respond (refer to Figure 2.6).

The Hullian view asserts that nonreward inhibits habitual behavior, thereby allowing the strengthening of other behaviors. However, this view does not accurately reflect the influence which nonreward has on instrumental behavior. Contemporary views of drive assert that frustration directly motivates behavior. Two frustration theories—Brown and Farber's (1951) and Amsel's (1958)—describe the mechanism which translates frustration into behavior.

Frustration state. The following example illustrates the central characteristics of both Brown and Farber's and Amsel's models of frustration. Suppose that you have 10 minutes to reach the gymnasium before the game begins. You get into your old car, but it will not start. Aroused, you leave it, but only after several hard kicks to its fender. Now even more determined to reach the game, you borrow a friend's bicycle, even though the gymnasium is 7 blocks away. Pedaling furiously, you reach the gym only several minutes late and proceed to watch the game. You might not drive in the future, but instead use a bike as your mode of transportation. Or you might trade in your car, which you now dislike, for a more recent model. This example demonstrates the major components of the drive model: (1) *Nonreward produces an intense internal state, called frustration.* (2) *Frustration motivates behavior; either this behavior can be the unsuccessful habit (or some other previously acquired behavior) which has produced reward in the past, or it can represent an attempt to escape from the aversive event.* (3) *If a specific behavior reduces frustration by producing reward, the stimulus conditions present during frustration become associated with the* *successful behavior.* In the future, the animal or human will exhibit this behavior when frustrated and when the appropriate stimulus conditions exist simultaneously with the frustration. Thus, habit strength can develop between frustration cues and behavior through the same mechanism responsible for the establishment of appetitive habits. (4) *Not only do environmental cues direct behavior when an organism is frustrated, but also this frustration state is conditionable.* In this view, the environmental cues associated with frustration become aversive, and therefore possess future motivational properties.

Experimental evidence.   Support for the frustration model comes from the work of many researchers; this chapter presents several important studies which demonstrate the main aspects of this view. Amsel and Rousell (1952) demonstrated the motivational aspect of frustration. They used a double runway apparatus (see Figure 2.7) in which the rats in the first stage of the study ran from the start box (SB) to the first goal box (GB₁) where they received a reward (food). After consuming their food, the rats were allowed to go to the second goal box (GB₂) for a second reward.. In the second phase of the study, the experimental group of rats received food only 50 percent of the time in GB₁, while a control group continued to receive a reward in GB₁ on every trial. Reward continued to be presented in every trial to all of the animals in the second goal box. The authors found that their rats ran to the second goal box more quickly if they had not been rewarded in GB₁ than if they had. Also, the experimental group animals ran faster after nonreward in the first goal box than did control animals after receiving reward in GB₁. The faster response in the experimental group was not due to lack of motivation in the control group; Wagner (1963) discovered that control animals that never received reward in the first goal box also ran more slowly than experimental animals. Apparently, frustration produced by the absence of anticipated reward in the first goal box intensified the rats' motivation to reach the second goal box.

According to the drive view, nonreward in a situation previously associated with reward is aversive, and escape from this aversive event is reinforcing. Adelman and Maatsch (1955) provided evidence of the aversiveness of frustration and the reinforcing quality of escape from a frustrating situation. They found that animals jumped out of a box previously associated with reward and up onto a ledge within 5 seconds if they were not rewarded. In contrast, animals which had been rewarded with food for jumping across the ledge took 20 seconds to jump. Additionally, although the reward animals stopped jumping after about 60 extinction trials, the frustrated animals did not quit responding after 100 trials, even though their only reward was escape from a frustrating situation.

An experiment by Daley (1969) provided evidence of the aversive quality of cues associated with frustration. She presented a cue (either a distinctive box or a light) during nonreinforced trials in the first phase of her study; during the second part of the experiment, the rats learned a new response—jumping a hurdle—which enabled them to turn off the light or to escape from the box. Apparently the cues (distinctive box or light) had acquired aversive qualities during nonreward trials; the presence of these cues

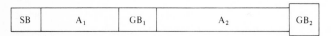

Figure 2.7
Double runway like the one used in Amsel and Rousell's study (1952). The rats placed in the start box (SB) ran to the first goal box (GB). After a short confinement in GB₁ the rats were allowed to go to the second goal box (GB₂).

subsequently motivated the new response. Termination of these cues reinforced the acquisition of the hurdle jump response.

Two frustration theories. Brown and Farber's and Amsel's theories present two different views of the nature of frustration. In Brown and Farber's model, frustration operates by increasing the general drive (D) level. According to this view, the closer an animal or person is to the completion of a task, the stronger the approach motivation, the greater the frustration when the goal is blocked and, therefore, the stronger the motivation to reach the goal. Haner and Brown's study (1955) supports this view. Haner and Brown required children to place 36 marbles in holes and varied the level of frustration by interrupting the children after they had completed either 25, 50, 75, 89, or 100 percent of the holes. When the task was interrupted, the marbles fell to the bottom of the apparatus. The subjects could begin their task again by pushing a plunger. The results of this study were in accordance with Brown and Farber's model: the closer subjects were to attaining their goal, the stronger their response to start again. Thus, as our motivation to obtain a goal becomes stronger, our frustration increases if we are unable to attain the goal, and thus our motivation to attain the goal is heightened.

Abram Amsel (1958) proposed that frustration is different from appetitive drive. Nonreward presented in a situation in which reward has occurred produces an innate (unconditioned) frustration response (R_F). This frustration response has motivational properties: the stimulus aftereffects (S_F) energize escape behavior. The cues present during the frustration (R_F) become conditioned to produce an anticipatory frustration response (r_F). The anticipatory frustration response also produces internal stimuli (s_F); these stimuli (s_F) motivate an animal or human to avoid a potentially frustrating situation. Thus, you might sell your old car after it failed to start, and therefore avoid future frustration. Although Amsel's r_F-s_F mechanism is conditioned as the r_G-s_G mechanism is, the two systems differ: whereas the s_G motivates you to approach reward, the s_F causes you to avoid nonreward.

You might think that Brown and Haber's and Amsel's models present opposite views of the influence of frustration on behavior. However, these two theories do not necessarily conflict; frustration could increase appetitive behavior if an animal's or person's escape response is either similar to or compatible with the attainment of reward. A frustrated individual could become conditioned to exhibit appetitive behavior if this behavior has reduced frustration in the past. The next section presents a similar matching of approach and avoidance processes in response to painful events.

Avoidance Behavior

Mowrer's two-factor theory. Recall our earlier discussion of Neal Miller's classic study (1948) showing that rats learned to escape a fear stimulus (which had previously been presented with electric shock) by running from a white chamber through a doorway into a black chamber. This and similar studies posed a problem for drive-oriented psychologists. Did the rat behave in this manner to avoid being shocked again? If so, then these types of studies would confirm the cognitive view that the purpose of avoidance behavior is to influence a future event. Mowrer's two-factor theory provided a mechanism by which the drive approach could explain avoidance behavior. He proposed that although it appears that the rats were avoiding shock, their behavior was an escape response from a feared object—not an avoidance response. The rats simply escaped from the white compartment and were not avoiding shock. According to Mowrer, fear was first conditioned to the white compartment and then reduction of fear, not avoidance of shock, reinforced the rats' behavior. Thus, when Miller's rats ran into the black compartment, the fear stimulus (the white compartment) was no longer present and the rats' fear declined. Fortunately for the rats, the environment was structured so that a by-product of an escape response was that the aversive event did not occur. However, Mowrer believed that the motivation was to escape fear, not to avoid a future aversive event.

   Supporting evidence.   Initial research evaluating Mowrer's theory was positive. Several studies (for example, Miller, 1948; Brown & Jacobs, 1949) observed that once fear of a distinctive cue is established, an animal learns a new response to escape from the fear stimulus. Perhaps the strongest support—and the evidence which Mowrer used to develop his view—came from his experiment with Lamoreaux (Mowrer & Lamoreaux, 1942). They used three groups of rats in their study. The CS (fear stimulus) was terminated in the experimental group immediately after the avoidance response. In the first control condition, called a *trace conditioning procedure,* the fear stimulus was removed before the rats' response; in the second control condition, the conditioned stimulus remained after the rats' avoidance behavior. Mowrer and Lamoreaux (1942) reported that the rats in the experimental group learned the avoidance response more quickly than did two control groups and that the experimental group's final performance was higher than that of the two control groups. The authors contended that the superior avoidance learning of the experimental group demonstrated that reduction of fear reinforces the avoidance response, because only in the experimental group did the rats' behavior immediately terminate the fear stimulus.

   Drive theorists (see Miller, 1951) believed that they had discovered the motivational basis of avoidance behavior. However, some problems with Mowrer's view surfaced during the 1950s and 1960s. The next section describes these problems, the reasons for them, and possible solutions. The problems identified with Mowrer's theory stimulated the development of two different views of avoidance behavior. A contemporary drive view proposed by Michael D'Amato (1970) is discussed in this chapter; the cognitive view of Robert Bolles (1972) is discussed in Chapter 3.

   Criticisms of two-factor theory.   Several problems exist with Mowrer's two-factor theory of avoidance learning. First, although exposure to the conditioned stimulus should eliminate avoidance behavior, avoidance behavior is often extremely resistant to extinction. Solomon and Wynne (1954) reported that their dogs, even after receiving over 200 extinction trials, failed to extinguish a previously established avoidance response. The apparent failure of extinction represents a problem for the two-factor theory: if fear is acquired through classical conditioning and is responsible for motivating the avoidance behavior, then presentation of the CS during extinction should cause a reduction of fear and a cessation of avoidance behavior. Levis, Smith, and Epstein (1978) offered an answer to this problem: it is not the number of extinction trials but rather the duration of exposure to the CS that determines the elimination of an avoidance response. Very little extinction will occur if an animal or human quickly responds to a fear stimulus. Levis, Smith, and Epstein found that the likelihood that avoidance behavior will occur depends upon the duration of exposure to the fear stimulus: the longer the exposure, the weaker the avoidance response. Thus, Solomon and Wynne's extinction results do not necessarily contradict the two-factor theory.

   A second problem for the two-factor theory concerns the apparent absence of fear in a well-established avoidance response. An example is the research of Kamin, Brimer, and Black (1963). These authors observed that a CS for a well-learned avoidance behavior did not suppress an instrumental response for food. The failure of the conditioned stimulus to reduce responding is thought to reflect an absence of fear since one indication of fear is the suppression of appetitive behavior. However, it is possible that the absence of suppression does not indicate that an animal shows no fear in response to the CS, but rather indicates that an animal's motivation for food is stronger than the fear induced by the CS. In addition, strong fear is not necessary to motivate a habitual avoidance response, an observation consistent with Hull's idea that the tendency to respond is a joint function of drive and habit strength. However, the next two problems cannot be explained with Mowrer's drive view of avoidance behavior.

The frequent observation that some animals, even under optimal conditions (see Turner & Solomon, 1962), fail to learn to avoid an aversive event creates yet another problem for the traditional drive view. These studies showed that a CS associated with shock (or with another aversive event) terminates with the appropriate response—but the animal does not learn. For example, D'Amato and Schiff (1964) found that over half of their subjects, even after having participated in more than 7,000 trials over a 4-month period, failed to learn an avoidance response. These animals escaped but did not learn to avoid the shock—a result not predictable from Mowrer's two-factor theory.

Kamin's classic experiment (1956) demonstrating the importance of the avoidance of the aversive event during conditioning is perhaps the most damaging evidence against Mowrer's view. Kamin compared the effectiveness of avoidance learning in rats whose response both terminated the CS and prevented the UCS ("normal condition") with that in animals which were shocked at a predetermined time but whose behavior terminated the CS ("terminate CS" group) and with that in rats which avoided the UCS while the fear (CS) stimulus remained on for a short time after the response ("avoid UCS" group). Although the two-factor theory would predict that the "avoid UCS" group would not learn, owing to the fact that their fear remained after their response, these subjects showed greater avoidance responding than control animals given CS and UCS but not allowed either to escape or avoid the shock ("classical-conditioned" group). Also, the "avoid UCS" subjects responded as well as the rats whose behavior terminated, but did not prevent, shock. The animals whose behavior both terminated the fear stimulus and avoided the shock demonstrated the highest performance level. Figure 2.8 presents the results of Kamin's study, which indicate that two factors—the fear reduction and the avoidance of the aversive event—play an important role in avoidance learning.

A contemporary drive view. *Basic principles.* Michael D'Amato (1970) developed a new drive view to explain why the prevention of the aversive event is important in avoidance behavior. According to D'Amato, an aversive event (for example, shock) elicits an unconditioned pain response (R_P); the stimulus consequences of the pain response (S_P) motivate escape behavior. Through classical conditioning, the environmental cues present during shock acquire the ability to produce an anticipatory pain response (r_P), with its stimulus aftereffects (s_P) also motivating escape behavior.

D'Amato's r_P-s_P mechanism motivates an animal or human to escape from the conditioned stimulus, just as Amsel's r_F-s_F system causes an animal to escape from a situation associated with frustration. You may have noticed a similarity between D'Amato's r_P-s_P system and Mowrer's conditioned-fear theory. In both views, the conditioned stimulus associated with an aversive event motivates avoidance behavior. The difference between the two views lies in the reinforcement mechanism responsible for avoidance behavior.

In D'Amato's view, the termination of an aversive event (the UCS; for example, shock) produces an unconditioned relief response (R_R). The stimulus consequences (S_R) of the relief response are reinforcing. According to D'Amato, the stimuli associated with the termination of the aversive event become capable of producing an anticipatory relief response (r_R), and the stimulus consequences (s_R) of this anticipatory response (s_R) are

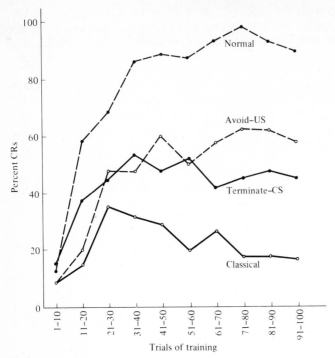

Figure 2.8
Percentage of avoidance responses as a function of the rats' ability to terminate the CS, avoid the UCS, or both. (From Kamin, L. J. The effects of termination of the CS and avoidance of the US on avoidance learning. Journal of Comparative and Physiological Psychology, 1956, 49, 420–424. Copyright 1956 by the American Psychological Association. Reprinted by permission.)

also reinforcing. In addition, the sight of the cues associated with anticipatory relief stimulates approach behavior in a manner closely resembling Spence's description of the approach response to anticipatory goal-related cues. This idea suggests a second motivational basis of avoidance responding; the animal or human is not only escaping from an aversive situation but also approaching a reinforcing one. The avoidance of the aversive event is important, D'Amato claims, because if the animal does not avoid, the r_R-s_R mechanism will not develop. Let us consider how D'Amato's theory would explain the motivational basis of some young children to do homework.

For many children, failure to complete homework leads to punishment by their parents. This punishment, if in the form of a spanking, produces an unconditioned pain response (R_P). Thus, an unfinished homework assignment becomes associated with punishment. The result of this conditioning is that a homework assignment produces an anticipatory pain response (r_P). The r_P-s_P mechanism motivates most of these children to finish their homework. Additionally, since the presence of an unfinished assignment is an aversive event, completion produces an unconditioned relief response (R_R). The relief that these children experience upon completing their homework acts to strengthen the habit of finishing their homework. D'Amato suggested that the anticipation of relief, as well as pain, motivates avoidance behavior. In the homework example, a completed assignment becomes associated with relief and can produce an anticipatory relief response (r_R). Thus, when homework is assigned again, the thought of a completed task produces the r_R-s_R complex which acts to motivate the child to finish the assignment. Therefore, the anticipation of both pain and relief motivates many children to complete homework. In the next section, evidence will be considered that supports D'Amato's drive view of avoidance behavior.

Empirical support.   Two lines of evidence support D'Amato's contemporary drive view in avoidance behavior. First, D'Amato, Fazzaro, and Etkin (1968) maintained that the reason for an animal's not learning to avoid when a trace conditioning procedure is used (in this technique, the CS terminates before the UCS is presented) is that there is no distinctive cue associated with the absence of the UCS. If there were a cue present when adversity ended, an avoidance response would be learned. In order to demonstrate this idea, D'Amato, Fazzaro, and Etkin presented a second cue (in addition to the CS) when their subjects exhibited an avoidance response. Although learning was slow—reaching the level observed with the traditional delayed procedure (in which CS and UCS terminate at the same time) only after 500 trials—these subjects performed at a higher level than rats which did not receive the second cue (see Figure 2.9). According to D'Amato's view, once the rat associated the second cue with the absence of shock, the r_R-s_R mechanism was acquired and then acted to reinforce avoidance behavior.

In D'Amato's view, we are motivated to approach situations associated with relief, as well as to escape those associated with adversity. Furthermore, the relief we experience following avoidance behavior reinforces that response. M. Ray Denny's research (see Denny, 1971) demonstrates the motivational and reinforcing character of relief. Let us examine Denny's evidence validating each aspect of D'Amato's view.

Denny and Weisman (1964) demonstrated that animals anticipating pain approach those events associated with the greatest amount of relief. They trained rats either to escape or to avoid shock in a striped shock compartment of a T maze by turning either right into a black compartment or left into a white one. One of the chambers was associated with a 100-second intertrial interval, the other, with only a 20-second

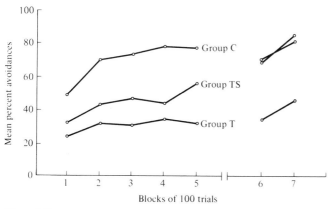

Figure 2.9
Percentages of avoidance responses during 700 trials for standard delayed conditioning group (group C), trace conditioning group (group T), and group receiving a cue for 5 seconds after each avoidance response (group TS). The break in curves indicates that a 24-hour interval elapsed between the fifth and sixth blocks of trials. (From D'Amato, M. R., Fazzaro, J., & Etkin, M. Anticipatory responding and avoidance discrimination as factors in avoidance conditioning. Journal of Experimental Psychology, 1968, 77, 41–47. Copyright 1968 by the American Psychological Association. Reprinted by permission.)

interval. Denny and Weisman found that their rats learned to go to the color associated with the longer interval. Apparently, when the rats anticipated adversity, they did not go to just any place but rather were motivated toward an environment which was associated with the longest relief.

Denny asserts that the amount of relief depends upon the length of time between aversive events: the longer the nonshock interval (or intertrial interval, ITI), the greater the conditioned relief. In Denny's view, the greater the relief, the faster the acquisition of an avoidance habit. To test this idea, Denny and Weisman varied the time between trials from 10 to 225 seconds and observed that acquisition of an avoidance response was directly related to intertrial interval: animals allowed a longer interval between trials learned the avoidance response more readily than those given a shorter time between trials. These results show that the longer the period of relief after an aversive event, the more readily the rats learned to avoid adversity.

Denny believes that extinction of an avoidance response occurs when an animal begins to relax in the shock (fear) compartment. This happens if the shock and nonshock environments share common characteristics. In support of this view, Denny, Koons, and Mason (1959) observed that extinction of an avoidance response is faster if the shock compartment and nonshock compartment are similar rather than dissimilar. Additionally, extinction eventually takes place, even in a dissimilar environment, as a result of the higher-order conditioning of relaxation to the aversive (shock) compartment; it happens once the relaxation produced in the shock chamber can successfully compete with the anticipatory pain response (fear). The next section describes how the relaxation response has been employed to extinguish phobic behaviors in humans.

Recall the spider phobia described at the beginning of the chapter. In the contemporary drive view, the anticipatory pain response produced at bedtime motivates John's ritual, while his sense of relief after the bedtime ritual reinforces his phobic behavior. John's relief occurs because he associates his mother's search-and-spray operation with the absence of spider bites. Let us now turn our attention to two clinical treatments of phobic behavior based on a drive model of avoidance behavior.

Clinical Applications

Some psychologists, beginning with Watson, have hypothesized that human phobias are learned avoidance behaviors. On the basis of this assumption, techniques which are effective in eliminating avoidance behavior in animals should be effective in treating phobic behavior in humans. The contemporary drive approach suggests several approaches to extinguish human phobias. Since the anticipatory pain response system which motivates avoidance behavior is acquired through classical conditioning, the presentation of the conditioned stimulus in the absence of the unconditioned stimulus should extinguish the response. The problem with this technique when used for human phobic behavior is not that it is unsound but that a human's avoidance behavior motivated by the anticipation of pain prevents the person from experiencing the CS alone and, therefore, extinction cannot occur. Two treatments of human phobias, flooding and systematic desensitization, have been used to overcome this problem. *Flooding* prevents the occurrence of the avoidance response; it forces patients to extinguish their fear. (This treatment is referred to as *implosion therapy* by psychoanalysts.) The second technique, *systematic desensitization,* induces a response (relaxation) antagonistic to the anticipatory pain response (fear). The patient does not avoid the CS, because the cues which previously elicited the anticipatory pain response now produce an anticipatory relaxation response. The reinforcing aspects of conditioned relaxation counter the aversive elements of anticipated pain, and so the person is no longer motivated to avoid.

The next section briefly describes flooding and desensitization and the evidence supporting their effectiveness as therapies. Also, several animal studies are cited to illustrate the generality of the behavioral principles upon which these techniques are based. [Refer to Rimm and Masters (1979) for a more detailed description of these methods.]

Response prevention, or flooding.   The characteristic distinguishing response prevention, or flooding, from the typical extinction procedure is the inability of an animal or human in response-prevention therapy to escape from the fear stimulus. Otherwise, the two procedures are identical: the animal or human is exposed to the conditioned fear stimulus without an aversive consequence. In animal studies, the experimenter prevents avoidance behavior. Solomon, Kamin, and Wynne's experiment (1953) represents the first use of this procedure. These psychologists shocked their rats in the presence of a distinctive cue and then allowed them to learn an avoidance response; this enabled them to escape the fear stimulus, so that the aversive event (shock) was prevented. After establishing the avoidance response, the experimenters exposed the rats to the fear stimulus and prevented them from escaping from it. They did not present shock during this last phase of the study. Solomon, Kamin, and Wynne reported that the fear to the CS was extinguished (the rats were no longer "anxious"), and then the animals stopped attempting to escape from the CS (that is, to avoid the UCS). Research investigating response prevention, or flooding, has demonstrated it to be an effective technique for eliminating avoidance behavior in animals (see Baum, 1970). Baum found that the effectiveness of flooding increased with longer exposure to the fear stimulus. In addition, Coulter, Riccio, and Page (1969) found that flooding suppressed an avoidance response faster than a typical extinction procedure did.

Clinical effectiveness.   Malleson (1959) first reported the successful use of flooding to treat phobic behavior in humans. Since Malleson's experiment, a large number of studies demonstrated the effectiveness of flooding to eliminate a wide variety of behavior disorders, including phobias (for example, Yule, Sacks, & Hersov, 1974), anxiety and neurosis (see Girodo, 1974), and obsessive-compulsive behavior (for example, Hackman & McLean, 1975).

Flooding seems to be especially effective in treating obsessive-compulsive behavior. The following case history, reported by Meyer, Robertson, and Tatlow in 1975, provides an example of the technique and its successful implementation. An adult female client had become extremely disturbed about anything associated with death—even the newspaper obituary column elicited anxiety. When anxious, she compulsively washed herself and changed her clothes. Treatment began by developing a hierarchy of anxiety-inducing stimuli. The most aversive stimulus was dead bodies. Thus, the therapist and the patient handled a corpse at a local hospital mortuary. She encountered other aversive stimuli—for example, a picture of a dead man. In order to prevent her ritualistic compulsive behavior, the therapist remained with her following her exposures to the feared stimuli. The authors reported that on the second treatment day the patient was completely able to suppress the rituals. Eight months after the therapy, the woman had no inclination to exhibit ritualistic behavior and demonstrated only a low level of anxiety to death-related stimuli.

Some flooding treatments have employed *imaginal* rather than real-life or in vivo exposure to the fear stimulus. The use of an imagined feared object is based on the demonstration that human patients can realistically imagine an aversive experience (see Grossberg & Wilson, 1968). Grossberg and Wilson reported a positive relationship between their patients' perceived clarity of the feared object and physiological measures of fear. However, the correlation was not perfect, as some subjects imagined the feared object but did not experience the emotional effects. According to Wolpe (1969), only one of ten patients does not experience the aversiveness of an imagined stimulus; for such a subject, in vivo treatment procedures are necessary. Although imagined treatment does seem to be effective, therapy usually progresses more readily with the in vivo treatment (Emmelkamp & Wessels, 1975).

Nature of the flooding process. Investigations of flooding indicate that extinction of a fear response is not completely responsible for the effectiveness of flooding (see Mineka, 1979, for a review of this literature). Mineka and Gino (1979) showed that animals receiving enough flooding (20 trials) to extinguish a well-learned avoidance response did not show reduced fear of the conditioned stimulus. Horne and Matson (1977) made parallel observations of college students' anxiety over tests: Although flooding did suppress their avoidance of tests, the students still thought that tests were aversive.

Mineka and Gino (1979) reported that additional flooding eliminates the fear of the CS. Also, Monti and Smith (1976) observed that response prevention produced faster extinction of the CS-induced fear than did the typical self-exposure extinction procedure. These results indicate that although flooding can eventually extinguish a fear response, the suppression of avoidance responding occurs independently of fear extinction when the flooding technique is used.

The precise mechanism responsible for the effectiveness of flooding remains unsettled. Baum suggested in 1970 that the conditioning of the relaxation response during flooding causes the elimination of avoidance responding. A study by Hawk and Ricco (1977) supports this view. They demonstrated that the introduction of a stimulus associated with the absence of shock facilitated the flooding-induced suppression of avoidance behavior; the cue associated with the absence of shock produced relaxation, and therefore enhanced conditioning of the relaxation response to the feared environment. Hussain's observation (1971) that the use of relaxing drugs increased the effectiveness of flooding also supports Baum's view. However, our earlier discussion indicated that with a moderate level of flooding treatment fear persisted even though the avoidance behavior did not occur. It may be that relaxation is responsible for the eventual elimination of fear but does not cause the suppression of avoidance behavior. An understanding of the mechanisms responsible for the success of flooding may lie in the cognitive approaches to avoidance behavior; these cognitive views are discussed in Chapter 3.

Systematic desensitization. Recall our previous discussion of the contemporary drive view of avoidance behavior in which avoidance behavior reflects both an escape response from the aversive state of anticipatory pain (fear) and an approach response to the stimuli associated with relief (or relaxation). According to this view, the presentation of a relaxing event should reduce an animal's or human's motivation to avoid by (1) *suppressing the anticipatory pain response* and (2) *eliminating the motivation to obtain relaxation (since it is already occurring).* In addition, the conditioning of relaxation to the feared environment should extinguish future avoidance response. Joseph Wolpe's systematic desensitization therapy (see Wolpe, 1958, 1969, 1973) provides support for this drive-based view of avoidance behavior. Wolpe observed that relaxation which occurred during anxiety-inducing situations reduced or extinguished the aversiveness of the situation and eliminated a person's motivation to escape from the previously feared object.

Original animal studies. Wolpe's therapy evolved from his animal research. In an initial study (see Wolpe, 1958), he shocked one group of caged cats after they heard a buzzer. For the other cats, he paired the buzzer with eating in their cages and then shocked them. Both groups of cats later showed extreme fear of the buzzer. One indication of their fear was their refusal to eat when hearing the buzzer. These results indicated to Wolpe that conflict—as proposed by Masserman in 1943—was not essential to produce neurotic reactions; Wolpe felt that human neurosis represented a classically conditioned fear response to a specific stimulus.

Since fear inhibited eating, Wolpe reasoned that eating could—if sufficiently intense—suppress fear. Also, Wolpe proposed that the repeated pairing of the reinforcing aspects of eating with the feared stimulus would cause the fear stimulus to become a permanent inhibitor rather than an elicitor of fear. The process of establishing a response which competes with a previously acquired response is called *counterconditioning*. Wolpe suggested that counterconditioning represented a potentially effective way of treating human phobic behavior. He based this idea on three lines of evidence: (1) Sherrington's statement (1906) that an animal can experience only one emotional state at a time, a process Wolpe termed *reciprocal inhibition* (refer to Chapter 4); (2) M. C. Jones's report (1924) that she had successfully eliminated a young boy's conditioned fear of rabbits by presenting the feared stimulus (a rabbit) while the boy was eating (see Chapter 1); and (3) Wolpe's own research using cats in which he employed a graduated counterconditioning process.

Wolpe's counterconditioning process worked as follows. He initially placed his phobic cats in a cage with food; this cage was quite dissimilar to their "home" cage. He used the dissimilar cage (which produced only a low level of fear from generalization) because use of the home cage would produce too intense a fear and therefore inhibit eating. Wolpe observed that his cats ate in the dissimilar cage and did not appear afraid after eating. Wolpe concluded that in the dissimilar environment the eating response had replaced the fear response. Once the fear of the dissimilar cage was extinguished, the cats were less fearful in another cage more closely resembling the feared home cage than they were before the elimination of fear in the dissimilar cage. The reason for this reduced fear is that the inhibition of fear conditioned to the dissimilar cage generalized to the second cage. The counterconditioning was now employed with this second cage, and Wolpe found that presentation of food in this cage quickly reversed the cats' fear. Wolpe continued the gradual counterconditioning treatment by slowly changing the characteristics of the test cage until the cats could eat in their home cage without any evidence of fear. Wolpe also found that a gradual exposure of the buzzer paired with food modified the cats' fear of the buzzer.

Clinical treatment. Wolpe (1958) asserted that human phobias could be eliminated in a manner similar to that which he employed with his cats. Wolpe chose not to use eating to inhibit human fears but instead used three classes of inhibitors: relaxation, assertion, and sexual responses. The discussion in this chapter is limited to the use of relaxation. (The basic procedures with assertion and sexual response are identical to those with relaxation, and their use is discussed in Chapters 6 and 8.)

Wolpe's therapy using relaxation to counter human phobic behavior is called *systematic desensitization*. Desensitization requires a patient to relax and to imagine anxiety-inducing scenes. To induce relaxation, Wolpe used a series of muscle exercises developed by Jacobson in 1938. These exercises involve tensing a particular muscle and then eliminating this tension. It is assumed that tension is related to anxiety and that reduction of tension is relaxing (or reinforcing). The patient tenses and relaxes each major muscle group in a specific sequence. Rimm and Masters (1979) indicated that relaxation is effective when the tension phase lasts approximately 10 seconds and is followed by 10 to 15 seconds of relaxation for each muscle group. The typical procedure requires about 30 to 40 minutes to complete; however, later in therapy less time is needed as the patients become able to experience relaxation more readily. Once relaxed, patients are required to think of a specific word (for example, *calm*). This procedure, called *cue-controlled relaxation* by Russell and Sipich in 1973, causes the development of a conditioned relaxation response which enables relaxation to be elicited promptly by a specific stimulus; the patient is then quickly able to inhibit any anxiety occurring during therapy.

Therapy can begin after the patient has learned to relax. The desensitization treatment consists of three separate phases: (1) *the construction of a hierarchy of fears*, (2) *the pairing of relaxation with the feared stimuli*, and (3) *an assessment of whether the patient can successfully interact with the phobic object*. In the first stage, the patients are instructed to construct a graded series of anxiety-inducing scenes related to their phobia. The level of induced anxiety must differ for the scenes; a list with 10 to 15 items of low-, moderate-, and high-anxiety scenes is typically employed. Using index cards, a patient writes descriptions of the scenes and then ranks them in a hierarchy from those which produce low anxiety to those which produce high anxiety. To provide an evaluation of the level of anxiety elicited, the therapist then reads the descriptions while the patient imagines the scenes.

Paul (1969) identified two major types of hierarchies: thematic and spatial-temporal. In *thematic hierarchies*, the scenes are related to a basic theme. Table 2.1 presents a

Table 2.1
An Example of Thematic Hierarchy of Anxiety

Level	Scene
1	You are in your office with an agent, R. C., discussing a prospective interview. The client in question is stalling on his payment, and you must tell R. C. what to do.
2	It is Monday morning and you are at your office. In a few minutes you will attend the regularly scheduled sales meeting. You are prepared for the meeting.
3	Conducting an exploratory interview with a prospective client.
4	Sitting at home. The telephone rings.
5	Anticipating returning a call from the district director.
6	Anticipating returning a call from a stranger.
7	Entering the Monday sales meeting unprepared.
8	Anticipating a visit from the regional director.
9	A fellow agent requests a joint visit with a client.
10	On a joint visit with a fellow agent.
11	Attempting to close a sale.
12	Thinking about attending an agents' and managers' meeting.
13	Thinking of contacting a client who should have been contacted earlier.
14	Thinking about calling a prospective client.
15	Thinking about the regional directors' request for names of prospective agents.
16	Alone, driving to prospective client's home.
17	Calling a prospective client.

Note: In the anxiety hierarchy, a higher level represents greater anxiety. (Higher numbers indicate higher levels.)

From: Rimm, D. C., & Masters, J. C. *Behavior therapy: Techniques and empirical findings* (2nd ed.). New York: Academic Press, 1979.

Table 2.2
An Example of Spatial-Temporal Hierarchy of Anxiety

Level	Scene
1	Four days before an examination.
2	Three days before an examination.
3	Two days before an examination.
4	One day before an examination.
5	The night before an examination.
6	The examination paper lies face down before the student.
7	Awaiting the distribution of examination papers.
8	Before the unopened doors of the examination room.
9	In the process of answering an examination paper.
10	On the way to the university on the day of an examination.

Note: In the anxiety hierarchy, a higher level represents greater anxiety. (Higher numbers indicate higher levels.)

From: Wolpe, J. *The practice of behavior therapy.* Oxford: Pergamon, 1969.

hierarchy detailing the anxiety experienced by an insurance salesman when anticipating interactions with coworkers or clients. It is an example of a thematic hierarchy; each scene in the hierarchy is somewhat different, but all are related to his fear of possible failure in professional situations. In contrast, a *spatial-temporal hierarchy* is based on a phobic behavior which has intensity determined by distance (either physical or temporal) to the feared object. The test of anxiety hierarchy shown in Table 2.2 indicates that the level of anxiety is related to the proximity (in time) of the examination.

One important aspect of the hierarchy presented in Table 2.2 needs to be mentioned. Perhaps contrary to your intuition, this student experienced more anxiety en route to the test than when actually at the test area. Others have a different hierarchy; they experience the most fear when taking the test. These observations indicate that each individual phobic response is highly idiosyncratic and dependent on one person's unique learning experience. Therefore, a hierarchy must be specially constructed for each patient. Some phobias are a combination of thematic and spatial-temporal hierarchies. For example, a person with acrophobia (fear of heights) can experience varying levels of anxiety at different heights and at different distances from the edge at these heights.

After the hierarchy is constructed, the counterconditioning phase of treatment begins. The patient is instructed to relax and imagine as clearly as possible the lowest scene on the hierarchy which the therapist is describing. Since even this scene elicits some anxiety, Rimm and Masters (1979) suggested that the first exposure be quite brief (5 seconds). The duration of the imagined scene can then be slowly increased as counterconditioning progresses. It is important that the patient not become anxious while picturing the scene; otherwise, additional anxiety rather than relaxation will be conditioned. The therapist instructs the patient to signal when anxious by raising a finger, and the therapist terminates the scene. After a scene has ended, the patient is instructed to relax. The scene can again be visualized when relaxation is reinstated. If the individual can imagine the first scene without any discomfort, the next-highest scene in the hierarchy is imagined. The process of slowly counterconditioning each level of the hierarchy is continued until the patient can imagine the most aversive scene without becoming anxious.

Clinical effectiveness.   The last phase of desensitization evaluates the success of the therapy. To demonstrate the effectiveness of desensitization, the patient is required to encounter the phobic object. The success of desensitization as a treatment of phobic behavior is quite impressive. Wolpe (1958) reported that 90 percent of 210 patients showed significant improvement with desensitization; by comparison, the rate of success with psychoanalysis was 60 percent. The comparison is more striking because desensitization produced a rapid extinction of phobic behavior (according to Wolpe, an average of 31 sessions was effective) compared with the slower cures obtained with psychoanalysis (3 to 5 years of therapy). Although Lazarus (1971) reported that some patients showed a relapse 1 to 3 years after desensitization therapy, their renewed anxiety could be readily reversed with additional desensitization. The list of phobias successfully treated or extinguished by desensitization is striking: fears of height, driving, snakes, dogs, insects, tests, water, flying, rejection by others, crowds, enclosed places, and injections are a few in a long list. In addition, desensitization apparently can be used with any behavior disorder initiated by anxiety. For instance, desensitization should be used to treat an alcoholic whose drinking occurs in response to anxiety.

Besides evaluating the effectiveness of desensitization, clinical research has determined the necessity of including relaxation or graded exposure into the desensitization treatment. In some studies (for example, Davison, 1968) no improvement was found when relaxation was not part of the desensitization process, although others (for example, Miller & Nowas, 1970) indicated that relaxation was not essential. Schubot (1966) reported that only extremely phobic individuals need relaxation. Rimm and Masters (1979) suggested that only severely phobic people and not those who are mildly afflicted seek treatment; thus relaxation should be included in the desensitization therapy. Additionally, Krapft (1967) discovered that presentation of the hierarchy of scenes in a descending order was approximately as effective as presentation in ascending order, which is typically employed. The reduction in phobic behavior with use of the descending order is not surprising; the flooding technique described earlier demonstrated that exposure to the feared stimulus is sufficient to eliminate phobic behavior. However, Rimm and Masters (1979) pointed out that intense fear is experienced if the items at the top of the hierarchy are presented first. In contrast, the generalization of relaxation occurring during the standard desensitization procedure reduces the anxiety level produced when the patient reaches the items at the top of the hierarchy. Thus, the exposure in graded ascending order is needed because it reduces the aversiveness of the therapy. Perhaps the most positive aspect of desensitization treatment is that it represents a relatively painless method of suppressing phobic behavior.

This discussion suggests an interaction of fear with relaxation; the stronger of these two emotional states determines an animal's or person's behavior. We saw a similar interplay of the emotional response produced by reward and nonreward: the approach response elicited by the anticipatory goal response contrasts with avoidance produced by the anticipatory frustration response. Rescorla and Solomon (1967) have developed a theory describing the dynamics of the interaction of appetitive and aversive states. Let us now take up their theory.

Central Motivational States

Rescorla and Solomon's theory.   Consider the following two situations: (1) You are eating lunch when you hear a fire alarm. The alarm causes you to stop eating and rush from the cafeteria. (2) You are studying for an examination to be taken tomorrow; your best friend arrives. You stop studying to chat. Both examples contain a particular element (the fire alarm in one case; the friend in the other) which suppressed one behavior and caused you to exhibit a different behavior. The fire alarm motivated you to terminate your eating and then escape from the cafeteria. In contrast, your friend acted to inhibit your studying and motivate your social behavior.

Rescorla and Solomon's motivational theory (1967) offers an explanation of these two examples. In this view, two central motivational states govern behavior. Arousal of an appetitive state motivates approach behavior; activation of an aversive state arouses avoidance behavior. Two types of conditioned stimuli stimulate the appetitive state and inhibit the aversive state. Since you associate your friend with past social reward, your friend's presence can excite the central appetitive state and suppress the aversive state as a conditioned response. Spence (1956) called this response the *anticipatory goal response;* Tarpy (1975) called it *hope.* The other conditioned stimulus activating the central appetitive motivational state and inhibiting the aversive state is one associated with the absence of an aversive event. For example, if you ran out of the cafeteria after the fire alarm had sounded, you would probably reenter when the alarm ended and attempt to locate your lunch. Rescorla and Solomon would assert that through conditioning, the termination of a stimulus (fire alarm) associated with the absence of an aversive event (fire) stimulates the appetitive state and suppresses the aversive state as a conditioned response. D'Amato (1970) termed this response an *anticipatory relief response;* Tarpy labeled it *relief.* Thus, *hope* and *relief* motivate appetitive behavior and suppress escape behavior by influencing the functioning of the two central motivational states.

Two types of conditioned stimuli also stimulate the central aversive state and inhibit the appetitive state. Since the fire alarm had been associated with fire, the alarm activated the aversive state and inhibited the appetitive state as a conditioned response in Rescorla and Solomon's view. Mowrer (1956) referred to this response as *fear;* D'Amato called it an *anticipatory pain response.* When a stimulus is associated with the absence of reward, the conditioned response produced by this stimulus is also an excitation of the central aversive state and an inhibition of the appetitive state. Amsel (1958) labeled this an *anticipatory frustration response;* Tarpy referred to it as *disappointment.* Thus, both *fear* and *frustration* stimulate avoidance behavior and suppress appetitive responding by influencing the functioning of the two central motivational states.

Interaction studies.   Many studies support Rescorla and Solomon's view that two central motivational states control instrumental behavior. To validate the theory, a study must separately classically condition a response to a specific stimulus and establish an instrumental behavior; then it must show that the presentation of that stimulus influences the instrumental behavior. Figure 2.10 presents a diagram of the behavioral predictions of Rescorla and Solomon's theory. The figure indicates the predicted direction of behavioral change produced by each type of conditioned response. For example, hope and relief should increase appetitive behavior (cells 1 and 7) and decrease aversive behavior (cells 2 and 8). Trapold and Winokur's study (1967) shows the influence which a conditioned stimulus paired with food has on instrumental appetitive bar-pressing behavior. The authors found, as predicted in cell 1, that the CS previously paired with food increased bar-pressing behavior. In contrast, Trapold and Winokur observed that another stimulus paired with the absence of food decreased the instrumental appetitive bar-press response. These results are in accord with the prediction seen in cell 3. Bolles, Grossen, Hargrave, and Duncan (1970) made a similar observation: hope increased rats' appetitive instrumental alley running; disappointment decreased it.

A study by Grossen, Kostansek, and Bolles (1969) illustrates the influence which hope (cell 2) and disappointment (cell 4) have on avoidance behavior. In the first phase of the study, they trained rats to postpone shock by running from one compartment of a

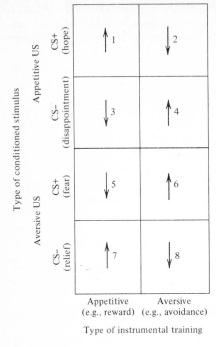

Figure 2.10
Matrix illustrating the interaction between conditioned stimuli and instrumental behavior. Arrows indicate whether the conditioned stimulus facilitates (↑) or suppresses (↓) behavior. The terms in parentheses show the conditioned emotional response elicited by a particular conditioned stimulus (Adapted from Rescorla, R. A., & Solomon, R. L. Two-process learning theory: Relationships between Pavlovian conditioning and instrumental learning. Psychological Review, 1967, 74, 151–182. Copyright 1967 by the American Psychological Association. Reprinted by permission.)

shuttle box to a second compartment and then back to the original compartment. Following the establishment of the avoidance response, they gave one group a tone paired with food and gave another group a tone with no food. Results indicated that the tone suppressed avoidance behavior when paired with food, but increased avoidance behavior when paired with no food. Apparently, the emotional response of hope inhibits an aversive instrumental behavior. Disappointment, in comparison, increases avoidance behavior.

The emotional responses (fear and relief) acquired in aversive situations also influence instrumental behavior. A study by Annau and Kamin (1961) demonstrated the effect of fear on an appetitive bar-press response. The authors observed that a stimulus previously paired with shock suppressed their rats' bar-press behavior for food. These results support the prediction of cell 5: the aversive state, when activated by a fear stimulus, suppresses appetitive behavior. In contrast to this suppression of appetitive behavior by fear, the emotional response of fear enhances avoidance behavior (cell 6). The influence of fear on avoidance behavior is exemplified in a study by Martin and Riess (1969). Following the pairing of a light with shock, these experimenters found that the conditioned light stimulus increased the level of a previously learned instrumental bar-press avoidance response. Rescorla and LoLordo (1965) demonstrated that a stimulus associated with the absence of shock suppressed an instrumental avoidance response. These results support the prediction of cell 8: the emotional relief response suppresses avoidance behavior by activating the central appetitive state. Finally, Hammond (1966) showed that a stimulus paired with the absence of shock enhanced appetitive responding for food (see cell 7).

This discussion indicates that emotional responses acquired through classical conditioning influence instrumental behavior. It should not be surprising that an appetitive emotional response (hope or disappointment) affects appetitive behavior or that an aversive emotional response (fear or relief) influences aversive behavior. What is surprising is the influence of appetitive conditioned responses on aversive behavior and aversive conditioned responses on appetitive behavior. Why should your relief, which occurred when the fire alarm stopped ringing, stimulate your return to the cafeteria and your food? Or why should your anticipation of a pleasant social evening reduce your aversive studying behavior? In asserting that two central motivational states exist, Rescorla and Solomon's theory provides an answer to these questions. The aversive state is activated by stimuli which produce fear and dissappointment, and the appetitive state is activated by stimuli which arouse hope and relief. An aversive conditioned response motivates avoidance behavior and suppresses approach behavior. On the other hand, an appetitive conditioned response initiates approach behavior and inhibits avoidance behavior. These observations suggest an antagonism between the approach and avoidance motives. The strongest support of this antagonism is perhaps the research which investigates conflict; this discussion of drive approaches to motivation concludes with an overview of this research.

Conflict. Each of us has experienced occasions on which we must choose between conflicting motives; we would like to satisfy both motives, but attaining one prevents us from attaining the other. Often, the choice is clear and the conflict easily resolved. At other times, the choice is extremely difficult and we experience considerable anxiety coping with conflicting motives.

Types of conflict. Dollard and Miller's theory (see Dollard & Miller, 1950) assumes that when two opposing goals are simultaneously pursued, conflict results. Dollard and Miller named this type of discord an *approach-avoidance conflict.* It takes place when an event contains both positive and negative aspects. For example, a person may want to date a certain man or woman but fear being rejected. Another type of conflict—an *avoidance-avoidance conflict*—occurs when we must choose between two unpleasant situations. A third conflict is the *approach-approach conflict,* which occurs when two rewarding goals are mutually exclusive. These conflicts not only are extremely unpleasant but also can be difficult to resolve. In Dollard and Miller's view, failure to resolve persistent conflict can lead to neurotic behavior—for example, excessive fear, anxiety, or depression.

Now let us focus on Miller's approach (see Miller, 1959) to the mechanisms responsible for either the success or the failure of efforts to resolve conflict. The discussion in this section is limited to approach-avoidance conflict, for it illustrates the antagonism between appetitive and aversive motives. The rules describing the resolution of an approach-avoidance conflict also apply to the other two types of conflict—approach-approach and avoidance-avoidance conflicts.

The following example illustrates the approach-avoidance conflict. A teenage girl was invited to a "boy-girl" party and told to ask a boy. Torn between her desire to invite a "special" boy and her fear of being rejected, for several days the girl would begin to dial his telephone number, only to stop before completing the call. She was quite distressed by her conflict. After some encouragement from her parents, however, she called the boy. Much to her parents' relief, he accepted her invitation. Let us now consider the process creating this girl's conflict, why she had such a problem resolving it, and why she was finally able to make her choice.

Establishing conflict. Miller (1959) developed a set of assumptions describing the establishment of approach-avoidance conflict. According to Miller, the girl's motivation to phone the boy increased the closer she came to completing her call. Thus, her tendency to approach grew as she neared her goal (see Figure 2.11). In addition, her fear of rejection increased as she came closer to that potentially aversive event. In Miller's view, since the girl's fear became stronger when she started to telephone, her motivation to escape from the situation increased during the call. However, Miller proposed that the avoidance gradient is steeper than the approach gradient. The tendency to approach and avoid will be equal at some point in the gradients, and the animal or human will be unable to decide whether or not to approach or avoid the event. The behavior in this conflict zone vacillates between approach and avoidance. The point of indecision, or conflict, depends upon the relative strengths of the approach and avoidance tendencies; the conflict can be experienced either near or far from the goal. The conflict will be experienced near the goal if the motivation to approach is stronger than the motivation to avoid; it will occur far from the goal when the motivation to avoid is more intense than the motivation to approach. No conflict will take place if there is no overlap in the gradients.

Conflict resolution.   Miller's analysis could also explain how the girl resolved her conflict. Miller suggested that the level of the gradients can be raised by changing either the strength of the motive or the number of reinforced or punished trials. If a change in motivation or learning raises one gradient enough to eliminate the conflict zone, an animal or human can then respond to the dominant motive. It is possible that the encouragement of her parents raised the girl's approach motivation enough to enable her to complete her call.

Experimental evidence.   Judson Brown's classic research (1948) supports Miller's analysis of conflict situations. Brown attached a calibrated spring to a harnessed rat in

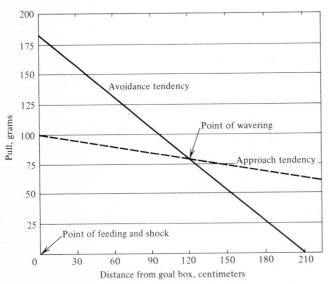

Figure 2.11
Graphic representation of approach-avoidance gradients. The rat will move toward the goal box until it reaches a point 120 centimeters from the goal. At this point—the conflict zone—the approach and avoidance tendencies will be equal and the animal will waver. If the rat is closer than 120 centimeters from the goal, it will move away from the goal, since the avoidance motivation is stronger than the approach tendency.

order to record the strength of pull toward or away from a goal. He trained some rats to run down an alley to obtain food. After the approach behavior was established, these rats were stopped either near the goal (30 centimeters away) or far from it (170 centimeters away). The strength with which the rat pulled toward the goal indicated its motivation to approach. The approach gradient (refer to Figure 2.11) illustrates the slightly greater pull close to the goal. Other rats trained in this apparatus received shock at the end of the runway. After an avoidance response was established, these rats were placed either close to or far from the aversive environment. Brown discovered that the rats pulled away with greater intensity when near to the goal than when far from it. These results demonstrate that the avoidance gradient is steeper than the approach gradient. To illustrate the conflict between the tendency to approach and the tendency to avoid, Brown first trained a third group of rats to approach food in the alley, and then shocked them when they touched the food container. Combined approach and avoidance tendencies caused the rats to run down the alley until they reached the conflict zone. At this point, the animals vacillated.

As mentioned earlier in this chapter, displaced activity (for example, grooming) is frequently observed at the decision point. However, if the level of motivation changes, one motive then controls behavior. In the situation just described, the rat may wait in the alley until its hunger increases, so that the approach motivation is strengthened throughout the entire alley. Kaufman and Miller (1949) demonstrated that conflict does not necessarily occur in approach-avoidance situations. They gave their rats more approach training than Brown's rats had received; this reduced the conflict, and the rats approached the goal box where they had previously been shocked.

SUMMARY

In this chapter we discussed two drive approaches—the ethological and Hull's drive theory—to motivation. Each view expressed the concept that behavior is motivated by an intense internal arousal, or tension, and that behavior will continue until this tension is reduced. However, the theories differ in several important ways.

The ethological approach developed by Lorenz and Tinbergen stresses the instinctive aspects of motivated behavior. According to these ethologists, a specific internal tension (or action-specific energy) exists for each major instinct. The energy accumulates constantly; an internal block prevents the release of this stored energy. The accumulation of internal energy motivates appetitive behavior which continues until a specific environmental cue called a *sign stimulus* is obtained. This sign stimulus can activate an innate releasing mechanism (IRM) to open the block. The elimination of the internal block causes the release of stored energy, and then the appropriate fixed action pattern occurs. As energy accumulates, the importance of the environmental cues for the release of the appropriate fixed action pattern diminishes. In fact, if sufficient energy accumulates, the block is bypassed and vacuum behavior occurs in the absence of an effective sign stimulus. The ethological model asserts that displacement activity is another example of behavior which occurs without a releasing stimulus.

The instinctive motivational system is not inflexible; the releasing stimuli or the instinctive behavior (or both) can sometimes be altered by experience. According to Lorenz, this adaptability is programmed into the genetic structure. In some cases, the modification involves altering the effectiveness of the existing releasing mechanism or instinctive action. At other times, new releasing stimuli, new behaviors, or both enable an animal or human to adapt.

Evolution occurs when a species incorporates additional energy or knowledge into its genetic programming through natural selection. This new energy or knowledge enhances adaptability. The evolution of social as well as physical knowledge is thought to be responsible for the great advances seen in human cultures.

The ethological view of behavior has enhanced our understanding of the instinctive basis of motivation. This influence is apparent throughout the text.

In contrast to the ethological approach stressing the instinctive aspects of motivation, Hull's drive theory emphasizes the learned aspects of motivation. Hull theorized that a nonspecific intense internal arousal, called *drive*, energizes behavior. Several stimuli (deprivation-induced, intense environmental events and hormonal changes) appear capable of innately initiating this internal drive. In addition, two types of learned motives (drive and incentive) also produce internal arousal and energize behavior. According to Hull, once arousal is induced, the specific prevailing stimulus conditions direct behavior. A specific stimulus is capable of eliciting several behaviors, and the strength of each of these stimulus-response bonds varies.

Hull thought that the behavior with the strongest bond (or habit strength) occurs when drive exists. The bond strengthens if the behavior reduces drive. However, the persistence of drive temporarily inhibits all behavior, a process called *reactive inhibition*. The continued failure of the dominant habit to produce reinforcement causes a permanent inhibition known as *conditioned inhibition*. The conditioned inhibition antagonizes the excitatory potential of the dominant habit and allows the next behavior in the habit hierarchy to be released. The success of this response leads to the establishment of a new dominant habit.

Hull's theory focuses on the unlearned or primary sources of drive and the development of habit strength; on the other hand, more recent drive theories emphasize the importance of acquired or secondary motives. Kenneth Spence developed his incentive motivation system to explain an animal's or human's approach response to reward. According to Spence, the presentation of reward elicits an unconditioned emotional response (R_G); the internal stimulus consequences (S_G) of the R_G motivate consummatory behavior. The association of environmental events with reward causes the development of a conditioned anticipatory goal response (r_G). The internal stimuli (s_G) produced by this conditioned response motivate the approach to reward. As environmental events distant from reward become capable of eliciting the r_G-s_G mechanism through higher-order conditioning, approach behavior toward the goal is activated by these cues.

Abram Amsel described another secondary motivational system to explain the influence of nonreward on behavior. According to Amsel, the presentation of nonreward in a situation previously associated with reward produces an unconditioned frustration response (R_F). The internal stimulus consequences of frustration (S_F) motivate the escape from the frustrating situation. Just as the conditioning of the r_G-s_G mechanism motivates approach behavior toward potential reward, the anticipatory frustration response mechanism (r_F-s_F), conditioned to the cues associated with unconditioned frustration, motivates avoidance of a potentially aversive frustrating situation.

Michael D'Amato proposed additional secondary motivational systems— anticipatory pain and relief—to describe the mechanism responsible for avoidance of painful events. D'Amato asserted that the classical conditioning of the anticipatory pain response mechanism (r_P-s_P) to the environmental cues associated with an aversive painful event motivates the animal or person to escape from this environment. Furthermore, the anticipatory relief response mechanism also motivates the avoidance behavior mechanism. According to D'Amato, the termination of pain produces an unconditioned relief response (R_R). The internal stimulus consequences (S_R) of relief motivate further appetitive behavior. The establishment of the anticipatory relief response mechanism

(r_R-s_R) motivates the approach to the cues associated with unconditioned relief in a manner similar to the conditioning of approach to a potential reward.

Unlike Hull's single motivational system, the research summarized by Rescorla and Solomon suggests the existence of two central motivational systems. One system motivates approach (or appetitive) behavior; the other system motivates aversive (or avoidance) behavior. The appetitive system appears to be activated by stimuli associated with either reward or the absence of adversity and inhibited by stimuli associated with the absence of reward or with aversive events. In contrast, stimuli associated with nonreward or adversity stimulate the aversive system, whereas stimuli present during reward or relief suppress the aversive state. Additionally, these two central states appear to be antagonistic; this antagonism is readily observed in approach-avoidance conflict. Chapter 4 will discuss the two biological systems—reward and punishment—which translate these conditioned emotional responses into motivated behavior.

The drive approach inspired two therapies for the treatment of human phobic behavior: flooding and desensitization. The use of flooding prevents avoidance behavior in order to extinguish a fear response. Desensitization therapy assumes that, since relaxation or relief suppresses fear, the association of relaxation with a feared stimulus should reduce phobic behavior. Each therapy appears to treat phobias successfully, although desensitization is less aversive and seems to be more effective than flooding. However, some observations regarding each therapy are inconsistent with the view that avoidance behavior exclusively reflects a drive process. These observations suggest that cognitive and biological mechanisms are also involved in avoidance motivation. We will study the role of cognitive and biological processes in avoidance as well as other motivated behavior in Chapters 3 and 4.

The drive view of motivation initially proposed by Hull and later modified and expanded by contemporary psychologists has enhanced our understanding of the emotional determinants of motivated behavior. Although the drive approach does not describe the entire motivational process, it does reflect an important influence on motivated behavior. That influence is reflected throughout the discussions of specific motivated behaviors later in this text.

COGNITIVE APPROACHES

CHAPTER 3

The insurmountable barrier

*M*athematics has always been an obstacle for Helen. Her distaste for arithmetic was evident even in elementary school: she dreaded working with numbers and soon realized that mathematics was the subject in which she earned the lowest grade. Helen's high marks in her other classes came without much effort, but she always had to struggle to earn an acceptable grade in mathematics. In college, she avoided high-level mathematics courses and chose only the courses which other students said were easy. She did well in these courses, since they resembled high school mathematics. During her junior year in college, Helen decided to major in political science. Only two B's, in mathematics, marred her superior grade record. But to earn her political science degree, Helen would have to complete a statistics course during the fall semester of her junior year. She did not. In the fall, she said that the hour of the class was not right; the next spring, she said she did not like the professor who was teaching the courses. Finally,

Helen enrolled in the statistics course during the fall of her senior year—only to drop out 3 weeks later. She could not comprehend the material, and so she had failed the first examination.

Helen knows that she cannot get her degree in political science without passing the statistics course, and only one semester remains until she is scheduled to graduate. On the other hand, she does not believe that she can pass the course. She has even begun to wonder if she is capable of exerting enough effort to attend the classes and to study the material. She has discussed her problem with her parents and friends, and they, in turn, have regularly offered encouragement. Unfortunately, their good wishes could not make her problem go away.

Yesterday, Helen learned from a friend that he had a similar problem with chemistry and that a psychologist at the university counseling center helped him overcome his "chemistry phobia." The friend suggested to Helen that the counseling center might help her, too. Helen has never considered her aversion to mathematics as a psychological problem and is reluctant to accept the idea that she might need clinical treatment. But she knows that she must decide before next week's registration whether or not to seek help at the center.

If Helen does go for help, she will learn several things. First, her fear of the statistics course is caused by her attribution of past failures to a lack of ability to perform well in mathematics. Second, on the basis of this attribution, Helen expects to fail in the future. Third, Helen expects to be unable even to attend the class regularly; her sense of incompetence in this area has been aggravated because of her recent inability to remain in the course. Later in this chapter we will examine several cognitive treatments which have successfully modified the expectations that maintain the phobic behavior of people like Helen.

THE MIND WITHIN US

In Chapter 2, we looked at the mechanistic drive approaches to motivation. Instead of the view that an intense internal force automatically motivates our behavior, many psychologists now think that cognitive processes motivate behavior. There are two classes of cognitions: *expectations* and *attributions*. Expectations have to do with our understanding of our environmental structure. Thus, in a certain environment we believe that our behavior will have a specific consequence. These expectations are based on attributions concerning our past experiences. In other words, attributions represent our beliefs about why specific events in our past have occurred.

Consider the following example, which illustrates this cognitive approach. You are a star high school baseball player who has been recently drafted by the New York Yankees. Your expectation of soon playing professional baseball motivates you to work hard in spring training. You base your expectation of future success on the attribution that ability and effort lead to success. A first-string player throughout many years of baseball, you know that you have ability; only hard work stands between your dream and playing in Yankee Stadium.

Recall the discussion of cognitive approaches to motivation which were described in Chapter 1. Although Edward Tolman proposed a cognitive view of motivation during the 1930s and 1940s, this approach was not acceptable to most psychologists. Hull's and Freud's mechanistic views represented the accepted view of motivation during that period. The cognitive views gained some acceptance during the 1950s as other psychologists expanded Tolman's original approach. However, only in the past decade has the cognitive approach represented the major motivational view in psychology. This discussion begins with Tolman's work. His research stands as a remarkable achievement; while Hull and his students were diligently working to disprove Tolman's view, he alone developed what was to become modern cognitive psychology. Later in the chapter, we'll look at the ideas and research of these contemporary cognitive psychologists.

TOLMAN'S PURPOSIVE BEHAVIORISM

Theoretical Approach

Basic principles.   Edward Tolman's view of motivation (1932, 1959) contrasts with the drive views described in Chapter 2. Tolman did not envision behavior as automatic responses to environmental events but rather believed that behavior has both direction and purpose. According to Tolman, our behavior is goal-oriented; we are motivated either to approach a particular object or to avoid a specific aversive event. In addition, we are capable of understanding the structure of our environment. There are (1) *paths leading to our goals* and (2) *tools which we can employ to obtain these goals*. Through experience, we gain an expectation of how to use these paths and tools in order to reach goals. Although Tolman used the terms *purpose* and *expectation* to describe our motivated behavior, he did not mean that we are aware of either the purpose or the direction of our behavior. He theorized that we act *as if* we expect a particular action to lead to a specific goal.

According to Tolman, not only is our behavior goal-oriented, but we expect specific outcomes to follow specific behaviors. If we do not obtain our goal, we continue to search for it and are not satisfied with a less-valued goal. Also, certain events in the environment convey information about where our goals are located. Tolman thought that we can reach our goals only after we have learned the signs leading to reward or punishment in our environment.

Tolman suggests that we do not have to be reinforced in order to learn. However, our expectations will not be translated into behavior unless we are motivated. Thus, from Tolman's perspective, we may have acquired substantial knowledge but unless we are motivated, our learning will not be evident in our behavior. Tolman proposed that motivation has two functions: (1) *it produces a state of internal tension which creates a demand for the goal object; (2) it determines the environmental features to which we will attend.* For example, if we are not hungry, we are less likely to learn where food is located than if we are starving. However, tension does not possess the mechanistic quality which it has in Hull's theory. According to Tolman, our expectations control the direction of our drives. Therefore, when we are motivated, we do not respond in a fixed, automatic, or stereotyped way to reduce our drive; rather, our behavior will remain flexible enough to enable us to reach our goal. In Tolman's view, only the end product (or goal) is fixed; the means (or behavior) necessary to reach a goal can vary.

Consider the following example to illustrate Tolman's proposal. Your goal is to clean your room. Although you typically complete this task successfully, the disarray in your room differs every day, and you do not use the same motor movements with each cleaning. Your behavior varies each time, but your knowledge of the means necessary to obtain your goal will enable your drive to be converted into successful behavior.

Motivational processes.   Tolman proposed two classes of motivators. *Deprivation conditions* produce an internal drive state which increases our demand for the goal. The value of the goal also influences the intensity of our motivations; we are more motivated to obtain a large reward than a small one. Tolman referred to the motivational qualities of a reward as *incentive motivation*. In addition, Tolman (1959) suggested that environmental events can acquire motivational properties through association with either a primary drive or a reinforcer. Suppose that a hungry child sees a cheeseburger (primary drive). According to Tolman, the ability of hunger to motivate behavior transfers to the cheeseburger. Tolman called this transference process *cathexis*, a concept he borrowed from psychoanalytic theory. As a result of cathexis, the cheeseburger is now a preferred goal object, and this child, even when not hungry, will be motivated to obtain a cheeseburger in the future. The preference for the cheeseburger is a positive cathexis. In contrast, avoiding a certain person could reflect a negative cathexis. In Tolman's opinion, association of a person with an unpleasant experience leads us to think of that person as an aversive object. Recall the discussion of conditioned drives in Chapter 2; Tolman's idea of cathexis is very similar to Hull's idea of acquired drive. Tolman's principle of belief in "equivalence" is also like Hull's concept of acquired incentive. Animals or people react to a secondary reinforcer (or subgoal) as they do to an original goal object. For instance, our motivation to obtain money reflects our belief in the equivalence of money to a desired goal object such as food.

Much research has been conducted to evaluate the validity of Hull's drive-based approach. In comparison, the research effort to validate Tolman's cognitive-oriented theory has been meager. Tolman and his students conducted several key studies providing support for his approach. The next sections examine these studies and describe what they tell us about motivated behavior. Despite the fact that the results of Tolman's studies seriously challenged some of the postulates derived from Hull's drive approach, the cognitive view was forgotten by all but a few psychologists during the 1950s and early 1960s, when the drive approach dominated American psychology. The psychologists who continued to use Tolman's cognitive approach provided more evidence for a cognitive view by describing additional cognitive processes involved in motivated behavior. The influence of this contemporary cognitive psychology which became evident in the late 1960s will be examined later in this chapter.

Empirical Support

Studies of place learning.   Tolman asserted that we expect reward to occur in a certain place and then follow the paths leading to that place. In contrast, Hull proposed that environmental cues elicit specific motor responses which have led to reinforcement in the past. How do we know which view is valid? Under normal conditions, we cannot determine whether our expectations or habits will lead us to reward. Tolman designed his studies of place learning to provide us with an answer. Consider the following story to illustrate the rationale behind Tolman's experiments. Every day you walk the same route from your dormitory to class. You can awaken 10 minutes before class and still be prompt because you take the shortest route. However, before your first class today, you have another course assignment which must be taken to a professor's office across campus. Afterwards, you will not have enough time to return to your dormitory before your first class. Although you have been to that part of the campus before, you have never gone from there to your first morning class. Necessity now causes you to use this new route. Will you arrive on time for your class? Tolman would believe that without much difficulty, you would be prompt; your prior experience with the campus has provided you with a "cognitive map." Using important landmarks as a guide, you would walk in the direction in which you expect to find your classroom. Hull's view, on the other hand, predicts that you would probably be late for class, since the responses you must use on the new route differ from those of your usual route. As we will discover next, Tolman's initial studies of place learning predict a prompt arrival; but later experiments by other psychologists have indicated that there are some conditions in which habit, not expectation, governs behavior. Let's briefly examine these studies.

T-maze experiments.   Tolman, Ritchie, and Kalish (1946) designed a study to distinguish behavior based on habitual movements from behavior based on spatial expectations. Figure 3.1 depicts their apparatus. For half of the trials, they placed the rats in place S_1; for the other trials, the rats began in place S_2. In the "place learning" condition, reward was always in the same location, but the turning response necessary to produce reward differed for each trial. In contrast, in the "response learning" condition, rats received reward in both places, but only one response—either right or left—produced reinforcement. Tolman, Ritchie, and Kalish found that all animals in the "place

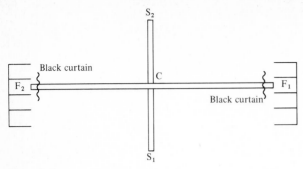

Figure 3.1
Schematic diagram of a typical apparatus for a place-learning study. The rat can start at either S_1 or S_2 and receive reward in either F_1 or F_2. (From Tolman, E. C., Ritchie, B. F., & Kalish, D. Studies of spatial learning: II. Place learning versus response learning. Journal of Experimental Psychology, *1946, 36, 221–229. Copyright 1946 by the American Psychological Association. Reprinted by permission.)*

learning" condition learned within 8 trials and continued to behave without errors for the next 10 trials. None of the rats in the "response learning" condition learned as rapidly; even after responding correctly, they continued to make errors. The results of Tolman, Ritchie, and Kalish's study illustrate that superior learning occurs when we can obtain reward in a certain place rather than by using a habit.

A second study by Tolman, Ritchie, and Kalish (1946) demonstrated that a rat will go to a place associated with reward even though an entirely new motor response is required to reach it. During the first phase of their study, they always put their rats in location S_1 and placed the reward in F_1. For the rats in this condition, both a habit (right turn) and an expectation of where food is located (F_1) produced reinforcement. During the second phase of their study, they placed the rats at location S_2. In this stage, the rats reached the goal only by turning left toward F_1; the habitual response of turning right led to an empty goal box. Tolman, Ritchie, and Kalish reported that their subjects turned left and went to F_1, the place associated with reward. These results indicate that expectancies, not habits, controlled behavior in this study.

Numerous studies have compared place learning with response learning. Many of these studies demonstrate that spatial relationships govern behavior; however, others indicate that response learning is superior to place learning. Fortunately, there are several likely reasons for these differing results. The presence of cues to guide behavior is one cause of the conflicting results (see Blodgett & McCutchan, 1947, 1948). Place learning is superior to response learning when extra cues are present to allow spatial orientation in a maze and thereby guide the rats to the correct location. Without extra cues, the animals are forced to rely on motor responses to produce reward.

Degree of experience with the task is another cause of the different results. I have sometimes experienced the following situation while driving home. Instead of turning from my typical path to run a planned errand, I continue past the turn and arrive home. Why did I follow the signs leading home rather than those leading to my errand? One likely answer is that I have driven home so often that the response has become habitual; an automatic-response process controls my behavior unless I exert considerable effort to inhibit it and take a less-habitual route. Kendler and Gasser's study (1948) indicates that well-learned behavior is typically governed by mechanistic processes rather than cognitive ones. They found that with fewer than 20 trials, rats responded to place cues; with greater training, the animals exhibited the appropriate motor response.

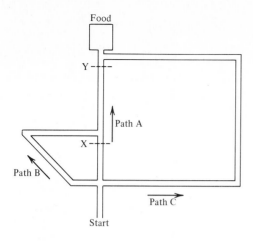

Figure 3.2
Apparatus used in Tolman and Honzik's alternative-path experiment. Obstacle Y blocks not only the shortest path A but also the middle-distance path B. With paths A and B blocked, the only available route to the goal is the longest route, path C. (From Tolman, E. C., & Honzik, C. H. "Insight" in rats. University of California Publications in Psychology, 1930, 4, 215–232.)

Alternative-path studies.   Examine the map in Figure 3.2. Let's pretend that these paths represent routes to school. Which path would you choose? In all likelihood, you would typically use path A, the shortest path. However, what would you do if path A was blocked at point Y? If you were behaving according to spatial knowledge, you would choose path C. Even though path C is longer than path B, your cognitive map would produce the expectation that B is also blocked and thus motivate the choice of C. In contrast, a drive interpretation predicts that you would choose B, since it represents the second dominant habit. Path C is your choice if you behave like the rats in Tolman and Honzik's study (1930a). In this study, the animals were familiar with the entire maze but usually chose path A to reach the goal. However, most rats chose path C when path A was blocked at point Y. These results point out that knowledge of our environment, rather than blind habit, often influences our behavior.

Although other psychologists have replicated Tolman and Honzik's study (see Calwell & Jones, 1954), animals have not always chosen path C. For example, Keller and Hill (1936) discovered that changing the width of the alleys caused their rats to respond according to habit and choose the blocked path. Unfortunately, there has been no definitive evaluation of why the blocked path is sometimes chosen. We can conclude from the foregoing discussion that the salience of cues leading to reward and the degree of experience with the paths probably determine the processes controlling our behavior; if we are attentive to paths leading to reward and the paths have not been employed frequently, expectations rather than habits will determine our action.

Studies of response alteration.   Suppose that your car has stalled 3 miles from school. Could you walk to school, even though you have always driven? The drive and cognitive approaches predict different outcomes. Changes in both the environmental stimuli and the motor responses which occur when you switch from driving to walking should, according to a drive view, lead to a difficult trip. However, since the paths leading to reward are not altered, a cognitive view suggests that you will have no problem with your walk. The results of several studies support Tolman's cognitive approach. Let's look at several of these experiments.

Macfarlane (1930), one of Tolman's students, filled a maze with several inches of water and then trained his rats to swim through the maze to obtain a reward (food). After the rats had learned to go through without errors, Macfarlane drained the maze. This change altered the stimulus characteristics of the maze (for example, the floor was now solid) and the motor response (walking instead of swimming) necessary to obtain the reward. But Macfarlane did not change the spatial design of the maze; the same paths led to reward in both mazes. Macfarlane reported that his rats encountered no difficulty with the altered maze. Apparently, the cognitive map acquired in the water maze was still valid in the dry maze. In an interesting variation of these studies of altered responses, McNamara, Long, and Wike (1956) initially gave their rats a ride on a small cart which went through a maze. Later, they found that their rats experienced no difficulty walking through the maze to obtain a reward.

Is reinforcement necessary for learning?   Recall the discussion of the law of effect in Chapter 1. According to Thorndike, S-R associations are established when the response leads to a satisfying state of affairs. Hull (1943) expanded Thorndike's early view and asserted that habit strength increases when a particular response decreases the drive state. Tolman (1932) felt that reinforcement is not necessary for learning to occur; the simultaneous experiencing of two events is sufficient. In Chapter 2 you learned about the development of the incentive motivation process initially detailed by Hull in 1952 and then later described by Spence in 1956. The research of Tolman and his students strongly influenced the concept of incentive motivation. The next section examines Tolman's experiments and then points out how the drive and cognitive approaches have explained them.

   Studies of latent learning.   Tolman felt that knowledge of the spatial characteristics of an environment can be acquired merely by exploring the environment. Reinforcement is not necessary for the development of a cognitive map; reward influences behavior only when we are required to use that information to obtain it. Tolman distinguished between learning and performance by asserting that reward motivates behavior but does not affect learning.
   Tolman and Honzik's classic study (1930b) directly assessed the importance of reinforcement on learning and performance. Tolman and Honzik assigned their subjects to one of three conditions: (1) Rats in the HR group were hungry and always received reinforcement (food) in the goal box of a 22-unit maze. (2) Rats in the HNR group were hungry but never received reward in the goal box. (3) Rats in the HNR-R group were hungry, were not rewarded until the eleventh trial, and thereafter continued to be rewarded on subsequent trials. Tolman and Honzik found that animals rewarded on each trial (the HR group) showed a steady decrease in the number of errors during training, whereas animals which were not rewarded (the HNR group) showed little imporvement in their performance (see Figure 3.3). Does this failure of the unrewarded rats to perform indicate a failure to learn? Or have the unrewarded rats developed a cognitive map which they are not motivated to use? The behavior of the rats which did not receive a reward until the eleventh trial answers this question. Since the development of a habit was envisioned by Hull (1943) as a slow process, animals in the HNR-R group should have showed a slow decline in errors when the reward began. However, if learning had already occurred by trial 11 and all these rats lacked was motivation, they should have performed well on trial 12. The results indicate that on trial 12 and all subsequent trials, there was no difference in performance between animals in the HR group (which were always rewarded) and the HNR-R group (which were rewarded only beginning at trial 11). Apparently, HNR-R animals were learning during the initial trials although they did not receive any apparent reinforcement.
   The studies of latent learning presented the Hullian drive view with a problem. To

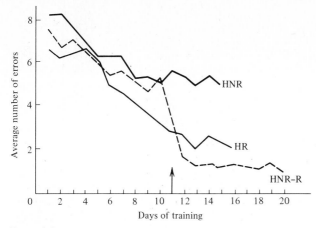

Figure 3.3
Results of Tolman and Honzik's latent-learning study. Animals in the HNR group received no reward during the experiment; those in the HR group received reward throughout the study; and those in the HNR-R group received reward only from day 11 through day 20. (From Tolman, E. C., & Honzik, C. H. Degrees of hunger; reward and nonreward; and maze learning in rats. University of California Publications in Psychology, 1930, 4, 241–256.)

deal with it, many drive-oriented psychologists initially attempted to show that latent learning was not a real phenomenon. When it became clear that latent learning can be reliably produced under some conditions, the drive view was modified to explain it. Next are discussed the conditions under which latent learning will or will not occur; following is a description of the changes brought about by Tolman and Honzik's studies.

MacCorquodale and Meehl (1954) reported that 30 of 48 studies were able to replicate latent learning. Although latent learning appears to be a real phenomenon, there are some conditions when it is likely to occur and other circumstances when it probably will not occur. MacCorquodale and Meehl observed that latent learning was typically found when reward was present for nondeprived animals during initial trials and motivation was introduced during later trials with the same reward. However, latent learning was not typically found when the reward present during the initial trials was irrelevant to the motivation existing at that time and became relevant only during later trials. These results suggest that a motivated animal will ignore the presence of a potent but irrelevant reward; thus, the results agree with Tolman's belief that motivation narrows an animal's attention to those cues which are salient to its motivational state.

Johnson's study (1952) provides direct support for this interpretation. Johnson varied the level of deprivation during initial exploration in a T-maze and found that as deprivation increased, the likelihood of observing latent learning decreased. Apparently, we will learn about the general aspects of our environment unless our motivation restricts our attention to some specific part of it.

The drive response. Although Hull's view (1943) was that drive reduction is necessary before learning can occur, the most consistent latent learning occurs when the animal is not deprived when it is initially exposed to reward. The r_G-s_G mechanism, described in Chapter 2, was developed to explain the results of these studies of latent learning. The anticipatory goal response (r_G-s_G) is established during initial exposure with reward but is not apparent until the motivating influence of deprivation is added. There are studies of latent learning—the original study by Tolman and Honzik is one example—in which no obvious reward is employed. However, the nonrewarded animals in those studies do show a slight improvement in their performance, which has indicated to advocates of the drive view (see Kimble, 1961) that reward was present for these animals. It has been suggested that handling the animals or removing them from the strange maze and returning them to the familiar home cage sometimes represents sufficient reward to establish the r_G-s_G mechanism during initial nonreward. The inconsistent results found with Tolman and Honzik's procedure provide support for this conclusion. Although the studies of latent learning did not alter the dominance of the drive view, they definitely changed its character.

Not every reward will do. Often after playing outside, my oldest son is thirsty. However, unless juice or a soft drink is available, he will not drink anything. Although water will satisfy his thirst, he is motivated to obtain a specific reward and does not find a less desirable reward satisfactory.

My oldest son's behavior is an example of Tolman's assertion that we are often motivated to obtain a specific reinforcer. If we do not receive it, we will not accept a less valued reinforcer, and we will continue to act until we obtain the desired reward. Many animal studies demonstrating the incentive motivational process have been reported since Tinklepaugh's study (1928; see Chapter 1 of this text). In Tinklepaugh's study, monkeys learned to obtain a banana by choosing the container which had a banana under it. The subsequent placement of a piece of lettuce, rather than a banana, under the correct container produced a typical response: the monkeys refused to eat the lettuce, a food less preferred than bananas, and continued to search the room for the expected banana. Sometimes the monkeys seemed quite disturbed by the absence of their expected banana and shrieked at the experimenters to indicate their displeasure. The behavior of these monkeys closely resembles my oldest son's negative response to water.

Recall the discussion of frustration in Chapter 2. We saw that the absence of an anticipated reward produces the aversive emotional state of frustration. Frustration can motivate avoidance of a less preferred reward and continued search for the desired reinforcer. Therefore, like latent learning, motivation for a specific reward can be incorporated into drive theory.

An Overview

Edward Tolman believed that the expectation of future reward or punishment motivates our behavior. He also believed that this behavior is guided by our knowledge of the paths and tools which lead us to obtain the reward or avoid the punishment. Research designed by Tolman and his students did not provide conclusive evidence for his cognitive approach, but it did force major changes in Hull's drive view. The idea that a conditioned anticipation of reward motivates us to approach a goal is clearly similar to Tolman's view that our expectation of reward motivates behavior which we believe will obtain it. However, once these changes were made, most psychologists ignored Tolman's cognitive view, and the drive view of motivation continued to be generally accepted. A few psychologists continued the cognitive tradition in the 1950s and 1960s; and as problems developed with the drive approach, the cognitive view gained wider approval. Psychologists began to use a cognitive approach to explain various forms of motivated behavior. Evidence of the value of this approach appears throughout this text. In the next two sections of this chapter we'll examine a contemporary cognitive view of motivation. Later in the chapter a cognitive explanation of human phobic behavior will be explored to illustrate one example of the cognitive approach.

EXPECTANCY-VALUE THEORY

Cognitive approaches emphasize the importance of sensory information on motivated behavior. According to these views, the way in which we interpret environmental stimuli plays an important role in determining our actions. This active interaction with the environment contrasts with the mechanistic view of the passive reception of environmental events. Neisser (1966) proposed that stimuli do not automatically elicit behavior but rather represent a source of information about our environment. We process this information into beliefs about the nature of the physical stimuli in the environment. These beliefs act to guide our actions but do not impulsively motivate our behavior. The contemporary cognitive views are similar to Tolman's view, described previously in this chapter. Besides providing additional evidence that expectations guide our motivated behavior, recent cognitive theories have expanded Tolman's general framework to explain how we form the beliefs which motivate our behavior.

Psychological investigations have revealed two components of the cognitive process that governs motivated behavior: *expectations* and *attributions*. Our expectations represent the anticipated consequences of our behavior and a perceived ability or inability to exhibit a particular behavior. Attributions reflect our belief in why we acted in a particular way as well as our perceived understanding of the relationship between our behavior and the consequences of our actions. Whereas expectations guide our behavior, attributions determine the character of our expectations. The following example illustrates the distinction between expectations and attributions. I plan to take my family to the movie *Star Wars III* when it is released, and I expect to enjoy the film. I do not expect any conflicts to prevent me from going, and my expectation of reward undoubtedly motivates me. Why do I expect a movie I have not seen to be enjoyable? I saw *Star Wars I* and *Star Wars II* and liked them both. I attribute my enjoyment of them to a liking for science fiction and to my perceived expectation that they would be quality films. Since the new movie will employ the same director and cast, and since my taste for science fiction has existed for years, my attributions of why I enjoyed *Star Wars I* and *II* represent the basis for my generalized expectation of future enjoyment.

The following discussion of contemporary cognitive approaches begins with expectancy-value theory, and then the attribution process is described.

Rotter's Approach

Julian Rotter's social-learning theory (1954) was based on Tolman's cognitive approach. Rotter expanded Tolman's view by describing the types of expectations we develop. In addition, his interest in clinical psychology led Rotter to describe how certain expectations can lead to pathological behavior.

Basic tenets.   There are five ideas expressed in Rotter's expectancy theory. *First, Rotter suggested that our preference for a particular event is determined by its reinforcement value.* According to Rotter, the value of a particular event is relative; its value reflects a comparison with other events. Thus, some of us may find an event highly reinforcing because we have not experienced many similar reinforcing events; but people who have experienced many reinforcing events may not find it as reinforcing. Perhaps the high reinforcement value which I placed on the *Star Wars I* and *Star Wars II* reflects an absence of quality in other films rather than a high artistic level in *Star Wars I* and *II*. Rotter also suggested that a reinforcer can change its value when new reinforcers are introduced. A restaurant you have valued may lose its appeal when compared with a new and better restaurant.

The second component of Rotter's expectancy-value theory is that each person has a subjective expectation concerning the likelihood of obtaining a particular reinforcer. We believe that there is a specific probability of reaching a desired goal which may not actually reflect reality. For example, you may believe that someone whom you like will not accept your dinner invitation, even though he or she would, in fact, go if you extended an invitation. The actual probability that the event will occur does not influence your behavior; you simply will not ask, since the expected probability is low. Thus, in Rotter's view, even if you are motivated, you will not behave if you do not expect reward. Attractive women who are not asked for dates because men expect to be rejected are another example of the influence of belief on motivated behavior.

The third aspect of Rotter's expectancy-value theory is that our expectation of obtaining reinforcement is determined by the situation. We may expect to receive a reward in one setting but not in another. Our past experiences determine this situational dependence; we acquire the expectation that a particular goal is more likely to occur under some circumstances than under others. For example, suppose that you have a strong preference for Italian food. You would then be more likely to expect reward in an Italian restaurant than a French one. Your relative expectations act to guide your behavior: if you had to choose, you would be more likely to choose the Italian restaurant.

Yet there are some occasions when we encounter a new experience. How do we respond to new events? *According to Rotter, generalized expectations from past experiences guide our actions.* Recall your initial feelings when you were a college freshman. You had never attended college and, therefore, had no direct experience upon which to base your expectations. Under these circumstances, your past expectations governed your behavior. Since you probably did well in high school, a generalized expectation of success motivated you to attend college.

Finally, Rotter's theory proposes that our behavior potential determines the likelihood that we will act in a particular way. Our behavior potential represents our expectation of obtaining reward in a particular situation and the value of that reward to us. In Rotter's view, we can predict our behavior if we multiply our expectation of reward by our valuation of the reward. This mathematical formula has proved useful in describing and predicting motivated behavior. Its application will be discussed in the chapters describing specific motivated behaviors later in this text.

Origins of psychopathology.   Rotter thought that unrealistic expectations often cause psychological disturbance. For example, if we expect that airplanes we ride will crash, we will avoid riding airplanes. Therefore, our phobia reflects an unrealistic expectation that airplanes are dangerous. One frequently occurring expectation leading to pathological behavior is a belief that a highly valued reinforcer has a low probability of being obtained. Consider the following example to illustrate Rotter's view. A student who wants to be admitted to law school does not expect to be admitted. This expectation not only causes the student to avoid applying to law school but also produces depression because of a perceived inability to obtain a highly valued reward. Therefore, the expectation motivates the student not to behave, and it ensures the development of his or her psychopathology.

According to Rotter, a clinical psychologist must modify a disturbed person's cognitions before treatment can permanently modify the psychopathology. The therapist must focus on altering both the person's expectations and the value he or she places on specific rewards. For example, a person whose depression is caused by an expectation that no member of the opposite sex will accept a date needs to be shown that this expectation is incorrect. Showing this depressed person similar people who have dated is one method of altering the incorrect expectation. Additionally, the depression could be caused by expecting a certain attractive person not to accept the date. Treatment of this depressed person will either provide the behavioral skills necessary to obtain reward (the date) or lower the reward value of the desired date, which results in the person's now attempting to locate acceptable alternative dates. Later in this chapter, we'll see how expectations lead to phobias and how clinical psychologists have modified the expectations which maintain phobic behavior. Cognitive approaches to modifying other behavioral disturbances will be addressed in other chapters.

Locus of control. Suppose that you would like to receive a high grade on your examination next week. Do you expect hard work to result in attaining this goal? Or do you feel that luck is necessary? According to Rotter (1966), if the first question describes your view, then you exhibit an *internal expectation.* An internal expectation represents your belief that obtaining your goal depends upon your own actions. Thus, your expectation that hard work brings success will motivate you to spend long hours studying for the test. However, you will not study much if you believe that luck will determine your grade. Rotter refers to this type of cognition as an *external expectation.* When you have an external expectation, you believe that events are beyond your control. For example, you are exhibiting an external expectation if you assume that luck, chance, or the power of others is responsible for you attaining a desired reward; since you believe there is little connection between your behavior and the reward, you will make no effort to obtain reinforcement.

There are environmental situations in which each expectation is appropriate. In tasks involving skills, you can obtain reward by exhibiting the appropriate ability. Chance tasks, in contrast, do not rely on any specific behavior for reward. Many of us are aware of the distinction between external and internal expectations and exhibit different expectations in each type of setting. In situations involving skill, we assume that our behavior can enable us to obtain reward. When we are successful in such tasks, we increase our expectation of future success; failure, on the other hand, often causes us to decrease our expectation of future reward. Our response during situations involving chance is quite different: since we assume that reward occurs independently of our actions, we are not likely to change our expectations of future reward following either success or failure.

A study by Phares (1957) illustrates the influence of success and failure on our expectations in situations involving skill or chance. Phares placed his subjects in an ambiguous setting and provided them information which indicated that they were participating in either a situation involving skill or one involving chance; but in fact all the subjects were dealing with a task based on chance. During the course of the study, the subjects received random experiences of success and failure. Before each trial, the subjects were asked to indicate how many chips they wanted to bet on their performance on the next trial. Phares assumed that the subjects' bets reflected their expectations of future successes or failures. He reported that subjects who believed they were in situations involving skill increased their bets after success and decreased them after failure. In contrast, the subjects who believed they were in a setting involving chance were unlikely to change their bets after either succeeding or failing. Phares' study is important for two reasons. First, he obtained the predicted differences in expectations between situations involving skill and those involving chance. Second, these differences occurred even though none of the subjects really had control over the attainment of reward. A belief in our ability to control events—not the actual contingencies which exist in our environment—determines our motivated behavior. Therefore, if our inappropriate actions are to be altered, our expectations must also be changed.

It is most appropriate for us to perceive each situation separately. We should attempt to obtain reward in settings where skill is important but either avoid or cope differently with situations in which success or failure occurs independently of our actions. However, many people show a generalized expectation by treating all situations alike. In Rotter's view, internally oriented persons believe that success or failure is caused by their own skills. Externally oriented persons, on the other hand, assume that they have no control over their fate. Rotter coined the term *locus of control* to refer to our generalized expectation that either internal or external factors control our behavior.

Rotter developed a personality test to indicate our degree of *internality* or *externality*. The test consists of 32 binary-choice questions. One alternative in each question reflects an internal orientation; the other alternative represents an external orientation. A person being tested receives a point for each external choice, and the total score reflects this person's locus of control. A high score on the I-E (internal-external) scale indicates an external person; a low score indicates an internal person.

The evidence indicates that internals typically act differently from externals. For example, Seeman and Evans (1962) found that internals suffering from tuberculosis not only asked their doctors more questions concerning their disease, but also were more knowledgeable about tuberculosis than externals were. Furthermore, internals evidently know more about critical political events than externals do (Ryckman & Sherman, 1976). Since internals, but not externals, believe that they can influence their successes and failures, it is not surprising that internals should be more interested than externals in obtaining information from the environment which can enable them to be successful.

Our locus of control also influences our actions in social settings. Lefcourt (1971) found that internals are more apt than externals to make independent judgments; externals tend to comply with social pressures exerted by others. Internals, believing that their actions can influence the behaviors of others, attempt to manipulate people more than externals do (Phares, 1965).

Overview.   Rotter developed his expectancy theory during a period when most psychologists were advocating a drive view of motivated behavior. In contrast to the idea that tension automatically motivates behavior, Rotter proposed that we act in a certain manner if we expect to receive a specific reward. The drive approach portrays us as responding to the environmental stimuli impinging upon us. Rotter's expectancy view assumes that our cognitions determine our motivated behavior. The idea that we are passive recipients of environmental stimuli and internal pressures contrasts sharply with Rotter's view that we play an active role in determining our actions. Although the drive approach continues to describe some aspects of the motivation process, the research of Julian Rotter and his associates indicates that a cognitive process also plays an important role in governing our behavior.

Expectancy and Animal Learning

Researchers using animal subjects have also provided evidence supporting an expectancy view. Much of this research does not directly validate a cognitive approach; rather, by rejecting the mechanistic reinforcement view, the results of these studies make a cognitive view more viable. However, some results indicate that animals play an active rather than a passive role in their interactions with the environment; this observation provides direct support for a cognitive approach to motivation. Robert Bolles, having reviewed this literature, developed a cognitive view which expands Tolman's earlier theory and is similar to Rotter's expectancy theory. The main difference between Bolles's approach and the views of Tolman and Rotter is that Bolles details the types of expectations which we develop. This section briefly describes Bolles's view and the research supporting his expectancy approach to motivation.

Basic principles.   Bolles (1972, 1979) proposed that during our interaction with our environment, two types of expectations develop which guide us to reinforcement. Bolles called the first type of expectation an *S-S* expectation.* According to Bolles, many environmental events (S) are present when a biologically important event (S*), such as food or shock, occurs. However, a particular event (S₁) happening simultaneously with the S* does not mean that we will expect S* when we encounter S₁. Bolles felt that S₁ must reliably predict the occurrence of S* in order for the S₁-S* expectation to develop. Contiguity, in Bolles's view, is not sufficient for learning: events must consistently occur together before we can acquire an S-S* expectation. Additionally, when two or more stimuli are present with S*, only the most reliable predictor of S* will become associated with it.

Bolles referred to the second type of expectation as an *R-S* expectation.* An R-S* expectation reflects our understanding of the response or responses which are necessary to produce reward or avoid punishment. Although R-S* expectations can be acquired through experience, Bolles stressed the importance of innate expectations which govern motivated behavior. Our R-S* expectations do not necessarily reflect the contingencies in the environment; we must believe that a specific response leads to reinforcement or prevents punishment. Although there are some conditions in which the attainment of reward or the presentation of an aversive event takes place independently of our behavior, in most circumstances reinforcements or aversive events depend upon our exhibiting a specific response. Under these conditions, our S-S* expectations predict the potential occurrence of a biologically important event, and our R-S* expectations lead us to the predicted goal—either the presence of an appetitive event (for example, food) or the prevention of an aversive event (for example, shock).

Consider the following example to illustrate Bolles's view of an S-S* and an R-S* expectation. Having refused to go to bed, a boy receives a spanking from his father. This father uses a belt to administer the punishment. Does the child expect to be spanked when his father removes the belt? If the boy usually sees his father remove his belt only before a spanking, the boy probably will expect a spanking (S*) when he sees the belt (S₁) being removed. The child's expectation of punishment activates the R-S* expectation which the child believes will prevent the spanking: the child starts to cry when his father removes the belt. Although not always effective, crying has frequently prevented spankings; the child's past experiences cause him to expect that crying (R) will prevent him from being punished (S*). The next section briefly examines research indicating that cues which are both reliable and consistent predictors of biologically important events guide our motivated behavior, while our R-S* expectations determine our behavior.

Studies of cue predictability.   Bolles's approach suggests that the predictive value of an event determines its ability to guide behavior. When a cue is consistently paired with an important event but does not reliably predict the occurrence of the event, the presentation of this cue will not have any effect on motivated behavior.

Robert Rescorla's research (1968) demonstrates the importance of cue predictability on our behavior. After his rats learned to press a bar for food, Rescorla divided the 2-hour training sessions into 2-minute segments. In each segment, (1) a distinctive cue (CS; tone) was paired with a shock (UCS), or (2) shock was presented without the distinctive cue, or (3) nothing happened. Rescorla varied the likelihood that the shock would occur with or without the tone in each 2-minute segment. He found that the tone suppressed bar pressing for food when the tone reliably predicted shock. However, the influence of the tone on the rats' behavior diminished as the frequency of experiencing shock without the tone increased. The tone had no effect on bar pressing when the shock occurred as

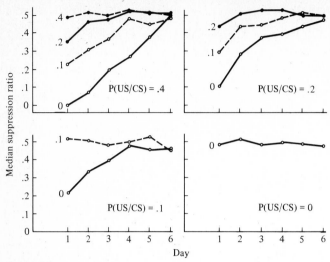

Figure 3.4
Suppression of bar-pressing behavior during six test sessions (a low value indicates that the CS suppressed bar pressing for food reward). The panels present the probability that the CS and UCS will occur in the 2-minute segment. The values within each panel indicate the probability that the UCS will occur without the CS. Notice that when the two probabilities are equal, the CS does not influence behavior. Only when the UCS occurs more frequently with the CS than without it does the CS suppress bar-pressing behavior. (From Rescorla, R. A. Probability of shock in the presence and absence of CS in fear conditioning. Journal of Comparative and Physiological Psychology, 1968, 66, 1–5. Copyright 1968 by the American Psychological Association. Reprinted by permission.)

frequently in the absence of the tone as it did when the tone was present. Figure 3.4 presents the results of Rescorla's study.

One important aspect of Rescorla's data is that even with only a few pairings, the presentation of the tone had a strong influence on motivated behavior if the biologically important event occurred only with the tone. However, when the shock occurred without the tone as frequently as with it, no conditioning was found even with a large number of tone-shock pairings. Apparently, the predictability, not the number of CS-UCS pairings, determines the ability of an environmental event to guide motivated behavior. Other investigators have documented the importance of cue predictability on our behavior; refer to a study by Bolles, Uhl, Wolfe, and Chase (1975) for another example.

Studies of cue blocking. In order for a cue to influence motivated behavior, Bolles suggested that it must not only predict the occurrence of an important event but also provide more reliable information than other cues present in the environment. The classic research of Leon Kamin (1968) demonstrates that the presence of a predictive cue will prevent, or *block*, the development of a predictive relationship between a second cue paired with a biologically important event. To demonstrate the importance of relative cue predictability, Kamin presented all his subjects (rats) with a distinctive cue (S_1, a light) paired with a shock (S^*) eight times during the first phase of the study. In the second phase of the study, the animals in the experimental group received eight exposures to the light (S_1), a new cue (S_2, a tone), and shock (S^*). Kamin observed that although presentation of the light (S₁) suppressed bar pressing for food reinforcement, the tone cue (S₂) had no influence on it. He gave the animals in the control group only tone (S₂)-shock pairings during the second phase of the study and noticed that strong suppression was caused by the tone (S₂).

Why did the tone suppress motivated behavior in the control animals but not in the experimental animals? Kamin (1969) offered two possible explanations. His first explanation was that the presence of the predictable light cue (S₁) caused the experimental group not to attend the tone (S₂). In the absence of the light, the control group paid attention to the tone and associated its presence with shock. A study by Wagner (1969) showed that animals in the "blocking" condition were aware of the presence of the tone but did not use this information. Wagner reported that when the light and tone cues together predicted no shock, the tone cue developed the ability to inhibit avoidance behavior.

Kamin's second explanation assumed that when animals first experience shock, they are surprised. *Surprise* causes them to associate a light cue with shock; learning, according to Kamin, occurs only when they are surprised. After conditioning, encountering the light cue causes no surprise. Since the light produced an expectation of shock in Kamin's experimental animals, the tone was not experienced when they were surprised, and therefore the tone did not develop the ability to motivate behavior.

A series of studies by Wagner, Rudy, and Whitlow (1973) demonstrates that conditioning occurs only when rats experience an unexpected (or surprising) event. One of their studies illustrates the importance of surprise in the development of S-S* expectation. In the first stage of the study, all of the animals received a series of paired presentations: tone with shock and vibration with no shock. In the second phase, either a surprising or a nonsurprising event followed light-shock pairings. A surprising event was either tone without shock or vibration with shock; a nonsurprising event was the same as either of the experiences (tone with shock or vibration with no shock) which had occurred in the first phase. Wagner, Rudy, and Whitlow found that the light cue developed the ability to suppress behavior when it was followed by an unexpected event; however, the light cue could not influence motivated behavior when an expected event followed light-shock pairings.

Why is surprise critical for the development of S-S* expectations? A cognitive view (refer to Bolles, 1979) suggests that surprise indicates to us that a new biologically important event has taken place. When surprised, we acquire new S-S* expectations in order to predict future biologically important events. An expected event, in contrast, does not arouse our surprise. Without surprise, new stimuli do not become associated with biologically important events; we do not need to develop new S-S* expectations when we are not surprised by the occurrence of expected events.

Superstitious behavior.   My youngest son's Little League baseball manager wears the same outfit to every game. He claims that it brings him good luck, although its value is questionable if you consider his team's record. This manager's actions exemplify *superstitious behavior*. Superstitious behavior can be defined as the actions of people who behave as if a relationship exists between their behavior and reinforcement when, in fact, no causal relationship exists.

The nature of superstitious behavior.   Does superstitious behavior reflect a habitual response which develops through coincidental reinforcement, or is it an expectation that our behavior will produce reinforcement? Skinner's description (1948) of pigeons' superstitious behavior seems to indicate an automatic response. All of Skinner's pigeons developed superstitious behavior when food was delivered at 15-second intervals, and the frequency of superstitious behavior increased as the pigeons received more reinforcements. The pattern of superstitious behavior differed from pigeon to pigeon: some walked in circles between food presentations; others scratched on the floor, while still others moved their heads back and forth.

Recent investigations seem to support a cognitive view of the motivational basis of superstitious behavior (refer to Bolles, 1978). Staddon and Simmelhag (1971) found that two different types of behavior are produced when reward (for example, food) is programmed on a regular basis: (1) *Terminal behavior* occurs during the last few seconds of the interval between food presentations, and it is reward-oriented. For example, their pigeons pecked on or near the food hopper which delivered food. (2) *Interim behavior*, in contrast, is not reward-oriented. Although contiguity influences the development of instrumental behavior, interim behavior does not occur contiguously with reinforcement. Terminal behavior falls between interim behavior and reward but does not interfere with the exhibition of interim behavior. The strange superstitious behavior described initially by Skinner is only one example of interim behavior. Animals exhibit a variety of other behaviors when reward occurs regularly (Staddon & Ayers, 1975). For example, Falk (1969) found that rats drink excessive amounts of water when they are allowed access to water on a fixed interval schedule of reinforcement. This excessive drinking is called *schedule-induced polydipsia.* Some other excessive behaviors produced by interval schedules of reward are grooming, running, and nest building.

Autoshaping.   What do animals or people expect to obtain from either terminal or interim behavior? The idea that terminal behavior produces reward is reasonable. However, this expectation does not have to be realistic. Research on *autoshaping* provides evidence that it is our belief that a specific behavior produces reward which motivates our behavior even when, in fact, no relationship exists between our actions and reinforcement. Brown and Jenkins (1968) discovered that the presentation of free-food reward at 15-second intervals produced quicker development of a key-peck response for food reinforcement in pigeons than did the traditional successive-approximation, or shaping, procedure detailed by Skinner (see Chapter 1). Brown and Jenkins named this self-shaping procedure *autoshaping.* Williams and Williams's (1969) study indicates that pigeons peck at a lighted key when they expect food; the lighted key indicates that food is available. Williams and Williams reported that the presentation of the cue which signaled food motivated the pigeons to peck at the key even though pecking reduced their reward.

Animal misbehavior.   According to Bolles (1979), autoshaping represents an example in which instinctive (R-S*) expectations can prevent the development of environmentally accurate expectations. For example, pigeons' instinctive expectation that pecking will produce food if food is available prevents them from learning that food will occur if they withhold pecking. Breland and Breland (1961) have detailed cases in which instinctive expectations interfere with learning. The Brelands, interested in training animals to perform exotic circus acts, found the Skinnerian shaping procedure ineffective in developing some behaviors. One example is presented here, and you may refer to the Brelands's article for other cases. The Brelands attempted to train raccoons to pick up two coins, walk across a stage, and deposit the money in a piggy bank. Although they were quite successful in training the raccoons to pick up a single coin and deposit it, they never trained the raccoons to pick up two coins and deposit them in the bank. The behavior of the raccoons when they reached the bank was quite intriguing: they rubbed the coins together and attempted to eat them. Finding the coins inedible, the raccoons threw the money away and did not deposit it in the bank. The Brelands called this inability to train a specific behavior by using the presumably effective reinforcement techniques outlined by Skinner an example of *animal misbehavior*.

Bolles (1972) suggested that animal misbehavior occurs because instinctive expectations prevent the development of environmentally effective R-S* expectancies. Consider the raccoons whose food was presented after they had deposited a single coin during the initial stages of training. The pairing of food with the bank created the expectation that food was available at the bank. Raccoons instinctively rub their food together before eating it; the instinctive response of the Brelands's raccoons to the expectation of food prevented reinforcement from having any influence on their behavior.

Can animals tell time? Although the discussion so far indicates that terminal behavior can be attributed to the inaccurate belief that a specific behavior produces reward, interim behavior appears to reflect a different type of expectation. When reward is programmed to be available after a specified interval of time, it is adaptive for an animal or person to be able to inhibit instrumental responding until the end of the interval and then respond when reward becomes available. An animal's behavior on a fixed-interval schedule indicates that such an effective timing mechanism exists. For example, after having received reward, rats stop pressing the bar; but they slowly increase their responding as the time approaches when reward will again be available (see Figure 3.5). In addition, the interval between responses increases with experience until responding only begins close to the end of the interval. Several lines of evidence point to the idea that interim behavior functions to aid timing ability: (1) The length of the interval between rewards governs the level of interim behavior; as the interval increases, the amount of interim behavior also increases. For example, Falk (1967) observed greater polydipsia when the fixed interval was increased up to 3 minutes. (2) Timing behavior is

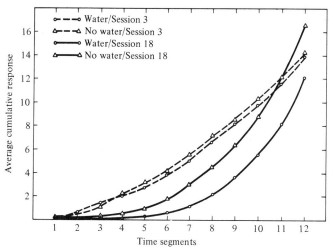

Figure 3.5
Cumulative bar-press responses during segments of a fixed-interval 1-minute schedule. Early in training (session 3) responding was equal throughout the interval, indicating an absence of timing behavior. After 18 sessions, the rate of responding increased during the interval. These results indicate an ability to withhold responding until reward is available. Notice that the presence of water improved timing ability on session 18. (From Cruser, L. G. Polydipsia's contribution to the temporal discrimination of rats. Unpublished master's thesis. Norfolk, Va.: Old Dominion University, 1980.)

improved when a frequently exhibited interim behavior is available. For example, Cruser (1980) observed that the timing behavior of animals on fixed-interval schedules was better when the animals were allowed access to water during an interval than when they did not receive water; the occurrence of schedule-induced polydipsia enhanced the ability to inhibit bar-press behavior until the end of an interval. Similar interim activities have been found to improve the accuracy of timing in humans (see Adams & Creamer, 1962; Treisman, 1963).

Why does interim behavior enhance the accuracy of timing? Bolles (1979) suggested a likely answer to this question. After receiving reward on an interval schedule, a rat does not expect the next reinforcement for a while. The expectation of no reward activates frustration-induced behavior. Excessive drinking is one example of behavior produced when a desired reward is not available. Also, frustration influences schedule-induced polydipsia; for instance, in support of Bolles's view, Thomka and Rosellini (1975) found that decreasing the reward magnitude—and thereby creating frustration—increased their rats' water intake.

It should not be concluded that reinforcement itself has no influence on interim behavior. Schwartz and Williams (1972) observed that changes in the contingency of reinforcement affected responding in the autoshaping situation. However, the influence of reinforcement as such is minor compared with the importance of the *predictability* of reinforcement (Trapold, Carlson, & Myers, 1965).

Avoidance behavior.   *Species-specific defense reactions.*   Bolles (1972) questioned the adaptive value of the drive-reduction interpretation of avoidance behavior which was proposed by Mowrer (this was described in Chapter 2). Although Bolles did not doubt that avoidance behavior could be acquired through a reinforcement mechanism, he thought that reduction of fear (that is, relief) represents too slow a process to enable animals or humans to respond readily to a dangerous situation. For example, if a deer has to learn to escape its predator before learning to avoid the predator, the deer probably will find itself as the predator's meal. Bolles proposed that animals and people have instinctive means of responding to danger; Bolles labeled these instinctive actions *species-specific defense reactions* (SSDRs). Rats employ three different species-specific defense reactions: running, freezing, and fighting. Rats attempt to run away from a distant danger; a close danger, however, motivates freezing. When these two responses fail, rats use aggressive behavior to attempt to escape danger.

A study by Bolles and Collier (1976) demonstrates that the cues which predict danger not only motivate defensive behavior but also determine which response rats will exhibit when they expect danger. Bolles and Collier's rats received shock in either a square box or a rectangular box. After they had been shocked, the rats either remained in the dangerous environment or were placed in the other box where no shocks were given. Bolles and Collier found that defensive behavior occurred only when the rats remained in the compartment where they had been shocked. These results indicate that the physiological state does not control avoidance behavior, since all of the rats were aroused; rather, it is the expectation of danger which motivates avoidance behavior. Also, Bolles and Collier found that one "dangerous" compartment—the square compartment—produced a freezing response; the other—the rectangular compartment—produced running behavior. Apparently, the particular SSDR produced depends upon the nature of the dangerous environment.

Response-narrowing process.   Bolles (1972) suggested that when experiencing danger, all species—animal and human—narrow their response repertoire to those behaviors which they expect will eliminate the danger. Since evolution has proved the species-specific defense reactions to be effective and other behaviors likely to produce failure, it is probable that behaviors other than the species-specific defense reactions would be nonadaptive.

Psychologists who have employed behaviors other than the species-specific defense reactions have experienced difficulty in training animals to avoid aversive events. The use of SSDR, in contrast, produces very rapid avoidance learning. Bolles (1969) reported that rats quickly learn to run in order to avoid electric shock but found no evidence of learning when his rats were required to stand on their hind legs to avoid shock. Although Bolles's rats stood on their hind legs in an attempt to escape from a compartment where they were being shocked, they did not learn the same behavior in order to avoid shock. According to Bolles, failure of the rats to stand on their hind legs is another example of animal misbehavior; their natural response in a small compartment was to freeze, and this innate SSDR prevented their learning a non-species-specific defensive reaction as the avoidance behavior.

To investigate principles of avoidance learning, many experiments have used bar pressing. Several hundred trials are typically needed to institute this avoidance behavior in rats, and many rats never learn to press a bar to avoid shock. Bolles (1972) argued that an animal learns a new avoidance response only by adapting an SSDR to the situation. In Bolles's view, if a rat is touching the bar when shock begins, the rat will freeze. The freezing activates the bar and terminates the shock. Although the reinforcement process can enable this rat to learn to press a bar if it is shocked, rats which do not freeze on the bar will never learn to press it. The large number of subjects which never develop this response to avoid shock supports Bolles's view.

Mischel's Integrative Approach

Although Bolles developed his theory on the basis of animal research, several psychologists have realized that his approach accurately describes certain aspects of the motivated behavior of humans. In 1973 Walter Mischel presented a personality theory which incorporates many of Bolles's ideas in order to explain the processes motivating our behavior. Mischel's theory also contains elements found in Rotter's expectancy-value theory and incorporates ideas expressed by other psychologists such as Albert Bandura and Aaron Beck. Therefore, Mischel's approach represents a comprehensive expectancy view of the processes motivating our behavior.

Do we have traits? Mischel (1973) found that the *trait* views which dominated personality theory described human behavior inaccurately. Although both psychologists and lay people have believed that we have central traits which govern our behavior, Mischel's clinical research indicates that we do not behave in the same way across differing situations. Mischel's article (Mischel, 1973) presents several case histories documenting his belief that behavior is situation-specific. One of these case histories is presented here to illustrate his view.

One of Mischel's female patients had been previously diagnosed as frigid. Did this woman's behavior reflect a central trait which she exhibited in all settings? Mischel found that the patient was capable of experiencing sexual pleasure in the dark but not under other environmental conditions. Therefore, her frigidity was not a central trait but reflected a behavior which was exhibited only under specific conditions. Mischel's view that specific environmental stimuli govern motivated behavior is consistent with Bolles's cognitive approach.

Types of expectations.   Mischel proposed that three types of expectations influence our actions. The first two, *stimulus outcome* and *behavior outcome,* are identical to the S-S* and R-S* which Bolles described. According to Mischel, stimulus outcome expectations reflect our belief in the consequences of the environmental stimuli which we experience. For example, Mischel's patient expected darkness to predict a safe sexual encounter. Behavior outcome expectations represent our belief in the consequences of our actions. However, we do not expect a particular behavior to have the same consequences each time we perform it; a particular behavior outcome expectation is activated only under specific environmental conditions. Thus, Mischel's patient expected sexual intercourse to produce pleasure, but only in the dark. In a lighted environment, this woman expected sexual intercourse to be aversive. This expectation caused her to avoid sex unless she was in a dark room.

Although we may expect to receive reward in a particular setting, we may still not behave. We will not exhibit a specific behavior unless we feel competent. *Competency* refers to a belief in our ability to behave in a certain fashion. (The concept of competency is identical to Bandura's concept of *self-efficacy.*) For example, suppose that you want to surf-fish. Good weather predicts good fishing, and you expect to make your catches by casting your rod into the surf. However, unless you feel able to place a worm on your hook, you will be unable to obtain reward. There are people who want to fish but cannot place worms on hooks. These people will be unable to experience the rewarding aspect of fishing unless they can change their feelings of incompetency.

Can we profit from the experience of others?   Mischel (1973) suggested that our expectations that we can perform a specific behavior can be developed both through personal experience and by observing the behavior of others. You can see support for this view in psychological research on *modeling* (see Bandura, 1971). Modeling is defined as behavior we learn by observing the action of another person without receiving explicit reinforcement. The classic experiment by Bandura, Ross, and Ross (1963) illustrates the influence of a model on motivated behavior. In this study, preschool children saw a model act aggressively toward a life-sized plastic doll called a Bobo doll. The model sat on this doll, punched it, hit it with a mallet, kicked it, and tossed it up and down. Other children in the study did not watch a model behave in this manner. After the initial phase of the study, all children first were allowed to play with attractive toys and then were frustrated by being required to leave these attractive toys for less attractive ones, including a Bobo doll. Bandura, Ross, and Ross recorded the level of imitative aggression (attacking the Bobo doll) and nonimitative aggression (behavior not performed by the model). They found that while all the children exhibited nonimitative forms of aggression when they were frustrated, only the children who had watched the model showed the imitative patterns of aggression. One striking aspect of this study is that a live model did not precipitate any more imitative aggression in these children than a filmed model did. We can apparently learn how to perform a particular behavior merely by watching others exhibit it.

Bandura's experiment (1965) shows that we can learn expectations about behavior outcome as well as expectations about competency by observing the consequences of others' actions. In Bandura's 1965 study, all the children watched a film of a model behaving aggressively toward a Bobo doll. In one film, children saw the model severely punished for aggressiveness; other children saw a different film, in which the model was rewarded for aggressive behavior. In a third film, still other children saw only the model's aggressive behavior. Bandura reported that the children who had watched the punished model displayed fewer imitative aggressive responses than the children who had seen the model receive no consequences for aggressive behavior. The children who had seen the model's aggression rewarded, in contrast, increased their level of imitative aggression above that observed for the children in the "no consequence" condition. These results indicate that by observing the actions of others we not only develop an expectation that we can exhibit a particular response but also learn what the consequences of that response will be. If the result is reinforcing, we will be more likely to use that response when we are motivated than we will be if we have not observed the outcome. Similarly, observing a negative outcome of a response causes us to avoid exhibiting that response. The recognition that modeling represents an effective way to change behavior has led to its use in cognitive behavior therapy. We will examine its use in treating phobic behavior later in this chapter. The importance of modeling in the development of our behavior, as well as in the modification of deviant behavior, will be apparent throughout the remaining text.

Additional characteristics of Mischel's theory. Three other aspects of Mischel's approach deserve mention. *First, Mischel proposed that the stimulus value of reinforcement influences the intensity of motivated behavior: the greater the incentive, the more intense our actions will be to obtain a reward.* This hypothesis is certainly consistent with the research on incentive motivation detailed in Chapter 2. *Second, not only is the likelihood of our exhibiting a specific motivated behavior dependent upon our expectation that the behavior will lead to reward, but the consequences of obtaining or failing to reach a specific goal must also be considered.* The following example illustrates this process. You are aware that you can obtain a desirable food from your refrigerator. However, the consequence of eating this food is that you will gain weight; thus, you avoid eating this food even though eating it will be pleasurable. *Finally, Mischel proposed that we have specific information-processing systems which determine how we perceive our environment and, therefore, determine the nature of the expectations we develop.* For instance, we may ignore environmental events which are inconsistent with our cognitions.

The importance of perception on motivation has been well documented by psychologists who have investigated the process of attribution. These psychologists have shown that our perception of the causes of our behavior determines our expectations and ultimately our motivated actions. Let's now turn to the types of attributions we make and how these attributions influence our behavior.

THE ATTRIBUTION PROCESS
Attribution theory, outlined initially by Fritz Heider in 1958, focuses on the processes leading to the development of our expectations. According to attribution theory, external events do not directly motivate behavior; rather, the perceived causes of our successes and failures determine how we will act. We can also develop attributions to describe the causes of our behavior. In this section, we will focus our attention on causal attributions of our experiences, keeping in mind that the same processes determine our behavioral attributions.

Our attributions do not have to reflect actual causes; as long as we believe that they do, they represent the basis for the expectations which govern our motivated behavior. Although expectancy-value theory referred to the importance of perception on motivated behavior, its contribution was not investigated by psychologists concerned with describing how expectancy affects our behavior. Let's now examine evidence that the attribution process plays a central role in determining our expectations and, thereby, our motivated actions.

Heider's Theory

Heider suggested that we examine our successes or failures to determine why we believe these events occurred. We might attribute our experiences to personal, or *internal*, causes—or, on the other hand, we might attribute them to environmental, or *external*, factors. Those factors to which we attribute our experiences have a profound influence on our expectations of future successes or failures, and these expectations then determine our subsequent motivated behavior. It is important to note that internal and external attributions differ from internal and external expectations. For example, a person might attribute failure to lack of ability (an internal causal attribution), which would lead to an expectation of being unable to succeed in the future (an external expectation).

Types of causal attributions.   According to Heider, there are two types of internal causal attributions. We can attribute our successes to *power* or to *motivation* and our failures to lack of power or lack of motivation. *Power* refers to our perceived level of such factors as ability, strength, and attractiveness. *Motivation* refers to the level of exertion or effort which we think we have exhibited to reach our goals.

We can also attribute success or failure to environmental factors. Heider proposed that environmental forces either impede or lead to our success. In Heider's view, environmental barriers frequently reduce the likelihood of our reaching goals, while some environmental forces aid us to obtain desired goals. The success or failure of others can provide us with information enabling us to judge the presence of these environmental forces. If most people have successfully completed a certain task, environmental events probably will enable us also to be successful at this same task. In contrast, the failure of most people to reach a certain goal may be attributed to the presence of environmental factors which would also block our success. Environmental forces also influence each of us differently. For example, the effect of the environmental event called *luck* fluctuates between people. We assume that good luck enables us to be successful, while bad luck prevents us from reaching our goals, or at least hinders us.

We are also concerned whether the factors to which we have attributed our successes or failures will or will not continue to influence our ability to reach our future goals. Heider (1958) assumed that some factors are *stable*, while others are *unstable*. When we attribute our success or failure in a certain task to a stable factor, we assume that this factor will continue to determine our future successes or failures in this specific task. In contrast, since the influence of unstable factors can change as time progresses, we are uncertain whether or not these factors will continue to influence our being able to reach a desired goal.

This dimension—stability—influences both internal and external attributions. Power is typically assumed to be a stable factor; motivation is often thought to be unstable. For example, most of us do not believe that our ability will change much in the course of time. In contrast, we *are* likely to feel that our level of motivation will fluctuate.

Environmental forces can also be stable or unstable. While we might believe that some environmental forces which either promote or prevent success will remain effective, other external factors may cease to have influence. For example, we assume that the difficulty of a task will not change. However, luck can change; good luck can become bad luck or vice versa.

The effects of our causal attributions.   Our specific attributions determine our expectation of future successes or failures as well as our subsequent motivated behavior. The following example illustrates the expectancy and behavioral outcomes of the eight possible attributions which we can make after either succeeding or failing. Table 3.1

Table 3.1
Causal Attributions of Success and Failure Experiences

| | Stable | | Unstable | |
	Success	Failure	Success	Failure
Internal	My good grade was due to high ability(1)	My poor grade was due to low ability (5)	My good grade was due to high effort (3)	My poor grade was due to low effort (7)
External	My good grade was due to an easy exam (2)	My poor grade was due to a difficult exam (6)	My good grade was due to good luck (4)	My poor grade was due to bad luck (8)

presents a real-world example for each attribution. You have received your grade for an English literature examination. Suppose that you received a good grade. (1) What would be the effect of believing that your ability, an internal stable factor, was responsible? If you make this attribution, you will expect to do well on future English literature tests and will study as diligently for the next one as you did for this last one. (2) Or you could perceive an external stable factor—the difficulty of the task—as the cause of your success: everyone in your class did well because the test was extremely easy. Considering your instructor's past record in this regard, you assume that the rigor of future tests will not change, and thus you expect to do well on them. You undoubtedly will study even less for your next literature test, since you expect it to be so easy that everyone will do well regardless of effort expended or ability. (3) You could also attribute success to an unstable internal factor. You might feel that studying hard was responsible for your success. As long as you maintain the effort which you exerted on the last test, your unstable internal attribution will cause you to expect success on the next literature test. In addition, your expectation will motivate you to study diligently for it. (4) Another alternative is that you think that luck caused you to do well on the test. As long as you think that you will remain lucky, your unstable external attribution will lead you to expect to do well on the next literature examination. Also, since you believe that luck rather than effort led to your success, you probably will reduce your effort on the next literature test.

Now suppose that you have received a failing grade. The consequences of failing also depend upon your attributions of why you failed. (5) You could attribute your failure to a stable factor: low ability. This internal stable attribution for your failure will then cause you to expect to fail the next literature examination. The lowered expectation of future success will probably result in your withdrawing from the course. (6) A stable external attribution for failure will have effects identical to those of the stable internal attribution: you would assume that the extreme difficulty of the test was responsible for your failure. The basis for this attribution is that your instructor is consistently known to give difficult tests which most students fail. As a result of your attribution of failure to a stable external factor, you expect to fail on future tests, and this expectation also can result in your deciding to drop the class. (7) Attributing your failure to an unstable internal factor (by contrast with stable attributions) increases your expectation of succeeding on the next test. This improved expectation of success is then translated into motivated behavior. Thus, if you believe that your own lack of effort caused failure, you probably will study harder in order to succeed on the next test. (8) Attributing failure to an external unstable factor—bad luck—will also cause you to study for the next test, since you believe that one cannot remain unlucky forever.

Empirical support.   This discussion points out that our expectations of future successes or failures and the behavior which results from these expectations depend upon the specific attributions we make for our successes and failures. As Table 3.1 shows, we can point to eight possible attributions. The next section describes research evaluating Heider's attributional approach. Psychologists have accumulated considerable evidence during the past 15 years to support Heider's attributional model, and several studies will be presented to document the validity of his view. Additional support for his theories will be evident during the discussion of specific motives.

Original studies of causality.   Heider demonstrated that we are capable of drawing causal judgments. The study of Heider and Simmel (1944) provides evidence of this ability. They projected three figures—a large triangle, a small triangle, and a circle—on a screen. The objects moved about the screen and occasionally touched each other. Heider and Simmel's subjects were then asked to indicate what they perceived to be the cause of these movements. The experimenters reported that their subjects were able to make causal attributions for these movements. Interestingly, these causal attributions seemed to represent human interactions rather than attributions for three inanimate objects. For example, if the objects moved together and then separated, the subjects reported that fighting caused the objects to move in different directions. We might draw a similar conclusion after having seen three children separate abruptly. The subjects also attributed human motives to the objects when the objects moved togerher: they said that a sense of belonging to a group was responsible. Similar results can be found in a series of experiments by Michotte (1946).

The causes of our experiences.   Heider's research demonstrates that we can make causal attributions; other studies (for example, Frieze, 1976) indicate the type of attributions we can draw from success or failure. The subjects in Frieze's experiment were instructed to indicate why certain events occurred. One part of the study required the subjects to suggest reasons why students had received high or low scores on an examination; in another part, they had to suggest why a game was won or lost. Frieze's results supported Heider's attributional model; her subjects reported that ability, effort, ease or difficulty of the task, and luck were the most common causes of success or failure. Other causal attributions reported by Frieze include (1) mood, fatigue, and illness (internal unstable attributions) and (2) other people and specific environmental circumstances (external unstable attributions). Consider the following examples to illustrate these last two attributions. Two friends came to your dormitory room while you were studying for an examination and you stopped to talk with them for several hours. If you failed the examination, you probably attributed your failure to your friends' visit. Or suppose that you did not study for an examination because an important political event which distracted you took place just before it. If you failed this test, you probably attributed failure to the political event.

Our expectations about the future.   Heider assumed that our attributions determine our expectations of future success or failure. Rosenbaum's study (1972) documents this influence. Rosenbaum told some of his subjects that a person working on a project had succeeded ("success" condition); he told other subjects that this person's project had failed ("failure" condition). All the subjects were given information which enabled them to make a causal attribution for the project's success or failure. Half of the subjects in each group were given a story which indicated that a stable factor—high or low ability—was responsible for the outcome. The other subjects were told that an unstable factor—high or low effort—was responsible. This was the first phase of Rosenbaum's study; in this phase, subjects were able to make a causal attribution for success or failure. In the second phase, Rosenbaum asked his subjects to indicate their expectation of this person's success on the next project. Although the expectation of future success is always greater after we have succeeded than after we have failed, the attribution of a stable factor was extremely important in this study (see Figure 3.6). Attribution of success to an unstable factor produced a lower expectation of future success than attribution to a stable factor. On the other hand, attribution of failure to an unstable factor produced a higher expectation of future success than attribution to a stable factor. As Heider predicted, our expectations of future success depend greatly on whether we attribute our successes and failures to stable or unstable factors.

Recall the discussion of Rotter's idea of "locus of control." Rotter assumed that our expectation of future success or failure depends upon whether we exhibit an internal or external expectation. The study of Phares described earlier seemed to confirm Rotter's prediction. Phares found that if we have succeeded in a task involving skill and a task involving chance, we are more apt to expect future success in the former than the latter. Similarly, after we have failed a task involving skill and one involving chance, we are more likely to expect future failure in the former than in the latter. However, Bernard Weiner (1980) points to a conceptual error in Rotter's theory. Skill is typically a stable factor, but chance is an unstable factor. Weiner suggested that our expectation of future success or failure depends not on whether we make an internal or external attribution but only on the stability dimension.

Weiner, Nierenberg, and Goldstein's study (1976) documents the importance of

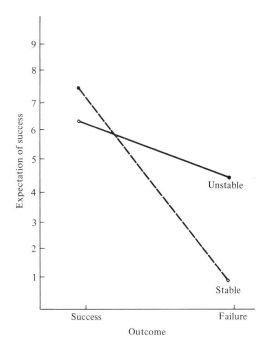

Figure 3.6
Subjects' expectation of success as a function of previous success or failure and the attribution of the outcome to a stable or unstable factor. (Adapted from Rosenbaum, R. M. A dimensional analysis of the perceived causes of success and failure. Unpublished doctoral dissertation. Los Angeles: University of California, 1972.)

stability in such attributions. These experimenters provided subjects with either 0, 1, 2, 3, 4, or 5 experiences of success on a block-design task and then collected data which indicated the subjects' causal attributions for success and also their expectations of future success. Although the subjects increased their tendency to expect success as they completed successful experiences, there was a greater expectation of success for subjects who made a stable rather than an unstable attribution. This observation was true regardless of whether subjects attributed success to an internal factor or to an external one. Apparently, the stability of an attribution—not its internality or externality—determines our expectation of future success.

The influence of attribution on our behavior. Heider's theory also assumes that our attributions determine our behavior. Meyer's study (1970) illustrates how our specific attributions influence motivated behavior. Meyer's subjects experienced a series of five consecutive failures on a task involving digit-symbol substitution. Failure was instituted by stopping every trial before each subject had completed the task. After each trial, Meyer assessed the subjects' causal attribution for failure and found that those subjects who had attributed their failure either to lack of ability or to the difficulty of the task showed a decline in performance on each subsequent trial. In contrast, subjects who believed that either lack of effort or bad luck had caused their failure increased the intensity of their behavior on following trials. Meyer's results demonstrate that our causal attributions determine our subsequent behavior.

Attributions also influence the intensity of our motivated behavior. Although locus of control may not influence our expectation of future success, it does influence our motivated behavior. We will work harder when we attribute success to an internal rather than an external factor. Breit's study (1969) illustrates this effect. Breit's subjects each composed an essay and then attributed the success of completing it to either an internal or an external factor. Breit reported that subsequent performance was better for those subjects who had made an internal attribution for their success in completing the essay than for those who made an external attribution. Breit's study again shows that our causal attributions determine our future actions.

Although Heider's approach represented an important breakthrough which increased our understanding of the motivational process, one major issue remained unanswered: What enables us to decide which attribution accurately reflects the cause of important events? Harold Kelley developed his theory to answer this question.

Kelley's Attribution Theory

Decision rules. Kelley (1967) suggests that a number of questions must be considered before we can formulate a causal attribution. The answers to these questions tell us to which factors we should attribute our successes or failures.

Distinctiveness. One question we ask following an event concerns the distinctiveness of our experiences: Is our success (or failure) unique to this setting or has it occurred in many situations? According to Kelley, we are more likely to attribute an experience to an external factor if we believe that it is unique than if we believe that it has happened in many settings.

Consider the following example to illustrate Kelley's view. You enjoyed yourself at a dance. To what factor do you attribute your enjoyment? If this is the first social gathering you have enjoyed, you probably will believe that the setting (an external factor such as meeting someone to whom you are attracted) produced your enjoyment. However, if you enjoy all social gatherings, you probably attribute your enjoyment to an internal factor; you might believe that you always exert the amount of effort needed to have a good time.

Consensus. We also ask about the experiences of others: have others had a similar experience, or are we alone in succeeding (or failing) at a certain task? Kelley suggests that we are more likely to attribute an experience to an external factor if we believe that others have also succeeded or failed at this task (high consensus) than if we know that we are alone in the experience (low consensus).

Recall the example of the dance. If you realize that others also enjoyed the dance, you are then apt to believe that some aspect of the situation, such as an exceptional band, was responsible for your enjoyment. If you believe that you alone had a good time, an internal factor will seem to be the logical causal agent. Perhaps you tried harder than the others to enjoy the dance.

Consistency. We also ask whether or not we typically succeed or fail in similar settings. Information about consistency allows us to determine the stability of factors to which we attribute our experiences.

Let's return to our example of the dance. If we enjoy most dances, we are likely to believe that a stable factor caused our enjoyment. We might feel that we have effective social skills (an internal, stable factor) which enable us to enjoy dances consistently. If our enjoyment is inconsistent, we will attribute our pleasure to an unstable factor. Perhaps we do not always exert the effort necessary to have a good time at dances.

The type of setting. You may have assumed from our discussion that a single factor determines how we react to an experience. It is true that in *usual*, or typical, situations, one factor is sufficient to produce a particular outcome; but in *unusual*, or atypical, situations, two or more factors are necessary. Consider a girl who asks to watch a favorite television show. If the child frequently watches the show, she attributes watching only to the request. However, if this child watches the show infrequently, she may then attribute the outcome—watching the show—both to the request and to some other fact (e.g., that she had not misbehaved during the day before the request). Only one factor (the internal stable social skill) is necessary to produce reward in a typical situation; but in an atypical situation, two factors (the internal stable social skill and the internal unstable appropriate behavior) are needed. Thus, the selection of our attribution depends upon the type of environmental setting to which we believe we are being exposed.

Empirical support. Considerable evidence has been gathered which validates Kelley's view of the attribution process. Let's briefly examine several key studies demonstrating this support.

McArthur (1972) tested the validity of Kelley's system of decision rules for making causal attributions. McArthur gave her subjects descriptions of a person's behavior in a number of situations. For example, one situation was "John laughed at the comedian"; here John's laughter reflects his enjoyment of the comedian. The description also contained information about the degree of distinctiveness, consensus, and consistency of the person's response to the situation. Table 3.2 presents items of high and low distinctiveness, consensus, and consistency for the comedian example. After receiving these data, McArthur asked all the subjects to pick from four alternatives the perceived cause of the person's reaction to the situation (see Table 3.3). McArthur found that subjects who had received information indicating low consensus, low distinctiveness, and high consistency chose a personal causal attribution (alternative a). Thus, the subjects believed that an internal factor was responsible for John's enjoyment when (1) no one

Table 3.2
Examples of Consensus, Distinctiveness, and Consistency Items

Consensus information took the form:
a. Almost everyone who hears the comedian laughs at him (high consensus).
or b. Hardly anyone who hears the comedian laughs at him (low consensus).
Distinctiveness information took the form:
a. John does not laugh at almost any other comedian (high distinctiveness).
or b. John also laughs at almost every other comedian (low distinctiveness).
Consistency information took the form:
a. In the past John has almost always laughed at the same comedian (high consistency).
or b. In the past John has almost never laughed at the same comedian (low consistency).

else but John laughed at the comedian, (2) John typically laughed at most comedians, and (3) John almost always laughed at this comedian. Subjects who had received information indicating high consensus, high distinctiveness, and high consistency picked an external causal attribution (alternative b). These subjects believed that an environmental factor was responsible for John's enjoyment when (1) everyone laughed at the comedian, (2) John did not usually laugh at other comedians, and (3) John almost always laughed at this comedian. Finally, subjects who received information indicating high distinctiveness and low consistency chose an unstable attribution (alternative c). These subjects assumed that an external, unstable factor caused John's enjoyment when he laughed only at this comedian and only some of the time. Orvis, Cunningham, and Kelley (1975) found that information about distinctiveness, consensus, and consistency has a similar influence on the specific causal attributions which we make for our experiences.

Cunningham and Kelley (1975) evaluated people's attributions in typical and atypical situations. The following example illustrates the two types of situations which they presented to their subjects. In a typical situation, a drama critic reviewed a new play positively. In an atypical situation, the critic said that the play was the best in a decade. Cunningham and Kelley asked their subjects to indicate whether the favorable review could be attributed to the play, to the critic, or to both. The results showed that in the typical situation the subjects found a single factor (i.e., either the play or the critic)

Table 3.3
Four Alternative Causal Attributions

a. Something about the person (John) probably caused him to make Response X (laugh) to Stimulus X (the comedian).
b. Something about Stimulus X probably caused the person to make Response X to it.
c. Something about the particular circumstances probably caused the person to make Response X to Stimulus X.
d. Some combination of a, b, and c above probably caused the person to make Response X to Stimulus X.

sufficient to produce success. In contrast, in the atypical example the subjects believed that both factors contributed to success. Cunningham and Kelley's results support the view that we assume that a single factor can cause a typical event but two or more causal factors are involved in determining an atypical event.

Attributional bias.   *Actor-observer bias.*   This discussion has suggested that we develop our attributions in a rational manner. However, it is clear that the decision-making process is not always a rational maneuver; bias exists which influences our attributions. One frequently investigated bias has to do with our attributions for the causes of our own experiences as opposed to our attributions for the causes of *others'* experiences. Jones and Nisbett (1972) suggest that we are apt to attribute the causes of our experiences to the environment; on the other hand, we are likely to make personal attributions concerning others' experiences. For example, a boy who has hit another child probably attributes his behavior to the other child's actions. However, the victim's parents might attribute this behavior to the aggressor's hostility. Our situational attributions can be self-serving, that is, they can be made in order to maintain self-esteem.

   Nisbett, Caputo, Legant, and Maracek's study (1973) demonstrates the difference between our causal attributions of our own experiences (called *actor attributions*) and those of other people (called *observer attributions*). These psychologists asked male college students to indicate why they and their friends had chosen their majors and their girl friends. Nisbett, Caputo, Legant, and Maracek discovered that for their own choices their subjects considered external reasons more important than internal ones. For example, in assessing their own choice of a girl friend, some students believed that luck rather than their own actions was responsible. But in assessing their friends' choice of girl friends and majors, they believed their friends' personal qualities to be more important.

   Jones and Nisbett (1972) suggested that attentional processes are probably responsible for the differences between actor and observer attributions. Because we cannot see our own actions, it is difficult for us to appreciate the influence which our behavior has on our experiences. Additionally, since we direct our attention toward the environment, it is easy to stress the importance of situational determinants for our experiences. Viewing other people's experiences causes us to focus our attention on those people and thus to ignore the situation influencing them. According to this view, our attention produces causal attributions that are personal rather than situational for the experiences of other people.

   Studies by McArthur and Post (1977) document the important role which attention plays in our causal attributions. Each subject in McArthur and Post's studies listened to a conversation between two men and then indicated perceived causes of the conversation. In one study, one of the men sat under a bright light; in a second study, one of the men sat in a rocking chair. According to the attentional view, these treatments should cause each subject to focus attention on one of the men and thus to perceive his behavior as governed by internal factors to a greater extent than that of the other man (to whom the subjects would not attend). The results were as predicted: the subjects felt that personality played a greater part in the conversation of the man on whom their attentions had been focused.

   Other attributional biases.   Although the actor-observer bias has frequently been reported in psychological literature, some studies (see Monson & Snyder, 1977, for a review of the literature) have found an opposite result: some experiments indicate that we attribute internal causes more frequently for our own experiences than for those of other people. Internal causal attributions for our experiences appear to reflect our typical attributions in achievement tasks (see Wiener, 1980). In achievement settings, we usually attribute our successes and failures to our ability, our efforts, or both. Perhaps our educational experiences cause us typically to focus on the internal rather than the external determinants of success or failure. Future research will undoubtedly clarify the conditions producing a particular attributional bias.

There are times when some people unjustifiably attribute successes to internal causes. For example, some people may feel that their high ability led to good grades when, in fact, an external factor was responsible. Ross (1977) suggested that this type of unjustifiable attribution serves to create a positive self-image. Langer and Roth's study (1975) demonstrates that some people do perceive internal causality when external factors are actually governing outcomes. Subjects in this study watched a person flip a coin and then had to predict the outcome of each flip (heads or tails). Although chance, an external factor, governed the outcomes, some subjects believed that they could anticipate the result of the next toss. Some persons' perception that they can predict outcomes in gambling settings represents an example of this attributional bias.

This discussion indicates that our attributions do not always accurately reflect the actual causes of our experiences. Sometimes we exaggerate the importance of personal factors, and sometimes we exaggerate the importance of situational factors. Attention appears to be an important determinant of our attributional bias; events which attract our attention may seem more important than those which do not.

How do you feel today?   One additional situation in which attributional processes influence our actions merits our attention. Psychological research indicates that the identification of emotional experiences is influenced by our causal attributions.

This morning my teenage daughter told me that she could no longer tolerate her youngest brother and that when he returned from playing, she was going to beat him up. Obviously, she was quite angry with him, and her emotional response would probably lead to aggression. Although he has angered her in the past, her anger usually subsides before he reappears. His usual response to her anger is amusement rather than fear or remorse; his actions merely act to increase her unhappiness with him.

James-Lange theory.   Why is my daughter angry? Many psychologists have attempted to answer questions similar to this one. The *James-Lange theory of emotion* which was proposed almost a century ago by William James and Carl Lange would assume that my son's actions caused a distinctive internal physiological response in my daughter. Her internal response created the emotional experience of anger. According to the James-Lange theory, our emotions, produced by our internal responses to environmental events, often occur following overt behavior. Thus, it is not because we are sorrowful that we cry; rather, the internal reaction that motivates crying produces the emotional response of sorrow.

Cannon's approach.   In 1929 Walter Cannon criticized the James-Lange theory. Cannon thought that the same visceral changes occur with different emotional states and that these visceral changes are often too slow to cause our emotional responses. Instead of believing that an internal response produces emotion, Cannon proposed that the environment independently produces both an emotional experience and a visceral reaction.

The James-Lange and Cannon theories of emotionality are quite different: according to the James-Lange theory internal responses to the environment produce our emotions; in Cannon's view, the environment causes our emotions. Unfortunately, the evidence does not provide definitive support for either view. However, there is research indicating that cognitive and biological processes influence perceived emotion. Let's now examine Schachter's cognitive theory of emotion. In Chapter 4, we will discover which biological systems are involved in our emotionality.

Schachter's attributional approach. In 1964, Stanley Schachter proposed an attributional theory of emotionality. Schachter asserted that when we notice that we are internally aroused, we are motivated to identify the cause of the arousal; and unless we know why we are aroused, we will attribute our arousal to the prevailing environmental conditions. For example, if we are internally aroused (or excited) at a party where those around us are having a good time, we attribute our arousal to the party and assume that we are also having a euphoric emotional response. We could experience a similar arousal in the form of fear if we are studying in anticipation of a very difficult examination.

THE MISATTRIBUTION OF AN EMOTION. An important aspect of Schachter's theory is his idea that internal arousal need not actually be produced by a particular environment but only experienced in that setting. Under some conditions, we will misattribute our arousal to our environment; in reality, another factor produced it. Consider the following example to illustrate this process. Many youngsters have "crushes" on opposite-sex school teachers. Since school can be a stressful experience, it is likely that these children misattributed their arousal and developed strong emotional attachments to their teachers. A similar misattribution may also be responsible in the example of my daughter's anger toward her brother. A telephone call awakened her today before she became angry at her brother. She probably attributed her arousal to her brother, whereas it was actually caused by the telephone call. We should not assume that my daughter is not often justifiably angry at her brother, but today's anger may reflect a misattributed cognition.

EMPIRICAL SUPPORT. Schachter and Singer's classic study (1962) points out the vital role of the attribution process on our emotional experiences. Schachter and Singer informed their subjects that the study was intended to evaluate the effects of a vitamin compound on visual skills. One group of subjects were injected with adrenalin (epinephrine), a drug which produces an internal arousal. A second group received a placebo injection. Schachter and Singer told some of the subjects in each group that the side effects of the "vitamin" would cause trembling hands, pounding hearts, and warm flushed faces—in fact, these are some of the symptoms produced by epinephrine. Other subjects in each group were informed that the side effects would produce numbness, itching, and a slight headache—symptoms different from those actually produced by epinephrine. Still other subjects in each group were not told anything about the side effects of the "vitamin."

In the second phase of the study, each subject waited with a confederate, believed to be another subject, for the experiment to begin. This phase required the confederate and the subject to answer a questionnaire, parts of which allowed the experimenters to assess the subjects' emotional responses. Each confederate acted in one of two ways while completing the questionnaire: the confederate either displayed a euphoric manner (for example, these confederates threw paper airplanes, shot paper wads, and played with a hula hoop) or displayed anger toward other subjects (these confederates complained about having to complete the questionnaires and finally shredded the forms and bolted from the testing room).

How did each actual subject report feeling after viewing a confederate's behavior? In accordance with Schachter's attributional approach, none of the subjects who received the placebo injection were emotionally affected by the confederate's behavior. The confederate's action was not sufficient to produce internal arousal, and without arousal the subjects had no reason to be influenced by the confederate's behavior. On the other hand, the subjects who received the epinephrine were internally aroused and needed an explanation for their arousal. Recall that some of these subjects had been told of side effects. Schachter and Singer predicted that these subjects would attribute their arousal to their injection and would not be influenced by the confederate's behavior; and the results were as predicted. But subjects who had been injected with epinephrine and were misinformed or uninformed about its effects would have to attribute their arousal to the confederate's behavior. Schachter and Singer reported that these subjects did report feeling more euphoric or angry than other subjects after viewing the confederate's actions. These results suggest that in order to have an emotional experience, we must first be aroused. Once aroused, we use environmental information to attribute a cause for our internal response. This attributed cause determines our emotional experiences, and the attributed cause does not have to reflect the actual environmental or internal factor which produces the arousal.

Although many psychologists have criticized Schachter and Singer's study for several methodological problems (see Plutchik & Ax, 1967), other experimenters, often using different procedures, have documented the relevance of the attribution process on emotionality, as well as on motivated behavior. Let's look at two of these studies.

Dienstbier and Munter (1971) gave their subjects a placebo, telling them that it was a drug. They then informed some of these subjects that the drug's side effects included pounding of the heart, sweating palms, and a tight feeling in the stomach, symptoms associated with internal arousal. Other subjects were told that they would encounter side effects unrelated to arousal. Following this phase of the study, all the subjects were provided the opportunity to cheat while they worked on an important test. Since the anticipated consequences of cheating are aversive for most people, these circumstances should have induced internal arousal for the majority of the subjects. Attributing our arousal to the setting causes us to avoid the negative consequences of cheating. As Dienstbier and Munter predicted, they found that those subjects who believed that their internal arousal was caused by the test environment and not the pill did not cheat. In contrast, the subjects who attributed their arousal to the pill instead of the test did not experience the emotional fear response and did cheat. It seems that when we do not attribute arousal to the negative aspects of a situation, we can concentrate on obtaining reward and ignore the potential danger inherent in the situation. Suppose that you want to ask someone for a date, a thought which is likely to induce arousal in you. If you attribute the arousal to anticipated rejection, you will experience fear and avoid asking for the date. But if you attribute your arousal to an anticipated rewarding evening, you will feel hopeful and ask for the date. The factors to which we attribute our internal arousal appear to determine both our emotional experiences and our subsequent motivated behavior.

Ross, Rodin, and Zimbardo (1969) used another technique to induce arousal. They told all their subjects that they were to receive a series of electric shocks. Some subjects were then informed that a loud noise would induce slight tremors, shaky hands, pounding hearts, and nervousness. The expectation of shock actually produced these symptoms; yet these subjects attributed their arousal to the loud noise. Other subjects were told that the noise would produce symptoms other than fear; these subjects could attribute their internal arousal only to expected shock. In the last phase of this study, Ross, Rodin, and Zimbardo allowed all the subjects to choose one of two tasks to work on. They could either attempt to avoid electric shock or try to obtain money. According to the attribution approach, subjects who had attributed their arousal to expected shock in the first phase of the study would now be motivated to avoid shock; subjects who thought that

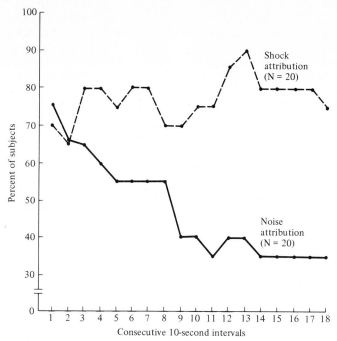

Figure 3.7
Percentage of subjects in the "shock attribution" and "noise attribution" groups who chose to work on the shock-avoidance task rather than attempt to obtain money. (From Ross, L., Rodin, J., & Zimbardo, P. G. Toward an attribution therapy: The reduction of fear through induced cognitive-emotional misattribution. Journal of Personality and Social Psychology, 1969, 12, 279–288. Copyright 1969 by the American Psychological Association. Reprinted by permission.)

the noise had caused their arousal would now work on the task which would enable them to obtain reward. As predicted, the subjects' attribution of their emotional responses determined their motivated behavior: subjects who had attributed their arousal to shock now avoided shock; subjects who had attributed their arousal to noise now worked on the task that would earn them money (see Figure 3.7). These results again demonstrate that attributions determine not only our emotional experiences but also our motivated behavior.

The influence of drive on human phobic behavior was discussed in Chapter 2; there we saw that the drive approach does not completely describe the motivational basis of phobic behavior. We'll now examine evidence which indicates that cognitive processes are important in motivating phobic behavior.

COGNITIVE INFLUENCE IN PHOBIC BEHAVIOR

Bandura's Approach

The phobic's expectations. Recall the description of Helen's mathematics phobia at the beginning of this chapter. In 1977 Albert Bandura presented a cognitive theory of phobic behavior; according to this theory, two classes of expectations—outcome and efficacy—maintain Helen's phobia. Outcome expectations reflect the perceived conse-quences of a behavior or an event. Helen expects a statistics class to be very aversive—a stimulus outcome expectation—and she believes that she cannot pass the course—a behavior outcome expectation. Also, Helen knows that she can prevent the aversive experience by not enrolling in the statistics course; this behavior outcome expectation motivates her phobic behavior.

Helen's phobia presents her with a dilemma typical of phobic situations. On the one hand, her phobia makes the statistics course aversive; on the other hand, the consequences of not taking the course are equally aversive—she cannot graduate without passing the course. She realizes that she must pass this course to graduate, but her phobic behavior prevents her from obtaining her desired goal. Unfortunately, this outcome expectation does not govern Helen's behavior: she avoids the course even though she cannot graduate without it.

Bandura's theory suggests that a second type of expectation is involved in motivating Helen's phobic behavior. According to Bandura's approach, Helen does not feel capable of enduring the aversive experience. Bandura labeled this belief that one can or cannot execute a particular action an *efficacy expectation*. (Bandura's efficacy expectation is identical to Mischel's concept of competency, described earlier.) Helen's lack of *self-efficacy* has left her unable to register for the course.

The importance of our experiences.   What factors are responsible for Helen's outcome and efficacy expectations? Helen's outcome expectation that she will fail the statistics course could have developed either from her own direct personal experiences, from observations of the experiences of other people, or from information provided by others. Since Helen has not failed this course or any other course, her outcome expectations cannot reflect any direct personal experience. It is likely that Helen has observed others, whom she perceived as similar to herself, fail. In addition, she probably has received information from other people that the course is difficult and therefore feels that she will fail it.

Bandura (1977) suggested that we use four types of information to establish an efficacy expectation. *First, personal accomplishments indicate our degree of self-efficacy.* Successful experiences generally increase our expectations of mastery; failure usually decreases our sense of self-efficacy. Bandura, Jeffrey, and Gajdos (1975) discovered that the influence of success or failure on efficacy expectations depends upon the difficulty of a task, the amount of effort expended, and the pattern and rate of success. We are more apt to feel competent if we usually succeed at a difficult task which requires considerable effort than if we succeed without trying. *Second, our sense of self-efficacy is developed by observing the successes or failures of other people whom we perceive as similar to ourselves.* Seeing others cope successfully with perceived aversive events enhances our belief that we also can be effective; observing others fail decreases our belief that we can cope with adversity. Several factors determine the effectiveness of a vicarious experience (that is observation of a model). The success of the other person's (the model's) behavior must be clear; we cannot develop a sense of self-efficacy if the outcome of this other person's behavior is ambiguous (Kazdin, 1974a). Also, we acquire a stronger expectation of mastery when we see several people rather than a sole person cope with an aversive situation (see Bandura & Menlove, 1968; Kazdin, 1974b). Finally, Meichenbaum (1972) discovered that we develop a greater sense of self-efficacy when we see another person struggle initially with adversity and gradually become effective than when the model succeeds immediately. *Third, we can be persuaded that we are either capable of coping or unable to deal with adversity.* For example, Helen's family or her peers could attempt to convince her that she could pass the statistics course if she would try. To test the idea that verbal persuasion can alter expectations, Lick and Bootzin (1975) suggested to their patients that they could successfully interact with a feared object. Unfortunately, they found little evidence of behavioral change with their use of verbal persuasion. Bandura (1977) proposed that the influence of verbal persuasion is shorted-lived unless personal experiences confirm it. *Fourth, emotional arousal determines our sense of competence; we feel less able to cope with an aversive event when we are agitated or tense.* Although Bandura feels that emotional arousal plays a part in motivating phobic behavior, his view certainly differs from the drive approach outlined in Chapter 2. Bandura does not believe that fear directly causes avoidance behavior: he suggests that fear and defensive action are correlated but do not reflect a causal relationship. We are more likely to display avoidance behavior when we are afraid, but only because fear makes us feel less effective. However, since emotional arousal is only one source of information which we use when developing a sense of self-efficacy, other information may enable us to feel competent even though we are afraid. Under these conditions, we will interact with a feared object while we are still afraid because we perceive ourselves as able to cope with adversity. Our emotional arousal extinguishes after we have interacted with an aversive event.

Remember the discussion of flooding therapy from Chapter 2. In this procedure, a patient is forced to interact with a feared object. We learned that patients, even though they are still fearful of a phobic object, can suppress phobic behavior. These results demonstrate that fear does not directly motivate phobic behavior. In all likelihood, flooding allows patients to discover that they are competent because of their successful personal interactions with aversive situations.

Bandura and Adam's study (1977) demonstrates the role which efficacy expectations play in phobic behavior. Patients with a snake phobia received the systematic desensitization therapy described in Chapter 2. Bandura and Adams discovered that when patients no longer became emotionally disturbed by an imagined aversive scene, differences still existed in their ability to approach a snake. In contrast, the patients' self-efficacy expectations corresponded closely to their ability to interact with the snake: the greater the patients' perceived efficacy, the more able they were to inhibit phobic behavior and approach the snake (refer to Figure 3.8). This relationship between self-efficacy and an absence of phobic behavior held true even after therapy when a new snake, different from the one in pretherapy testing and desensitization training, was employed. These results demonstrate that if we believe ourselves competent, we will generalize our self-efficacy expectations to new situations.

Modeling Treatments of Phobia
Our discussion points to the critical role of outcome and efficacy expectations in motivating phobic behavior. These expectations develop both through our experiences and through our observations of the experiences of other people. During the past 15 years, behavior therapists have employed models to interact with feared objects in order to treat phobic patients. The aim of this modeling treatment is to alter patients' phobic behavior by vicariously modifying their expectations.

Graduated modeling therapy.   In this therapy, the therapist employs a graduated treatment procedure; the patients see the model move closer and closer until the feared object is encountered. A study by Bandura, Grusec, and Menlove (1967) shows the effectiveness of modeling in treating phobic behavior. These psychologists allow children who feared dogs to watch a peer model interact with a dog. The children received eight

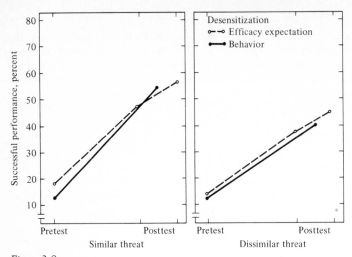

Figure 3.8
Influence of desensitization therapy on the subject's level of self-efficacy and ability to approach a snake. The success of therapy on the posttest was evaluated using both the same snake used in therapy ("similar threat") and a different snake ("dissimilar threat"). (From Bandura, A., & Adams, N. E. Analysis of self-efficacy theory of behavioral change. Cognitive Therapy and Research, 1977, 1, 287–310.)

10-minute therapy sessions during a 4-day period. At first, the children saw the model pat the dog while it was in a pen. During later observations, the children watched the model walk the dog around the room. In the final sessions, the model climbed into the pen and played with the dog. Other children did not see the model but saw only the dog, which occupied the pen for the first therapy session and was leashed in the last seven sessions. Bandura, Grusec, and Menlove assessed the effectiveness of modeling by determining if the phobic children could approach and play with either the dog seen in therapy sessions or a new dog. The results indicated that modeling reduced the children's phobic behavior and increased their interaction with the dog seen in the study or a new dog.

According to Bandura's approach, the success of modeling therapy must be attributed to the vicarious modification of a patient's expectations. Support for this view is evident in a study by Bandura, Adams, and Beyer (1977). They exposed adult snake phobics to models interacting with a snake and assessed the influence of this modeling treatment on the subjects' approach response to the snake and their efficacy expectation (that is, their expectation of being able to interact fearlessly with the snake). Bandura, Adams, and Beyer found that the degree of success of this modeling treatment corresponded to the increase in the phobics' self-efficacy expectation; the more the model's action altered a patient's efficacy expectations, the greater the patient's approach to the snake.

Participant modeling therapy.   In 1969, Bandura, Blanchard, and Ritter introduced a change in the modeling therapy which significantly enhanced its effectiveness. They suggested that in addition to the standard use of a patient observing a model (or therapist), the model (or therapist) should encourage the patient to interact with the feared object; they called this *participant modeling*. In the participant modeling procedure, the model slowly moves nearer and nearer to a phobic object. After each modeled behavior, the model (or therapist) asks the patient to imitate that action. During the imitation, the model (or therapist) either stands close to the patient or is in direct physical contact with the patient. After the model (or therapist) has helped the patient interact with the feared object, the success of the treatment is evaluated by having the patient encounter the feared object alone.

Bandura, Blanchard, and Ritter (1969) compared the degree to which participant modeling altered a fear of snakes with the degree to which symbolic modeling and systematic desensitization altered it. Patients who received symbolic modeling therapy saw a 35-minute film of children, adolescents, and adults with a snake. The desensitization treatment, identical to the procedure described in Chapter 2, employed a 35-item hierarchy. Control subjects who did not receive formal therapy were assessed for their level of fear. For patients being treated by means of desensitization, therapy continued until they could imagine the most feared item in the film without displaying any emotional response; for patients being treated by means of participant modeling, therapy continued until they could interact with their most feared item when the therapist was with them. The patients receiving symbolic modeling therapy had as much modeling exposure as patients receiving participant modeling therapy. Bandura, Blanchard, and Ritter found that with participant modeling, patients needed only 2 hours to reach the criterion; with desensitization, patients required 4½ hours of therapy to imagine the most-feared item in the hierarchy. In addition, with participant modeling 92 percent of patients could interact alone with a snake; with symbolic modeling, this figure was 33 percent; with systematic densitization patients, it was 25 percent; and for control subjects, it was zero percent. These results demonstrate that although symbolic modeling and desensitization are more effective than no treatment, both are much less effective than participant modeling. Other studies have also documented the effectiveness of participant modeling in treating phobic behavior. For example, participant modeling has successfully treated phobia of heights (Ritter, 1969) and phobia of water-related activities (Hunziker, 1972).

What factors contribute to the rapid elimination of phobic behavior when participant modeling is used? As you learned in the last section, the use of modeling provides a vicarious change in a patient's expectations. Two processes are likely to account for the enhanced effectiveness when participation is also included: (1) A model (or therapist) provides patients with a sense of security. Many psychologists have realized that other people's presence can reduce the emotionality produced by aversive events (refer to Chapter 9 for a discussion of the influence of other people on emotionality). Since Bandura's approach assumes that our level of emotionality influences our efficacy expectations, the reduction of arousal induced by a model's presence will increase our perceived efficacy, thereby enhancing our interaction with a feared object. (2) A model's (or therapist's) encouragement places social pressure on a patient to encounter a feared object (see Chapter 12 for a review of the social influence process). This personal experience enables patients to discover that they can interact with phobic objects without any aversive consequences.

This discussion suggests that because participation alters a patient's efficacy expectations, it increases the effectiveness of modeling therapy. Bandura, Adams, and Beyer's study (1977) supports this view. These experimenters discovered that the efficacy expectations of being able to encounter a snake were higher with participant modeling than with modeling alone (refer to Figure 3.9). Furthermore, the higher the level of self-efficacy produced by participant modeling, the more able each patient was to

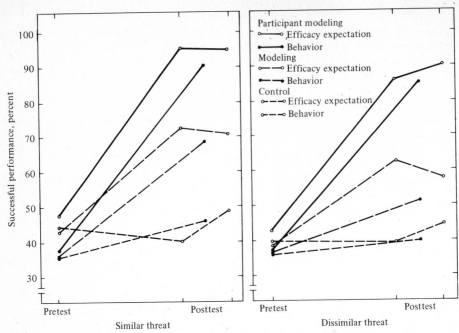

Figure 3.9
The influence of participant modeling, modeling, and control treatment on both the subjects' level of self-efficacy and their ability to approach a snake. The subjects' self-efficacy and avoidance behavior were measured before (pretest) and after (posttest) the treatments. In addition, the treatment effects were evaluated on the posttest with the same snake used in therapy ("similar threat") and a new snake ("dissimilar threat"). (From Bandura, A., Adams, N. E., & Beyer, J. Cognitive processes mediating behavioral change. Journal of Personality and Social Psychology, 1977, 35, 125–139. Copyright 1977 by the American Psychological Association. Reprinted by permission.)

approach the snake. Many clinical psychologists (for example, Franks & Wilson, 1974) suggest that participant modeling represents one of the most powerful ways of altering phobic behavior. Clearly, its effectiveness lies in its ability to modify a phobic's cognitions.

SUMMARY

During the past two decades, many psychologists have recognized the important role cognitive processes play in governing our motivated behavior. In contrast to the mechanistic view that we automatically respond to environmental events, the cognitive approach assumes that we play an active role in determining our response to environmental circumstance.

Cognitive psychology began in the 1930s and 1940s with Edward Tolman's ideas. Although Tolman's cognitive approach did not receive much initial acceptance, his views represent the foundation for current cognitive theories. Tolman proposed that our behavior is goal-oriented; we are motivated to reach specific goals and continue to search until we obtain them. Rather than believing that behavior represents an inflexible habit, Tolman assumed that our behavior remains flexible enough to allow us to reach our goals.

Our expectations determine the specific behavior we use to obtain reward or avoid punishment. According to Tolman, we expect that behaving in a particular fashion enables us to obtain reward or avoid adversity. In addition to understanding the means necessary to reach our goals, Tolman believed that certain environmental events direct our actions. The environment guides us to our goals, and we use this information to reach our goals.

Tolman theorized that although we may know how to obtain our goals and where these goals are located, we will not behave unless we are motivated. He proposed two classes of motives: (1) conditions of deprivation and (2) incentive motivation. According to Tolman, deprivation increases our demand for goal objects; greater reward value increases our motivation to obtain goals. Also, Tolman felt that associating environmental events with either deprivation or incentive motivation enabled these environmental stimuli to develop motivational properties.

Tolman's view altered the character of drive theory (for instance, the concept of the anticipatory goal mechanism was developed in response to Tolman's studies of incentive motivation and latent learning), but the drive-dominated psychology of the 1950s and 1960s all but forgot his cognitive approach. The importance of Tolman's views is now quite evident in the thinking of psychologists currently investigating the influence of cognition on motivated behavior.

Contemporary research has identified two critical components in the cognitive control of motivated behavior: attributions and expectations. An attribution reflects the processes which we believe cause us to behave in a particular way or to have a specific experience. Our expectations represent our perceived ability to exhibit a particular behavior as well as the anticipated consequences of our actions. Our causal attributions determine our expectations, and our expectations guide motivated behavior. Attributions and expectations do not always reflect actual environmental circumstances; as long as we believe that they are accurate, we will act in accordance with our cognitions.

Three types of expectations appear to influence motivated behavior: stimulus outcome, behavior outcome, and efficacy. Stimulus outcome expectations have to do with our understanding of the predictive relationships in our environment; we expect a particular stimulus to predict a biologically important event. Behavior outcome expectations represent our belief in the consequences of our actions; we expect a specific outcome when we behave in a particular way. Efficacy expectations reflect our perceived ability to execute a particular action; we feel competent when efficacy expectations are high and inadequate when they are low. Though stimulus outcome and efficacy expectations direct our behavior, behavior outcome expectations determine which behavior we will exhibit to obtain desired goals.

Our expectations are based on the causal attributions we make for our actions and experiences. We can attribute causality to personal internal factors, or we can assume that environmental external factors are responsible for our actions and experiences. Moreover, we can believe (1) that these factors are stable and will continue to influence us or (2) that other factors may determine our future behavior and experiences because of the instability of the processes we assume are now governing them.

We employ several rules when developing a causal attribution: we use the distinctiveness, consensus, and consistency of our behaviors and experiences as well as their frequency. A causal attribution may not reflect actual environmental circumstances; our attention or desire to enhance our self-image may bias our causal attributions.

Each motivated behavior discussed in this text is governed by cognitive processes. Often our attributions and expectations enable us to interact effectively with our environment. However, pathological behavior sometimes results when we develop inaccurate attributions or expectations. Cognitive behavior therapy attempts to provide disturbed persons with realistic cognitions. This approach has proved quite successful; the effectiveness of the modeling therapies used to alter phobic behavior is one example.

This chapter and Chapter 2 presented drive and cognitive approaches to motivation. These two approaches describe the psychological factors which determine our motivated behavior, but other research has focused on the biological systems which influence our motivated behavior. Chapter 4 describes these biological systems, which affect each of our specific motives, and the importance of these systems is evident throughout the remainder of this text.

BIOLOGICAL SYSTEMS

Do you have a light?

*F*or 2 days, Greg has resisted his urge to smoke. Having attempted to quit on more occasions than he can count, he's determined not to let his extreme nervousness and irritability keep him from stopping this time. His family tries to distract his thoughts from cigarettes, but these attempts work only temporarily. Anticipating tonight's televised championship boxing match helped him for a while, but this too cannot prevent his recurrent, intense impulses to smoke.

Greg began smoking cigarettes when he was 15. All his friends smoked, and so it seemed like the natural thing to do. At first, he did not like to smoke, for it made him cough and sometimes feel slightly nauseated. Greg smoked only with his friends and, to feel part of the group, pretended to inhale. However, as the unpleasant effects began to disappear, he learned to inhale and smoke more. By the age of 18, Greg smoked two to three packs of cigarettes each day.

He never thought about stopping until he met Paula. A nonsmoker, she tried to convince him to quit. Finding himself unable to break his habit, he simply did not smoke when dating Paula. After they married, Paula continued her plea for Greg to stop smoking. He has tried every now and then over the past 10 years to resist cigarettes, usually avoiding his habit for a day or two.

This time had to be different. At 35, Greg felt himself in perfect health, but a routine check-up with the family physician, Dr. Logan, 2 days ago proved Greg wrong. Greg learned that his extremely high blood pressure made him a prime candidate for a heart attack. Dr. Logan told Greg that the pressure must be lowered through special diet, medication—and no smoking. Continued smoking would undoubtedly interfere with the other treatments. The threat of a heart attack frightened Greg; he had seen his father suffer the consequences of an attack several years ago. Determined now to quit, he only hopes that he can endure his withdrawal symptoms.

Greg's intense motivation to smoke, as well as his record of being unable to stop, is shared by millions of other people. Their addiction, stemming from dependence on the effects of cigarettes, causes their actions. Evidence of this dependence can be seen in the aversive withdrawal symptoms which many people experience when they no longer have the effects of smoking. These withdrawal symptoms intensify as the time since these people have smoked increases. When strong enough, the withdrawal state motivates them to resume smoking.

Cigarette smoking is just one example of addictive behavior. People become addicted to many drugs which have quite different effects. For example, the pain-inhibiting effects of heroin contrast sharply with the arousing effects of the amphetamines. Although the effects of drugs may differ, the cycle of these effects, withdrawal symptoms, and resumption of addictive behavior characterizes all addictive behaviors. Addiction also can be the result of experiences unrelated to drugs. Some people's strong social reliance on others is one example; another is the intense motivation of some persons to watch television. Both physiological and psychological systems play important roles in motivating addictive behavior, although their relative contributions vary from person to person. We'll look at the factors which produce addiction later in this chapter.

Addiction is one example of the way biological systems influence motivated behavior. In fact, biological systems are important in motivating all behavior. This chapter emphasizes the influence of the nervous system in motivating our behavior. Although the functioning of all our biological systems affects our behavior, the nervous system is central to our effective interaction with our environment. The nervous system is a complex system divided into numerous segments, each with a different function; the actions of each segment (as well as our other biological systems) influence the functioning of the other segments. Thus, our motivated behavior reflects the integrative input of many different neural and nonneural systems. Some of these systems influence all motivated behavior. For example, the neural systems which control reward and punishment affect all motivated behavior. In this chapter we'll look at those systems which affect all our motives; the biological systems unique to a particular motive will be addressed when the factors producing that specific motivated behavior are discussed. (Before reading this chapter, you may find it helpful to review the basic principles of neural physiology and anatomy presented in the Appendix.)

THE NEURAL CONNECTION

Chapters 2 and 3 taught us that both external and internal stimuli have an important influence on our motivated behavior. However, we also learned that there is not a perfect correspondence between our environment and our behavior. Our past experiences modify our perception of environmental events. In addition, both our past and our current biological condition affect our motives. Individual differences in perception and motivation produce varied responses to the same environment. The nervous system not only connects us to our environment but also allows a flexible response to that environment.

The function of the nervous system is to process environmental information, both internal and external, and to execute the most effective response in order that we may adapt to our environment. Let's use the following example to illustrate the role of the nervous system in our interaction with our environment. Walking to your car after a night class, you notice a man holding an object; he's approaching you in the dimly lighted street. Suddenly you realize that the object is a knife. Panic-stricken, you look about for help, only to realize that no one is nearby. Your only escape is to run back toward the campus. Having run two blocks, you stop for a second to catch your breath. In a quick glance over your shoulder, you discover that the man is no longer there. You now feel enough relief to return to your car and go home.

Your escape from danger required effective functioning of many neural systems. There are five phases in the processing of information by the nervous system. *First, the sense organs must detect the presence of significant environmental stimuli.* In our example, the retinal cells of your eyes noticed that the man carried a knife. Environmental events are occurring constantly around us; we cannot sense all of them. Failure to detect the knife probably would have led to your being attacked. Although many factors determine which events we notice, novelty and past significance are two elements that determine which events will attract our attention. Detecting an important event is only the first step in processing environmental information.

Next, we must identify the significance of events. Our perceptual systems process environmental stimuli into an awareness of the meaning of detected events. In the foregoing example, the visual-association area located in the temporal-occipital regions of the cortex identified the object as a knife. Perceptual processing of information does not occur independently of other neural systems; the ability to identify an object requires information from our memory bank of past experiences.

In addition to recognizing an object (in our example, the knife), we must establish its motivational significance. A knife represents danger; we must detect this danger and then be motivated to respond to avoid potential adversity. In Chapter 2, we discovered that certain events, similar to the example here, activate an aversive motivational state. We will see in this chapter that arousal of the periventricular tract provides the motivational basis of our avoidance behavior.

Once we are motivated, we must identify the appropriate response to cope with the situation. In this example, you found no one to help, so running seemed the best response. Although the decision process appears to take place in the association areas of the cortex, input from other areas is important. For example, information about our general level of arousal influences whether or not we feel that we can exhibit a specific response. Activation of the appropriate area of the motor cortex produces the avoidance response.

After deciding the most effective response, we must activate the muscles which produce that response. In addition, the nervous system must ensure that no action occurs which might impair the effectiveness of our response. For example, you controlled your arm movements because flinging them haphazardly while running would have slowed your flight from the stranger with the knife.

To summarize: Our discussion has pointed to five key stages in the processing of information by the nervous system. First, sensory systems detect an event. Second, perceptual systems enable us to identify the event. Third, motivational systems assess the significance of our perception. Fourth, association systems make a decision concerning the appropriate response. Fifth, motor systems execute the desired behavior.

One further point deserves our attention. We are continually processing information and reassessing our response to the environment. Recall from our example that you stopped running after two blocks, looked back, and felt relief upon seeing that the man was no longer following you. This relief motivated you to return to your car and go home. The potential to alter our behavior is caused by the continuous functioning of the nervous system and its ability to change earlier decisions.

Thirst, the first topic in this description of biological approaches to motivation, is a relatively pure example of biologically controlled motivation. Later in the chapter we will look at the biological systems which influence all motivated behavior. In subsequent chapters, the biological processes which influence specific motivated behaviors are described.

THIRST

A Constant Fluid Level

Our body maintains a constant level of fluid within each cell, the intracellular fluid, and outside each cell, the extracellular fluid. The extracellular fluid is composed of the blood plasma and interstitial fluids which surround each cell. Approximately two-thirds of our body's fluid is inside the cells; the other one-third is outside the cells. This constant fluid level is essential for effective metabolic functioning; any change activates compensatory mechanisms which restore optimal fluid levels. We usually drink more water than we need; our kidneys excrete the excess. However, if our fluid level is lower than it should be, internal changes are activated which decrease the water contained in urine. In addition, specific brain receptors are stimulated, creating sensation—thirst—which, in turn, causes us to drink water in order to restore the optimal level of fluid.

Osmotic thirst. Fluids contain a small amount of sodium chloride. Increases in the concentration of sodium chloride in body fluids activate processes which restore normal sodium chloride levels. Sometimes internal conservation can reinstate the optimal level of sodium chloride, but it is often necessary to increase fluid intake. The thirst produced by increased sodium chloride levels is called *osmotic thirst.*

The following example illustrates this process. You have just eaten a very salty meal which raised the sodium chloride concentration in the extracellular fluid. To restore the optimal concentration, the extracellular fluid must increase its fluid volume. Where does this fluid come from? You lose intracellular fluid into the extracellular compartment by means of the diffusion process. Although this reaction raises the concentration of sodium chloride in the extracellular fluid, it decreases intracellular fluid, or *dehydrates* our cells. This cellular dehydration causes the internal changes which increase water retention and induce thirst.

Verney's classic experiment (1947) investigated the changes which occur when salt is injected into the bloodstream. He discovered that salt injections cause the posterior pituitary to secrete the antidiuretic hormone (ADH) which increases retention of fluid in the kidneys. Verney also noted that the salt injections cause rats to drink excessive amounts of water. Verney's results plus those of other psychologists demonstrate that increased salt concentration in the blood produces both an internal conservation of the water which is already present and a behavioral response which introduces additional fluid.

Why does salt cause ADH release and thirst? Verney (1947) suggested that the heightened osmotic pressure, caused by increased intracellular salt concentration, stimulates receptors located in the hypothalamus. These *osmoreceptors* produce thirst and initiate the release of ADH from the posterior pituitary. Many studies, several of which are presented next, have confirmed the existence of osmoreceptors in the medial area of the hypothalamus. These receptors, stimulated by increased intracellular salt concentration, produce both ADH and osmotic thirst.

Andersson (1953) discovered that injecting saline, a water and salt solution, into goats' medial hypothalamic area stimulated drinking. Electrical stimulation of this area motivated drinking (Andersson & McCann, 1955). In contrast, Andersson and McCann (1956) found that destruction of the *medial hypothalamus* of dogs and goats produced lowered water intake. Furthermore, Peck and Novin (1971) and Blass and Epstein (1971) observed that lesions in the medial hypothalamic area eliminated ADH release and the drinking response to saline injections. These observations indicate that neurons in the medial hypothalamus are stimulated when our cells become dehydrated.

Arousal of these *osmoreceptors* causes the release of ADH; this increases water retention and drinking which in turn introduces new fluid. Both ADH release and drinking restore optimal fluid levels.

Volumetric thirst. We have just seen that osmotic thirst is produced by the loss of intracellular fluid caused by increased salt concentration in the extracellular fluid. A second type, *volumetric thirst*, occurs when extracellular fluid is lost. Several circumstances can lead to loss of excellular fluid, or *hypovolemia:* (1) sweating during exercise (notice the salty taste of sweat; both salt and fluids are lost when we sweat), (2) diarrhea induced by illness, (3) bleeding as the result of an injury, and (4) absence of water. All of these conditions result in a lowered volume of extracellular fluid. The effect of hypovolemia is activation of internal changes which causes water retention and an increased motivation for water. Let's next consider biological changes which enable us to conserve bodily fluids, and then examine evidence that hypovolemia causes thirst.

When hypovolemia exists, the decreased volume of extracellular fluid lowers blood pressure. This lowered blood pressure stimulates the release of ADH from the pituitary. Recall that ADH increases water retention. In addition, the lowered blood pressure stimulates the kidneys to release an enzyme called *renin*. Renin causes the conversion of the blood protein *angiotensinogen* into *angiotensin*. Angiotensin, in turn, stimulates the adrenal cortex to release *aldosterone* hormones which cause increased salt retention. Figure 4.1 diagrams the changes which occur in response to the lowered blood pressure.

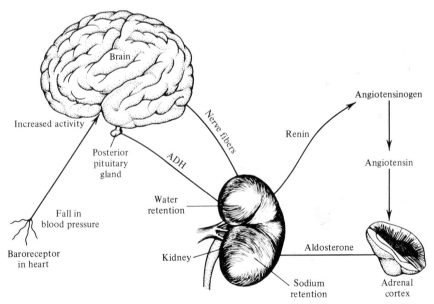

Figure 4.1
Hormonal changes initiated by a drop in blood pressure detected by heart baroreceptors. Stimulation of the hypothalamus causes the posterior pituitary to secrete ADH and the kidney to release renin. Renin secretion results in the conversion of angiotensogen into angiotensin. Angiotensin then stimulates the adrenal cortex to secrete aldosterone. ADH increases fluid retention, while aldosterone increases sodium retention. (From Carlson, N. R. Physiology of behavior. Boston: Allyn and Bacon, 1977.)

Loss of extracellular fluid not only increases fluid conservation but also produces thirst. Physiological evidence indicates that angiotensin activates neurons in the preoptic and anterior areas of the hypothalamus. Stimulation of these hypothalamic neurons produces volumetric thirst and drinking. To demonstrate the influence of angiotensin on drinking, Epstein, Fitzsimmons, and Rolls (1970) injected angiotensin into the *preoptic and anterior hypothalamic areas* of rats. They found that drinking occurred in response to angiotensin even in satiated animals. Furthermore, increasing the quantity of injected angiotensin caused the rats to drink more. These results suggest that under natural conditions the amount of fluid we drink corresponds to the amount lost, since the level of angiotensin released depends on the amount of extracellular fluid lost.

Osmotic and volumetric thirst often occur together, although different neural systems regulate them. Alan Epstein and his associates (see Epstein, Kissileff, & Stellar, 1973) proposed a *double-depletion hypothesis*: they theorized that both cellular dehydration and hypovolemia produce thirst and drinking. Consider this example to illustrate this double-depletion process. Having jogged for 2 miles, your body has lost water (hypovolemia) and your osmoreceptors have been dehydrated. You drink two glasses of water to quench your thirst.

The "dry mouth" theory.   In 1934 Walter Cannon proposed that we become thirsty and drink when the mouth is dry. Although a dry mouth may cause us to drink, it does not regulate the amount of drink. Only a few sips eliminate a dry mouth, but we usually drink much more to satisfy our thirst. In addition, neither removal of the salivary glands (which causes a permanently dry mouth) nor administration of drugs which causes excessive salivation have any influence on the amount of water we drink when we're thirsty. Apparently it is cellular dehydration and hypovolemia rather than a dry mouth which control the level of water intake required to eliminate thirst.

A good meal can make you thirsty.   Most of us drink during meals. The food we eat does create thirst: it dries the mouth and causes secretion of digestive juices and loss of extracellular fluid (hypovolemia); also, any salt in a meal leads to cellular dehydration. Le Magnen and Tallon (1966) determined that the change in osmotic pressure produced by a meal governs the amount we drink; the greater the change, the more we drink. Food containing protein is especially dehydrating.

Fitzsimmons and Le Magnen (1969) demonstrated that rats which consumed equal quantities of food and water on a carbohydrate diet consumed 1.47 times as much water as food on a protein diet. Although these results suggest that we drink as much as we need to compensate for the dehydrating effect of a meal, drinking during a meal—other than to eliminate a dry mouth—is probably learned. Support for this conclusion is obtained from a study by Oakley and Toates (1969) which shows that sufficient drinking occurs before eating in order to prevent dehydration. It seems that we can anticipate impending thirst and drink enough to counteract future dehydration.

Satiety

The factors which cause us to stop drinking have not been so clearly defined as those which initiate drinking. In all probability, rigid controls over the suppression of drinking are not as important as those producing thirst; any excess water can be readily eliminated. Evidence suggests that the amount of ingested water plays an important role in the inhibition of drinking. The mouth is thought to be like a meter: after a sufficient amount has been drunk, further fluid intake is suppressed. However, this oral meter is not a perfect regulatory device.

Bellows (1939) cut a dog's esophagus, bringing the cut ends out of the animal. The esophagotomized animal drank, but the swallowed water fell to the ground. Bellows discovered that his esophagotomized dogs drank two times as much water as they needed before they stopped drinking. Apparently, oral factors do contribute to the suppression of drinking but other factors are also involved.

One other important factor in the inhibition of drinking seems to be the presence of water in the stomach. Several experimenters (for example, Adolph, Barker, & Hoy, 1954) have placed water into the stomach of dogs through a tube, a procedure which enabled the experimenters to bypass oral factors. The results of these experiments show that drinking is suppressed; this suppression occurs even before the water can be absorbed into the bloodstream.

Neural systems which suppress drinking have been identified. Neurons located in the *parainfundibular hypothalamic area* control drinking. Researchers (for example, Witt, Keller, Batsel, & Lynch, 1952) have discovered that lesions in the parainfundibular hypothalamus produce polydipsia, excessive water intake. In the absence of the functioning of this hypothalamic area, inhibition of drinking is extremely difficult. In all likelihood, the neurons in this area are sensitive to the amount of ingested water. When a sufficient amount of water has been drunk, the cells are activated and further drinking is inhibited.

A number of psychologists have identified the areas of the brain controlling sleep and arousal and have also investigated the importance of sleep and arousal. Let's now see what these scientists have discussed.

SLEEP AND AROUSAL

The Circadian Cycle
Each of us experiences different levels of arousal every day. Typically, we have a long behavioral arousal period followed by a period of inactivity. Although some of us may occasionally nap, most of us establish a regular 24-hour cycle for sleeping and waking. This cycle can be tied to external events (for example, sleeping at sunset and rising at sunrise); however, the cyclical biological changes occurring within us during the 24-hour *circadian cycle* probably control the cycle for most of us. Many people think that their internal clock wakes them; their beliefs apparently are typically correct.

Not only do we have regular sleeping-waking patterns; in addition, our arousal levels differ while we are awake, and our inactivity levels differ while we sleep. While we are awake, we are sometimes alert and sometimes relaxed and less attentive to our environment; at other times we may be extremely aroused. Similarly, there are different levels of sleep: during light sleep we are easily aroused, but only a strong stimulus, like an emergency, can awaken us from deep sleep. Dreaming is more likely to occur during a distinct phase of sleep which is called *REM sleep* because of the rapid eye movements during this phase. In REM sleep, our cortex is aroused while behaviorally we are asleep. Evidently, distinct physiological differences exist during the many levels of sleep and alertness. Our EEG pattern provides one indication of these differences. The next section examines first the physiological and behavioral correlates of arousal, then of sleep.

Levels of Arousal
Three distinct cortical EEG patterns occur during different levels of behavioral arousal (refer to Figure 4.2). When we are awake and alert, the EEG shows a rapid desynchronized pattern of small voltage changes (approximately 18 to 24 Hz) which is

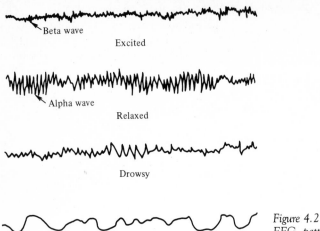

Beta wave

Excited

Alpha wave

Relaxed

Drowsy

Delta wave

Deep sleep

Figure 4.2
EEG patterns corresponding to various behavioral states.

referred to as *beta activity*. This cortical activity is more rapid when we become excited; the greater the arousal, the higher the activity level. Another EEG pattern, called *alpha activity*, is recorded while we relax with our eyes closed. The frequency of alpha activity is 8 to 13 Hz, and the waves are larger than those observed with beta activity. Alpha activity stops when we open our eyes and resume activity; beta activity is then observed again. The EEG pattern changes again as we sleep. These waves, called *delta waves*, occur frequently (1 to 3 Hz), are larger than those in alpha activity, and are synchronized.

RAS and arousal. Donald Lindsley's article (1951) detailed the importance of the *brain-stem reticular formation* or the *reticular activating system (RAS)* for both cortical and behavioral arousal. According to Lindsley, the RAS is central to both cortical and behavioral arousal. Stimulation of the RAS by environmental events produces the EEG arousal or activation pattern (beta waves) seen during behavioral arousal as well as during intense emotional arousal. In Lindsley's view, our behavioral arousal can be measured by recording the level of cortical arousal. Many studies support Lindsley's approach to arousal. Let's examine the classic study by Moruzzi and Magoun (1949) to document the role of the RAS in arousal.

Moruzzi and Magoun reported that stimulation of the reticular activating system (RAS) produced EEG arousal and behavioral alertness. In contrast, they also found that disruption of RAS functioning caused large-wave synchronized EEG recordings characteristic of sleep, and a low level of behavioral arousal. Stimuli presented when the RAS was not functioning reached the sensory cortex but produced neither EEG arousal nor behavioral alertness. Apparently, unless our RAS is activated, we are not aware of a particular environmental event. Moruzzi and Magoun's observations indicate that the RAS plays an important role in arousal; increased RAS activity causes us to be more attentive to our environment.

Why does the RAS affect our cortical and behavioral arousal? The RAS receives input from all sensory systems (refer to Figure 4.3). If this information is significant, the RAS alerts the cortex. In addition, the RAS maintains the muscle tonus necessary for a behavioral response to the environment. Suppose that you are listening to a dull lecture; your environment is devoid of perceptually arousing stimulation. Under these conditions,

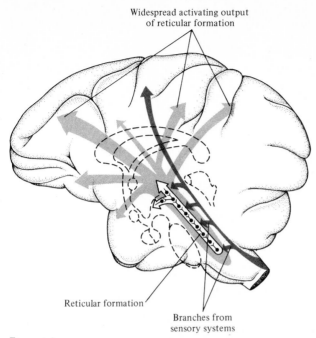

Widespread activating output
of reticular formation

Reticular formation

Branches from
sensory systems

Figure 4.3
Schematic drawing of the reticular activating system (RAS). The dark arrows represent input from specific sensory systems. The light arrows indicate the general activating effect of output from the reticular formation. (Adapted from Magoun, H. W. Brain mechanisms and consciousness. Oxford, England: Blackwell Scientific Publications Limited, 1954.)

your RAS will not be activated and no EEG will result. An inactive RAS is obviously causing the drowsiness which you are experiencing. Compare this with a stimulating lecture. Perhaps the content of the lecture stimulates the RAS, which arouses your cortex. You find yourself attending to the instructor's every word; this action reflects the behavioral alertness produced by a perceptually stimulating environment. However, the exciting lecture produces only a moderate level of RAS activation. In contrast, considerably greater RAS activation will be induced if your instructor is talking of an impending examination. This produces intense cortical and behavioral arousal. Such examples illustrate the important relationship between perceived environmental stimulation, RAS functioning, and both cortical and behavioral arousal.

Arousal theory.   Sports coaches sometimes complain that a team performed poorly because the players were not sufficiently motivated. This statement implies that increases in arousal will lead to better performance. Students occasionally make a rather opposite assertion when they do poorly on an examination: they say that they were too motivated (or aroused) and that this caused them to "draw a blank." This statement assumes that a high level of arousal impairs effectiveness. The classic Yerkes-Dodson law (see Yerkes & Dodson, 1908) offers an explanation for these opposing statements of the relationship between arousal level and performance.

According to the Yerkes-Dodson law, our ability to function effectively depends upon our level of arousal (see Figure 4.4). We perform poorly when our arousal level is

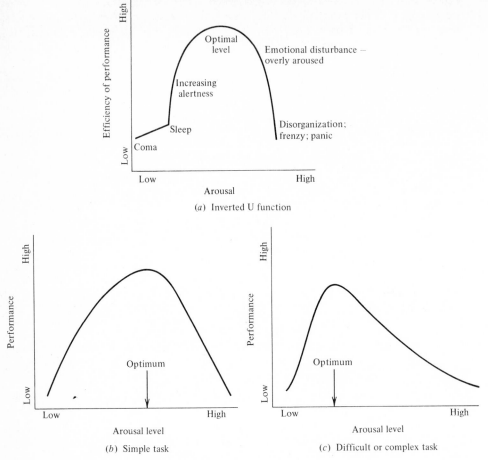

Figure 4.4
(a) *Inverted-U-shaped relationship between arousal and performance predicted in the Yerkes-Dodson law. The optimum level of arousal is higher in* (b) *a simple task than in* (c) *a complex task.*

either low or high; we perform effectively only with an optimum arousal level. The complexity of a task determines the optimum arousal level. In simple tasks, the optimum arousal level is high and, therefore, too high a level is not likely to occur. Thus, increased arousal will improve performance in a simple task. As the task becomes more difficult, the optimum level declines. In complex tasks, even a moderate arousal will produce poor performance.

Recall the examples presented earlier in this section. A coach might be able to improve a team's performance by increasing the players' arousal. However, many sports (for example, football) are complex tasks requiring the ability to adjust to changing conditions. Thus, a coach may actually impair the team's performance by increasing its already high arousal. Similarly, intense arousal probably can cause a student to "draw a blank" on an examination. Later, this chapter discusses methods of lowering arousal levels which are too high, thereby producing more efficient performance.

Arousal can be induced either by external or internal circumstances. Although evaluation of the Yerkes-Dodson law has generally supported this assumption, extreme arousal levels, either externally or internally produced, do not always impair behavioral effectiveness. In the next two sections we'll examine several of these studies and discuss why behavioral inefficiency does not always result from high arousal.

The influence of extreme arousal levels.   Arousal theory assumes that our arousal level depends upon environmental conditions: the greater the degree of environmental stimulation, the higher our arousal level.

LOW LEVELS OF AROUSAL AND BEHAVIORAL EFFECTIVENESS.   According to this view, sensory deprivation can produce a low level of arousal. Studies evaluating the influence of sensory deprivation have generally found that deprivation impairs behavior. Bexton, Heron, and Scott's study (1954) is one example. In this study, subjects received $20 if they agreed to be confined for several days to a small chamber containing only a bed. The subjects wore translucent glasses to reduce visual stimulation and an outfit like a spacesuit to eliminate other stimulation. Bexton, Heron, and Scott observed that subjects showed extreme emotional and intellectual impairments as a result of this sensory deprivation. However, not all experiments with sensory deprivation have yielded extreme behavioral deterioration. For example, Orne and Scheibe (1964) discovered severe impairment only when the subjects expected the experience to be aversive. Apparently, cognitive factors as well as low cortical arousal determine the effect of sensory deprivation.

HIGH LEVELS OF AROUSAL AND BEHAVIORAL EFFECTIVENESS.   We have discovered that exposure to a nonstimulating environment ordinarily impairs behavior. There is a similar detrimental influence on behavior when people are exposed to environments producing excessive RAS activity and cortical arousal. Scientists have shown that many excessively stimulating events (for example, excessive environmental noise, crowding) impair our interaction with the environment. Let's briefly examine the effects of *overcrowding,* or high population density.

Calhoun's classic study (1962) illustrates this effect in animals. In this study, Calhoun doubled his population of Norway rats by having no predators and an unlimited food supply. Calhoun observed both physiological and psychological abnormalities produced by overpopulation. For example, Calhoun discovered that some rats were extremely passive while others were abnormally aggressive.

Studies of humans living in overcrowded environments indicate that high population density may also precipitate physical and psychological disturbances. Observational research (for example, Gove, Hughes, & Galle, 1979) shows that many physical factors (for example, fertility and mortality) and psychological factors (for example, juvenile delinquency and admissions to mental hospital) increase as population density increases. Yet, although the correlation between population density and physical or behavioral factors is high, it is not perfect: some people in low-density environments are disturbed, and some in high-density areas are not. Moreover, though many variables (for example, race, education, income) have been statistically controlled, other noncontrolled factors could have been responsible for the effects. Laboratory studies have tried to solve this problem, but their results have been inconsistent. For example, Hutt and Vaizey (1966) found that aggression increases as crowding increases, whereas Hutt and McGrew (1967) reported no differences with crowding. Similarly, Sherrod (1974) observed that crowding impaired performance on tasks, but Freedman, Klevansky, and Enrlich (1971) found no relationship between crowding and performance.

Berkowitz (1980) suggested several reasons for the failure of overcrowding to induce physical and behavioral impairments. The nonsignificant labratory studies may not have lasted long enough to produce negative effects. In addition, the physical stimulation which we feel when near others may not affect us adversely if we can separate ourselves psychologically from these people. Invasion of personal space (Sundstrom, 1973) and lack of privacy (Altman, 1975) have been suggested as psychological factors contributing to crowding effects. We are less likely to consider high density a negative experience if we can establish privacy or do not feel that others are invading our space. Architectual design is one way to increase privacy. Archea (1977) compared architectual influence on people's sense of privacy and found that privacy can be experienced, even under crowded conditions, if environmental structures create privacy (for example, by use of partitions). It seems likely that by creating privacy, we reduce the amount of environmental stimulation and, thereby, produce a moderately arousing environment.

INTERNALLY INDUCED AROUSAL AND BEHAVIORAL EFFECTIVENESS. External environmental influence can be a source of arousal, but arousal can also be induced from within. People often attribute their poor academic performance to either a lack of motivation (arousal) or excessive motivation. Although low levels of internally created arousal will lead to behavioral inefficiency, high levels do not always have this effect. The Yerkes-Dodson law proposed that high levels of motivation impair performance only in complex tasks. Some studies (for example, Broadhurst, 1957) support the Yerkes-Dodson law; others do not (see Duffy, 1962). Apparently, internal motivation does not always accurately predict our response to an environment. This observation again illustrates the complexity of the motivational process.

CAUSAL VIEWS OF THE INFLUENCE OF AROUSAL LEVEL ON BEHAVIOR. Several psychologists (for example, Easterbrook, 1959; Hebb, 1955) have suggested why performance often depends on both arousal level and task complexity. Hebb (1955) proposed that our ability to discriminate correctly between important environmental cues depends upon arousal level: when arousal level is either low or high, we have difficulty responding correctly to environmental cues. The ability to discriminate is highest when arousal level is optimal.

In 1959, Easterbrook presented an alternative explanation to Hebb's view. According to Easterbrook, drive (or arousal) restricts the use of environmental cues in guiding our behavior. (A similar approach, advocated by Tolman, was described in Chapter 3.) Easterbrook assumes that increased drive initially reduces the use of cues irrelevant to the task. This improves behavioral efficiency, since attention is then focused more on relevant cues. However, as arousal increases beyond the optimal level, we stop using relevant cues; therefore, our proficiency falls. Easterbrook suggests that our poor performance when we are highly aroused is due to the fact that we are not utilizing any cues properly to guide our behavior.

Hebb's and Easterbrook's views of the influence of drive are not necessarily antagonistic. At low levels of arousal, the utilization of both relevant and irrelevant cues impairs effective discrimination. It is likely that at moderate levels of arousal, limiting attention to relevant cues can improve the ability to detect the important aspects of one's environment. However, any further reduction in attention produced by intense arousal impairs discrimination.

Many studies indicate that (1) *increased drive reduces utilization of cues*, and (2) *decreased attention to irrelevant cues occurs before failure to utilize relevant cues*. Let's briefly examine two of these studies.

Bruner, Matter, and Papanek (1955) initially trained rats to use several cues to guide their behavior. During the second phase of their study, only the least obvious cue was useful to the rats in obtaining reward. In this phase, they found that rats deprived of food for 36 hours performed better than rats deprived of food for 12 hours. According to Easterbrook's analysis, the rats which had been hungry longer had higher drive, which reduced their attention to irrelevant cues and thereby enabled them to attend only to the relevant cue.

In an experiment with humans, Bahrick, Fitts, and Rankin (1952) required their subjects to perform two tasks. The central task involved continuous tracking; the peripheral task was reporting the occurrence of occasional lights or the deflection of a needle on a peripheral display. Varying the level of motivation by offering either a small or a large bonus for good performance, Bahrick, Fitts, and Rankin discovered that increased motivation produced better work on the central task but poorer work on the peripheral tasks. Apparently, the increased arousal limited the range of cues utilized to only cues relevant to the central task.

What is the role of the reticular activating system in the relationship between arousal and behavioral efficiency? Recall that EEG arousal and alertness become stronger if RAS activity increases. Since a low level of RAS activity leads to a low level of cortical functioning, we cannot, under these conditions, react appropriately to our environment. This inability to attend to the relevant cues may contribute to the behavioral ineffectiveness often seen with low levels of arousal. When RAS activity is low, we fail to process information effectively; when RAS activity is very high, on the other hand, we try to process too much information. Extreme cortical activity, induced when RAS activity is high, allows us to notice so much of our environment that we cannot organize our experiences efficiently. This inability to process information effectively reduces our behavioral efficiency. Only with intermediate levels of RAS activity do we process our experiences effectively and thereby interact efficiently with our environment.

The aversiveness of extreme arousal levels.   Arousal theory also assumes that we usually avoid environments which cause either high or low levels of arousal. Furthermore, when we are exposed to these situations, we will be motivated to escape to a setting which induces an intermediate arousal level. This idea suggests that we prefer moderately stimulating environments (for example, the exciting lecture described earlier) which produce intermediate arousal levels. We find environments aversive which lack stimulation (for example, a dull lecture) or which are extremely stimulating (for example, an automobile accident).

You may have detected an inconsistency in arousal theory. Why would we find an environment devoid of stimulation to be aversive, since that environment would produce little RAS arousal? Routtenberg's theory (1968) provides one possible answer to this apparent inconsistency. According to Routtenberg, there are two arousal systems in the brain. Arousal system I, the RAS, produces a nonspecific arousal like that in Hull's drive concept. Stimulating this system produces cortical arousal and behavioral alertness. Routtenberg's arousal system II, located in the *limbic system* (see Appendix), is similar to Hull's concept of incentive motivation. Attractive environments activate arousal system II; this, in turn, motivates us to approach these situations. Recall that a dull lecture does not produce either cortical or behavioral arousal. Using this example, let's see how Routtenberg's theory explains why we avoid dull settings. A boring lecture, although it does not produce cortical EEG arousal, lacks incentive value. It was pointed out in Chapter 2 that we avoid low-incentive conditions and approach high-incentive conditions. Therefore, if we are in a dull situation, a more stimulating environment appears attractive and motivates us to leave the boring setting.

Berlyne (1960, 1966) offers an alternative explanation for avoidance of a nonstimulating environment. According to Berlyne, animals and people possess *curiosity* as an innate motive. An environment lacking interesting information stimulates curiosity, which then motivates exploratory behavior. Activated curiosity directs animals or humans toward the most salient, most complex, and most novel aspects of their environment.

Berlyne conducted many studies to demonstrate curiosity as a motive; let's examine

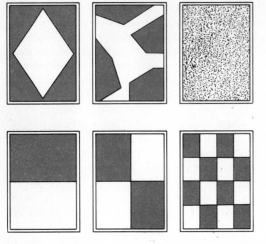

Figure 4.5
Berlyne presented these designs to infants and found that the babies looked first at the more complex stimuli on the right. (From Berlyne, D. E. Curiosity and exploration. Science, 1966, 153, 25–33. Copyright 1966 by the American Association for the Advancement of Science. Reprinted by permission.)

one of them. Berlyne presented babies with designs differing in complexity. (Figure 4.5 shows several.) Berlyne discovered that the infants spent more time looking at the complex designs than the simpler ones. According to Berlyne, the infants' preference for the complex patterns reflects the operation of the innate curiosity motive.

People are motivated not only to explore their environment but also to acquire knowledge of it. Berlyne calls this search for knowledge *epistemic curiosity*, a curiosity directed toward obtaining both cognitive and perceptual information about the environment. Recall the discussion of the self-actualization concept in Chapter 1. The humanists suggested that we have an innate motivation for growth which differs from our deficiency motives. The innate potential to grow motivates self-actualization.

Butler and Rice (1963) suggested that the self-actualization process reflects the operation of curiosity or *stimulus motivation*. In their view, psychopathology occurs when intense anxiety inhibits our stimulus motivation. They feel that the function of the therapist is to provide a safe psychological climate. In this safe setting, the patient can experience new stimuli and, thereby, create new cognitive structures. This new cognitive awareness will prevent further anxiety and allow the development of a competent individual. The process of self-actualization and competence is described in more detail in Chapters 8 and 9.

Our preference for moderately arousing situations.   Arousal theory also suggests that we avoid situations which create either low or high cortical arousal levels and approach those situations which produce moderate (or optimal) levels. Let's briefly consider several of these studies to illustrate our preference for moderately stimulating environments.

Butler and Harlow (1954) found that sensory-deprived monkeys learned to press a bar in order to open a window through which they could get a brief look at an electric train. We saw in Chapter 3 that Miller's rats (Miller, 1948) turned a wheel to escape a fear-producing environment. Finally, Haber (1958) asked human subjects who had adapted themselves to a water temperature of 68° Fahrenheit to rate their preference for various water temperatures. He reported that subjects found temperatures slightly above or below 68° Fahrenheit—moderately arousing temperatures—pleasant. In contrast, the subjects thought that temperatures much warmer or cooler than 68° were very unpleasant.

Though we clearly prefer moderately arousing situations, there are distinct differences in people's arousal response to a particular situation. For example, a movie which is terrifying to you may be stimulating to someone else and boring to yet another person. Experience is one factor influencing our responses; the more often we experience most events, the less stimulating these events become. You undoubtedly found a rollercoaster quite frightening the first time you rode on one; however, it probably became less arousing with each ride. Still, some of us refuse to ride even a first time, indicating that the situation is too aversive to be approached.

Dorfman's study (1965) shows the differences between individuals in initial reaction to a particular response as well as change in preference as they gained experience. Dorfman evaluated subjects' preference for six visual stimuli which varied in complexity. Some subjects preferred complex stimuli; others preferred less complex stimuli. As the subjects continued their experiences, Dorfman observed that they displayed decreased liking for their preferred stimuli.

Experience seems to determine the stimuli we prefer initially. Vitz (1966) discovered that musically experienced people preferred a complex tone sequence to a simple tone sequence. People who are musically inexperienced were attracted to the less complex tone sequences.

Why do we prefer moderately arousing environments? P. T. Young's *hedonic theory* (1961, 1966) provides a likely answer. According to Young, rewarding stimuli have the capacity to produce *primary affective arousal*, and the greater the affective arousal, the higher the reward (or incentive) value. Thus, our preference for a moderately arousing environment, in Young's view, reflects the strong positive affective arousal produced by stimulating environments. Consider your preference for a particular kind of music; Young's hedonic theory would assert that your preference is due to the primary affective arousal elicited by it.

Young's theory also suggests the process which motivates you to listen to your favorite music. Stimuli associated with the primary affective arousal (for example, a band you have heard playing your favorite music) become able to elicit a *conditioned affective arousal*. Exposure to these stimuli motivates approach behavior toward the object (music), thus producing the primary affective arousal. Therefore, you will attend a concert at which your favorite music will be played but not one at which another type of music will be played.

Young and Chaplin's study (1945) demonstrates conditioned affective arousal in a laboratory setting. Rats exposed to both sucrose (sugar) and casein (a protein) in a distinctive environment showed a preference for the palatable, arousing sucrose over the nonpalatable casein. Young and Chaplin then created a protein deficiency in these rats by removing protein from their diet. However, the rats continued to choose sucrose over casein.

Why did Young and Chaplin's protein-deficient rats choose the sucrose instead of the casein? Their choice did not reflect an inhibition of the need for casein because of the hedonic value of sucrose. Instead, the conditioned affective arousal elicited by the distinctive environment motivated the rats to choose sucrose. Evidence for this view can be seen in the behavior of these rats in a new environment in which they chose casein. Apparently, an environment does not motivate behavior indiscriminately; it motivates only a response toward an affectively arousing experience.

Young's hedonic theory assumes that primary affective arousal is responsible for the reinforcing value of pleasurable events. Also, stimuli associated with reward become able to elicit a conditioned affective arousal which functions to motivate us toward the reinforcing event. With respect to reinforcement and motivation, Young's theory has the same properties as Spence's concepts R_G and r_G, described in Chapter 2. Later, this chapter presents the brain mechanism responsible for the motivational and reinforcing function of reward.

The material we've just examined indicates that the difference in our arousal levels has an important influence on behavioral functioning. Extreme cortical arousal often impairs behavioral effectiveness; we typically perform most efficiently at a moderate arousal level. Also, we prefer moderately arousing situations and avoid situations producing either low or high arousal. There are also differences in levels of sleep, each level serving a vital function in our behavioral effectiveness when we are awake. Additionally, sleep deprivation often leads to behavioral deficits. The next section describes the stages of sleep as well as how they affect behavior and also looks at which brain system controls our ability to sleep.

Stages of Sleep

When we first fall asleep, our EEG pattern shows high-voltage, slow delta waves (see Figure 4.6). The EEG recordings change during the next hour: the waves become larger and slower as we progress into deeper sleep—through stage 2, on to stage 3, and finally to stage 4. Deepening sleep renders us increasingly more difficult to awaken. Approximately 90 minutes after we fall asleep, our cortical activity changes radically (with low-voltage, rapid desynchronized waves) to resemble that of our waking cortical activity. This sleep stage is called REM because of the rapid eye movements which occur in it; it is sometimes

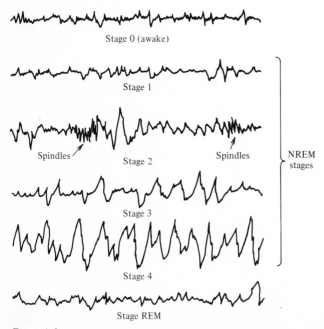

Figure 4.6
EEG patterns correlated with various stages of sleep.

referred to as *paradoxical sleep* because of the inconsistency between an aroused EEG pattern and an absence of motor activity.

REM sleep and non-REM (NREM) sleep differ in various ways. Our regulatory processes (for example heart rate, blood pressure) slow down during NREM sleep, but we maintain muscle tonus. In contrast, our internal physiological responses are aroused and irregular during REM sleep, but we lose muscle tonus (see Dement & Kleitman, 1957). Dement (1969) concluded that we are more likely to dream during REM sleep than during NREM sleep. Dement's subjects, awakened during REM sleep, reported 70 percent of the time that they had dreamed; subjects awakened during NREM sleep said 30 percent of the time that they had dreamed. Many people report that they do not dream. However, Faraday's research (1972) clearly shows that all people will report dreaming if awakened during REM sleep. Dement and Kleitman (1957) observed that the ability to recall a dream decreases the longer the sleep researcher waits after REM sleep to awaken the subject. It seems that the reason people say they do not dream is lack of recall rather than an absence of dreaming.

After our first REM period (approximately 10 minutes), we resume NREM sleep. During the remainder of our sleep we will go through three or four more cycles of NREM and REM sleep. In each successive cycle we spend more time in the lighter stages of sleep and REM sleep, and less time in the deeper stages of sleep. In fact, by the third or fourth cycle, we do not enter deep sleep, and REM may last for 30 minutes. Although the duration of REM and NREM sleep differs among people, a particular person's sleep pattern is typically consistent from night to night (Kleitman, 1963). The onset and termination of each period of NREM and REM sleep typically is regulated by biological changes programmed to occur during our 24-hour circadian cycle. Our sleep has a definite adaptive significance, and we alter our sleep pattern when we need additional sleep. The function of sleep is our next topic.

Why do we sleep?   Certainly all of us have stayed up several hours, if not many hours, past our usual bedtime. Tired and irritable by the end of the following day, we undoubtedly fell asleep early that night. The next day we felt rested. This example illustrates that sleep must serve a valuable function: feeling drained when we do not get our usual amount of sleep, we are motivated to make up lost sleep so that we can function normally.

The function of NREM sleep.   Contemporary research holds that the functional significance of REM sleep differs from that of NREM sleep. NREM sleep has a restorative function; it enables us to replenish physiological stores depleted during our waking hours. Several studies point to a restorative function for NREM sleep. Hartmann (1973) observed that strenuous physical exercise increased the time which his subjects spent in NREM sleep; in contrast, the subjects showed no change in REM sleep after they had exercised. Stage 4 appears especially important in restoring our biological system. Agnew, Webb, and Williams (1967) concluded that people deprived of only stage 4 sleep are physically lethargic but display no other behavioral changes. Also, Johnson and Naitoh (1974) found no decrease in the time their subjects spent in stage 4, even though total sleeping time was slowly decreased from 8 to 4 hours. Evidently we need NREM sleep in order to interact effectively with our environment.

The function of REM sleep.   REM sleep, or paradoxical sleep, also serves a valuable function. In contrast to the general restorative function of NREM sleep, REM sleep seems to restore the *norepinephrine* in the brain, which is depleted during stress. The importance of REM sleep in enabling us to cope with stress can be seen in the sleep patterns of people experiencing intense emotional trauma. Hartmann (1973) found that time spent in REM sleep increases after a death in the family, a major occupational change, or marital conflict.

Why does REM sleep aid our ability to deal with stressors? As will be seen shortly, the chemical transmitter norepinephrine is central in coping with stressors. When we deal with stress, norepinephrine is depleted. This depletion motivates increased REM sleep in order to restore norepinephrine to the normal level. Several studies support this view of REM function; here two are described. Hartmann, Bridwell, and Schildkraut (1971) injected rats with *alpha-methyl paratyrosine*, a drug which inhibits norepinephrine synthesis. They observed that the amount of REM sleep increased when levels of norepinephrine in the brain declined. Moreover, Holman, Elliot, and Barchas (1975) discovered that drugs which enhance the transmission of norepinephrine lead to decreased REM sleep.

People sometimes reduce their habitual sleep time to have more opportunity to work. The effect of a shortened sleep period is reduction of REM sleep. This loss of REM sleep appears to have both positive and negative consequences for motivated behavior. Positively, reduced REM sleep increases the intensity of many motivated behaviors (see Vogel, 1979). For example, Morden, Mullins, Levine, Cohen, and Dement (1968) reported that a loss of REM sleep increased sexual motivation in rats. Also, Hicks, Moore, Hayes, Phillips, and Hawkins (1979) observed an increased aggressiveness in rats following reduced REM sleep, while Dement (1965) found that loss of REM sleep intensified rats' motivation for food. These enhanced motivated actions returned to normal levels when REM sleep was increased to normal. However, a reduction in REM sleep also has negative consequences. Hicks and Sawrey (1978) reported that loss of REM sleep in their rats increased susceptibility to stressors; Hawkins, Phillips, Moore, Dunbar, and Hicks (1980) discovered that their animals' ability to cope with stressors was reduced. Apparently, the loss of REM sleep produces a heightened energy level and lowered ability to cope. Hartmann (1973) discovered that behavioral effects of reduced REM sleep disappeared when individuals were able to regain lost REM sleep.

Roffwarg, Muzio, and Dement (1968) suggested another function of REM sleep. According to Roffwarg, Muzio, and Dement, REM sleep provides the internal stimulation necessary for brain development, and as the brain matures, there is less need for REM sleep. In support of this view, Roffwarg, Muzio, and Dement (1968) reported that the amount of their subjects' REM sleep decreased steadily from infancy until adulthood. On the other hand, NREM sleep actually increased slightly until the subjects were 6 years old and then declined slighty until they became adults. Adults spend only slightly less time in NREM sleep than infants. It is interesting that Feinberg (1969) discovered that premature infants spend a greater percentage of sleep in REM than full-term infants. In all probability, the significance of REM sleep decreases as we get older; NREM sleep, on the other hand, continues throughout our lives to provide an important restorative function.

REM and NREM sleep apparently serve separate functions. In the next section we will see that two different brain systems control REM and NREM sleep.

Brain mechanisms controlling sleep.   Earlier in the chapter we saw that the RAS serves an important role in producing cortical and behavioral arousal. The RAS is also a critical area in controlling REM and NREM sleep. Jouvet's research (1967) demonstrates that two different parts of the RAS govern each sleep state: (1) the *raphe nuclei* control NREM sleep and (2) the *locus coerulus nuclei* govern REM sleep. Jouvet observed that stimulating the raphe nuclei increases NREM sleep but decreases REM sleep. In contrast, activating the locus coerulus nuclei produces the paradoxical EEG sleep pattern and decreases muscle tonus. Jouvet's research demonstrated that destroying raphe nuclei produces "sleepless" cats; destroying locus coerulus nuclei produces "dreamless" cats.

The neurotransmitter substance in the raphe nuclei—*serotonin*—differs from that in the locus corerulus. Jouvet's study (1969), providing support for involvement of the serotonin system in NREM sleep, concluded that an injection of the drug *para-chlorophenylalanine*, which decreases serotonin levels, reduces NREM sleep; injection of the chemical *tryptophan*, which can be converted to serotonin, produces normal sleep patterns. Also, Jouvet reported that selective destruction of neurons containing serotonin produces decreased ability to sleep. The chemical transmitter in the locus coerulus is norepinephrine. We saw in the previous section that the lowered levels of norepinephrine in the brain, which occur while we are awake, produce REM. In all likelihood, norepinephrine in the locus coerulus is not depleted during the day. Sensitive to norepinephrine levels in other brain centers, the locus coerulus produces the REM necessary to restore norepinephrine levels in these other systems to normal.

Other brain systems also influence our ability to sleep. The hypothalamus contains one area which produces, and another which inhibits, sleep. Stimulating the anterior hypothalamus produces sleep (Hess, 1957); destroying it produces insomnia (Nauta, 1946). The posterior hypothalamus, on the contrary, creates physiological and behavioral arousal (Hess, 1957). Destroying the posterior hypothalamus leads to continuous sleep (Feldman & Waller, 1962). Numerous areas in the frontal lobe, midline thalamus, and limbic system have been shown to facilitate sleep. Thus, many brain centers play an important role in producing both sleep and arousal.

This discussion of arousal has pointed out that through our biological processes, we have a natural capacity to adjust to changing environmental circumstances. However, one class of circumstances, called *stressors,* places unusual demands on us. A stressor represents any event which either strains or overwhelms our ability to adjust. Both psychological and physiological changes occur when we encounter a stressor. Some of us are able to cope with the stressor while others are not. In some instances, the response to stress is behavioral; in other cases, biological. We learned in Chapters 2 and 3 that our habits and expectations allow us to cope behaviorally with adversity. In the next section we'll discover the physiological systems which allow us to deal with a stressor.

Before the physiological consequences of experiencing a stressor are described, it is important to emphasize that psychological processes influence the stressfulness of an event. Noting that the severity of shock per se does not determine its stressfulness, Jay Weiss and his associates (see Weiss, 1972; Weiss, Stone, & Harrell, 1970) discovered that uncontrollable shocks produced a stronger reaction than controllable shocks of equal duration and intensity. Similarly, the reaction to unpredictable shocks was stronger than the reaction to predictable shocks. These results suggest that an event will be more stressful when it is perceived to be uncontrollable, unpredictable, or both.

OUR RESPONSE TO STRESSORS

General Adaptation Syndrome

Hans Selye (1956) described our biological reactions to a stressor. According to Selye, we exhibit a generalized pattern of internal changes when we are exposed to a stressor (refer to Figure 4.7). Selye called this physiological stress response the *general adaptation syndrome (GAS)*. All stressors, regardless of whether the stressor is physiological or psychological, activate the GAS. Examples of physiological stressors are extreme cold

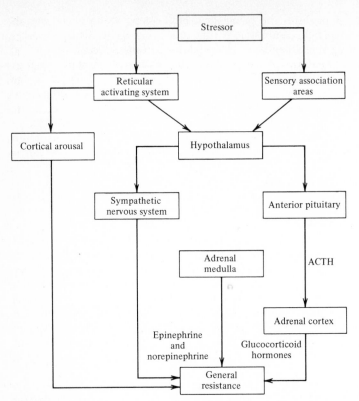

Figure 4.7
Diagrammatic representation of the internal physiological changes initated by an environmental stressor.
The event stimulates both the RAS system and specific sensory areas. Activation of the RAS produces
cortical arousal and hypothalamic stimulation. Activity in the hypothalamus leads to arousal of the
sympathetic nervous system and initiation of ACTH release from the anterior pituitary. The activation of
the sympathetic nervous system causes the adrenal medulla to release epinephrine and norepinephrine;
ACTH stimulates the release of glucocorticoid hormones from the adrenal cortex. All these physiological
changes provide general resistance to the stress. (Adapted from Buck, R. Human motivation and
emotion. *New York: Wiley, 1976.)*

or heat, invasion of dangerous microorganisms, and physical injury. Death of a relative or
friend, an impending examination, and being fired from a job are psychosocial stressors.
However, stressors are not always negative; the anticipation of a date can be as stressful as
fear of an examination. Any event which taxes our ability to adjust will activate the
GAS. Selye described three GAS stages: the *alarm reaction, resistance,* and *exhaustion.*

The alarm reaction. During the alarm reaction, the *sympathetic nervous system* is
activated under the control of the hypothalamus. Stimulation of the sympathetic nervous
system results in (1) increased respiration rate which enhances oxygen intake, (2)
heightened heart rate which allows more oxygen to be pumped, (3) release of stored red
blood cells to carry the increased oxygen, (4) redistribution of blood supply from the skin
and viscera to the brain and muscles, (5) increased conversion of glycogen into glucose
(sugar) and then release of glucose from the liver (the brain and muscles use this released

glucose as a source of energy), (6) secretion of epinephrine and norepinephrine from the adrenal medulla into the bloodstream, and (7) dilation of the pupils which enhances visual ability. In addition, the stressor activates the RAS which creates cortical arousal.

Why do stressful experiences cause these physiological responses? In 1915, Cannon referred to these internal changes as our *emergency reaction,* a biological reaction mobilizing our resources and preparing us for "flight or fight." Therefore, in Cannon's view, our immediate internal response to a stressor enables us to cope with stressful experiences.

Evidence does indicate that our alarm reaction often enables us to deal with adversity. Stimulating the sympathetic nervous system with norepinephrine enhances learning of escape and avoidance behavior; destruction of sympathetic nerves, a procedure known as *sympathectomy,* impairs our ability to escape or avoid stressors (see DiGusto, Cairncross, & King, 1971, for a review of this literature). However, this initial alarm response sometimes impairs our ability to cope. For example, many people "freeze" when confronted with an emergency; their intense internal responses prevent them, for example, from helping victims. The inability to recall information for examinations is another example. In fact, a stressor may be so severe as to cause death.

The alarm reaction lasts for only a short time—several minutes to several hours—and stops if the stressor stops. In these circumstances, the *parasympathetic nervous system* is dominant, enabling us to restore our physiological reserves to normal levels. For example, the parasympathetic nervous system hastens the digestive process, returning glycogen quickly to normal levels. However, if the stressor continues, we enter into the second GAS phase, the stage of resistance, in which we mobilize all of our resources to cope with the stressor. Systems designed to cope with extended stressors are activated, and all physiological systems not directly involved in our stress response are shut down. Let's now examine the biological changes which occur during the stage of resistance.

The stage of resistance. The adrenal gland secretes two classes of hormones involved in the body's response to a stressor. The catecholamines (norepinephrine and epinephrine) released by the *adrenal medulla* provide the intense general arousal and mobilization of energy which characterize the alarm reaction. The glucocorticoid hormones secreted by the *adrenal cortex* are involved in long-term resistance to stress. Activation of the hypothalamus by the stressor stimulates the release of *adrenocorticotrophic hormone* (*ACTH*) by the anterior pituitary gland. ACTH then causes the release of the *glucocorticoid hormones* from the adrenal cortex. This physiological system is often referred to as the *adrenocortical system.*

The glucocorticoid hormones. Glucocorticoid hormones (*hydrocorticosone, corticoster-one, cortisol*) enable us to remain mobilized in our fight against a continued stressor by stimulating the conversion of nonsugars (fats, proteins) to sugars and enhancing the rate of glycogen storage in the liver. The glucocorticoid hormonal effect provides us with the continued energy which we need to cope with the stressor. In addition, glucocorticoid hormones increase the effectiveness of epinephrine and norepinephrine, thereby allowing us to be able to continue to respond even with dimininished levels of epinephrine and norepinephrine. However, glucocorticoid hormones also antagonize inflammatory processes: they (1) delay the growth of new tissue around a wound or foreign substance in the skin, (2) inhibit the formation of antibodies, (3) decrease the formation of white blood cells, and (4) reduce the effectiveness of the thymus gland and other lymphoid tissues.

A susceptibility to disease. Glucocorticoid hormonal effects are surprising: they provide us with the resources needed to cope with a stressor but simultaneously antagonize our body's defense against it. The reduced resistance produced by glucocorticoid hormones can cause susceptibility to diseases which would not have occurred had the body not been responding to the original stressor and which may even result in death.

Psychological as well as biological stressors can predispose us to develop physical illnesses. Holmes and Rahe's research program (see Holmes & Rahe, 1967) demonstrates that changes in our lives can increase our sensitivity to disease. We may perceive these life changes as pleasant (for examples, a promotion, marriage, or a new house) or unpleasant (for example, death of a spouse, divorce, or loss of a job). Regardless of their nature, life changes are stressors and appear to be related to a wide variety of physical illnesses such as cancer, coronary disease, tuberculosis, skin disease, and kidney disorder. In addition, many studies (for example, Rahe, McKean, & Arthur, 1967; Wyler, Masuda, & Holmes, 1971) have shown that an increase in the stressfulness of life changes causes an increase in the probability that physical illnesses will develop.

How did Holmes, Rahe, and their colleagues demonstrate that life changes can enhance the likelihood of disease? They developed the *social readjustment rating scale* (SRRS) which could be used to indicate how severe a readjustment each life change requires. They arbitrarily assigned a value of 50 to marriage and then asked subjects serving as judges to rate the seriousness of other life changes by using marriage as a standard. Holmes, Rahe, and their colleagues found considerable agreement between adolescents and adults in several cultures regarding the severity of life changes. Table 4.1 presents the life-change units (LCU) for 43 experiences. Next, the experimenters asked other subjects to match certain events they had experienced during the preceding year with items on the *schedule of recent experience* (SRE) questionnaire. These incidents were then correlated with subjects' current physical illnesses. Not only did Holmes and Rahe discover that life changes increased the probability of illness but, using each subject's combined score in life-change units, they were able to estimate the probability of illness. For example, a score of 150 yielded a 30 percent likelihood of illness; a score of 150–300 yielded a 50 percent likelihood of illness; a combined score of over 300 yielded an 80 percent likelihood of illness. Thus, it seems that as the number of intense and different stressors which we experience during a year increases, the more likely we are to develop a physical illness.

Lazarus (1976) identified several methodological problems in Holmes and Rahe's research program. First, many of the studies used self-reports rather than direct observations of experiences and diseases. Second, many ill subjects may be more apt to perceive severe stress in their lives. Third, noncontrolled factors may have been responsible for the obtained results in this correlational research. For instance, environmental conditions could have caused the life changes and illnesses. Although methodological improvement will strengthen our confidence in the view that life changes predispose us to physical illnesses, the relationship between life changes and illnesses that Holmes and Rahe observed is certainly predictable from the physiological changes seen in the general adaptation syndrome.

In addition, animal research has shown that a psychological stressor can lead to physical illnesses. An experiment by Friedman, Ader, and Glasgow (1965) is one example of this research. They reported that rats frightened by exposure to electric shock became ill after receiving the *Coxsackie B* virus. In contrast, the disease did not occur in those animals which received only the virus or only the psychological stressor.

Davis and Read (1958) provided another example of reduced resistance to stress-produced disease when they injected their mice with the *Trichinella spiralis* worm larvae. All of the mice were housed individually for 15 days; however, half were crowded into groups of six for 3 hours per day. To minimize the transfer of worms, the animals had no

Table 4.1
Social Readjustment Scale

Rank	Life Event	Mean Value
1	Death of spouse	100
2	Divorce	73
3	Marital separation	65
4	Jail term	63
5	Death of close family member	63
6	Personal injury or illness	53
7	Marriage	50
8	Fired at work	47
9	Marital reconciliation	45
10	Retirement	45
11	Change in health of family member	44
12	Pregnancy	40
13	Sex difficulties	39
14	Gain of new family member	39
15	Business readjustment	39
16	Change in financial state	38
17	Death of close friend	37
18	Change to different line of work	36
19	Change in number of arguments with spouse	35
20	Mortgage over $10,000	31
21	Foreclosure of mortgage or loan	30
22	Change in responsibilities at work	29
23	Son or daughter leaving home	29
24	Trouble with in-laws	29
25	Outstanding personal achievement	28
26	Wife begins or stops work	26
27	Begin or end school	26
28	Change in living conditions	25
29	Revision of personal habits	24
30	Trouble with boss	23
31	Change in work hours or conditions	20
32	Change in residence	20
33	Change in schools	20
34	Change in recreation	19
35	Change in church activities	19
36	Change in social activities	18
37	Mortgage or loan less than $10,000	17
38	Change in sleeping habits	16
39	Change in number of family get-togethers	15
40	Change in eating habits	15
41	Vacation	13
42	Christmas	12
43	Minor violations of the law	11

From: Holmes, T. H., & Rahe, R. H. The social readjustment rating scale. *Journal of Psychosomatic Research*, 1967, *11*, 213–218.

food or water when in the stressor condition (crowding). Davis and Read found few worms in the nonstressed animals, but all of the crowded animals had worm infestation. A reasonable conclusion from both the animal and human studies is that a stressor can increase our susceptibility to physical illnesses.

A shutdown of nonessential systems.   Our body not only activates internal systems designed to resist a stressor but also inhibits all physiological systems not directly involved in resistance to stress. A prolonged stressor causes decreased secretion of the thyroid-stimulating hormone (TSH) and the growth hormone. Sexual and reproductive physiology are also inhibited. In males, a stressor produces a decrease in sperm and testosterone (the male sex hormone). In females, suppressed menstrual cycle (or suppressed estrus in nonhuman mammals), failure to ovulate, increased natural abortion, and reduced lactation are consequences of a prolonged stressor. Stressors can also precipitate disturbances in sexual behavior; a loss of sexual motivation frequently occurs with extended exposure to stressors. Decreased food consumption accompanied by weight loss occurs during our resistance to stressors. Bodily processes are apparently geared completely to defending against stressors, and all other biological and behavioral functions are inhibited during our attempts to cope.

The stage of exhaustion.   An animal or human eventually depletes all resources if a stressor does not stop; with no resources, all the body's defense systems fail, and the animal or person dies.

This section has covered our general biological responses to various stressors. There are also variations in our physiological responses to different stressors. These differences enable us to respond appropriately to each stressor. For example, a cold stressor elicits shivering, which generates heat; a warm stressor producers sweating, which decreases heat. Chapter 3 discussed the cognitive processes which allowed us to identify our emotional responses and provided the information telling us which behaviors are appropriate. Let's now examine the internal changes specific to different stressors. These internal changes also appear to influence our behavioral response to a stressor.

The Physiology of Fear and Anger
Recall that Cannon suggested that our emergency reaction prepares us for "flight or fight." Yet, how do we know whether to be angry and fight or to be afraid and flee? In Chapter 3 we saw that we usually attribute our emotional arousal to the behavior of those near us: if people with whom we associate act frightened, we are afraid; we are angry when those near us are also angry. However, some research indicates that when we are afraid, our internal response differs from when we are angry; this difference plays an important role in our motivated behavior.

Ax's experiment (1953) demonstrates that the adrenal medulla releases both epinephrine and norepinephrine when we are angry or fearful; however, more epinephrine than norepinephrine is released when we are afraid, while the opposite is true when we are angry. Although the effects of norepinephrine and epinephrine are mostly the same, there are some differences. For example, norepinephrine increases diastolic blood pressure (pressure when the heart is relaxed and filling with blood), whereas epinephrine increases systolic blood pressure (pressure when the heart is pumping blood). To illustrate that our physiological response to anger differs from that produced by fear, Ax exposed subjects to one of two treatment conditions. Some subjects were attached to a polygraph machine by a rude, arrogant experimenter; other subjects were presented with a polygraph machine from which sparks suddenly flared. Subjects in the former group became angry; those in the latter group were frightened. Ax discovered that angry subjects showed a physiological reaction similar to that which would have been produced by an injection of norepinephrine. In contrast, the frightened subjects' physiological response was identical to that which would have been produced by an injection of epinephrine.

Do these physiological differences between angry and frightened people influence their motivated behavior? Several studies indicate that the levels of secreted norepinephrine and epinephrine do affect our behavioral response to a stressor. Let's examine two of these studies. Elmadjian, Hope, and Lamson (1957) observed that aggressive psychiatric patients had high norepinephrine levels, but that patients frightened by a staff conference had high epinephrine levels. Funkenstein (1955) concluded that predatory animals, relying on aggression to survive, have greater norepinephrine levels than nonpredatory animals; animals which flee to survive (for example, rabbits) show higher epinephrine levels than norepinephrine levels. Although psychologists are not certain how these differences lead to flight or fight, these results do indicate that our internal responses when we are afraid are different from those when we are angry.

Diseases of Adaptation

You learned earlier that our body's response to a stressor increases our susceptibility to disease. In addition, the response itself can actually cause physical disease. Selye labeled diseases produced by our physiological stress response *diseases of adaptation*. These diseases, also called *psychosomatic diseases*, include essential hypertension, ulcers, and colitis. They are the side effects of our attempts to cope biologically with stress. Stress is implicated as capable of causing each of these illnesses and is also thought capable of intensifying their severity. Let's examine ulcers as an example of these diseases of adaptation.

Ulcers are small holes in the stomach or the upper part of the small intestine caused by the oversecretion of hydrochloric acid (HC1) over a period of time. In addition to being painful, ulcers can bleed and thereby cause death.

Mahl's experiment (1949) shows that psychological stress can cause increased secretion of hydrochloric acid. In order to measure this secretion, he had eight premedical students each swallow a balloon which contained measuring devices. Levels of hydrochloric acid were measured on nonstressful days and on the day of an extremely important examination determining admittance to medical school. In six of the eight subjects, Mahl found hydrochloric acid much higher before the examination than on the control days. The two subjects who did not have high secretion of hydrochloric acid appeared not to have been stressed by anticipating the examination. One of them had already been admitted to medical school; the other was only an average student and did not expect admittance in any event.

Stress has also been shown to cause ulcers. In Sawrey, Conger, and Turrell's study (1956) indicating that conflict (see Chapter 2) can precipitate ulcers, hungry rats had to cross a grid to receive food. This experiment employed several control conditions: (1) Some hungry animals were shocked only when food was not presented; thus, their two motives did not conflict. (2) Other animals either were not hungry when they were shocked or were hungry and received no shock. (3) Still other rats received no stress (no shock). Sawrey, Conger, and Turrell found that although both shock and hunger (control conditions 1 and 2) led to ulcers, it was the experimental condition—conflict—that caused the most severe ulcers.

Why did shock and hunger alone produce ulcers? Weiss (1968) offered a likely explanation. According to Weiss, it is not stress but the inability to control stress that causes ulcers. In Weiss's study, two groups of monkeys received electric shocks. Group 1 could escape shock by jumping onto a platform; group 2 could not control shock, which terminated independently of any behavior. To control for the duration of shock which the monkeys experienced, shock ended for a monkey in group 2 whenever its counterpart in group 1 escaped from the shock. Weiss discovered that monkeys unable to control shock developed ulcers; the monkeys able to escape shock had no ulcers.

Perhaps you have noticed a contradiction between Sawrey, Conger, and Turrell's study and Weiss's. Conflict led to ulcers in the Sawrey, Conger, and Turrell's study. Yet, their animals could control events (that is, they could choose whether or not to cross the shock grid); this should have prevented ulcers. Gray (1972) has suggested that the severity of conflict negated the influence of control. It is also likely that there is less perception of control in conflict situations than in nonconflict settings.

How Do You Cope with Stress?

Response differences.   Stress is in all of our lives. As students, you have examinations which provide frequent stressful experiences. Although some of you may develop psychosomatic disorder symptoms as a result, most of you will not. Why do some people develop psychosomatic illnesses while others do not? Evidence points out that people respond differently to the same stressor. Some persons exhibit an intense alarm reaction to a stressor to which other persons show only a low or moderate physiological reaction. These differences in responsivity to stressors influence the development of disease; the more we respond physiologically to a stressor, the more we are apt to develop a psychosomatic illness. Let's look next at the evidence demonstrating that how we respond to a stressor determines our susceptibility to disease.

Several researchers (see Friedman & Rosenman, 1974; Jenkins, 1976) have identified two types of people who differ in their responsivity to stressors. The response of *type* A persons to a stressor differs both behaviorally and physiologically from that of *type* B people. Compared with type B people, type A persons sense extreme environmental demands to excel, feel a strong urgency to achieve, are extremely competitive, and become impatient and hostile when success is not imminent. In addition, type A people show much stronger arousal to stressors than type B people do. In Dembroski, MacDougall, and Shields's study (1977) illustrating these differences, type A subjects performing a reaction-time task showed greater increases in heart rate and blood pressure increases than type B subjects. Friedman, Byers, Diamant, and Rosenman (1975) found that type A people, when exposed to a challenging task, displayed higher norepinephrine levels than type B people exposed to the same task.

However, the physiological and psychological differences between type A and type B individuals do not occur in all situations (see Glass, 1977). Glass reported that his subjects showed the type A behavior pattern (competitiveness, impatience, and hostility) and extreme physiological responsivity only in a challenging task or when esposed to an uncontrollable stressor. In nonstressful circumstances, there are no differences between type A and type B people.

One important difference between type A and type B persons is their differing susceptibility to coronary disease. For example, Rosenman, Brand, Jenkins, Friedman, Straus, and Wurm (1975) discovered during their 8½-year study that type A men were twice as likely as type B men to have coronary heart disease. Although these experimenters adjusted for other traditional risk factors (for example, cigarette smoking, high systolic blood pressure, and high serum cholesterol), type A men still showed a greater risk of coronary disease. Several studies (see Blumenthal, Williams, King, Schanberg, & Thompson, 1978) indicate that type A patients show more severe narrowing of the coronary arteries than type B people. Recall that type A people exhibit a higher norepinephrine response to a stressor than type B persons. Glass (1977) suggested that this greater stressor-induced release of norepinephrine in type A people plays an important role in the development of coronary disease. Several studies (Haft, 1974; Eliot, 1979) demonstrate that release of norepinephrine can accelerate arterial damage, enhance formation of thrombi, and produce cardiac arrhythmias; these studies provide strong support for Glass's view.

You can cope with stress. Is there any hope for people who are extremely sensitive to stressors? Fortunately, methods are available which can reduce their responses to acceptable levels. Some of these methods directly antagonize responses to stress. Other techniques decrease the perceived aversiveness of stressful experiences. By reducing the adversity of stress, physiological responses are indirectly attenuated. People who cope successfully with stressors use these techniques, and the use of these procedures by sensitive people can either decrease susceptibility to disease or curtail disease which has already developed. This discussion of stress ends by considering several ways to decrease our physiological response to stressors.

The inhibition of the stress response. Several ways of directly inhibiting our stress response have been used successfully. In Chapter 2, relaxation training as part of the desensitization treatment of phobias was discussed. Recall that relaxation training involves tensing and then relaxing all major muscle groups. This state of relaxation, assumed to inhibit fear, thus prevents the elicitation of avoidance behavior. Research has clearly indicated that relaxation is an effective antistress response. One example of this research is Benson's study (1975), in which he found that relaxation lowered heart rate and decreased blood pressure, muscle tension, and cortical activity.

Why is the relaxation procedure effective? Several aspects of this procedure contribute to its effectiveness. The quiet environment, closed eyes, and comfortable position decrease afferent sensory input. (We learned earlier that cortical arousal is related to sensory stimulation.) The relaxation response inhibits arousal of the sympathetic nervous system. By reducing cortical arousal and activity in the sympathetic nervous system, the relaxation response decreases our reaction to stress and facilitates our behavioral coping response.

Biofeedback is another successful technique which directly inhibits our physiological stress response. Operant conditioning principles (see Chapter 1) appear to be responsible for the effectiveness of biofeedback. Recall that reinforcement increases the frequency of behavior which precedes reward. In biofeedback, our physiological response is the behavior and the decreased stress response represents reinforcement. How do people experience reward, since they are not aware of their level of physiological functioning? Electronic recording devices are used to record physiological responses, and subjects (or patients) are usually shown a visual record of their responses. When a person alters the stress reaction, this change is reinforced. Biofeedback for hypertensives works like this: their blood pressure is recorded and then shown to them; when they lower their blood pressure, they are told that they have done so and are thus reinforced.

Schwartz's experiment (1973) demonstrating the effectiveness of biofeedback found that hypertensive patients showed lowered blood pressure, lowered heart rate, and decreased muscle tension. Other clinical applications of biofeedback include: (1) Engel and Blecker's study (1974), in which biofeedback controlled patients' cardiac irregularity or arrhythmia if the arrhythmia was capable of being aided by increasing or decreasing their heart rates; and (2) Friar and Bealtley's experiment (1976), which concluded that decreasing the dilation of blood vessels in the brain effectively treated migraine headaches.

However, Stoyva (1976) argued that biofeedback merely represents another method of training people to relax. He showed that biofeedback training, though it did provide a more rapid change in physiological responding than relaxation training did, was not more effective than relaxation training. Since biofeedback requires sophisticated recording devices, whereas the relaxation procedure needs no equipment, relaxation therapy appears preferable at this time.

Maybe it isn't so bad.   Richard Lazarus (1974) suggested that cognitive processes can alter our physiological and behavioral responses to a stressor. Since a stressor does not always produce psychosomatic illness or behavioral pathology, Lazarus believed that how we perceive the events which influence us determines our response. According to Lazarus, our *cognitive appraisal* of situations can either increase or decrease the effects of stressors.

There are three methods which we employ to minimize the impact of a stressor. *First, we can deny its aversiveness. Second, we can believe others who tell us that it is not aversive. Finally, since a stressor we have never experienced often seems aversive, we can reduce its impact if we imagine that it has happened before.* On the other hand, cognitive processes can increase the aversiveness of a stressor. *First, we can exaggerate its aversiveness. Second, we can receive information indicating that it is very aversive.* We learned in Chapter 3 that our cognitive processes serve an important role in our behavioral responses. Next, several studies are described which indicate that our environmental perceptions influence our physiological reactions.

A study by Wolff, Friedman, Hofer, and Mason (1964) demonstrates that denying the aversiveness of a stressor reduces the physiological response to it. They examined how the parents of children dying of leukemia coped with their child's disease. Some parents accepted that their child would die; others denied it. Wolff, Friedman, Hofer, and Mason discovered lower levels of hydrocortisone in parents who denied the situation than in those parents who accepted it.

Many studies have shown that the information we receive from our environment influences our physiological responses; let's examine several of them. In a study by Lazarus, Speisman, Mordkoff, and Davison (1962), subjects saw one of three films depicting a primitive circumcision ritual. The video was identical for the three films but their sound tracks varied. Some subjects heard the film narrator deny any aversive effects of circumcision, other subjects heard a detached technical discussion of the ritual, and a third group heard horrible details of the rite. The experimenters discovered that the physiological responses to the film were lower in those subjects who heard the denial and the intellectual presentation than in those who heard the aversive commentary. In a similar study, Speisman, Lazarus, Mordkoff, and Davison (1964) learned that the denial and the intellectual description produced lower physiological responses than a silent film; in contrast, they noted greater stress reactions when the sound track emphasized the dangers than when the film was silent. Also, Lazarus and Alfert (1964) observed that denial of aversiveness presented before the film rather than during it was more effective in reducing stress reactions.

Stressful experiences which we view do not have to be as unusual as an initiation rite to affect our physiological responses. Lazarus, Opton, Numikos, and Rankin (1965) found that denial or intellectual information affected the physiological responses to viewing a filmed accident. The subjects in this study saw a film of a man being hit by a wooden plank while he operated a saw in a woodworking shop. Lazarus and his colleagues observed that presenting a taped denial of aversiveness and intellectual information lowered the subjects' physiological responses; a soundtrack emphasizing danger heightened the stress reaction to the film.

We can also influence physiological responding by imagining events before they occur. Folkins, Lawson, Opton, and Lazarus (1968) discovered less stress reaction in subjects who imagined the accident in the woodworking shop before they saw the film than in subjects who did not imagine the accident beforehand.

This discussion has indicated that information can reduce our physiological response to a stressor. Auerback, Kendall, Cuttler, and Levitt's study (1976) demonstrates one example of a clinical application of the cognitive appraisal orientation. Before being hospitalized to undergo dental surgery, two groups of patients received different information. One group was given typical, general information about the hospital; the other group received specific information about the upcoming operation. The study concluded that patients who were given specific information showed less emotional response than those who received general information. In an earlier experiment, Egbert, Battit, Welsh, and Bartlett (1964) found that surgery patients who received both description of the pain involved and a description of the medication which the doctor would probably prescribe went home almost 3 days earlier than patients who were given only general information about hospitalization. Evidently, knowledge of what to expect from a future stressor reduces our physiological reaction when we actually encounter it.

Relationship between Arousal and Stress

In this chapter, arousal and stress have been treated as separate concepts. Arousal represents a nonspecific internal activation, primarily consisting of the RAS and the limbic system. We learned that we function most efficiently at intermediate arousal levels and prefer moderately arousing environments. A stressor, in contrast, not only taxes our ability to adjust, but also can, if sufficiently intense and prolonged, result in disease or even death. We saw that a stressor stimulates specialized internal systems which mobilize our resources to cope. Unfortunately, the central characters in our body's reaction to stress—the adrenal glucocorticoid hormones—actually decrease our resistance to disease and often lead to illness or death.

Although the distinction between arousal and stress seems logical, it appears to reflect different psychological viewpoints of the same process. According to arousal theory, we prefer moderately arousing situations. What type of events lead to moderate arousal levels? Since most people apply for jobs, it seems reasonable to conclude that this is a moderately arousing circumstance experienced by most of us. Yet, it is also stressful and increases the probability of disease. In contrast, most people avoid the extremely arousing and stressful situation of mountain climbing. Although sometimes we have no choice but to endure aversive stressful events, we often deliberately expose ourselves to many situations that lead to psychosomatic illness. Hennessey and Levine's review article (1979) presents convincing evidence that identical physiological systems mediate both arousal and stress. Let's briefly consider this evidence.

Berlyne (1971) reported that novel, uncertain, or conflicting events produce strong RAS and cortical arousal. Since these situations are also stressful, animals and humans are motivated to avoid them. Hennessey and Levine described many studies supporting the idea that novelty, uncertainty, and conflict also activate the adrenocortical system.

Let's look at three studies illustrating, respectively, the influence of novelty, uncertainty, and conflict on adrenocortical functioning. (1) *Novelty:* An article by Barrett, Cairncross, and King (1973) showed that exposure to novel events (for example, handling by experimenters or confinement in an experimental chamber) produced large elevations in rats' plasma cortisol levels. (2) *Uncertainty:* Hennessey, King, McClure, and Levine (1977) compared both plasma corticosterone and behavioral arousal in rats exposed to highly predictable aversive events, moderately predictable aversive events, unpredictable aversive events, or nonaversive events. They reported high corticosterone levels and a high degree of fear in animals exposed to either predictable or unpredictable adversity. Less fear and lower corticosterone levels were observed when aversive events were moderately predictable; the lowest physiological and behavioral responses were noticed with nonaversive events. Apparently, both an intense stress reaction and behavioral arousal are produced when we are either certain that an aversive event is going to occur or do not know when to expect that aversive event. The least stressful and arousing situation is certainty that adversity will not occur. (3) *Conflict:* Smotherman, Hennessey, and Levine (1976) evaluated plasma corticosterone secretion in an approach-avoidance conflict. In the first phase of this study, rats learned to drink sweetened milk from a water bottle. After four exposures to the milk, each rat was injected with lithium chloride, a drug which induces illness. Thus, the animals were in conflict between their approach to their desired food and avoidance of illness. The authors discovered heightened corticosterone secretion in this conflict situation.

This discussion points to strong adrenocortical involvement in arousal and stress (refer to Figure 4.7). Other physiological systems also contribute to our stress and arousal response. As you can see from Figure 4.7, an environmental event activates the reticular activating system and the sensory association areas. Stimulation of the RAS produces cortical and hypothalamic arousal. Hypothalamic stimulation activates the sympathetic nervous system and the adrenocortical system. This reaction provides our internal resistance to stress. Yet we have omitted one important concept in this discussion of stress and arousal. Our stress and arousal responses produce the motivational force behind our behavior, but these responses do not determine which behavior we will exhibit. We learned in Chapters 2 and 3 that the environment directs our behavior—we approach reinforcers and avoid aversive events. In those chapters we also discovered the psychological factors which control our incentive to approach reinforcers and avoid adversity. The biological systems which motivate our approach and avoidance behavior are described next.

THE BIOLOGY OF REWARD AND PUNISHMENT

We differ considerably in our responses to reward and punishment: Some of us are intensely motivated to obtain reward; others show a lack of interest in reinforcement. Similarly, punishment can readily modify some persons' behavior; other persons seem totally oblivious to punishment. Although psychological factors can clearly affect our sensitivity to reward and punishment, physiological research during the past 25 years demonstrates that several brain systems are significantly involved in our responses to both reinforcers and adversity. Effective functioning of these systems allows us to obtain socially acceptable rewards and avoid potential punishment. Malfunctions in these systems lead to pathological behavior. The next section takes up the brain systems which mediate reward and punishment, and later discusses evidence that behavioral disorders result when these systems operate improperly.

Olds and Milner's Studies

James Olds and Peter Milner's research (see Olds & Milner, 1954) is a significant contribution to psychology. Olds and Milner found that stimulating some areas of the brain is reinforcing; stimulating other areas is aversive. It is interesting that they made their classic observations accidently when trying to determine the effects of activating the reticular formation. Their electrode placement mistakenly swung forward into the hypothalamus. When this area was aroused, their rats behaved as if stimulation was reinforcing. For example, the rats strongly preferred the place on the long table where they received the stimulation.

In order to evaluate their findings further, Olds and Milner made the electrical stimulation contingent upon pressing a bar in a Skinner box (see Figure 4.8). They found that the rats learned to press a bar to receive brain stimulation. The animals' behavior to obtain brain stimulation is called either *electrical stimulation of the brain (ESB)* or *intracranial self-stimulation (ICSS)*. Many species, including pigeons (Goodman & Brown, 1966), rats (Olds & Milner, 1954), cats and dogs (Stark & Boyd, 1963), primates (Brady, 1961), and humans (Heath, 1955), have demonstrated that brain stimulation can be reinforcing.

Although Olds and Milner found that stimulating many brain areas provided reinforcement, activation of other brain areas was aversive. Animals receiving this aversive stimulation learned a new behavior to terminate or avoid it. For example,

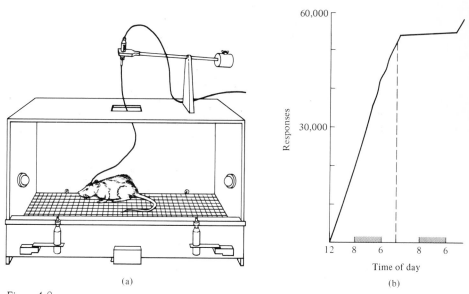

(a)   (b)

Figure 4.8
(a) *Rat pressing a bar for electrical brain stimulation (ESB).* (b) *Sample cumulative record. Note the extremely high rate of responding (over 2,000 bar presses per hour) which occurred for more than 24 hours and was followed by a period of sleep. [Adapted from Olds, J. Self-stimulation experiments and differentiated rewards. In H. H. Jasper, L. D. Proctor, R. S. Knighton, W. C. Noshav, & R. T. Costello (Eds.), Reticular formation of the brain. Boston: Little, Brown, 1958. Copyright 1958 by Little, Brown and Company.]*

Delgado, Roberts, and Miller (1954) discovered that cats learned to turn a paddlewheel to terminate brain stimulation, just as they would have done to escape an electrical shock to the feet.

The Anatomical Location of Reward and Punishment

Larry Stein and his associates (see Stein, 1969) presented evidence indicating that a group of nerve fibers, the *medial forebrain bundle* (MFB) located in the limbic system, is the brain's reward center (see Figure 4.9). Stimulation of the MFB motivates us to approach reward. Additionally, another limbic system fiber tract, the *periventricular tract* (PVT), represents the brain's punishment center. Activation of the PVT motivates us to avoid punishment.

Stein also described how the reward (MFB) and punishment (PVT) systems exert control over motivated behavior (refer to Figure 4.9). Activity in the PVT inhibits our tendency to approach events. Stimulation of the MFB—either by internal activation or the presence of a reinforcing event—inhibits the amygdala. The amygdala excites the PVT through the medial thalamus and hypothalamus; inhibiting the amygdala lessens this excitation and thereby suppresses the effectiveness of the PVT punishment system. Stein's theory portrays animals and humans as normally cautious when encountering new events. The reward system inhibits our hesitancy and motivates approach behavior.

Why is the PVT not directly inhibited by the MFB? Recall the discussion of information processing; it was pointed out that although one system may be controlling a particular aspect of behavior, input from other areas is essential. For example, cortical information must be considered before any decision to behave or not to behave is reached. The location of the amygdala in the brain provides a mechanism for this cortical input. Let's now consider evidence for Stein's view that these two brain systems control

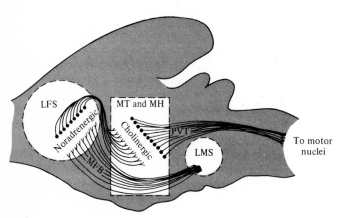

Figure 4.9

Schematic diagram of the reward and punishment systems. Stimulation of the medial forebrain bundle (MFB) by stimuli associated with reward or internal drive states causes the release of norepinephrine into the amygdala and other forebrain areas. Norepinephrine has an inhibitory influence on these forebrain neurons: the reduced activity in these forebrain structures results in a decreased activity in the periventricular system (PVT). The lowered arousal of the PVT system causes a lessening of behavioral suppression and an increased motivation for reinforcement. [From Stein, L. Chemistry of purposive behavior. In J. T. Tapp (Ed.), Reinforcement and behavior. New York: Academic Press, 1969.]

reward and punishment, and in addition, let's look at the processes which influence the effectiveness of these two systems.

The Reward System of the Medial Forebrain Bundle

Is this the site of reward?   Not only are most of the brain sites for reward located in the MFB, but MFB stimulation causes more intense reinforcing effects than stimulation of other brain areas does. For example, Olds, Travis, and Schwing (1960) found that rats press a bar up to 10,000 times per hour for MFB stimulation and only 500 times per hour for septum and amygdala stimulation.

Lesion studies also demonstrate the importance of the MFB in motivating reward-seeking behavior. These experiments (see Morgane, 1961; Teitelbaum & Epstein, 1962) showed that destruction of the MFB impairs reward-seeking behavior. Apparently, the MFB must be intact if we are to be motivated by reward.

The nature of the MFB's influence.   Chapter 2 described Rescorla and Solomon's concept of the central appetitive motivational state. In this section we will see that this is in fact stimulation of the MFB.

The appetitive motivational state and stimulation of the MFB share four characteristics: (1) *Activation of the central appetitive motivational state elicits behavior. Psychologists have discovered that MFB arousal motivates behavior, too.* (2) *Stimulation of the MFB is highly reinforcing; animals will exert considerable effort to activate this system. We exert considerable effort to obtain stimuli (secondary reinforcers) which stimulate the central appetitive motivational state, indicating that arousal of this state is also reinforcing.* (3) *We learned that reward and stimuli associated with reward activate the central appetitive motivational state. Evidence collected by numerous psychologists shows that reward enhances MFB functioning.* (4) *Deprivation increases the intensity of the approach behavior which is activated by the central appetitive motivational state. A similar influence of drive is found in MFB effectiveness.*

The MFB's reinforcing and motivational abilities should not be surprising; conventional reinforcers (for example, money) also possess motivational properties. For example, the extreme measures taken by many children to obtain ice cream indicates that ice cream reinforces them. And, the presence of ice cream often motivates them to consume large servings of it. Evidence which indicates that MFB stimulation is both reinforcing and motivating follows in the next section.

The reinforcing power of stimulation of the MFB.   Stimulation of the MFB is extremely reinforcing. Valenstein and Beer's study (1964) illustrating the impact of brain stimulation on rats found that for weeks, rats pressed a bar continuously up to 30 times per minute, stopping for only a short time to eat and groom. These rats responded until exhausted, fell asleep for several hours, and awoke to resume bar pressing. In addition, electrical stimulation of the brain (ESB) is more powerful than conventional reinforcers such as food, water, or sex. To illustrate that ESB has greater reinforcing value than other rewards, Routtenberg and Lindy (1965) constructed a situation in which pressing one lever caused brain stimulation and pressing another level produced food. The experimental animals (rats) were placed in this situation for only 1 hour a day and had no other food source. Yet all of the rats spent the entire hour pressing for brain stimulation and eventually starved to death.

The pleasurable aspect of brain stimulation has also been demonstrated in humans. For example, Ervin, Mark, and Steven (1969) reported that MFB stimulation not only eliminated pain in cancer patients but also produced a euphoric feeling (approximately equivalent to the effect of two martinis) lasting several hours. Sem-Jacobson (1968) found brain stimulation to be pleasurable to patients suffering intense depression, fear, or physical pain; patients who felt well experienced only mild pleasure.

The powerful reinforcing effect of ESB in animals has raised fears of its potential use in behavioral control (see Valenstein, 1973). Although brain stimulation appears pleasurable, it has not yet been proved to control human behavior effectively. Carlson (1977) argued that the use of brain stimulation as a method of behavioral control is not even feasible; a complex technology would have to exist to ensure that appropriate behaviors produce brain stimulation. Carlson believed that the extremely reinforcing effect of drugs (for example, heroin) poses more danger from misuse than brain stimulation does.

The motivational influence of MFB stimulation. The research of Elliot Valenstein and his associates (see Valenstein, Cox, & Kakolewski, 1969) demonstrated that activation of the reward system also motivates behavior. The specific response motivated by brain stimulation depends upon the prevailing environmental conditions. Thus, brain stimulation will motivate eating if food is available or drinking when water is present. This phenomenon is named *stimulus-bound behavior* to indicate that the stimulus environment determines which action is motivated by brain stimulation.

Electric brain stimulation motivates behavior even when no internal deprivation exists. Why would brain stimulation cause an animal to eat food when it is not hungry or to drink when it is not thirsty? Mendelson's study (1966) suggests that MFB activity makes environmental events more reinforcing and thereby motivates us to obtain these events. Mendelson placed his rats in a T maze (see Chapter 2); if the rats went to one side they received ESB; going to the other side produced both ESB and food. What did Mendelson's rats do in this situation? The previous discussion pointed out that animals will learn a new behavior to obtain ESB. Thus, we might predict that Mendelson's rats would favor both sides equally since they were not hungry. However, Mendelson reported that his subjects learned to go to the side producing both ESB and food.

Mendelson's rats first received the brain stimulation and then ate their food. It appears that receiving pleasurable brain stimulation motivated eating behavior. This observation indicates that the influence of reinforcement is to increase the reinforcing ability of other events.

This section has discussed the reinforcing and motivational effects of MFB stimulation. Yet, we do not have electrodes implanted in our reward system to motivate us; naturally occurring processes must activate our reward system. The next two sections point out that reward and drive stimulate the MFB and motivate our approach behavior.

The influence of reward. Many people report that sexual intercourse is more pleasurable after watching an erotic film (see Chapter 6). According to our view of MFB functioning, the movie activates the MFB reward center which then increases the reinforcing quality of sex. A number of studies have demonstrated that the presence of reward or stimuli associated with reward increases the reinforcing value of MFB activity. Let's examine several of these studies.

Mendelson's study (1967) illustrates the influence of water on the reward value of ESB. Mendelson compared how often his rats pressed a bar to obtain brain stimulation when water was available with how often they pressed it in the absence of water. His results showed that rats pressed significantly more with water present than without it. Coons and Cruce (1968) found that the presence of food increased the effort expended to obtain brain stimulation; and Hoebel (1969) discovered that a peppermint odor or a few drops of sucrose in the mouth produced a heightened self-stimulation response. These results indicate that the presence of reward makes brain stimulation more reinforcing.

Suppose that you can choose either vanilla or chocolate ice cream. Which will you pick? Some of us undoubtedly like vanilla ice cream and will select it. Others will select chocolate. We face many choices of rewards; usually our selection is based on differential reward values. Similarly, animals must choose between rewards which have different values. Two potential rewards (for example, food and water) can illustrate animals' preferences. The stimulus-bound behavior of some rats is eating; for other rats, it is drinking (see Valenstein, Cox, & Kakolewski, 1969). If our understanding of MFB functioning is accurate, a preferred reward should increase the value of brain stimulation more than a less preferred reward. DeSisto and Zweig's experiment (1974) supports this view. DeSisto and Zweig identified rats ("killers") which, following brain stimulation, killed but did not eat frogs; other rats ("feeders") ate frogs which were already dead but did not kill. The experimenters found that the presence of food increased ESB in the "feeders" but not in the "killers." In contrast, the presence of frogs intensified ESB in "killers" but had no effect on "feeders." Apparently, one reason for our preferences is that highly valued rewards produce more activity in the reward system than less valued rewards; thus, we choose the highly valued rewards.

The influence of drive.   Drinking ice water is very satisfying on a hot day, yet on a cold day ice water has little reinforcing quality. This example illustrates one characteristic of deprivation: drive increases the value of rewards. In this example, the presence of thirst on a hot day enhances the reward value of ice water. Increasing the activity of the brain's reward system is one probable mechanism responsible for this drive effect. Studies which show that drive increases the value of brain stimulation definitely support that view. Let's look at several of these demonstrations.

Using rats, Brady (1961) showed that the rate of self-stimulation depends upon the level of hunger; the longer his rats were deprived of food, the more intense was their rate of brain stimulation. Using water deprivation, Olds (1962) found that a similar effect enhanced the value of brain stimulation in rats deprived of water, as compared with nondeprived rats. We will see in Chapter 6 that the male sex hormone testosterone and the female sex hormone estrogen increase sexual motivation. Caggiula and Szechtman (1972) discovered that injecting rats with testosterone increased ESB; Prescott (1966) reported that the rate of brain stimulation increased in rats when estrogen levels increased during the estrus cycle and decreased when estrogen levels declined.

This discussion has indicated that MFB activity is pleasurable. Environmental reinforcers and internal drives activate the MFB system, and the effect of stimulating this reward system is to motivate approach behavior in order to obtain reward. However, we also avoid aversive events. The brain system which mediates our response to adversity is explained next.

The Punishment System of the Periventricular Tract

Chapter 2 detailed Rescorla and Solmon's central aversive motivational state, which is activated by aversive events and the anticipation of adversity. This stimulation results in terminating approach to reward and avoiding aversive and potentially aversive events. Much research indicates that the periventricular tract (PVT) is the site of Rescorla and Solomon's punishment system. Let's examine some of this evidence.

Stimulation of the PVT produces three effects identical to those induced by aversive events such as electric shock (see Olds, 1962). *First, PVT stimulation in animals elicits jumping, biting, and vocalizations, all behaviors which electric shock and other painful agents can produce. Second, both PVT stimulation and conventional punishers suppress reward-seeking behavior. Third, animals are motivated to terminate PVT stimulation as well as to acquire behaviors which prevent activation of the PVT. Shock and other aversive events also motivate escape and avoidance behaviors.*

Destruction of the PVT produces animals insensitive to aversive events. For example, Margules and Stein (1969) noted that rats with PVT lesions showed large deficits in their ability to avoid electrical shock. Apparently, as is true with the MFB and reward-seeking behavior, effective avoidance and escape from aversive events depend upon the effective functioning of the PVT. In the next section we will see that malfunctions in the MFB and PVT can lead to behavioral disturbances in humans.

The Influence of the Reward and Punishment Systems in Behavior Pathology

Many prominent psychologists (see Snyder, 1974; Stein & Wise, 1971, 1973; Valenstein, 1973) have suggested that behavioral disturbances can result from failure of the reward and punishment systems to operate effectively. Three major categories of abnormal behavior—schizophrenia, depression, and phobias—have been linked to malfunctions in the reward and punishment systems. Contemporary evidence implicates an overresponsive reward system in schizophrenia, a disorder characterized by disoriented thought, lack of emotion, and withdrawal from people and reality. A low level of functioning of the reward system is believed to produce depressives' failure to obtain satisfaction from reward. Phobics' extreme fear is thought to be caused by intense arousal of the punishment system. The discussion turns next to the chemical transmitter substances in the MFB reward system and the PVT punishment system, since the experimental evidence which shows that malfunctions in the reward and punishment systems cause behavioral disturbances comes primarily from chemically induced alterations in MFB and PVT functioning. This experimental evidence will be presented after the chemistry of reward and punishment is described.

The chemistry of reward and punishment.   *The MFB reward system.*   Many studies support the idea that two catecholamine substances, *norepinephrine* and *dopamine,* are the chemical transmitter substances in the MFB reward system (see Stein, 1969; Stein & Wise, 1969). Several of these studies are briefly described.

Margules (1969) found that an injection of *amphetamine,* a drug which stimulates the release of both norepinephrine and dopamine, enhances the reinforcing value of ESB. Olds (1970) and Stein and Wise (1974) made similar observations. Other experiments (see Olds, 1975; Stein & Wise, 1973) have discovered that direct administration of the catecholamines into the MFB reward system also increases the rate of brain stimulation.

Drugs which inhibit the MFB reward system decrease the reinforcing effect of self-stimulation. Stein and Wise (1969) reported that administration of *alpha-methylparatyrosine (AMPT),* a drug which prevents the synthesis of both norepinephrine and dopamine, decreases the rate of brain stimulation. Also, administration of *chlorpromazine,* a drug which blocks both norepinephrine and dopamine neural transmission, attenuates the reinforcing value of ESB. Other experiments (for example, Cooper, Cott, & Breese, 1974; Liebman & Butcher, 1974; Wauguier & Niemegeers, 1975) have also concluded that drugs which antagonize noradrenergic and dopaminergic neurons (those neurons for which dopamine is the transmitter substance) either reduce or eliminate responding aimed at brain stimulation.

The PVT punishment system. The chemical transmitter substance *acetylcholine* has been implicated in the motivation of escape and avoidance behavior (see Carlton, 1969; Stein, 1969). Injections of drugs which activate cholinergic neurons (those neurons for which acetylcholine is the transmitter substance) increase the influence of punishing agents. In contrast, drugs which block cholinergic activity reduce the effectiveness of punishment.

The experiments by Margules and Stein (1967) provide direct evidence of cholinergic transmission in the PVT punishment system. They injected directly into the punishment area drugs which either increase cholinergic activity (for example, *carbachol*) or decrease it (for example, *atropine*). Before being injected, their rats had been trained to press a bar for a reward (milk) and had experienced a tone paired with electric shocks. Margules and Stein administered the injections while presenting this tone. They reported that drugs which aroused cholinergic neurons increased the effectiveness of the tone in suppressing bar pressing. Drugs which inhibited cholinergic neurons decreased the suppressive ability of the tone.

The pharmacology of behavioral disturbance. We have seen that noradrenergic and dopaminergic neurons in the MFB reward system are activated when we seek reward. Moreover, cholinergic neurons in the PVT punishment system are aroused when we avoid adversity. Under ideal conditions, the effective functioning of these two systems enables us to obtain reward and avoid punishment. Evidence suggests that malfunctions in either the reward or the punishment system are involved in schizophrenia, depression, and phobic behavior.

Schizophrenia. Numerous studies have suggested that overresponsive dopaminergic neurons in the reward system are involved in producing schizophrenic behavior (see Carlson, 1977). Yet, why should an excessive concern for reward contribute to schizophrenia? Carlson suggested that schizophrenics are so attentive to reward that they process excessive environmental information. This sensory overstimulation confuses schizophrenics and causes them to withdraw from reality.

Several types of evidence indicate that the dopaminergic reward system contributes to schizophrenia. First, antipsychotic drugs (for example, *chlorpromazine*) block dopaminergic neural activity (Carlson, 1977). Second, drugs (such as amphetamine) which stimulate dopaminergic neurons can produce schizophrenic symptoms. Davis (1974) illustrated the influence of dopaminergic activation on schizophrenic behavior when he injected *methylphenidate*, a drug which causes the release of dopamine and prevents it from being taken up again, into schizophrenic patients when they were not exhibiting disturbed symptoms. Davis reported that these patients displayed extreme schizophrenic behavior within a minute after being injected. The type of schizophrenic symptom which the drug produced depended upon each particular patient: some had delusions and hallucinations; others became catatonic. Finally, Anden and Stock (1973) noted the effectiveness of *clozapine*, a specific antipsychotic drug which influenced only dopaminergic neurons in the limbic system.

Depression. A central characteristic of depression is lack of interest in reward. Considerable evidence indicates that lowered responsivity of the catecholamine neurons in the MFB reward system contributes to the development of depression in humans. This evidence is examined briefly next; Chapter 8 discusses in greater detail the role of catecholamines in producing depression.

Studies demonstrating that the MFB system is involved in depression fall into three categories. (1) Some studies show that depressives' blood and urine have an abnormally low level of catecholamine. This suggests that less catecholamine neurotransmitter is available for neural communication. (2) In some studies, drugs which lower brain catecholamine levels have produced depressive behavior in humans. Recall from the last section that these same drugs administered directly into the MFB area decreased the effect of brain stimulation. (3) Some studies show that clinically effective drug treatments for depression elevate brain catecholamine levels. You learned in the last section that chemicals which activate the MFB area increase the motivation to obtain reward. Apparently, normal functioning of the catecholamine neurons in the MFB reward system is necessary for us to appreciate reinforcing events.

Phobic behavior.   Recall from Chapters 2 and 3 that phobics are intensely motivated to avoid adversity. You learned that both fear and expectation play an important part in the development of human phobias. There is also evidence indicating that an overresponsive PVT punishment system contributes to a phobic's preoccupation with avoiding a particular aversive event.

Suppose that you feel extremely anxious about your forthcoming examinations and do not know whether you can take them. Your doctor might prescribe a tranquilizer as treatment for this excessive fear. Two frequently prescribed tranquilizers used to treat anxiety are *chlordiazepoxide* (*Librium*) and *diazepam* (*Valium*). Other common antianxiety drugs are the barbiturates (for example, *pentobarbital*) and *alcohol.* These drugs provide only temporary relief from fear and anxiety, which reappear as soon as the effect of the drug dissipates. The behavioral therapies described in Chapters 2 and 3 represent the only permanently effective treatment of phobic behavior.

Animal research clearly demonstrates the capacity of the antianxiety drugs to reduce fear (see Gray, 1971). Let's examine one of these experiments. Conger (1951) trained rats to run down an alley to obtain food and then shocked them before they entered the goal box. This procedure established an approach-avoidance conflict. Conger discovered that an alcohol injection reduced the suppressive effects of the electrical shock: the animals that received alcohol ran into the goal box. In contrast, animals which were given a control injection of water would not approach the goal box. It is possible that the effect of alcohol was not to reduce fear but to increase hunger. Conger used Brown's concept of strength of approach-avoidance tendencies (described in Chapter 2) to test this assertion. He measured his rats' approach to reward or the avoidance of punishment. Testing either mildly drunk or sober rats, he found that alcohol reduced the aversiveness of punishment but had no effect on the attractiveness of reward. These results demonstrate that alcohol directly antagonizes the suppressive effects of punishment. Bailey and Miller (1952) discovered that the barbiturate *sodium amytal* also reduced the influence of electric shock in an approach-avoidance situation.

Recall the description of Rescorla and Solmon's aversive motivational state. We saw that both fear and frustration activate this system and motivate escape and avoidance behavior. Alcohol and barbiturates also antagonize the influence of frustration on aversive motivated behavior. For example, Wagner (1963) reported that alcohol increased responding for reward which was being inhibited by a cue associated with nonreward. Ison and Rosen (1967) found a similar reduction of frustration with the use of sodium amytal.

The observation that the antianxiety drugs antagonize both fear and frustration suggests that these drugs affect the PVT punishment system. Margules and Stein (1967) provided additional direct evidence by finding that the barbiturate *oxazempam* not only reduced the suppressive effects of conventional aversive events (for example, electric shock, nonreward, or bitter quinine) but also antagonized the punishing effects of brain stimulation.

This section has pointed out that activation of the MFB reward area is pleasurable and that activation of the PVT punishment system is unpleasant. Also, extreme effort is exerted to stimulate the reward system or to prevent activation of the punishment system. The next section considers addiction and indicates that the intensity of addictive behavior resembles the extreme effort which animals or humans exert to obtain reinforcing brain stimulation or to terminate punishing brain stimulation.

ADDICTIVE BEHAVIOR

Earlier in this chapter we learned that *addiction* reflects an extreme dependence on drug-related or non-drug-related events (for example, social interaction). We also learned that after repeated exposures, addicts develop *tolerance,* a need for greater amounts of a certain drug or event to satisfy their dependence. In addition, addicts deprived of a drug or experience to which they are addicted exert intense motivation to obtain it. The *withdrawal symptoms* experienced when the drug or event terminates initiate the search for it. An addict often feels intense craving when the drug or experience is unavailable.

A common thread links the many different forms of addiction. Richard Solmon's elegant analysis of addiction (1977, 1980) described the process responsible for the three dominant characteristics of addiction: tolerance, withdrawal, and craving. The present discussion of addiction focuses on Solmon's theory. Three drug addictions are described to illustrate the physiological changes which they produce; non-drug-related addictions (for example, excessive social dependence) will be discussed in Chapter 9.

Addicting Drugs

Alcohol. *Alcohol* reduces fear and frustration. This reduction in aversive emotions produces a sense of well-being, motivates approach behaviors (for example, sex), and enhances the reinforcing value of these experiences. These effects occur because alcohol inhibits the brain's punishment system. Consuming large quantities of alcohol causes disruption in thought processing and motor coordination because alcohol acts as a depressant.

Although some of us may have had an occasional hangover, heavy drinkers experience severe withdrawal symptoms—tremors, confusion, sweating, nausea, restlessness, insomnia, and a craving for alcohol. These symptoms begin 12 to 48 hours after a final drink and may last for days. Withdrawal symptoms for an alcoholic are even worse—psychomotor agitation, hallucinations, memory loss, and severe autonomic arousal accompany *delirium tremens.*

Our culture's social acceptance of alcohol, perhaps the most abused drug, is undoubtedly responsible for the extent of its abuse. Many of us drink alcohol with meals and consider it an integral part of social interaction; alcohol is a way of occasionally obtaining pleasure. However, millions of Americans are alcohol addicts, or *alcoholics;* they cannot control their drinking, which disrupts their effective interaction with the environment. For example, they have difficulty keeping jobs and often have troubled relationships with friends and relatives. But the most severe sequence is probably physical damage to their bodies. Alcohol produces poisonous *aldehydes* which eventually damage the organs. Even these negative consequences of excessive drinking do not deter alcoholics from drinking. Most alcoholics attempt to stop drinking, but their intense motivation for alcohol usually undermines their efforts. In support of this observation, Hunt and Matarazzo (1973) reported that only 50 percent of alcoholics who entered therapy remained and that of those alcoholics who abstained for a few months, 80 percent had resumed drinking within a year (see Figure 4.10).

Opiates.   *Opiates* are a group of highly addictive drugs which produce sedation and reduce pain (reduction of pain is called *analgesia*). *Opium*, the dried milky juice of the opium poppy, is a mixture of 18 alkaloids. *Morphine*, a more potent opiate, is a single alkaloid obtained from opium. *Heroin*, the most potent opiate, is derived from morphine. All the opiates induce euphoria, although several injections are typically necessary to produce pleasure. Additionally, heroin creates an initial feeling of ecstasy called a *rush*. The addictiveness of the opiates appears to be related to the rapidity and intensity of their action; of all the effects of opiates, that of heroin is the most rapid, has the greatest intensity, and is the most addicting.

Withdrawal effects from the opiates develop very quickly; several doses followed by abstinence produce severe physiological and psychological symptoms. Within 12 hours after the effects of opium dissipate, addicts experience muscle pains, sneezing, sweating, and increased emotionality. The symptoms become more severe after 36 hours since the last dose: at this point they include uncontrollable muscle twitching, cramps, chills which alternate with excessive flushing and sweating, and increased autonomic-nervous-system arousal. All these symptoms persist for 72 hours and then decline over a period of 3 to 5 days.

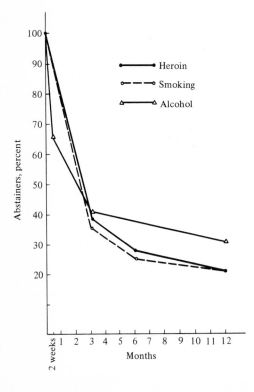

Figure 4.10
Level of abstinence during the first 12 months after "successful treatment" of addiction. (From Hunt, W. A., & Matarazzo, J. P. Three years later: Recent development in the experimental modification of smoking behavior. Journal of Abnormal Psychology, 1973, 81, 107–114. Copyright 1973 by the American Psychological Association. Reprinted by permission.)

Several researchers (see Goldstein, 1976; Synder & Simantov, 1977) have isolated opiate receptors in the brain. In addition, the brain produces a natural opiate, an *endorphin*. Stimulated by pain, endorphins provide us with a protective analgesic reaction. In all likelihood, the ability of the opiate drugs to activate the brain's opiate receptors causes their effect.

Unlike the alcoholic (who deteriorates), the opiate addict can function effectively as long as the drug is available to prevent withdrawal symptoms. Solomon (1977) suggested that the opiate receptor system in the brain probably has a built-in compensatory mechanism to prevent overstimulation from either internally produced or externally induced activation. However, opiate addicts are no more successful in breaking their habit than alcoholics (see Figure 4.10; Hunt & Matarazzo, 1973).

Nicotine.   The vignette of the beginning of this chapter described an addiction to *nicotine*. Greg, who smokes several packs of cigarettes each day, has repeatedly tried to quit, only to find himself unable to do so because of the physical and mental consequences. Greg's addiction is typical of nicotine addicts. Tolerance develops rapidly: the pleasure experienced during smoking declines with repeated use. The cessation of smoking creates aversive withdrawal symptoms which include headaches, irritability, increased motor activity, anxiety, tension, and a strong craving for nicotine.

Nicotine addicts do not have any more success overcoming their habit than alcoholics or opiate addicts. Hunt and Matarazzo found that only a small percentage (20 percent) of people who stopped smoking during therapy had not resumed smoking 1 year later (refer to Figure 4.10). Our discussion points to the dilemma facing all addicts: they want to stop because the consequences of addiction are aversive; but they find that the consequences of stopping—intense withdrawal symptoms and craving—are also aversive. The next section focuses on what causes the aversive consequences of taking drugs and when drugs lead to addiction.

Opponent-Process Theory

Our initial reaction.   Solomon and Corbit (1974) proposed that all experiences (both biological and psychological) produce an initial affective reaction, *A state* (see Figure 4.11). This A state can either be pleasant or unpleasant. For example, drinking alcohol produces a pleasurable A state. In contrast, a scheduled examination creates an aversive A state. According to Solomon and Corbit's view, the strength of the A state depends upon the intensity of the experience; the stronger the event, the more intense the A state.

The A state arouses a second affective reaction, the *B state*. The B state is the opposite of the A state; if A state is positive, then B state will be negative and vice versa. Thus, the pleasurable A state aroused by drinking automatically initiates an opposing, or opponent, aversive affective state. Similarly, the pain produced during the examination creates a pleasurable relief response. In Solomon and Corbit's view, our biological systems automatically initiate an opposite, or opponent, response to counter the initial effect of all events.

Several important aspects of the opponent process must be described in order to understand the changes depicted in Figure 4.11. First, the B state is always less intense than the A state. Second, the B state builds up strength more slowly than the A state. Finally, after an event has terminated, the strength of the B state is reduced more slowly than that of the A state.

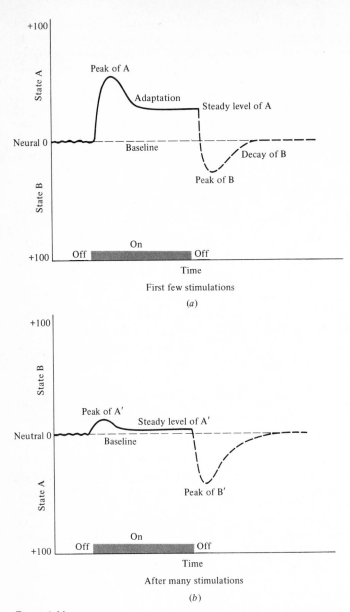

Figure 4.11
Schematic diagram of the affective changes during and after an environmental event. (a) Changes for the first few presentations. Notice the large initial A-state reaction and the small opponent B-state reaction which occurred after termination of the event. (b) Affective responses after many presentations. There is a small A-state response (tolerance) and a large and long B-state reaction (withdrawal). (From Solomon, R. L., & Corbit, J. D. An opponent-process theory of motivation: Temporal dynamics of affect. Psychological Review, 1974,   81,   119–145. Copyright 1974 by the American Psychological Association. Reprinted by permission.)

Consider the following example to illustrate the operation of these rules. A friend whom you have not seen for some time arrives. This friend's presence activates a pleasant A state—social pleasure. Automatic arousal of the opponent aversive B state—loneliness—causes your initial A state (social pleasure) to diminish during your friend's visit. When your friend leaves, the A state declines quickly, and you experience the B state (loneliness), which will slowly diminish with time.

The intensification of the opponent B state. Solomon and Corbit discovered that repeated experience with a certain event often increases the strength of the opponent B state (see Figure 4.11), which in turn reduces the affective reaction (the A state) experienced during the event. Thus, the strengthening of the opponent B state is thought to be responsible for the development of tolerance. Furthermore, termination of this event causes a strong opponent B state.

Let's return to our example of social pleasure versus loneliness to illustrate this intensification of the B state process. Your friend arrives for the fifth time in a week, causing you to experience only a mild A state of social pleasure. However, you feel intense prolonged loneliness when the friend leaves.

Katcher, Solomon, Turner, LoLordo, Overmeir, and Rescorla's study (1969) demonstrates this process. These experimentors observed physiological reactions in dogs during and after the termination of electric shock. As the number of shocks increased, the intensity and frequency of yelping declined during the shock. After the termination of shock, physiological response (for example, heart rate) declined below preshock levels. Thus, the heart rate declined to 80 beats per minute for 2 minutes before returning to baseline. After many presentations, the decline was greater and lasted longer. After shock terminated, heart rate dropped to 45–50 beats per minute and took 5 to 10 minutes to return to normal. These observations show (1) a strong A state and a weak opponent B state during the first presentations of shock and (2) a diminished A state (tolerance) and an intensified B state (withdrawal) after many experiences.

The opponent process operates in many different situations; let's look at two of them. Wikler (1953) reported that his subjects' first few self-administered doses of an opiate produced a peak A state (rush) followed by a reduced A state (euphoria). After the opiate's effect wore off, an aversive B state (craving state) occurred which diminished with time. The opponent process when a person administers opiates to himself or herself frequently differs from the drug's initial affect. A lessened rush occurs when the drug has been experienced many times; this is followed by a reduction in the euphoric feeling, or an absence of euphoria, while the drug is still acting. However, the more a drug is used, the more intense and longer the withdrawal B state.

In the examples so far, the initial A state was reinforcing and the opponent B state aversive. Yet, there are also many circumstances in which the A state is aversive and the B state is reinforcing. Epstein's description (1967) of the affective changes which military parachutists experienced illustrates this type of situation. Epstein reported that during the first free fall all the parachutists showed an intense aversive A state (terror). This A state diminished after they had landed, and they looked stunned and stony for several minutes. Then, the parachutists began to talk enthusiastically with friends. This opponent B state (relief), which lasted for about 10 minutes, was quite different from the affective response of experienced parachutists. During the free fall, they seemed tense, eager, or excited, reporting only a mildly aversive A state. Their opponent B state was exhilaration. Having landed safely, experienced parachutists showed (1) a high level of activity, (2) euphoria, and (3) intense social interaction. This opponent B state (exhilaration) decreased slowly, lasting for several hours. In the next section, we will learn that the opponent process appears to be responsible for the development of addictive behaviors.

The addictive process.   Solomon's theory (1977, 1980) presents a single explanation for all addictive behaviors. Solomon asserts that addiction reflects the activation of instrumental behaviors (such as taking a drug) which occur in response to the withdrawal reaction. In Solmon's view, addictive behavior reflects a coping response to an aversive opponent B state. Addictive behavior, then, is another example of aversive-motivated behavior; the addict acts to terminate (or prevent) the unpleasant withdrawal state.

Most people who are heavy drinkers do not become alcoholics. Similarly, people who consume other drugs do not always become drug addicts. Solomon suggests that in order for addiction to develop, people must recognize that abstinence causes their withdrawal symptoms and that the resumption of the addictive behavior after abstinence eliminates or prevents their aversive feelings. People who think that the discomfort they experience with abstinence is caused by factors other than the absence of the substance or event are not motivated to resume the addictive behavior. Under these circumstances, addiction does not develop. *Thus, one reason that addiction sometimes does not occur despite excessive exposure to a substance or event is failure (1) to connect the absence of the substance or event with the onset of withdrawal symptoms or (2) to connect the addictive behavior with the elimination of withdrawal symptoms.*

There is another reason why addiction may not occur following repeated exposure. The number of exposures to a substance or event alone does not determine the intensification of the B state. If sufficient time intervenes between experiences, there is no increase in the opponent state. And without the aversive withdrawal B state, the motivation for addiction does not exist. In support of Solomon's view, Starr (1978) discovered that young ducklings showed no distress to the absence of the mother when a 5-minute interval lapsed between separations. In contrast, with a 1- or 2-minute interval, strong withdrawal symptoms occurred. The importance of frequency in strengthening the opponent state suggests why some people can take one drug infrequently and never experience intense withdrawal symptoms after its effect has ended.

Once addiction is established, an addict focuses all of his or her attention on preventing or terminating withdrawal symptoms and craving. One consequence of addiction is the sacrifice of potential reinforcers (for example, friends or a job). Most addicts recognize the serious consequences of their addiction and try to stop their self-destructive behavior. Now let's examine why it is so difficult for addicts to break their habits.

The conditioning of the opponent state.   This discussion suggests that two opposing affective states occur during an experience. These two emotional states are unconditioned responses (UCRs) produced by a drug-related or non-drug-related event. Furthermore, the environmental cues surrounding the event can develop the capacity to elicit both the initial reaction A state and the opponent process B state. The development of antagonistic conditioned responses was described in Chapter 2. For example, the conditioned relief response antagonizes the conditioned fear reaction. In the context of addiction, the conditioned opponent reaction is thought to contribute to the development of tolerance and withdrawal and, therefore, to increase the likelihood of addiction. In addition, the conditioning of the opponent state is part of the reason why it is so difficult for an addict to break a habit permanently.

Let's use the nicotine addict to illustrate the role of the conditioned withdrawal state in addictive behavior. You learned that abstinence produces nervousness, irritability, and craving for nicotine. The conditioning of this unconditioned withdrawal state acts to increase the intensity of these symptoms. The opponent response, in turn, reduces the pleasure of smoking (that is, increases tolerance) and causes extreme discomfort when an addict is not smoking. Suppose an addict has stopped smoking for a few days. Under these circumstances, the unconditioned withdrawal state has dissipated and will not be reactivated unless this person smokes again. Then, why is it so difficult for nicotine addicts to quit smoking permanently? Unfortunately, whenever addicts encounter the cues associated with smoking, a conditioned withdrawal reaction will be elicited. For instance, if the addict sees someone else smoking (a lighted cigarette serving as a conditioned release of both the initial pleasure reaction and the opponent withdrawal response), the withdrawal state will be activated and the motivation to resume smoking will return. Thus, it is the conditioned withdrawal reactions which make eliminating addictions so difficult. To ensure a permanent cure, an addict must not only stop "cold turkey" and withstand the pain of withdrawal but also recondition all of the cues associated with the addictive behavior. Psychologists who ignore these conditioned withdrawal reactions doom addicts to eventual resumption of their addiction. Consider the alcoholic who goes to a bar just to socialize. Even though this alcholoic has abstained for weeks, the environment of the bar can produce a conditioned withdrawal reaction and motivate this person to resume drinking.

Shepard Siegel's research (see Siegel, 1975, 1977) provides convincing evidence of the conditioning of the opponent withdrawal state. Siegel paired a distinctive environmental cue (for example, a tone) with morphine injections. One A state reaction to morphine is *analgesia* (decreased sensitivity to pain); the opponent B state response is *hyperalgesia* (increased sensitivity to pain). Siegel defined the threshold of pain as the temperature necessary to make an animal withdraw its paw from a hot plate. He reported that the tone elicited a conditioned opponent hyperalgesic response.

Wikler and Prescor (1967) demonstrated that the conditioned withdrawal reaction can be elicited even after months of abstinence. They injected dogs with morphine when the animals were in a distinctive cage. The addicted dogs were then allowed to overcome their unconditioned withdrawal reaction in their home cages and were not injected for several months. When placed in the distinctive cages again, these dogs showed a strong withdrawal reaction, including excessive shaking, hypothermia, loss of appetite, and increased emotionality.

Siegel argued that the development of the conditioned opponent response is partly responsible for the development of tolerance; the conditioned B state antagonizes the unconditioned A state reaction. To demonstrate this point, Siegel extinguished the CR elicited by the environmental cue (a tone) associated with morphine injection. (Recall that to extinguish a CR, the CS must be presented alone.) After extinction of the opponent CR, Siegel noted an increased response to morphine. The amount of time the dogs spent without an injection did not cause this decreased tolerance; animals which did not receive tone presentations continued to show drug tolerance.

The influence of other aversive events.   There is one additional reason why it is so difficult for addicts to be cured. The aversive withdrawal reaction is a nonspecific unpleasant affective state. Therefore, any event which arouses the aversive state will motivate the addictive behavior. For example, multiple problems face alcoholics who attempt to stop drinking. Inhibiting drinking in the presence of the conditioned and unconditioned B state is only part of the problem. Some alcoholics lose their jobs; termination of this reward also activates the aversive motivational state. The stress of losing a job increases the motivation for the habitual addictive behavior. The aversive state does not have to be a withdrawal B state; the direct exposure to aversive events can also activate an aversive A state. Suppose that an alcoholic's mother-in-law arrives, and that her presence is a very aversive event. Under these conditions, the mother-in-law's presence will also activate the aversive motivational state, thus intensifying the pressure to drink. It is not surprising that it is so difficult for addicts to overcome their addiction. Solomon feels that all potential aversive events must be prevented in order for addicts to break their habits.

The search for pleasure. Most of us equate addictive behavior with situations in which people are motivated to terminate the aversive withdrawal state and reinstate a pleasant initial state. However, there are also occasions during which some people deliberately expose themselves to an aversive A state in order to experience the pleasant opponent B state (Solomon, 1977, 1980). The behavior of most experienced parachutists exemplifies this process. Most people anticipating the occasion to parachute from an aircraft never jump at all or quit after one jump. However, those who do jump and experience a strong reinforcing B state are often quite motivated to jump again. Epstein reported that some experienced jumpers become extremely depressed when bad weather cancels a jump. The behavior of these parachutists when denied the opportunity to jump definitely resembles that of drug addicts who cannot obtain the desired drug. Other behaviors in which the positive opponent state may lead to addiction include running in marathons (Milvy, 1977) and jogging (Booth, 1980).

Craig and Siegel (1980) discovered that introductory psychology students taking a test felt apprehensive and experienced a positive euphoric feeling when the test ended. However, it is unlikely that students' level of positive affect after having taken a test is as strong as that of an experienced parachutist after jumping. Perhaps most students are not tested often enough to develop a strong opponent reinforcing B state. You might suggest that your instructor test you more frequently to decrease your initial aversive apprehension and to intensify your positive affective relief when the test ends.

Overview. Unfortunately, psychologists (see Davison & Neale, 1978) attempting to identify the causes of specific drug addictions have not been successful. Mello and Mendelson's remarks about alcoholism (1978) illustrate this failure: "It is, in part, the inconsistency and unpredictability of the behavioral effects of alcohol that defies our best efforts to describe and understand it (alcoholism)."

Solomon's theory of addiction suggests that a single motivational process is responsible for all addictions. The same opponent-process motivational system which controls other addictions also controls drug addiction, according to Solomon. For example, the same process controls the behavior of alcoholics and of people who are extremely socially dependent. The differences are only in the labels for the emotional states ("pleasure-pain" for the alcohol-dependent person versus "attachment-loneliness" for the socially-dependent person) and the behaviors used to terminate the withdrawal state (the alcoholic drinks; the socially-dependent person intensifies efforts to reinstate social relationships). The underlying opponent process governs both forms of addictive behavior. Although psychologists have not thoroughly tested the opponent-process theory of addiction, it is consistent with the motivational literature presented here. It is to be hoped that applying this theory will produce a brighter future in the treatment of addiction.

SUMMARY

Our biological systems play an important role in our ability to execute motivated behavior. The peripheral nervous system detects important external and internal events, while the central nervous system identifies the significance of these events and our motivational reaction to them. Finally, the CNS arouses the appropriate muscles which perform the appropriate response to the event.

Thirst occurs when the body's fluid balance is disrupted. Several factors—a dry mouth, cellular dehydration, and hypovolemia—produce this fluid imbalance and create an internal thirst. Thirst induces drinking, which restores fluid levels to normal. Other oral and gastric factors produce the satiety which inhibits drinking. In addition, neurons in the medial, anterior, and preoptic hypothalamic areas initiate drinking, whereas parainfundilar hypothalamic neurons suppress drinking.

Our level of cortical arousal influences the effectiveness of motivated behavior. We perform most efficiently when moderately aroused; extremely high or low levels of arousal impair behavioral functioning. The cortical arousal level depends upon environmental circumstances: the more stimulating the environment, the higher the level of cortical arousal. However, the environment does not directly cause cortical arousal. Sensory information from the environment is transmitted to a specific sensory association area in the cortex and to the reticular activating system (RAS). Activation of the RAS produces the cortical arousal necessary to execute motivated behavior.

Our interaction with the environment depletes our physiological resources. During sleep these resources are restored; failure to sleep can cause behavioral disorders. There are two major categories of sleep: REM and NREM. The cortex is relatively inactive during NREM sleep, which is the time when we restore general biological resources. During REM sleep, the cortex is increasingly aroused; this is the time when we restore the resources depleted by stress.

Stressors in the environment elicit a general reaction pattern to stress which taxes our ability to respond efficiently. Selye labeled this response the *general adaptation syndrome* (GAS). An initial alarm reaction is characterized by arousal of the sympathetic nervous system and release of catecholamines from the adrenal cortex. Although this reaction provides the internal basis motivating escape from a stressor, if it is too intense, it can actually impair our effectiveness.

If the stressor persists, we enter into the second GAS stage, the stage of resistance, during which the adrenocortical system dominates our biological reaction. The release of the glucocorticoid hormones mobilizes all of our resources to cope with the stressor. However, our responding during this stage of resistance has several negative aspects. The glucocorticoid hormones reduce our inflammatory response, thus decreasing our resistance to certain other stressors (such as infections). In addition, the biological responses occurring during the resistance stage are responsible for such adaptation diseases as asthma, essential hypertension, ulcers, and colitis.

We cannot resist a continuous stressor indefinitely. Reduced eating and inhibition of the parasympathetic nervous system prevent us from restocking our resources. Eventually there are no remaining biological reserves, and we enter the exhaustion stage, during which death occurs if the stressor is not terminated.

We not only perform most effectively while moderately aroused but prefer environments which induce moderate arousal levels and avoid situations which produce either low or high cortical arousal. In addition, many stressors which induce moderate levels of arousal are actually experienced as rewarding. Thus, we approach many events which can lead to disease, and we avoid many nonstressful events because they evoke the less-pleasurable low levels of arousal.

Specialized neural systems control our responses to reinforcers and punishers. Arousal of the medial forebrain bundle (MFB), the brain's reward system, is pleasurable. Research indicates that the presence of rewards activates the MFB; arousal of the MFB motivates us to seek the reward. Drive also increases MFB activity, thereby increasing the value of reinforcers. In contrast, activity in the periventricular tract (PVT), the brain's punishment center, is unpleasant. Punishers activate this system, motivating escape and avoidance behavior.

Some people become addicted to pleasurable experiences even though arousal decreases with repeated experience. Richard Solomon proposed that one form of addiction occurs when addicts learn that their addictive behavior terminates an aversive opponent withdrawal state. Unfortunately, resumption of addictive behavior guarantees that this aversive state will be experienced as soon as the pleasurable effect wears off. Environmental events associated with the withdrawal state, as well as other aversive events and the termination of other pleasurable experiences, also play a part in motivating the addictive behavior. Only by eliminating all conditioned and unconditioned withdrawal reactions can the addictive cycle be broken and the addict cured.

A second form of addiction occurs when a person learns that an intense pleasurable opponent state can be produced following exposure to an initial aversive state. Although early experience with the event was unpleasant, the "pleasure addict" now finds the initial affective response only mildly aversive and the opponent state very pleasurable. Anticipated pleasure motivates the addict to experience the aversive event deliberately.

There are biological systems which influence a specific motivated behavior. In Chapter 5, we'll look at the biological processes which control eating and the physiological processes which motivate it.

$\mathcal{P}$ATTERNS OF EATING BEHAVIOR

The fat kid on the block

Eleven-year-old Bruce is slightly under 5 feet tall, weighs 125 pounds, and is gaining more weight. He is a rotund, lonely child who spends much of his time watching from his window as the other boys in the neighborhood play. His earlier attempts to play with them were met with the cruelty common in the young. He was rejected and taunted and became the target of preadolescent wit. Some "fatties" overcome such aggression with humor, but Bruce achieved survival through retreat. He now rarely asks to play, typically preferring to remain alone in his house. Bruce usually spends his time watching television, playing with his toys—and eating. He particularly loves banana splits, cookies, and candy bars.

Last summer Bruce's parents sent him to camp, hoping that the experience would enable him to become more sociable. Although their wish was in vain, Bruce did lose 10 pounds. Bruce said that the camp food was "crummy"—none of his favorite foods were served. Everyone hoped that Bruce would not regain his lost weight, but this wish was also in vain. Searching for a solution to his weight problem, Bruce's parents recently took him to the family doctor. The doctor found no physical problems and informed them that Bruce simply had to stop eating junk food. He restricted Bruce to a diet, but just as with his preceding attempts, Bruce quit in frustration after several days.

Last night Bruce's mother, trying as always to soothe her child's hurt, made his favorite dinner, lasagna. Bruce ate three portions before his parents had finished their first. His parents have concluded that Bruce simply does not have any "willpower," and they do not have the "heart" to refuse his requests for second or third servings. Bruce has one especially bad habit: he yells from his room for his mother to bring him a bowl of ice cream or a candy bar. His mother delivers his food, hoping to make him "happy." When she arrives with his food, he is often standing by his window, watching the boys play outside. His anguish soon dissolves as he eats the ice cream.

Bruce's eating behavior is typical of obese persons. The research of Stanley Schachter at Columbia University has revealed a set of behaviors that characterize the eating habits of the obese. Schachter's work shows that obese people are often unwilling to exert much effort to obtain food, are extremely sensitive to the sensory appeal of food, have difficulty stopping once they begin to eat, and are stimulated to eat by the presence of food or food-related cues. This chapter discusses why Bruce is overweight, what biological and psychological processes motivate his eating habits, and what can be done to help Bruce reduce his food intake. In addition, the systems which initiate and inhibit eating in people of normal weight are described.

THE STIGMA OF OBESITY

Our society admires the "thin" and scorns the "heavy." Social psychologists have found that overweight people are generally considered unattractive by others, not only because of their physical appearance but also because of their lack of self-control (Cahnan, 1968). Overweight children are cruelly tormented by their peers. Although the scorn experienced by the overweight adult is more subtle, it is obvious to "heavies" that others think poorly of them (Schachter & Rodin, 1974). The overweight person is frequently discriminated against at school and at work. "Fat people" jokes are the mainstay of many comedians, and to many, Robert Redford and Farrah Fawcett embody the American dream.

In order to realize this dream, people will go to extraordinary lengths. A close family friend, for example, diets constantly, even though she is thin. She perceives herself as fat, always needing to lose several pounds to be attractive. A more extreme form of this behavior is seen in victims of *anorexia nervosa*, a behavioral disease which is considered to be a consequence of our society's obsession with thinness (see Bruch, 1973). Anorexia nervosa occurs most commonly among adolescent girls and young women. The anorexic is extremely emaciated, exhibiting approximately a 35 percent weight loss after the onset of the illness. Although anorexics before the onset of illness are frequently chubby, they are never obese and are sometimes thin. Anorexics seem totally unaware that their bodily appearance is painfully scrawny. They are excessively preoccupied with not becoming fat and often weigh as little as 60 to 80 pounds. Anorexics seem totally unaware of hunger and feel full after only several small bites of food. Occasionally the anorexic has an eating binge but deliberately vomits the ingested food.

Hilde Bruch (1973) proposed that the fear of becoming fat is the major force precipitating anorexia. The main aspect of her therapeutic approach lies in the modification of the anorexic's self-image. The importance of body build as a determinant of self-esteem is deemphasized, and the individual's feelings of self-worth and self-initiative are enhanced. These changes in self-esteem lead to a resumption of normal eating behaviors. Bruch has reported moderate success with her treatment.

Bruch's view that excessive concern with obesity produces anorexia is not the only explanation that has been proposed. Many investigators suggest that anorexia is caused by a physiological or chemical disturbance; others feel that an intensely unpleasant event, such as the death of a loved one, produces the anorexic's refusal to eat. Although the origin of anorexia remains unresolved, reinforcement therapy appears to be another successful treatment. Garfinkel, Kline, and Stancer (1973) rewarded hospitalized anorexics for eating (for example, by giving them a weekend pass or an opportunity to socialize with friends). Their patients gained 20 to 30 pounds during the 2 to 10 weeks of treatment.

The desire to lose weight is intense in overweight persons, yet they seem unable to control their eating habits. They spend millions of dollars each year on diet foods and books and constantly try new diets that result in a few lost pounds which are quickly regained. A little "internal fortitude" is the common remedy offered by the well-meaning layperson. Yet the extraordinary number of overweight Americans (25 to 45 percent of the population are 20 percent or more overweight, according to the Public Health Service) suggests the problem requires an effective method of dealing with overweight, rather than mere will power. Apparently many people would like to control their eating but cannot. Their failure to inhibit their motivation to eat leads typically to obesity. This chapter focuses on the motivational factors which produce eating and, in addition, discusses the disturbances leading to an inability to control food intake and obesity.

Bruch (1973) identified two classes of obesity—developmental and reactive. *Developmental obesity* originates in early childhood. It is characterized by misperceptions of hunger and satiety, as well as by an inability to control food intake. *Reactive obesity*, on the other hand, typically develops during early adulthood when overeating occurs in response to stress.

Let's begin by examining the research of Stanley Schachter. Many of the behaviors Schachter observed in obese college students resemble the characteristics associated by Bruch with developmental obesity. Later in the chapter we'll turn our attention to reactive obesity by considering the influence of stress on eating behavior.

EATING HABITS OF OBESE AND NORMAL-WEIGHT PEOPLE

A number of behavioral differences in the motivation for food have been observed between obese and normal-weight individuals. The research effort of Stanley Schachter and his associates (Schachter, 1971a, 1971b) has established a set of behaviors which typically differentiate obese people from people of normal weight. The obese person's eating behavior is stimulated by external processes: the presence of food or food-related cues causes the obese person to eat. In contrast, the person of normal weight is influenced more by internal cues: eating is usually stimulated by internal hunger rather than by the presence of food. Additionally, the obese are often less motivated to work for their food, are more particular about what they eat, and are less able to inhibit eating than persons of normal weight. Although these characteristics are *typical*, not all fat persons show them. There are other factors (for example, those associated with stress) which can cause a person to overeat. In addition, Schachter discovered that some normal-weight people have eating habits which resemble those of typical fat people. Many of these thin people were overweight at one time. This observation indicates that in the proper environment, a fat person can become thin.

All of Schachter's laboratory experiments share a common methodology. In his research, Schachter defined obesity as a weight 15 percent above the norm established by the Metropolitan Life Insurance Company for a specific height and body build. A maximum of 10 percent above the norm was established as the upper limit for a subject to be classified as of normal weight. Schachter's subjects were led to believe that their performance on a problem-solving task or some similar task was the main objective of the experiment. The task usually lasted until the subject's normal lunch or dinner time, or later. Some food (for example, crackers, sandwiches, ice cream) was either in front of the subject or readily available. In order to determine various aspects of the eating behavior of normal-weight and overweight persons, each experiment differed slightly.

Such experimental studies can demonstrate causal relationships, but they lack external validity. That is, there is a possibility that obese persons do not behave in the real world as they did under Schachter's laboratory conditions. Fortunately, observational findings from field research done by Schachter are consistent with his laboratory findings. In addition, he gathered some entirely new information concerning behavioral differences between obese and normal-weight subjects by employing observational methods.

Internal–External Control of Eating

Environmental influence. Some of Schachter's studies evaluated the misconception that obese people eat constantly. Schachter's research suggests that the amount of food that the overweight person consumes depends upon the presence of food-related environmental cues. In the absence of these environmental stimuli, the overweight person is not disturbed by his or her failure to eat. Normal-weight persons typically eat only when biologically hungry; the presence of food has less effect on normal than on overweight persons.

Support for a differential influence of environmental factors on eating for overweight and normal-weight persons can be seen in the following two studies. In the first study (Schachter, 1971b), subjects had participated in the experiment for several hours and relied entirely on a wall clock for the time. At one point, crackers were offered. Some subjects were led to believe that their normal dinner hour had not arrived; others thought it was their dinner time. Schachter found that subjects of normal weight ate an equal number of crackers in either case. Overweight subjects ate considerably more when they thought it was dinner time than when they thought it was earlier. Schachter interpreted these results as indicating that time is one external cue which can initiate eating in overweight people but has no influence on the eating behavior of normal-weight people. Another aspect of Schachter's study concerned the correspondence between the perceived and biological time. Schachter found that regardless of perceived time, normal-weight subjects ate when their biological dinner hour arrived. Thus, we can conclude that the person of normal weight eats when hungry, not when the clock suggests that it is time to eat. The overweight person, on the other hand, eats when the clock suggests that it is time to eat; actual biological time has little or no influence on his or her behavior.

Ross's study (1969) documented additional support for environmental initiation of eating behavior in overweight people. Ross's subjects were seated at a table with a tin of almonds. For some subjects, a 40-watt bulb in an unshaded lamp provided a bright illumination; other subjects were at a table poorly illuminated by a 7½-watt red bulb in a shaded lamp. Ross felt that high illumination would focus attention on the presence of food and increase the amount consumed in overweight subjects. The results of his study are presented in Figure 5.1. Ross found that the prominence of food-related cues did not influence the eating behavior of normal-weight subjects; they ate an equal amount of nuts under both lighting conditions. However, obese subjects ate more nuts under high illumination than under low illumination. Apparently, overweight persons will eat more if food is extremely obvious or directly in front of them.

In his laboratory studies, Schachter found that the eating behavior of overweight subjects depended upon environmental cues. The field studies described below add support to his view. Goldman, Jaffa, and Schachter (1968) compared the ability of obese and normal-weight people to fast (inhibit eating) on Yom Kippur, an extremely important religious holiday on which orthodox Jews remain primarily in synagogue. Their results indicated that the obese were better able to maintain fasting than people of normal weight. Schachter also observed that the longer the obese remained in synagogue, the less aversive fasting became; for people of normal weight, fasting remained unpleasant

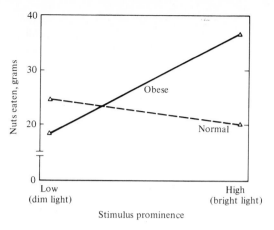

Figure 5.1
Effects of stimulus intensity on amount eaten. (From Ross, L. D. Cue and cognition-controlled eating among obese and normal subjects. Cited in Schachter, S. Some extraordinary facts about obese humans and rats, American Psychologist, 1971, 26, 129–144. Copyright 1971 by the American Psychological Association. Reprinted by permission.)

throughout the entire day. Apparently, the absence of food-related cues in the synagogue was responsible for the greater ability of the obese to maintain their fast.

In another field study, Schachter (1971a) compared the regularity of dinner times among obese and normal-weight undergraduates at Columbia University. He discovered that during the week, obese students were more consistent than students of normal weight with regard to dining time. According to Schachter, students' activities during the week are highly routine. Various activities regularly occur before eating, and the obese person, dependent upon external cues to initiate eating, is stimulated by these activities. Eating patterns of normal-weight persons are less consistent because they are independent of external cues associated with meals. During weekends the presence of food-related cues is less predictable. Schachter observed that eating habits of overweight and normal-weight students are equally inconsistent under weekend conditions.

Responsivity to environmental stimuli. The greater influence of environmental events on the eating behavior of obese compared with normal-weight persons is probably due to the fact that obese people are more readily distracted by external stimuli (Rodin, 1973). Rodin evaluated the ability of both obese and normal-weight persons to proofread an article. Some of her subjects were undistracted as they read the material; others were exposed to one of several distracting tape-recorded stimuli, varying from nonemotional (for example, random numbers) to extremely emotional (for example, a description of death from leukemia). The proofreading of the normal-weight subjects was not adversely affected by these external events; but the performance of the obese subjects declined as the distractors became more emotional in nature. These observations suggest that obese people are more responsive to all external cues, even those unrelated to food. Thus, when nonfood cues are present, the obese person responds to them and does not think of food.

Additional support for the influence of environmental events on eating behavior was demonstrated by Judith Rodin (1977). In one study, Rodin and Slochower (1976) measured changes in weight of young girls at summer camp. The food was abundant and attractively prepared. In addition, the girls were sent goodies by their parents and were allowed to purchase candy from the canteen after dinner. The authors found that the greater a girl's degree of externality, as measured by responsivity to environmental distractors, the larger the weight change. Typically, externally motivated girls gained weight; but some "externals" actually lost weight. Rodin and Slochower proposed that for these girls, the food at camp was not presented in as obvious a fashion and did not appear as desirable as food in their homes. In an earlier study, Rodin (1976) found that an obese girl's externality did not change, even though she lost weight at a diet camp. Apparently, obesity does not make a person more responsive to food; rather, one's externality causes overeating and obesity.

Food-Seeking Behavior

The motivation to obtain food.   Additional evidence gathered by Schachter concerns the validity of the common conception that fat people have an internal craving for food, an intense motivation which causes them to do anything in order to obtain it. Contrary to the popular notion, the results of Schachter's research indicate that if much effort is required to obtain food, obese persons will under some circumstances actually work less than normal persons. Schachter has suggested that many of the processes initiating eating in the obese spring from the external environment.

The following study (Schachter, 1971a) demonstrates the lack of interest of overweight individuals in exerting effort to obtain food. In Schachter's study, subjects took several personality tests at a desk. On top of the desk was a bag of almonds. The experimenter took one of the nuts, telling the subject to have some. Half of the subjects received nuts with shells; the other half, nuts without shells. The results of this study are shown in Table 5.1. Although the effort demanded is not monumental, some work is required to remove an almond shell. Half of the normal subjects were willing to expend this effort in order to nibble. While all but one of the fat students ate the nuts without shells, only 1 of 20 fat subjects ate the nuts with shells. Obviously, the obese people in this study preferred indolence to shelling almonds.

In a real-world analogy, Schachter (1971a) recorded the use of chopsticks by obese and normal-weight Americans in a number of Chinese and Japanese restaurants in New York City. Schachter noted that five times as many normal-weight people as obese people ate with chopsticks. Apparently the effort required to use chopsticks is too great for many obese Americans.

Effort requirement.   The amount of effort necessary to obtain food does not appear to be a critical determinant of the obese person's willingness to work for food; rather, the

Table 5.1
Effect of Work on the Eating Behavior of Obese and
Normal Subjects

Subjects	Nuts Have:	Number who:	
		Eat	Don't Eat
Normal	Shells	10	10
	No shells	11	9
Obese	Shells	1	19
	No shells	19	1

From: Schachter, S. Some extraordinary facts about obese humans and rats. *American Psychologist*, 1971, *26*, 129–144. Copyright 1971 by the American Psychological Association. Reprinted by permission.

obese individual is willing to work for food only if the effort expended does not exceed that which he or she normally exerts (Singh & Sikes, 1974). Singh and Sikes found that wrapping chocolates in aluminum foil did not affect the eating behavior of obese subjects. They were accustomed to obtaining chocolates in this manner and therefore were as willing to unwrap chocolates as normal people were. However, in Singh and Sikes' study, obese subjects unwrapped fewer cashew nuts than normal-weight subjects did. The obese were not willing to expend the extra effort needed to unwrap the cashews, which are typically presented unwrapped. This observation may be compared with the fact that obese orientals, but not Americans, use chopsticks when eating. The use of chopsticks requires more effort than usual only for obese Americans; for orientals the use of chopsticks is the typical manner of obtaining food.

The presence of food.   However, there are some circumstances when the overweight person will work harder than the normal person to obtain food. The presence of food appears to be capable of engendering this additional motivation. Johnson (1970) required his subjects to pull a string 50 times (on the average) in order to obtain a quarter of a sandwich. After 12 minutes of participation, each subject could eat the food he or she had earned. In one condition, the promised sandwiches were not visible. Johnson found that normal-weight people in this condition made more responses than overweight persons. In the other condition, a sandwich was placed beside the subject before the trials began, and a quarter of a sandwich was added after each 50 responses. The presence of food did not influence the behavior of normal-weight people; their response was the same with food absent or present. However, the presence of food increased the overweight subjects' motivation to obtain food. The overweight subjects worked harder for food when it was visible than the subjects of normal weight. An interpretation of this research suggests that when food or food-related cues are present, the obese person initiates food-producing behavior. For example, the presentation of an attractive food (for example, cheesecake) on a television commercial probably produces sufficient motivation to cause the obese person to go to the refrigerator for food. In contrast, individuals of average weight seem to be less motivated to work for their food unless they are biologically hungry.

Sensitivity to Food

Some studies have investigated the influence of taste on the amount eaten by overweight and normal-weight subjects. Decke (1971), one of Schachter's students, gave her subjects either a good, but not superb, vanilla milk shake or a bad, but not awful, vanilla milk shake (which was laced with a small amount of quinine). The results of her study are shown in Table 5.2. Decke discovered that, in comparison with the subjects of normal weight, the overweight people consumed more of the good-tasting milk shake but less of the unsavory milk shake. Decke's results present the overweight person as a finicky eater, preferring good-tasting foods and avoiding bad-tasting ones. In an earlier study, Nisbett (1968) found that while obese people like good food, they are not gourmets. He observed that obese people ate an equal amount of either good or superb ice cream; in contrast, normal-weight people ate more ice cream when they thought it was superb rather than merely good. Demonstrating that both groups were capable of discrimination, he found that neither the obese nor the normal subjects ate terrible-tasting ice cream.

Field observations have confirmed the laboratory findings that obese people are more particular about their food than people of normal weight. For example, Schachter (1971a) noted that obese freshmen at Columbia University were more apt than normal-weight students to drop their meal contracts in the university dining hall, and less

Table 5.2
Effect of Taste on Eating

Subjects	Ounces Consumed in:	
	Good Taste	Bad Taste
Normal	10.6	6.4
Obese	13.6	2.6

From: Decke, E. Effects of taste on eating behavior of obese and normal persons. Cited in S. Schachter, *Emotion, obesity, and crime.* New York: Academic Press, 1971.

likely to renew their contracts the next year. University food is not known for its appeal, and therefore we are not surprised that the overweight students looked elsewhere for food. Such studies indicate that Bruce's strong preference for rich food and his dislike of bland food, described in the story at the beginning of this chapter, appear to be typical reactions of overweight people.

In an interesting clinical study, Hashim and Van Itallie (1965) combined a bland diet with an unusual mode of presentation. Their subjects were obese and normal-weight hospital patients. The authors found that while obese patients typically ate all of a standard hospital diet, they consumed only a few hundred calories a day when a bland unappetizing liquid diet obtained from a dispenser was the only food available to them. In contrast, patients of normal weight consumed an equal number of calories on the liquid diet and the standard diet.

A Lack of Control
Although they eat less often than normal-weight people, obese people have more difficulty inhibiting their eating once it begins. Nisbett (1968) notes that obese people ate more spoonfuls of ice cream per minute than normal subjects did; Schachter (1971a) discovered that overweight persons were more likely to clean their plates than normal persons. Apparently, the three portions of lasagna that Bruce ate before his parents had completed their first serving represents eating behavior which conforms to that of other obese people.

A Genetic Origin?
The eating behavior of obese humans (finickiness, less willingness to exert effort to obtain food) has been observed in both genetically obese mice and chubby human infants. Fuller and Jacoby (1955) found that genetically obese mice consumed more of a palatable food but less of an unplatatable one than nonobese mice did; Rytand (1970) reported that young genetically obese mice were less willing than nonobese mice to gnaw at their food through wire mesh. In addition, when their milk was sweetened, heavy human infants increased their consumption more than lighter infants (Nisbett & Gurwitz, 1970). Nisbett and Gurwitz also discovered that when a standard nipple opening was used, heavy infants consumed more milk than lighter infants. However, when the nipple opening was reduced to half of the normal size, so that food was more difficult to obtain, the heavy infants' consumption decreased significantly. Not surprisingly, the size of the nipple opening had no influence on the milk intake of the lighter

infants. These results suggest that for many obese humans, their eating habits probably were present during infancy and may have a genetic origin.

Implications for Weight Control

The typical obese person is often unmotivated to work for food, is stimulated to eat only by the presence of food or food-related cues, likes only good-tasting food, and cannot inhibit eating once it begins. The following five rules, based on Schachter's research, will enable the obese individual to reduce intake and lose weight.

1. *Overweight persons should vary their eating times from day to day.* Since they are extremely sensitive to environmental cues, this procedure will reduce the importance of the clock as a cue for eating.
2. *Overweight persons should reduce the number of situations in which they eat.* Probably the first thing that most obese persons do while watching television is to start eating. They should keep a record of the places they eat and should limit eating to one regular dining area in the home.
3. *Overweight persons should be required to work for their food.* Their families should not wait on them, and they should avoid places like restaurants where little effort is required to obtain food. In fact, overweight persons might be helped by cooking their own food. Any method which makes food more difficult than normal to obtain will reduce intake.
4. *Overweight persons should eat bland food which is neither rich nor tasty.* Since they are extremely sensitive to taste, they will eat less food if it is less appealing.
5. *Overweight persons should receive only a single portion of food, and second servings should be kept out of sight.* They probably will not miss what they do not see.

BIOLOGICAL SYSTEMS

The ability of animals or people to survive depends upon the effectiveness of the biological systems controlling their eating. These systems must protect against starvation by being able to initiate eating when the animal or human is deprived, and they must be able to suppress eating to prevent excessive weight gain. The control mechanism which governs the animal's or person's eating habits lies within the central nervous system (CNS). Information gathered from the peripheral biological systems concerning the animal's or human's well-being plays an important role in enabling the CNS to maintain an adaptive body weight. Malfunctions in these systems have been shown to cause either an excessively low level of food intake (*aphagia*) or an excessively high level (*hyperphagia*). Evidence collected by Schachter indicates that the eating behavior of overweight people can be the result of malfunctions in the biological systems that usually inhibit eating. Let's now focus on the biological systems which govern an animal's or human's motivation to eat.

Hypothalamic Theory

Early evidence indicated a central control of eating behavior, located in the hypothalamus (see Appendix); initiation of eating was held to be determined by the *lateral hypothalamus* (LH), and inhibition of eating by the *ventromedial hypothalamus* (VMH). Refer to Figure A.8 in the Appendix for the anatomical location of the LH and VMH in the hypothalamus.

The pioneer research of Anand and Brobeck (1951) indicated that the "feeding" center of the brain was located in the lateral hypothalamus. After its lateral hypothalamus had been destroyed, an animal that had not eaten for some time (for example, 24 hours) would not eat anything. Additional evidence was provided by the observation that electrical stimulation of the LH produced eating in a satiated animal (Anderson & Wyrwicka, 1957).

Other research located a "satiety" center in the ventromedial hypothalamus. Hetherington and Ranson (1940, 1942) found that destruction of the VMH produced a dramatic increase in food intake with a rapid doubling to quadrupling of weight. This strongly suggests that the VMH is important in suppressing eating. The demonstration that electrical stimulation of the VMH inhibited eating in hungry rats (Margules & Olds, 1962) provided additional support for the view that the ventromedial hypothalamus is the "satiety" center. The patterns of behavioral changes produced by destruction of these brain regions have been called the *LH-lesion syndrome* and the *VMH-lesion syndrome*.

LH-lesion syndrome. Anand and Brobeck (1951) reported that destruction of the lateral hypothalamus severely disrupted laboratory rats' normal eating and drinking behavior. The animals immediately stopped eating (aphagia) and drinking(adipsia) after surgery and would die within a week unless force-fed. However, Teitelbaum and Epstein (1962) discovered that with appropriate treatment, some of the LH-lesioned animals would regain their normal eating habits and to a lesser extent regain drinking behaviors.

Teitelbaum and Epstein (1962) identified four stages in these animals' recovery from surgery; Table 5.3 summarizes them. In stage 1, the animal will neither eat nor drink; to survive, it must be force-fed through a gastric fistula opening directly into the stomach. The rat enters stage 2 approximately 20 days after surgery. During this stage it eats palatable food but is not able to regulate food intake to meet its needs. It will not eat dry food and will not drink. During stage 3, which begins about 40 days after surgery, the ability to regulate food intake to meet nutritional needs reappears. It will eat dry food if

Table 5.3
Stages of Recovery in Animal with LH-Lesion Syndrome

	Stage I: Adipsia Aphagia	Stage II: Adipsia Anorexia	Stage III: Adipsia Dehydration-Adipsia	Stage IV: Recovery
Eats wet palatable foods	No	Yes	Yes	Yes
Regulates food intake and body weight on wet palatable foods	No	No	Yes	Yes
Eats dry foods (if hydrated)	No	No	Yes	Yes
Drinks water; survives on dry food and water	No	No	No	Yes

From: Teitelbaum, P., & Epstein, A. N. The lateral hypothalamic syndrome: Recovery of feeding and drinking after lateral hypothalamic lesions. *Psychological Review*, 1962, 69, 74–90. Copyright 1962 by the American Psychological Association. Reprinted by permission.

hydrated but still will not drink water. A large percentage of LH-lesioned rats die before reaching stage 4, but those who survive this long will start drinking water and eating dry food.

Even an animal which survives to stage 4 still has a number of problems. First, although it will drink while eating, it does not drink without eating even when deprived. Second, it is extremely sensitive to the quality of its food: it will not consume any food that does not taste good. Finally, it never regains the weight lost during the initial stages of the disorder but eats only enough food to maintain its postoperative weight.

The pattern of recovery of eating and drinking behavior in the LH-lesioned animal resembles the sequence of the development of eating and drinking in the normal animal (Teitelbaum, Cheng, & Rozin, 1969). The newborn rat drinks milk (essentially a wet food) but refuses water, a pattern of behaviors which resembles stage 2. A slightly older animal will eat dry food and drink water while eating, but will not drink without eating even after it has been deprived of water for any length of time, a pattern resembling stage 3. Apparently, the brain possesses sufficient flexibility to use other biological systems to initiate eating and drinking behavior.

VMH-lesion syndrome.   Hetherington and Ranson (1940) observed that destruction of the ventromedial area of the hypothalamus produces several impairments in eating habits. The most prominent of these impairments is the excessive intake of food (hyperphagia) which leads to obesity. The VMH obesity syndrome occurs in two stages (Brobeck, Tepperman, & Long, 1943). The first, the *dynamic stage,* is characterized by a steady increase in food intake, reaching four times the normal level over the first 10 to 20 days following surgery. After this the hyperphagic rat shows a steady but slower increase in weight which peaks at two times the normal weight about 40 days following surgery. Figure 5.2 shows both physical appearance and body weight of a hyperphagic rat and a normal rat. Weight stabilizes during the second stage—the *static stage.* Apparently, once their new weight stabilizes, lesioned animals consume only enough food to maintain it. Bray and Gallagher (1975) reported a similar change in the eating behavior of clinical patients when a pathology (for example, tumor or disease) developed in the VMH area. These patients exhibited the traditional VMH-lesion syndrome—hyperphagia and obesity.

Characteristics of hyperphagic animal.   The hyperphagic rat exhibits several behavioral impairments besides overeating. Teitelbaum (1955) discovered that VMH-lesioned rats are very finicky eaters. They will not eat any bad-tasting food such as stale chow or food

Figure 5.2
Comparison of normal and hyperphagic rat. Before lesion of ventromedial nucleus both rats weighed the same. In their present condition the normal rat weighs 175 grams and the hyperphagic rat 800 grams.

mixed with quinine, and they eat more sweet-tasting or highly palatable food than normal rats eat. The VMH-lesioned rats become less willing to work for food as their weight increases (Miller, Bailey, & Stevenson, 1950), and the obese rat is considerably less willing to exert effort to obtain food than the normal rat. In addition, Gladfelter and Brobeck (1962) found that the VMH-lesioned animal is less active than a nonlesioned animal in a quiet environment, but more active in a noisy one (for example, during the time when the animals are tended). Apparently, the environment is more influential in determining the level of activity in VMH-lesioned animals than in nonlesioned ones. These similarities to the behavioral characteristics of obese people are indeed food for thought.

Singh (1973) compared the intensity of food-seeking behavior acquired before destruction of the ventromedial hypothalamus with that of food-seeking behavior acquired after destruction. He found that VMH-lesioned animals, compared with nonlesioned animals, exerted more effort to obtain food when the behavior required had been learned before lesioning, but less effort when a new behavior was necessary. Singh suggested that the development of a new behavior requires more effort than the obese animal is willing to exert, whereas a habitual behavior involves an acceptable level of effort. It is also likely that when conditioning occurred before lesioning, the environmental cues present during conditioning became associated with eating; therefore, these cues can later act to motivate the hyperphagic animal to work for food. When training takes place after conditioning, the environmental cues are not related to food, and the lesioned rat is operating in an environment that does not contain food-related cues.

Similarity to obese humans.   Schachter (1971a) conducted an extensive examination of the results of studies investigating either the effect of a VMH lesion in animals or the behavioral characteristics of obese humans. A comparison was made of eating habits in obese and normal-weight subjects (animals and humans), and the extent of such observed differences was noted. First, Schachter presented the comparisons of habits as a "batting average," a ratio in which the number of studies that showed differences was contrasted with the total number of studies conducted. Second, he expressed the average percentage difference between the behavior of fat and normal subjects (animals and humans) as a "fat" to "normal" (F/N) ratio. The results of Schachter's analysis are presented in Table 5.4.

Schachter's comparisons clearly demonstrate that both hyperphagic animals and obese humans ate more food during a day, ate fewer meals per day, ate more per meal, ate faster, liked good-tasting food more, and disliked bad-tasting food more than normal-weight animals or humans. Especially impressive were the F/N ratios, which were almost identical in humans and animals for each particular aspect of eating. For example, obese humans ate 29 percent more per meal than humans of normal weight; hyperphagic animals ate 34 percent more than normal animals. Schachter also noted that both obese humans and animals will not exert as much effort to obtain food as their normal-weight counterparts. Furthermore, obese humans and rats continue to eat with a full stomach (a procedure called *preloading*); normal-weight animals and humans will not eat with a full stomach.

The hyperphagic animal and the obese human also share a number of behavioral characteristics unrelated to eating: both are more emotional, exhibit greater sensitivity to pain, and are more responsive to non-food-related stimuli than their normal-weight counterparts. The remarkable similarity of eating habits between many obese humans and hyperphagic animals led Schachter to conclude that the physiological locus of the major cause of human obesity must lie, as it does in the rat, in the ventromedial area of the hypothalamus.

Table 5-4
Eating Habits of Animals and Humans

	Batting Average		F/N ratio	
	Animals	Humans	Animals	Humans
Amount of food eaten ad lib	9/9	2/3	1.19	1.66
No. meals per day	4/4	3/3	0.85	0.92
Amount eaten per meal	2/2	5/5	1.34	1.29
Speed of eating	1/1	1/1	1.28	1.26
Good taste	5/6	2/2	1.45	1.42
Bad taste	3/4	1/2	0.76	0.84

Note: Batting average refers to number of studies showing a difference to all studies conducted; F/N refers to ratio of fat to normal behavior.
From: Schachter, S. Some extraordinary facts about obese humans and rats. *American Psychologist*, 1971, 26, 129–144. Copyright 1971 by the American Psychological Association. Reprinted by permission.

The brain does not control feeding in isolation from other biological systems. The central control mechanisms which initiate and suppress eating must rely on other biological systems for information regarding the animal's or person's nutritional condition.

Hunger

An animal's or human's ability to survive depends upon the maintenance of an adequate energy balance and an optimal body weight. The animal or person regulates energy balance and an optimal body weight, maintaining approximately the same weight throughout adulthood. Energy balance is regulated in animals or humans on a short-term, meal-to-meal basis; control of body weight occurs on a long-term, day-to-day basis. Any deficiency in these regulatory systems produces the sensation of hunger, leading the animal or person to eat to satisfy its needs. This discussion of hunger begins by describing the systems responsible for the regulation of energy balance. Later, the chapter describes how an animal or human maintains optimal body weight.

Energy needs. The operation of all bodily functions requires energy. The normal animal or person has only limited reserves of glucose (sugar), fat, and protein—three substances that it can convert to energy. Food is consumed to reinstate any deficiency to the energy level necessary for optimal physiological functioning, with any excess energy being stored as fat. The metabolism of energy nutrients is illustrated in Figure 5.3. An animal or human can effectively monitor its nutritional levels and regulate its food intake to correct any nutritional deficiencies. For example, Kissileff (1971) observed that animals increase their food intake to meet higher nutritional energy needs in a cold environment. Also, as Janowitz and Grossman (1949) showed, an animal increases its intake in order to maintain a constant caloric level (energy) when fed a nonnutritive substance.

Le Magnen's research (1971) indicated that a nutritional deficiency initiates eating, but the amount consumed in a meal depends upon nonnutritive factors (for example, the desirability of the food). Le Magnen also discovered that an animal waits longer to eat again after a large meal than after a small meal. Obviously, the larger the meal, the longer

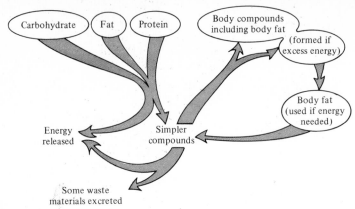

Figure 5.3
Energy nutrients (carbohydrates, fats, proteins) can convert either directly to energy or to simpler compounds (for example, glycogen, fatty acids, amino acids). These compounds can also be either used to generate energy or combined into essential body compounds (for example, muscles, bones). The energy generated when the nutrients are transformed into the simpler compounds is then used either to form these body compounds or to execute other bodily processes. Any excess energy can be stored as fat; this fat can be transformed to simpler compounds or energy to be used in case of future nutritional deficiency. (Reproduced by permission from Understanding nutrition *by Eva May Hamilton and Eleanor Whitney, copyright © 1977, West Publishing Company. All rights reserved.)*

the elapsed time before a deficiency develops that triggers hunger and causes the animal to eat. Nonetheless, the size of an animal's meal does not depend upon how much time has passed since it last ate. The taste of the food, rather than the amount of deficiency, will determine how much an animal will eat at one feeding; the more desirable the food, the larger the meal. Food-deprived animals allowed to feed freely on less desirable foods do not eat more but do eat more often to alleviate their deficiency. Apparently the initiation of eating depends upon a nutritive deficiency, whereas the continuance of eating depends on other factors. The biological systems which determine why these nutritional variables initiate and maintain eating are reviewed next.

Peripheral cues. Two classes of peripheral cues, stomach contractions and oral sensations, have been associated with hunger and eating. Apparently, pangs in your stomach do not make you hungry; but the oral sensations derived from desirable food do keep you eating.

   Cannon (1934) suggested that stomach contractions signaled the presence of hunger and initiated eating. In a classic experiment, Cannon and Washburn (1912) had normal subjects swallow a balloon which recorded stomach contractions. They found a close relationship between the presence of these contractions and the subjects' subjective hunger pangs. However, more recent evidence indicates that gastric factors do not play a significant role in the initiation of eating. Tsang (1938) found that removing rats' stomachs did not alter the daily intake of food, although they did eat more frequently and their meals were smaller. The same observation was true of human patients whose stomachs had been removed for medical reasons. Apparently, the information coming from the stomach is not what makes animals or humans hungry.

   Although the quality of food does not initiate eating, it does appear to control the continuance of eating. An animal will eat more of a good-tasting food than a neutral or

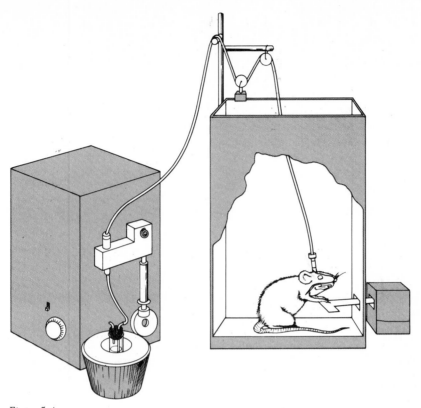

Figure 5.4
Schematic illustration of the apparatus used to administer intragastric self-injection by the rat. When the rat presses the bar, the pipetting machine delivers the liquid diet through the gastric tube directly into the rat's stomach. (Adapted from Teitelbaum, P., & Epstein, A. N. Regulation of food intake in the absence of taste, smell, and other oropharyngeal sensations. Journal of Comparative and Physiological Psychology, *1962, 55, 753–759. Copyright 1962 by the American Psychological Association. Reprinted by permission.)*

undesirable food. The nuts or chips you simply cannot stop eating serve as a good example of the influence of taste on feeding behavior. The importance of taste (oral) cues on the maintenance of feeding was indicated in a study by Snowden (1969). Snowden implanted a tube into rats' stomachs. The technique, developed by Teitelbaum and Epstein (1962), is illustrated in Figure 5.4. The rat was trained to press a bar to deliver food directly to the stomach. The rat eventually learned, although the training was slow, and oral supplements had to be used during training. The animal lost weight during training and never regained its preoperative weight. The bar-pressing responses were brief, and amount eaten at a meal was small. The presence of hunger caused these rats to initiate feeding, but in the absence of oral cues, they were unable to maintain eating.

Metabolic cues.   Since oral factors have been shown to be important in the maintenance of eating but not in its initiation, other factors must elicit hunger and eating. The evidence indicates that a deficiency in substances (such as sugar and fat) which can be converted to energy provides the hunger signal. The CNS, stimulated by these deficiencies, initiates eating.

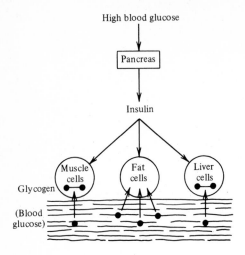

High blood glucose

Glucostatic view.   Jean Mayer (1953) proposed that low levels of blood *glucose*
(sugar) produced the sensation of hunger by stimulating specialized *glucoreceptors* in the
lateral area of the hypothalamus, thus initiating eating. Evidence supporting Mayer's
view was provided by studies investigating the effect of insulin on eating and the
relationship between blood glucose level and activity of the lateral hypothalamus. The
administration of *insulin,* a hormone which lowers blood glucose levels, was found to
initiate eating in animals (for example, Mackay, Callaway, & Barnes, 1940) and to
induce sensations of hunger in human subjects. The influence of insulin on blood glucose
level is presented in Figure 5.5.

A serious problem existed with Mayer's early view. It was recognized that individuals
with *diabetes mellitus* overeat despite high blood glucose levels. The explanation of this
phenomenon lies in the fact that, lacking insulin, the untreated diabetic cannot convert
glucose to energy. One major function of insulin is to promote the entry of glucose into
the body's cells for subsequent metabolism and release of energy. These observations led
Mayer to revise his model in 1955, when he suggested that the availability of glucose for
metabolism rather than its quantity in the bloodstream determines the presence of
hunger. Thus, when glucose is either low or unavailable for use as an energy source, an
animal is stimulated to eat.

An investigation of the role of the availability of glucose on eating was made by
Smith and Epstein (1969). They injected rats with the substance *2-deoxy-D-glucose*
(2-DG). This form of glucose cannot be metabolized and blocks the availability of glucose
to the cells. Smith and Epstein found that the rats injected with 2-DG overate although
their blood glucose levels remained high. These animals, like diabetics were both hungry
and hyperglycemic (i.e., they had high blood sugar). Providing related evidence,
Oomura, Ono, Oogama, and Wagner (1969) injected 2-DG into the LH area of rats and
observed an increase in food consumption. A deficiency in the availability of glucose as a
source of energy appears to be one cue motivating eating behavior.

Lipostatic view.   A high level of fatty acids present in the blood system during
deprivation has been proposed as another stimulus responsible for the initiation of eating
(Kennedy, 1953). When an animal has been deprived of food, it uses stored fats as an
energy source. During deprivation, growth hormones are released from the anterior
pituitary (see Figure A.7). The presence of growth hormones causes the breakdown of fats

into *free fatty acids* which can be used as an energy source until new sources are found. According to Kennedy, the high level of fatty acids stimulates the LH, which then prompts eating.

Set-point theory.   Animals are capable of maintaining a constant body weight through-out their lifetime when maintained on a free-feeding diet. Keesey and Powley (1975) suggested that a *critical set point* (or level) of stored fat exists within the animal. When the animal's stored fat falls below this set point, the brain activates food-seeking behaviors. This system will remain active until the animal's body weight exceeds its set point.

Normal animals deprived of food for several days will regain the lost weight when provided access to food. The animal does not eat enough at one time to regain the lost weight but instead will gain weight slowly over several days of eating. Short-term satiety may temporarily inhibit eating, but the animal will eventually regain the lost weight by eating more frequently.

Keesey and Powley proposed that the set point for initiating eating to maintain body weight is lowered by destruction of the LH area. In order to activate the feeding system in the LH-lesioned animal, its body weight must drop to a level lower than necessary in the normal animal. Powley and Keesey (1970) deprived some of their animals of food before lesioning the LH area. Their results are shown in Figure 5.6. They observed no additional weight loss as the result of the LH lesion in these rats. In well-fed lesioned rats, postoperative aphagia was observed, and their weight dropped to a level comparable to that of the rats which had been starved before the operation. Thus, LH lesioning appears to reduce set point rather than directly cause aphagia. Aphagia is a by-product of the lowered set point induced by the lesion.

Satiety

As we have seen, an animal or human inhibits eating to regulate its energy balance and body weight. The evidence indicates that internal events occurring during and after eating stimulate the brain to inhibit further eating. Becker and Kissiloff (1974) proposed two types of inhibiting processes: a short-term inhibition which suppresses ongoing

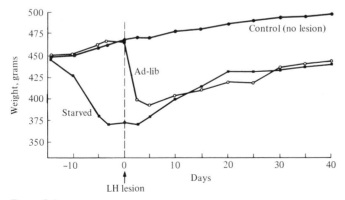

Figure 5.6
Influence of preoperative starvation on the LH-lesion syndrome. (Adapted from Powley, T. L., & Keesey, R. E. Relationship of body weight to the lateral hypothalamic feeding syndrome. Journal of Comparative and Physiological Psychology, *1970, 70, 25–36. Copyright 1970 by the American Psychological Association. Reprinted by permission.)*

feeding, and a long-term inhibition which suppresses feeding between meals. Let's now examine the two major classes of events (peripheral and metabolic) which appear to inhibit eating.

Peripheral cues.   A full stomach has been identified as one event inhibiting eating. Preloading the stomach with food produces a significant reduction in eating. This suppression of eating occurs before digestion, indicating that the short-term inhibition does not depend upon metabolic changes.

Two events occur in the stomach during eating which cause the rat to stop eating. First, the presence of food distends the stomach, and this distention suppresses eating. Berkun, Kessen, and Miller (1952) injected either a liquid food or saline (salt solution) directly into the stomachs of hungry rats. Regardless of which substance was used, these animals consumed less than animals with empty stomachs. Second, in addition to pressure detectors, there are also nutrient detectors in the stomach. Janowitz and Hollander (1953) found that when liquid food, rather than saline, was injected into the stomach, a smaller volume was needed to suppress eating.

The VMH satiety area appears to be involved in the suppression of eating produced by preloading the stomach. Sharma, Anand, Dua, and Singh (1961) observed electrical activity in the VMH area, but not in the LH area, when a balloon in the stomach was filled with water. The VMH area receives input from the gastric region. The pressure and nutrient receptors within the stomach are probably responsible for activating the VMH area, which in turn suppresses eating. Thus gastric factors appear to play an important role in the termination of eating.

Stimuli arising from the oral area are also involved in the suppression of food intake. Janowitz and Grossman (1949) cut a rat's esophagus, bringing the cut ends out of the animal. The animal ate, but the swallowed food fell to the ground. The meal consumed by the *esophagotomized* animal was only slightly larger than a normal meal. These results indicate that oral factors can suppress eating. The suppression of eating is short-lived: an esophagotomized animal soon returns to the food and resumes eating. Since there are no additional satiety factors, eating is resumed once the oral cues are no longer effective.

Metabolic cues.   *Glucostatic view.*   An animal will not eat when information is available that its energy needs have been met. The presence of glucose is one such source of information. Mayer (1953) suggested that the increase in blood glucose which follows food intake acts to suppress eating. Injections of *glucagon*, a pancreatic hormone which increases blood glucose, produced a rapid decrease in hunger and stomach contractions in human subjects (Stunkard, Van Itallie, & Reiss, 1955) and suppressed food intake in a deprived animal (Mayer, 1955). Figure 5.7 presents the influence of glucagon on blood glucose level.

The VMH satiety system responds to this increase in blood glucose by suppressing eating. Anand, Chhina, and Singh (1962) found that a rise in the blood glucose level coincides with increased electrical activity in the VMH area and the suppression of eating. However, the glucoreceptors sensitive to heightened blood glucose are not located in the VMH satiety system. In demonstrating this point, Stricker, Rowland, Saller, and Friedman (1977) injected rats with insulin, producing hypoglycemia (low blood glucose). An injection of glucose or fructose (another sugar) produced satiety and inhibited eating. As fructose cannot enter the brain, the animal should have been hungry if the glucoreceptors were located in the brain. Epstein (1960) found that injections of glucose directly into the VMH do not suppress eating in a hungry rat. Apparently, the VMH satiety system receives information from other systems before inhibiting eating.

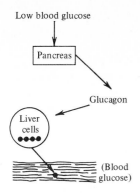

Low blood glucose

Pancreas

Glucagon

Liver cells

(Blood glucose)

Figure 5.7
When blood glucose level is low (hypoglycemia), glucagon is released from the pancreas. Glucagon converts liver glycogen into glucose, and then releases it into the bloodstream for use as an energy source. (Reproduced by permission from Understanding nutrition *by Eva May Hamilton and Eleanor Whitney, copyright © 1977, West Publishing Company. All rights reserved.)*

The receptors that respond to increased blood sugar are located in the liver. Maurcio Russek (1971) proposed that the presence of food in the duodenum activates neurons which excite the VMH area. Stimulation of the VMH system inhibits eating and causes the release of glucagon from the pancreas. Glucagon is responsible for the breakdown of glycogen to glucose in the liver. The amount of glucose released by the liver depends on the stored glycogen. Since a food-deprived animal will have little stored glycogen, it will resume eating quickly. The animal with free access to food will have sufficient stores of glycogen and will not resume eating again until its blood glucose decreases to the LH set point. In support of his view, Russek found that administration of glucose into the liver suppressed eating. He implanted a cannula (a small tube) in either the hepatic portal vein (a vein which goes to the liver) or the jugular vein of a food-deprived dog. Administration of glucose into the portal vein suppressed eating; administration of glucose into the jugular vein had no influence on eating. In addition, Schmitt (1973) found that an infusion of glucose into the liver increased neural activity in the VMH satiety center. The VMH center inhibits eating as long as a positive energy balance persists.

Lipostatic view. Kennedy (1953) suggested that VMH cells are also sensitive to the level of fat stored in the adipose tissue. The release of insulin during eating enhances the use of glucose as a source of energy and decreases free fatty acids as an energy source. The body then converts the free fatty acids into fat and stores them in adipose tissue. The increase in fat reserves stimulates the VMH, inhibiting further eating. The animal will not resume eating as long as the satiety system is stimulated by the presence of adequate lipid (fat) stores.

Set-point theory of satiety. One critical aspect of an animal's feeding system is the limitation of excessive body weight. As was noted earlier, Keesey and Powley (1975) proposed that an animal could govern its body weight by limiting the amount of stored body fat. The maximum amount of stored body fat is called the *critical set point* and varies from individual to individual. Once the amount of adipose tissue reaches the critical set point, the VMH satiety center is activated and in turn inhibits further eating.

VMH lesions appear to establish new and higher critical set points. An animal which ate to maintain a certain adipose tissue level before VMH lesioning would find after VMH lesioning that it no longer had enough adipose tissue to meet the criterion of the new set point. The VMH-lesioned animal becomes obese because it eats until it has stored enough lipids to satisfy the new set point. This hypothesis also explains Hoebel and Teitelbaum's finding (1966) that VMH-lesioned rats did not subsequently overeat if they were made obese by force feeding prior to surgery. According to the set-point theory, their fat stores were already above the critical set point and their satiety system inhibited further eating.

New Directions
Traditionally, physiological psychology has focused on the neurological disturbances which induce overeating and obesity. However, in the past 10 years there has been a shift away from a pure neurological approach. Other systems have been implicated in the disruption of the normal pattern of eating. Some of these new ways of viewing eating and overeating are discussed in the following sections.

A metabolic view.   Obese people, especially those who are dieting, will admit that they are typically receptive to eating. In fact, a metabolic disturbance produces an elevated level of insulin in both obese humans (Solomon, Ensinck, & Williams, 1968) and hyperphagic rats (Frohman, Goldman, & Bernardis, 1972), causing them to be in a constant state of hunger. Their hunger usually causes them to eat whatever is placed before them, but their obesity often prevents them from working for their food. If the hyperphagic rat is prevented from becoming fat, it will be as motivated to work for food as a normal animal (for example, Sclafani & Kluge, 1974). Apparently, the effort required to obtain food is often too much for the obese animal or person.

Friedman and Stricker (1976) suggest that the hyperphagic animal eats because food is its only available source of energy. The elevated insulin level found in the hyperphagic rat promotes the storage of digested food as glycogen and fat, while preventing the obese animal from effectively using its fat reserves as an energy source.

In hyperphagic rats which have been kept at normal weight, an elevation in blood insulin level occurs shortly after VMH destruction, although rats recently lesioned have lower blood insulin levels than obese lesioned animals (Tannenbaum, Paxinos, & Bindra, 1974). It is interesting that these nonobese VMH-lesioned animals continue to gain weight even on a restricted diet: their elevated levels of insulin cause them to store more of their ingested food as fat than normal animals do (Han & Liu, 1966).

Overweight people typically quickly regain weight lost by dieting. Since nonobese VMH-lesioned animals store more food as fat than nonlesioned animals, the weight gain seen in previously overweight individuals after dieting probably reflects the inherent tendency of overweight people to gain weight on the same caloric intake as people of normal weight. Thus, unless the overweight person's food intake is severely limited, additional methods must be used to maintain lost weight.

Jean Mayer (1978) suggested that exercise must be an integral part of a successful weight-reduction program. He compared many obese adolescents and adults to static-stage hyperphagic animals: having reached their maximal weight, they eat only enough to maintain it. These obese people are typically less active and often consume fewer calories in a day than their normal-weight counterparts. Exercise enables overweight individuals to use their excess calories rather than store them as fat. Mayer reported the successful implementation in a large city public school system of a weight-loss program involving diet and exercise. The overweight children were placed on a balanced but not restrictive diet and were given psychological counseling on how to improve their dress, their walk, and their general appearance. They attended special physical education classes and followed an independent exercise program during weekends and holidays. Mayer found improvement in the majority of the children enrolled in his program: their activity increased, and they lost weight. Apparently, an effective exercise plan should be included in a successful weight-loss program for those who are more than just a few pounds overweight.

A reflexive approach. *Cephalic reflex.* When an animal or human is exposed to food, it exhibits a set of responses which prepares it to digest, metabolize, and store ingested food. These internal preparatory responses are called *cephalic reflexes* by Terry Powley (1977). (A reflex is said to be cephalic when input to the brain originates in the head region, output to the periphery goes to the autonomic nervous system and endocrine system, and the CNS mediates the input and output.) These *cephalic responses* are elicited by the taste and smell of food and include the secretion of saliva, gastric juices, pancreatic enzymes, and insulin. The intensity of these cephalic responses is directly related to the palatability of food: the more palatable the food, the greater the cephalic autonomic and endocrine responses and the larger the animal's meal. Table 5.5 presents a summary of cephalic response amplitudes as a function of the sensory characteristics of food.

The lateral hypothalamic feeding center appears to be involved in this cephalic reflexive initiation of eating (see Figure 5.8). The LH area receives direct input from the olfactory and gustatory systems (Norgren, 1970; Pfaff & Pfaffman, 1969), and the intensity of the LH response is directly related to the palatability of food (Burton, Mora, & Rolls, 1975). Stimulation of the LH area produces eating behavior; therefore, one reason palatable foods are eaten in greater amounts is that they are able to generate

Table 5.5
Cephalic Response Amplitude as a Function of Sensory Quality of Food

Cephalic Responses and Afferent Stimuli	Foods Compared	Subjects
Salivary secretion:		
Sight of food	Pickled plum > orange > apple > biscuits (approx.: 6:3.4:1.2:1)	Man (Japanese)
Sight and smell of food	Banana split or pizza > unappealing pizza (approx.: 7:1)	Man
Gastric secretion:		
Sham feeding	Self-selected meal > hospital meal > gruel (approx.: 1.8:1.4:1)	Man
Sham feeding	Meat > milk > bread (approx: 7:6:1)	Dog
Sham feeding	Fish > meat (approx.: 1.8:1)	Man (Russian)
Sham feeding	Meat > milk > bread (approx.: 2.2:2:1)	Dog
Exocrine pancreas secretion:		
Sight and smell of food	Usual French breakfast > forced beefsteak at breakfast (approx.: 4:1)	Man (French)
Sham feeding	Pard dog food > rat chow	Rat

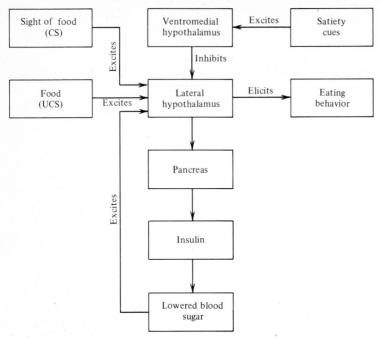

Figure 5.8
Hypothalamic-cephalic feeding system. The sight of food (CS), the presence of food (UCS), or both can activate the lateral hypothalamus which then elicits eating. Stimulation of the lateral hypothalamus also causes the pancreas to release insulin, which acts to lower blood glucose level. The lowered blood glucose level continues the stimulation of the lateral hypothalamus. Eating will continue until the satiety cues activate the ventromedial hypothalamus which in turn inhibits the lateral hypothalamus. The human or animal then stops eating.

greater LH responses. In addition, activation of the LH area was observed to initiate the cephalic reflexes (increased salivary and gastric secretion, enhanced intestinal contractions, and heightened insulin release). In circular fashion, these cephalic responses continue the activation of the LH area (Anand, Chhina, & Singh, 1962), which in turn causes the animal to continue eating.

Although this cycle explains the comparative effectiveness of palatable foods in stimulating eating, we must look to an additional set of responses (which have recently been identified as cephalic) for explanations of active rejection of food. Doty (1967) found that taste cues could also elicit a rejection reflex consisting of ejection, gagging, and vomiting. The rejection reflex is produced by unpalatable food (for example, quinine) and is elicited by stimulation of the hypothalamus feeding center in the presence of unpalatable foods (Robinson & Mishkin, 1968).

A lack of control. Powley (1977) proposed that one major function of the VMH area is to modulate or inhibit the intensity of the cephalic response to food. According to Powley, the destruction of the VMH area eliminates VMH inhibition and causes an exaggeration of LH-induced cephalic responses. In a VMH-lesioned animal, palatable foods produce a heightened preparatory response, thereby increasing the LH-induced eating; an unpalatable food increases the cephalic rejection response and causes an increased avoidance of unpleasant foods. Powley feels that this exaggeration of the cephalic response to food is responsible for both the excessive eating and the finickiness about food exhibited by VMH-lesioned animals.

Several recent studies demonstrate this greater cephalic response in VMH-lesioned rats. Strubble and Steffens (1975) measured insulin release in VMH-lesioned and normal rats beginning within the first minute after feeding. The rapid onset of this response indicates that a cephalic reflex is involved. The insulin response of VMH-lesioned animals was four times faster than that of normal animals. Weingarten and Powley (1977) showed a significantly larger secretion of gastric acid in VMH-lesioned animals than in normal animals; Rozkowska and Fonberg (1973) found a higher salivary response in VMH-lesioned rats than in normal animals. Also, Weingarten and Powley (1977) compared food intake and weight gain in VMH-lesioned and nonlesioned animals exposed to two diets. One of these diets (Purina rat pellets) elicits little cephalic response; the other (Pard dog food) produces a large cephalic response. Weingarten and Powley noted that none of the animals overate or gained weight on the Purina diet, but the VMH-lesioned animals became hyperphagic and gained weight over a 2-week period when switched to the Pard diet. When returned to the Purina diet, these animals reduced their intake and stopped gaining weight. Evidently, one reason why VMH-lesioned animals overeat is that they are overresponsive to palatable foods.

The exaggerated toxic consequences (for example, illness) of unpalatable foods, not their taste, cause VMH-lesioned animals to avoid a certain substance. Sclafani, Aravich, and Schwartz (1979) fed VMH-lesioned and normal rats either a quinine diet or a *sucrose octa-acetate* (SOA) diet. Although both diets taste bitter, quinine produces toxic effects after ingestion, while SOA has no aversive aftereffects. The experimenters found that VMH-lesioned rats ate less of the quinine diet but more of the SOA diet than normal rats. Apparently, it is not the bitter taste of food but an overresponsive cephalic rejection reflex produced by nonpalatable foods which is responsible for the obese animal's avoidance of undesirable foods.

This discussion indicates that VMH-lesioned animals prefer palatable foods and cannot inhibit eating because of an overresponsive cephalic reaction to food. Although a heightened cephalic response has not been demonstrated in obese humans, the fact that the other characteristics of the VMH-lesion syndrome have been seen in obese people provides support for the view that obese people, like hyperphagic animals, are physiologically overresponsive to food. This overresponsivity, producing the finickiness seen in obese people, is due to the failure of the VMH area to inhibit the internal metabolic reaction initiated when we eat.

Stress-induced eating. How often have you found yourself going to the refrigerator during periods of stress? Recent evidence has implicated stress as one event precipitating overeating. Rowland and Antelman (1976) exposed rats to a series of mild, nonpainful pinches (to the tail) in the presence of sweetened milk. They discovered that this mild stress induced hyperphagia and an increase in weight. Rowland and Antelman proposed that these results indicate that stress could be one cause of obesity. The effect of the stress in this study appears to operate through activation of the LH feeding system. Antelman, Sehzechtman, Chen, and Fisher (1975) showed that tail pinching increases the activity of the animal's CNS feeding system.

It is surprising that tail pinching elicited eating, since fear has been consistently observed to suppress eating in animals (see Chapter 4). Antelman, Rowland, and Fisher (1976) suggested that the animals ate to suppress the aversive aspects of this stress. In support of their interpretation, the authors found that the amount consumed during tail pinching was related to the *hedonic* value of the food; the more palatable the food, the greater the increased consumption. For example, the stress produced a greater intake of sweet milk than plain milk as compared with the intake of either milk by nonstressed animals. Stress had no effect on water intake: both stressed and nonstressed animals consumed approximately the same amount of water.

The influence of stress on eating behavior has also been investigated in humans. Schachter, Goldman, and Gordon (1968) compared the number of crackers consumed during apprehension of either mild or severe electric shock. They noted that the intake of crackers by subjects of normal weight was lower in the "high threat" condition than in the "mild threat" condition. In contrast, under both conditions obese subjects consumed equal quantities of either crackers (Schachter, Goldman, & Gordon, 1968), chocolate chip cookies (McKenna, 1972), or ice cream (Herman & Polivy, 1974). The failure of fear to suppress eating in obese persons is an unexpected result, as fat persons tend to be more emotionally responsive than normal-weight persons (Rodin, Elman, & Schachter, 1974). Rodin, Elman, and Schachter found that obese people reported greater nervousness when threatened with painful shocks and were more emotionally distressed when exposed to disturbing tapes (for example, a description of death by leukemia) than normal-weight people. It is likely that emotional reactivity of obese people causes them to learn to eat in order to prevent emotional distress. The observation that moderate fear can be suppressed by eating in both animals (for example, Wolpe, 1958) and humans (for example, Jones, 1924) indicates that people can inhibit stress by eating. In some obese persons, extreme anxiety, restlessness, and irritability occur during prolonged dieting (for example, Glucksman & Hirsch, 1968); this may reflect the removal of their method of coping with stress.

PSYCHOLOGICAL SYSTEMS

The animal's or human's biological systems recognize the presence of a nutritional deficiency: the psychological systems locate and obtain desirable foods, while avoiding undesirable foods. An animal or person learns where desirable food is located through classical conditioning. The environmental stimuli that are regularly associated with eating act to motivate feeding behavior. In addition, classical conditioning enables the animal or human to learn what foods and places produce illness and are to be avoided. In this case the presence of the environmental cues and foods associated with illness acts to motivate the termination of feeding behavior. Those behaviors that are successful in obtaining desirable foods are strengthened through instrumental conditioning. An animal or person will exhibit these instrumental behaviors to obtain food when deprived, and the strength of the animal's or human's instrumental behaviors is directly related to the level of deficiency and the value of the anticipated reward. This discussion begins by considering how classical conditioning enables an animal to learn where food is located and whether the food should be consumed. Later in the chapter we will see how the animal or human learns to obtain food.

Classical Conditioning

The classical conditioning process enables an animal or person to learn how to respond to an event. (The reader is referred to the discussion of classical conditioning in Chapter 1.) Before conditioning, an *unconditioned stimulus* (UCS) will elicit an unlearned or *unconditioned response* (UCR). Pavlov (1927) found that when a neutral event was repeatedly presented with a UCS, the neutral stimulus (called a *conditioned stimulus* or

CS) also developed the capacity to elicit a response (called the *conditioned response* or CR). Psychologists over the past 50 years have studied the relationship between classical conditioning and eating.

Conditioned hunger. Almost everyone has experienced hunger in the absence of any nutritional deficiency. A cream puff in the window of the local bakery or a piece of cheesecake starring in a television commercial can trigger overwhelming hunger responses in the most sensible eater. Burton, Mora, and Rolls (1975) found that the sight of an animal's most preferred food produced the greatest activity in the lateral hypothalamic feeding center, while an unpalatable food did not elicit any response. Often, simply the thought of some delectable food is sufficient to initiate hunger. What mechanism is responsible for this psychological hunger?

In 1943, Hull suggested that psychological, or conditioned, hunger reflects a classical conditioning process. A physiological deficiency produced a hunger reaction capable of initiating eating. Hull thought that any neutral environmental cue, when consistently paired with hunger, will become a conditioned stimulus capable of initiating both hunger and eating.

Empirical support. During the 1940s and 1950s, a number of researchers sought to demonstrate the existence of *conditioned hunger* in the laboratory. A study by Calvin, Bicknell, and Sperling (1953) is typical of these studies. They observed that when their animals had been deprived of food in a distinctive environment, eating occurred in that environment even when the animals were satiated. Although several studies did indicate that satiated rats would eat when in the presence of environmental cues associated with hunger, most research on conditioned hunger failed to find empirical support for the phenomenon (see Cravens & Renner, 1970, for a review of the literature).

The failure to obtain a reliable conditioned hunger effect (using amount consumed as the index of hunger) may not be too surprising: the presence of deficiency (hunger) merely acts to initiate eating; the amount consumed is determined by the palatability of the food (Le Magnen, 1971). In addition, a number of studies show that the influence of deprivation declines as environmental cues associated with eating develop the capacity to initiate feeding behavior. In one of these studies, Birch, Burnstein, and Clark (1958) maintained their animals in a specially constructed cage and fed them from a food trough for 2 hours every 24 hours. As conditioning progressed, the animals began to approach the trough as feeding time grew near. If they were not fed after 24 hours, their feeding behavior declined over the next several hours; it reappeared as the forty-eighth hour without food approached. The environmental cues associated with eating began to initiate eating behavior, and the actual deprivation level of the animal lost its influence as the determinant of eating.

Conditioned cephalic reflex. Animals' motivation to eat intensifies during eating because the cephalic responses elicited by food stimulate the LH feeding center and maintain eating until the satiety factors inhibit eating (Powley, 1977). Palatable foods produce a greater cephalic response and cause the animal to eat more than unpalatable foods do. Weingarten and Powley (1977) found in rats that a light-and-tone CS, when paired with a high-fat food (UCS), developed the capacity to recreate gastric acid as the CR. Furthermore, Booth, Coons, and Miller (1969) observed that a CS paired with LH stimulation produced hypoglycemia (decreased blood glucose) as the CR. Further, Booth and Miller (1969) observed that administration of novocaine to the LH area blocked the hypoglycemic CR. Earlier, you saw that the amount consumed is increased by these cephalic responses to either a palatable food or LH stimulation. Apparently, environmental stimulation associated either with palatable foods or LH stimulation can also produce this cephalic feeding response (refer to Figure 5.8).

As you saw earlier in this chapter, the research of Stanley Schachter consistently underscores the importance of environmental cues in initiating eating by obese humans. Weingarten and Powley (1977) found that VMH-lesioned animals showed a greater cephalic response to a conditioned stimulus than nonlesioned rats. Unfortunately, no researcher has yet demonstrated that VMH-lesioned hyperphagic rats show increased food-seeking behavior to conditioned stimuli compared with nonlesioned rats. On the basis of Schachter's observation of externalization of feeding in obese humans, such a comparatively stronger motivational response to a CS would be predicted. Finding such parallel responses between species is important in order to identify the determinants of human obesity.

Taste aversions.   I have a friend who refuses to walk down an aisle in a supermarket where tomato sauce is displayed; he says that even the sight of cans of tomatoes makes him ill. My oldest son once got sick after eating string beans, and now he refuses to touch them. I once was very nauseated several hours after eating at a local restaurant, and I have not returned since. Almost all of us have some food that we will not eat or a restaurant that we avoid. Often the reason for this behavior is that at some time we experienced illness after eating a particular food or in a particular place, and associated the event with the illness through classical conditioning. Such an experience engenders a *conditioned aversion* to the taste of the food or the place itself. Subsequently, we avoid it.

Conditioning principles.   Animals have a strong preference for saccharin, consuming large quantities even when nondeprived; nonetheless, animals will not subsequently drink saccharin if illness has followed its consumption. John Garcia and his associates (Garcia, Kimeldorf, & Koelling, 1955; Garcia, Kimeldorf, & Hunt, 1957) discovered that rats made ill by such agents as *x-ray irradiation* or *lithium chloride* after consuming a palatable substance will subsequently avoid that taste. Their subjects developed aversions to taste cues even when the taste stimulus preceded illness by several hours. A number of important characteristics of flavor (or conditioned) aversion learning have been uncovered over the past 20 years (see Logue, 1979). An animal experiencing a new taste consumes only small quantities of the food. This "bait-shyness," or neophobic response, protects the animal from eating lethal amounts of poison. After several hours without illness, the animal assumes that the food is safe and returns to eat more of it (Kalat & Rozin, 1973). The failure of poison to control rodents is due to this protective neophobic response.

Animals develop aversions to novel tastes more readily than to familiar tastes. Revusky and Bedarf (1967) paired a novel and a familiar taste cue with illness. They observed that their subjects developed an aversion to the novel taste but not to the familiar taste. Later research has shown that animals can develop an aversion to a familiar taste if the taste and illness are paired frequently enough (Fenwick, Mikulka, & Klein, 1975). Kalat's study (1974) demonstrates the importance of novelty in the development of a taste aversion. Kalat raised some rats on water and others on a high sucrose concentration, and then paired both a low and a moderate sucrose concentration with illness. The rats raised on water avoided the moderate sucrose concentration; the rats raised on the high sucrose concentration developed an aversion to the low sucrose concentration. Apparently, when the offending substance cannot be clearly identified, animals avoid the more unfamiliar taste.

In a classic study, Garcia and Koelling (1966) exposed rats to either a saccharin taste

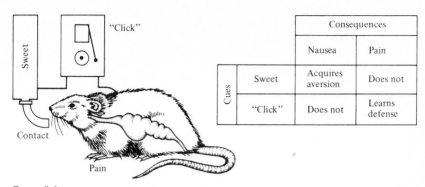

Figure 5.9
Effects of pairing a gustatory cue or an auditory cue with either external pain or internal illness. [Adapted from Garcia, J., Clark, J. C., & Hankins, W. G. Natural responses to scheduled rewards. Cited in P. P. G. Bateson, & P. H. Klopfer (Eds.), Perspectives in ethology *(Vol. 1). New York: Plenum, 1973.]*

cue or a light and tone compound stimulus. Following exposure to one of these cues, animals received either an electric shock or irradiation-induced illness. Figure 5.9 presents the results of the study. The animals exhibited an aversion to saccharin when it was paired with illness but not when it was paired with shock. In addition, they developed a fear of the light and tone stimulus when it was paired with shock but not when it was paired with illness. Seligman proposed, on the basis of this study, that rats have an evolutionary predisposition (preparedness) to associate illness with taste cues but cannot learn (contrapreparedness) to avoid food-induced shock (1970). Similarly, Seligman feels that animals have inherited biological systems enabling them to associate an environmental cue (for example, a light and tone cue) with shock, but they cannot become afraid of a light and tone cue paired with illness. His hypothesis has been challenged by a number of recent studies which demonstrated that rats have the ability to associate a taste cue with shock (Krane & Wagner, 1975) and a place (environment) with illness (for example, Best, Best, & Mickley, 1973; Revusky & Parker, 1976). Best, Best, and Mickley found that rats avoided a distinctive black compartment previously paired with an illness-inducing apormorphine injection; Revusky and Parker observed that rats did not eat out of a container which had been paired with illness induced by lithium chloride.

Applications. John Garcia (Garcia, Rusiniak, & Brett, 1977) discovered an effective way to help ranchers in the southwest prevent coyotes from killing their sheep. These researchers injected lithium chloride into a few lamb carcasses and left the poisoned carcasses at various places on the open range. The authors noted a rapid decline in the number of sheep killed by coyotes. Furthermore, they noted that coyotes approaching the poisoned meat for a second time exhibited retching movements and "conditioned disgust responses" (urinating or rolling on the meat or burying it). They also observed that coyotes approaching live sheep showed strong conflict responses before leaving the area, still hungry. The use of this classical conditioning procedures has proved to be an effective deterrent against the predators of domestic animals.

Unfortunately, the use of illness in the treatment of obesity has not been shown to be effective (see Little & Curran, 1978). *Covert sensitization* (a form of behavior therapy; see Cautela, 1972) has typically been the form of aversion therapy used in the treatment of obesity. Rather than actually suffering a drug-induced illness, patients receiving covert sensitization are required to imagine eating and savoring preferred but fattening foods and then becoming disgustingly ill. A study by Diament and Wilson (1975) represents a typical experiment evaluating the effectiveness of covert sensitization. Three groups of subjects were included in their study: (1) one group was treated by covert sensitization; (2) a second group received a covert sensitization "placebo" (pleasant rather than aversive scenes were paired with eating); (3) a third group was kept on the waiting list, as a control. Subjects in group 1 ("covert sensitization" condition) were asked on aversion trials to imagine eating a preferred food and subsequently suffering nausea and vomiting. On escape trials, these subjects experienced relief (see Chapter 2) when they did not eat the target food. On some trials the therapist described the scene to the patient in order to increase the vividness of the experience; on other trials the patients imagined their own scenes. Diament and Wilson reported that the use of covert sensitization did not significantly reduce the patients' weight or alter their food preferences.

Little and Curran (1978) concluded from their review of the studies using covert sensitization as a treatment of obesity that each study suffered from one of several procedural problems. *First, insufficient attention was paid to controlling the level of arousal experienced during the imagined illness experience.* Janda and Rimm (1972) found that the effectiveness of covert sensitization depended on the patient's level of arousal. *Second, the use of relaxation during aversive scenes served to decrease the level of arousal rather than to increase the vividness of the scene (as predicted by Cautela, 1972).* Wolphin and Kirsch (1974) observed that relaxation reduced the aversiveness of illness, thus demonstrating that this procedure also may have confounded the results. *Finally, in this design, the patients do not have an acceptable alternative to eating the preferred food.* Animal studies have found that a taste aversion is significantly stronger when animals can choose an alternative food (Grote & Brown, 1965).

Despite these results, the use of aversion therapy theoretically should be an effective treatment of obesity. Schachter's research indicates that obese humans avoid unpalatable foods. The effect of taste aversion is to change preferences, thus making target food unpalatable. The use of actual illness as opposed to imaginary illness may represent a more effective treatment of overeating in obese humans. Evidence supporting this idea is the loss of appetite typically seen in cancer patients receiving radiation therapy (Morrison, 1976). In addition, Bernstein (1978) found that children in the early stages of cancer acquired an aversion to a distinctively flavored Mapletoff ice cream (maple and black walnut flavor) consumed before toxic chemotherapy in the gastrointestinal (GI) tract. Instead of eating Mapletoff ice cream, these children preferred either to play with a toy or to eat another novel-flavor ice cream. In contrast, children who had previously received the toxic therapy to the GI tract without the Mapletoff ice cream and children who had been given the Mapletoff ice cream before toxic chemotherapy not involving the GI tract both ate the Mapletoff ice cream. It appears that a learned taste aversion is one factor contributing to anorexia and weight loss in cancer patients. Additional clinical research should evaluate whether or not the procedures leading to the development of a flavor aversion can produce a change in the eating habits of obese humans.

Specific hunger.   Richter (1936) proposed that animals possess specialized receptors capable of detecting the presence of a dietary deficiency. For example, we know that animals whose adrenal glands are removed have an increased need for salt. Richter found that *adrenalectomized* rats show an increased preference for salt, consuming levels that normal rats avoid. Animals show an increased consumption of a large number of substances (for example, calcium, phosphorus, vitamins, and proteins) when their diets are deficient in these substances, or when a biological malfunction creates an additional need for them.

Recent evidence indicates that an animal's increased intake of the needed substance does not reflect an innate biological sensory system which can detect the presence of the nutrient, but rather reflects a learned preference for a diet containing the deficient substance (Rozin & Kalat, 1971). According to Rozin and Kalat, an animal becomes ill owing to the deficiency and develops an aversion to the deficient diet. The animal's taste aversion to its familiar diet causes it to search for and consume a new diet. If the new diet contains the needed nutrient, it will enable the animal to recover. The animal then associates the new diet with recovery from illness and develops a strong preference for it. In Rodgers and Rozin's study (1966), rats deprived of *thiamine* (vitamin B_{12}) rejected their diet, dug the food out of their dishes without eating it, and chewed on other objects in their cages. This behavior is identical to that of animals given unpalatable quinine. The old, deficient diet had apparently become aversive. When rats were given a new diet containing thiamine, they consumed large quantities of the new foods. When offered another new diet as an alternative to the old deficient diet, they showed a preference for the second new diet.

The development of the preference for the new diet evolved because of an association between the new diet and recovery from illness. Garcia, Ervin, Yorke, and Koelling (1967) also placed animals on a thiamine-deficient diet. After several days of the deficient diet, they paired saccharin with an injection of thiamine. The thiamine injection produced a rapid recovery from the deficiency, and these animals consumed more saccharin than control animals that were not deficient when they received the saccharin-thiamine pairing. Also, Garcia, Hankins, and Rusiniak (1974) found that any taste presented during a rat's recovery from illness induced by lithium chloride will become a preferred taste. Animals are apparently capable of learning which foods produce a recovery from illness, as well as which foods induce illness. One might speculate that many of our homemade remedies for illness (for example, chicken soup) may have coincidentally been paired with our natural recovery from illness. The treatment we think will make us well may merely reflect a "conditioned medicine effect."

Conditioned satiety. Earlier in the chapter we saw that environmental cues can become associated with food and produce a conditioned appetite response. It is also true that animals or humans can associate cues with the cessation of eating. Booth (1977) proposed that stimuli which occur at the end of a meal become associated with the unconditioned nutritional changes that occur after an animal has eaten. These conditioned stimuli elicit a conditioned satiety response, thus producing a short-term inhibition of eating. The unconditioned nutritional changes continue the inhibition until the next meal. The observation that animals or people stop eating before the actual nutritional effects of eating occur supports the idea that classical conditioning is involved in satiety.

Booth (1972) gave rats experience with both a dilute and a rich diet. A different flavor was associated with each diet. At the beginning of his experiment, animals ate an equal amount of each diet and displayed an equivalent preference for each flavor. During the course of the study, the animals ate less of the rich diet and more of the dilute diet. Booth felt that a greater conditioned satiety response was produced for the rich diet than for the dilute diet because the rich diet produced a stronger unconditioned satiety effect. In support of this model, Booth found that when the flavor associated with the rich diet was changed to the dilute diet, the rats ate small meals and lost weight; if the flavor associated with the dilute diet was switched to the rich diet, the animals ate large meals and gained weight. Booth, Lee, and McAleavey (1976) observed a similar phenomenon in human subjects. These results indicate that conditioned satiety plays an important role in the regulation of food intake.

Animals other than humans typically eat only a single type of food at a time; this enables them to learn what flavors are linked to satiation or to illness. The wide variety of different foods eaten during a meal probably is partly responsible for the high level of overeating seen in humans. Support for this conclusion can be found in a study by Le Magnen (1971). He observed that rats at mealtime ate more when allowed access to four different-flavored foods than if they were given only a single food—that is, a single flavor. We might be able to regulate our eating more easily if we were to limit the number of foods consumed in one meal.

Overview.   Classical conditioning plays an important role in motivating the initiation and suppression of food intake. Even in the absence of a nutritional deficiency, stimuli associated with the early stages of eating or with recovery from illness motivate eating. The regimentation of our eating habits (for example, having a specific dinner hour) is one indication of a conditioned appetite response. Neutral stimuli can also become conditioned inhibitors of eating. The association of stimuli with illness produces a conditioned aversion, and the stimuli present during the later stages of eating become associated with the unconditioned nutritional effects of eating, thereby producing conditioned satiety. These inhibitory stimuli enable us to avoid poisoning and overeating.

Instrumental Conditioning

We may be hungry, but unless we have learned what behaviors produce food (for example, purchasing food at the grocery store and cooking food), we will remain hungry. The function of instrumental (or operant) conditioning is to develop behaviors that are effective in obtaining food. Psychologists for the last 75 years have investigated the instrumental conditioning process. Thorndike's puzzle-box studies (1932) demonstrate that food-seeking behavior can be modified (see Chapter 1). He placed cats in a small cage and put their food outside it. Several potential behaviors could release the cat to obtain food: it might escape by stepping on a pedal, pulling a string, or manipulating the wooden bars with its paws. Food-deprived cats eventually exhibited behaviors which allowed them to escape the cage and thereby obtain food. With continued exposure to the puzzle box, the cats were quicker in escaping and limited their behavior to a single successful pattern. A hungry cat can obviously learn a new behavior to obtain food.

Hull's drive theory.   According to Hullian learning theory (see Chapter 2), an animal's or person's levels of learning (or habit strength), motivation, and inhibition determine the intensity of instrumental behavior. This section examines the influence of drive and incentive on instrumental behavior performed to get food as a reinforcer.

Clark Hull (1943) proposed that drive (D) represents an intense internal arousal which energizes instrumental (learned) behavior; the greater the drive, the more intense the response. The evidence indicates that as its drive level increases, an animal does behave more intensely to obtain food. Weiss (1960) investigated the influence of deprivation time on how rapidly a rat ran down an alley to obtain food and concluded that the rat ran faster as deprivation increased from 2 hours to 48 hours. The difficulty of eliminating (extinguishing) an instrumental behavior also increases as drive increases. Perin (1942) found that resistance to extinction was greater with higher levels of deprivation. These observations support Hull's concept: the intense internal arousal produced by deprivation energizes our instrumental food-seeking behavior.

The incentive motivation of an animal or human is an unconditioned reaction to food and a conditioned motivation produced by the association of external stimuli with reward (Hull, 1952). Environmental events that occur when a reward is given become capable of eliciting an anticipatory reward (or goal) response. This anticipatory goal response produces the incentive motivation to respond. According to Hull, the level of incentive motivation increases with the magnitude of the reward. Although earlier research had demonstrated that an animal will respond more intensely for a greater food reward (Crespi, 1942), Hull's concept of incentive motivation has been proven inadequate. The evidence has not consistently shown that anticipatory behavior precedes instrumental behavior. For example, Kintsch and Witte (1962) made two observations. They noted that rats salivate before bar-pressing on a fixed interval schedule (in which a reward is given after a fixed time). They also observed that bar-pressing occurs before salivation (r_G) on a fixed-ratio schedule (in which a reward is given after a fixed number of responses). Obviously the animal's conditioned salivation response cannot, as Hull proposed, provide the motivation for fixed-ratio behavior. As a result of these experiments, it appears that our overt anticipation of food does not motivate food-seeking behavior; rather the motivation produced by external events seems to be within the CNS (see Chapters 2 and 4).

Bindra's central motive state. Bindra (1974) proposed that a central representation (within the CNS) of an environmental cue associated with food is created during conditioning (see Chapter 1). This internal representation then becomes a central anticipation of food when the environmental cue associated with food is presented. The central anticipation of food stimulates a central motive state (CMS). Arousal of the CMS elicits appetitive food seeking or consummatory behavior. In Bindra's model the anticipation of food is central, requiring no overt response to produce incentive motivation.

You may have noted the similarity of Bindra's central motive state and Rescorla and Solomon's central appetitive motivational state detailed in Chapter 2. Although both views suggest that a central state motivates appetitive behavior, they differ in one important respect: Bindra describes a motivational state specific to eating behavior, whereas Rescorla and Solomon's central appetitive state provides the motivational basis of all appetitive behavior.

An animal appears to respond to an environmental stimulus associated with food as if it were food (Brown & Jenkins, 1968). In Brown and Jenkins's study, pigeons received 160 presentations of a lighted white key followed by food. The pigeons learned to peck at the key, even though no relationship existed between pecking and food. In the pigeon's mind, the white key represented food and activated the same consummatory behavior as food did. Furthermore, the central representation is of a specific food. The presentation of an alternative food will alter the animal's feeding behavior. Tinklepaugh (1928) trained monkeys to respond to one of two containers to obtain a banana. When lettuce (normally a desirable food) was placed in the container instead of the banana, even deprived monkeys refused it. Instead, they began to explore the room, apparently searching for the anticipated banana. Elliott (1928) observed a similar disruption of behavior when rats were given sunflower seeds instead of bran mash. In addition to a disruption in level of performance when the reward magnitude is shifted downward (negative contrast effect; Crespi, 1942), a greater performance is produced when the reward magnitude is increased (positive-contrast effect). Mellgren (1972) observed that rats trained on one pellet perform better when shifted to eight pellets than animals which have always received the larger reward. The anticipation of a banana split is more motivating to a person whose choice has been limited to vanilla ice cream than to a person who normally indulges in banana splits. Conversely, the anticipation of vanilla ice cream is not very motivating to a person who previously ate only banana splits.

Self-control of eating.   During the past 10 years, clinical psychologists have employed operant techniques to motivate obese persons to reduce their food intake. The operant methodology used by clinical psychologists utilizes a self-reinforcement procedure: the patients themselves administer reinforcement when they successfully reduce food intake (see Rimm & Masters, 1979, for a thorough review of self-control methodology and experimental evaluative research). Psychologists were initially skeptical of the efficacy of *self-control* in behavioral management. They felt that self-reinforcement would not modify instrumental behavior (Skinner, 1953). Bandura and Perloff (1967) demonstrated that the self-control operant technique was as effective in changing behavior as the typical method of reinforcement (given by the therapist). In addition, even though overweight individuals are intensely motivated to lose weight, they receive no immediate reinforcement for reducing their intake, since significant weight loss will not occur for days or weeks. The absence of immediate reinforcement prevents instrumental behavior change, since the reinforcement contingency cannot be established (see Renner, 1964). The use of self-control methods and self-reward allows the individual to receive immediate reinforcement for behavior change and thus encourages successful modification of instrumental responses.

   Clinical treatment.   The self-control procedure involves two separate stages: *self-monitoring* and *self-reinforcement.* During the self-monitoring stage, the patients record the frequency of eating behavior, including the quantity and caloric content of all food that is eaten. Surprisingly, overweight people typically are unaware of the amount they consume. The self-monitoring procedure serves to enlighten the patients concerning the extent of their overeating. Often patients lose weight in the self-monitoring phase (Green, 1978), probably because it simply allows them to recognize the extent of food intake. Patients are also required to record the stimulus conditions that precede eating and the consequences of eating. The self-monitoring stage establishes the baseline level of eating performance and provides an evaluation of the behavior change produced by the self-control treatment.
   The operant methodology is implemented in the self-reinforcement phase. Reinforcement (for example, money or some enjoyable activity) is provided when the person reduces intake sufficiently to meet the requirement. The patient is given realistic goals, recognizing that behavior cannot change quickly. A shaping procedure is usually employed by slowly reducing caloric intake. The self-monitoring phase reveals that the obese person eats in a large number of situations (for example, while watching television, driving, or at the movies), and therefore the situations where eating can occur must be limited. Thus, the patient is allowed to eat only in the dining room. The patient is also rewarded for avoiding situations leading to eating. Competing responses must be identified and reinforced. For instance, the patient should provide some other form of reinforcement when reading a book rather than eating. Finally, the self-control procedure reinforces the behavior itself rather than the effect of the behavior. For example, the patient's reward (going to a movie) would be earned after limiting his or her daily intake to only 1,000 calories rather than being made contingent on the loss of 1 pound. The objective of the therapy is to develop new, permanent, and effective modes of eating which will continue after treatment ends and after the weight goal has been met.

   Effectiveness.   Generally, self-control methods have produced modest weight losses over the typical 10-week therapy period. Some experiments have yielded more impressive effects. For example, Musante (1976), working with 229 overweight patients at Duke

University, reported an average weight loss per week of 3.5 pounds in males and 2.3 pounds in females; Stuart (1967) observed an average weight loss of 38 pounds during a 20-week session. However, most studies indicate an average loss of 1 pound per week. Follow-up studies show that 55 percent of the patients regain weight and 43 percent lose even more weight after the study ends. Social support (Mahoney, 1974) and periodic maintenance sessions (Stuart, 1967) are two factors which seem important in maintaining or continuing weight loss. The idea of self-control is based on sound psychological principles leading to behavior change. The substantial difference in amount of weight loss among studies suggests that the most effective implementation of the self-control procedure remains to be discovered.

SUMMARY

The main function of eating is to regulate energy balance and to maintain an optimal body weight. The normal animal or person possesses effective systems for obtaining nutritional needs. As a result of food deprivation, internal physiological changes occur which motivate food-seeking behaviors. When the animal or human eats palatable foods, the act of eating stimulates internal changes which maintain the animal's consummatory behavior. Environmental cues, present during the internal changes, become conditioned to elicit a conditioned appetite response and serve to stimulate eating. Thus, in the normal animal or person, both psychological and biological cues stimulate feeding behavior.

During the course of eating, internal nutritional changes produced by food act to suppress eating, while cues produced by food become become associated with these internal nutritional changes and, thus, produce a conditioned satiety response. Therefore both biological and psychological stimuli operate to inhibit eating. In addition, an animal or person can also learn to inhibit eating to prevent poisoning as well as initiate eating to prevent illness.

The hypothalamic area of the brain appears to play a central role in the control of food intake. Destruction of the lateral hypothalamus produces a loss of appetite and weight loss. This change in food intake is apparently induced by a reduction in the ability of hunger cues to initiate eating. In contrast, a ventromedial hypothalamic malfunction causes an animal or human to overeat and become obese. A diminished ability of the animal's or human's satiety cues to inhibit the lateral hypothalamus appears to be responsible for the changes in food intake occurring after the disturbance in VMH functioning.

Obese humans and VMH-lesioned animals exhibit similar feeding behaviors (finickiness with regard to taste, inability to inhibit eating, and extreme sensitivity to environmental initiation of eating) which lead to obesity. Heightened physiological responsivity causes an increased intake of desirable foods and a greater rejection of unpalatable foods. Thus, the obese person's finickiness and excessive eating are apparently due to increased sensitivity to the taste of food. In addition, an elevated insulin level in obese animals and humans causes them to be constantly hungry, but their obesity prevents them from exerting unusual effort to obtain food. In the presence of food-related cues, the hungry obese animal or person will be motivated to obtain food; and the presence of food initiates eating in obese rats and humans. The remarkable similarity of the behavior of obese humans and VMH-lesioned animals strongly suggests that the major cause of human obesity lies in the malfunctioning of the ventromedial area of the hypothalamus.

Many overweight people are intensely motivated to lose weight but seem totally unable to control their overeating. Clinical psychology has made some progress in the development of effective techniques; for weight control, self-reinforcement appears to be the most promising method at this time, but additional research is necessary to indicate the influence of aversive events on the eating habits of obese people. Since our understanding of the causes of obesity has increased considerably during the last several years, the future holds great promise for helping more people with problems of weight control.

*H*UMAN SEXUALITY

CHAPTER 6

The pleasures of sex

*I*n high school, Paula dreamed of marriage and children. Today, that seems a distant memory. After graduating from high school, she met Doug while she worked as a waitress. Tall and handsome, he fit her ideal; they married the next year. Their first years of marriage were happy. Doug's promotion to supervisor at the automobile plant allowed them to buy a small house. Soon their first child was born; another baby followed in 2 years.

Everything progressed according to Paula's plans until Doug lost his job 2 years ago. Even after not having worked for 6 months, Doug refused to look for another job: he was certain that the economy would improve and he would be recalled. Another 6 months passed before the plant reinstated Doug. During this time, Doug's umemployment had put a strain on their marriage. Bills mounted, and Paula resumed her job as a waitress. Doug resented this and became very moody. In an attempt to escape his unhappiness, he began to drink a six-pack of beer each night and then fall asleep while watching television. The warmth and closeness of their early years of marriage now waned and were replaced with arguments about finances and whether Doug should look for another job. Also, Paula was bitter and hostile toward Doug because he offered no help in caring for their young children, even after she had returned to waiting tables. This added to the destruction of their marriage.

Paula also missed the sexual aspects of her early marriage. Even though Paula's mother had told her that sex was an unpleasant task which a wife performed to satisfy her husband's animalistic needs, Paula found sex with Doug pleasurable. Doug did not behave like a "hungry animal" but rather was gentle and considerate. Paula felt that intercourse, a frequent part of her life with Doug, strengthened their love for each other.

Paula's sexual experience changed when Doug became unemployed. His interest in sex decreased; the frequency of their lovemaking dropped to once or twice a week.

Doug was no longer gentle and concerned during intercourse; he now seemed interested only in relieving his tension. The touching that had once preceded intercourse was replaced by a quicker, mechanical procedure. After Doug ejaculated, he dressed and returned to what occupied most of his hours at home—television. Paula no longer experienced pleasure during sex; in fact, she actually came to dread sex with Doug.

Paula longs for the beautiful sexual relationship of her early marriage. Now, masturbation helps to satisfy her sexual

drive; however, she does not find it as fulfilling as intercourse. Paula needs to talk to someone about her problem. She and her parents have never been able to discuss sex without embarrassment. She has thought of discussing her problem with her best friend, Vera. But, never having discussed sex with anyone except in a few awkward conversations with her parents, Paula is not certain that she could overcome her embarrassment and talk with Vera. She desperately wants to talk to someone about her feelings—but she does not know who.

Paula's sexual desire is not unique. Sex is a powerful human motivation. In this chapter we'll look at the complex biological and psychological processes involved in motivating sexual behavior. Although many people like Paula find that sex can be extremely pleasurable, others perceive it as an aversive event to be either tolerated or avoided. Still other people, like Doug, seem to be uninterested in sexual activities. We'll also examine the physiological changes which occur during arousal and intercourse—and which are responsible for their pleasurable aspect—as well as the psychological processes responsible for people's varied responses to sex.

THE VARIED EXPRESSIONS OF HUMAN SEXUALITY

The concept of sexuality reflects more than a person's level of sexual desire. People have various ways of satisfying their sexual motives. For example, although *heterosexual intercourse* is the typical method of expression, *homosexuality* represents an effective response for many people. The acceptability of varied sexual behaviors differs considerably among cultures. In some cultures, only heterosexual response is appropriate; other cultures permit, or even encourage, other ways of satisfying one's sexual needs.

A person's culture also defines the appropriate behavior for each sex. Sexuality is judged by adherence to the sex role established by the culture. For example, aggressiveness is equated with masculinity in some cultures but not in others. A male who fails to exhibit sufficient aggressiveness in a society in which aggression reflects manhood is considered effeminate. Similarly, an overly aggressive female in such a culture is either avoided or punished. The exhibition of appropriate *sex role behaviors* determines both sexual satisfaction and nonsexual rewards (for example, a job).

In Chapter 2 Lorenz's view of human tradition was discussed. Lorenz asserts that we inherit only a sensitivity to express our innate motives according to the culturally acceptable form of expression. The powerful effects of both cultural and sexual motives provide support for Lorenz's view of instinct. Additional evidence for this ethological approach is the similar variation of sexual expression among primates. Apparently, primates also have strong sexual motives and have evolved varied ways to satisfy their sexual needs. In all likelihood, our mammalian heritage has provided us with strong sexual motives—but with no specific behavioral patterns to resolve sexual needs.

Clellan Ford and Frank Beach (1951) described the sexual practices of 191 human societies as well as many primate species. They observed wide variations in *(1) types of behavior (or behaviors) used to obtain sexual gratification, (2) tolerance by the culture of deviant forms of sexual expression, and (3) physical characteristics considered sexually attractive.* Let's now briefly consider these differences in the sexual behavior of humans and primates.

Heterosexual Behavior

Humans.   Although heterosexual intercourse is the most frequent behavior used to satisfy sexual motives, there are substantial differences in heterosexual techniques between cultures. In our culture, kissing is a common prelude to sexual intercourse. Ford and Beach also observed this to be true in many other societies (for example, the Alorese of Indonesia, the Hopi of Arizona, and the Trukese of the Carolina Islands). However, some cultures—including the Chewa of central Africa and the Manus of New Guinea—do not kiss.

Stimulation of the female breast is another common type of precoital activity. Kinsey and his associates (see Kinsey, Pomeroy, & Martin, 1948; Kinsey, Pomeroy, Martin, & Gebhard, 1953) reported that the majority of American males manipulate the female's breasts before intercourse. Ford and Beach observed breast stimulation in some cultures (for example, the Haitians and the Marquesans of the central Pacific) but not in others (including the Kwakiutl of Vancouver Island and the Sirionians of Bolivia).

Some forms of sexual foreplay used in some societies but not others include manual or oral stimulation of the partner's genitals. In addition, physical pain is sometimes inflicted on a partner either before or during intercourse. For example, the Apinaye women of South America bite off bits of their partner's eyebrows, and Ponapean men tug at the women's eyebrows, occasionally yanking out tufts of hair. Some people in our culture and some other societies may pinch, scratch, or bite their partner during intercourse.

Married couples' frequency of intercourse also differs greatly among cultures. In some cultures, intercourse occurs infrequently: the Keraki of the South Pacific, for instance, copulate only about once a week. In certain other societies, the frequency of intercourse is considerably higher. For example, the Aranda of Australia engage in intercourse as often as three to five times a night; they sleep between sex acts. Ford and Beach asserted that American culture, in comparison with other societies, is sexually "restrictive." The low incidence of marital sex is one indication of this sexual restrictiveness. Kinsey and his associates reported in 1948 that in young adults (16 to 25 years old), marital sex occurs approximately 2½ times a week. Although Hunt's more recent research (1974) indicates an increase to 3½ times a week, this is still low compared with many societies. The frequency of sexual intercourse drops steadily as the married partners' age increases. But while aging does have some deleterious effect on sexual capacity, many elderly adults in our culture continue to engage in sexual intercourse. Interestingly, frequency also decreases in more permissive societies, but old people in these cultures still engage in sex more often than young adults in American society. For example, Gorer (1938) observed that Lepcha men over the age of 30 still copulate at least once every night. Apparently, the intensity of sexual motivation, as well as the behaviors employed to satisfy sexual desires, are strongly influenced by one's culture.

Primates.   Three patterns of sexual behavior (kissing, genital stimulation, and infliction of pain) which often precede sexual intercourse in humans also occur in many primate species. Bingham (1928) reported that chimpanzees kiss before and during copulation. Hamilton (1914) also observed kissing in macaques.

Genital stimulation before coitus has been reported in many primate species.

Hamilton noted that the male macaque monkey first inspects his female partner's genitals and then uses his mouth and fingers to stimulate them. The level of this precopulatory behavior increases with cohabitation; the longer the male and female are together, the greater the amount of precopulatory stimulation. Hamilton suggests that the male's behavior increases the female partner's sexual arousal, as well as the male's sexual arousal, since vigorous copulations follow the male's stimulation of the female. Similar behavior, producing increased arousal, has also been observed in other primate species.

Although the female primate is less likely to stimulate the male's genitals, this does occasionally occur. Hamilton reported that female chimpanzees sometimes squeeze and pull on male chimpanzee's penis. This stimulation usually causes the male to attempt copulation. Other female primates also occasionally manually stimulate a nonaroused male primate to arouse him.

We have seen that pain is inflicted before sexual intercourse in some human cultures. This is also true of some primate species (for example, baboons and macaque monkeys), though not of others (for example, howler monkeys and spider monkeys). Pain before intercourse appears to provide sufficient sexual arousal to induce copulation. In support of this view, Hamilton found that after a male macaque chased and bit a nonresponsive female, she became eager for intercourse. Since the female displayed the same signs of excitement (lip smacking and convulsive arm movements) as shown by females aroused without infliction of pain, the behavior of this female is not merely submission to the male but actual sexual arousal.

Our discussion points to the relationship between sexual arousal and aggressive behavior. However, the importance of aggression in sexual behavior differs in primates and humans. In primates, a male's aggression increases the female's sexual responsivity. The opposite is not true of female primates: they do not inflict pain upon males before intercourse. In contrast, human males and females both sometimes inflict pain on a partner before intercourse. Ford and Beach suggest that the larger size of the male and the rear-entry coital position typical of primates is responsible for the failure of female primates to inflict pain on males before intercourse. Apparently, the emotional arousal produced by mild pain can increase people's sexual arousal; each individual's culture determines whether or not aggression is an acceptable way of increasing arousal and satisfaction.

Homosexuality

Humans. Ford and Beach (1951) reported a wide variation in the incidence of homosexuality in different societies. In western culture, the level is low. The classic data collected by Kinsey in the late 1940s and early 1950s indicated that 3 percent of adolescent girls and 22 percent of adolescent boys had at least one homosexual experience. However, Sorensen's more recent evidence (1973) suggests that approximately 10 percent of men and 5 percent of women have homosexual experiences; also, many of these have only one homosexual experience (or only a few experiences) and display heterosexual behavior as adults.

The level of homosexual behavior in a particular society appears to reflect its acceptability. Homosexuality is low or absent in cultures which disapprove of it and occurs often in cultures which encourage or condone it. Societies which do not allow homosexuality severely punish its occurrence in children. For example, Chiricahau children of Arizona engaging in homosexual play are severely beaten and Sanpoil children of northeastern Washington are thrashed if they exhibit any behavior suggesting homosexual tendencies. In other societies, adults' homosexual behavior results in extremely severe consequences. Any adult male or female of the Rwala Bedouin of the northern Arabian desert who commits a homosexual act is executed.

In contrast to societies which disapprove of homosexuality, many other cultures consider it normal and socially acceptable for some or all of their members. Usually, certain people called *berdache* or *transvestites* adopt the sex role of the opposite sex. Thus, the male berdache dresses like a female, assumes women's tasks, and engages in anal intercourse with other males. The Siberian Chuckchu male who dons women's clothing may become the "wife" of another male. Adoption of the male sex role by a female is much less prevalent. In some societies, a social institution exists for homosexuality, but without a change in sex roles. In the aborigines of Australia, homosexual relationships occur between unmarried adult males and 10- to 12-year-old boys. These attachments end when the boy reaches manhood; but because homosexuality is thought to keep men young and strong, bachelors engage in homosexual relationships until marriage. Some societies which do not institutionalize homosexual relationships nevertheless accept homosexual behavior. For example, all Siwan males of Africa engage in homosexuality. Although homosexuality is more rare in women than men, it is present in many cultures. To induce orgasm, Australian Aranda women characteristically stimulate each other's genitals. The Mbundu and Nama women of Africa use an artificial penis to stimulate their partner. Our observations point to the importance of culture in the incidence of homosexual behavior.

Primates. Homosexual behavior has been observed frequently in primates and other mammalian species (see Ford & Beach, 1951). Hamilton (1914) and Kempf (1917) noted anal intercourse between male macaque monkeys. Recently, Erwin and Maple (1976) observed homosexual behavior in male rhesus monkeys. Male baboons have been seen exhibiting mutual grooming, genital examination, and sexual mounting (Zuckerman, 1932). Although homosexual behavior occurs in most male mammals, including rats, rabbits, cattle, sheep, cats, and dogs, there is a distinct difference in the cause of homosexuality for primates and lower mammals. Adult male primates typically prefer heterosexual intercourse, but some male monkeys will, as the result of homosexual experience, exhibit homosexual behavior even when a heterosexual contact is available. In contrast, male homosexuality in lower mammalians reflects only a compensatory sexual response which occurs because no female is present when the males are aroused.

Although homosexual behavior has been observed in female primate species, it is much rarer than in male members of the same species (Ford & Beach, 1951). Bingham (1928) reported that two female primate cage mates exhibited mutual masturbation and intense physical contact. Hamilton (1914) observed a similar homosexual response between a mother and daughter. However, the typical female homosexual response involves one female mounting another female; this behavior is an expression of a masculine sexual response. Zuckerman (1932) suggests that the homosexual response of the typical female primate reflects an expression of dominance since it often occurs in the absence of sexual excitment. Similarly, Hamilton (1914) believes that female monkeys are sexually aroused by another female only infrequently.

Masturbation

Humans. Ford and Beach (1951) reported that societies differ in their toleration of masturbation in children. For example, Pukapukan boys and girls of Polynesia masturbate in public while their parents simply ignore their behavior. A similar tolerance of masturbation exists in the Nama Hottentot tribe of southwest Africa. Other cultures punish masturbation in young children. In the Kwoma of New Guinea, any boy found masturbating has his penis beaten with a stick. Although Kwoma girls are told not to touch their genitals, they are not punished for doing so. The Cunas of Panama whip any child, boy or girl, who is observed masturbating.

In contrast to the wide variability in the acceptance of childhood masturbation, cross-cultural studies indicate that most cultures have a negative view of masturbation by adults (see Ford & Beach, 1951), generally viewing it as an inferior sexual activity. For example, the American Crow Indians believe that masturbation reflects an inability to obtain a lover. Also, Lepcha men of the southeastern Himalayas never masturbate, regarding semen as a "soiling substance," while the Trobriand islanders assume that masturbation by men or women is undignified and unworthy.

In some societies adult masturbation occurs despite stringent social disapproval. For example, Trukese men masturbate secretely while watching women bathe. African Azande women commonly use an artifical phallus for self-stimulation even though they risk being beaten by their husbands if discovered. These cross-cultural comparisons of masturbation again indicate a significant influence of one's culture on the expression of sexual motivation.

Primates.   Primates frequently manipulate their genitals. Their masturbatory behavior appears to be motivated to induce orgasm. In 1942, Carpenter conducted natural observations of the sexual behavior of new world and old world male monkeys and reported that they manipulated their sexual organs with the tip of the prehensile tail until ejaculation occurred. Similar self-stimulation has been observed in male baboons (Zuckerman, 1931) and chimpanzees (Yerkes, 1939). Both immature and adult male primates masturbate. In addition, Carpenter (1942) reported that adult male rhesus monkeys may masturbate even when females are available. Zuckerman (1932) reported that male baboons at times prefer self-stimulation to mating with a female.

Observations of the sexual behavior of female primates indicate that females, as well as male primates, masturbate. However, genital stimulation is less frequent in the female than in the male. Also, there appears to be wide differences between primate species in the level of female masturbation. Although female great apes, particularly chimpanzees, masturbate less frequently than males, they do occasionally stimulate their genitals, sometimes with their fingers and sometimes with objects. Bingham (1928) provided evidence of masturbation in female apes. For example, he found that one female at times turned her back to the grill of her cage and vigorously rubbed her genitals. Another female primate used the corner of a packing box to stimulate herself. Although Bingham's observations were with captive primates, Jane Goodall (1968) reported self-stimulation in wild female chimpanzees.

In contrast to the masturbation found in the apes, Zuckerman (1932) reported no evidence of self-stimulation in female baboons other than anogenital examination. Carpenter (1942) found a similar absence of masturbation in free-living rhesus monkeys.

Ford and Beach (1951) do not feel that masturbation in humans is abnormal or perverted but that it evolved from an adaptive biological tendency to examine, manipulate, and clean the external genitals. Masturbation became a supplement to or substitute for sexual intercourse, and the importance of this learning experience evolved in the great apes. According to Ford and Beach, the significance of masturbation increased in humans as it became linked with fantasy and imagination.

Attracting a Sex Partner

Humans. *Standards of attractiveness.* What type of person do you consider sexually attractive? In our society there are wide variations in the physical characteristics which people find attractive. One male may prefer tall, thin women; another may prefer big-bosomed women. Some men are attracted to blondes; others like brunettes. Women have similar differences: some women are drawn to athletic, muscular men, others to tall, trim men.

There are also enormous differences between cultures in the physical characteristics which are considered attractive. Ford and Beach (1951) sampled the standards of 60 societies. In contrast to our own culture, many societies (for example, the Abelam tribe of north Guinea; the Gandas of Uganda; the Maricopa Indian tribe of southern Arizona) prefer plump women rather than thin ones. Other female characteristics which some societies prefer include a broad pelvis and wide hips, small ankles, shapely and fleshy calves, long and pendulous breasts, large breasts, and upright, hemispherical breasts. Other cultures judge female sexual attractiveness on the basis of the physical appearance of the external genitals. Ford and Beach found eight cultures (for example, the Kusaians of the eastern Caroline Islands in the Pacific Ocean and the Nama tribe of southwest Africa) which considered an elongonated labia major (the pads of fat on either side of the vaginal opening) to be attractive. In these societies, women often pull on their labia major to make them longer.

Methods of inviting intercourse. Our discussion suggests that cultures determine the physical characteristics which stimulate sexual arousal. Societies also influence what cues indicate willingness to engage in intercourse. In our society, the cues are often subtle; a phrase or gesture may indicate desire. There are times when the cue is quite specific (for example, when a woman puts on a black negligee to indicate her sexual arousal), but sexual motivation typically is not that explicit.

In other cultures, people display their sexual desire quite obviously. The Lesu women of New Ireland expose their sexual organs to seduce a man. When Dahomean women of west Africa desire sex, they drop their skirt, exposing their genitals. Blackwood's description (1935) of the customs of the Kurtatchi women of the Solomon Islands leaves no doubt about their intentions:

> A woman desiring sexual intercourse with a man who does not make advances to her will, when opportunity arises, lie down in his presence with her legs apart, a position otherwise regarded as indecent. . . . If a woman exposes her genitals, even unwittingly, as in sleep, the situation is liable to be taken advantage of by any man whose passions may thereby be aroused.

Odor is another cue which often indicates sexual arousal. Cayapa men of Ecuador use sweet-scented herbs to attract women; western Apache women wear aromatic plants to arouse Apache men. Also, many societies employ musical instruments and songs to evoke erotic feelings in a potential partner; for example, Hopi women sing love songs to their lovers and Crow Indian men blow on flutes to entice women to have intercourse with them. Infugao men and women of the Philippine Islands play the lover's harp as a sign of sexual desire.

Primates. *Standards of attractiveness.* Like humans, many primates also show preferences in their choice of sexual partner. For the male primate, the female's sexual responsivity is an important determinant of her attractiveness. Carpenter (1942) reported that dominant male macaque monkeys, when given their choice of mates, choose only females in the middle of the estrus cycle, who are the most receptive. Subordinate males must be satisfied with females at other stages of the cycle, who are less responsive and therefore less attractive mates.

However, receptivity is clearly not the only determinant of preference. Yerkes and Elder (1936) discovered that many male chimpanzees will refuse intercourse with a receptive female and wait for a preferred partner. Facial appearance seems to be another determinant of attractiveness. Tinklepaugh (1931) observed that a male and female macaque caged together for several years and then separated for several weeks displayed behavior illustrating the role of facial appearance in attractiveness. Tinklepaugh reported that when reunited, the male noticed that the female's eyebrows and cheek tufts had grown, thus changing her appearance. The male, evidently disenchanted with this new appearance, pulled out her eyebrows and the long hairs of cheek tufts. The male frequently observed the results of his actions and stopped when he was satisfied with her altered appearance.

Female primates, like males, prefer certain characteristics in an opposite-sex mate. The appearance of the male's penis is one determinant of attractiveness. Yerkes (1943) found that the majority of female chimpanzees prefer a male with a long penis, who copulates for long periods of time, making a large number of thrusts during intercourse. The male's dominance also influences his attractiveness. Zuckerman's research (1932) with baboons and Carpenter's work (1942) with macaque monkeys revealed that receptive females prefer to mate with only the dominant male in their group. Evidently, the male primate's attractiveness is determined by his social position.

Methods of inviting intercourse.   Like humans, primates also employ specific behavioral techniques to attract and arouse a potential mate and motivate intercourse. The receptive female primate can indicate her desire by exposing her genitals; she turns her back to the male, bending forward to expose her sexual organs. In some primate species, there is a pronounced swelling or bright coloration of the receptive female's *sex skin,* an epidermal area adjacent to the external parts of the sexual organs. These signs, revealed when the female exposes her genitals, also indicate receptivity.

Vocal gestures also play an important role in motivating intercourse. Carpenter (1942) noted that receptive female macaques make a rhythmic mouth movement called "smacking of the lips." Male macaques, too, exhibit this vocal response before intercourse, and Carpenter suggests that it represents a way of inviting the female to have intercourse. Zuckerman (1932) observed that baboons use similar vocal gestures to arouse a partner. In addition to lip smacking, baboons make a clicking sound by placing their tongue against the upper front teeth and then pulling the tongue away quickly. This sound emitted by the female baboon causes a male to have an erection. The male also utters these dental "clicks" before copulating with the female.

THE BIOLOGY OF SEX

Biological systems play an important role in sexual motivation and behavior, although this influence is definitely weaker in humans than in lower animals. In this section, we will study the physiological changes which occur during sexual stimulation. These physiological changes influence the detection of sexual motivation and produce the characteristic pleasurable aspects of sex. Although in some ways the biological aspects of sex differ between males and females, many aspects are similar. We will examine both the similarities and the differences. The male's sexual response begins the description of the biological aspects of sexuality; it is followed by a description of the sexual response in females.

The Male's Sexual Response

The physiology of the male sexual response.   Since the beginning of recorded history, people have acknowledged the importance of sexual motives and behavior; yet only since about 1965 have we isolated the physiological changes which occur during sexual intercourse. Despite the significance of sexual physiology on effective sexual functioning or sexual dysfunction, the sexual act was not considered a proper topic for scientific investigation. Fortunately, within the past few decades, sexual research has become more legitimate in the academic and nonacademic communties. Only in a climate of tolerance would the classic research of William Masters and Virginia Johnson have been accepted.

Physiological changes.   Masters and Johnson's publication of *Human Sexual Response* (1966) represented 12 years of research on the physiology of the human sexual response. Masters and Johnson reported observations of the physiological changes occurring during sexual behavior in 382 women and 312 men. Over 10,000 cycles of sexual arousal and orgasm were recorded to provide a clear picture of the human sexual response.

Masters and Johnson's research indicates that two major physiological changes— vasocongestion and myotonia—occur in response to sexual stimulation. *Vasocongestion* refers to the increased flow of blood into the pelvic area when the blood vessels in that area dilate. *Myotonia* occurs when the muscles contract throughout the body. Masters and Johnson discovered that these changes take place during sexual activity, regardless of whether masturbation, intercourse, or reading erotic literature produced the arousal.

Stages of sexual response.   According to Masters and Johnson's research, there are four phases in the human sexual response: *excitement, plateau, orgasm,* and *resolution.* Although different physiological changes occur during each phase, there is no detectable shift from one phase to another; the sexual response is a continuous process. The distinction between phases merely reflects a method of illustrating the changes which occur during sexual behavior. Let's now examine these changes as they occur in the male.

EXCITEMENT.   The male becomes aroused during the excitement phase. Vasocongestion of the penis produces an *erection,* which takes place within a few seconds after stimulation when the penis fills with blood. Other physiological changes which occur in some males during the excitement phase include (1) *erection of the nipples,* produced by contractions of muscles and vasocongestion of the blood vessels around the nipple, (2) *sex flush,* resembling a rash on the skin of the upper abdomen and chest, and (3) tensing of the scrotal sac which causes the scrotum to be pulled closer to the body and the spermatic cords to shorten, causing an elevation of the testes.

PLATEAU.   Sexual arousal intensifies during the plateau phase if the sexual stimulation persists. The physiological changes which began in the excitement phase continue and increase: the penis becomes fully erect and the glans, because of vasocongestion, may swell to over 1½ times its normal size; the skin flush continues. In addition, generalized muscle tension develops, and breathing, pulse rate, and blood pressure rise. As the tension necessary for orgasm is established, the male senses the peak of sexual arousal.

ORGASM.   The male's orgasm occurs in two stages. In the first stage, the male senses the inevitability of ejaculation when the vas deferens, seminal vesicles, and prostate contract. This contraction forces the ejaculate into the urethra. The urethra and the penis contract rhythmically at 0.8-second intervals in the second stage, forcing the semen out of the urethra. In the second phase, the pleasurable aspects of orgasm are experienced as the sex organs contract.

During an orgasm, pulse, blood pressure, and breathing increase rapidly. Other muscles throughout the body may also contract during orgasm. Masters and Johnson report that males describe an orgasm as a highly pleasurable experience.

RESOLUTION.   After an orgasm, the male slowly returns to the nonaroused state during the resolution phase, which generally lasts from 15 to 30 minutes. After orgasm, several other changes occur, including a rapid loss of erection, a slow reduction in the size of the penis, and a gradual reduction to normal levels of pulse, blood pressure, and breathing. Also, the sex flush disappears. In many males, perspiration covers the body.

The most significant aspect of the resolution phase is a loss of sexual responsivity. In this *refractory period*, males cannot be sexually aroused and, therefore, are incapable of having an erection. The refractory period varies among men, lasting only a few minutes for some and up to 24 hours for others.

Biological systems controlling male sexual behavior.   The male's ability to become sexually aroused and exhibit appropriate sexual behavior depends partly upon the effective function of biological processes. Biologically, both hormonal and neural systems influence sexual motivation and behavior. The effect of these biological systems is twofold: *First, they provide a general activating effect for sexual behavior. Second, these systems are involved in producing the male's sexual arousal and response.*

Hormonal influence.   The male sex hormone, *testosterone*, plays a significant role in producing the arousal necessary for sexual behavior in both animals and humans. In adults, the level of testosterone typically remains constant, so that the adult male (animal or human) is sensitive to those environmental events (for example, the presence of a receptive female) which can initiate sexual behavior. The importance of testosterone becomes apparent only when it is eliminated by removing the testes (*castration*). The loss of testosterone typically renders a male less able or unable to be sexually aroused. These observations indicate that testosterone critically influences sexual motivation. Let's briefly examine evidence which shows that testosterone provides the sensitivity necessary for sexual behavior and then describe the biological systems which control testosterone production as well as the manner in which testosterone produces sexual arousal.

Castration, removal of the testes, is one way to assess the impact which testosterone has on the male's sexual motivation. A loss of sexual motivation in both animals and humans is the typical effect of castration. However, the rapidity of this loss varies considerably among members of a species. Davidson (1966a) discovered that while most rats lost their sexual interest within a few weeks after castration, some male rats remained sexually motivated for as long as 5 months. Following castration, men also show a variable loss of sexual drive and behavior (see Money & Ehrhardt, 1972). Bremer's observations (1959) of 157 legally castrated Norwegian males document this variability: 49 percent showed rapid *asexualization*, or loss of sexual motivation; 18 percent lost their interest within 1 year; and the remaining males displayed the slowest reduction in sexual motivation, taking several years before it was extinguished. As Carlson (1977) points out, the data for male rats and male humans are quite comparable if we consider the differential life spans of each species. The rat's average life span is approximately 2 years; therefore, retaining some sexual motivation 5 months after castration does compare favorably with retention of motivation for some years in a human. However, many rats and humans do lose interest in sex immediately after castration. Cats

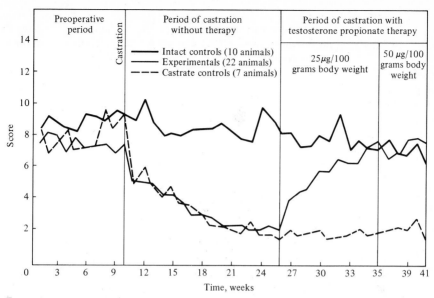

Figure 6.1

Effects of castration and subsequent testosterone replacement therapy on the sexual activity of male guinea pigs. (From Grunt, J. A., & Young, D. C. Differential reactivity of individuals and the response of the male guinea pig to testosterone proprionate. Endocrinology, 1952, 51, 237–248.)

(Rosenblatt, 1965), dogs (Schwartz & Beach, 1954), and primates (Beach & Fowler, 1959) have shown a similar loss of sexual interest after castration.

Administering testosterone to castrated animals and humans produces a rapid gain of sexual responsivity. Grunt and Young's experiment (1952) with male guinea pigs illustrates the influence of testosterone therapy (see Figure 6.1). During 16 weeks following castration, the guinea pigs typically showed a gradual reduction in sexual behavior. Testosterone injections then produced a steady increase in sexual motivation which reached the level of uncastrated control animals approximately 6 to 9 weeks after the administration of testosterone began. Castrated control animals which did not receive testosterone injections showed no resumption of sexual behavior. These results demonstrate that hormone-replacement therapy can reinstate sexual behavior after castration. Similar results have been obtained with castrated rats (Beach & Holtz-Tucker, 1949), cats (Rosenblatt, 1965), dogs (Beach, 1969), primates (Beach & Fowler, 1959), and humans (Money, 1961).

One interesting result of Grunt and Young's study (refer to Figure 6.1) is that doubling the effective dose of testosterone did not increase sexual motivation. Bermant and Davidson (1974) made a similar observation in castrated men. Apparently, a critical level of testosterone is necessary to produce sexual responsivity. Once this critical level is reached, no additional testosterone will affect sexual motivation.

Why does the rapidity with which male animals and humans lose sexual motivation vary so greatly? A male's sexual experience seems to be one critical factor. Hart (1968) discovered that when compared with other castrated rats, mature and sexually experienced castrated rats had the slowest decline in sexual interest. Beach's study with dogs (1969) and Rosenblatt's research with cats (1965) also found that sexual experience influenced the effect of castration on sexual motivation. Although many men would like to believe that psychological processes entirely govern their sexual motivation, the evidence clearly indicates that hormones are a central factor in motivating men's sexual behavior. (We'll soon see that women also depend a great deal upon hormones for their sexual arousal.)

Neural influence. Testosterone cannot directly produce sexual behavior. The central nervous system determines if the testosterone-induced sexual responsivity will be translated into sexual activity. In males, the hypothalamus controls the secretion of gonadotrophic-stimulating hormones, detects the presence of testosterone which provides the receptivity necessary for sexual arousal, and inhibits sexual activity until encountering an appropriate sexual stimulus. The cortex detects the presence of an acceptable sexual object and then releases sexual activity.

HYPOTHALAMUS. The hypothalamus serves three important functions in sexual motivation. *First, the tuberal area of the hypothalamus (see Appendix, Figure A.8) stimulates the manufacture of testosterone and its release.* However, the control of testosterone production is indirect. Activation of this tuberal region causes the release of the gonadotrophic-releasing hormones which, in turn, are transmitted to the anterior pituitary by the *hypothalamic-hypophyseal portal system,* causing the anterior pituitary gland to secrete *luteinizing hormone* (LH). LH, one gonadotrophic-stimulating hormone, stimulates the Leydig cells of the testes to manufacture testosterone and then release it. (Another gonadotrophic-stimulating hormone, *follicle-stimulating hormone, or FSH,* enables the testes to produce sperm cells.)

Harris's experiment (1955a) provides support for hypothalamic control of the release of gonadotrophic-stimulating hormones. Harris removed the anterior pituitary of rats and transplanted it in different locations (for example, the kidney). The transplanted pituitary glands did not secrete the gonadotrophic-stimulating hormones. However, placing a removed gland in its typical location in another animal whose pituitary had also been removed caused the vascular (blood) connections between the hypothalamus and anterior pituitary to regenerate, and the pituitary then resumed its secretion of gonadotrophic-stimulating hormones. Harris (1955b) also found that stimulating the tuberal region increased the secretion of the gonadotrophic-stimulating hormones.

Second, testosterone stimulates the anterior area of the hypothalamus; this produces the sexual responsivity necessary for sexual behavior. VanDis and Larsson (1971) discovered that electrical stimulation of this anterior hypothalamic area increased male rats' sexual behavior, and destruction of this area abolished their sexual motivation (Heimer & Larsson, 1966/1967).

The hypothalamus, moreover, appears to be involved in producing the human male's sexual motivation. Roeder and Mueller (1969) discovered that hypothalamic lesions decreased the activity of sex offenders, while the drive of homosexual men with a long history of *pedophilia,* a sexual interest in children, declined following hypothalamic lesions (see Whalen, 1977).

Our discussion suggests that the anterior hypothalamus contains testosterone-sensitive neurons. Two types of research support this view. First, Davidson (1966b) and Lisk (1967) implanted testosterone into the anterior hypothalamus of castrated rats and reported that testosterone injections reinstated sexual motivation. Second, testosterone-replacement therapy does not reinstate sexual motivation in anterior-hypothalamic-lesioned animals (see Heimer & Larsson, 1966/1967). These results suggest that the destruction of the anterior hypothalamus prevents male animals from sensing the presence of testosterone and they thus are rendered unable to respond to sexual stimulation.

The lateral and medial mammilary portions of the hypothalamus (see Appendix, Figure A.8) provide the third function in sexual motivation by inhibiting sexual behavior. To illustrate this role, Lisk (1966) lesioned the lateral and medial portions of the mammilary hypothalamus of rats. He found that destruction of this area produced a sharp increase in sexual behavior. People with hypothalamic damage have shown a similar disturbance in sexual behavior. Bauer (1954) reported that 43 of 60 patients with hypothalamic injury showed sexual abnormalities. These results indicate that the hypothalamus is able to suppress sexual behavior until an appropriate sexual object causes its release. Malfunctions in an animal's or human's inhibitory areas reduce the ability to control sexual responses.

CORTEX. The cortex plays a critical role in sexual behavior. Beach (1958) suggested that the cortex provides (1) *organization of motor responses involved in sexual activity,* (2) *interpretation of the sexual appropriativeness of sensory information, and (3) storage of past sexual experiences.* The failure of the cortex to function properly can lead to either misdirected sexual behavior or failure to engage in sexual activity.

The effect obtained from cortical destruction depends upon which area has been destroyed and the extent of the destruction. Large neocortical lesions, especially in the frontal cortex, produce a loss or absence of sexual behavior (see Beach, Zitrin, & Jaynes, 1955). The larger the destruction, the greater the loss of sexual responsivity. The influence of cortical damage also varies among the mammalian species. For example, comparable destruction in cats and rats produces greater loss of sexual behavior in the cats. Male primates and men receiving cortical damage would have even a more severe loss of sexual behavior than cats or rats which had received similar destruction. The greater role of the cortex in higher-order mammals indicates that they rely on experience in sexual activity more than lower mammals do.

One cortical area crucial in sexual behavior is the temporal lobe, which receives and interprets sensory information to determine the presence of an appropriate sexual object. When the temporal cortex operates effectively, animals or humans exhibit sexual behavior only toward an appropriate object. However, malfunctions in the temporal lobe of the cortex result in sexual behavior toward unnatural objects (for example, a member of another species or an inanimate object). Let's examine some evidence which shows that the temporal cortex assures the male of obtaining acceptable sexual satisfaction.

The classic experiment by Kluver and Bucy (1939) demonstrates the disruptive effect that malfunctioning of the temporal lobe has on the sexual behavior of male primates. Kluver and Bucy discovered that male primates, following lesioning of their temporal lobe, mounted and attempted to copulate with many inappropriate sexual objects. For example, these lesioned males exhibited sexual behavior to other males of their species, members of another primate species, or inanimate objects.

Males of other species receiving temporal-lobe damage have also shown aberrations. For example, Schreiner and Kling (1956) observed that lesioned male cats tried to copulate with anything they could mount, exhibiting sexual behaviors toward objects ranging from a teddy bear to a piece of furniture. Terzian and DalleOre in 1955 reported that men with temporal-lobe damage exhibited a similar sexual response to inappropriate objects. Also, Kolarsky, Freund, Macheck, and Polak (1967) found a strong relationship between sexual disorders and temporal cortical dysfunction.

Although temporal-lobe malfunction results in misdirected sexual behavior, the disturbance is a perceptual problem—not a motivational one. Temporal-lesioned animals do not show an increase in either the frequency or the intensity of sexual behavior. Apparently, the temporal lobe functions only to direct an aroused male toward an appropriate sexual object.

The Female's Sexual Response

The physiology of the female sexual response. *Physiological changes.* Recall that vasocongestion and myotonia are the two major physiological changes which take place during the male's sexual response. Vasocongestion and myotonia also represent the two major physiological changes which lead to sexual arousal and pleasure in the female.

We also learned that during the resolution stage males show a reduction of sexual responsivity. Masters and Johnson (1966) reported that women do not necessarily experience a loss of responsivity after orgasm, and with proper stimulation many can have *multiple orgasms*. Masters and Johnson discovered that once a woman experiences an initial orgasm, additional orgasms are easily induced. The limit seems to reflect physical endurance rather than a ceiling on the ability to experience pleasure. Masters and Johnson found that some women using a vibrator had 50 orgasms in one session.

Stages of sexual response. Although a standard response is shown by all males, females' responses occur in several patterns. Masters and Johnson reported that during sexual stimulation all males experience the four phases of sexual response. This same four-stage response is typical for most females, but some show other patterns. Some females do not experience a distinct plateau and orgasm but exhibit a series of sustained orgasms. Some females move from excitement to orgasm without experiencing a plateau. Still, even though not all women exhibit the four separate stages associated with sexual stimulation, Masters and Johnson's model provides a clear description of the physiological changes which do take place during sexual arousal as well as the typical sequence of such changes.

EXCITEMENT. When a woman is sexually stimulated, she experiences profound physiological changes. Many important changes occur in the excitement phase: (1) Vasocongestion of the clitoris causes it to increase in length and diameter, a response similar to the male's erection. (2) Seepage of fluid through the vaginal walls, which is caused by blood engorgement of the genitals, provides the vaginal lubrication necessary for intercourse. This vaginal lubrication occurs within 10 to 30 seconds after exposure to arousing stimuli. (3) Vasocongestion causes the inner lips of the vagina to swell and open, allowing the erect penis to enter the vagina. (4) The upper two-thirds of the vagina expands outward, allowing it to accommodate the erect penis. (5) The cervix and uterus pull up; this enlarges the cervical opening, permitting the sperm to enter the uterus more easily. In addition, contractions (myotonia) of muscles around the nipple cause the female's nipples to become erect, and vasocongestion causes them to swell. The sex flush begins, and heart rate and blood pressure increase. All these physiological changes reflect the fact that the female's sexual arousal is produced during the excitement phase.

PLATEAU. Vasocongestion and myotonia begin during the excitement phase and reach their peak during the plateau phase. This intensified physiological response indicates a high level of sexual arousal which occurs in response to continued sexual stimulation. The thickening of the tissues surrounding the vagina causes the *orgasmic platform* which develops during the plateau phase; an increased flow of blood to the genital area produces this swelling, or thickening, which in turn causes the vaginal opening to become smaller, increasing the pressure on the male's penis. Other physiological changes which occur during the plateau phase are (1) further swelling of the breasts and uterus, (2) retraction of the clitoris into the body as the shaft becomes 50 percent shorter, and (3) a change in the color of the inner lips from bright red to a deep wine color in women who have given birth and from pink to bright red in women who have not. These color changes indicate that a woman is near orgasm; continued sexual stimulation during this period results in orgasm. These physiological changes taking place in the plateau phase produce the subjective feeling of intense sexual arousal as well as the tension necessary for producing the orgasmic experience. Some women mistakenly assume that the intense arousal experienced during the plateau stage is an orgasm.

ORGASM. The physiological changes (intense muscle contractions) which happen during a women's orgasm resemble those which occur during a male's orgasm. During the female's orgasm, the orgasmic platform and uterus contract rhythmically at approximately 0.8-second intervals. Other muscles, especially those around the anus but also those in the arms, thighs, and back, may also contract. A mild orgasm may have three or four contractions, while a dozen may occur in a very strong, prolonged orgasm. In addition to these muscle contractions, pulse rate, blood pressure, and breathing rate increase sharply during an orgasm.

Although the male's ejaculation provides evidence of orgasm, the female has no such concrete evidence. The woman may be able to feel the contraction of the muscles around the vaginal entrance. The sensation is very intense and is more than a warm glow or a pleasant tingling. Hyde (1979) described an orgasmic experience as a "spreading sensation that begins around the clitoris and then spreads outward through the whole pelvis." There may also be sensations of falling or opening up. Interestingly, Vance and Wagner's study (1976) concluded that the sensations of an orgasm are not different for males and females. Experts (for example, obstetricians, gynecologists, and clinical psychologists) asked to indicate whether they thought a description of an orgasm had been written by a man or a woman could not detect a description written by a male from one written by a female.

RESOLUTION. After an orgasm, a women enters the resolution phase during which sexual arousal diminishes. However, in the female, unlike the male, no refractory period follows orgasm. With sufficient stimulation, a woman can experience another orgasm.

A tremendous release of blood from the engorged blood vessels (loss of vasocongestion) produces the physiological changes occurring in the resolution stage. The first change in this phase is reduced swelling of the breasts. This reduction may cause the nipples to appear erect and serves as an indication of an orgasm. Within 5 to 10 seconds after an orgasm, the clitoris returns to its normal position, although it usually takes a longer period of time to resume its normal size. Also, the orgasmic platform and uterus relax and begin to shrink slowly to normal size. Finally, pulse rate, blood pressure, and respiration rate gradually return to normal.

Biological systems controlling female sexual behavior. Effective functioning of the biological systems involved in sexual activity enables the female to be sexually aroused and to inhibit sexual behavior until encountering an appropriate sexual object. Several hormonal and neural systems affect a female's sexual behavior. These systems provide the sensitivity necessary for sexual activity and also produce sexual arousal and behavior.

Hormonal influence. Two hormones, *estrogen* and *progesterone*, are involved in female sexual behavior. In males, sex hormones typically remain constantly high; in females, by contrast, the level of sex hormones changes dramatically during the *estrus cycle*, or *menstrual cycle*, in many primate species and humans. Estrogen level is high in the middle of each cycle, but low at the beginning and end of the cycle. For most mammals, sexual arousal and behavior occur only when the level of the female sex hormone estrogen is high; the intense sexual motivation which most mammals exhibit during this period is called *heat*. Although the females of many primate species and women will respond sexually throughout the menstrual cycle, evidence shows that their greatest period of responsivity is during the time when estrogen level is high. This observation indicates that estrogen does influence human sexual motivation. The sex hormone progesterone has an inhibitory effect on sexual behavior, mainly preparing and maintaining the uterus before and during pregnancy. Let's look at the sequence of hormonal changes which occur during the estrus (or menstrual) cycle and then at evidence documenting the role of sex hormones in female sexual behavior.

The estrus (or menstrual) cycle is divided into two phases: the *follicular phase* and the *luteal phase*. In women, each phase lasts approximately 15 days, and different physiological responses occur in each phase. At the beginning of the follicular phase, the anterior pituitary gland begins secreting the *follicle-stimulating hormone,* FSH (see Figure 6.2), which causes (1) one or several ovarian follicles, a small sphere of cells surrounding the ovum (or egg), to grow into a *Graafian follicle,* (2) the ovum to mature, and (3) the Graafian follicle to secrete estrogen.

The released estrogen has three different effects. First, it inhibits the release of FSH. Second, it stimulates the anterior pituitary to release a second hormone, called *luteinizing hormone,* or LH. As estrogen levels rise, FSH concentrations fall and LH concentrations increase. Finally, when estrogen level is highest, it produces an intense sexual arousal in estrus animals.

Toward the end of the follicular phase, the follicle containing the mature ovum moves toward the ovarian surface and then becomes embedded under it. When LH level is highest, the walls of the follicle rupture and the egg is released into the fallopian tube. The release of the egg is called *ovulation* (see Figure 6.2).

After ovulation, the second or luteal phase begins. LH causes the ruptured follicle to become a corpus luteum or "yellow body" (see Figure 6.2). The corpus luteum begins to secrete the sex hormones estrogen and progesterone. The secreted estrogen and progesterone prepare the uterine lining for implantation. This preparation involves the growth of the *endometrium,* the inner lining of the uterus. If fertilization does occur, the corpus luteum continues to secrete estrogen and progesterone in order to maintain the endometrium throughout pregnancy. However, if the ovum does not implant on the uterine wall, the uterine lining is either reabsorbed or expelled, a process known as *menstruation.*

Another effect of progesterone is inhibiting LH release. Unless the developing placenta secretes hormones which continue the secretion of progesterone by the corpus luteum, the reduced LH will result in a regressing corpus luteum. This regression causes production of progesterone to cease, and the luteal phase ends. Now a female animal or a woman is ready for a new cycle.

Our discussion indicates that profound physiological changes occur during the estrus (or menstrual) cycle. Do these changes affect the female's sexual behavior? There are three ways to assess the influence of sex hormones on female sexual motivation: (1) *correlating the incidence of sexual behavior with changes in hormonal levels,* (2) *administering the hormones during periods when they are absent in the body,* and (3) *removing the ovaries and assessing the influence which this surgical removal of sex hormones has on sexual behavior.* Combining the results of these three methods will give a good indication of the effect of female sexual hormones on sexual activity.

In estrus animals (for example, rats and cats), sexual activity occurs only when estrogen levels peak just before ovulation (see Beach, 1947). This period of receptivity lasts for several days before ovulation. The receptive female secretes vaginal *pheromones,* hormones released into the external environment, which make her very attractive to males. Once a male is attracted to her, the estrus female will readily accept his advances and sexual activity will ensue. However, when the female is not in heat, she lacks pheromones and thus is unattractive to males. In addition, if any male does make sexual advances, this female will resist his attempts to engage in sexual intercourse. Apparently, the estrus female's sexual motivation depends upon her level of estrogen.

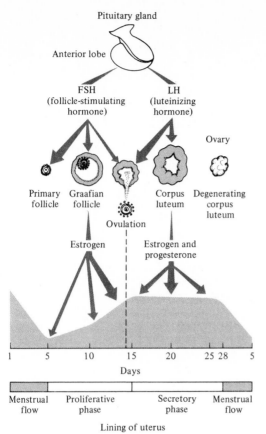

Figure 6.2
Changes which occur in the pituitary hormones, ovaries, and uterine wall during the
menstrual cycle. The width of the arrows
illustrates the hormonal level at that time
during the cycle, and their direction shows the
cause-effect relationships. [From Volpe, E.
Peter. Man, nature, and society (2nd ed.).
© 1975, 1979 Wm. C. Brown Company,
Publishers, Dubuque, Iowa. Reprinted by
permission.]

We find support for the importance of estrogen on sexual activity in studies in which estrogen was administered when it was normally low (refer to Beach, 1947). Estrogen injections in animals will produce a period of intense sexual receptivity identical to that which normally occurs before ovulation. The female's sexual motivation lasts for as long as the estrogen level remains high. In contrast, removing the ovaries, a surgical procedure called *ovariectomy*, produces a rapid, permanent loss of sexual receptivity. Beach reported that the loss of sexual motivation can be reversed by administering estrogen-replacement therapy to an ovariecotomized animal.

Although the influence of estrogen is less in female primates than in lower animals, it is still important. Females of many primate species will copulate throughout the entire menstrual cycle (see Chapter 9; also Ford & Beach, 1951), though the highest incidence of sexual activity occurs during the few days before ovulation. One effect of a high estrogen level in primates is increased sexual receptivity. In 1943, Young and Orbison observed that female chimpanzees demonstrate this increased responsivity before ovulation, moving toward the male more frequently and exhibiting a sexual presentation posture to serve as an invitation to a potential mate. Another effect of estrogen is genital swelling, which makes a female primate extremely attractive to males; in fact, males generally prefer the female with the greatest swelling, although some males will copulate with any willing female. Vaginal pheromones also increase the male's attraction to the female. Increased responsitivity, genital swelling, and vaginal phermone secretion all cause a higher frequency of sexual activity during the period of high estrogen level.

The importance of estrogen can also be seen in ovariectomized female primates. Beach (1958) reported that ovariectomy produces a loss of sexual activity in most female primates, although a few show infrequent sexual activity. Estrogen replacement can reverse this loss; however, some female primates do not completely regain sexual receptivity even with estrogen therapy. Although estrogen is important in the female primate's sexual motivation, other factors—which will be discussed later in the chapter—clearly influence sexual activity.

Estrogen does affect women's sexual activity, but its effect is clearly less, and more variable, than in female primates (see Money & Ehrhardt, 1972). Udry and Morris's study of human sexual behavior (1968) shows a sharp increase in reported sexual activity between the end of menstruation and ovulation; this indicates that estrogen can influence women's sexual behavior (see Figure 6.3). Udry and Morris also noted that women showed increased sexual activity just before menstruation. Although it is unclear why this increase occurs, one answer is perhaps that since many women become tense and irritable during the premenstrual period because of a drop in the level of progesterone, this increased arousal motivates sexual behavior (see Chapter 7). It is important to note that Udry and Morris's observations reflect only general tendencies; many women report no change in sexual activity during the cycle. Also, sexual behavior does occur throughout the cycle, although less frequently at some times than others. Obviously, factors other than estrogen influence female sexual behavior. Additional evidence for this view is the fact that sexual motivation for many women is not diminished by ovariectomy (surgical removal of an ovary) or *menopause* (a natural ceasing of estrogen production by the ovaries). It is also difficult to assess whether loss of libido reflects a lack of estrogen or an expected loss of sexual motivation after either surgery or menopause.

After a hysterectomy-ovariectomy or during menopause, women often receive testosterone, the male sex hormone (see Foss, 1951). This acts to increase their sexual responsivity. You might wonder why testosterone influences female sexual behavior. The answer is that women secrete *androstenedione*, an androgen similar to testosterone. Androstenedione, produced in low levels by the adrenal gland, affects women's sexual

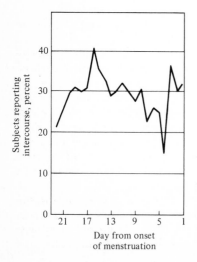

Figure 6.3
Percentage of women engaging in sexual intercourse during the female menstrual cycle. Note that estrogen levels are highest about 15 days after the onset of the cycle and lowest just before menstruation. (From Udry, J. R., & Morris, N. M. Distribution of coitus in the menstrual cycle. Nature, 1968, 220, 593–596.)

behavior. Removal of the adrenal gland produces a sharp reduction in sexual motivation (see Money, 1961). Androstenedione also appears to produce sexual receptivity in female monkeys. Everitt and Herbert (1969) injected female primates with *dexamethasone,* a hormone that decreases blood levels of androstenedione, and noted that the dexamethasone treatment also produced a rapid loss of sexual receptivity.

Although androstenedione clearly affects women's sexual arousal, it is important for us to know why this is true. As Chapter 9 will point out, many primatologists believe that the evolution of continuous sexual responsivity enabled primates and humans to establish stable pair bonding to protect the defenseless young. The evolution of an increased sensitivity to adrenal androgen, which is secreted continuously rather than cyclically, gives the primate or human female a hormonal basis for the occurrence of sexual responsivity throughout the menstrual cycle. (It should be noted that the level of androgen secreted by the adrenal gland is obviously too low to produce masculinization.)

In contrast to estrogen and androstenedione, which have an arousing effect, progesterone has an inhibitory effect. Young (1961) discovered that progesterone given to ovariectomized animals antagonized the arousing effects of estrogen. Many women using birth-control pills, which contain progestin, a synthetic form of progesterone, report a decrease in sexual desire (Grant & Meyers, 1967).

Neural influence. The CNS of the female animal or human (1) controls the release of the gonadotrophic-stimulating hormones, (2) is sensitive to the presence of female sex hormones, and (3) inhibits sexual behavior until such behavior is released by an effective arousing stimulus. For example, a female animal will not display a *lordosis response*—a posture that exposes her genitals—until a male approaches her. The female's hypothalamus controls the release of gonadotrophic hormones and produces sexual receptivity when detecting the presence of estrogen. The cortex inhibits sexual activity until a sexually arousing stimulus is encountered. Next, the influence of the hypothalamus is described; this is followed by a description of the effect of the cortex on female sexual activity.

HYPOTHALAMUS. The hypothalamus serves three essential functions in female sexual activity. *First, the tuberal region of the hypothalamus controls the release of the female sex hormones (see Appendix, Figure A.8).* Recall that hypothalamic control in males is indirect; this is also true of females. Neural activity in the tuberal region stimulates the secretion of the gonadotrophic-releasing factors. The hypophyseal portal system then conveys these releasing hormones to the anterior pituitary gland, which is stimulated by these releasing factors to release the gonadotrophic-stimulating hormones—these, in turn, cause the ovaries to produce and release the female sex hormones.

Several types of evidence indicate that the tuberal region controls secretion of gonadotrophic hormones by the anterior pituitary. Sawyer (1960) discovered that basal tubular hypothalamic lesions in cats or rabbits completely abolished both sex hormone production and sexual activity. Estrogen-replacement therapy reinstated sexual motivation but not hormonal production. These observations point out that the basal tuberal hypothalamic region controls the release of gonadotrophic-stimulating hormones; another hypothalamic area is sensitive to the influence of estrogen on sexual behavior. We can find support for the idea that the tuberal area influences sex hormone production from Harris's observations (1955b). Harris found that stimulation of the basal tuberal region increases the secretion of the gonadotrophic-stimulating hormones.

Actually, two centers in the basal tuberal region regulate the release of gonadotrophic-stimulating hormones: one area stimulates the release of FSH, and the other causes the secretion of LH. Estrogen inhibits the area which controls FSH release; low estrogen levels cause the release of FSH. Estrogen activates the other area, releasing LH.

In contrast to the basal tuberal region, which controls hormonal production and secretion, the anterior hypothalamus detects the presence of estrogen and stimulates sexual receptivity when the estrogen level is high. Many studies indicate that stimulating the anterior hypothalamus with estrogen produces sexual receptivity. Let's consider two of them.

Michael (1962) injected estrogen directly into the anterior hypothalamus of ovariectomized female cats, and noted an intense sexual response in previously nonresponsive cats. Lisk (1962) also observed the sexually arousing effects of estrogen in ovariectomized female cats.

Destruction of the anterior hypothalamus abolishes sexual responsivity. This has been observed in many species, including cats (Sawyer & Robinson, 1956), rats (Singer, 1968), guinea pigs (Brookhart, Dey, & Ranson, 1941), and rabbits (Sawyer & Robinson, 1956). Loss of receptivity after lesioning is caused by the inability of these animals to detect the sexually arousing action of estrogen. Evidence supporting this view is the fact that administration of estrogen in these lesioned animals has no effect on their sexual behavior.

The hypothalamus also exerts an inhibitory influence on sexual behavior. Law and Meagher (1958) discovered that mammilary hypothalamic lesions caused female rats to be sexually responsive to males throughout the estrus cycle. Goy and Phoenix (1963) observed a similar result in female guinea pigs with mammilary hypothalamic lesions: these animals exhibited lordosis randomly throughout their estrus cycle.

CORTEX.   Earlier in the chapter, we learned that neocortical lesions either reduced or disrupted male sexual behavior. This suggests that the cortex has a facilitative role in male sexual behavior. However, its influence on female sexual behavior appears to be primarily inhibitory. Beach (1944) discovered that cortical ablation increased lordosis in female rats. Clemens, Wallen, and Gorski (1967) made a similar observation when they chemically depressed rats' cortical functioning.

Why is the role of the cortex in sexual activity different in male and female animals? Carlson (1977) suggested that the male animal's sexual behavior is more complex than that of the female and thus requires more motor coordination. In addition, a male's sexual arousal relies heavily on the sight and smell of a receptive female, whereas a female animal's sexual arousal depends very much upon her hormonal state.

The cortex does appear to provide some organization in lower animals. The sexual response of cortically lesioned female rats, rabbits, cats, and dogs is not as integrated as that of their normal counterparts (see Ford & Beach, 1951). However, the sexual behavior of these lesioned animals is sufficiently organized to permit copulation.

There are no comparable data for the role of the cortex in the sexual behavior of female primates and humans. However, since experience has a more critical influence in the sexual activity of primates and humans, it seems reasonable to assert that the cortex has a more active role for primates and humans than for lower animals. Without appropriate experience, sexual behavior will not occur, regardless of the hormonal state.

PSYCHOLOGICAL PROCESSES GOVERNING SEXUAL ACTIVITY

An Arousing Experience

Psychological processes also have an important influence on sexual motivation and activity. Through classical conditioning, environmental cues are capable of arousing and inhibiting sexual motivation. In addition, the classical conditioning process is involved in the development of our sexual preferences. Furthermore, our experiences teach us when we can expect sexual satisfaction and provide us with the development of effective behavior which allows us to engage in successful sexual activity. Our discussion of the psychological processes governing sexual activity begins by examining the influence of classical conditioning on sexual motivation. Later in this chapter we will look at the influence which experience has on obtaining sexual satisfaction.

The influence of erotic stimuli.   Exposing humans to sexually explicit material provides one indication that environmental factors are important in eliciting sexual arousal. In a study by Howard, Reifler, and Liptzin (1971), male subjects watched an erotic movie and changes in the size of the penis were recorded (see Figure 6.4). During the first few minutes of the film, most of the males showed a rapid increase in the size of penis, which indicates that a sexually explicit movie can cause penile erection. For most of the subjects, sexual arousal continued throughout the movie (which lasted 20 minutes) and rapidly decreased when the movie ended. Geer, Morokogg, and Greenwood (1974) exposed female subjects to an erotic movie in order to measure female sexual arousal. They reported that most of the subjects responded with rapid vasocongestion and that their sexual arousal continued until the movie ended. It is important to note, however, that not everyone is aroused by erotic material. Some people find sexually explicit material either disgusting or boring (see Griffitt, May, & Veitch, 1974).

Sexually explicit stimuli need not be presented visually to elicit sexual arousal. In a study by Heiman (1975) subjects—male and female college students—listened to either sexually explicit or nonexplicit but romantic tapes while physiological arousal of the penis or the vagina was recorded. When the tapes ended, Heiman asked the subjects to rate their arousal. Both the physiological and the psychological measures indicated that most subjects found the explicit material, but not the nonexplicit material, to be sexually arousing. By varying the content of the tapes, Heiman discovered that the most sexually arousing situation, for both male and female subjects, involved a female initiating intercourse. Exposure to erotic stimuli, then, sexually arouses most men and women.

However, sexual arousal can be elicited without actual environmental stimuli:

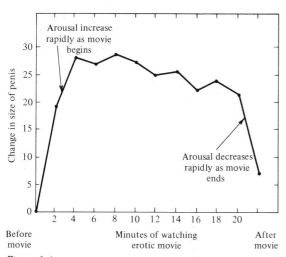

Figure 6.4
Changes in size of penis during exposure to an erotic movie. (From Howard, J. L., Reifler, C. B., &
Liptzin, M. B. Effect of exposure to pornography. In Technical report of the Commission on Obscenity
and Pornography. *Vol. VIII. Washington, D.C.: U. S. Government Printing Office, 1971.)*

imagining sexually explicit material can arouse people (for example, Heiman, 1977; Miller, Byrne, & DeNinno, 1980). Numerous studies have demonstrated that imagining sexual activity leads to sexual arousal. In fact, arousal is sometimes more intense when a person fantasizes sexually explicit material than when he or she is experiencing erotic stimuli. This observation suggests that fantasy can be an effective way to produce sexual arousal and maintain it during sexual activity.

Exposure to sexually arousing stimuli also motivates sexual activity. Cattell, Kawash, and DeYoung (1972) illustrated the sexually motivating effects of erotic stimuli. They showed their subjects—married men—either 40 erotic slides or 40 slides of geometric forms and found that the subjects who viewed the erotic stimuli were as a group more aroused than the others. However, the arousal level produced by the erotic material differed among subjects: some were highly aroused, and some were not aroused at all. Interestingly, two-thirds of the highly aroused subjects had intercourse with their wives when they went home after the experiment, in contrast to only one-fourth of the subjects who saw the erotic slides but were not aroused by them. Other studies also show that exposure to sexually arousing stimuli often leads to sexual activity. For example, Mann, Berkowitz, Sidman, Starr, and West (1974) discovered that exposure to sexually arousing stimuli motivates married people to have intercourse, and Amoroso, Brown, Pruesse, Ware, and Pilkey (1971) found that unmarried persons are more apt to masturbate after viewing erotic material than similar subjects who have been exposed to nonerotic material.

Earlier we saw that fantasy leads to sexual arousal. It also influences the likelihood of sexual behavior. Several studies (for example, Hariton & Singer, 1974; Hessellund, 1976) demonstrated that imagining sexually explicit situations often produces orgasm. In addition, Giambra and Martin (1977) reported that the more people fantasize about sex, the higher their rate of intercourse will be.

Acquired sexual motives. We have seen that either overt or imagined exposure to sexually explicit material produces sexual arousal, which in turn often motivates sexual activity. How does such material become able to produce sexual arousal? Since not all people become aroused when viewing erotic material, it seems reasonable to conclude that these stimuli develop the ability to elicit sexual arousal through conditioning (see Chapter 1). More direct support for this view can be seen in studies which have paired neutral stimuli with sexually arousing cues. These studies have shown that neutral cues, when associated with sexual arousal, sexual satisfaction, or both, can become conditioned to produce sexual arousal in both animals and humans. Thus, our arousal elicited by explicit stimuli probably reflects the development of an acquired motive. Consider the following example to illustrate this conditioning process.

Imagine that you are sitting with your spouse (or date) beside a warm glowing fire and listening to your favorite music. In this setting you might become sexually aroused because of past associations. You have been sexually aroused and have received sexual satisfaction in a situation such as this before. However, this situation is not likely to produce sexual arousal if you have not been aroused and experienced satisfaction in a similar setting. Let's now consider evidence that environmental stimuli can acquire the ability to produce sexual arousal because of past associations.

Denniston (1954) did a study with male rats in which turning a wheel would cause a receptive female rat to be dropped into the training environment. He observed that all the male rats learned to turn the wheel to obtain a female and that response time decreased from 100 seconds on the first conditioning trial to 30 seconds on the last trial. When turning the wheel no longer provided a female, the latency to turn the wheel steadily increased during 6 extinction days. Why did the rats learn to turn the wheel when they could not see a receptive rat? The only reasonable answer is that the males associated the training environment with sexual arousal produced by the receptive female and the satisfaction of intercourse. As a result of this conditioning, the test environment developed motivational properties; that is, when the rats were placed in the training cage, they became sufficiently motivated to turn the wheel, which caused a receptive female to appear. Also, conditioning probably caused the extinction of the rats' response: when their behavior no longer produced reward—a receptive female—they began to associate the environment with the absence of reward, and the frustration produced by the training environment motivated them to stop turning the wheel. Using male rats, Schwartz (1956) observed similar conditioning of a bar-press response which provided access to a receptive female; and Bermant (1961a, 1961b) discovered that sexually responsive female rats quickly learned to press a lever in order to obtain a sexually active male rat. Apparently, environments associated with sexual activity can produce the arousal necessary to motivate sexual behavior.

Researchers also have examined the conditioning of sexual arousal in humans by pairing neutral stimuli with sexually arousing stimuli. The result of this conditioning is that these neutral cues, when later presented alone, elicit arousal. Rachman's experiment (1966) provides evidence of this. Rachman instructed male subjects to view pictures of nude females together with pictures of women's shoes. After several conditioning trials, Rachman's male subjects exhibited arousal when the shoes were presented without the pictures. This study shows that a neutral event, as the result of its association with a sexually arousing event, can elicit sexual arousal. Rachman and Hodgson (1968) replicated this study and observed the same results.

We should note that imagination appears to play an important role in the strength of sexual arousal produced by a particular stimulus. After a conditioning experience, a person probably imagines the event. This fantasizing recreates the experience and intensifies the ability of the conditioned stimulus to produce sexual arousal. Recall the example presented at the beginning of this section: you and your spouse (or date) are sitting by the fire. Imagine that on the following day, you visualize this pleasant scene. When you imagine the arousal and pleasure that you experienced, this event becomes more able to elicit future sexual arousal.

Fetishes. When someone requires the presence of a particular object in order to become sexually aroused, this behavior is known as a *fetish*. Fetishes are thought to be caused by classical conditioning (see McGuire, Carlisle, & Young, 1965) and to reflect an intense exaggeration of conditioned arousal which people typically experience when exposed to erotic stimuli. According to McGuire, Carlisle, and Young, this exaggeration develops because the fetish object is repeatedly imagined during masturbation, which, in turn, increases the ability of the fetish object to produce sexual arousal. Thus, a person with a fetish can experience sexual satisfaction only in the presence of the fetish object.

Classical conditioning experience with aversive events appears to represent an effective method of eliminating fetishes. In aversive therapy (or counterconditioning) the fetish object is paired with an unpleasant event. Psychologists have successfully eliminated fetishes by using either drug-induced illness (for example, Cooper, 1964; Raymond, 1956; Raymond & O'Keefe, 1965) or electric shock (for example, Kushner, 1965; Marks and Gelder, 1967; Marks, Gelder, & Bancroft, 1970).

Let's examine Raymond's study (1956), which effectively used aversion therapy to treat a male client's fetish for handbags and baby carriages. During therapy, the patient was shown pictures of handbags, baby carriages, or both. Immediately thereafter, he would receive an apomorphine injection which induced intense nausea. The treatment occurred every 2 hours for 1 week. At the end of the week, none of the pictures produced arousal. Raymond also noted that the fetish was not present 6 months after treatment. These results indicate that an undesirable sexual arousal response can be successfully eliminated—as well as acquired—through classical conditioning. It is also likely that some people acquire their aversions to erotic stimuli through past associations with negative experiences.

Why do erotic stimuli motivate sexual behavior? The information just presented indicates that sexual arousal reflects a drive which automatically motivates sexual activity. However, other research, which we will look at next, demonstrates that cognitive processes also influence our sexual motivation.

Cognitive influence.   Many people believe that alcohol increases sexual responsivity because they are more motivated when drinking. The research of G. Terrance Wilson and his associates (Briddell & Wilson, 1976; Wilson, 1977; Wilson & Lawson, 1976a, 1976b) shows that these people expect alcohol to produce sexual arousal and that it is this expectation rather than any pharmacological effect of alcohol which causes them to become aroused. In fact, either moderate or high consumption of alcohol impairs sexual responsiveness; small amounts, however, have no pharmacological effect. The following evidence points to a cognitive influence in sexual arousal.

The critical point at which alcohol begins to influence sexual responsivity is 50 to 60 miligrams per 100 milliliters (mg percent) of blood alcohol, a level which can be produced by consuming two or three drinks within an hour. Although levels of blood alcohol below 50 mg percent have no direct influence on sexual behavior, levels of blood alcohol above 50 mg percent impair sexual arousal (Briddell & Wilson, 1976; Wilson & Lawson, 1976a). Briddell and Wilson's male subjects and Wilson and Lawson's female subjects demonstrated that above 50 mg percent of blood alcohol, the greater the alcohol level, the lower the sexual arousal produced by an erotic movie.

Wilson and Lawson (1976b) reported that cognitive factors can influence sexual arousal. Half of their subjects (who were all males) were given 20 minutes to drink one glass of alcohol containing 1 part 80-proof vodka to 5 parts tonic water, an amount which produces a blood alcohol level of 40 mg percent. The rest of their subjects drank only tonic water. There were four groups in this study. Subjects in group 1 were given the alcoholic drink and were told that it did, in fact, contain alcohol. Subjects in group 2 were also given the alcoholic drink but were told that it contained only tonic water. Subjects in group 3 received the nonalcoholic drink but were told that it contained alcohol. Subjects in group 4 were given the nonalcoholic drink and were correctly informed that it was nonalcoholic. To reinforce their belief about what they had drunk, the subjects were given a simulated breath-analyzer test; the test was rigged so that the results corresponded with what the subjects had been told. For example, the test showed a blood alcohol level of 40 mg percent for subjects who thought that they had had an alcoholic drink even when in fact they had drunk only tonic water; and it showed zero blood alcohol for subjects who thought that they had drunk only tonic water even when in fact they had drunk alcohol.

Next, the subjects viewed an erotic movie. Wilson and Lawson found that the movie produced greater sexual arousal in subjects who *believed* that they had drunk alcohol than in subjects who *believed* that they had not. *Actual* consumption of alcohol, as opposed to beliefs (or expectations), had no direct effect on these subjects' response to erotic films. The subjects who believed that they had received alcohol when in fact they had not (group 2) showed as much sexual arousal as subjects who had been given alcohol (group 1). Similarly, consumption of alcohol did not affect the sexual arousal of subjects who had received alcohol but who did not think that they had drunk alcohol (group 3) as compared with subjects who neither expected nor received alcohol (group 4). Briddell,

Rimm, Caddy, Krawitz, Sholis, and Wunderlin (1978) also reported that *expectations* about the effect of alcohol—*not* its actual physiological effect—enhanced sexual responsiveness to an erotic movie. (Their study used a malt beverage laced, or not laced, with alcohol.) Evidently, it is people's expectations about the effects of alcohol rather than the physical actions of alcohol which influence the level of sexual arousal.

Sexual Preference

We have seen that environmental cues can acquire the ability to produce or inhibit sexual arousal through the classical conditioning process. In addition, our expectations influence the impact of these stimuli on sexual arousal. Exposure to these sexually arousing stimuli can motivate sexual activity. Once aroused, we are likely to seek sexual satisfaction. It seems logical to examine next those factors which determine to whom we are sexually attracted. Recall from earlier in the chapter that most people in western cultures engage only in heterosexual intercourse. Yet, some people prefer sexual activity with those of their own gender. Most Americans believe that heterosexuality is the natural sexual preference and that homosexuals and bisexuals are sick (see Hyde, 1979). Until recently, psychiatry shared this view and labeled homosexuality as a personality disorder. However, the evidence clearly indicates that homosexuals are not any more likely to be maladjusted than heterosexuals. For example, Hooker (1957) asked male heterosexuals and homosexuals who were not undergoing therapy and were comparable in terms of age, education, and intelligence to take the Rorschach personality test. Two clinical psychologists rated the adjustment level of respondents. Hooker found no differences in the adjustment of heterosexual and homosexual males. Other studies (for example, Dean & Richardson, 1964; Gagnon & Simon, 1973) have also found that male homosexual subjects were as well adjusted as heterosexual subjects. Rosen (1974) reported similar findings with female subjects. Apparently, one's sexual preferences does not influence whether or not psychopathology will develop. In 1973, the American Psychiatric Association decided not to consider homosexuality a psychiatric disorder any longer. It will probably be a long time before our society accepts the APA's opinion, however.

Psychologists have conducted a great deal of research in an effort to explain individual sexual preferences. You may wonder why sexual preference is being discussed in this section. Although both biological and psychological theories of sexual preference have been proposed, research clearly indicates that there are no biological differences between homosexuals and heterosexuals. The same biological processes which we described in the section on biology operate in the sexual motivation of both homosexuals and heterosexuals. Psychological processes appear to govern sexual preference, although the basis of this control has not been completely resolved. Let's now examine several biological and psychological views of the causes of individual sexual preferences.

Biological theories.   Two biological theories have been offered to explain the differences in sexual preferences between homosexuals and heterosexuals: one based on genetics and one on hormonal imbalance. As will be noted, neither approach accurately describes the causes of homosexuality.

A genetic view.   Irving Kallman (1952) proposed that a genetic predisposition produces homosexuality and provided initial support for his view. Kallman showed that if one identical twin was homosexual, the other twin would also be homosexual. Among fraternal twins, there was no relationship in sexual preference. Others have criticized Kallman's research because the twins in his study lived in the same environment;

therefore, social factors could have been responsible for his observations. In addition, other researchers (for example, Heston & Shields, 1968) have since found instances in which only one identical twin was homosexual. Furthermore, it can be argued that natural selection would quickly eliminate a homosexual gene, since most homosexuals will have no children. Thus, it seems unlikely that genetic factors produce sexual preference.

A hormonal-imbalance approach. A second biological theory assumes that a hormonal imbalance produces homosexual behavior. A lower-than-normal level of testosterone is thought to be responsible for male homosexuality (see Hyde, 1979). However, research (for example, Meyer-Bahlburg, 1977; Rosen, 1975) suggests that there is no hormonal difference between homosexual males and heterosexual males. Some psychiatrists and clinical psychologists have attempted to treat homosexuality with testosterone injections. However, this treatment does not alter sexual preference, although it sometimes increases sex drive. (This observation is not surprising; we learned earlier that testosterone administration can increase sexual receptivity in both male primates and humans when levels are below normal.) A study by Loraine, Adampopoulous, Kirkhan, Ismail, and Dove (1971) indicated that homosexual women (lesbians) had higher testosterone levels and lower estrogen levels than heterosexual women. However, this study had not been replicated. Furthermore, it is unclear how this pattern of hormonal levels could influence sexual preference: testosterone injections do not produce homosexual behavior in heterosexual women; rather, androgen merely increases sexual arousal.

Psychological theories. There are two psychological views to explain the origins of homosexuality. The first view, suggested by Freud, assumes that failure to develop appropriate gender identity during the phallic stage leads to homosexuality. A second approach proposes that learning is responsible for the development of either a homosexual or a heterosexual preference.

Freud's view. What, in Freud's view, causes homosexuality? According to Freud (1910), the determination of sexual preference occurs in the phallic stage (see Chapter 1). Freud's theory asserts that children direct their sexuality toward members of both sexes. They become heterosexual if they only respond to opposite-sex people and repress their attraction to any same-sex person. Children unable to repress their attraction to same-sex people become homosexual.

During the phallic stage, a male encounters two conflicts. First is his Oedipus complex—his strong sexual attraction to his mother, coupled with fear of castration by his father because of this desire. Second is his attraction to his father, a process which Freud called the *negative Oedipus complex.* The way in which a boy resolves these two conflicts governs whether he becomes a homosexual or heterosexual. Males who resolve the Oedipus complex by identifying with the father and developing a masculine gender identity will be heterosexual. This masculine sex role will direct their sexual attraction to females. However, males must also suppress their attraction toward other males (the negative Oedipus complex) if they are to become heterosexual.

According to Freud, males who do not repress their attraction to the father become homosexual. The continued love for the father causes the male to identify with his mother and develop a feminine gender identity. The boy's feminine sexuality directs his sexual behavior toward other males rather than toward females. Freud views homosexuality as a pathology: the homosexual male cannot resolve his negative Oedipus complex and is thereby fixated at the phallic phase.

What determines whether males resolve conflicts of this phallic stage and become heterosexual or fixate at the phallic stage and become homosexual? According to psychoanalytic theory, the home environment determines sexual preference. The research of Irving Bieber (1962) suggests that male homosexuals have a dominant mother and a weak or absent father. This family pattern causes a male to become homosexual because of fear of women, resulting from both his mother's possessive jealousy of others who give him attention and his attraction to men whom he hopes will satisfy his unresolved love of his absent father. However, Bieber's view has two flaws (see Janda & Klenke-Hamel, 1980). First, he drew his conclusions from observations of homosexual males in therapy, and there is no assurance that homosexuals generally show this family pattern. Second, the pattern of the strong mother and the absent father is characteristic of urban blacks; yet, black males do not show any higher incidence of homosexuality than white males.

The young girl also experiences two conflicts during the phallic stage. First, she desires a penis and blames her mother for this deficiency. This "penis envy" also causes the girl to be attracted to her father because he has the organ she desires. Freud labeled this conflict the *Electra complex.* Second, the young girl is also attracted to her mother (the *negative Electra complex*) and will be attracted to males only if she resolves her Electra complex by identifying with her mother and developing a feminine gender identity. Also, to become heterosexual, she must repress her attraction to her mother; if she cannot she will become a homosexual—the continued attraction to the mother will cause her to identify with the father and adopt the masculine gender identity. A masculine sex role will motivate her to seek female sex partners and thus will be responsible for her homosexuality. Like the male homosexual, the female homosexual is deviant because she cannot resolve her negative Electra complex and is therefore fixiated at the phallic stage.

Charlotte Wolff (1971) conducted an evaluation of the family background of 100 nonpatient lesbians and 100 nonpatient heterosexual women. The two groups were comparable in family background, social class, and profession. She found that homosexual women were more likely than heterosexual women to have a rejecting or indifferent mother and a distant or absent father. According to Wolff, homosexual women seek to obtain from other women the love which they failed to obtain from their own mother and reject men because they do not know how to relate to them.

Hyde (1979) points to two major weaknesses in Freud psychoanalytic theory. *First, Freud equated "gender identification" with "choice of sexual partner."* In other words, the male homosexual's identification with his mother causes him to develop a feminine gender identity which allows him to be attracted to men. Similarly, the female homosexual's identification with her father causes her to develop a male gender identity which motivates her toward women. However, the evidence does not indicate that homosexual males consider themselves feminine or that lesbians believe they are masculine. Rather, most male homosexuals have a masculine gender identity and most lesbians have a feminine gender identity. Apparently, homosexuals do not have an errant gender identification as Freud assumed. *Second, the Freudian approach proposed that homosexuality reflects a pathology and that all homosexuals are poorly adjusted.* As we learned earlier, the data indicate that homosexuals are not any more likely to be maladjusted than heterosexuals.

Since we have seen that Freud's psychoanalytic theory has not fared well, we'll turn our attention to the only remaining view, the learning approach. Unlike the other views, learning theory seems to reflect a realistic approach to homosexuality.

Learning theory. The learning approach assumes that sexual preference is an example of an acquired sexual motive (see McGuire, Carlisle, & Young, 1965).

Homosexuality, according to this view, is not deviant, but rather reflects the development of sexual preference through conditioning.

Sexual preference can develop through positive reinforcing experiences. For example, young males or females may find their first homosexual experience to be very reinforcing and fantasize about it whenever they masturbate. Using homosexual fantasy increases the erotic value of members of the same sex and results in the development of a homosexual preference. Similarly, males or females who experience a pleasurable first heterosexual encounter will have heterosexual fantasies and, thereby, develop a preference for members of the opposite sex.

Sexual preference need not be learned only through a positive reinforcing experience. A person can develop a sexual preference in response to a negative experience. For example, if someone's first heterosexual encounter is aversive, members of the opposite sex will develop aversive qualities. Under these conditions, a person may be motivated toward members of the same sex in order to receive sexual satisfaction. If the ensuing homosexual experience is reinforcing, an attraction to members of the same sex will develop, and the person will become a homosexual. The observation that *as the result of experience* some male primates prefer sexual activity with another male rather than a receptive female supports this view of sexual preference as a matter of conditioning.

You may wonder what motivates a first heterosexual or homosexual experience. Remember from the beginning of the chapter that homosexuality frequently occurs in societies which approve of it; by contrast, cultures which punish homosexuality have few homosexuals. This observation suggests that an individual's social expectations are one factor influencing whether or not he or she is apt to engage in heterosexual or homosexual intercourse. A second factor concerns the availability of a sexual partner. If a member of the opposite sex is not present, the likelihood of homosexual behavior increases. The higher incidence of homosexuality which occurs in single-sex environments (for example, prisons) supports this view.

Although using the learning theory to account for homosexuality is consistent with literature on motivation described in this text, it still remains an untested theory. However, it has been demonstrated that aversive counterconditioning can alter homosexual preference effectively (see Rimm & Masters, 1979, for a detailed review). The ability of behavior therapy to modify sexual preference provides indirect support for the importance of learning in the development of sexual preference. (It is important to emphasize that psychiatry no longer views homosexuality as a pathology; therefore, only people who want to change their preference should receive the treatment described below, or any other form of therapy to modify sexual preference.)

MacCulloch and Feldman (1967) gave 43 male homosexuals 18 to 20 aversive counterconditioning sessions which lasted 20 to 25 minutes each. During every session the subjects saw a series of pictures of nude males. Immediately after each picture was presented, the subject would receive an electric shock. To prevent the shock, the subject could press a button which caused the picture of the nude male to be replaced with one of a nude female. MacCulloch and Feldman evaluated the success of their therapy in terms of their patients' ability to avoid homosexual activity; they reported that it was successful with 70 percent of their patients.

Feldman and MacCulloch (1971) conducted several other studies comparing the effectiveness of aversive counterconditioning therapy with a comparable control treatment, psychotherapy. *Success* was defined as a change in sexual preference lasting 1 year. The success rate for aversive counterconditioning was 70 percent, as compared with only 20 percent for psychotherapy. Evidently, people's sexual preference can be influenced by their conditioning experiences.

However, a change from homosexual to heterosexual *preference* does not necessarily mean that heterosexual *intercourse* will follow. For example, Birk, Huddleston, Millers, and Cohler (1971) found that although aversive counterconditioning produced a significant change from homosexual preference, it did not produce any increase in heterosexual activity when compared with a placebo control condition (see Figure 6.5). These results suggest that sexual preference and the attainment of sexual satisfaction are not related; a sexually motivated person must develop effective means of obtaining satisfaction.

Our discussion has portrayed people as being either heterosexual or homosexual; however, many people, who are called *bisexuals*, engage in sexual activity with members

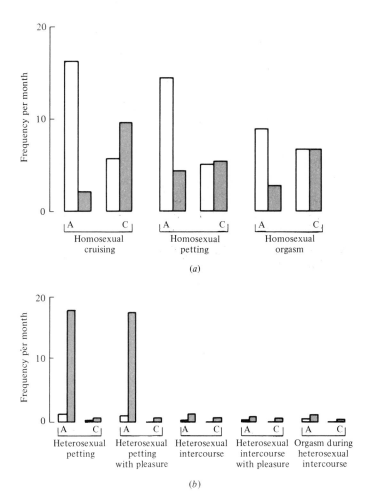

Figure 6.5
Changes in the frequency of sexual activity in homosexuals receiving either aversive conditioning (A) or placebo control (C) treatment: (a) homosexual behaviors; (b) heterosexual activity. (From Birk, L., Huddleston, W., Millers, E., & Cohler, B. Avoidance conditioning for homosexuality. Archives of General Psychiatry, 1971, 25, 314–323. Copyright 1971, American Medical Association.)

of both sexes (see Blumstein & Schwartz, 1974, 1976). Blumstein and Schwartz noted that the classification is often difficult to make, because some people label themselves *bisexual* even though they have limited heterosexual or homosexual experience, and some who do have frequent sexual contacts with both sexes consider themselves to be either heterosexual or homosexual. Apparently, a person's sexual identity and sexual preference are not always equivalent. Blumstein and Schwartz reported that many bisexuals had their first homosexual experience when they were between 30 and 40 years of age, but they continued their heterosexual as well as their homosexual behavior afterwards. Furthermore, Blumstein and Schwartz found that the development of an intimate friendship with a member of the same sex, or the absence of a member of the opposite sex, or both, preceded the establishment of bisexual behavior. These observations again point to the important role of experience in sexual preference.

SEXUAL DYSFUNCTION

Two separate processes are involved in producing sexual pleasure. *First, people must form the types of social attachments which will lead to sexual activity. Second, they must be able to perform sexually.* Thus, failure to obtain sexual satisfaction can result from either the absence of interpersonal attachments or ineffective sexual functioning. Our discussion of human sexuality continues by describing the types, causes, and treatment of *sexual dysfunction,* the inability to perform effectively. The nature of interpersonal attachment and its role in obtaining sexual pleasure will be described in Chapter 9.

Masters and Johnson's *Human Sexual Inadequacy* (1970) suggested that "at least half of marriages (in the United States) are either presently sexually dysfunctional or imminently so in the future" and also indicated that with appropriate treatment, sexual dysfunction need not exist. Although recently criticized for methodological flaws, their work has contributed to an acceptance of the legitimacy of research on sexual disorders and the use of psychotherapy to treat sexual dysfunction.

Forms of Sexual Dysfunction

There are several different types of sexual dysfunction in males and females. Masters and Johnson (1970) found *erectile dysfunction,* or *impotence,* to be the most common form of sexual dysfunction in males. Masters and Johnson reported that 245, or 54 percent, of the 448 males in their study suffered from chronic inability to have an erection sufficient to achieve penetration, although most had been able to engage in intercourse on at least one occasion.

Premature ejaculation, the second most common form of male sexual dysfunction, accounted for 186, or 41 percent, of the male patients in Masters and Johnson's study. Hyde (1979) suggested that premature ejaculation is probably the most frequently occurring form of sexual inadequacy in males but that males with this disorder are less likely to seek therapy than those with erectile dysfunction. This may partly reflect a greater difficulty in recognizing premature ejaculation than erectile dysfunction. How does a man know if he ejaculates too soon? Masters and Johnson do not think that time is the crucial issue; they define premature ejaculation as a male's inability 50 percent of the time to delay ejaculation until his partner attains orgasm. However, some psychologists (see Hyde, 1979) have not agreed with this figure. Hyde suggests that it may be too high in some cases and too low in others; she believes that an ejaculation dysfunction occurs in those males overly concerned about their lack of control and its effect on their partner's satisfaction.

Retarded ejaculation, or the inability to ejaculate, is the third major form of sexual dysfunction in males. Some males with this dysfunction can ejaculate with manual stimulation; others cannot. Although Masters and Johnson found this to be a rare disorder (only 17, or 4 percent, of their subjects were in this category), others (see Kaplan, 1974) now think that it is fairly common. Kaplan reported that many male patients seeking therapy suffer from ejaculatory incompetence.

There are also several forms of sexual dysfunction in females, although *orgasmic dysfunction* is by far the most prevalent. Masters and Johnson found that 342, or 92 percent, of the 371 females patients in their study were unable to experience an orgasm. The majority of these women, 56 percent, never had an orgasm (primary orgasmic dysfunction); the others were able to experience an orgasm only under certain conditions (secondary or situational orgasmic dysfunction). Hyde (1979) believes that situational orgasmic dysfunction probably is more common than primary orgasmic dysfunction but less likely to be reported. In support of this view, Hunt's survey (1974) indicates that 10 percent of American women have never experienced an orgasm and 20 percent have orgasms only infrequently.

Masters and Johnson reported that 29, or 9 percent, of the sexual dysfunction of their female patients was caused by involuntary contractions of the muscles surrounding the vagina. In this condition, known as *vaginismus,* the muscle contractions cause the entrance to the vagina to close, therby preventing intercourse.

Masters and Johnson's research indicates that several different processes—including organic problems, certain drugs, and psychological factors—can cause sexual dysfunction. It is important to note that while one process may lead to sexual problems, the dysfunction itself may act to create an additional disturbance which intensifies or maintains the dysfunction. For example, as the result of an emotional problem, a person takes a drug which produces sexual inadequacy. This person then develops a fear of sexual activity, and this psychological factor will now increase the inadequacy as well as maintain the dysfunction if the drug is discontinued.

Causes of Sexual Dysfunction

Organic causes. Sexual dysfunction is undoubtedly a complex phenomenon. There is evidence that both biological and psychological processes can lead to inadequacy. Masters and Johnson reported that organic factors cause about 10 to 20 percent of cases of sexual dysfunction. Hyde (1979) described several organic causes of sexual dysfunction. Erectile failure can occur because of (1) severe illness, especially diseases of the heart and circulatory system, (2) diabetes mellitus [although most diabetics do not experience erectile dysfunction, it is two to five times more likely to occur in diabetics than nondiabetics (Marmore, 1976)], (3) damage to the lower spinal cord which controls the erectile center, (4) severe stress or fatigue, and (5) some diseases of the reproductive system. Although premature ejaculation and retarded ejaculation are primarily caused by psychological processes (see Kaplan, 1974), diseases of the nervous system may precipitate these dysfunctions. For example, degenerative disorders such as multiple sclerosis may lead to premature ejaculation, and Parkinson's disease seems to be related to retarded ejaculation.

Although most cases of orgasmic dysfunction in women appear to be psychological in origin, severe illness or fatigue can cause a women's failure to attain orgasm. Fear of pain is primarily responsible for vaginismus, or painful intercourse; but several organic factors may produce painful intercourse and lead to involuntary muscle contractions (Kaplan,

1974). These organic causes include (1) disorders of the vaginal entrance (for example intact hymen or irritated remnants of the hymen, (2) irritation of the clitoris, (3) disorders of the vagina (for example, infections), and (4) pelvic disorders (for example tearing of uterine ligaments).

The influence of drugs.   Many drugs can cause sexual inadequacy (see Kaplan, 1974, and West, 1975, for a detailed description of the nature of their effects). Opiates appear to impair sexual functioning. For example, Chein, Gerard, Lee, and Rosenfeld (1964) found that of 100 heroin addicts, almost half had erectile dysfunction. Moderate or high doses of alcohol also cause sexual dysfunction. Jones and Jones (1977) discovered that alcoholics frequently had sexual problems. Anticholinergic drugs, primarily used in treating peptic ulcers and glaucoma, can produce erectile dysfunction by inhibiting the parasympathetic nerves which normally produce an erection. Sexual dysfunction, especially ejaculatory problems, can be created by the use of antiadrenergic drugs— medicine prescribed to treat hypertension and other vascular disorders. These antiadrenergic drugs block the sympathetic nerves which normally initiate an ejaculation. Other drugs which can lead to sexual dysfunction include *chlorphentermine* (or *preste*), usually used for weight reduction, and antihistamines, ordinarily taken to treat colds and allergies.

Psychological causes.   The psychoanalytic view suggests that intrapsychic conflict causes sexual dysfunction. According to Freud, sexual dysfunction originates in the phallic stage and involves an inability to resolve phallic conflicts. These unconscious conflicts make it impossible to experience sexual satisfaction.

In the psychoanalytic view, when a man who has erectile dysfunction prepares to have intercourse with a woman, the situation arouses his childhood castration anxieties, causing a loss of an erection. A different process causes premature ejaculation. Males with this dysfunction have an intense unconscious hatred of women. They experience sexual pleasure but ejaculate prematurely in order to prevent their partner from having an orgasm. According to the psychoanalytic view, women who suffer from vaginismus hate men because of their own inability to resolve their penis envy. This unconscious hatred causes these women to deny men sexual pleasure.

Learning theory does not assume that unconscious conflict causes sexual dysfunction; rather, it proposes that sexual dysfunction develops through conditioning. Learning theorists believe that the principles which enable people to be sexually effective are also responsible for the development of sexual inadequacies. According to this view, sexual dysfunctions result from negative experiences.

What kinds of experiences, from this viewpoint, could lead to sexual dysfunction? *First, consider people who, as the result of an aversive sexual experience, become afraid of sexual activity.* This fear will then interfere with their effective sexual functioning and can even motivate them to avoid sexual activity. *Second, frustration over the failure to receive pleasure from intercourse can also lead to sexual dysfunction.* Most people expect sexual intercourse to be a rewarding experience. If the pleasure derived from sexual activity is not as reinforcing as someone has expected it to be, the anticipated failure which results from this experience either reduces sexual effectiveness or motivates avoidance of sex.

Several types of evidence seem to provide support for the learning view. First, it is consistent with the motivational principles described in Chapters 2 and 3. Second, since learning appears to play an important role governing effective sexual functioning, it seems reasonable to conclude that experience also affects the failure to function effectively. Third, the influence of experience which decreases sexual functioning (for example, punishment by parents for sexual activity; aversive sexual encounters, such as rape; unrewarding sexual activity, as, perhaps, with a prostitute) is predictable from a learning approach. However, we must be aware that all such evidence is indirect; furthermore, any experimental study using humans in an attempt to produce sexual dysfunction would obviously be unethical. Animal research might provide evidence revealing the psychological causes of sexual dysfunction, but I know of no studies in this area.

One way to determine the psychological mechanisms which cause sexual dysfunction is to compare psychoanalytic and behavioral treatments of sexual dysfunction. The effectiveness of one approach or the other would provide evidence of the origins of sexual dysfunction.

Treatment of Sexual Dysfunction

Before the therapies are described, it should be noted that most research evaluating sex therapies consist of case studies; that is, a patient receives a given treatment, and the outcome is reported (see Janda & Klenke-Hamel, 1980). This type of research suffers from several deficits. First, the relative effectiveness of different treatments cannot be assessed, since no control treatments are employed. Second, the conditions necessary for the treatment to be effective cannot be determined. For example, without an experimental comparison, the length of an effective treatment cannot be assessed. In addition, there is no control for nonspecific factors such as expectancy effects or placebo effects. Finally, there are varied definitions of *success* as well as frequent failure to report the continued ability to maintain sexual effectiveness after the termination of treatment. As you will soon learn, there is a definite need to use more rigorous scientific methods in this area. Also, since organic factors and drugs can cause sexual dysfunction, these factors must be considered before any psychological treatment is employed. Our discussion begins with the psychoanalytic approaches; these are followed by a description of behavior therapies.

Psychoanalytic approach. A sexually dysfunctional patient undergoing psychoanalysis would be helped to identify and understand the conflict which created the dysfunction. Once the patient no longer represses the conflict, the problem can be resolved, and the dysfunction will no longer be evident.

Evidence points out that psychoanalysis is sometimes effective, but the conditions during which it is either successful or unsuccessful are not evident (see Janda & Klenke-Hamel, 1980). O'Connor and Stern's study (1972) illustrates the occasional success of this treatment. O'Connor and Stern evaluated the success of psychoanalysis in 61 dysfunctional women and 35 dysfunctional men. They reported that 25 percent of the women and 57 percent of the men were no longer dysfunctional following treatment.

Behavioral approaches. Psychologists have employed a number of behavioral therapies to treat sexually dysfunctional persons. Systematic desensitization, one frequently used behavioral technique, aims at reducing the fear which inhibits sexual arousal and behavior (see Chapter 2). It has been reported to be successful with erectile dysfunction (Friedman, 1978; Lazarus, 1961), premature ejaculation (Ince, 1973; Razani, 1972), orgasmic dysfunction (Farmer, 1969; Kraft & Al-Issa, 1967), and vaginismus (Eysenck & Rachman, 1965; Lazarus, 1963).

Modeling has also been employed to treat sexual dysfunction (see Chapter 3). Robinson's study with nonorgasmic women (1974) illustrates the use of modeling. He exposed his subjects to videotapes of sexual scenes. After this experience the women not only acquired novel sexual behaviors but also dramatically increased the frequency of sexual activities; they had rarely engaged in any sexual behaviors before the modeling treatment.

The best-known and most frequently employed behavior therapy for sexual dysfunction is Masters and Johnson's 2-week intensive treatment. Although Masters and Johnson do not label themselves *behavior therapists,* their approach to treating sexual dysfunction definitely is behaviorally oriented. They believe that sexual dysfunction has been learned and can be unlearned with proper treatment. Masters and Johnson used many behavioral techniques which had been developed in the 1960s but also created some innovations themselves. For example, their sensate-focus exercises inhibit fear in a manner similar to that of systematic desensitization treatment. Let's continue in more detail with Masters and Johnson's therapy program.

Masters and Johnson's treatment.   Masters and Johnson's *Human Sexual Inadequacy* (1970) describes their therapy approach, which uses general goals for all patients as well as specific treatment for particular dysfunctions. Before their treatment program is described, two unique aspects of their sex therapy need to be mentioned. *First, for several reasons, their therapy uses cotherapists—a male and female therapist together—to treat sexual dysfunction.* This procedure provides a same-gender therapist for each client, decreases the opportunity of a patient's perceived bias or a therapist's informational bias toward a patient, and minimizes the likelihood of an emotional relationship between client and therapist. *Second, also for several reasons, only couples are treated in therapy.* Sexual exercises, an integral part of the program, require a trained cooperative partner. Masters and Johnson feel "that there is no such thing as an uninvolved partner in any marriage in which there is some form of sexual inadequacy." Thus, their therapy treats not only the dysfunction but also the interpersonal relationship. Masters and Johnson use a surrogate who is trained to be a patient's partner only when a dysfunctional person does not have a partner. Although this procedure is controversial, it is, according to Masters and Johnson, as effective as the use of a spouse.

Masters and Johnson's therapy consists of four phases. *In the first phase, the patients' medical and psychological history is taken in order to identify the type and cause of their sexual dysfunction.*

The second phase involves a reeducation program in which the patients are given factual information about human sexuality and causes of sexual dysfunction. This knowledge corrects many misconceptions concerning sexual arousal and behavior which can lead to inadequacy; it also provides information which can enhance sexual functioning.

Many patients believe that they have failed unless their sexual performance reaches a particular level. To alleviate this attitude, *the third phase of Masters and Johnson's program employs sensate-focus exercises in which patients provide each other with sensual pleasure other than intercourse.* The sensate-focus exercises are structured to provide patients with successful sexual experience and eliminate anxiety and the expectation of failure. In order to accomplish this goal, patients are forbidden to engage in any unassigned sexual activity. Therapists first assign simple sensate-focus exercises which will lead to pleasure. For example, patients initially touch each other in a nongenital area and experience pleasure because they are not anxious about intercourse nor embarrassed about past failures. Having succeeded in these initial touching exercises, patients add more sexual aspects to the procedure to increase their pleasure. They are instructed to communicate their feelings to their partner; this procedure allows them to learn how they can please each other. In addition, these exercises teach patients to focus their attention on their pleasure—not on outside activities or their performance.

Specific techniques to treat a particular dysfunction are employed during the last phase of Masters and Johnson's therapy. With the fear of intercourse removed, many males with erectile dysfunction occasionally have an erection during sensate-focus exercises. These males are then trained how to suppress an erection. Once the male learns to control his erection, his partner helps him gradually to engage in sexual intercourse. Masters and Johnson reported a 65 percent "nonfailure" rate in the treatment of erectile dysfunction: this means that 65 percent of their patients improved during therapy.

The squeeze technique is used to treat premature ejaculation. When a male's partner squeezes his penis for 3 to 4 seconds, he will lose the urge to ejaculate. This procedure is continued until the patient can be aroused for 15 to 20 minutes without ejaculating. Next, he is instructed to engage in intercourse with his partner, who prevents an ejaculation whenever the patient feels the urge. Masters and Johnson reported a 97 percent "nonfailure" rate in treating premature ejaculation.

A partner of a patient with retarded ejaculation first manually stimulates the penis until ejaculation occurs. She then stimulates him until just prior to ejaculation, whereupon she inserts his penis into her vagina. Once the male has experienced an ejaculation during intercourse, he requires less and less manual stimulation before intercourse. Masters and Johnson discovered that only 18 percent of their patients who had ejaculatory incompetence did not improve by the end of therapy.

The treatment of orgasmic dysfunction in females begins with instructions on how the male can give his partner sexual pleasure. Once the female can experience pleasure through manual stimulation, the couple is instructed to use two intercourse positions (female superior and lateral coital) which provide maximal sensations for the woman. Masters and Johnson reported a 78 percent "nonfailure" rate in the treatment of nonorgasmic female patients.

The treatment of women who have vaginismus begins with a demonstration of the involuntary vaginal spasms to both partners. The woman is placed in the gynecological examination position and the physician inserts a finger into the vagina. After the severity of the spasm has been demonstrated, the couple is given a set of graduated dilators. The male is instructed to begin with the smallest dilator and gradually go on to the larger ones. Within several days, this procedure eliminates the involuntary spasms, and intercourse can occur. Masters and Johnson reported a 100 percent "nonfailure" rate in treating vaginismus, and within 6 months after treatment 90 percent of their patients became orgasmic.

Masters and Johnson also reported that even 5 years after successful treatment most of their patients were able to maintain effective sexual functioning. A 5-year follow-up study of 225 patients showed that only a few (7 percent) had become dysfunctional over that period. These results seem to suggest that Masters and Johnson's therapy produces long-lasting behavioral change.

Criticisms of Masters and Johnson's therapy. You might think that Masters and Johnson's treatment is effective because most sex therapists use it, or a variation of it. Evaluating the effectiveness of a clinical treatment requires that others use the same procedures and find similar results. Unfortunately, no critical evaluation has been conducted since the publication of *Human Sexual Inadequacy* in 1970 (see Zilbergeld & Evans, 1980).

Why have laypeople and psychologists uncritically accepted Masters and Johnson's approach? Why were hundreds of people trained to use an unscientifically evaluated treatment? Zilbergeld and Evans (1980) offer two reasons for the widespread acceptance of the effectiveness of Masters and Johnson's treatment. *First, Masters and Johnson's extensive research into human sexual response initiated an acceptance of sex research.* Other researchers are perhaps hesitant to criticize those who contributed to the establishment of that field. *Second, a young field is generally less critical than better-established disciplines.* For example, although many sex therapists who employ Masters and Johnson's treatment approach indicate "a success rate" comparable to that of Masters and Johnson, they do not report any statistical data to support their claim. Thus, failure to adopt rigid standards has led to the acceptance of an untested therapy.

Zilbergeld and Evans (1980) believe that a close examination of the effectiveness of Masters and Johnson's treatment program is necessary. The impetus for their inquiry was observations—by themselves and of others who were using Masters and Johnson's techniques—which indicated less therapeutic effectiveness than had been reported in *Human Sexual Inadequacy*.

Zilbergeld and Evans decided to duplicate Masters and Johnson's results. However, they were unable to conduct an evaluative study of Masters and Johnson's 2-week therapy program because of the imprecise and difficult writing style used in *Human Sexual Inadequacy*. They could not, for example, find answers to certain essential questions. First, Masters and Johnson did not describe their screening techniques; *Human Sexual Inadequacy* noted only that psychotics and couples who were not in agreement about altering a dysfunction were rejected. It was unclear how psychosis or lack of agreement was determined or how the decision to reject was made. Second, Masters and Johnson did not indicate whether or not any patients left before the treatment was completed, although they did say that some were asked to leave. However, the basis of this decision and the number of patients asked to leave therapy was not apparent. Finally, Masters and Johnson did not state how many hours of therapy were involved in their treatments. Patients from the St. Louis area seemed to have received 3 weeks of less intense therapy than patients from other localities. It was noted in *Human Sexual Inadequacy* that patients encountering problems could call Masters and Johnson's foundation as well as make regularly scheduled calls. Although Masters and Johnson did not consider telephone calls to be part of therapy time, Zilbergeld and Evans think that they should have done so, since patients who called received help. If, during the many months following formal treatment, such calls were frequent and of long duration, the Masters and Johnson program may not actually be a short-term intensive program.

Zilbergeld and Evans found other serious problems. Masters and Johnson define *success* as the "absence of failure" (hence their term *nonfailure rate*), and *failure* to mean that a patient did not "initiate reversal of the basic symptomatology of sexual dysfunction." Yet Zilbergeld and Evans could not detect in *Human Sexual Inadequacy* what "initiating reversal" meant. They point out that it could mean several different things. For example, was a woman with orgasmic dysfunction classified as a "nonfailure" if she learned to reach an orgasm while masturbating, or did this classification mean that she experienced orgasm during intercourse? Unfortunately, Masters and Johnson did not clearly define "nonfailure" for any dysfunction. In addition, Zilbergeld and Evans felt that if *success* is defined as "absence of failure," considerable differences in the level of change should have been noticed. Again, Masters and Johnson did not indicate the degree of change which had occurred in their "successful" patients. How Masters and Johnson conducted the evaluation of "nonfailure" is also unclear. Finally, recall that Masters and Johnson reported very low relapse rates for patients 5 years after their therapy. Yet, they failed to state either the questions which were asked in the follow-up or how they evaluated continued sexual effectiveness.

It seems reasonable to conclude that Masters and Johnson successfully treated some—perhaps many—of their patients, since their program combined many techniques which are often effective alone. However, the essential elements of an effective sex therapy have yet to be delineated. Since most sexually dysfunctional people seeking help receive Masters and Johnson's treatment (or therapy believed to be similar to it), an experimentally sound investigation of this therapy is obviously necessary.

SUMMARY

Our sexuality reflects not only our level of sexual desire but also our sexual preference, the type of interpersonal situation in which we obtain sexual pleasure, and also the exhibition of nonsexual behaviors considered appropriate to our sex. Our sexuality is determined by the interaction of biological, sociological, and psychological factors.

Biological processes determine our ability to be sexually motivated, to exhibit sexual behavior, and to experience sexual pleasure. From a sociological standpoint, there are enormous cross-cultural differences in sexual motivation and behavior. A person's culture influences the types of behavior used to obtain sexual gratification, the tolerance of deviant forms of sexual preference, the physical characteristics considered to be sexually attractive, and the kinds of interpersonal relationships which can be established to gain sexual pleasure. Many of the forms of sexual expression which are found in humans also occur in primate species; this observation suggests that our mammalian heritage provides the potential for the variety of sexual practices observed in different societies.

Our biological systems play an important role in sexual arousal and behavior. During sexual activity, powerful physiological changes take place in the sex organs. Vasocongestion of the genitals occurs during sexual excitement and indicates sexual arousal; and the intense myotonia which takes place during an orgasm provides the sensations of sexual pleasure.

Hormones influence whether or not a person is sexually receptive. The male's ability to be aroused depends upon the presence of testosterone; estrogen, progesterone, and the adrenal androgen androstenedione affect the female's sexual responsivity.

The production of the sex hormones and the detection of their presence is controlled by different areas of the hypothalamus: the tuberal region governs hormone secretion; the anterior portion detects the presence of a hormone and produces sexual responsivity. A third area of the hypothalamus, the mammilary area, inhibits sexual activity until an appropriate sexual object is encountered. In the male, the cortex identifies a sexually appropriate object, thereby releasing sexual behavior. The role of the cortex in female sexual behavior appears to be primarily inhibitory, although in higher mammals it also may have a facilitative influence.

Psychological processes also have an valuable function in sexual arousal. Environmental stimuli develop the capacity to produce sexual arousal through the classical conditioning process. Our sexual preference also appears to reflect a conditioned reaction developed through experience. Sometimes inappropriate objects arouse people; sometimes people want to alter their sexual preference. Aversive counterconditioning seems to represent an effective behavior therapy to decrease intense sexual arousal or alter sexual preference.

Many persons are able to obtain desired levels of sexual satisfaction; yet many others are not able to experience sexual pleasure. Men's sexual dysfunctions include erectile dysfunction, premature ejaculation, and retarded ejaculation. Women's sexual dysfunctions are orgasmic dysfunction and vaginimus. Several different causes—organic factors, drugs, and psychological processes—can produce sexual dysfunction. Although many dysfunctional people have been successfully treated, we do not know at present how effective the sex therapies are or what conditions are necessary to ensure their success. It is to be hoped that these questions will soon be answered.

$\mathscr{A}$GGRESSION

CHAPTER 7

A cause for concern

*T*om's promise to his wife Claire that he will control his temper and stop beating their sons has been broken many times. Tom's temper flares easily; he often spanks the boys for even slight misbehavior. Whenever Claire tries to reason with Tom, in the hope of showing him how harmful his behavior could be, he becomes hostile and asserts that the boys need discipline. In fact, she has recently become somewhat frightened by his hostility and, even though Tom has never struck her, she simply no longer questions his disciplining of their sons when he is hostile. Tom's irritability subsides several minutes after he has spanked his boys; he usually realizes that he has acted too harshly and promises to control his temper in the future.

During the past 2 months, the problem has intensified. Lately, Tom has become violently angry at something or someone at least daily. Claire suspects that Tom's increased inability to control his temper stems from additional pressures at work. Tom was recently promoted to supervisor of his company's warehouse, and he often works late in an attempt to establish a more efficient operational system. Tom finds this challenge frustrating, and it usually leaves him tired and irritable when he arrives home.

Yesterday evening seemed particularly exasperating to Tom. The boys bickered over their toys, which television show to watch, and who would do what chores. Three-year-old Barry's refusal to go to bed triggered a reaction in Tom which caused him to strike Barry's arm violently. Tom was terrified by his own behavior; he had never seriously hurt anyone and certainly had never imagined that his spankings would result in physical injury to either of his sons. Claire rushed Barry to the hospital emergency room. When an examination revealed that Barry's arm was broken, Claire told the doctor that Barry had fallen off a chair. She was ashamed of her lie, but she did not want Tom to be prosecuted. Although Claire did *not think that the doctor believed her story, fortunately he did not question her further. Once again Tom has promised Claire that he* | *will change his behavior; and once again Claire can only hope that he will keep his promise.*

Tom's aggressive actions have obviously inflicted great physical and psychological harm on his sons. Claire's intuitive feeling that her husband's frustration is causing his aggressiveness toward their children is probably accurate. In this chapter, we'll learn that frustration can motivate aggressive behavior although it does not automatically lead to aggression. Also, we'll look at the variables which determine whether or not frustration induces aggression and discuss what factors other than frustration can cause aggression.

THE NATURE OF AGGRESSION

A Definition of Aggression

We often refer to a person's behavior as *aggressive*. What do we mean when we talk of aggressive behavior? Table 7.1 presents a list of behaviors which are often considered aggressive. It is interesting that the list is quite diverse. For example, businesspeople who hire a professional killer to assassinate a business rival contrast sharply with businesspeople who vigorously struggle to improve their business in order to drive out competition; yet we call both types of behavior *aggression*.

Can a single definition of aggression encompass each of the aggressive behaviors presented in Table 7.1? Many psychologists (see Berkowitz, 1962; Buss, 1961; Frank, 1967; Kaufman, 1970; Montagu, 1966; Moyer, 1971) have struggled to develop an acceptable definition of aggression. The most frequent definition is that aggression is behavior motivated by the intent to harm a creature or, under some conditions, an inanimate object. Thus, any behavior which has malicious intent is considered aggressive. Most psychologists prefer this definition because it includes most behaviors which we intuitively think are aggressive and conveys what we typically believe an aggressive act to be. Thus, a person who knocks a flower pot off a fifth-story windowsill and hits a passerby (example 3 in Table 7.1) has acted aggressively if the act was deliberate but nonaggressively it was accidental.

How can we infer intent from observing human or animal behavior? We could determine people's intent from their verbal behavior. However, verbal reports are unlikely to represent an accurate indication of intent; we are not apt to tell others about our deliberately aggressive acts. Obviously, also, we cannot detect intent from animals' verbal behavior. Moyer (1976) suggests an indirect way of assessing intent. According to Moyer, we can infer intent by observing the persistence of animals' or humans' "destructive acts toward the same or similar stimulus objects at different times." Thus, if the woman in example 3 in Table 7.1 consistently behaves in a manner which harms other people, we could with some degree of confidence infer that her behavior is aggressive. Similarly, a cat which stalks, tosses, and eventually kills a mouse is acting aggressively if it persistently kills mice (example 7 in Table 7.1).

Our definition based on intent does not include some behaviors which are often regarded as aggressive. For example, an energetic, hardworking executive (example 16) is not considered aggressive unless his or her behavior is intended to harm someone else. Moreover, this definition includes some behaviors which we do not usually consider aggressive. The parent who punishes a child is displaying aggressive behavior (example

Table 7.1
Samples of Potentially Aggressive Behaviors

1. A man who cannot start his car smashes his hand into the dashboard.
2. A debater belittles an opponent.
3. A woman knocks a flowerpot off the fifth story window ledge, and it hits a passerby.
4. A bombardier presses a button, and thousands of people below are killed.
5. A hunter kills a tiger and mounts its head on the mantle as a trophy.
6. A frightened boy, caught stealing but unable to escape, shoots his discoverer.
7. A cat stalks, catches, and kills a mouse.
8. A mother spanks her son for not doing his homework.
9. A mugger stabs a victim during a robbery.
10. An assassin attempts to kill the President, but the shot misses.
11. A Boy Scout trips an old woman while helping her across the street, and she sprains her ankle.
12. One child makes another child cry by taking away a toy.
13. A football player makes a vicious tackle which injures another player's knee.
14. A dominant male rhesus monkey threatens a less dominant male, causing him to flee.
15. A farmer kills a chicken for dinner.
16. An energetic executive works hard to establish a company and drive out competitors.
17. A wife plans to, and does, kill her husband, who has repeatedly beaten her.
18. A boy dreams about beating up the neighborhood bully but never fulfills this wish.

From: Beck, Robert C. *Motivation: Theories and principles,* © 1978, pp. 286–287. Adapted by permission of Prentice-Hall, Inc., Englewood Cliffs, N. J.

8). Although punishment of a child by a parent may represent a socially acceptable method of controlling children's behavior, the parent does intend to inflict harm. Likewise, hunters who kill wild game are behaving aggressively (example 5).

We should recognize that for a behavior to be considered aggressive, its consequences do not have to be harmful. Behavior is aggressive as long as people or animals try to hurt another creature. Thus, the assailant who inaccurately fires a shot in an attempt to kill the President is exhibiting aggressive behavior even though the shot misses (example 10). Moreover, the harm can be psychological as well as physical. Suppose that one child causes another child to cry by taking away his or her toy (example 12). The psychological trauma of losing the toy can be as harmful as physical trauma. Consider a dominant male primate threatening a submissive male that has begun to eat a piece of fruit (example 14). If the threat is effective and the submissive male gives up the fruit, he will experience frustration (owing to inability to obtain a desired goal). As you learned from Chapter 2, frustration can be as aversive to primates as physical injury.

People can display aggressive behavior covertly, rather than overtly. Consider example 18 in Table 7.1: thinking about hurting someone else is being aggressive. Although the boy is not verbalizing his thoughts of beating up the bully, he does fantasize about hurting someone. Thus, we would define his behavior as aggressive.

However, some psychologists (see Feshbach, 1971; Johnson, 1972) do not agree with the definition of aggression based on intent. They assume that many aggressive behaviors occur without intent; for example, a farmer who kills a chicken for dinner (example 15 in Table 7.1) is being aggressive but does not want the chicken to suffer. Similarly, a robber who uses force to obtain money may not intend to injure the victim (example 9). Although this approach seems reasonable, it can be argued that intent is present in these examples. The farmer did deliberately kill the chicken, an act which certainly inflicted harm. Likewise, the robber who constrained a victim to gain money deliberately acted in a way that hurt the victim physically, emotionally, or both. Thus, the view that aggression occurs when people or animals deliberately harm others seems to be most accurate.

Are All Aggressive Acts Alike?

Our examples of aggressive behavior have indicated that many different responses can be classified as aggressive and that these aggressive acts can occur in various situations. You might wonder what process or processes motivate these varied patterns of aggressive behavior. Kenneth Moyer (1971, 1976) presented a detailed analysis of aggression. He asserted that there are eight types of aggression: (1) predatory, (2) intermale, (3) maternal, (4) sex-related, (5) fear-induced, (6) irritable, (7) instrumental, and (8) territorial. Table 7.2 presents a brief description of these forms of aggression, which will be examined in greater detail after a look at the general characteristics of Moyer's view.

Moyer asserts that the motivational system, as well as the psychological system controlling each form of aggression, differs for each type of aggression. Instrumental aggression is the only exception to Moyer's rule; it can involve the biological system which controls any of the other forms of aggression. In addition, a specific releasing stimulus exists for each form of aggression; however, the effectiveness of a particular releasing stimulus depends upon the efficient functioning of the physiological systems which are relevant to that stimulus. In other words, the releasing stimulus for predatory aggression will not release predatory behavior unless the biological systems which control that form of aggression are functioning effectively.

In animals, a different pattern of aggressive behavior characterizes each type of aggression. For example, while a natural prey and an unfamiliar male *conspecific* (that is, another male of the same species) both release aggressive behavior, an animal's predatory aggressive response is quite different from its intermale aggressive response. People, on the other hand, appear to have different biological systems and releasing stimuli for each type of aggression; yet the same aggressive response can be activated by different types of

Table 7.2
Moyer's Eight Types of Aggression

Type	Description
Predatory	An animal stalks, catches, and kills its natural prey.
Intermale	A male attacks a strange male conspecific.
Maternal	A mother assaults a perceived threat to her young.
Sex-related	A male becomes aggressive when encountering sex-related stimuli.
Fear-induced	An animal cornered and unable to escape from danger becomes aggressive.
Irritable	An annoyed person attacks another person or object.
Instrumental	An individual employs aggressive behavior to obtain a desired goal.
Territorial	An animal defends his territory against intrusion.

aggression. Consider a male debater who belittles an opponent's qualifications (example 2 in Table 7.1). This could be a reflection of many factors, such as instrumental aggression (contending for a women's attention), fear-induced aggression (fear induced by the opponent's attack), and irritable aggression (anger at the opponent, induced by an incident just before the debate). These observations indicate that different motives can produce identical aggressive behavior in a person. Moyer's theory also points out that a single type of aggression can motivate many different patterns of aggressive behavior; for example, irritable aggression can cause someone either to abuse verbally or to hit another person.

Although there appears to be a consensus that many different motives are responsible for aggressive behavior, some psychologists (see Adams, 1979), do not completely agree with Moyer's classification system. As you'll discover in this chapter, there is some overlap in both the biological and the psychological processes which motivate several forms of aggression in Moyer's classification system. However, there are still important differences between the aggressive motives identified by Moyer. His approach, compared with any other research in this area, currently seems to be better-defined, more thoroughly investigated, and supported better by empirical evidence. Our discussion focuses on the motives which Moyer identified; but the similarity between the motivational processes of several forms of aggression and some unanswered questions about Moyer's approach will also be addressed in this chapter.

PREDATORY AGGRESSION

The Prey

Predatory aggression occurs when animals attack and kill their natural prey. Predators are highly selective, attacking only the limited number of species which constitute their natural prey. For example, different strains of rats prey on various animals. Some rats do not attack mice but will attack hamsters and small rabbits (Kreiskott, 1969). Even those rats that will attack mice do not exhibit a predatory aggressive response toward rat pups (Myer & White, 1965). Other species also show stimulus-specificity. Levison and Flynn (1965) reported that their cats attacked rats but did not respond aggressively toward a toy dog or a stuffed rat.

A specific attribute of the prey usually releases predatory aggressive behavior. Tinbergen (1955) observed that predatory water beetles reacted to the olfactory cues of their prey—tadpoles—but did not react to a visual pattern of the prey. Eibl-Eibesfeldt (1970) found that although toads' predatory aggressive behavior is elicited by a movement of any object which equals the size of their prey—insects—toads do not respond to a motionless object which resembles their prey.

The Aggressive Response

The prey objects of animals elicit an aggressive behavior which differs from other forms of aggression. Predators typically attack the anterior portion of the prey in a manner which is quiet and efficient and involves little affect. Eisenberg and Leyhausen (1972) studied many carnivorous species and identified several discrete components of the attack response: an initial approach followed by a biting, shaking response or a biting, tossing response, or both.

Predatory aggressive behavior reflects an instinctive species-specific response which can be improved by experience—experience appears to increase an animal's ability to aim the biting response toward the desired part of the prey (see Eibl-Eibesfeldt, 1970) and to attack motionless prey (see Fox, 1969; Eibl-Eibesfeldt, 1961). Predators, according to Eibl-Eibesfeldt, learn to limit their attack to the anterior portion of the prey in order to avoid being bitten.

The Motive for Predatory Behavior

Since prey objects are predatory animals' food, you might perceive the predatory aggressive response as dependent upon hunger; that is, only hungry animals attack prey. Although food deprivation does shorten the killing latency (De Sisto, 1970), satiated predatory animals will attack prey (Huston, DeSisto, & Meyer, 1969; Kruuk, 1972). Apparently, the predatory aggressive motive and the hunger motive are separate but interrelated.

Why do different motives control predatory aggressive behavior and feeding behavior? Young animals must learn to kill their prey effectively at a time when they are being cared for by their parents. If predation depended upon hunger, animals would wait too long to develop an efficient predatory aggressive response. By separating the hunger motive and the predatory motive, the young animal can become an efficient predator before it has to obtain its own food.

Although nonpredatory animals can learn to kill other animals for food, they do not exhibit the response pattern which characterizes predatory aggression. For example, Moyer reported in 1972 that while nonpredatory rats can be trained to kill and eat mice, they can never acquire the neck-biting aggressive response shown by predatory rats. Apparently, as was noted above, predatory aggression is an instinctive behavior pattern in which efficiency can be modified through experience. The killing response of nonpredatory animals reflects an example of instrumental aggression; that is, aggressive behavior functions to enable these animals to obtain reward.

The Pleasure of the Kill

Intrinsically, predatory aggressive behavior is highly reinforcing. Many studies have demonstrated that predatory animals will acquire certain behaviors if these behaviors give them the opportunity to kill prey. For example, Van Hemel (1972) discovered that mice-killing rats learned to press a key which activated a motorized wheel which, in turn, provided access to a caged mouse. Similarly, De Sisto (1970) observed that frog-killing rats learned to press a bar which produced a frog; and Roberts and Kiess (1964) reported that cats placed in a T maze could acquire the appropriate response which led to a rat. The inherently reinforcing property of predatory aggressive activity undoubtedly is responsible for the occurrence of this behavior in satiated animals.

The Physiological Basis of Predation

John P. Flynn and his associates (see Chi & Flynn, 1971; Flynn, 1967, 1972; Levison & Flynn, 1965; MacDonnell & Flynn, 1966; Wasman & Flynn, 1962) identified the neural system of cats which is activated by natural prey and initiates predatory aggressive behavior. The neural circuit begins in the lateral hypothalamus, travels through the medial forebrain bundle, and terminates in the ventral tegmentum. Stimulating any segment of this circuit initiates predatory aggressive behavior in cats which would not normally attack rats. The predatory aggressiveness of these cats is identical to that of a natural killer; that is, it is quiet and efficient, lacks affect, and is directed toward the victim's neck. Destruction of the neurons in the predatory aggression circuit will eliminate predatory behavior in animals which typically attack natural prey. An identical neural circuit has been shown to control predatory aggression in rats (DeSisto, 1970; De Sisto & Huston, 1969; Karli, Vergnes, & Didiergeorges, 1969; King & Hoebel, 1968; Panksepp, 1969; Vergnes & Karli, 1969) and opposums (Roberts, Steinberg, & Means, 1967). We have learned that predatory aggression is intrinsically reinforcing. The involvement of the medial forebrain bundle (the reward system of the brain; see Chapter 4) is undoubtedly responsible for the highly reinforcing character of predatory aggression. Let's examine the evidence that this neural circuit controls predatory aggression.

Stimulating the lateral hypothalamus of cats that would not typically attack a rat, Wasman and Flynn (1962) noted that the cats attacked and killed the rat during 97.6 percent of 2,500 trials. The aggressive behavior of cats is stimulus-bound; that is, in the absence of a rat, cats do not exhibit attack behavior. Instead, they pace around the cage; this indicates arousal but is not predatory behavior. The ability of lateral hypothalamic stimulation to elicit predatory aggressiveness in cats has been reported by other researchers (for example, Hutchinson & Renfrew, 1966; Roberts & Kiess, 1964). Furthermore, many studies (see King & Hoebel, 1968; Vergnes & Karli, 1969) have documented that lateral hypothalamic stimulation arouses predatory aggressive behavior in rats. We should note that these animals ceased their aggressive attacks when stimulation stopped—regardless of whether or not the prey had been killed. These observations indicate that lateral hypothalamic activity is essential to predatory aggressiveness.

Further support for this view comes from studies of lesions. Panksepp (1971) and Karli and Vergnes (1964) found that destruction of the lateral hypothalamus eliminated predatory aggression in predatory rats.

Attack behavior during lateral hypothalamic stimulation is directed only toward a natural prey. For example, as was noted earlier, Levison and Flynn (1965) observed that while lateral hypothalamic stimulation caused cats to attack a rat, these cats rarely attacked a toy dog or a stuffed rat. Similarly, De Sisto (1970) observed that during lateral hypothalamic stimulation, frog-killing rats would attack a live frog but not a dead frog, a small rubber mouse, or a live mouse. However, some rats do attack mice (Karli, Vergnes, & Didiergeorges, 1969). Lateral hypothalamic stimulation of these mice-killing rats produced predatory aggressiveness against a mouse.

We have seen that although predatory aggression and hunger are not controlled by the same neural systems, lateral hypothalamic stimulation produces both predatory aggressiveness and eating (Chapter 5). However, while the control of both predation and feeding reside in the lateral hypothalamus, separate neurons govern each motive. Flynn, Vanegas, Foote, and Edwards (1970) discovered that the stimulation of different sites in the lateral hypothalamus of rats results in attack and eating behavior. Even though predatory aggression and hunger are separate motives, the proximity of the control center for both motives obviously enables adaptiveness: predatory aggressiveness is essential for hungry predatory animals in natural environments.

Stimulation of the other areas in the predatory circuit will also elicit predatory aggression. For example, Bandler (1971a, 1971b) found that stimulation of the ventral tegmentum area produced aggressive attack behavior in nonpredatory rats. Other studies (see MacDonnell & Flynn, 1964, 1968; Bandler, Chi, & Flynn, 1972) reported elicitation of predatory aggression in cats during ventral tegmentum stimulation.

Destruction of the ventral tegmentum causes an elimination of predatory aggressive behavior (see Bernston, 1972).

INTERMALE AGGRESSION

Two males of the same species sometimes engage in a ritualistic hostile conflict with each other. Although two females occasionally exhibit this form of aggression, it is found primarily in males. Also, males rarely use this form of aggression against females.

The Releasing Stimulus

What cues arouse a male person or animal, causing him to fight with another male of his species? Although many events can influence the likelihood of intermale aggression, the presence of a "strange" male conspecific is the stimulus which releases this form of aggression. According to Moyer, a "strange" male is someone to whom (or some animal to which) the attacker has not become habituated; that is, the attacker is not aware of the stranger's intentions. Once males have learned what to expect from other males, they are no longer strangers and, thus, intermale aggression does not occur. It is important to note that once the attacker responds in an aggressive manner toward the stranger, the victim sometimes reciprocates the attack. Numerous observations document the ability of a strange male to release aggression in another male; the next section examines some of this evidence.

However, it should first be noted that two familiar people (or animals) may fight, sometimes violently. This aggressive behavior is not an example of intermale aggression: intermale aggression represents only an unprovoked confrontation between two strangers. Carpenter (1940) reported that while male gibbons do not tolerate the close presence of strange male gibbons, they will live peaceably with familiar male gibbons or with males of other primate species. Although male rodents (for example, the Mongolian gerbil) make excellent pets because they do not react aggressively toward humans, they will exhibit an intense aggressive response when caged with another male of their species (see Ginsberg & Braud, 1971).

Two characteristics of the strange male have been identified as the sign stimuli which release intermale aggressive behavior. In many species, a unique odor of the strange male elicits intermale aggression; in other species, visual cues elicit it. Mackintosh and Grant's research (1966) indicates that a pheromone secreted in the urine of strange males is the olfactory cue which releases intermale aggression in mice. Although two familiar mice do not ordinarily fight, rubbing the urine from a strange mouse on the perineal region of one of the familiar mice initiates fighting between the two familiar mice. In contrast, intermale aggression can be prevented between two strange mice if one of them is rubbed with the urine of a third mouse which is familiar to both of them. Archer (1968) discovered that two familiar mice will fight when placed in a cage soiled by strange mice.

Studies in which the olfactory bulbs of aggressive males are removed also document the importance of odor in the initiation of aggressive fighting. Ropartz (1967, 1968) discovered that a reduction in intermale aggressive conflict between aggressive male mice followed lesions of the olfactory bulbs. Similarly, Richardson and Scudder's male mice (1970) and Murphy and Schneider's male hamsters (1970) which had had their olfactory bulbs removed showed a sharp decrease in aggressiveness.

We saw in the last section that males do not typically attack a strange female. The reason for this is that females secrete an aggression-inhibiting odor. Rubbing urine of a female on an aggressive male mouse will prevent him from being attacked by another aggressive male (Connor, 1972; Dixon & Mackintosh, 1971).

Visual cues release intermale aggression in many species. For example, Tinbergen (1948) noted that the red underbelly of the male stickleback is the releaser of aggressive attack from another male stickleback. He found that even a crude model of the male which contained a red area like the underbelly elicited attack. Also, Lack (1943) observed that male English robins attacked the tuft of red breast feathers of other male English robins and showed intermale aggression even when the feathers were placed on a model.

The Aggressive Response

Intermale aggressive behavior is a highly stereotyped, ritualized action comprising several distinct phases. The males usually approach each other cautiously in a defensive position. One (or both) males will then exhibit a species-specific threat posture intended to induce withdrawal in the adversary. If the threat is ineffective, fighting ensues, continuing until one male flees, indicates defeat, or dies. Many studies (see Eibl-Eibesfeldt, 1970) have observed intermale aggressive behavior in animals. Let's look at the intermale aggression of rats and baboons.

Barnett (1963) observed with rats that the attack begins when both the attacker and the newcomer adopt a defensive position (see Figure 7.1). The males then exhibit the arched-back threat posture. An ineffective threat (one which does not cause the opponent to withdraw) causes the attacker to leap at his opponent, biting either an ear, a limb, or the tail. The two males exhibit violent movement during this leaping and biting attack, which lasts only a few seconds. After the initial attack, the rats adopt either a boxing stance or the defensive position. This defensive phase also lasts only a few seconds; if one rat is not defeated, another attack begins. The fight ends when the defeated rat flees, dies, or adopts a *submissive posture* indicative of defeat. In the submissive posture, the defeated rat sits on his rump, rears without displaying an aggressive fall, and emits a series of 25-kilohertz ultrasounds of 3,400-millisecond duration. This submissive behavior causes the other male to cease attacking and leave the defeated animal. However, if the defeated male tries to flee rather than submit, the victor follows in pursuit, frequently biting his victim on the rump. Apparently, submission is often better than flight.

Kummer's observations (1968) of intermale aggression in baboons show that ritualistic intermale aggressive behavior also occurs in primates. Male baboons display their fighting response by attempting to bite each other's shoulder or neck and mockingly hitting one another with their fists. Interestingly, Kummer discovered that baboon males only rarely hit, and almost never bite, their adversary. The sparring continues until one male flees or exhibits the submissive posture. In primates, the defeated male usually turns in a manner which presents his hindquarters to the victorious male. This submissive display, identical to the posture of an receptive female, causes the victorious male to exhibit a perfunctory mounting response. The loser's submissive posture and the victor's mounting behavior act to inhibit further attack. However, if the loser attempts to flee, the victor will chase him and upon catching him will occasionally scratch him in the anal region.

Intermale aggression seldom results in serious injury. The defeated male typically exhibits the submissive display to prevent the victorious male from harming him. A submissive male that has recognized the greater aggressiveness of the dominant male will exhibit the submissive posture just before the attack, thus causing the dominant male to

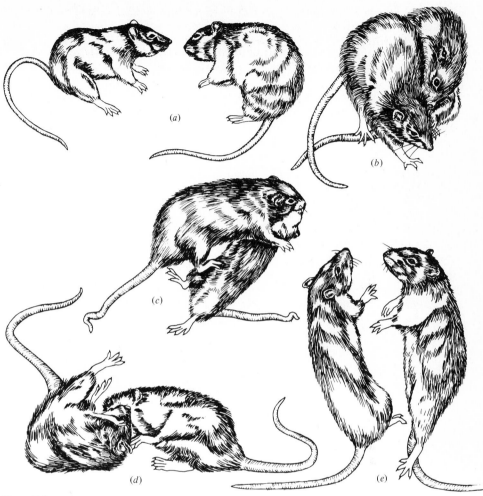

Figure 7.1
The rat's intermale aggressive behavior. (a) The attacker (right) and the newcomer adopt defensive position. The attacker shows raised hair. (b) The two males then exhibit the arched-back threat posture. (c) If the threat is ineffective, fighting ensues. The attacker leaps on and bites the strange male. (d) The attack often causes both rats to fall. (e) Following the attack, the rats show boxing position. (From Barnett, S. A. The rat: A study in behavior. Chicago: Chicago University Press, 1975.)

leave. This action not only prevents submissive males from being exposed to stressful conditions and to possible injury but also provides social stability within an established group by minimizing intergroup conflict.

Learning does not appear to influence the ability of males to exhibit either aggressive or submissive responses (see Eibl-Eibesfeldt, 1961). Rats raised in isolation are able as adults to exhibit effective aggressive or submissive actions. Eibl-Eibesfeldt concluded that ritualistic intermale aggressive behavior is an instinctive, fixed action pattern which is not changed by experience. However, experience does influence the likelihood that males will engage in aggressive conflict with other males. Defeated animals are significantly less aggressive than other males of their species; furthermore, the more times they are defeated, the less likely they are to exhibit intermale aggression (see Kahn, 1951; Lagerspetz, 1964). In contrast, victorious males become more willing to fight with other males. Also, experience enables submissive males to learn to anticipate conflict and, thereby, avoid actual fighting.

Harlow and Harlow's research with primates (1962) provides a vivid demonstration of the importance of experience in intermale aggressiveness. They found that socially deprived male rhesus monkeys directed attacks toward dominant male monkeys (nondeprived primates were not so foolish); the dominant males were very abusive of these socially deprived males. The deprived males also exhibited other behaviors which nondeprived monkeys did not exhibit: harming themselves (for example, head beating) and attacking infants. These observations indicate that social experience provides the direction for intermale aggression.

The Motive for Intermale Aggression

Why do males of the same species fight? To win the affection of a female is one seemingly logical reason. However, evidence clearly indicates that the motivation to engage in intermale aggression is not sexually induced. *First, sexual satiation does not reduce the aggressive tendencies of mice* (Lagerspetz, 1964; Gustafson & Winokur, 1960) *and rats* (Hall & Klein, 1942). *Second, young males behave aggressively toward other males when they are both sexually immature* (Harlow, 1965; Goy, 1968). This aggressiveness takes the form of threat responses, rough-and-tumble play, and sham biting. But the presence of a receptive female does increase the likelihood of intermale aggression. Barnett (1967) assumed that males encountered each other because they approached a receptive female to which they were attracted. This situation initiated intermale hostility.

Competition for available food or water is another possible reason for intermale fighting. But research has demonstrated that the biological need for food or water is not responsible for intermale aggression. Ginsburg and Allee (1942) discovered that neither hunger nor thirst increased intermale fighting. Although two males will fight over food, the level of aggression in this type of situation is actually less than that which occurs in spontaneous intermale encounters (Fredericson, 1950). In addition, the pattern of aggressive behavior of males competing for food differs from that of males fighting with each other.

We might speculate that fear is the force which motivates intermale aggression. However, fear usually inhibits aggressive behavior. Davis (1933) observed that male rats were more apt to attack a strange rat in their home cage than when placed in the stranger's cage with him. Davis suggested that the fear aroused in the novel environment inhibited aggressive behavior. Jones and Nowell (1973) varied the degree of novelty of the environment and discovered that intermale aggression increased as the attacker's familiarity with the environment increased. The only exception to this rule involves fear-induced aggression, a form of aggression which is quite different from intermale aggression. Intermale aggression represents an offensive attack initiated by either a stranger's presence or a reaction to a stranger's threat; fear-induced aggression is a defensive reaction which happens only when escape from danger is impossible. Although fear-induced aggression can occur in response to a threat from a member of the same species, it often reflects perceived danger from another species. Fear-induced aggression will be described in greater detail later in the chapter.

If hunger, thirst, sex, and fear do not motivate intermale aggression, then what does? It seems that fighting is intrinsically reinforcing; that is, males enjoy fighting with each other as long as they do not expect to lose. Strong evidence (see Moyer, 1976) indicates that intermale aggressive behavior is highly reinforcing. One example of the reinforcing property of aggressive responding is Scott's observation (1958) that male mice learned the correct position habit in a T-maze in order to gain the opportunity to attack another mouse. Similarly, Robinson, Alexander, and Bowne (1969) found that male primates learned to press a bar when this behavior resulted in their being allowed to fight with another male.

Lagerspetz (1964) let males fight but interrupted the fight before it was over. Interestingly, the rats would cross an electrified grid if the only reward was being able to continue the conflict. However, rats will not respond to reinitiate the fight if they expect to lose (Fredericson, 1949, 1951). In Fredericson's studies, a match between two male mice was interrupted by placing one of the mice in another compartment of the maze. If this mouse was either winning or evenly matched with his opponent, he pushed open a door and ran through the maze to reach his opponent. However, if he was losing, he remained in the compartment and did not attempt to engage in combat again (a control group of mice not involved in fights behaved the same way). Apparently, males often find conflict reinforcing.

The Function of Intermale Aggression

Intermale aggression appears to serve several important functions (see Johnson, 1972; Lorenz, 1966). This form of aggression is responsible for the establishment of *dominance hierarchies*. Once formed, the dominance system produces a stable social climate in which dominant males can assert their authority or gain possession of objects without resorting to actual fighting. They can dwell close together without the danger of continuous conflict. DeVore (1965) observed that although adolescent male baboons living in the wild fought often, little aggression occurred among adult males that had established their dominance relationships. The absence of conflict enables the group to focus attention on the survival of the group. In addition, the dominance structure influences which males will mate. As we learned in Chapter 6, dominant males are more likely to mate than nondominant males. Since dominant males presumably possess adaptive traits, the greater sexual activity of dominant males increases the group's probability of surviving. The dominance system also reduces the likelihood that males will fight over receptive females. Apparently, intermale aggression represents an adaptive behavioral system which aids in the survival of a species.

Is Intermale Aggression a Trait Found in Humans?

While walking with several friends, my youngest son was approached by an unfamiliar boy who was approximately his age. Having exchanged a few hostile comments, they threw several punches before the other boy ran away. Although this is not a frequent occurrence, my son and his friends do occasionally fight with others boys who live in the neighborhood. These isolated occurrences imply that under some circumstances, people exhibit hostile intermale aggression. A number of psychologists (see Freud, 1930; Lorenz, 1966; Morris, 1967) have suggested that hostile threats and attacks between strangers do occur in humans.

In 1930, Freud pointed to the problem of strangers who meet. He wrote:

> Not merely is this stranger on the whole not worthy of my love, but to be honest I must confess he has more claim to my hostility, even to my hatred. He does not seem to have the least trace of love for me, does not show me the slightest consideration. If it will do

him any good, he has no hesitation in injuring me. . . . What is more, he does not even need to get an advantage from it; if he can merely get a little pleasure out of it, he thinks nothing of jeering at me, insulting me, slandering me, showing his power over me. The bit of truth behind all this—one so eagerly denies—is that men are not gentle, friendly creatures wishing for love, who simply defend themselves if they are attacked, but that a powerful measure of desire for aggression has to be reckoned as part of the instinctual endowment. . . . Anyone who calls to mind the atrocities of the early migrations, of the invasion by the Huns or by the so-called Mongols under Jenghiz Khan and Tamurlane, of the sack of Jerusalem by the pious Crusaders, even indeed the horrors of the last world war, will have to bow his head humbly before the truth of this view of man. (Sigmund Freud Copyright Ltd. The Institute of Psycho-Analysis, and the Hogath Press, Ltd., for permission to quote from the Complete works of Sigmund Freud, *translated and edited by James Strachey, Vol. 21. London: Hogath Press, 1959.)*

Morris (1967) argued that humans signify their intentions by using various gestures, some indicating hostility and others submission or appeasement. According to Morris, the stare, a threat gesture, is common among humans and primates.

Moore and Gilliland's study (1921) implies that the ability to maintain a stare is related to the level of aggressiveness. To identify the 13 most aggressive and the 13 least aggressive students at Dartmouth College, the faculty rated the aggressiveness, reliability, and personality of 1,480 students, the whole student body. Moore and Gilliland reported that the president of the senior class, the quarterback of the football team, and the track manager were among the 13 students rated most aggressive. The "low aggression" group, according to the investigators, were "decidedly without prominence." These two groups of students were asked to perform mental arithmetic problems while simultaneously staring at the experimenters. Moore and Gilliland found that the subjects in the "low aggression" group shifted their stare an average of 5.5 times during each problem, in contrast to those in the "high aggression" group, who stopped staring only 0.5 times during each problem. Also, the "high aggression" subjects were more likely than the "low aggression" subjects to shock another subject. The results of their study suggest that highly aggressive people more readily employ threats and are more willing to act aggressively than nonaggressive people. After examining subjects of high and low dominance, Strongman and Champness (1968) reported results comparable to those of Moore and Gilliland.

Threat gestures provoke attack; appeasement gestures, by contrast, inhibit attack. Morris (1967) speculated that some contemporary human rituals (for example, bowing, bending over when being spanked, and lowering one's head during prayer) are related to primitive gestures of submission.

Our discussion suggests that intermale aggression is an instinctive trait found not only in animals, but also in humans. However, while it is clear that males fight with strangers, it is possible that this fighting reflects either irritable or instrumental aggression. The influence of these other motives could be controlled by ensuring that fighting occurs only between males who are not irritated. Unfortunately, no direct investigation has indicated that fighting between unfamiliar human males reflects intermale aggression. Several types of indirect evidence, however, seem to provide support for this view. First, males are typically more aggressive than females (see Blurton, 1969; McIntyre, 1972; Sears, 1965); yet, this difference may reflect only greater irritable aggressiveness, which is more likely to occur in men than in women. Furthermore, as will be seen in the next section, the male sex hormone testosterone has an important effect on aggressiveness in male animals and humans. However, testosterone also has an influence on irritable aggressiveness. In male animals testosterone definitely influences intermale aggression as well as irritable aggression, but no research has attempted to determine its effect on these two aggressive motives in humans. Further research is necessary to allow us to know whether human males have an innate tendency to fight with strangers.

The Physiological Basis of Intermale Aggression

The likelihood that one male will attack another, the intensity of his aggressiveness during a fight, and the probability that he will be successful in combat are influenced by several hormonal systems. The central nervous system detects the presence of a stranger and, under appropriate environmental conditions, initiates attack. In addition, the CNS must anticipate possible defeat so that the submissive posture can be exhibited to prevent injury. The following discussion begins by describing the hormonal systems involved in intermale aggression; this is followed by a description of the influence of the CNS.

Hormonal influence.   One hormone, *testosterone*, provides the aggressiveness necessary to engage in successful combat. Three hormones—*ACTH, progesterone, and estrogen*—inhibit intermale aggression. Let's now examine evidence which indicates the excitatory influence of testosterone and the inhibitory affect of ACTH, progesterone, and estrogen.

The effect of testosterone.   There is substantial evidence that testosterone plays a critical role in the development and maintenance of intermale aggressive behavior. The results of three types of studies document the influence of testosterone on intermale aggression.

First, studies have investigated naturally occurring differences in the level of testosterone. These experiments have shown that higher levels of testosterone correlate with greater intermale aggressiveness. Several methods can be used to assess changes in the level of testosterone. One technique examines the changes which occur during intermale aggression at puberty, when testosterone levels rise. Although prepubescent males do engage in intermale aggression, their aggressive behavior is clearly different from that of adult males. Young males' intermale aggressiveness involves more vigorous physical activity but is less serious and emotional than that of adult males. For example, Seward (1945) noted that after puberty male rats engaged in more intense, emotional combat with other rats. Similar results have been reported in mice (Lagerspetz & Talo, 1967) and mink (MacLennon & Bailey, 1969). Experimenters have also compared the correlation between the level of testosterone in adults and the frequency, intensity, and success of intermale aggression. This research points out that a male's intermale aggressive tendencies are strongly related to his level of testosterone.

A study by Rose, Holaday, and Bernstein (1971), which demonstrated the significant influence of the level of testosterone in adult male rhesus monkeys, observed the intensity of aggressive behavior (threatening and chasing) and both the reception and the exhibition of submissive behavior. In addition, they determined dominance rank by observing interactions among the monkeys and by measuring their plasma testosterone level. Rose, Holaday, and Bernstein discovered that the intensity of aggressive behavior directed toward another male was significantly correlated with the level of testosterone; that is, the higher the level, the more aggressive the behavior which the male exhibited while fighting and the more dominant he was (see Figure 7.2). Furthermore, the male primates submitted to threats of males that were more dominant, but their own threats

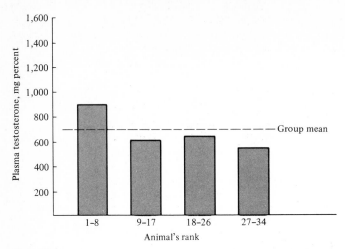

Figure 7.2
Mean level of plasma testosterone for each quartile of the dominance hierarchy in male rhesus monkeys. The most dominant males had a significantly higher testosterone level than those in the lower quartiles. (From Rose, R. M., Holaday, J. W., & Bernstein, I. S. Nature, 1971, 231, 366–368.)

caused less dominant males to submit. These observations indicate that the level of testosterone influences both the dominance and the aggressiveness of male rhesus monkeys.

Similar results have been reported with human males (see Sheard, 1979). For example, Scarumella and Brown (1978) compared the level of serum testosterone in hockey players with their coaches' rating of their aggressiveness. They found that the most aggressive hockey players had the highest testosterone levels. However, we must note again that it is unclear whether in human males testosterone influences intermale aggression or other forms of aggression, or both.

Second, there have been experiments which reduce the level of testosterone. In such studies, a lowered level of intermale aggressiveness has been found. The most frequently employed method of reducing the level of testosterone is removing the testes. Although castration does reduce both the intensity and the frequency of intermale aggression, its influence in primates and humans is quite variable (see Moyer, 1976, for a review of this literature). This section briefly presents several studies to illustrate the effect of castration on intermale aggression in lower animals and humans.

A classic study by Beeman (1947) examined whether the castration of mice affected intermale aggressive behavior. She evaluated several measures of aggression, such as tail rattling, parrying, attacking, and fighting, and found that while uncastrated mice showed intense intermale aggression, no castrated mice exhibited any aggressiveness when placed with another mouse. Timidity following castration has also been observed in many other species, including the rat (for example, Barfield, Busch, & Wallen, 1972; Beach, 1945), the gerbil (Sayler, 1970), and the hamster (Vandenberg, 1971).

On the other hand, marked individual differences do occur in adult primates (Wilson, 1968; Phoenix, Slob, & Goy, 1973) and in humans (Bremer, 1959; Stürup, 1972). After castration, some male primates and humans are docile; others seem to be only slightly affected. Although the reason for this variability has not been firmly established, the effect of castration seems to depend upon social experience. Wilson (1968) discovered that 10 castrated young rhesus monkeys living on Cayo Santiago Island off the coast of Puerto Rico were less aggressive and dominant than uncastrated rhesus monkeys, but, interestingly, several of these castrated monkeys formed a coalition and successfully fought together against more dominant males.

Why is social aggressive experience important? In all likelihood, once a male has engaged in conflict with another male, he has learned whether he can expect future aggression to be successful or unsuccessful. Since intermale aggression is intrinsically reinforcing and since all but the least dominant male has had some successful aggressive experience, males will continue to fight even after castration if they expect to succeed. Thus, under these conditions, hormonal influence diminishes and the importance of psychological processes increases. In contrast, immature males have not gained sufficient experience to compensate for the reduced aggressiveness caused by castration.

Third, some studies have investigated the influence of treatments which increase the level of testosterone. This research indicates that the administration of testosterone can intensify intermale aggressiveness. Many studies have shown that administering testosterone to castrated mice (for example, Beeman, 1947; Sigg, 1969; Luttge & Hall, 1973), rats (for example, Beach, 1945; Barfield, Busch, & Wallen, 1972), gerbils (Sayler, 1970), and hamsters (Vandenberg, 1971) increases intermale aggressive tendencies. Furthermore, Suchowsky, Pergressi, and Bonsignori (1971) discovered that testosterone injections intensified aggressiveness in uncastrated male mice. The influence of testosterone on primates appears to depend upon social experience. While Mirsky (1955) found that testosterone given to adult macaque monkeys had no effect, Kling (1968) reported that in some juvenile macaque monkeys the level of intermale aggression doubled after testosterone injections.

Inhibitory hormones. Three hormones appear to suppress intermale aggression. One of these hormones is *adrenocorticotrophic hormone, ACTH.* Earlier it was noted that fear inhibits intermale aggressive behavior. One consequence of exposure to fearsome circumstances is the release of ACTH from the anterior pituitary gland (see the Appendix, Figure A.8); this suppresses intermale aggression.

Several types of evidence document the inhibitory influence of ACTH on intermale aggression. Mice which have been given direct administration of ACTH have a significantly lower level of intermale aggressiveness than control mice (Brain, Nowell, & Wouters, 1971; Leshner, Walker, Johnson, Kelling, Kreisler, & Svare, 1973). *Adrenalectomy,* surgical removal of the adrenal gland, produces a significant increase in ACTH because the adrenal hormones no longer inhibit its release. Numerous studies (see Brian, Nowell, & Wouters, 1971; Harding & Leshner, 1972; Svare & Leshner, 1972) indicate that adrenalectomized mice are significantly less aggressive in combat with another mouse than normal mice. In contrast, the glucocorticoid hormones released by the adrenal gland inhibits ACTH release; this in turn causes a significant increase in intermale aggressiveness. For example, Brian, Nowell, and Wouters (1971) discovered that mice which had been injected with dexamethasone showed increased fighting. Similarly, hydrocortisone enhances the level of aggressiveness in male mice in conflict with another male (see Banerjee, 1971; Kostowski, Rewerski, & Piechocki, 1970).

Recall that males are more likely to fight than females. One reason for this is the inhibitory effect which the female sex hormones *estrogen* and *progesterone* have on intermale aggression. Researchers using male mice (for example, Anton, Schwartz, & Kramer, 1968; Suchowsky, Pegressi, & Bonsignori, 1971) have shown that estrogen reduced the occurrence of intermale aggression. Similarly, Suchowsky, Pergressi, and Bonsignori (1969) reported that a progesterone injection also suppressed intermale aggression in male mice.

We have seen that hormones influence the level of intermale aggressive behavior. The central nervous system translates the influence of these hormones into the elicitation or inhibition of intermale aggression. Let's now focus on the CNS areas which govern the level of fighting behavior.

Neural influence.   Several areas in the CNS initiate attack behavior. The *anterior portion of the lateral hypothalamus* appears to be one area which arouses intermale aggression. Adams (1971) reported that male rats lesioned in this area displayed no aggressive response to another male placed in their home cage. In contrast, Robinson, Alexander, and Bowne (1969) electrically stimulated the anterior portion of the lateral hypothalamus in male rhesus monkeys to induce vicious attack behavior. The hypothalamic stimulation caused these male primates to attack males of higher dominance—an aggressive reaction which was not exhibited before the stimulation. The stimulated males were not motivated to attack a female monkey or an inanimate object; thus, their behavior clearly represents an example of intermale aggression. During each stimulation, a dominant and a stimulated male engaged in intense fighting. After several episodes of intermale aggression, the dominance roles reversed: the formerly dominant male exhibited submissive behavior, and the stimulated male became aggressive. As an indication of his new dominance, the stimulated male would pace freely around the cage, mount the female consort of the other male, and be groomed by her. Similar results were reported by Alexander and Perachio (1973).

In the last section, we saw that testosterone stimulates intermale aggression in the presence of an appropriate attack object. Christie and Barfield's study (1973) demonstrated that testosterone implants in the lateral hypothalamus of castrated male rats aroused intense aggressive behavior in those rats when they were placed with another male rat. These observations indicate that through its stimulating effect on the lateral hypothalamus, testosterone can arouse intermale aggression.

Several other areas, especially the amygdala, appear to be involved in the initiation of intermale aggression. Miczek, Brykczynski, and Grossman (1974) discovered that intermale aggression between rats was significantly reduced by destroying either the *periamygdaloid cortex,* the *cortical amygdaloid nucleus,* or the *bed nuclei of the stria terminals.* Miczek, Brykczynski, and Grossman noticed that these lesions did not affect either irritable aggression or predatory aggression and concluded that these areas appear to control only intermale aggression. It is important to note that stimulation of some areas of these excitatory brain systems is also highly reinforcing; that is, animals will learn a behavior in order to obtain this stimulation. Apparently, the intrinsically reinforcing property of intermale aggression is due to the involvement of the reward system of the brain.

Other brain areas inhibit intermale aggression. The *midbrain reticular formation* seems to be an important area in the control of aggressive tendencies. Kesner and Keiser (1973) observed an increase in intermale fighting which followed destruction of the midbrain reticular formation at the level of the inferior colliculus [MRF (IC); see Appendix, Figure A.7]. In contrast, lesions of the midbrain reticular formation at the superior colliculus level did not affect intermale aggression, and lesions at the inferior colliculus level did not disrupt irritable aggression or predatory aggression. Kesner and Keiser's results indicate that the MRF (IC) neurons specifically function to inhibit intermale aggression.

MATERNAL AGGRESSION

A mother perceiving a threat to her young will attack the source of the perceived danger. Many animal species display maternal aggression, including squirrels (Taylor, 1966), langurs (Jay, 1963), baboons (DeVore, 1963), chimpanzees (Chance & Jolly, 1970), rabbits (Ross, Swain, Zarrow, & Dennenberg, 1963), sheep (Hersher, Richmond, & Moore, 1963), weasels (Lockie, 1966), cats (Schneirla, Rosenblatt, & Tobach, 1963), rats (Barnett, 1964), mice (King, 1963), and cows (Altman, 1963). But not all animal species are maternally aggressive. For example, King (1963) found that some strains of mice do not exhibit maternal aggression. A similar observation was made with rats (Flandera & Novakova, 1971) and rabbits (Ross, Swain, Zarrow, & Dennenberg, 1963).

The likelihood of maternal aggression is related to the mother's level of maternal behavior; that is, the more maternal attention the mother shows her young, the more likely she is to attack any animal which she perceives as harmful to her young. As you'll see in Chapter 9, after giving birth, mothers show a high degree of maternal care for a short period of time. Once offspring begin to mature and explore the environment, the level of maternal behavior declines, as does the tendency of the mother to protect her young.

Gandelman (1972), observing the importance of the age of the infant on the intensity of maternal aggression, discovered that during the first 14 days postpartum, female mice are extremely aggressive toward any intruder. From day 14 to day 21, the likelihood of maternal aggressive behavior declined; on day 21, the mothers did not attack any intruder. Other species also show this time-dependency. For example, Revlis and Moyer (1969) found that female rats exhibited intense maternal aggression during the first five days postpartum and that the incidence of aggression toward an intruder declined from day 5 to day 15.

The Releasing Stimulus

Several variables appear to play a vital role in the initiation of maternal aggression. *First, a mother is much more apt to attack a strange animal of her species than a familiar animal.* Svare and Gandelman (1973) found that nursing female mice readily attacked an unfamiliar mouse but refused to attack a familiar mouse. Female mice nursing their young will even attack a strange male mouse—a behavior which they are not otherwise likely to exhibit. Calhoun (1962) observed similar selectiveness in rats.

Second, lactating females are more likely to attack an adult than a young member of the species. For example, Svare and Gandelman (1973) noted that nursing mice did not attack a 1- or a 10-day-old intruder but did attack a 14 and a 20-day-old intruder.

Third, mothers typically are more protective of young in the nest than in other places. Calhoun (1962) reported that any alien rats that neared the mothers' burrow were attacked; but these females were much less likely to attack alien rats in other places (for example, the food pen).

Although nursing mothers of many species are aggressive only if other animals approach their young, the nursing mothers of some species will attack all intruders. Hersher, Richmond, and Moore (1963) found that female sheep are not selectively aggressive and will attack all approaching animals, regardless of age or sex. Schneirla, Rosenblatt, and Tobach (1963) observed similar behavior in cats. However, female sheep or cats, even if their young have been removed, will attack all other animals. Schneirla, Rosenblatt, and Tobach suggest that increased irritability following parturition is responsible for the nonspecific aggressiveness of nursing mothers in some species.

The Aggressive Response

The maternal aggressive response differs greatly from intermale fighting. Herrero (1970) noted that a sow bear with cubs exerts considerable effort to stay several hundred yards away from other animals but will attack an approaching intruder even if this intruder has not cornered her. Altman (1963) made a similar observation with female moose.

Maternal aggressive behavior represents a direct attempt by mothers to harm intruders. Gandelman (1972) noticed that—unlike intermale aggression, which is preceded by warning behavior—maternal aggression included no warning. He observed that nursing female mice continue their aggressive attack response—biting the flanks and the neck region of an intruder—until the intruder either leaves or dies. Apparently, females will exhibit intense aggressive behavior to protect their young.

Although women will allow strangers to approach their children, most mothers are protective of their offspring and will not allow them to encounter danger. In all likelihood, women have a greater ability than animals to anticipate danger. It is this ability which allows women who are mothers to avoid dangerous circumstances that might require aggressive action. Yet, most women undoubtedly would be intensely aggressive if their children were threatened.

The Physiology of Maternal Aggression

Unfortunately, we have limited knowledge about the physiological processes which are responsible for maternal aggression. While we do know that the loss of maternal aggressive tendencies coincides with a reduced level of *prolactin* (see Gandelman, 1972), there has been no experimental evaluation of the role of this hormone in the control of maternal aggression. Future research is necessary to identify the biological systems which control maternal aggression.

SEX-RELATED AGGRESSION

The Releasing Stimulus

Moyer (1976) asserted that sex-related aggressive behavior and sexual behavior are aroused by identical stimuli. According to Moyer, males show primarily sex-related aggression, and the male's aggressiveness is typically elicited by a female of his species. In many species, sex-related aggression is an integral part of the courtship process. For example, Etkin (1964) reported that before copulation, a male and a female ferret engage in intense fighting for a period of 1 hour or longer. Eisenberg and Leyhausen (1972) noted that a similar intense aggressive response occurrs before intercourse in a number of mammalian species. However, in some species, sex-related aggression does not always precede sexual activity. For example, recording the incidence of sex-related aggression in rhesus monkeys, Carpenter (1942) found that an aroused male occasionally attacked a receptive female. We saw in Chapter 6 that some humans inflict pain on their partner during sexual activity; thus, sex-related aggression also occurs in people.

The Aggressive Response

The intensity of sex-related aggressive behavior is typically controlled; thus, serious injury does not occur. For example, MacLennon and Bailey (1969) reported that the male mink will grab the scruff of the female's neck during copulation in a manner which resembles his response during intermale aggression. However, the female will not be seriously injured during intercourse, even though she is very vulnerable. The gray fox also displays this intense aggressive behavior during sexual activity (Fox, 1969). Evidently, while the aggressive behavior of male animals can be quite intense during sexual activity, they usually control it to prevent serious harm.

However, under some conditions sex-related aggression is violent and results in serious injury. Carpenter (1942) observed 22 attacks by male rhesus monkeys and noted that 6 inflicted serious injury on the female. One female was severely cut on her arm and face; another received a gash on her hip which damaged a motor nerve, leaving her premanently crippled. Although sex-related aggression in humans often occurs between consenting adults and does not produce serious injury, there are occasions—called *rape*—during which a sexually aroused male harms an unwilling female. There were 56,090 reported cases of rape in the United States in 1975; this illustrates the frequency of this extreme form of sex-related aggression (FBI, 1975). In addition, it is estimated that only one rape out of five is reported (see Amir, 1971).

The Aggressive Motive

Our discussion suggests that sexually related stimuli arouse aggressive behavior. A number of psychologists have investigated the relationship between sexual cues and aggressive behavior by measuring the level of hostile fantasy in subjects after they have been exposed to sexually arousing stimuli. Some studies (for example, Barclay, 1971; Clark, 1953) reported that aggression, reflected in subjects' written stories, increased more after exposure to erotic stimuli than after exposure to nonerotic stimuli. However, other studies (for example, Clark & Sensiber, 1955; Mosher & Katz, 1970) have not found increased aggressiveness in this situation. Although there is no definitive explanation for these contradictory results, it may be that only in some persons will sexually related stimuli arouse aggressiveness. We saw in Chapter 6 that some, but not most, sexually aroused men behave in an overtly aggressive fashion. Thus, the theory that sexual stimuli arouse aggression only in some men seems to be a reasonable conclusion. We do not know why most men do not become aggressive in sexual situations. This absence of sex-related aggression may reflect the inhibition of aggressive tendencies or the absence of an aggressive motive. Future research should seek to identify the conditions under which people respond aggressively to sex-related stimuli.

We must also emphasize that rape may often reflect the expression of irritable or instrumental aggression (or both) rather than sex-related aggression. Murray Cohen and his colleagues (see Cohen, Garofalo, Boucher, & Seghorn, 1971) identified four major types of rapists. The *aggressive-aim rapist* attempts to injure his victim but usually does not engage in intercourse with her. Anger characterizes the emotional state of the aggressive-aim rapist and in all likelihood, his aggressive actions represent an example of irritable aggression. In contrast, the *sexual-aim rapist* is highly aroused sexually and uses the minimal level of violence needed to accomplish his sexual aim. The sexual-aim rapist is not angry and his aggression is probably a case of instrumental aggression. The *sex-aggression-fusion rapist* is both sexually aroused and motivated to harm his victim. The *impulse rapist* will seize the opportunity, perhaps during a robbery, to rape a victim. These last two types of rape may reflect the operation of sex-related aggression.

The Physiological Basis of Sex-Related Aggression

In Chapter 6, we saw that castration effectively reduces sexual motivation. Castration also appears to be a useful therapeutic technique to eliminate the aggressiveness of sexually violent men (see Moyer, 1976). For example, Hawke (1950) observed this phenomenon in 330 prison inmates in Kansas, all sex offenders. According to Hawke, after castration, some of these sex offenders were paroled and others became cooperative in prison. Furthermore, none of them later committed a sex crime. Stürup (1961) studied Danish male sex offenders; he found that after they were freed, the likelihood of repeating the crime was 10 times higher for noncastrated men than for castrated men.

The effects of castration appear to be limited to sexual and aggressive behavior. Bremer (1959) evaluated the effects of castration on 224 Norwegian sex offenders. Although castration eliminated both sexual motivation and sex-related aggression, it did not alter any serious psychological disturbance (for example, schizophrenia) which existed before the operation.

Drugs which decrease the level of testosterone have been successfully used in recent years for treating sex offenders. Blumer and Migeon (1973) reported that *medroxyproges-terone* (Provera), a drug which resembles natural progesterone and which lowers testosterone level, administered for 10 days to males with sexual deviations, successfully reduced sexual arousal and sex-related aggressive behavior. Money (1970) also found that Provera is an effective treatment for sex offenders.

FEAR-INDUCED AGGRESSION

The Releasing Stimulus

In Chapter 2, we saw that exposure to dangerous environmental conditions arouses the intense, internal emotional state of fear. Fear motivates animals or people to attempt to escape from aversive situations. However, aggression often occurs if the escape response fails. This aggressive behavior continues until the adversity terminates or until the animal or the person is unable to fight.

What conditions motivate fear-induced aggression? According to Moyer (1976), a barrier causes an escape response to be ineffective and necessitates the use of an aggressive reaction to an adversity. For example, normally docile animals or humans confined to an inescapable environment will become aggressive if frightened by an anticipated attack from another animal or person. Consider the following example. Suppose that while you are walking to class at night, someone approaches from behind and places one hand over your mouth and the other around your waist. How would you respond to this attack? First, you probably would attempt to escape; but if this escape response fails because the attacker's grasp is too tight, in all likelihood you will become aggressive. Your aggressive response might be biting the hands or stomping the feet of the attacker. If this behavior frees you, you could kick the person in the groin or scream for help. You are apt to continue your aggressive behavior until either the attack stops or you can no longer resist.

Fear-induced aggression clearly differs from the other forms of aggression described in this chapter. Fear-induced aggressive behavior is a defense reaction exhibited by animals or humans only when they feel threatened and perceive escape to be impossible. Thus, the aggressive behavior of a cornered or captured animal or person is a final reaction to a perceived life-threatening situation. On the other hand, animals or people showing other forms of aggressive behavior do not feel threatened. Under these conditions, non-fear-induced aggression reflects an immediate response rather than a last recourse.

The Aggressive Response

Animals unable to escape danger will exhibit intense aggressive behavior. For example, Leyhausen (1965) described the defensive aggressive responses of cats. He noted that if cornered cats cannot escape danger, they face the threat and hiss; they also show piloerection (erection of fur) and pupillodilation (dilation of the pupil). Eibl-Eibesfeldt (1970) observed that frightened squirrels emit a clattering sound with their front teeth and lay their ears back. They also display a posture, such as rearing on their haunches and stretching, which causes them to appear larger; the intent to this threat is to terminate danger.

Fox and Apelbaum (1969), studying the fear-induced aggressive reaction of several rabbit species, observed that frightened rabbits first oriented themselves toward danger and then emitted a loud noise. The attack continued with stabbing, reaching movements of the forelegs; striking the ground repeatedly with the hindlegs; and biting the attacker, the source of the danger. Only frightened squirrels and mothers protecting their young display such aggressive behavior. Moyer (1976) noted the similarity between fear-induced aggression and maternal aggression. The mother may perceive danger, but the presence of her young prevents her escape. It may be that maternal aggression is a special category of a fear-induced aggression.

It is often difficult to distinguish between fear-induced aggression and irritable aggression. There are several reasons for this. The behavior patterns of these two forms of aggression not only are similar but also involve strong affective reaction. The biological systems which mediate each type of aggression differ, but these differences cannot be detected by observations of overt behavior. The main observable distinction is that fear-induced aggression occurs only after escape is perceived to be impossible, whereas irritable aggression is an aggressive reaction produced directly by frustration or anger. Yet, detecting whether an escape response was attempted before aggressive behavior is often impossible.

Fear-induced aggression is not the only response which occurs in extremely frightened animals or humans. Perceiving that escape is impossible may cause animals or humans to freeze or to assume a submissive posture. As we saw in Chapter 3, the species-specific defensive reaction determines what behavior is exhibited in threatening situations. However, conditions can alter this behavior. If frightened animals do not expect aggressive behavior to be successful, they employ other defensive responses to terminate danger. The submissive behavior which nondominant males display when threatened by a dominant male provides support for the view that circumstances determine whether or not fear will motivate aggressiveness.

The Physiology of Fear-Induced Aggression

We have seen that the releasing stimulus of fear-induced aggression differs from those of other types of aggression. The brain systems which control fear-induced aggression are also separate from those governing other aggressive behaviors. Excitatory areas implicated in the activation of fear-induced aggression include the temporal lobes and several areas of the amygdala. Several amygdala areas and the septal area appear to be involved in the inhibition of fear-induced aggressive behavior.

The temporal lobe. Kluver and Bucy's classic study (1937) using rhesus monkeys indicated that lesions of the temporal lobes significantly reduced fearfulness. This has also been found with human schizophrenic patients (see Terzian & DalleOre, 1955). Other studies have shown that destruction of the temporal lobes reduced fear-induced aggression. For example, Myers (1972) and Franzen and Myers (1973) found that a lesion of either the anterior third of the temporal lobes or the prefrontal cortex severely disrupted the fear-induced aggressive response of rhesus monkeys.

Amygdala.   The *central amygdaloid nucleus* and the *dorsal section of the basal amygdaloid nuclei* appear to be the excitatory areas for fear-induced aggression. Two types of evidence support this view. *First, stimulation of these areas produces increased fear-induced aggressive behavior.* For example, Fonberg (1965) discovered that stimulation of the central amygdaloid nucleus produced aggressive behavior in confined dogs. Similarly, Anand and Dua (1956) and Wood (1958) noted that arousal of the central nucleus and the dorsal section of the basal nuclei motivated fear-induced aggression in cats; and Ursin (1972) found this in primates.

Second, destruction of these excitatory amygdaloid areas produces a fearless animal that will not show aggressive behavior when in danger. There is strong evidence that lesions of these exitatory areas lead to an absence of both fear and fear-induced aggression in threatening situations in many animal species, such as cats (for example Schreiner & Kling, 1953; Shealy & Peale, 1957), wild Norway rats (for example Galef, 1970a; Wood, 1958), dogs (Fonberg, 1965), and primates (for example, Rosvold, Mirsky, & Pribam, 1954; Kling, Dicks, & Gurwitz, 1968). Blanchard and Blanchard's observations (1972) of the behavior of albino rats following *amydalectomy* provide a dramatic illustration of the importance of these areas in motivating fear and fear-induced aggression. An albino rat which sees a cat will freeze and remain immobile as long as the cat is present. On the other hand, an amygdalectomized rat shows no fear of cats. One of Blanchard and Blanchard's amygdalectomized rats climbed upon a cat's head and nibbled the cat's ear. Even after being attacked and released by the cat, the rat attached itself to the cat's back.

The *ventral portion of the basal* and the *lateral nucleus of the amygdala* appear to play an inhibitory role in fear-induced aggression. Fonberg (1965, 1968) reported that stimulation of these amygdala areas inhibits both fear and fear-induced aggressive behavior in cats and in dogs.

Evidence also indicates that the amygdala has an important influence on fear and fear-induced aggression in people. Hitchcock (1979) reported that stimulation of the medial amygdala produced fear and fear-induced aggressive reactions; Kaada (1972) observed that destruction of this area of the amygdala reduced fear and fear-induced aggressiveness.

However, the precise anatomical location of these areas of the amygdala which affect fear-induced aggression in people have not been identified. Some studies (see Heath, 1964, Heath & Mickle, 1960) have even indicated that fear (and fear-induced aggression) and anger (and irritable aggression) can be elicited by stimulating the same anatomical location. Moyer (1976) suggested one likely reason for this observation. The centers of the amygdala which control fear-induced aggression and irritable aggression in animals are located very close to each other. It is quite likely that in these studies, which used humans as subjects, some of the electrodes were placed in an area which could activate both aggressive centers. Although further research is obviously necessary, a reasonable conclusion based on present data gathered from animal and human subjects is that a distinct fear-induced aggressive system exists which is probably located in the identical anatomical structure for all mammalian species.

Septum.   The function of the septal area is to inhibit fear-induced aggression. Several studies have found that septal lesions in rats produce an increased tendency to escape and an aggressive response to threat (see Brady & Nauta, 1955; King & Meyer, 1958). Schnurr (1972) identified the *anterior septal areas* as being critical in the inhibition of fear-induced aggression. She discovered that mice lesioned in this area showed both intense attempts to escape danger and vigorous biting when restrained.

IRRITABLE AGGRESSION

Last week my family decided to see a movie; but upon arriving at the theater, we were informed that the show had been canceled because of a defective copy. I expressed my displeasure harshly to the ticket seller, even though she was not at fault. My hostile behavior exemplifies irritable aggression; perhaps you have also become aggressive in a similarly annoying situation.

Irritable aggression is elicited by one of several affective reactions which include frustration and anger. Specific environmental circumstances arouse these emotional responses, which in turn produce irritable aggressive behavior. In a mild form, irritable aggression involves an overt display of annoyance or a halfhearted threat. In contrast, extreme cases of irritable aggression involve destructive, uncontrollable rage.

Situations Which Arouse Irritable Aggression

Frustration-aggression hypothesis. In 1939, Dollard, Doob, Miller, Mowrer, and Sears proposed that blocking of ongoing, goal-directed behavior produces an internal emotional state called *frustration*. According to their view, "frustration always leads to some form of aggression" and "aggression is always a consequence of frustration." Although it is now clear that frustration does not always motivate an aggressive reaction and that other annoying circumstances can arouse aggression, considerable research in both animals and humans points out that frustration can activate aggressive behavior (see Buss, 1961; Berkowitz, 1969; Miller, 1941). Let's look at several studies which indicate that frustration can arouse aggressive behavior.

Azrin, Hutchinson, and Hake (1966) trained hungry pigeons to peck a key for food. After the pigeons had learned the pecking behavior, the experimenters alternated periods of reinforcement and nonreinforcement. Throughout both periods, one pigeon was restrained at the back of the chamber. Only during the nonreinforced trial did the other pigeons attack the restrained pigeon, pecking its head and the throat, pulling its feathers, bruising its skin, and sometimes seriously injuring it. Other investigators have shown that nonreward motivates attack behavior in pigeons (Flory, 1969; Gentry, 1968), mice (Lagerspetz & Nurmi, 1964), rats (Gallup, 1965; Thompson & Bloom, 1966), and primates (Seay & Harlow, 1965).

Frustration can even motivate aggression directed toward an inanimate object. For example, Keller and Schoenfeld (1950) observed that during the extinction of a bar-pressing response, rats attacked the bar. In addition, Hutchinson, Azrin, and Hunt (1968) reported that primates attacked a rubber hose more frequently during periods of nonreward than during periods of reward.

Researchers have consistently observed aggressive behavior in humans who are frustrated. For example, consider a study by Kelly and Hake (1970). Their subjects, 14- to 18-year-old males, pulled on a knob to receive a monetary reward (see Chapter 1). There was a fixed-ratio schedule of reinforcement. At various times during the study a noxious 68-decibel tone was presented. Subjects could terminate the tone by either pressing a button (this required 1.5 pounds of pressure) or punching a padded cushion (this required 20 pounds of force). Kelly and Hake felt that punching the cushion constituted an aggressive reaction. During the portion of the experiment when the subjects were being rewarded, they rarely punched the cushion. In contrast, there was a significant increase in the frequency of punches when the knob-pulling behavior was no longer rewarded. Harrell (1972) replicated the results of Kelly and Hake's study and also showed that the force of the punches increased in response to frustration.

Barker, Dembo, and Lewin (1941) found an even more obvious influence of frustration on aggression. In their study, some children were led to a playroom containing many attractive toys. However, these children were not immediately allowed to play with the toys; instead, for several minutes they could only look at the toys through a window. Barker, Dembo, and Lewin assumed that this treatment would frustrate these children. Other children could go immediately to the toys and thus were not frustrated. Barker, Dembo, and Lewin reported that when they finally were given access to the toys, the frustrated children played destructively with the toys, frequently smashing them; the children who had not been frustrated played quietly with the toys.

Anger and irritable aggression.   Several aversive events appear to produce anger and, thereby, impulsively activate aggressiveness. These include physical pain, unpleasant environmental conditions (for example, extreme heat or cold), and psychological threat or insult.

Physical pain.   A number of psychologists have investigated pain-induced aggressive behavior in rats (see Moyer, 1976; Ulrich, 1966). In a typical study, two rats placed in a small chamber are given a series of periodic electric shocks to the feet. These rats adopt the boxing posture: they face one another and rear up on their hind legs. But they do this only when they are being shocked; after the shock has terminated, the rats avoid any social interaction. Although psychologists have used laboratory rats in research to explain the causes of human behavior, it is clear that laboratory rats and humans respond quite differently to painful events. Laboratory rats react by adopting the defensive threat posture. They do not physically attack one another except when they are trying to avoid contact with the shock grids by climbing on top of each other. In contrast, other animals and humans respond with an intense overt attack.

Azrin, Hutchinson, and Sallery (1964) observed that when primates are shocked, they attack other monkeys, rats, or mice. In addition, monkeys which are being shocked will attack a toy tiger (Plotnick, Mir, & Delgado, 1971), a stuffed doll, or a ball (Azrin, 1964). Shock-induced aggressive attack has also been reported in cats (Ulrich, Wolff, & Azrin, 1964), wild rats (Galef, 1970a, 1970b; Karli, 1956), and gerbils (Dunstone, Cannon, Chickson, & Burns, 1972).

During the past 20 years, Leon Berkowitz and his associates (see Berkowitz, 1962, 1969, 1971, 1978) have conducted research supporting the theory that anger induced by exposure to painful events can lead to aggression in humans. In one of these studies (Berkowitz & LePage, 1967), subjects were asked to list, within a period of 5 minutes, ideas which could be used by a publicity agent to increase sales of a product. A confederate then rated some subjects' performance as poor by giving these subjects seven electric shocks; this confederate shocked other subjects only once, to indicate a positive evaluation. According to Berkowitz and LePage, the seven-shock evaluation angered subjects, but the one-shock evaluation did not. Next, all the subjects evaluated the confederate's performance by giving the confederate from one to seven shocks. Table 7.3 presents the results of this study. (As will soon be shown, this experiment was more complex; but we are now interested only in the "no object" conditions.) Subjects who had received seven shocks retaliated by giving the confederate significantly more shocks than the other subjects did. These results clearly indicate that painful events can motivate aggressive behavior.

In an experiment by Berkowitz, Cochran, and Embree (1980), cold water (6° Celsius) rather than shock created the painful event. Subjects were told that they were participating in a study evaluating the degree to which harsh environmental conditions affect work performance. Each subject's task was to supervise a partner's solutions to a

Table 7.3
Mean Number of Shocks Administered to Confederate

Condition	Nonangered	Angered
Associated weapons	2.60	6.07
Unassociated weapons	2.20	5.67
No object	3.07	4.67
Badminton racquets	—	4.60

From: Berkowitz, L., & LePage, A. Weapons as aggression-eliciting stimuli. *Journal of Personality and Social Psychology*, 1967, 7, 202–207. Copyright 1967 by the American Psychological Association. Reprinted by permission.

number of problems; the partner, who was in fact a confederate, occupied an adjacent room. The subject was either to reward or to punish the partner; reward consisted of five-cent coins, punishment of blasts of noise. To create harsh working conditions, the actual subject was required to keep one hand submerged in a tank of water. For half of the subjects the water was very cold (6° Celsius); for the other subjects it was more comfortable (18° Celsius). Berkowitz, Cochran, and Embree found that the subjects who were exposed to the extremely cold water administered significantly more "punishments" to their partners than subjects exposed to water of a moderate temperature. These results again document the assertion that pain can motivate aggressive behavior.

Other annoying environmental events. Painful stimuli are not the only annoying physically aversive events which can arouse an aggressive response. Recent studies demonstrate that several kinds of objectional environments, such as those with unpleasant odors and elevated temperatures, produce aggressiveness.

Jones and Durbin (1978) evaluated the level of aggressiveness in subjects who occupied a room filled with cigarette smoke and subjects who were in a room with no smoke. They reported that the subjects in the smoke-filled room, compared with subjects in the other room, displayed more punitive behavior toward another person. Rotton, Barry, Frey, and Soler (1978) found that subjects were more aggressive in a foul-smelling environment than in a normal environment. Apparently, the annoyance produced by an unpleasant environment arouses an aggressive reaction.

Other studies (see Baron & Ransberger, 1978; Goranson & King, 1980; Griffitt, 1970) have suggested that temperature affects the level of aggressiveness. Goranson and King (1980) noted that a sharp increase in temperature occurred on the day preceding the major riots in 17 American cities in 1967. It would appear that the temperature played a role in this aggression. In addition, Goranson and King observed that the length of the riot depended on how long the temperature had remained abnormally high; that is, the longer riots corresponded to longer periods of heat. In addition, Baron and Ransberger (1978) found that the level of violence which took place in United States cities from 1967 through 1971 correlated with temperature. In a laboratory study (Griffitt, 1970), subjects showed more hostility to another person when they were together in a hot room (91° Fahrenheit) than when they occupied a more comfortable setting (68° Fahrenheit). These observations again suggest that annoying environmental circumstances can lead to aggressiveness.

Psychologically irritating circumstances. Evidence also indicates that verbal threats and verbal insults can provoke an aggressive reaction. For example, Goldstein, Davis, and Herman (1975) observed that mild taunts often lead to aggressive retaliation which can escalate quickly, resulting in a stronger and stronger exchange of provocation between the people involved. Other researchers (see Kimble, Fitz, & Onorad, 1977; Dengerink, Schnedler, & Covey, 1978) found that after unprovoked verbal abuse, people will show aggression against their attacker. In addition, other researchers (Greenwell & Dengerink, 1973; Dyck & Rule, 1978) discovered that when people believe that someone intends to harm them, they will initiate the attack.

The Releasing Stimuli

Berkowitz (1964, 1970, 1974, 1978) asserts that *aggression cues*, environmental events which are associated with the source of frustration or anger, influence the intensity of aggressive behavior. For example, seeing the person who is responsible for our arousal typically releases a stronger aggression reaction than seeing someone who is not involved in the annoyance. This aggression cue, according to Berkowitz, can also be anything associated with aggression. For example, a gun that has been associated with violence can increase the intensity of aggressive behavior in a frustrated or an angry person.

Our discussion has suggested that the presence of an aggression cue can intensify aggressive behavior. Such a cue can also increase the likelihood that aggressive behavior will occur. If the level of anger or the level of frustration is not sufficient to motivate aggressive behavior, the presence of an aggression cue may produce enough arousal to elicit an aggressive response. Considerable evidence indicates that aggression cues can influence irritable aggressive behavior. Several studies which document this influence are presented next.

The influence of watching violence.   Many people intuitively think that violence depicted on television and in movies influences people's aggressiveness. The behavior of some youths who had seen the movie *The Warriors* confirms this viewpoint (see *Time*, March 19, 1979). When this movie, which portrayed gang warfare in New York City, was shown in early 1979, it was directly linked to at least three real-life violent incidents there; for example, after viewing the film, 12 youths terrorized and assaulted subway passengers. In California, two people were killed by youths who had seen the movie.

Some people might feel that these incidents would have occurred whether or not these youths had seen a violent movie. However, the research of Berkowitz and his colleagues (see Berkowitz, 1980) has provided additional evidence that watching violence can lead to aggression in frustrated or angry people. Parke, Berkowitz, Leyens, West, and Sebastian (1977) recorded the levels of aggressive interactions of delinquent boys who lived in a reformatory. The boys were observed before and after some of them viewed a violent movie. Those psychologists reported that the youths who had watched the violent movie showed a much greater increase in the level of both physical and verbal aggression than the other boys in the study. Leyens, Camino, Parke, and Berkowitz (1975) observed an increase of aggressive responses in delinquent Belgian boys shortly after they had viewed a violent film.

We must recognize, however, that not everyone who watches a violent film like *The Warriors* becomes aggressive. Why is it that some people react aggressively to violent television shows or movies while others do not? According to Berkowitz, people do not become violent merely by viewing violence: such people must first be either angry or frustrated, and they must have an appropriate target for the aggressive act. Berkowitz and Geen (1966) illustrated how the emotional state of a person affects the ability of a violent movie to stimulate aggression. In their study, a confederate was first introduced to each subject as "Mr. Anderson" and was then asked to evaluate the subject's solution to a problem. For half of the subjects, the confederate indicated he did not like the solution by shocking them seven times; for the rest of the subjects, the confederate demonstrated approval by shocking them only once. All the subjects were then shown one of two movies. One was a violent movie in which the star, Kirk Douglas, was badly beaten during a brutal prizefight; the other was nonviolent and showed a 1-mile foot race. Half of the subjects saw the violent movie, while the other half saw the nonviolent one. After seeing the movie, half of the subjects in each condition were told that the confederate's name was *Kirk Anderson*; the other subjects were informed that his name was *Bob Anderson*. The subjects were then allowed to shock the confederate in order to indicate their judgment of his task performance. According to the aggression-cue model, the subjects should associate the name *Kirk* with the violent movie and, thus, be more aggressive against a confederate named Kirk.

Berkowitz and Geen discovered that angry subjects who had viewed the violent movie showed more punitive behavior toward the confederate than angry subjects who had seen the nonviolent movie (see Table 7.4). On the other hand, the violent movie did not influence the aggressive behavior of subjects who were not angered. As predicted by the aggression-cue hypothesis, the name affected the intensity of aggression only in angry subjects who viewed the violent film. These angry subjects were more aggressive toward the confederate named Kirk than the one named Bob; the angry subjects who did not view the violent movie were equally agressive to all the confederates. Therefore, the greatest level of aggression was demonstrated by angry subjects toward the confederate named Kirk after viewing the violent movie.

Geen and Berkowitz's experiment (1967) showed that a violent movie and a target associated with aggression can also increase aggression in people who are aroused by frustrating circumstances or psychological insults as well as physical pain. Berkowitz (1965) also noted that angry subjects who had viewed a violent movie were more punitive toward a confederate whom they believed to be a member of their school's boxing team than to a confederate who was assumed to be a speech major. According to the aggression-cue model, boxers will elicit more aggressive behavior than speech majors because of the association of boxers with aggression.

The results of these studies provide strong support for the aggression-cue model. According to this model, environmental cues associated with aggression can increase the level of aggressive behavior in people who are angry or frustrated. We have just seen that both violent movies and people associated with aggression can increase aggressive behavior in people who are predisposed to become aggressive; it appears that objects associated with aggression have a similar effect on such persons. One particularly important kind of object associated with aggression appears to be weapons. Although many people think that "guns don't kill people; people do," the research of Berkowitz and

Table 7.4
Mean Number of Shocks Administered to Confederate

Accomplice's Name	Aggressive Film		Track Film	
	Angered	Nonangered	Angered	Nonangered
Kirk	6.09	1.73	4.18	1.54
Bob	4.55	1.45	4.00	1.64

From: Berkowitz, L., & Geen, R. G. Film violence and the cue properties of available targets. *Journal of Personality and Social Psychology*, 1966, 3, 525–530. Copyright 1966 by the American Psychological Association. Reprinted by permission.

other psychologists suggests that weapons are not neutral objects. Instead, weapons can stimulate aggressive behavior in angry or frustrated people.

The weapon's effect. Recall Berkowitz and LePage's study, which demonstrated that angry subjects were more aggressive toward a confederate than subjects who were not angry. This study used four conditions for the angry subjects and three for the "nonangry" subjects. The "no object" condition was described earlier. Two other groups of angry subjects and two other groups of nonangry subjects saw a 12-gauge shotgun and a .38-caliber revolver while shocking the confederate. For these subjects, both objects lay on a table near the shock key. Subjects in the "associated weapons" condition were told that the guns belonged to another subject who, in fact, was the confederate. Subjects in the "nonassociated weapons" condition were told that the guns were being used in other research. Subjects in a fourth condition, the "badminton racquet" condition, found badminton racquets rather than guns on the table. Berkowitz and LePage observed that the presence of the guns significantly increased the punitiveness of the angry subjects but not the nonangry subjects (refer to Table 7.3). In contrast, the presence of the objects not associated with violence did not influence the aggressiveness of angry subjects. (Subjects' beliefs about the ownership of the weapons were not important to the outcome of the study.) Berkowitz and LePage's results clearly demonstrate that weapons can increase the intensity of aggressive behavior in angry people.

The "weapons effect" came under attack during the early 1970s. Conducting several experiments, Buss, Booker, and Buss (1972) were unable to show that the presence of guns increased aggressiveness in angry people. In addition, Page and Scheidt (1971) attributed the subjects' behavior when a gun was present to the fact that the subjects anticipated how they were expected to react and acted accordingly; that is, they behaved more aggressively when the gun was present simply to please the experimenter.

However, recent evidence has provided additional support for the "weapons effect," indicating that it does not occur because subjects comply with their expectations of the experimenter's wishes. Two lines of evidence support this view. First, Turner and Simons (1974) reported that subjects who suspected that the intention of a study was to evaluate aggressiveness did, indeed, inhibit their aggressive behavior so as not to appear maladjusted. Apparently, laboratory research which evaluates subjects' aggression finds that subjects behave aggressively in spite of their suspicions rather than because of them. Second, naturalistic observations also demonstrate that the presence of weapons increases aggressiveness. For example, Simons, Finn, Layton, and Turner (1977) evaluated the level of aggressive behavior exhibited by male students who were participating in a college carnival. The students were invited to one of the booths and asked to purchase a pail of wet sponges to throw at a target person who stood at the back of this booth. While half of the subjects participated, there was a rifle on the counter; no weapon was present while the other subjects participated. The experimenters reported more aggressive behavior occurred when the rifle was present than when it was absent. Once again, results have shown that cues associated with aggression can arouse aggressive reactions.

The Aggressive Response

The specific behavior patterns which occur during irritable aggression have not been extensively evaluated. Flynn, Vanegas, Foote, and Edwards's description (1970) of the irritable aggressive behavior of cats provides one of the best pictures of this form of aggression. They observed that irritable aggressive behavior comprises both an intense affective arousal, *feline rage,* and an aggressive attack. In cats, the response of the autonomic nervous system includes pupillary dilation, piloerection (particularly along the middle of the back), and the appearance of a bushy fluffed tail. The cat has its back arched and claws unsheathed and is hissing and breathing deeply when it approaches a target (for example, a rat). After closing in on the target, the cat often strikes with its paw in a series of swift, accurate blows and then leaps on the target and claws it. If the annoyance continues, the cat will savagely bite the target. In humans, the irritable aggressive reaction is characterized by intense autonomic arousal but not by any specific behavioral reaction. People use a variety of effective aggressive responses which allow them to harm the target of the aggression.

The Motive for Irritable Aggression

The drive to be aggressive. We have seen that frustration or anger can result in aggressive behavior. However, this aggressive reaction is not motivated by the expectation of gaining reward; rather, it reflects an impulsive act energized by the emotional arousal which is characteristic of frustration and anger. The drive aspect of irritable aggression can be seen in an animal's or a human's aggressive reaction which follows a loss in a competitive situation. Since the loser in competition does not obtain a desired reward, frustration is aroused. The aggressive response elicited by frustration is often directed toward an animal or a person that neither possesses the desired goal nor is involved in the competition.

Hamburg's observations (1971) of the irritable aggressive behavior of baboons illustrate the impulsive character of frustration-induced aggression. He found that male baboons will often harass adult male chimpanzees in order to get them to relinquish bananas; however, these attempts are rarely successful. Male baboons will even frequently attack female or juvenile chimpanzees without bananas. These observations point out that frustration-induced aggression is often directed toward either animate or inanimate objects which are not responsible for the frustration. It seems that only an unthinking, mechanistic reaction could be the explanation for the male baboons' attack on defenseless female or juvenile baboons. Similarly, the aggressive reaction of the frustrated children in Barker, Dembo, and Lewin's study could not have been motivated by the desire to obtain a toy, because their aggressiveness actually destroyed attractive toys. Since anger can also motivate displaced aggressive behavior, a drive view of anger-induced aggression seems to reflect the most reasonable view of anger-initiated irritable aggression.

The pleasure of being aggressive. The expression of aggressive behavior in irritated animals or people appears to be highly reinforcing. Many studies show that annoyed animals will learn a behavior which allows them the opportunity to be aggressive. For example, Azrin, Hutchinson, and McLaughlin (1965) discovered that squirrel monkeys loosely restrained in a chair bit inanimate objects (for example, a ball) after being shocked. However, if no object was present, they learned to pull a chain which provided them with a ball to bite. Similarly, Dryer and Church (1970) reported that shocked rats chose the appropriate arm in a T-maze which provided another rat to fight.

Bramel, Taub, and Blum (1968) reported that irritated people report "feeling good" after being aggressive. During the early 1960s, Hokanson and his colleagues (see Hokanson & Burgess, 1962a, 1962b; Hokanson, Burgess, & Cohen, 1963; Hokanson & Shetler, 1961) found that angry people who were either verbally or physically aggressive toward the instigator of their anger showed a rapid decline in the level of systolic blood pressure until it reached the initial resting level. In contrast, the decline in systolic blood pressure was much slower in angry subjects who were not given the opportunity to be aggressive. Evidently, aggressive behavior reduces arousal.

However, several researchers have proposed that the drive-reducing aspect of aggressive behavior typically occurs only in males; that is, most women do not feel better after having been aggressive. While Baker and Schaie (1969) and Gambaro and Rabin (1969) reported that their male subjects showed a rapid reduction in physiological arousal after behaving aggressively, Holmes (1966) and Vantress and Williams (1972) observed that female subjects did not feel better after aggressive behavior.

Although angry males but not females show a reduced arousal following aggressive behavior, a completely different pattern emerges when angry males and angry females reward rather than punish the instigator of their anger. In Hokanson and Edelman's study (1966), male and female subjects chose either to shock, reward, or not respond to a confederate who had just shocked them. Systolic blood pressure was recorded before and after the subjects' response and then for 20-second intervals until it reached baseline levels. Hokanson and Edelman discovered that the males were more likely than the females to shock the confederate; females were more likely to reward the confederate. In addition, Hokanson and Edelman found that their male subjects recovered more quickly following an aggressive reaction than after they had either given a reward or not responded. In contrast, females recovered more rapidly after they had rewarded, rather than attacked, the confederate or had not responded.

Other research has consistently shown that under annoying circumstances, males are more aggressive than females. For example, Bandura, Ross, and Ross (1963) discovered that when boys were frustrated, they showed significantly more aggressive behavior toward a "Bobo" doll than girls who had been frustrated.

The influence of punishment.   Why do males and females differ in their behavioral and physiological response pattern during annoying situations? According to Hokanson (1970), people's experiences determine their reactions. Someone whose irritable aggressive behavior has been rewarded will become aggressive when angered and will feel better after the aggressive behavior. This reduced arousal is assumed to be due to a conditioned response, caused by the association of aggressive activity with past reward; to the intrinsic reinforcing property of aggression; or to both. However, someone whose irritable aggressive reactions have been punished typically will not become aggressive when angered and will not show a reduced arousal after acting aggressively. The failure to show reduced arousal following aggressive behavior is believed to reflect an association of aggressive behavior with punishment. According to Hokanson, males have learned that aggressive behavior reduces irritating circumstances, whereas females have found that responding aggressively leads only to further annoyance. In contrast, males are likely to be punished for unaggressive behavior, whereas females have discovered that responding unaggressively can reduce frustration or anger.

Hokanson, Willers, and Koropsak (1968) conducted a direct test of the view that experience determines a person's response to anger. In their study, male and female subjects were allowed to choose either an aggressive or a rewarding response to a confederate's annoying action. After each subject responded, the confederate either rewarded or punished the subject's response. During the baseline phase of the study, the confederate gave reward and punishment at random, regardless of the subject's behavior. On baseline trials, the males' and the females' behavior was identical to that reported in Hokanson and Edelman's study. The males were more likely to shock than to reward the confederate who had angered them and showed a faster reduction of arousal after they had responded by shocking the confederate than after rewarding the confederate. In

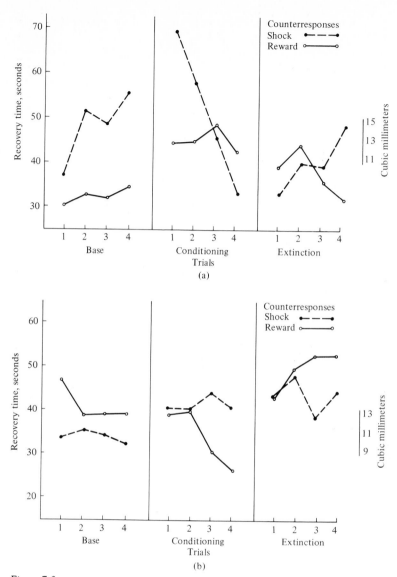

Figure 7.3
Recovery latency following aggressive and nonaggressive reaction in (a) females and (b) males during baseline, conditioning, and extinction phases of study. (From Hokanson, J. E., Willers, K. R., & Koropsak, E. The modification of autonomic responses during aggressive interchange. Journal of Personality, *1968, 36, 386–404. Copyright 1968, Duke University Press, Durham, N.C.)*

contrast, the females were more apt to reward than to shock the confederate who had angered them and exhibited a faster decline in their arousal when they had rewarded the confederate than when they had reacted aggressively (see Figure 7.3).

In the conditioning phase of their experiment, Hokanson, Willers, and Koropsak had the confederates reward the subjects' sex-atypical behavior. Thus, male subjects were punished for aggressive behavior and rewarded for nonaggressive behavior; females who responded nonaggressively were shocked and females who responded aggressively were rewarded. The confederate's behavior during the conditioning phase of the study caused the subjects to alter their responses. Males became more nonaggressive; females began to show more aggression. In addition, males' arousal decreased rapidly following nonaggressive behavior, and females exhibited faster recovery after aggressive behavior (see Figure 7.3). These results indicate that the consequences of irritable aggression influence how we respond when annoyed as well as how we feel after having been either aggressive or nonaggressive.

During the extinction phase of the study, the confederate no longer selectively rewarded sex-atypical behavior and no longer selectively punished sex-typical behavior. The males' and the females' overt behavior and their postresponse physiological reactions returned to a level identical to that observed in the baseline phase (see Figure 7.3).

It should be noted that not all males feel better after having been aggressive, and some females show a reduced level of arousal after an aggressive act. Hokanson, Willers, and Koropsak's results portray males' and females' typical pattern of physiological reaction during annoying circumstances. This physiological response reflects people's past experiences during which their aggression has been rewarded or punished. For example, some males who have been punished for being aggressive are not apt to demonstrate reduced arousal after an aggressive act, while some females who have not been punished for aggressiveness are likely to show reduced arousal after acting aggressively. In support of this view, "high guilt" subjects (those who have been punished for aggression) show less reduction of tension after being aggressive than "low guilt" subjects. This observation is true of both males (Gambaro & Rabin, 1969) and females (Schill, 1972).

Are You Angry or Frustrated?

Although an impulsive process motivates irritable aggressive behavior, cognitions do affect irritable aggression. In Chapter 3, we learned that environmental circumstances allow us to label our emotional arousal. If we are aroused when working on a task which we cannot complete, we attribute our arousal to frustration; yet if we are insulted by another person, we attribute our arousal to anger. The research of Dolf Zillman and his colleagues (see Zillman, 1971; Zillman & Bryant, 1974; Zillman, Katcher, & Milavsky, 1972; Zillman, Johnson, & Day, 1974) indicates that people may often misattribute emotional arousal to anger or frustration which, in turn, motivates aggressive behavior. Yet, at other times when frustration or anger actually does produce arousal, we may attribute that arousal to another emotion which, in turn, causes us not to be aggressive.

Zillman and his associates have demonstrated that cognitive processes do influence whether or not we feel anger or frustration but that once we have attributed our arousal to one of these emotions, we impulsively behave aggressively. Their research also points out that the level of aggressive behavior depends upon arousal level; that is, the higher the arousal, the more intense the irritable aggressive response will be.

To illustrate the effect of both the level of arousal and the emotional attribution on anger-induced aggression, Zillman (1971) chose three types of films—a violent film, a sexually arousing film, and an interesting, unarousing documentary—and showed one type to each of three groups of subjects. After viewing the movie, some subjects in each group were angered by a confederate, while other subjects were not angered. The subjects were then given the opportunity to evaluate the confederate on performance of a task by shocking him. Zillman also recorded the subjects' blood pressure during the study. Although viewing a film did not influence the nonangry subjects' aggressiveness toward the confederate, the content of the film did affect the angry subjects' level of aggression. In the angry subjects, the erotic movie produced the greatest physiological arousal and motivated the most intense aggressive response; the documentary produced the least arousal as well as the least aggression. Evidently, the greater the level of arousal, the more intense a person's aggression will be. Why, then, do erotic movies increase angry subjects' aggression? According to attribution theory, the confederate's actions caused the arousal produced by the erotic movie to be misattributed to anger. Attributing sexually induced arousal to anger served only to increase the subjects' anger, which in turn intensely motivated these subjects to shock the confederate.

Other studies have also shown that emotional misattribution can increase anger-induced aggression. For example, Zillman, Katcher, and Milavsky (1972) and Zillman, Johnson, and Day (1974) reported that angry subjects were more aggressive after strenuous exercise than before it. In addition, Mueller and Donnerstein (1977) noted that exposing angry subjects to highly arousing humor increased their aggressive behavior compared with subjects who had been exposed to mildly arousing humor. Finally, several experiments (see Donnerstein & Wilson, 1976; Geen & O'Neal, 1969) indicate that arousing noise intensifies angry people's aggressive behavior but does not affect nonangry subjects.

We have seen that people's aggressiveness increases if emotional arousal is incorrectly assumed to reflect anger. In contrast, aggressive behavior decreases if arousal caused by annoying circumstances is misattributed to another emotion. For example, in Geen, Rakosky, and Pigg's study (1972), a confederate shocked subjects who were reading erotic material. The subjects were then led to believe that their arousal was due to shock, or to the sexually arousing story, or to a drug they had just taken. The subjects who attributed their arousal to either the erotic material or the drug felt less angry and were less aggressive toward the confederate than subjects who assumed that their arousal was due to being shocked by the confederate. Other studies (Baron, 1977; Harris & Huang, 1974; Zillman, Johnson, & Day, 1974) also found reduced aggressive behavior when emotional arousal caused by an irritating situation had been misattributed. These observations provide additional evidence for the combined influence of drive and cognitive processes in motivating our aggressive behavior.

The Physiological Basis of Irritable Aggression

Several CNS areas have been identified as having an influence in the control of irritable aggression. Some brain systems arouse irritable aggressive behavior, while others inhibit it. Certain hormones, drugs, and illnesses also appear to play an important role in the expression of irritable aggression.

CNS influence. *Temporal lobe.* The classic research by Kluver and Bucy (1937) showed that destruction of the temporal lobes in primates produced a permanent docility and demonstrated that the temporal lobes are involved in the initiation of irritable aggression. On the basis of this study, some surgeons (see Terzian & DalleOre, 1955) removed the temporal lobes of excessively aggressive people. Although this surgical treatment did reduce irritability, it unfortunately produced the other aspects of the "Kluver-Bucy syndrome": socially inappropriate sexual activity, decreased ability to recognize people, and memory deficits. To replace this radical surgical procedure, other, more restrictive treatments which produce only a reduction of irritable aggressiveness are now preferred. It must be noted that any psychosurgical procedure is radical and to be employed only if other treatments have been proved ineffective.

Amygdala.   The amygdala appears to influence the excitation and suppression of irritable aggressiveness. The area of the amygdala which seems to excite this form of aggressiveness is the medial nucleus. In support of this theory, MacLean and Delgado (1953) reported that stimulation of the *medial amygdaloid nucleus* in cats produced intense affective and behavioral arousal which included hissing, growling, claw extension, and pupillary dilation but not the attempt to escape. Ursin and Kaada (1960) reported similar effects of amygdala stimulation in cats; and Fonberg (1965) discovered that stimulation of the medial amygdaloid nucleus aroused irritable aggressiveness in dogs. In addition, Fonberg discovered that the lesioning of this amygdala area produced tameness or a lack of irritable aggressiveness in dogs.

In contrast to the excitatory influence of the medial nucleus, the *central amygdaloid nucleus* appears to inhibit irritable aggressiveness. In support of this view, Deci, Varszegi, and Mehes (1969) found that stimulation of the central area of the amygdala in cats inhibited a rage reaction. Wood (1958), also using cats, reported that lesioning of this area increased irritability. Fonberg (1965) made an analogous observation about lesioned dogs and also reported that once these animals had become annoyed, the intensity of their rage reaction continued to increase. Fonberg called this an *avalanche syndrome.*

Our discussion has suggested that there are separate nuclei in the amygdala for exciting and for inhibiting irritable aggression. Significant documentation, such as observations that epileptic seizures initiated in the amygdala have been associated with extremely violent behavior, indicate that the amygdala plays an important role in human irritable aggressiveness. During a seizure, the amygdala is extremely active and irritable aggressiveness is intense. Many studies have shown a relationship between activity in the amygdala which occurs during a seizure and hostility in humans (see Mark & Ervin, 1970, for a detailed review of this literature).

The following two case histories provide a vivid illustration of the role of the amygdala in irritable aggression. Mark and Ervin (1970) reported the case of a teenage girl who behaved as a model child except for occasional extremely destructive acts initiated by circumstances which annoyed her (for example, being criticized for playing records too loudly). This girl was institutionalized for smothering a baby to death because the crying annoyed her. Mark and Ervin implanted electrodes in her amygdala and recorded activity before, during, and after the presentation of a recording of a baby's crying. They found that this recording evoked intense, localized activity in the amygdala (see Figure 7.4) as well as the arousal of intense anger. Evidently, an annoying circumstance can elicit both anger and amygdala activity.

Sweet, Ervin, and Mark's description (1969) of the violent behavior of a 34-year-old man provides even more vivid evidence of the relationship between irritation, aggression, and the amygdala. With the exception of extremely violent behavior, usually precipitated by an argument with his wife, this man appeared to be reserved. He often became so angry during his outbursts that he beat and injured his wife and children. After 7 years of therapy had failed to alter his aggressiveness, EEG tests revealed abnormal brain activity in the temporal lobes and amygdala. When the use of antiseizure drugs had failed to curtail his violent behavior, electrodes were implanted in the lateral and medial amygdala. This man reported that he "felt one of his fits coming on" when the medial amygdala was stimulated. In contrast, stimulation of the lateral nuclei inhibited his rage.

Surgical treatment of this man and others like him whose extreme aggressive

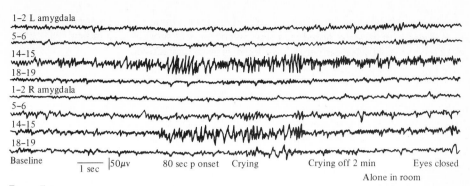

Figure 7.4
Electrical activity of a teenage girl who had smothered a baby whose crying annoyed her. The electrical activity was recorded in four sites of right and left amygdala before, during, and after a tape of a baby crying. Note the intense activity recorded from electrodes 14-15 of right and left amygdala which began when crying started and ended when crying stopped. The crying had no effect on other areas. (From Mark, V. H., & Ervin, F. R. Violence and the brain. New York: Harper and Row, 1970.)

violence can be linked to an amygdaloid malfunction is an *amygdalectomy*. This psychosurgery procedure destroys selected neurons in the amygdala. Sweet, Ervin, and Mark reported that following this surgery, their male subject returned to normal life and experienced no further attacks.

Many other clinical observations (see Hitchcock, Laitinen, & Vaernet, 1972, for a review of this literature) have indicated that amygdalectomy reflects an effective treatment of excessively violent people. For example, Narabayaski (1972) found that 85 percent of 51 hostile people who had received amygdala lesions showed a marked reduction in irritability. Heimburger, Whitlock, and Kalsbeck (1966) destroyed half of the amygdala in 25 violent patients and reported that 23 showed a significant reduction in destructiveness, hostility, and aggression toward other people. A final example of the effectiveness of an amygdalectomy is Mark and Ervin's description (1970) of a 62-year-old woman who at the age of 33 had sustained a head injury which led to epileptic seizures. She became physically aggressive, attacking her husband, mother-in-law, and other people. Her seizures and aggression, intensifying during the years following her injury, caused her to be hospitalized. Forty electrodes were implanted in the amygdala, and its activity was recorded for several months. When several electrodes recorded abnormal activity, the area surrounding the electrode was destroyed. The woman then showed a total absence of rage and was able to return to a normal life.

Hypothalamus. The hypothalamus is also vital in controlling irritable aggression. Stimulation of the *anterior lateral region of the hypothalamus*, the area apparently involved in the arousal of irritable aggressive behavior, has been reported to elicit irritable attack by rats on live mice or on other rats (see King & Hoebel, 1968; Panksepp & Trowill, 1969).

The *ventromedial hypothalamus* has a suppressive effect on irritable aggressive behavior. A number of studies (see Grossman, 1972; McAdam & Kaebler, 1966) have observed that animals show intense irritability following VMH lesions. In addition, hyperirritability has been reported in people who have tumors in the hypothalamic area (Wheatley, 1944; Vonderahe, 1944). Scalafani's research (1971) indicates that the VMH inhibits irritable aggressive behavior by directly suppressing the anterior lateral hypothalamus of rats. He cut the neural connections between these two areas and reported a hyperirritability identical to that which is produced by VMH lesions. Paxinos and Bindra (1972) observed a similar effect of the destruction of this neural connection on irritable aggression.

Hormonal influence.   *Testosterone.*   Several types of evidence support the view that the male sex hormone testosterone appears to affect a male's irritability. First, males of most species engage in more aggressive fighting and threatening behavior than females, an observation which does not merely reflect intermale aggression. For example, male domestic animals, such as the bull and stallion, are as aggressive with people who handle them as they are with other males of their own species (see Moyer, 1976). In addition, men commit a significantly greater number of violent crimes than women (see Cressey, 1961). Second, castrating male animals and men reduces their irritability. Many observations of domestic animals which show that docility follows castration have also pointed out that castration not only reduces men's intermale and sex-related aggression but also decreases their hostility. For example, Hawke (1950) noted that castration of sex offenders reduced their destructiveness as well as their sexual aggressiveness. Furthermore, administration of testosterone reinstated their antisocial behaviors, including attacking small children, instigating fights, breaking windows, and destroying other property. The irritability decreased when testosterone was no longer injected. Finally, amygdalectomy produces both reduced irritable aggressiveness and testicular atrophy (see Goddard, 1964). Kling (1968) reported that amygdalectomy caused juvenile rhesus monkeys to be less aggressive, while testosterone injections increased their level of irritability.

Female sex hormones.   We saw earlier in the chapter that the female sex hormones, estrogen and progesterone, inhibited intermale aggressive behavior. Some researchers suggest that estrogen arouses irritability and that progesterone inhibits irritable aggressive behavior. Kohler (1925) observed that sexually receptive female chimpanzees become irritable, and Michael (1969) reported increased aggressiveness in sexually receptive female rhesus monkeys as well as baboons. (Recall from Chapter 6 that the level of estrogen is highest when the female is sexually receptive.) In addition, Michael reported that estrogen injections produced a significant increase in the amount of irritable aggressive behavior displayed by female rhesus monkeys and baboons.

In contrast to estrogen, progesterone inhibits irritable aggression. The increase in the level of irritability of females during the premenstrual period has been attributed to the lack of progesterone which occurs at this time. Many investigators (see Coppen & Kessel, 1963; Dalton, 1961; Ellis & Austin, 1971; Hamburg, 1971; Moos, 1968) have reported that their subjects showed irritable aggressiveness during the premenstrual period. For example, Hamburg (1971) interviewed 1,100 women and discovered that they had significantly greater feelings of irritability during the premenstrual part of the cycle than at other stages. Documenting additional support for the effect of progesterone, Dalton (1961) noted that 49 percent of reported crimes committed by women had been done during the offenders' premenstrual period. Female rhesus monkeys also show a heightened irritability during the premenstrual period (Sassenrath, Rowell, & Hendricks, 1973).

Research (see Dalton, 1964; Hamburg, Moos, & Yalom, 1968; Lloyd, 1964; Wiseman, 1965) shows that progesterone can decrease the irritability and the hostility which often occur during the premenstrual period. Dalton (1964) found that the administration of progesterone decreased premenstrual hostility and aggressiveness. It is interesting to note that Hamburg, Moos, and Yalom (1968) discovered that women who took oral contraceptives containing progesterone showed much less premenstrual irritability than women who did not take them.

Disease and irritable aggression. A number of diseases have been identified as being responsible for intensifying the levels of irritability, hostility, and overt aggressiveness. Three diseases—brain tumors, epilepsy, and allergic reactions—seem to play a significant role in people's irritability. Let's now focus on evidence which explains the influence of these diseases in irritable aggression.

Brain tumors. When a tumor grows, it activates the brain cells in the immediate area of the tumor. Eventually, the cells are destroyed, and thus the neurons do not function. There are many instances of a reported link between violence and tumors present in the excitatory areas controlling irritable aggression. The case of Charles Whitman is perhaps the best-known instance of this relationship. Whitman was an extremely angry young man whose anger had slowly intensified over a period of years. After this anger finally culminated, causing him to kill his wife and mother, he took a high-powered rifle with several hundred rounds of ammunition to the tower at the University of Texas in Austin. Whitman killed a receptionist, barricaded the door of the tower, and within 90 minutes had wounded 24 people and killed 14 others before he himself was killed. An autopsy revealed a malignant tumor in the area of the amygdaloid nucleus (see Sweet, Ervin, & Mark, 1969). Other investigators have reported cases in which extremely violent persons were found to have temporal-lobe or amygdaloid tumors (Malamud, 1967; Sweet, Ervin, & Mark, 1969).

Epilepsy. Epilepsy is a disorder which causes various neural systems to become abnormally active; this in turn produces seizures. If a seizure consists of generalized muscular contractions and a loss of consciousness, it is called a *grand mal seizure*. A seizure characterized by temporary loss of consciousness with no muscle contractions is known as a *petit mal seizure*. A third type of seizure, *psychomotor epilepsy*, does not involve overt symptoms but, instead, is detectable from subjective experiences.

There is considerable evidence (see Mark & Ervin, 1970) that epileptic seizures which are initiated in the brain areas controlling irritable aggression often precipitate aggressiveness. In support of this view is Williams's observation (1969) that rage is likely to follow epileptic activity in the anterior temporal lobe. Deltaas (1963) and Monroe (1970) also reported that aggressive behavior usually followed intense spontaneous activity in the temporal lobe. It is important to mention that many epileptics, instead of being angry and violent after a seizure, become frightened or depressed. Unfortunately, the reason for the occurrence of these different behavioral responses is unclear, even though experience may determine how someone reacts to a seizure.

Abnormal EEG activity occurring in the irritable aggression neural system has also been associated with extreme violence. Bayrakal (1965) reported that of 200 problem children, 100 had abnormal EEGs. Among these 100 children, most showed disturbances in the temporal lobe and subcortical areas as well as a typical behavioral pattern: poor control of impulses, inadequate social adaptation, and hostility. Monroe (1970) reported that 50 to 60 percent of children with behavioral problems show EEG disturbances, compared with 5 to 15 percent of normal children.

Individuals who commit impulsive crimes are also likely to have abnormal EEG patterns (see Bonkalo, 1967). Knott (1965) found that psychopaths, compared with the general population, show a significantly greater number of EEG abnormalities. Yoshii, Ishiwara, and Tani (1963) observed this in juvenile delinquents compared with the rest of the population. Furthermore, delinquents with EEG abnormalities are likely to show habitual violent tendencies.

Allergic tension-fatigue syndrome.   In 1954, Speer introduced the term *allergic tension-fatigue syndrome* to describe the behavioral disturbances which often accompany an allergic reaction. The most common behavioral response to an allergic reaction is irritability. Investigating this syndrome, some studies have shown that irritability can be caused by an allergic reaction to pollens (Kahn, 1927), inhalants (Eisenberg, 1970), drugs (Gottieb, 1970), and many foods, such as milk, chocolate, cola, corn, and eggs (Speer, 1970).

Several processes seem to play a role in this allergic reaction. Campbell (1970) described evidence which suggests that the allergic reaction is related to epileptic seizures initiated in subcortical areas. In addition, angioedema, a noninflammatory swelling of the brain, is also involved in allergy-induced irritability (see Gottieb, 1970). It should be noted that allergic reactions are highly idiosyncratic; that is, many people have aggressive allergic reactions, while others do not. Unfortunately, the reason for this varied response is not clear.

In addition to the several diseases which we have learned are linked to increased irritable aggressive behavior, other diseases, including rabies, hyperkinesis, Lesh-Nyhan syndrome, hypoglycemia, and some types of poisoning often produce irritability. Our irritability can also be affected by some drugs, and our discussion of irritable aggression ends with a brief discussion of several of them.

Drugs and irritable aggression.   *Amphetamine.*   While moderate use, and even occasional abuse, of amphetamine does not appear to influence aggressiveness, long-term abuse has been linked to extreme irritable aggressive behavior. Kalant (1966) noted that people are hyperirritable and extremely aggressive during acute amphetamine intoxication. Furthermore, Cohen (1969) found amphetamine abusers to be impulsive and violent; and Tinklenberg and Stillman (1970) observed a progressive inability of amphetamine users to control their destructive behavior.

Alcohol.   Strong evidence indicates that alcohol and aggression are related. For example, Wolfgang (1958) discovered a correlation between drinking alcohol and a high percentage of homicides. Similar observations linking alcohol and aggression have been noticed in cases of rape (Blum, 1969) and assault (Molof, 1967). However, it is also apparent that not all people who drink alcohol become aggressive. Many people report a feeling of euphoria after drinking alcohol (see Wallgren & Barry, 1970).

Why is it that alcohol produces aggression in some people while it reduces irritability in others, increasing their feelings of relaxation and self-satisfaction? The effect of alcohol on aggressive behavior appears to depend upon people's emotional state as well as the amount consumed. If someone is annoyed, low doses of alcohol seem to decrease irritability and enhance sociability, while high doses appear to increase aggressiveness. Several studies conducted by Taylor and his associates (see Shuntich & Taylor, 1972; Taylor & Gammon, 1975; Taylor, Gammon, & Capasso, 1976) provide direct support for this relationship between the dose of alcohol, the emotional state, and the level of aggressiveness. In their studies, subjects competed with a confederate in the performance of a reaction-time task. Before the task, some subjects were given a high dose of alcohol (1.5 ounces per 40 pounds of body weight, or the equivalent of three or four drinks); other subjects received a low dose of alcohol (0.5 ounces per 40 pounds); and a third group did not get any alcohol. At the beginning of the task, the subjects were instructed to select the intensity of shock that they would apply to the confederate if they won the competition. During the study, the confederate acted so as to anger some subjects but not others. Alcohol did not influence the aggressive reaction of nonangry subjects toward the confederate, but it did significantly influence the aggressiveness of angry subjects. Angry subjects who had been given a high dose of alcohol administered shocks of greater intensity to the confederate than control subjects who had received no alcohol; and subjects who had received a low dose of alcohol were less punitive than the control subjects. Apparently, in angry people, low doses of alcohol inhibit aggressiveness, but high doses intensify it.

Why do high doses of alcohol increase aggressiveness? According to Lang, Goeckner, Adesso, and Marlatt (1975), cognitive processes are involved: we expect to feel better after a few drinks, and we expect that aggressive behavior will be permissible after many drinks. In Lang, Goeckner, Adesso, and Marlatt's study, half of the subjects were told that they would receive alcohol and half that they would be given tonic water. However, only half of these subjects actually did receive the drink which they had expected to receive. Some subjects who believed that they would receive alcohol did not; and some subjects who believed that they would receive only tonic water were actually given enough alcohol to render them legally intoxicated. The researchers found that the *actual* dose of alcohol did not affect how punitive a subject was toward a confederate. What affected the subjects' aggression was their *beliefs*: subjects who believed that they had been given alcohol were more aggressive than subjects who believed that they had received none. These results provide another indication of the importance of cognitive processes on aggressive behavior.

Aggression-inhibiting drugs. A number of drugs reduce irritable aggressive behavior. These drugs include the phenothiazines, dilantin, benzodiazepines, and lithium.

The *phenothiazines*, the major tranquilizers, represent an important drug treatment for patients who exhibit destructive, assaultive behavior (see Brill, 1969). For example, *thioridazine* has successfully decreased aggressive tendencies in psychotics (see Kamm & Mandell, 1967; Wolpowitz, 1966), disturbed adolescents (Rosenberg, 1966), mentally retarded persons (Abbott, Blake, & Vincze, 1965), and hyperactive children (Alderton & Hoddinott, 1964). In addition, the phenothiazines seem primarily to affect hostility. Cole, Goldberg, and Davis (1966) discovered that the effectiveness of the phenothiazines in reducing hostility and uncooperativeness in schizophrenic patients was greater than its effect on anxiety, tension, and agitation in these patients.

Dilantin, or *sodium diphenylhydantoin,* a drug which successfully controls seizures, can also decrease hyperexcitability and hostility in epileptics as well as nonepileptics. For example, Stephens and Shaffer (1970) reported that dilantin reduced the feelings of anger, irritability, and impatience in neurotic patients. Resnick (1967) observed a similar effectiveness of dilantin in decreasing the aggressive behavior of prisoners and juvenile delinquents.

The *benzodiazepines* also seem to be a clinically effective treatment of irritable aggressive behavior. Gleser, Gottschalk, Fox, and Lippert (1965) found that *chlordiazepoxide,* or *Librium,* significantly reduced the hostility of juvenile delinquents. Similarly, Mans and Senes (1964) reported that Librium decreased the irritability of neurotic patients. The other major benzodiazepine, *diazepam* (or *Valium*), has been used successfully to treat neurotic patients (Barsa & Saunders, 1964) and psychotic criminals (Kalina, 1964).

The clinical disorder *mania,* characterized by hostility and hyperaggressiveness (see Chapter 8), can be effectively treated with the drug *lithium* (see Gattozzi, 1970). Several studies (for example, Sheard, 1971; Turpin & Clanon, 1976) have observed that lithium significantly reduced the aggressiveness of chronically assaultive prisoners. In addition, Sheard (1970a, 1970b) reported that lithium decreases the irritable aggressiveness of animals.

INSTRUMENTAL AGGRESSION

Suppose that you have been attacked and robbed by a mugger. What motivated the mugger to assault you? Although it is possible that the mugger was motivated by anger or frustration, the act was probably an example of instrumental aggression rather than irritable aggression. *Instrumental aggression,* an aggressive reaction aimed at obtaining reinforcement, is motivated by any of the usual incentives that arouse nonaggressive behavior. For example, hungry people can employ either an aggressive or a nonaggressive response in order to obtain food. Similarly, aggressive as well as nonaggressive behavior can be used to gain money, status, a mate, or victory in a competitive situation. Although anger or frustration may be present during instrumental aggression, this type of aggression can occur in the absence of irritation. However, anger and frustration can intensify an aggressive act; under these circumstances, the aggressive behavior represents a combination of two separate motives.

It is assumed that the same learning principles which affect the development of nonaggressive behavior also affect the establishment of instrumental aggressive behavior. Thus, aggressive behavior which produces reward increases in frequency. In addition, the motivational processes which govern nonaggressive instrumental acts are thought to control the occurrence of an aggressive instrumental act; that is, the greater the motivation, the higher the level of aggressive behavior.

Animal Studies

The real world supplies many examples of instrumental aggression in animals. For example, dogs can be trained to attack certain people or animals if these aggressive acts are reinforced. Similarly, cats can learn to use aggressive behavior to obtain another cat's food, such as a mouse.

Laboratory studies also illustrate the effectiveness of reward in establishing an aggressive behavior as the means of obtaining reinforcement. Although nonpredatory rats caged with a live mouse will starve to death, Moyer (1968) discovered that these rats can learn to kill a mouse as a source of food. Moyer reported that most food-deprived rats will eat a dead mouse which has its back skin slit. After having been exposed to several dead mice, these rats will eat a totally anesthetized mouse. Then, after several experiences with a totally anesthetized mouse, they will attack, kill, and eat a sluggish but mobile slightly anesthetized mouse. Eventually, these hungry, nonpredatory rats will attack, kill, and eat a nonanesthetized mouse. The shaping procedure described in Chapter 1 obviously enables these nonpredatory rats to learn to kill live mice for food. Zagrodzka and Fonberg (1979) observed a similar ability of nonpredatory cats to acquire an instrumental aggressive behavior which enabled them to use the mouse as food.

Reinforcing brain stimulation has also been used to increase the level of aggressive behavior. Stachnik, Ulrich, and Mabry (1966a, 1966b) were able to motivate a rat to attack other rats by reinforcing successive approximations to aggressive behavior. These researchers also reported that this procedure could cause rats to attack monkeys or cats.

Human Studies

A 12-year-old boy makes a violent tackle while playing football, and his coach praises him for his aggressiveness. If the boy values his coach's praise, his next tackle will also be violent. This situation is one example of instrumental aggression. Thieves who are often successful in their robberies and businesspeople whose advertisements attack competitors in order to gain customers are merely two of many cases of instrumental aggression which can be readily observed in the real world.

The literature has consistently reported that the consequences of human aggressive behavior influence the likelihood of aggressive acts (see Bandura, 1977). Persons whose aggressive behavior results in obtaining desired rewards increase the frequency of instrumental aggressive activity; but this form of aggression decreases if the aggressive response is unsuccessful. To provide a vivid illustration of the impact of success on aggressive behavior, let's examine a study of Patterson, Littman, and Bricker (1967).

Patterson, Littman, and Bricker observed children's behavior for 10 weeks and recorded the occurrence of interpersonal aggression as well as the events which followed the aggressive acts. Three types of aggressive consequences were observed: (1) reinforcers (victim winced or cried), (2) punishment (victim counterattacked), or (3) neutral reactions (victim ignored the aggressor). Patterson, Littman, and Bricker noted that positive reinforcement was the most frequent consequence of aggression. In addition, they found that children who initially were passive but whose occasional counteraggression stopped an attack became less defensive and more likely to initiate their own attacks. In contrast, passive children whose occasional counteraggression was unsuccessful remained typically submissive when being attacked. Furthermore, Sallows (1973) discovered that parents of problem children were more likely to provide positive consequences for aggression than parents of normal children. These results indicate that the effects of aggressive behavior play an important role in its use as a way of obtaining reward.

Many people believe that parents' attention, shown in the form of punishment, will increase a child's aggressiveness rather than inhibit it. According to this view, children act aggressively in order to receive punishment from their parents. Tyler and Brown's study (1967), in which boys were verbally punished for aggressive actions, supports this theory. This punishment caused the boys' aggressiveness to increase rather than decrease. In contrast, if boys were quickly and calmly removed from the aggressive situation and placed in a room where they could not receive any reinforcement, their future aggressive behavior was reduced. Apparently, aggressive behavior can be inadvertently reinforced by punitive actions which attempt to discourage it. These observations again illustrate that controlling aggressive behavior is often difficult.

One effective method of inhibiting instrumental aggression is to reward nonaggressive but not aggressive behavior. Smith (1977) discovered that highly aggressive 8-year-old children behaved less aggressively toward another child who rewarded their nonaggressive behavior than toward a child who did not give a reward. In addition, Patterson (1978) and Patterson and Fleischman (1978) reported that training parents to provide fewer positive consequences of aggressive behavior and to reward prosocial responses produced a significant reduction in problem children's aggressive behavior and an increase in the occurrence of nonaggressive acts.

TERRITORIAL AGGRESSION

My local newspaper recently reported the following story: A young man discovered an intruder in his house. Having secured his gun, this young man confronted the burglar, warning him not to move while he called the police. When the intruder tried to escape, the young man shot and killed him.

The Territorial Instinct

What motivated this young man to attack the intruder? In 1966, Konrad Lorenz suggested in his book *On Aggression* that animals and humans possess an instinctive territorial motive which causes them to establish and defend their territory. According to Lorenz's view, our homes are our territory, and thus the young man was defending his territory when he killed the intruder. The young man's aggressive defense of his territory is called *territorial aggression*. Many ethologists (for example, Ardrey, 1966; Jewell, 1966; Morris, 1967; Wynne-Edwards, 1962) advocate the existence of an instinctive territoriality.

It is not surprising that most ethologists support the existence of an instinctive territorial aggressive motive. The literature portrays many animals or humans defending a land area (see Ardrey, 1966, for a review of this literature). For example, lions which enter another lion's territory will be attacked and often killed (see Schaller, 1969). Similarly, mice (see Eibl-Eibesfeldt, 1950), rats (see Archer, 1970), primates (see Carpenter, 1964), and many other species will become aggressive in defense of their territory.

What is a territory? Although you might equate *territory* with *home*, that is not an adequate definition. Most ethologists (see Ardrey, 1966; Jewell, 1966) have merely assumed that a territory is "any defended area," because the home is not the only territory which may be defended. For example, people often defend their place of business, their rights, their beliefs, or their nation, as well as their home; and children will undoubtedly become aggressive when their play area is invaded by another child. To explain the fact that people will defend various areas, Stea (1965) introduced the concept of *territorial unit*.

Animals also defend a variety of areas. Burt (1943) proposed that territories be classified on the basis of function. One territory defended by mammals is their breeding area. Other regions which mammals will defend are those functioning in the rearing of the young, the attainment of food, or the provision of shelter. Nice (1941) classified the territories of birds into types, each based on the combination of feeding, breeding, and nesting behavior. Other ethologists (see Hatch, 1966) have proposed the existence of communal territories; that is, animals will defend areas which they share with other animals.

According to the ethological view, animals "resent" intrusion into their territory (see Ardrey, 1966). This motivational state provides territorial animals with a significant psychological advantage in the protection of their territory. Animals defending their territory are almost always successful in evicting the intruder. The consistent success of the defender is thought to reflect this psychological advantage of the instinctive territorial aggressive motive.

The Defense of One's Territory

You might have the impression that all animals are territorial, automatically defending their territory. However, it is clear that territorial aggressive behavior is highly variable (see Carpenter, 1958). According to Carpenter, species differ in the expression of territorial defense: some species defend their territories, but others are nonterritorial. In addition, the likelihood that a specific member of a particular species will protect a territory from intrusion depends upon the sex of the defender, the characteristics of the intruder, climatic conditions, population density, social organization, availability of food supplies, and various other factors. Let's briefly examine the evidence for these wide variations in the occurrence of territorial aggressive behavior.

Many ethologists (see Ardrey, 1966) have been impressed by the extent of the occurrence of territoriality in the animal kingdom. However, Moyer (1976) argued that it is not universal, and an experiment by Heller (1971) supports this idea. Heller studied four chipmunk species and discovered that two species were territorial while the other two were not. Other species which have been identified as nonterritorial include black rhinoceros (Schenkel & Schenkel-Hilliger, 1969), genus *Phoca* seals (Wynne-Edwards, 1962), red deer of the island of Rhum (Ryzkowski, 1966), ungulates (Wynne-Edwards, 1962), baboons of Rhodesia (Washburn & DeVore, 1961), gorillas (Schaller, 1963), and monkeys of the forest fringes and the savannahs (see Crook, 1968).

Territorial defense is limited to the males of many animal species; however, both males and females of numerous other species will attack intruders of their territory. For example, Carpenter (1940) observed that the female gibbon is as territorial as the male gibbon. Territorial defense has also been reported in female rhesus monkeys (see Wilson, 1968), female lions (Schenkel, 1966), and female weasels (Lockie, 1966).

Animals also differ in their selection of intruders which will be attacked. Some species will attack any intruder; for example, the vole will become aggressive when it encounters any other vole, except during a restricted mating period. However, only certain members of the same species of most territorial animals will elicit territorial aggressive behavior. Sometimes an intruding male of a certain species is attacked while an intruding female of this species is not. Examples of animals which show selective territorial defense include the male wildebeest (Estes, 1969) and the Uganda kob (Buechner, 1961). Still other animal species, such as the lion, will defend their territory only against unfamiliar intruders. Lions live in prides of 4 to 15 members. Although all lions have their own territory, they will not attack a member of their pride entering their territory; they will attack only an unfamiliar intruder. Other studies have documented defense against unfamiliar conspecifics in rabbits (Mykytowycz, 1968), rats (Archer, 1970), mice (Eibl-Eibesfeldt, 1950), and many primates (Carpenter, 1964).

Many external conditions and internal physiological processes affect an animal's tendency to defend its territory. First, territoriality does not occur if (1) space is insufficient, (2) escape cover is inadequate, or (3) high population density exists (see Archer, 1970). In addition, many animal species limit their territorial defense to certain periods of the year, particularly the breeding season (see Wynne-Edwards, 1962). Finally, a limited food supply for which a large number of animals are competing will increase the likelihood of territorial defense (Lockie, 1966).

The Value of the Territoriality Concept

Is there an innate motive which is responsible for the defense of one's territory? Many ethologists believe that there is and find it an attractive explanation of both territorial defense and the psychological advantage of the defender. However, Moyer (1976) argued that the aggressiveness of animals or people in their own territory does not necessarily imply the existence of a territorial instinct. Moyer maintains that so-called territorial aggression actually reflects other forms of aggression; for example, a male in his own territory attacking an intruding male could be showing intermale aggression, irritable aggression, or even instrumental aggression.

Moyer does not think that the typical success of the defender confirms the existence of a territorial motive. He asserts that this success occurs because the area which is familiar to the defender is unfamiliar to the intruder. In an unfamiliar setting, investigatory or escape motives will be elicited, which in turn will inhibit the intruder's hostility. In contrast, since the defender's only motive is aggression, the defender, compared with the intruder, is more likely to be successful.

In Moyer's view, the concept of territoriality does not allow us to understand the causes of animal or human behavior. He asserts that we must look for other causes of aggressive behavior rather than relying on the notion of territorial defense. The wide variety of conditions which influence the occurrence of aggressive behavior within a territory seems to support Moyer's approach.

SUMMARY

When an animal's or human's actions are intended to harm another animal or person, that animal or human is behaving aggressively. Aggressive behavior need not actually inflict damage to be considered aggressive: as long as the intent is to impose harm, the behavior may be labeled *aggression*. This definition does not limit aggression to socially inappropriate acts; punishment and murder are both considered to be aggressive behaviors. In addition, actions which are unintentional but do harm someone else are considered nonaggressive.

According to Moyer, there are seven different causes of aggressive behavior. Each form of aggression, with the exception of instrumental aggression, has a different physiological basis. In animals, each type of aggression has a different behavioral pattern; however, instrumental aggression can employ any of the other forms of aggressive acts in order to obtain rewards. Although in humans the different forms of aggression are not associated with different behavioral patterns, people's aggressive behavior can reflect one or more of these aggressive motives.

Predatory aggression occurs when a predatory animal attacks and kills its natural prey. The aggressive response is characteristic of the predator's species and involves little affective reaction; yet, its occurrence is highly reinforcing. Although predatory aggressive behavior is related to hunger and the attainment of food, its occurrence does not depend upon deprivation. In addition, different areas of the lateral hypothalamus control predatory aggression and hunger. Since learning plays a significant role in the refinement of the instinctive predatory aggressive behavior, the separation of these two motives has obvious adaptive significance.

Intermale aggression occurs when two unacquainted males of the same species encounter each other. The males exhibit a species-specific fighting reaction during this type of aggression. The aggressive response usually takes the form of a threat display at first; this is followed by actual fighting if the threat proved ineffective. An attack will continue until one male either submits or escapes; however, actual physical harm rarely occurs during intermale aggression. The male sex hormone testosterone appears to be an important factor in providing the arousal which is necessary for the exhibition of intermale aggression. In addition, the anterior portion of the lateral hypothalamus seems to be the neural center which activates this form of aggression. The male is not competing for food, a mate, or shelter; this form of aggression is intrinsically reinforcing. However, successful intermale aggressive behavior leads to dominance as well as the attainment of attractive environmental rewards. Once the dominance hierarchy is established, little fighting occurs and social tranquillity exists.

Maternal aggression occurs when a mother attacks any animal which is a perceived threat to her young. The more maternal attention a mother shows her young, the more likely it is that she will show maternal aggression. The maternal aggressive reaction is species-specific, intensely affective, and aimed at inflicting the greatest amount of harm on its target.

Sex-related aggression occurs before and during sexual activity. It is released by the same stimuli that arouse sexual behavior. In some species, sex-related aggression is an integral part of courtship; in other species, it occurs only in certain members. This form of aggression is related to the level of testosterone. Castration eliminates sex-related aggression in animals and has been an effective treatment of human sex offenders.

Fear-related aggression is elicited when an animal is cornered with no possible escape. This form of aggression involves intense autonomic arousal and defensive threat display. If the threat is unsuccessful, a vicious attack ensues. A number of CNS areas, especially the temporal lobes and several areas of the amygdala, arouse fear-induced aggressive behavior; other neural systems in the amygdala and in the septal area inhibit fear-induced aggression.

Irritable aggression reflects an impulsive aggressive reaction elicited by anger and frustration. The aggressive behavior can be directed toward the source of the annoyance or be displaced to either an animate or an inanimate object. The irritable aggressive reaction involves intense autonomic arousal as well as vicious attack behavior. The exhibition of this form of aggressive behavior is highly reinforcing in both annoyed animals and people. After the occurrence of irritable aggressive behavior, autonomic arousal quickly declines unless the aggressive act has been punished in the past. The likelihood that aggressive behavior will occur in an annoyed animal or person is influenced by reward and punishment: if past aggressive acts have been rewarded, irritability will probably arouse aggressiveness; if past aggressive behaviors have been punished, irritability is likely to cause the occurrence of other behaviors. The intensity of irritable aggression also depends upon the presence of aggression cues. These cues associated with aggressive behavior can arouse aggressiveness when an animal or a person is annoyed. Neural systems located in the temporal lobes, several areas of the amygdala, and the anterior lateral hypothalamus initiate irritable aggressive behavior. In contrast, the ventromedial hypothalamus and certain areas of the amygdala inhibit irritable aggressive behavior. Malfunctions in the excitatory areas have been related to extremely violent behavior in humans; surgical destruction of these areas has been an effective treatment of hostile and destructive people. Several diseases, including epilepsy, tumors, allergic reactions, and several drugs (particularly alcohol and amphetamine), can increase irritability. Other drugs, especially tranquilizers, reduce irritable aggressiveness.

Instrumental aggression reflects an aggressive reaction aimed at obtaining reward. This form of aggression is increased when reinforcement is contingent upon aggressive behavior. It can be acquired through direct experience or by observing the acts of others.

Territorial aggression occurs when animals or humans defend their territory from an invader. There is wide variation in the occurrence of territoriality between species. In addition, in territorial animals, not all members of a certain species may be territorial, and territorial defense often depends upon environmental circumstance. When territorial aggression does occur, the defender is usually successful in chasing away the intruder. However, Moyer denies the existence of a territorial motive, maintaining instead that the so-called territorial motive reflects the other forms of aggression.

***D**EPRESSION*

CHAPTER 8

A lack of identity

*T*omorrow is Sarah's fortieth birthday. Thoughts of this impending day have disturbed her for weeks, although her friends assure her that she should be very happy. She and her husband, Charles, recently promoted to sales vice president of his company, occupy an exquisite, large home in an exclusive neighborhood. To celebrate her birthday, Charles bought Sarah an expensive car. Sarah's children also seem successful. Her oldest son, a freshman at the state university, is on the dean's list; her daughter, a senior in high school, is a basketball star; her youngest son, a high school freshman, is class president. Sarah seems to have everything necessary to secure happiness. Yet she does not see a promising future.

Sarah did not attend college; instead, she married Charles the summer after she graduated from high school. Her secretarial job supported them while Charles earned his college degree. Although their first child was born when Sarah was twenty, she continued to work while her mother cared for the baby. When she became pregnant again, Charles had just finished college and had begun to work for a clothing company. Sarah then quit her job to devote herself to her family.

Sarah enjoyed her children's early years; their dependency made her feel needed and important. She felt quite content helping them learn to dress themselves, ride their bicycles, and read. Their needs—someone to help with homework, to chauffeur them to their various activities, and to provide comfort and security—fulfilled Sarah's needs. Sarah and Charles also felt that she had contributed to Charles' advancement in his career—for example, by her successful dinner parties, which enabled Charles to interact pleasantly with his coworkers and superiors. However, now that Charles has become a vice president, Sarah no longer gains much satisfaction from her ornate social gatherings. Also, as the children have matured, their dependency upon their mother has markedly decreased, and they spend much of their time with peers.

Sarah's depression began about a year ago. Her initial infrequent feelings of apathy have changed over the past 2 months to a more intense depression. She not only feels useless and unneeded but also realizes that she does not have the training to get a good job. The thought of going to college after so long an absence from school frightens her. Sarah lacks a sense of identity; she has been a wife and mother for so long that she has no idea of who she is. Feeling helpless and unable to cope with her situation or solve her problems, she has begun to isolate herself from others. She rarely attends social gatherings, preferring to remain home with her problems. Sarah had enjoyed reading, but lately extreme difficulty in concentrating has thwarted this pleasure. Also, Sarah's appetite has dwindled, and she has lost 10 pounds during the past month. Charles, very much concerned about his wife's welfare, has suggested that she discuss her depression with their family physician. She cannot decide whether or not she should seek help.

Sarah's depression is not uncommon in our society. Many people share Sarah's feelings of being unable to cope with their problems. In this chapter we will discuss the processes which produce depression and what people like Sarah might do to overcome their feelings of helplessness.

You might wonder why the topic of depression is included in a motivation text. Sarah's inability to initiate behavior is clearly different from the overt responding which produced the various rewards described in the preceding chapters. Yet not all depressives exhibit an absence of motivated behavior; in fact, some depressed people show excessive levels of responding. Sadness because of their real or imagined inability to obtain desired rewards or to prevent failures is the only characteristic found in all depressives. Thus, rather than reflecting an absence of motivation, the central component of depression represents an emotional response produced by failure to reach one's goals. As you will discover in this chapter, the psychological and biological processes which motivate other behaviors also govern the occurrence of depression. We begin by describing the behavioral symptoms of depression and follow with a discussion of the causes of depression.

THE SADNESS OF DEPRESSION

Martin Seligman (1975) has described depression as the "common cold of psychopathology." No one is immune to the sense of despair indicative of depression; each of us has become depressed following a disappointment or failure. For most, this unhappiness quickly wanes and normal activity resumes. For example, athletes may become depressed following the loss of an important game; yet in a few hours or days the depression is gone, and they are ready to play again. Wallace's account (1956) of the behavior of victims of a tornado in Worcester, Massachusetts, illustrates the typical healing power of time. Wallace noted that although these people functioned well immediately after the tornado, they were extremely distraught 24 to 48 hours later—they wandered aimlessly or just sat in the rain. However, within several days most of them showed no evidence of their previous depression and were able to undertake the task of rebuilding their town. Helplessness persisted for some who were unable to resume normal functioning.

Woodruff, Goodwin, and Guze (1974) estimated that approximately 5 percent of men and 10 percent of women in the United States suffer from severe depression at least once during their lives. These profoundly depressed people, like Sarah in our opening story, are unable to cope with life's stresses; their clinical disturbance prevents them from experiencing the pleasures available to people who are not depressed.

Behavioral Characteristics of Depression

Eight behavioral symptoms are characteristic of depression: (1) *a mood of sadness*, (2) *a negative self-concept*, (3) *social withdrawal*, (4) *loss of appetite*, (5) *recurrent thoughts of death or suicide*, (6) *problems with concentration*, (7) *a change in level of activity*, and (8) *a change in level of hostility*. There are substantial behavioral differences between depressives; for example, one depressed person may be extremely aggressive while other shows a complete lack of aggression. Although each depressive may not exhibit all of the signs of depression, sadness is central to depression and, therefore, present in all depressed people. Let's briefly discuss the eight behavioral characteristics of depression.

1. Depressives feel sad over their inability to obtain desired goals. This sadness does not accurately reflect a personal experience; depressed people, thinking that they are more ineffectual than they are, see their prospects as limited and themselves as unable to make correct decisions. This sense of gloom pervades the entire personality.

2. Many depressed persons assume that their plight has resulted from their own inadequacy. This creates a negative self-image.

3. A depressed person may also withdraw from social relationships and prefer to remain alone.

4. Depressives often lose interest in activities which have been pleasurable or exciting to them. Their loss of appetite causes them to eat less and lose weight. A reduced interest in sex also occurs frequently; impotence or frigidity often accompanies severe depression. Although lack of interest in pleasurable activity causes the reduced appetite of many depressed people, some depressives have a heightened response to rewarding events (see Mathew, Largen, & Claghorn, 1979). These depressives show hyperphagia, or excessive eating, and hypersexuality.

5. One frequent behavior pattern in many depressed people is recurrent thoughts of death or suicide. Lack of hope causes these depressives to consider drastic means, such as suicide, to overcome their plight. Some depressed persons actually do commit or attempt suicide; however, their thoughts of death and suicide do not typically lead to this. (It should be noted that nondepressed people also commit suicide; see Leonard, 1974. Apparently, the process which causes depression differs from that which produces suicide.)

6. Problems with concentration, or extreme difficulty with intellectual tasks, often occur in depressives. For example, Payne (1961) found that his subjects' scores on intelligence tests dropped during periods of depression and rose as their depression waned. Miller and Seligman (1973) reported that depressives performed even a simple task poorly. For example, depressed people solved fewer anagrams (familiar five-letter words to be unscrambled) and required more time to solve them than nondepressed persons.

7. Many depressives show a change in their level of activity; some become lethargic while others become agitated. Seligman (1975) proposed that depressives are less able to initiate voluntary responses than nondepressives. Evidence of this inability is their slower reaction time on psychomotor tasks. For instance, Klein and Seligman (1976) exposed depressed and nondepressed students to an unpleasant noise and found that depressed subjects escaped more slowly than nondepressed subjects. In addition, depressives show a reduced sensitivity to social intercourse—for example, depressives took longer to respond to the social courtesy "good morning" than nondepressed persons (Lewinsohn, 1974). However, Depue and Monroe (1978), observed that this reduced activity is representative only of *endogenous depression,* a form of depression thought to be caused by an internal biological or psychological process. In contrast, individuals whose depression is reactive or exogenous are more active and agitated than nondepressed persons. *Reactive or exogenous depression* is thought to occur in response to an environmental trauma such as the death of a parent or spouse. The research of Kendall (1972) and Mendels and

Cochrane (1968) supports the view that lowered initiation of voluntary responses (or psychomotor retardation) occurs with endogenous depression, whereas active pacing and agitation are characteristic of reactive (exogenous) depression.

8. A change in the level of hostility is the eighth behavioral characteristic which often occurs in depressed people. Freud (1917) noted that depressed persons exhibit a lack of overt hostility toward others. The lack of aggression is still considered typical of depression (see Jacobson, 1971). In addition, Kurlander, Miller, and Seligman (1975) discovered that depressed college students were less competitive than nondepressed ones. Seligman (1975) suggested that the absence of aggressiveness in depressives is another example of their failure to initiate voluntary action. As we learned from our discussion of activity, not all depressives act alike and many are not "drained of overt hostility" (Depue & Monroe, 1978). The absence of aggression is representative of endogenous depression and most reactive depressives; however, Paykel (1971) noted that one group of reactive depressives—a hostile type—were extremely aggressive compared with nondepressed or other depressed people.

The Distinction between Endogenous and Exogenous Depression: Fact or Fiction?

The endogenous-exogenous classification system is frequently used to distinguish between types of clinically depressed people; internal factors cause endogenous depression, whereas an external crisis is thought to cause exogenous depression. However, a review of the literature does not indicate that precipitating environmental stressors affect only exogenous depressives. Leff, Roatch, and Bunney (1970) failed to observe differences in the type of frequency of stresses preceding the onset of either endogenous or exogenous depression. The differences between endogenous and exogenous depression seem to reflect behavioral differences rather than the presence or absence of a precipitating event. Even when a specific situation (for example, loss of job) appears to precede depression, it may be difficult to determine if the depression is the reason for or the result of the situation (Mendels, 1970): depression may have caused the person to lose his or her job. Briscoe and Smith (1975), in support of this view, found that depression is often the cause rather than the result of a divorce. Therefore, while endogenous depressives are more likely than reactive exogenous depressives to exhibit withdrawal from the environment, the causal agent may be identical for each category of depression. In fact, Klerman and Paykel (1970) believe that the behavioral differences between these two types of depressives merely reflect the greater severity of depression in the endogenous depressive.

Although it may be difficult to detect the actual cause of a particular person's depression, psychologists have identified several processes which influence the development of depression. Theories describing these processes fall into five categories: (1) *genetic*, (2) *biochemical*, (3) *psychoanalytic*, (4) *reinforcement*, and (5) *cognitive*. Contemporary research indicates that no single process determines every case of depression, but that the causes of depression differ among individuals (see Figure 8.1). In many cases, more than one cause may be responsible for depression. We now turn to these processes. Later in the chapter we will focus on methods of motivating depressed persons which enable them to resume normal activities.

GENETIC INFLUENCE

Some depressives exhibit periods of an emotional state, *mania*, which is the opposite of depression. Individuals in this manic state display the following symptoms: (1) *they seem*

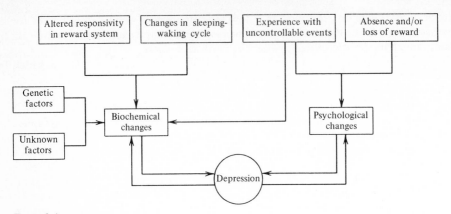

Figure 8.1
Psychological and biochemical factors which influence the occurrence of depression. Once depression occurs, the depressive's behavior can intensify the biochemical and psychological changes associated with depression and thereby increase its severity.

elated and overconfident of future success, (2) *they speak rapidly, often of grandiose plans*, (3) *they are quite active and easily agitated*, (4) *they have difficulty sleeping*, and (5) *they have difficulty concentrating and are easily distracted*. This disorder, previously termed manic-depression, has been renamed *bioplar depression* in the current clinical labeling system (DSM-III) of the American Psychiatric Association. This label seems more appropriate, as depression is the major component of this disorder. Bipolar depressives do not typically go through a regular pattern of manic and depressive states; their depression usually lasts for a period of several weeks or months, followed by a period of normality. A limited period of mania (of unpredictable length) usually occurs between the normal period and the next depression. However, in some instances the manic phase may not occur, and the person simply becomes depressed again. The absence of manic episodes makes it very difficult to distinguish *bipolar depressives* from *unipolar depressives*, those exhibiting only depression. In the absence of mania, the classification of bipolar or unipolar depression is based on family history. A depressed person who has not exhibited manic states is classified as bipolar if mania and depression have appeared in this person's first-degree relatives. This system is used because there is substantial evidence that bipolar depression has a strong genetic component. On the other hand, unipolar depression appears to occur independently of inheritance.

Family History
Evidence supporting the view of genetic influence on bipolar depression comes from studies analyzing the *concordance rate* between first-degree relatives. Rosenthal (1970) summarized these studies and reported that the concordance rate between identical twins ranged from 50 to 100 percent (see Table 8.1). This means that if one twin has bipolar depression, the likelihood that the other twin will have this disorder is between 50 and 100 percent. The concordance rate for fraternal twins ranged from 0 to 40 percent; most studies reported from 20 to 30 percent. Since identical twins are genetically identical, whereas fraternal twins are no closer genetically than ordinary siblings, the higher concordance rate for identical twins implies that bipolar depression

Table 8.1
Concordance Rates for Bipolar Depression in Monozygotic (Identical) and
Dizygotic (Fraternal) Twins

Study	Monozygotic Twins		Dizygotic Twins	
	Pairs	Concordance Rate	Pairs	Concordance Rate
Luxenburger, 1930	4	75.0	13	0.0
Rosanoff et al., 1934–1935	23	69.6	67	16.4
Kallmann, 1952	27	92.6	55	23.6
Slater, 1953				
(only manic-depressive)	7	57.1	17	23.5
Other affective disorders	1	0.0	13	18.8
Dafonseca, 1959	21	71.4	39	38.5
Harvaid and Hauge, 1965	10	50.0	39	2.6

Adapted from: Rosenthal, D. *Genetic theory and abnormal behavior.* New York: McGraw-Hill, 1970.

has a strong genetic component. The concordance rate between first-degree relatives is between 10 and 20 percent; this indicates a moderate risk of bipolar depression when a close relative suffers from it. In comparison, the likelihood that two nonrelated persons will suffer from bipolar depression is 1 to 2 percent (see Davison & Neale, 1978). In contrast, the concordance rate of unipolar depression between first-degree relatives is equal to the incidence of depression between nonrelated persons. For example, Perris (1969) found a concordance rate for unipolar depression between first-degree relatives of 7.4 percent; this is equivalent to the level of depression in the general population. Apparently, the likelihood of unipolar depression is not related to genetic background.

Sex-Related Genetic Transmission

The genetic mechanism responsible for the inheritance of bipolar depression remains unsettled. Winokur and Clayton (1967) suggest that bipolar depression is caused by a dominant gene on the X chromosome, one of the two chromosomes determining sex. If this view is correct, then male offspring of bipolar fathers should not exhibit bipolar depression, since they do not receive the X chromosome from their fathers. To support this view, Winokur, Clayton, and Reich (1969) investigated the family history of bipolar depressives. One comparison was the percentage of fathers and sons who exhibited bipolar depression. Results of this comparison indicated no instances of father-son bipolar depression. They next evaluated father-daughter pairs and found a 13 percent concordance rate; mother-offspring pairs (mother-son and mother-daughter) showed a 17 percent concordance rate. These results support the idea that the X chromosome influences bipolar depression; offspring who receive the X chromosome from a bipolar depressive parent are likely to suffer from the same disorder, whereas offspring who do not receive the X chromosome will not exhibit bipolar depression. However, Goetzl, Green, Whybrow, and Jackson (1974) and Hays (1976) did discover evidence of father-son pairs of bipolar depressives. The precise genetic mechanism responsible for bipolar depression awaits future investigation.

BIOCHEMICAL INFLUENCE

Brain Amine Deficiency

Contemporary research indicates that disturbances in the functioning of the brain amine chemical transmitter systems (the *catecholamines* and *indoleamines*) are involved in human depression. The two amine transmitter substances implicated in depression are *norepinephrine* and *serotonin*. A deficiency in one (or both) of these substances correlates with depression; an elevation of either reverses depression. In addition, unusually high levels of norepinephrine appear to be related to the manic state. In this section, we will present the evidence which indicates that these substances are related to depression. (Refer to the Appendix for a review of the chemical transmission process.) Also, we will discuss why changes in these brain amine systems lead to depression.

Studies evaluating amine levels have demonstrated a deficiency in depressed individuals (see Depue & Evans, 1976). For example, Ashcroft, Crawford, and Eccleston (1966) measured the level of a serotonin metabolite (*5-hydroxyindole acetic acid* or 5HIAA) in the cerebrospinal fluid of depressed and nondepressed persons and found lower levels of 5HIAA in the depressives. Similarly, several other studies (for example, Maas, Dekirmenjian, & Fawcett, 1971) point to a low level of the cerebrospinal metabolite (*3-methoxy-4-hydroxyphenylethylene glycol,* or MHPG) of norepinephrine in depressives. In addition, Bunney, Goodwin, and Murphy (1972) found that urinary levels of norepinephrine increased as their patients became manic and decreased when they became depressed.

Drugs which decrease brain amine levels induce depressive behavior. Lemieux, Davignon, and Genest (1956) reported that reserpine, a drug which reduces levels of serotonin and norepinephrine, produced depression. In contrast, drugs which elevate brain amine levels are able to decrease depressive symptoms. Two classes of drugs— *tricyclic compounds* and *monoamine oxidase* (MAO) *inhibitors*—which increase brain amine levels appear to provide clinical relief for many depressed individuals. The tricyclic compounds increase brain norepinephrine by interfering with its reuptake after the neuron fires. Davis, Klerman, and Schildkraut (1967) found the tricyclic drugs effective in the treatment of some depressives. Additionally, people with severe endogenous depression seem to benefit most from use of these drugs (Lapolla & Jones, 1970). The MAO inhibitors increase levels of norepinephrine and serotonin by preventing their breakdown and thus prolonging their effectiveness during neural transmission. Davis, Klerman, and Schildkraut (1967) discovered that MAO inhibitor *plenelzine* decreased depression.

Additional support for the importance of the brain amines comes from research which evaluates the effect of *lithium carbonate* on bipolar depressives. Recall that Bunney, Goodwin, and Murphy (1972) observed that urinary levels of norepinephrine increased during mania. Since lithium carbonate acts to decrease brain levels of norepinephrine, it should provide an effective treatment of mania (see Frazer & Winokur, 1977). The clinical effectiveness of lithium carbonate seems well established. For example, Prien, Caffey, and Klett (1973) conducted a double-blind study to evaluate the influence of lithium on bipolar depressives. Some patients received lithium; others were given a placebo treatment. This 2-year study indicated that the group treated with placebos displayed a strong tendency to stop treatment and be hospitalized. In contrast, the group treated with lithium showed a significant reduction in manic episodes. Also, lithium reduced the intensity of depression. Other studies (see Dunner, Stallone, & Fieve, 1976) showed that lithium decreased the frequency of depression. Apparently, mania is involved in producing depression—a result consistent with the opponent-process model (see Chapter 4).

Causes of Biochemical Disturbance

The biochemical changes in depressed persons probably result from genetic processes, experiential processes, or both. Although no direct evidence indicates that genetic factors produce depression, the importance of inheritance in bipolar depression and the clinical effectiveness of lithium in treating bipolar depression strongly suggest this. The research of Jay Weiss and his associates (see Weiss, Stone, & Harrell, 1970) suggests that experience might also cause the biochemical changes related to depression. They noted that exposing rats to uncontrollable events produced many of the biochemical and behavioral symptoms characteristic of depression. They gave rats a shock from which the rats could not escape; one-half hour later these rats failed to escape an electrical shock from which they could have escaped. Other rats were exposed to shocks which they could escape or control; these rats did not show any behavioral impairment. Weiss observed that uncontrollable events produced a greater reduction in brain norepinephrine than controllable events. According to Weiss, depression occurs when uncontrollable events lower brain norepinephrine levels. The lowered norepinephrine prevents the animal from being able to initiate overt behavior. Depression diminishes as norepinephrine levels rise—either naturally with time or because of chemical intervention—and the animal is able to resume normal responding.

CNS Reward System and Depression

The behavioral and chemical changes during depression indicate that the CNS reward system is involved in depression (see Chapter 4). Norepinephrine is the chemical transmitter substance in the medial forebrain bundle (MFB). Activity in the MFB is reinforcing, and the function of the MFB is to motivate an animal to seek reward. A loss of interest in reinforcement occurs in many depressed people. Drugs which decrease the norepinephrine level reduce responsivity to reward, whereas the antidepressant drugs (tricyclics, MAO inhibitors) increase both the brain norepinephrine level and the motivation to obtain reinforcement.

The research of Thomas and Balter (1975) provides support for the role of the MFB in depression. The *septum area* of the limbic system inhibits the MFB. The chemical transmitter within the septum is *acetylcholine*. Thomas and Balter found that chemical stimulation of the septum produced the behavioral passivity characteristic of depression. In another study, Thomas and Balter noted that if rats which had received uncontrollable shocks were injected with *atropine*, their behavioral passivity was reduced. Since atropine blocks acetylcholine activity, the lowered depression produced by atropine supports the idea that the central reward system is involved in depression. Janowsky, El-Yousef, Davis, Hubbard, and Sekerke (1972) noticed a similar influence of cholinergic drugs in humans. Injecting nondepressives with *physostigmine*—a drug which increases acetylcholine level by blocking its breakdown during neural transmission—produced feelings of helplessness and suicidal wishes. Atropine reduced their feelings of depression.

Our discussion indicates that the reward system plays an important role in elevated (manic) and reduced (depressed) emotional states. However, it is clear that affective disorders are influenced by other biological systems. There are substantial behavioral differences among depressed individuals: some depressives are agitated; others are withdrawn. The mania seen in many bipolar depressives is not found in unipolar depressives. Also, depressives vary in their responsivity to different drugs. For instance, the sedative action of the tricyclic *amitriptyline* is especially effective with anxious depressives. The activational effect of the tricyclic compound *protriptyline* helps withdrawn depressives (see Frazer & Winokur, 1977). Interestingly, Frazer and Winokur also found that only 20 percent of depressed patients who responded to the MAO inhibitors reacted favorably to the tricyclic drugs. The same is true of depressives who responded to a tricyclic drug; the MAO inhibitors probably will not reduce their depression. Apparently, in addition to the reward center, other biological systems are involved in depression.

Recent evidence suggests that a disturbance in the cycle of sleeping and waking can also produce depression. Let's now examine some of this research.

Sleep and Depression

Recall the discussion of REM and NREM sleep in Chapter 4. We learned that the frequency and latency of REM sleep increased during the latter half of the sleep cycle and that the circadian rhythm regulates the onset, pattern, and termination of sleep. The research of several investigators (for example, Kupfer, 1976) indicates that many depressives show a disturbance in the typical waking-sleeping cycle: REM sleep occurs earlier than normal in the sleep period and total sleeping time is shortened. Also, Wehr, Wirz-Justice, Goodwin, Duncan, and Gillin (1979) discovered that some of their bipolar depressives' sleeping patterns changed as their mood improved. Furthermore, advancing sleep 6 hours for those patients produced temporary remission of depressive symptoms.

Studies altering the sleeping-waking cycle in nondepressed people also demonstrate the important role which sleep plays in depression. For example, Weitzman, Kripke, Goldmacher, McGregor, and Nogeire (1970) showed that the disturbed sleep response seen in many depressives can be produced in nondepressed people by shifting the onset of sleep from 10 P.M. to 10 A.M. Also, an experimentally altered sleeping-waking cycle is associated with depression, hostility, and suicide in some healthy individuals (see Cutler & Cohen, 1979).

According to Wehr, Wirz-Justice, Goodwin, Duncan, and Gillin (1979), a disturbance in the circadian rhythm of some depressive people causes biological changes which initiate REM sleep earlier in the sleep cycle than in nondepressives. This advanced REM sleep produces the altered sleep pattern observed in some depressives. In support of this view, Wehr, Muscettola, and Goodwin (1980) discovered that changes in oral temperature and motor activity which normally occur in the circadian cycle took place 3 hours earlier in some depressives than in nondepressives.

Sleep serves an important restorative function. Thus, disruption in the normal sleep pattern impairs our ability to interact with the environment and, thereby, increases the likelihood of depression. However, advanced REM sleep, while related to depression in some people, reflects only one of many biochemical factors which appear to be involved in producing depression. Support for this view can be seen in the observation that not all depressives show a sleep disturbance. Further, an altered sleeping-waking cycle does not always induce depression in nondepressed people. Thus, the biochemical substrates of depression vary among depressed persons. The biological systems responsible for these differences remain unsettled.

The importance of biochemical systems in depression is striking; yet psychological events also play an important role in the development of depression. Although it may be difficult in a specific instance to determine whether biological or psychological processes have precipitated depression, psychotherapy can reverse both the behavioral and the biochemical correlates of depression. We will next study the psychological determinants of depression. In the last section of this chapter, we will discuss several psychological methods of motivating depressed individuals to resume their normal functioning.

PSYCHOLOGICAL APPROACHES

Three psychological views, each stressing the importance of environmental influences, have emerged to explain depression. In the *psychoanalytic view,* early unresolved conflict is thought to predispose an individual to depression. The *reinforcement approach* suggests that the absence of reinforcement or effective methods of obtaining reward (or both) produces depression. The third approach is a *cognitive view* of depression. Although there are several different cognitive approaches, the core component of each is the depressed person's belief that goals are unattainable. We begin our discussion of psychological approaches to depression with the psychoanalytic approach.

Psychoanalytic View

In 1917, Freud suggested that the origin of depression lies in the oral stage of psychosexual development (refer to Chapter 1 for a review of his theory). According to Freud, during this stage children experience conflict between their instinctual needs and environmental forces. Their dependency on others for the satisfaction of their strong oral needs conflicts with their anger when these needs are thwarted. In some cases this intense conflict causes children to fixate at the oral stage and therefore to remain dependent upon their parents. The fixation produces children who continue during childhood and adolescence to be excessively dependent upon parents. Because of this dependency upon parents, they fail to develop a sense of self which is independent of the evaluation of others. The absence of self-esteem causes dependent persons to hate themselves; either they will remain dependent upon their parents or they will develop a new dependency relationship with others. These dependent people see love as the support provided by others.

The distinction between grief and depression. This external support enables excessively dependent persons to function as they mature. However, they will become extremely depressed following the death of the loved one who has provided support. Let's begin by examining the psychoanalytic view of grief to understand why dependent persons become depressed when loved ones die. After the death of a loved one, a mourner first *introjects.* According to the psychoanalytic view, introjection is an unconscious process in which the grieving person incorporates into his or her ego structure the dead person's values, attitudes, and qualities in an effort to maintain the bond with the dead person. The mourner also has negative feelings toward the deceased, which stem from resentment over the loved one's desertion. These negative feelings lead to experiencs of guilt for real or imagined crimes committed against the loved one or the loved one's wishes. For most people, this introjection period is short-lived. Memories of the deceased are recalled during this time, enabling the mourner to break the bond imposed by the introjection period. Once the bond is weakened, the mourning ends and the person is able to resume normal social relationships.

The separation process enables most people to overcome their grief; however, for the excessively dependent person grief is so intense that the bond cannot be broken. Under these circumstances, grief becomes depression. In the psychoanalytic view, depression reflects anger turned against oneself. The depressive's guilt, self-hatred, and anger over desertion remain. The depressed person attempts to overcome guilt by becoming manic; the childlike adoration of oneself typical of mania represents a defense against depression. Unfortunately, mania only temporarily overcomes self-hatred, and depression recurs. Several periods of alternating mania and depression will ensue as the dependent person continues to attempt to overcome his or her depression. However, the continued presence of intense grief makes it more difficult for a person to inhibit depression by using the self-love characteristic of mania. The failure to defend against depression results in longer and more intense periods of depression, until eventually depression is the only emotional state experienced.

Apparent support for the psychoanalytic view of depression comes from studies which demonstrate that the loss of a parent, close friend, or relative sometimes produces intense *anaclitic depression* (see Chapter 9 for a detailed discussion of the process responsible for producing anaclitic depression). However, Depue and Evans's review (1976) of the literature did not indicate that depression always occurs in response to the loss of a loved one. They reported that there are many instances in which people become depressed in the absence of loss. Contemporary psychoanalytic thinking, in an attempt to account for the absence of a loss preceding depression, suggests that a dependent individual will view rejection as a "symbolic loss" of the support of a loved one.

Criticism of the psychoanalytic approach.   Davison and Neale (1978) point to one major flaw in the psychoanalytic view. If during the introjection period mourners are reexperiencing their feelings toward their loved ones, why do anger and resentment dominate to produce depression, since many of their previous feelings are pleasant? Psychoanalytic thinking suggests that the overly dependent person views the death of a loved one as a rejection or withdrawal of love. These feelings of rejection cause the negative emotions to dominate and produce depression. However, there is no evidence that depressives view the death of a loved one as rejection. Davison and Neale agreed with Mendels's theory (1970) that there is little support for the psychoanalytic view "other than the often-repeated assertions by adherents that things are as they conceive them to be."

Many aspects of the psychoanalytic approach do not seem to reflect the processes leading to depression accurately; yet the loss of a loved one may represent a causal agent in depression. Rather than creating self-hatred and guilt, the death may represent one type of loss of reward; this source of reinforcement may be especially difficult for the dependent person to replace. We now turn to the reinforcement approach to depression. In this view, the absence of reward or of an effective method of obtaining reward produces depression.

Reinforcement Theory

Peter Lewinsohn (see Lewinsohn, 1974) proposed a reinforcement explanation of depression. According to Lewinsohn, a low rate of positive reward naturally elicits depression. Thus, those who have experienced little or no reinforcement become depressed. Three types of circumstances produce an absence of reward: (1) *Positive reinforcers are unavailable to some as a result of their personal characteristics such as age, race, sex, or attractiveness.* One obvious example is an unattractive person who is unable to get dates and, lacking this important source of social reinforcement, becomes a victim of depression. Another is a middle-aged person who is denied jobs because of age. (2) *There is an absence of reinforcers in the environment.* Here there is no discrimination against certain people; rather, there are situations in which nobody is able to obtain reinforcement, because it is not available. For example, many people are likely to lose their jobs during a recession; the reinforcement of working and earning money is no longer available, and this absence of reward subsequently elicits depression. Similarly, the death of a loved one produces depression because the loss removes an important source of reinforcement for those who are bereaved. (3) *The lack of effective skills results in little or no reinforcement.* In the vignette at the beginning of this chapter, Sarah's depression is an example of the influence of instrumental behavior in producing depression. It is Sarah's lack of adequate training that prevents her from obtaining reinforcement and, according to Lewinsohn, produces her depression.

A depressed person's behavior is also likely to decrease the amount of reinforcement further. Others usually avoid someone who is depressed; and a depressive's typically reduced activity and concentration makes it unlikely that he or she will obtain reinforcement. Therefore, a depressed student probably will not excel in school. In a vicious circle, the lowered level of reinforcement produced by depression acts to increase the intensity of the depression.

Social reward of depression. One further point in Lewinsohn's theory deserves our attention. Close relatives may provide depressives with social reinforcement (for example, sympathy or concern) for a while. The effect of this social reward is that the depression acts like any instrumental behavior and, having been reinforced, increases in intensity. This increase, however, reduces the likelihood that the depressive will obtain other sources of reinforcement. Eventually, even this social reward will no longer be available, as close relatives begin to avoid the extremely depressed person. For example, family and close friends provide comfort to someone whose parent has died. The depression is short-lived in most instances, and the mourner resumes normal reinforcing activity. However, if the depression continues (possibly owing to a lack of sufficient outside reinforcers), this attention from family and friends will diminish until the depressive is finally avoided by even close relatives and friends. Lewinsohn and Shaffer (1971) observed the social interactions between depressed people and their spouses in their homes. They found that those depressed people elicited less attention and interest from their mates than nondepressed people. Figure 8.2 presents a schematic representation of Lewinsohn's model of depression.

Empirical evidence. Support for Lewinsohn's theory is indirect but does indicate that reinforcement plays an important role in the development and maintenance of depression. The only way to demonstrate causality would be for an experimenter to

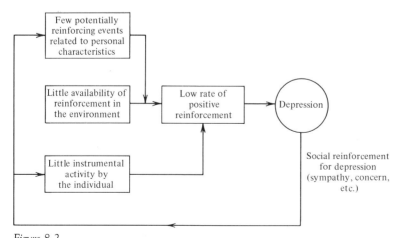

Figure 8.2
Lewinsohn's reinforcement model of depression. In Lewinsohn's view, a low rate or absence of reward elicits depression. Once the person becomes depressed, social reinforcement of the depressive decreases the likelihood of obtaining other rewards and thereby prolongs the depression. [From Davison, G. C., & Neale, J. M. Abnormal psychology: An experimental clinical approach (2nd ed.). New York: Wiley, 1978.]

reduce the level of reinforcement in nondepressed humans. This type of research is unethical and fortunately psychologists have not pursued it. However, the correlational research of Lewinsohn and his associates does provide evidence of the relationship between reinforcement and depression. Lewinsohn and Libet (1972) noticed a significant positive correlation between the number of pleasant (reinforcing) experiences and the mood of depressed and nondepressed persons; the larger the number of pleasant experiences, the better the reported mood of both depressed and nondepressed people. These results demonstrate the importance of the level of reinforcement on perceived emotionality. In accord with Lewinsohn's theory, a reduced level of reward appears to be related to poorer mood.

According to Lewinsohn, as was noted earlier, depressives receive less reward than nondepressives because depressives (1) interact less frequently with the environment, (2) have fewer rewards available, and (3) possess less effective skills for obtaining reward. MacPhillamy and Lewinsohn's data (1974) supported the first two of these characteristics. MacPhillamy and Lewinsohn compared clinically depressed patients, psychiatric nondepressed patients (persons experiencing psychological disorders but not depression), and nondepressed normal persons in terms of observed frequency of obtaining reward and their potential for receiving reinforcement. The results indicated that depressed people participated in fewer reinforcing activities and had fewer available reinforcers than either nondepressed psychiatric patients or normal people. Also, depressed persons experienced less pleasure from reward than either nondepressed psychiatric patients or normal people. These data demonstrated not only that depressives receive less reinforcement than nondepressives but also that a lowered level of reward is related to depression but not to other behavioral disturbances. Interestingly, the data revealed that depressed people desire reward as much as others but unfortunately receive less reinforcement. Table 8.2 presents the results of MacPhillamy and Lewinsohn's study.

In Lewinsohn's view, lack of skills also reduces the amount of experienced reward. Libet and Lewinsohn (1973) evaluated the level of social skills in depressed and nondepressed people. They observed that, compared with nondepressed persons, depressed individuals in group settings initiated fewer social interactions and were less likely to reciprocate the positive social responses of others. Depressives' lack of social skill very likely causes others to provide little social reinforcement for them.

Lewinsohn recognized that these observations do not prove that lack of reinforce-

Table 8.2
Mean Scale Scores for Obtained Pleasure, Activity Level,
Reinforcement Potential, and Desired Pleasure in Depressed
and Nondepressed Individuals

Scale	Group		
	Depressed	Psychiatric Control	Normal Control
Obtained pleasure	.196	.271	.262
Activity level	.323	.414	.405
Reinforcement potential	.479	.528	.526
Desired pleasure	.662	.714	.722

Adapted from: MacPhillamy, D. J., & Lewinsohn, P. M. Depression as a function of levels of desired and obtained pleasure. *Journal of Abnormal Psychology,* 1974, 83, 651–657. Copyright 1974 by the American Psychological Association. Reprinted by permission.

ment causes depression. It is possible that depressive behaviors produce the lack of reinforcement and that other processes actually cause depression. However, Lewinsohn and his colleagues (see Lewinsohn & Atwood, 1969; Lewinsohn, Weinstein, & Alper, 1970) demonstrated that behavioral procedures which increase the frequency of reinforcing activities represent an effective treatment for depression. The ability of a change in experienced reinforcement to influence depression provides support for the importance of using reinforcement to treat depression. We will examine Lewinsohn's behavioral approach to the treatment of depression later in this chapter.

CNS punishment state and depression.   Lewinsohn's reinforcement theory resembles the drive view of nonreward described in Chapter 2. The absence of anticipated reward elicits an intense emotional state called frustration or disappointment; this emotional state motivates avoidance behavior. The withdrawal observed in many depressed individuals is similar to the effects of nonreward seen in animal studies. In Chapter 2, we learned that frustration activates a central aversive motivation state. The stimulation of this system increases the motivation to avoid potentially painful events. Lewinsohn, Lobitz, and Wilson (1973) found depressives more responsive than nondepressives to painful events (for example, mild electrical shock). These results support the idea that a central aversive motivational system is involved in depression.

An overview.   Although loss of reinforcement plays an important role in depression, it clearly is not sufficient cause for clinical depression. Many persons who lose important rewards do not become depressed. In the next section we will see that for a person to become depressed, there must also be either a real or an imagined inability to regain lost rewards. Moreover, no evidence exists indicating that failure to obtain one's goals precipitates the biological changes related to depression. However, once someone becomes depressed, he or she is likely to lose additional rewards and, thereby, deepen depression. Our discussion portrays depression as being governed by several processes. We now turn to the cognitive processes which influence it.

Cognitive Approaches

The American Psychiatric Association stated in 1952 that depression is an affective disorder in which cognitive processes play a minimal or secondary role. However, contemporary evidence indicates that cognitive systems represent a major factor in the development of depression. Two cognitive views emerged during the late 1960s to explain the role of expectations in the development of depression. Aaron Beck (1967) based his approach on clinical observations; a second view, described by Martin Seligman(1975), evolved from experiments with animals and college students. Each theory assumes that depressed individuals' expectations about the future produce the emotional and motivational disturbances characteristic of depression. Geer, Davison, and Gatchel's experiment (1970) is an example of the studies which demonstrate the influence of expectations on emotionality. These experimenters found that subjects who believed that they had control over the occurrence of painful stimulation were less aroused than those who felt that they had no control over it. Geer, Davison, and Gatchel noticed this lowered arousal even if the subjects' belief that they would control events was inaccurate. Apparently, what we believe affects how we feel. Although both Beck's and Seligman's cognitive views enhanced the understanding of the processes producing depression, these views were too simplistic and did not accurately reflect the role of cognitive processes in depression. In 1978, Martin Seligman (see Abramson, Seligman, & Teasdale, 1978) reformulated his expectancy approach into an attributional model of depression. His attributional approach, although still in its infancy, appears to represent a major advance in correctly describing the complex cognitive processes which produce depression. In addition, Beck's early cognitive view fostered the development of several effective cognitive treatments of depression; we will discuss these therapies later in this chapter. We begin our discussion with Aaron Beck's cognitive theory of depression.

Beck's perceptual view.   As was noted earlier in this discussion, depressives have a negative self-image; they think very poorly of themselves. Some approaches assume that depression produces this poor self-image; Beck (1967), on the contrary, believes that the cognitive structure of the depressive causes the emotional and motivational symptoms. According to Beck, people become depressed because they interpret experiences in a negative way. These people think of themselves as inadequate, blaming themselves for their failures and assuming that their own incompetence causes them to fail. In addition to their feelings of inadequacy, they do not expect to be successful in the future; this bleak prospect causes depression. Nondepressed persons may also feel responsible for failure, of course, but they do not assume that failure is the result of their inadequacy. Instead, they might suppose that they need to work harder to produce future success. After a failure, depressives expect future failure; this attitude sharply contrasts with that of nondepressives, who are hopeful after failure.

A distortion of reality.   What differences in cognitive processes exist between the depressed and the nondepressed? Beck assumes that people become depressed because they draw illogical conclusions from their experiences. Everyone has a perceptual processing system, or *schema* (plural, *schemata*). According to Beck, a depressed person's schema is based on self-deprecation and self-blame. These people interpret failure by employing a distorted perceptual processing system. They become depressed after saying to themselves, "What a jerk I am for causing my failure," or "How hopeless the future is." In Beck's view, depressives are victims of their illogical judgments about themselves.

Yet, even the most depressed have sometimes succeeded in the past. According to Beck, these people do not believe that they were ever responsible for their success. For example, if they received an A on a test, they assume that they were lucky or that the teacher was nice to them. Thus, while depressives attribute failure to their own incompetence, they attribute success to outside forces. In contrast, nondepressives assume themselves responsible for both their successes and their failures.

Recall our discussion of Sarah's depression at the beginning of the chapter. According to Beck's cognitive view, Sarah's distorted perceptual processing is responsible for her depression. Sarah believes that her incompetence has caused her to fail to obtain training; also, if she reentered school, her feelings of inadequacy would cause her to expect to fail. She does not view the advancement of her husband and children as partially due to her efforts; she feels that her family would have succeeded just as well without her. Sarah's distorted cognitive processes cause her to experience the aversive emotional state of depression.

Empirical evidence.   The support for Beck's cognitive view, like Lewinsohn's reinforcement approach, is indirect. However, a number of studies report correlations between cognitive processes and emotional states; the results implicate cognitive systems in depression. For example, Minkoff, Bergman, Beck, and Beck (1973) found a significant positive correlation between hopelessness and depression. Furthermore, Beck (1976) reported that changes in the cognitive processing of depressed individuals produced a reduction in the other symptoms characteristic of depression.

The cognitive view of depression proposed by Beck indicates that depressed people blame themselves for their failures and expect future failure to occur as the result of their incompetence. Martin Seligman's learned-helplessness theory (see Seligman, 1975) contrasts sharply with Beck's view. According to Seligman, depressed persons assume that their failures are due to uncontrollable events and expect to continue to fail as long as these events are beyond their control: depression develops because these people believe that they are unable to control their own destiny. Whereas Beck attributes depression to an internal belief of incompetence, Seligman attributes it to an external assumption— that one has no control over events. We will shortly discover that each approach is valid—but only in specific circumstances: an internal assertion of incompetence produces depression in certain situations; in other instances, people may become depressed despite general feelings of competence if they believe that events cannot be controlled. We will examine the appropriateness of each view when Seligman's attributional model of depression is described in the next section. First, let's discuss Seligman's learned-helplessness approach to depression.

Learned-helplessness theory. Imagine that your dream since childhood has been to be a physician, but none of the medical schools to which you have applied has admitted you. You certainly would feel distressed for a while. If you are like most people who are at first rejected, you might decide to enroll in some additional courses, study harder, and apply again. Or you could search for an alternative future occupation. Suppose, however, that you do become severely depressed. According to Seligman, in this case your depression would not be caused by self-depreciation; you probably believe that you are very capable of succeeding in medical school. Seligman proposed that depression emerges when you think that failure is inevitable—thus, you become depressed because you feel that there is nothing that you could do to be accepted; you expect that if you reapply, you will be rejected again. You base this expectation on your assumption that no matter how well you perform in school, you will be rejected. Depression, according to Seligman, is produced when people come to believe that events are independent of their behavior. The expectation that events are uncontrollable Seligman labeled *learned helplessness*.

Original animal research. Seligman developed his learned-helplessness theory of depression from his animal studies (see Maier & Seligman, 1976, for a review of this literature). The original studies (Overmier & Seligman, 1967; Seligman & Maier, 1967) used dogs as subjects. The dogs in one group were strapped in hammocks and then exposed to a series of 64 intense inescapable shocks. The dogs in the second group received a series of 64 escapable shocks; shock terminated when a dog pressed a panel with its head. The amount of shock received in both groups was equivalent: for dogs in the first group, shock ended whenever their counterparts in the second group had succeeded in terminating shock. A third group of dogs did not receive any shock. In the next phase of the study, 24 hours after this first phase, the experimenters placed each of the dogs in the three groups into a shuttle box where it received 10 training trials, the object being to establish either an escape or an avoidance response (see Chapter 2). Once the CS (the signal) was presented, each dog had 10 seconds to jump over a hurdle to avoid shock. At the end of the 10-second interval, the shock was presented; the dogs could terminate (escape) the shock by jumping the hurdle. The shock remained on for 50 seconds or until the dog escaped. The experimenters reported that two-thirds of the animals which had received inescapable shocks 24 hours earlier did not learn either to avoid or to escape shock (refer to Figure 8.3). These dogs appeared helpless: they did not respond to the signal, and they sat in the box and endured the intense shock for the entire 50 seconds. A few of these helpless dogs occasionally jumped the hurdle and either escaped or avoided shock. However, these dogs again acted helpless on the next trial;

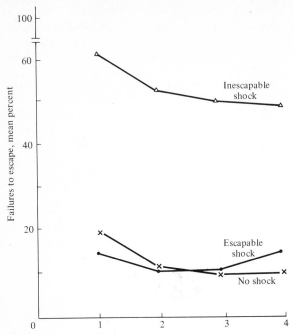

Figure 8.3
Percentage of trials on which dogs failed to escape shock in the shuttle box after receiving either escapable shock, inescapable shock, or no shock in a harness. (From Seligman, M. E. P., & Maier, S. F. Failure to escape traumatic shock. Journal of Experimental Psychology, 1967,   74, 1–9. Copyright 1967 by the American Psychological Association. Reprinted by permission.)

apparently, they did not benefit from their successful experiences. In contrast, the dogs which had been given either escapable shock or no shock in the earlier phase quickly escaped shock during their initial trials in the shuttle box; and in their later trials they learned to respond to the signal and thereby avoid shock.

A wide range of animal species are susceptible to the negative impact of uncontrollable experiences. Psychologists have observed helplessness in cats (Seward & Humphrey, 1967; Thomas & Dewald, 1977), fish (Frumkin & Brookshire, 1969; Padilla, 1973), rats (Maier & Testa, 1975; Seligman, Rosellini, & Kozak, 1975), and humans (Fosco & Geer, 1971; Glass & Singer, 1972; Hiroto, 1974; Hiroto & Seligman, 1976; Klein & Seligman, 1976; Miller & Seligman, 1975; Rodin, 1976; Roth & Kubal, 1975). Although the studies of humans have demonstrated an aversive influence of uncontrollable experiences, the effects are small in comparison with those found in lower animals. These results are not surprising; the aversive stimuli used with humans are considerably less unpleasant than those used with nonhumans. Exposing individuals to a treatment which can induce intense helplessness is unethical. Thus, human experiments in this area are *analog* studies; the intent is merely to demonstrate a similar directional influence of uncontrollable experiences in humans and lower animals.

Helplessness in human subjects.   Hiroto's experiment (1974) with human subjects provides a good duplication of the original studies, which used dogs. Hiroto also employed the three-group design. Let's briefly examine Hiroto's study to illustrate the influence of uncontrollable experiences on human subjects. College students who volunteered to participate were assigned to one of three treatment groups. Subjects in group 1 could terminate an unpleasant noise by pushing a button four times. Subjects in group 2 heard the same noise and were told that a correct response would end it; but there was actually no response which could terminate the noise. As in the animal studies, for a subject in group 2 the noise actually ended when his or her counterpart in group 1 had successfully terminated it. Finally, subjects in group 3 were a control; they did not participate in this first phase of the study. In the second phase, Hiroto trained all the subjects to avoid or escape noise in a finger shuttle box. The noise ended when a subject moved his or her finger from one side of the shuttle box to the other. Hiroto reported that subjects in group 2, who had been exposed to uncontrollable noise in the first phase, failed to learn either to escape or to avoid the noise in the shuttle box; they listened passively until the noise terminated at the end of a trial. In contrast, subjects in group 1 (who had earlier been exposed to controllable noise) and group 3 (the control group) quickly learned to escape and then avoid noise in the shuttle box. Apparently, uncontrollable experiences produce a similar negative effect on·learning in both humans and lower animals.

Characteristics of helplessness. Seligman (1975) proposed that exposure to uncontrollable events produces helplessness because of the development of an expectation that these events are independent of behavior. Once animals or humans acquire the belief that they cannot influence the occurrence of aversive events, helplessness ensues. Thus, the behavioral symptoms characteristic of helplessness are caused, according to Seligman, by the expectation of lack of control. In Seligman's view, there are three major behavioral components of helplessness: (1) *motivational deficits,* (2) *cognitive deficits,* and (3) *emotional disturbance.*

MOTIVATIONAL IMPAIRMENTS. After the establishment of helplessness, animals or humans are unable to initiate voluntary behavior. The passivity of dogs or humans following uncontrollable events is thought to reflect an inability to initiate motivated behavior. Many different motivated behaviors appear susceptible to the influence of uncontrollable events. For example, Braud, Wepman, and Russo (1969) observed that mice exposed to uncontrollable shock were later significantly slower to escape from a water maze than mice receiving controllable shock. Rosellini and Seligman (1974) found that rats which had previously received inescapable shock did not escape from a frustrating situation; these rats also sat passively in a situation formerly associated with reward. In contrast, rats which had received either escapable shock or no shock readily learned to escape from the frustrating situation.

The absence of motivation following uncontrollable events also occurs in appetitive situations. Engberg, Hansen, Welker, and Thomas (1973) trained one group of pigeons to jump on a pedal for food; for a second group, provision of food was independent of behavior. A third group of pigeons did not receive either treatment. In the second phase of this study, the pigeons had to peck at a key to obtain grain. The experimenters reported that the pigeons which had received food independently of behavior (the "learned-laziness" group) took significantly longer to learn to peck the key for food than the pigeons in the other two groups. Apparently, the development of helplessness does not depend upon the nature of the uncontrollable events; rather, in order for learned helplessness to occur, an animal or human must believe that it has no control over events.

Hiroto and Seligman's study (1975) readily exhibits the nonspecific character of helplessness. Human subjects were exposed to uncontrollable experiences in either a cognitive task (unsolvable problems) or an instrumental task (inescapable noise). In the next phase, Hiroto and Seligman evaluated the effect of these uncontrollable events on performance of a cognitive task (unscrambling anagrams) or an instrumental task (a finger shuttle box). Results indicated that poorer performances followed uncontrollable events than controllable events; this effect was found regardless of the nature of the uncontrollable events or the type of test situation. In addition, Hiroto and Seligman found that the uncontrollable experience and the test situation did not need to be similar. For example, subjects who received uncontrollable experience in a cognitive task (unsolvable problems) performed an instrumental task more poorly (anagram problems) than subjects exposed to solvable problems.

Aggressive behavior perhaps illustrates the most striking motivational deficit which follows uncontrollable events. Seligman (1975) reported a study in his laboratory in which he placed dogs that had received inescapable shocks as puppies into competition over food with dogs which he had given either escapable shock or no shock. A single coffee cup filled with dog food was placed in the same room with two dogs. Since only one of the dogs at a time can obtain food in this situation, competitive aggression typically occurs. Seligman found that the helpless dogs did not compete for food as well as the other dogs. Kurlander, Miller, and Seligman (1975) observed a similar phenomenon with humans. In their study, human subjects initially received either solvable discrimination problems, unsolvable discrimination problems, or no discrimination problems. After the first stage of the study, the experimenters placed two subjects together to obtain reward in a social-psychological game, "prisoner's dilemma" (see Chapter 13 for a detailed description of this game). Simply, the subjects can cooperate or compete to obtain a reward, or they can withdraw from competition and lose the reward. In this situation, most subjects will compete; but in this study subjects who had received unsolvable problems competed infrequently and withdrew from the game significantly more often than other subjects. In conclusion, our discussion indicates that regardless of the nature of the uncontrollable event, a motivational deficit will be produced following the uncontrollable experience. This motivational deficit can be noticed in any situation involving voluntary responding.

INTELLECTUAL IMPAIRMENTS.   Cognitive deficits are also characteristic of helplessness. The creation of an expectation by animals or people that they have no control over environmental events renders them incapable of benefiting from experience. When animals or humans do not expect their lack of control to change, successful experiences fail to influence subsequent behavior. Overmeir and Maier (1967) and Seligman and Maier (1967) reported that their helpless dogs occasionally jumped over the hurdle and either escaped or avoided the electric shock. Despite this successful experience, these dogs did not change their behavior on subsequent trials; instead, they remained on the shock side of the shuttle box. On the other hand, dogs who were not helpless—those who had not been shocked or had experienced controllable shock—learned from success: after a successful avoidance response they were more likely to respond correctly on the next trial. In addition, normal dogs changed their ineffective behavior; helpless dogs continued not to respond even though they received punishment on each trial.

Miller and Seligman's study (1975) shows that (1) a similar failure to change behavior is seen in human subjects who were previously exposed to uncontrollable events and (2) the reason for this failure is that the subject expects future events to be uncontrollable. In the first phase of this study the subjects (college students) were exposed to escapable noise, inescapable noise, or no noise. In the next phase, the experimenters required all the subjects to sort 15 cards into 10 categories within 15 seconds and told them that the rapidity of sorting depended upon their skill. In reality, the experimenters controlled the subjects' success or failure on this task; all subjects succeeded on 50 percent of the trials and failed on the other 50 percent. The experimenters controlled the length of each trial so that the subjects experienced a predetermined sequence of successes and failures. At the end of each trial, they asked all subjects to rate their expectation of their success on the next trial (on a scale of 0 to 10). Miller and Seligman discovered that subjects who had earlier been exposed to inescapable noise showed little change in expectation after either success or failure; those subjects did not believe that their behavior influenced future events. In contrast, the subjects who had been exposed to escapable noise or no noise displayed large changes in expectation after each trial: a successful trial increased their expectation of future success; a failure decreased it. Apparently, our expectations about future events depend upon our beliefs about our control over present and past experiences. It is the *perceived* ability to control events that is important, since in reality none of Miller and Seligman's subjects controlled the likelihood of success and failure.

EMOTIONAL TRAUMA. The expectation that events are uncontrollable, according to Seligman (1975), produces emotional disturbance. Animals exposed to uncontrollable events are obviously experiencing a traumatic emotional state. For example, the dogs in the original helplessness studies sat in a corner of the shuttle box and whined until the shock ended. Human helplessness studies show a similar emotional response. For example, Roth and Kubal (1975) administered questionnaires to their human subjects following uncontrollable experiences and reported increases in feelings of helplessness, incompetence, frustration, and depression. In addition, Gatchel and Proctor (1976) found that helplessness training lowered electrodermal activity; this lowered activity is thought to be correlated with lowered motivational level (Malmo, 1965) and occurs with clinical depression (McCarron, 1973).

Similarities of helplessness and depression. The importance of learned helplessness lies in its proposed relationship to the clinical disorder of depression. Although a direct causal test cannot be ethically conducted, the correlational evidence supports Seligman's statement that the expectation of an inability to control events produces human depression. These comparisons show that depressed people display the cognitive characteristics of learned helplessness. Let's now examine this evidence.

Animals and humans exposed to uncontrollable events exhibit motivational deficits. For example, college students who had previously been subjected to uncontrollable noise failed to learn to escape noise in the finger shuttle box (Hiroto, 1974). The depressed subjects in Klein and Seligman's study (1976) similarly failed to escape noise in the shuttle box (see Figure 8.4). Klein and Seligman had four groups of subjects: the subjects in one group had been classified as depressed according to the Beck Depression Inventory; the subjects in the other three groups were not depressed. Klein and Seligman exposed one group of nondepressed subjects to uncontrollable noise—a procedure which produces helplessness. The second group of nondepressed subjects were exposed to escapable noise. The last group of nondepressives and the group of depressives received no noise treatment. The results indicated that the nondepressed subjects who were exposed to inescapable noise (the "helpless" group) and the depressed subjects escaped more slowly than nondepressed subjects who had been exposed to either escapable noise or no noise. Evidently, the nondepressed subjects, as a result of uncontrollable laboratory experiences, behaved like the clinically depressed subjects. We should not assume that this treatment produced clinical depression, but rather that both groups did not expect to be able to control laboratory noise. Depressives have a generalized expectation of no control; their failure to escape in the study merely reflects this generalized expectancy.

Our prior discussion indicates that subjects exposed to uncontrollable events do not benefit from their experiences: such subjects do not change their expectations of future

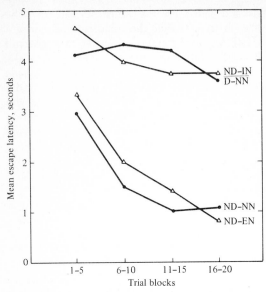

Figure 8.4
Escape latency to terminate noise for depressed subjects (on Beck Depression Inventory) who were not previously exposed to noise (group D-NN), nondepressed subjects who were not previously exposed to noise (group ND-NN), nondepressed subjects who were previously exposed to inescapable noise (group ND-IN), and nondepressed subjects who were previously exposed to escapable noise (group ND-EN). (From Klein, D. C., & Seligman, M. E. P. Reversal of performance deficits and perceptual deficits in learned helplessness and depression. Journal of Abnormal Psychology, 1976, 85, 11–26. Copyright 1976 by the American Psychological Association. Reprinted by permission.)

success after experiencing either success of failure. Depressives show a similar failure to change their expectations after a successful experience (see Miller & Seligman, 1973). Miller and Seligman classified college students as either depressed or nondepressed and then exposed them to one of two tasks (refer to Figure 8.5). The first task involved a test of skill: the subjects had to move a platform upward in an appropriate manner to prevent a steel ball from falling. The second task, a game of chance, requested the subjects to guess which one of two slides would be presented on a given trial. Since the presentation of slides was random, success on this task was due simply to chance. All subjects estimated after each trial whether or not they expected to be successful on the next trial. Miller and Seligman reported that success in the first task increased nondepressed subjects' expectation of future success. On the other hand, depressed subjects showed significantly less change in expectations after having performed this task successfully. Thus, the depressed subjects behaved like persons exposed to uncontrollable events: success did not change their expectations. Why don't depressed and helpless subjects increase their expectation of success after a successful experience? The answer lies in behavior of both depressed and nondepressed subjects on the task involving chance. After a successful trial on this second task, neither depressed or nondepressed subjects increased their expectation of future success. There was no reason to increase it, since all of the subjects in this task knew that their success was due to chance and therefore beyond their control. Depressed and helpless subjects, in Seligman's view, assumed that

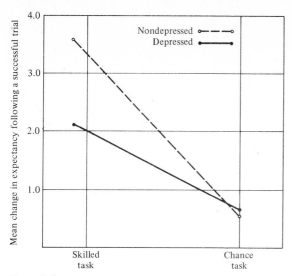

Figure 8.5
Average change in the expectation of future success in depressed and nondepressed subjects after success on either a skill task or a chance task. (From Miller, W. R., & Seligman, M. E. P. Depression and the perception of reinforcement. Journal of Abnormal Psychology, *1973, 82, 62–73. Copyright 1973 by the American Psychological Association. Reprinted by permission.)*

chance must be credited for any of their successful experiences on the first task, since they believed that these events were uncontrollable.

Criticism of the learned-helplessness approach. Seligman's original learned-helplessness model generated interest in the role of cognitive processes involved in depression. However, his theory has encountered difficulties; it was too simplistic and did not precisely reflect the process which produces depression. Therefore, Seligman (see Abramson, Seligman, & Teasdale, 1978) developed a revised theory of helplessness to provide a more accurate model of human depression. We will examine the problems with Seligman's original theory and follow with a discussion of his reformulated attributional model of helplessness, which resolves these problems.

We have seen from the prior description of Seligman's original theory that human subjects, after exposure to uncontrollable events, did not change their expectations about success in a task involving skill even after having already succeeded at it. These results suggest that the helpless subjects believed that their success was due to chance. In contrast, nonhelpless subjects increased their expectation of future success after having succeeded; this indicates that they thought that their behavior produced success. Helpless subjects during the experiment behaved as if tasks involving skill were really tasks involving chance; however, when questioned after the experiment both helpless and nonhelpless subjects described the situation correctly, as one involving skill. The original helplessness model cannot explain why helpless subjects responded as if they had no control over events when they were aware that other prople were able to control these same events.

A second problem with the original helplessness model is that some other studies have not observed performance deficits following uncontrollable experiences. In fact, several (see Roth & Kubal, 1975; Tennen & Eller, 1977) have demonstrated improved performance after exposure to unsolvable problems; their human subjects actually did better on subsequent tasks than those who were exposed to solvable problems. This is inconsistent with Seligman's original model of helplessness, which maintains that uncontrollable experiences should create expectations which impair—not improve— later behavior.

A third problem occurs when subjects generalize their expectation of no control to a dissimilar situation. This generalization is inappropriate: subjects have no reason to believe that all tasks are uncontrollable. Unfortunately, the original helplessness model does not explain why inappropriate generalizations appear during some circumstances but not others.

Rizley's study (1978, experiment 1) illustrates a final problem with Seligman's original helplessness theory. Rizley presented depressed and nondepressed subjects with a series of 50 numbers (either 0 or 1) and instructed the subjects to guess the number that would be presented next. Although there was no pattern to the numbers, Rizley told his subjects that there was, and that their score would be above chance if they were aware of it. After the presentation of 50 numbers, the subjects were told whether they had passed the test (by scoring 26 or more) or failed (by scoring 25 or less). (Since there were only two choices, a score of 25 meant performance at the chance level.) The subjects were then told to indicate the reason for their score, choosing from a list of several possibilities—luck, difficulty of the task, effort, or ability. Rizley's results demonstrated that depressed people attributed success to external factors (luck and ease of the task) and failure to internal factors (lack of effort and ability). On the other hand, nondepressed people thought internal factors were responsible for success and external factors were responsible for failure. Thus, depressives attribute their failures to internal processes—a result consistent with Beck's cognitive view of self-blame. Yet, they also feel helpless because they can do nothing to prevent future failures. Since neither Beck's nor Seligman's original cognitive views could explain Rizley's observations, a new cognitive theory was needed. Fortunately, Seligman's attributional model of learned helplessness provides an answer to problems inherent in earlier cognitive theories.

An attributional model. Abramson, Seligman, and Teasdale (1978) found that the attributions which people make for their failures determine whether or not they become depressed. (Refer to Chapter 3 for a description of the attribution process.) Causal attributions of failure can be made on three dimensions: personal (internal)–universal (external), global–specific, and stable–unstable. The combination of these three dimensions produces eight possible attributions for failure. Table 8.3 provides an interpersonal example of these eight possibilities. The specific attribution that a person makes for failure will determine whether (1) *depression occurs,* (2) *depression generalizes to other situations,* and (3) *the depression is temporary or permanent.* In one of the examples presented in Table 8.3, the woman attributes her rejection to an internal, stable, global factor (I'm unattractive to all men) and becomes depressed. In contrast, the woman will not become depressed if she attributes rejection to an external, unstable, specific factor (he was in a rejecting mood). This attribution model, while certainly complex, gives us an accurate view of peoples' varied responses to uncontrollable experiences. Let's see how the specific causal attributions for our failures affect us.

Personal versus universal helplessness. Consider the two following examples: (1) There is a downturn in the economy, and poor sales of automobiles force several assembly plants to close. An automobile worker loses his or her job and becomes depressed. (2) A sixteen-year-old who wants to play for the high school basketball team has diligently

Table 8.3
The Attributional Model of Depression: A Woman Rejected

| Dimension | Internal | | External | |
	Stable	Unstable	Stable	Unstable
Global	I'm unattractive to men.	My conversation sometimes bores men.	Men are overly competitive with intelligent women.	Men get into a rejecting mood.
Specific	I'm unattractive to him.	My conversation bores him.	He's overly competitive with women.	He was in a rejecting mood.

Note: The attribution of uncontrollability to internal causes produces personal helplessness, while an external causal attribution results in universal helplessness.

From: Abramson, L. Y., Seligman, M. E. P., & Teasdale, J. D. Learned helplessness in humans: Critique and reformulation. *Journal of Abnormal Psychology*, 1978, 87, 1, 49–74. Copyright 1978 the American Psychological Association. Reprinted by permission.

practiced summer and fall; this student is not selected for the team and becomes depressed. In both examples, depression occurs, according to Abramson, Seligman, and Teasdale (1978), because of each person's perceived inability to control events: the automobile worker does not have a job, and the student is not on the team. However, the helplessness of the automobile worker and that of the student are quite different. The attributional model has two kinds of helplessness: personal and universal. The student's failure to be picked for the team is an example of *personal helplessness:* this student's inability caused failure; yet other, more competent students were selected for the team. *Universal helplessness* occurs when the environment is structured so that no one can control events: the automobile worker cannot control the economy; therefore, loss of a job is attributed to external forces.

Abramson (1977) ascertained from her experiments that both personal and universal helplessness produced both the cognitive deficits (expectation of future inability to control events) and the motivational deficits (lack of ability to initiate voluntary behavior) which are characteristic of depression. In addition, Abramson and Sackeim (1977) examined the attributions of depressed people and found that those who were personally depressed made internal attributions for failure, while those who were universally depressed made external attributions.

The nature of helplessness determines whether or not loss of esteem appears. People who attribute their failure to external forces—universal helplessness—experience no loss of self-esteem, since they do not believe themselves responsible for their failure. However, the attribution of failure to internal factors which is seen with personal helplessness produces loss of self-esteem; those people see their own incompetence as the cause of their failure. In support of this view, Abramson (1977) found that lowered self-esteem occurs only with personal helplessness.

A feeling of personal helplessness need not be acquired through direct experience; watching others similar to ourselves fail can render us helpless (Brown & Inouye, 1978). Brown and Inouye asked pairs of subjects to estimate their expected success on an anagram task and then provided them with a score which indicated how they rated their own and their partner's perceived ability to solve the problem. Each pair contained only one actual subject; the other was a confederate. Except in the control condition, the confederate always attempted but failed to solve the problem before the actual subject tried it. The three experimental conditions were as follows. In the first condition, subjects were given information leading them to believe that their ability was comparable to that of their partner. In the second condition, subjects were given information leading them to believe themselves more capable than their partner. In the third condition, subjects received no information about their partner's ability. In the control condition, subjects had not observed their partner fail before they themselves attempted the task. Brown and Inouye found that subjects in the first condition (partners of comparable ability) and the third condition (no information) persisted less after failure than control subjects or subjects in the second condition (subject more competent than partner). These results suggest that we can become helpless by watching others fail—but only if we feel that their abilities equal ours.

Global verus specific causal attributions.   People who are exposed to uncontrollable events may not become depressed; they could believe that their failure could be attributable to a *specific situation,* and helplessness will not occur in other circumstances. Or these persons could feel that their helplessness is *global* and will happen at other times. The automobile worker might believe that a job exists in another company and actively search for it. The student could attribute failure to make the team to the coach, could change schools, and could try again next year. Thus, the attribution of lack of control to global rather than to specific factors will produce helplessness which will generalize to new situations; yet, helplessness will be limited to a single situation if the attribution is specific.

Roth and Kubal's experiment (1975) supports the idea that global–specific attributions are important when determining whether people are helpless in new situations. College freshmen volunteered to participate in Roth and Kubal's study. Two separate, very different experiments were conducted on the same day and in the same building. The first experiment was designed to fail all students. In this first experiment, one group of subjects were told that the task was a good predictor of college grades (the "important" condition); the second group of students were told that they were participating in an "experiment in learning" (the "unimportant" condition). Next, all the subjects proceeded to the second experiment. Since both groups had experienced failure on the first experiment, the original helplessness model would predict that both groups would perform poorly in the second. However, the subjects who had been told that the first experiment was a study of learning did significantly better on the second experiment than subjects who thought that the first experiment was a predictor of their future success. According to the attributional model, the subjects in the "important" condition attributed their failure to a more global factor (absence of ability to succeed in college) than subjects in the "unimportant" condition, who attributed their failure to the nature of a single task. As a result, the helplessness generalized to the new situation for subjects in the "important" condition but not for those in the "unimportant" condition.

Stable versus unstable causal attributions.   Abramson, Seligman, and Teasdale (1978) proposed that a person's attribution of helplessness to a stable or unstable factor also influences the effect of uncontrollable experience on behavior. Ability is considered a stable factor; effort, an unstable one. If someone attributes failure in an uncontrollable experience to lack of effort, this attribution will increase this person's subsequent effort. However, attribution of failure to lack of ability—a stable factor—will lead to helplessness, since people can change their effort but not their ability. As an example of this approach, recall the high school student who failed to make the team. Suppose that this student attributes failure not to lack of ability but rather to insufficient effort. Under this condition, failure might increase rather than decrease motivated behavior. Thus, the facilitation which follows uncontrollable experiences in some studies probably is due to the subjects' belief that increased effort leads to success. However, continued failure will eventually cause an expectation of no control over failure. A test of this view is found in Roth and Kubal's study (1975). Roth and Kubal gave their subjects either one or two learned-helplessness training tasks and found that those who received one such task showed more motivation than control subjects, but those who had two such tasks exhibited helplessness.

The idea that stability or instability of the perceived cause influences helplessness also explains why depression is temporary under some situations and permanent under others. Let's return to the example of the automobile worker. The attribution of the problem to an external factor—a poor economy—causes depression which will remain if the economy remains poor. However, the depression will be temporary if the economy recovers (which is typical) and the worker gets a job. (If the economy improves but the worker fails to find employment, the worker may then attribute that failure to uncontrollable personal stable factors and continue to be depressed).

The severity of one's depression. Helplessness can apparently follow several different types of uncontrollable experiences. However, severe depression typically appears when individuals attribute their failure to internal, global, and stable factors. Their depression is intense because they perceive themselves incompetent (internal attribution) in many situations (global attribution) and believe that their incompetence is unlikely to change (stable attribution). In support of this notion, Hammen and Krantz (1976) found that depressed women typically attributed interpersonal failure (for example, being alone on a Friday night) to internal, global, and stable factors. In contrast, nondepressed women usually blamed their failure on external, specific, and unstable factors. Rizley (1978) observed a similar difference in causal attribution of failure on a cognitive task between depressed and nondepressed people.

Depressives' attributional style. Seligman's attributional model assumes that *attributional style* (perceived causes of events) influences the likelihood that a person will become depressed. In order to validate the attributional model, it is necessary to show that the differences in attributional style between depressed and nondepressed people was present before the onset of depression. Although it is possible that depression causes the attributional style which is characteristic of depression, recent evidence presented by Seligman and his associates provides more direct support of the attributional model. Semmel, Peterson, Abramson, Metalsky, and Seligman (1981) found that knowledge of a person's attributional style allowed prediction of suceptibility to depression following failure. In their study the attributional style of college students was measured at the beginning of a semester. They discovered that those students who attributed past failures to internal, global, and stable factors were more likely to become depressed after earning a poor grade (in the student's view) on a midsemester examination than students who had attributed past failures to external, specific, and unstable factors. Apparently, a person's attributional style influences the likelihood of becoming depressed when he or she fails.

AN OVERVIEW

For several reasons, Abramson, Seligman, and Teasdale's model represents a potentially important breakthrough in enhancing our understanding of the causes of depression. First, nondepressed people who have experienced uncontrollable events and clinically depressed people have identical causal attributions of failure. Second, after Beck's behavior therapy is detailed later in this chapter, we will discover that changing a depressive's cognitions represents an effective treatment of depression. The success of Beck's therapy indicates that cognitive processes play a significant role in depression. However, as we learned earlier in this chapter, there are many behavioral and physiological differences between depressed people. While the attributional model predicts the cognitive aspects of depression, it cannot explain the varied behavioral and biological responses seen in depressives. Everyone has an individual physiological and behavioral response to stress. Perhaps these individual differences are responsible for the observation that not all depressives show the same set of symptoms. Additional research is obviously necessary to indicate why depressives respond differently to events perceived as uncontrollable.

Our discussion has indicated that several processes—both biological and psychological—participate in human depression. However, after the depression is established, depressives' experiences intensify whatever causal agent produced the depression. For example, some people's depression may be the consequence of the expectation that events cannot be controlled; these depressives do not attempt to secure reward or avoid punishment, and this passivity merely confirms and strengthens their expectation of an inability to control events. In addition, even though a particular process may now have caused depression, other disturbances are created by the depression. Suppose that a biological disturbance produces depression. Because of the symptoms characteristic of depression (sadness, withdrawal), the behaviors necessary for reward do not appear, and even if someone tries to obtain reward, success will be unlikely. Thus, depression which is produced by a biochemical imbalance creates psychological disturbances; the addition of new causal factors which are capable of producing depression decreases the likelihood that depressives' pathology will wane with time. The poor prognosis for recovery from severe depression if no therapy is employed probably reflects the fact that multiple factors produce depression.

The observation that depression involves several factors suggests that the elimination of one causal agent is not likely to eliminate depression; all factors must be resolved to treat depression successfully. Helplessness is an example of this view. Recall from our earlier discussion Jay Weiss's argument that norepinephrine depletion, which is caused by exposure to uncontrollable events, produces helplessness. Evidence for a physiological interpretation of helplessness comes from the results of the original helplessness studies: there was no helplessness if 48 rather than 24 hours intervened between the inescapable shocks and escape-avoidance training. Norepinephrine depletion is transient; its level increases as the animal recovers from trauma. Since norepinephrine depletion is only temporary, the presence of helplessness 24 hours but not 48 hours after inescapable shocks is thought to represent support of a physiological view of helplessness.

However, an animal's or human's physiological recovery does not automatically indicate that the feelings of helplessness will decline. The experiences produced by this helplessness may create psychological disturbances which will remain after an animal's or person's physiological recovery. In support of this view, Overmeir and Seligman (1967) found that their dogs, after having received two experiences with uncontrollable events, were helpless even a month after the second experience. The physiologically induced helplessness can result in the development of a psychologically based helplessness. Psychological processes must be responsible for the helplessness which was observed after the month-long interval, since the depletion of norepinephrine could not have persisted so long.

Our earlier discussion indicated that antidepressant drugs represent an effective treatment of depression. Yet, these drugs do not cure all depressives. The inability of the antidepressant drugs to treat all depressives effectively may be due to the multidimensional character of depression. The influence of the antidepressants apparently is to stimulate the CNS reward system, which increases an animal's or human's motivational level. The results of this enhanced motivation may be the production of reward or a change in the expectation of control. In this situation, depression probably will not reappear when the drug treatment is eliminated. However, failure may occur when a depressed individual attempts to obtain reward. The consequence of this failure is a strengthened psychological foundation for depression. Thus, failure of a particular antidepressant to control depression in certain people may reflect the continued presence of these psychological systems which can cause depression—as well as an inability of that antidepressant to modify the biological disturbance which exists in a specific depressed person. Attention to the psychological changes accompanying drug treatment might indicate the psychological procedures which are necessary to reverse depression if antidepressant drugs fail. We will discuss these psychological therapies in the next section.

We have focused on the processes responsible for depression. In order to overcome depression, people must feel that they can successfully interact with their environment. This confidence must accurately reflect these persons' abilities if depression is not to recur. It is important now to turn our attention to the creation of a sense of competence which enables people who have been depressed to resume normal activities. Also, this establishment of a feeling of competence can reduce the chances that a person will become depressed.

COMPETENCE

Effectance Motive

In 1959, the psychologist Robert White suggested the existence of an innate *effectance motive*. This motive, aroused when a person encounters a novel environment, enables the person to master the new environment. According to White, mastery is acquired as the person gains knowledge about the environment as well as the effective skills necessary to cope with any problems existing in it. White based his view on his observations of children's exploratory play in a novel environment. He noted that the children persisted with exploratory behavior until they mastered their new surroundings. In contrast to White's view that an innate drive is responsible for producing competence, Albert Bandura (1977) proposed that people become competent when they perceive themselves capable of interacting effectively with their environment. Bandura's concept of self-efficacy (see Chapter 3) reflects the idea that if persons believe that they can cope with and control external events, they will engage in specific motivated behavior. However, if persons lack a sense of self-efficacy, they will avoid participating in certain situations. Thus, people will not approach, explore, and deal with novel situations because of an innate effectance motive as White suggested, but rather will participate only in those events which they perceive to be within their capacities and avoid those in which they feel unable to cope.

Self-Efficacy

Bandura views competence not as a disposition existing independently of environmental influence but rather as a perceived ability to cope with a specific environment. There is evidence to support Bandura's contention that competence does not reflect either a global personality trait or a motive of effectance. People do not feel competent in all situations; they may feel able to cope with some situations but not others. Self-efficacy can be established in ways other than through direct exploratory activities with novel environments. A person can develop a sense of ability to control events by observing the behavior of others. Bandura found modeling an effective way to increase someone's feelings of competence. One child, for instance, may watch another climb a tree and, as a result, develop the belief that the tree can be climbed. The child will then proceed to climb the tree because of the vicariously acquired self-efficacy. Although direct experience provides a stronger sense of self-efficacy, competence can be acquired by observing the behavior of others. Further, the establishment of a sense of self-efficacy increases the probability that a person will engage in novel but related activities. For example, once a person feels competent to ask a specific individual for a date, this person will also be likely to ask others for dates in the future. Bandura suggests that participation in a new situation does not reflect an innate effectance motive; it occurs because of a belief in self-efficacy.

A Multidimensional Treatment Approach

Bandura (1977) suggested that our interactions with our environment create two separate expectations (see Chapter 3). The *efficacy expectation* represents our perceived ability to cope, while the *outcome expectation* reflects our belief that a particular behavior has certain outcomes such as reward or punishment. According to Bandura, people become depressed either because they lack a sense of self-efficacy strong enough to foster success or because they expect that their behaviors will not produce the desired outcomes. These two expectations of futility are produced by different antecedent conditions and require different remedial procedures. To change efficacy expectations, a person must develop the expectation of personal effectiveness. In contrast, to change outcome expectations a person must develop effective skills to produce reward, or the environment must provide reward for existing skills. This discussion suggests that two types of procedures are necessary for successful treatment of the psychological components of depression. *First, behavioral and environmental changes are necessary to increase the level of obtained reinforcement.* This observation is in accord with Lewinsohn's view that the reduction or absence of reward elicits depression. *Second, cognitive changes need to occur in order to correct the depressive's inaccurate or irrational beliefs.* This prediction receives support from Seligman's attributional model of helplessness; in this theory, the expectation of being unable to control events produces depression.

Two successful behavioral treatments for depression have emerged during the past decade. Reinforcement therapy focuses on increasing obtained reward; a cognitive therapy restructures the depressed individual's expectations. However, recent evidence suggests that the most effective treatment employs a combination of these two approaches. We will next briefly examine both approaches and at the end of the section explore the need for a multidimensional treatment.

Reinforcement approach. Reinforcement treatment aims to increase the level of obtained reward. This goal is accomplished in three ways: (1) *reinstate previous adaptive behaviors or teach new behaviors which produce reinforcement,* (2) *extinguish inappropriate behaviors which decrease the likelihood of obtaining reward,* and (3) *restructure the environment to administer reward when appropriate behavior occurs.* In a traditional therapy situation, contingent attention from the therapist appears to represent one effective reward (Liberman & Raskin, 1971). Liberman and Raskin observed a decrease in the incidence of depression when the therapist ignored complaints about depression and attended to the possible solution of problems. Also, Burgess (1968) gave depressed patients tasks to accomplish and reinforced them when they succeeded. The tasks, structured in a graded sequence, increased in frequency and difficulty until the target behavior occurred. For example, a person who is unable to present a speech may become depressed. A therapist would first reinforce this person for saying a few words of the speech. As therapy progresses, reinforcement is made contingent upon a longer and more difficult speech. This procedure appears quite effective. Beck (1976) reported an example of this approach. His hospitalized patient had refused to move from bed for one year. This patient had received antidepressant drugs, but they had been ineffective. Beck's encouragement enabled his patient to get out of bed and walk just 10 yards. The patient was then reinforced by Beck's approval for his behavior and urged to complete the next task, walking 20 yards. After having completed this task, the patient again received reinforcement. In 45 minutes the patient was walking throughout the ward where he could obtain available reinforcers (for example, a candy machine). The patient was discharged after another month.

Depressives' emotional state may prevent them from experiencing the reinforcing aspects of events. It is necessary under these conditions to institute an emotional state to counter the depressive's emotionality. Assertiveness is an emotional state which can compete with the depressive's mood (Wolpe, 1958). Assertiveness training requires patients to express their feelings—such as affection, disagreement, and anger—in an honest, straightforward, yet socially appropriate way. Behavioral rehearsal of these feelings is the central component of assertiveness training. A patient disagreeing with the boss (who is "played" by the therapist) or saying no to an imaginary friend asking for a favor is an example of behavioral rehearsal. Assertiveness training seems to represent a positive treatment for depression. LaPointe and Rimm (1979) reported assertiveness training as more effective than cognitive training in reducing their parents' subjective ratings of their own moods. Furthermore, both therapies were more effective than a control therapy—insight. Taulbee and Wright (1971) discovered an interesting method of creating an emotional state which antagonizes depression. They asked their hospitalized clients to perform a monotonous task—sanding a block of wood—for hours. This procedure induced anger, and all of their patients eventually refused to continue. Taulbee and Wright then praised their patients and moved them to a more pleasant ward environment. The induction of anger significantly reduced the depression.

Lewinsohn and his associates (see Lewinsohn & Atwood, 1969; Lewinsohn & Shaw, 1969) described an extremely effective home intervention treatment program for depression. They observed interactions between depressed persons and their families and found that depressives emitted few voluntary responses, received few reinforcements, and were either ignored or verbally punished. The clients and families received instructions concerning the appropriate target behaviors and contingent reinforcers. For example, the clients' increased affectionate responses, participation in new or previously enjoyed activities, and initiation of conversation were reinforced by social approval and attention; on the other hand, when they tried to discuss their problems, they were ignored. This therapeutic intervention produced both significantly increased social interaction and decreased depression.

Our discussion has suggested that reinforcement therapy can reduce the emotional aspects of depression and increase the incidence of behaviors which produce reinforcement. However, it is also clear that depressives' cognitions require modification; their inaccurate expectations need to be replaced by more objective cognitions. We now focus on the cognitive approaches of treating depression.

Cognitive approach. In 1976, Beck described a cognitive restructuring therapy designed to develop rational adaptive expectations of future events. The therapy consists of four phases: (1) *Patients become aware of their thoughts,* (2) *they learn to understand why these thoughts are inaccurate or distorted,* (3) *they replace these irrational perceptions with accurate,* *more objective cognitions,* and (4) *they test the validity of these cognitive beliefs.* Beck developed a 20-hour standardized program of specific procedures for modifying depressives' cognitions. Among these procedures are distancing, decatastrophizing, and decentering. In *distancing,* patients must distinguish between a belief and a fact. Once patients recognize that their beliefs may not reflect reality, they can modify them. Patients learn to separate their experiences from those of others in *decentering.* For example, depressives must recognize that they will not lose their job because others do. *Decatastrophizing* enables patients who feel that the occurrence of certain events are catastrophic to recognize the fact that the consequences of certain events are not disastrous. Moreover, in Beck's cognitive therapy, depressed people learn to substitute workable solutions for apparently unsolvable problems and to identify the variables which produce failure. Patients are also required to test new ideas. For example, someone who has felt unable to present a speech but now feels capable is encouraged to discover the validity of these new cognitions.

Beck's cognitive restructuring therapy appears to represent a very effective treatment for depression. A study by Rush, Beck, Kovaks, and Hollon (1977) demonstrated both the success of the cognitive approach with severely depressed individuals and its superiority to a tricyclic drug treatment. Their 12-week cognitive and drug treatments revealed that although both procedures reduced depression, patients receiving cognitive restructuring therapy showed greater improvement on self-ratings (the Beck Depression Inventory) and clinical ratings (the Hamilton Rating Scale). On the nonbiased, blind clinical ratings, the group receiving cognitive treatment achieved a 97 percent improvement compared with only 23 percent for the group receiving drug treatment. The cognitively treated patients maintained their superiority on follow-up evaluations after 3 and 6 months. These results are quite impressive for several reasons. First, the cognitive treatment was compared against a recognized, effective treatment. The success of the drug therapy was equivalent to previous clinical evaluations of tricyclic antidepressant therapy. Second, these therapists were not biased toward the cognitive treatment; in fact, they had received their clinical training in the traditional forms of psychotherapy. Two additional results of this study need mention. Whereas only 1 of 19 patients withdrew from the cognitive therapy, 8 of 22 patients withdrew from drug therapy. Most of those who dropped out of drug therapy reported that their failure to respond to treatment was their reason for leaving. These two therapies also differed in terms of how many patients required further treatment: 68 percent of those who had received drug therapy resumed treatment for depression, compared with only 16 percent of those who had received cognitive therapy. McLean and Hakstian (1979) also found the cognitive therapy superior.

Our discussion has indicated that changes in cognitive functioning are essential for a depressive's recovery. The high incidence of the return of depression in many who have received drug therapy may occur because the drug-induced change did not result in permanent cognitive changes. Therefore, expectations of helplessness resumed, and depression returned, when the drug treatment was discontinued.

Multimodal approach.   Lazarus suggested in 1974 that the most effective therapy for depression incorporates drugs with reinforcement and cognitive therapies. His multimodal depression therapy consisted of seven interactive treatments aimed at modifying the patients' inappropriate overt behavior, affective processes, sensory reactions, interpersonal relationships, and cognitions. In addition, antidepressant medication was typically included. Lazarus reported that after 3 months of his multimodal treatment, 22 of 26 chronically depressed patients showed significantly reduced depressive symptoms.

The study by Taylor and Marshall (1977) demonstrates the enhanced therapeutic effectiveness of a unified approach. Taylor and Marshall provided one of four types of treatments for mild to moderately depressed patients. The first treatment consisted of cognitive restructuring procedures. The second employed a reinforcement therapy. The third combined reinforcement and cognitive therapy. The fourth was no treatment: patients receiving no treatment were on a waiting list and served as a control group. Although Taylor and Marshall found better results for all three therapy conditions than for the control group, the combined therapy was superior to either the cognitive or the reinforcement therapy alone. These results suggest that maximal therapeutic gain occurs when each component of the depressive's behavior is directly modified during therapy.

THE IMMUNIZATION PROCESS

Two people working together lose their jobs; one person becomes depressed, while the other searches for a new job. It is clear that the same uncontrollable event does not produce identical or even similar effects in different people. What personality characteristics enable one person to cope with an uncontrollable experience when another individual cannot? This is an extremely important question. Knowledge of the factors predisposing some people to attempt to cope with the same events which produce depression in others provides psychologists with a strategy for preventing depression in those experiencing uncontrollable events. Our society does not typically try to prevent behavioral problems before they develop, but rather attempts to modify inappropriate behavior after it occurs. However, the emotional tragedies experienced by both depressives and their families and friends require the implementation of any technique which can prevent depression. Although a successful prevention program has not yet been developed, the research and writings of Martin Seligman (1975) indicate that prevention is possible and suggest the direction that a prevention program must take.

A History of Control

The key to prevention lies in the past history of those who have successfully overcome the effects of uncontrollable experiences. According to Seligman (1975), individuals having prior experience with control become *immunized* to the influence of future uncontrollable happenings. The result of a past history of successful experiences is the creation of an expectation that events are controllable. Thus, when these persons encounter uncontrollable occurrences, they do not become depressed, because their expectation of control prevents them from viewing their current experience as uncontrollable.

Evidence from both animal or human studies supports the contention that past experience with control can prevent—or at least reduce—the probability of depression. Seligman and Maier (1967) gave some of their dogs experience with controlling shock in a shuttle box before the dogs received inescapable shock in a hammock. Other dogs were given only the inescapable shock. Then both groups were observed in a shuttle box. In contrast to the helplessness exhibited by the dogs which received only the uncontrollable shocks, Seligman and Maier observed no motivational impairment in dogs which had a past history of control. Recall from our earlier discussion that only two-thirds of the dogs in Seligman's original helplessness study exhibited behavioral impairments following uncontrollable experiences. Seligman (1975) suggests that since the dogs in his initial experiments had an unknown history of control, many of them probably had had considerable experience with control and were immunized to the effects of uncontrollable experiences. To test this idea, Seligman and Groves (1970) compared the susceptivity to helplessness in dogs of unknown history and dogs raised singly in laboratory cages with few experiences of control. They found that fewer exposures to uncontrollable events were necessary to produce helplessness in dogs raised under laboratory conditions than in dogs with unknown backgrounds (which probably had involved some experience with control).

A similar immunization process appears to occur in humans who have a past history of control. Hiroto (1974) provides experimental support for this view: individuals who have an internal locus of control believe that they control their destiny, whereas "externals" think that events occur by chance or luck and therefore are not controllable (see Chapter 3 for a review of Rotter's idea of locus of control). It is generally assumed that "internals" have learned from experience that their skill and effort can produce success and cause them to avoid failure. On the other hand, "externals" have learned from past experience that their abilities and effort could not obtain success or avert failure; thus, "externals" believe that luck or chance determines success and failure. Hiroto discovered that more externals than internals failed to escape noise in a shuttle box after exposure to inescapable noise. Apparently, people with an expectation of being able to control events (internals) are less likely to become helpless than those who expect to be unable to control events (externals).

A Sense of Mastery

How can we develop an expectation of control to immunize us against depression? Childhood experiences, according to Seligman, are critical to the development of an internal locus of control. Children must be allowed to experience successes and attribute them to their own effort and skill. Parents who make all of their children's decisions rob them of the opportunity to develop a sense of efficacy. Seligman believes that these choices need not be monumental; a child deciding which type of cereal to eat is learning that he or she can successfully choose between alternative outcomes. An expectation of being able to control success is established if the child chooses a good-tasting cereal. And, if the child picks a bad-tasting cereal and then chooses a better-tasting cereal the next time, the child develops an expectation that failure can be prevented. Obviously, a single situation is not likely to create the belief that events are controllable; however, repeated experiences which enable a child to produce success and avoid failure will create an "internal" person. Parents should not, of course, let their children behave in unsafe ways, but, they should allow choice in situations that are not dangerous. For example, the choice of whether to wear a coat in subfreezing weather is certainly risky (although if no coat is worn, this choice probably will not occur again); but the child could be allowed to choose which coat to wear. The knowledge of how to immunize people against depression seems clear. However, it is society's task to ensure that this knowledge is implemented to reduce future depression.

Childhood Depression

Carol Dweck's research (Dweck, 1975; Diener & Dweck, 1978) demonstrated that depression also occurs in childhood; her observations point to the importance of the immunization process in preventing children, as well as adults, from becoming depressed. She found that many children attributed their failure to lack of ability and therefore did not continue to try after failing. Helplessness in these children was identical to that observed in depressed adults. In contrast, Dweck noticed that mastery-oriented children worked harder after failing—indicating that they attributed failure to insufficient effort. Dweck (1975) instructed the helpless children's teachers to explain to them that their failure was due to their lack of effort and that they should try harder. The teachers' aim, according to Dweck, was to modify each child's causal attribution of failure and produce greater motivation. Dweck found that this training produced significant improvement in the children, as compared with helpless children who did not receive it. Diener and Dweck (1978) also observed that mastery-oriented children focused their attention on potential solutions in order to prevent future failure. This suggests that in order to modify childhood helplessness, treatment should entail training in mastery. We have seen that successful cognitive therapy includes components which modify causal attributions and enhance competence. Dweck's research indicates that these cognitive approaches would also effectively treat childhood depression.

SUMMARY

Depression is a psychological experience familiar to each of us. The dominant feature of depression is a sense of sadness. Other characteristics include a negative self-image, social withdrawal, loss of appetite, recurrent thoughts of death and suicide, problems with concentration, a shift in activity, and a change in hostility. Although some depressives exhibit each of these characteristics, most show only some of them. For most people, depression is mild and short-lived; for others, it is intense and wanes slowly or not at all.

Several processes appear to produce depression. Genetic factors predispose an individual to develop bipolar depression; people having a close family member who has experienced periods of mania and depression are also likely to have bipolar depression. In contrast, inheritance does not appear to influence the occurrence of unipolar depression.

Biochemical changes are also correlated with depression. During periods of depression, there is a reduction in the brain amine transmitter systems (norepinephrine, serotonin). The psychological disturbances characteristic of depression can be produced by decreasing the effectiveness of these neurotransmitters; drugs which increase the amine level represent an effective treatment for many depressives. The antidepressant drugs probably decrease depression by activating the CNS reward system; the effect of this stimulation is to increase both a depressed person's motivational level and the value of reinforcement. A disturbance in the biochemical systems controlling the sleeping-waking cycle also appears to be involved in depression.

Lewinsohn proposed that reduction of reinforcement elicits depression. Such reduction can occur because a person does not possess the skills needed to obtain reward, because the person avoids interacting with others, or because rewards are not available. A worsening of mood is correlated with a reduction in reinforcement, although it is unlikely that loss of reward alone can produce clinical depression. Behavioral therapies which increase the level of obtained reward reduce the symptoms characteristic of depression.

Depression can also result when someone expects to be unable to obtain reward and prevent failure. The importance of cognitive processes in causing depression is demonstrated by the similarities between the behavior of depressed people and the behavior of animals and humans exposed to uncontrollable events. Severe depression occurs when people believe that (1) their personal inabilities rather than external forces cause events to be uncontrollable, (2) their inability to control events will happen in many different situations, and (3) their inability to obtain reward and avoid failure will not change with time. Changes in the cognitive functioning of depressed persons represent one effective method of treating depression.

A single factor may produce depression, but a depressive's behavior, once established, causes disturbances in the other processes correlated with depression. The multidimensional character of depression suggests that the most effective therapy must employ several different approaches. Recent evidence indicates that a multimodal approach is the ideal treatment for depression. Our understanding of the causes of depression has dramatically increased over the past decade. This knowledge has fostered both an improved outlook for helping depressed people and a strategy for preventing depression. It is society's responsibility to implement effective programs to reduce the incidence of depression.

AFFILIATIVE MOTIVATION

CHAPTER 9

Mama's boy

Kevin arrived at college last week. As he was an excellent high school student, the challenge of college excited him. In fact, anticipation colored everything he did last summer. Unhappily, though, after only one week of classes, Kevin is extremely frightened by his new surroundings, has been unable to develop any new friendships, and is contemplating returning home.

Acting on the recommendation of his advisor, yesterday Kevin went to the university counseling center. Dr. Johnson, one of the center's psychologists, discovered not only that Kevin has never been away from home before but also that he is very attached to his family—his parents and his sister Gloria. Kevin was not popular in high school; his studies consumed him, leaving little time for friends or for school activites. His parents, especially his mother, rewarded him for his good grades; but, fearing that other youngsters might be a bad influence, had not allowed him to date until his junior year of high school. Even then Kevin dated very infrequently, preferring to stay at home with his family. He had a couple of friends from his neighborhood, but shared no real contact with other young people at school. His outings were with the family rather than with other young people. Dr. Johnson concluded that Kevin is an overly insecure person who had not developed any effective social skills and informed Kevin that he must develop a greater sense of self-esteem. An appointment was scheduled for Kevin to begin therapy.

Kevin, very much disturbed by Dr. Johnson's analysis, returned to his dormitory; his anxiety heightened his need for his parents. However, last night, when Kevin's parents telephoned, he did not tell them of his misery. They told him that they missed him and looked forward to his return home during the Thanksgiving holiday. Their call only intensified his loneliness.

Kevin wants to excel in school, but his feelings of isolation prevent him not only from making friends but even from being able to study. Today, believing that he can no longer remain in college, he has decided to return to the security of home and family.

Our social motives serve a very valuable function: they enable us to experience satisfaction and security through social experience. Yet excessive dependency on others can interfere with our effective adjustment. A lack of feelings of self-worth, low self-esteem, and an absence of initiative can result from too much dependency upon others. For some people, social needs dominate their personality. Such socially dependent people require excessive attention and support from others in order to satisfy their own social motives.

In this chapter, you will learn why Kevin developed his strong attachment to his parents, why he experienced such extreme loneliness when he left home, and why he was unable to develop relationships with other people. The different ways in which psychologists have conceptualized the attachment process will be described in the second section of this chapter. Later in the chapter, we will examine the processes motivating us to be with other people.

THE PAIN OF LONELINESS

My grandmother died nineteen years ago, yet the thought of her still inflicts some hurt. My relationship with my grandmother was an extremely rewarding one, and I felt a deep sense of loss when she died. I have developed other strong attachments since her death, but none can replace that special relationship. Everyone except the most socially isolated has experienced pain when a close friend or loved one moves away or dies. We seem to have strong social needs which are satisfied only through the development of attachments. Some of these bonds are casual, while others are deep and meaningful. We are motivated to develop close friendships and are disturbed if someone rejects our friendship. The loss of a friend or loved one provokes a sense of isolation and loneliness. For some people, the pain quickly wanes and it is possible to return to the comfort of existing social attachments or form new ones. In other people, the sense of loss may remain for a long period of time and may even, in extreme cases, result in severe depression or suicide.

The loneliness and depression resulting from withdrawal of social support can become extreme in socially dependent people. Even the threat of departure is likely to intensify their possessive behaviors. Socially dependent persons often seem addicted to a friend or loved one; they demand ever-increasing levels of affection from the friend or loved one in order to satisfy their needs while showing excessive concern over the loss of social support.

Solomon and Corbit's opponent-process theory (Solomon & Corbit, 1974) offers a viable interpretation of the addictive behavior of the socially dependent person. (A description of opponent-process theory was presented in Chapter 4, but its relationship to social attachment was not explored.) According to this view, the presence of social support causes a strong pleasurable state (A). When the friend or loved one leaves, the pleasurable state terminates; it is followed by an opponent aversive withdrawal state (B). When the friend or loved one returns, the pleasurable state is reestablished. As the cycle of presence and loss proceeds, the intensity of the pleasurable state (now A') diminishes, and the person needs more support to reinstate the intensity of the initial social attachment. This increased demand for attention reflects the development of *social tolerance*, and, according to Solomon and Corbit, it is the natural effect of frequent repeated attachment and withdrawal experiences. The decreased pleasurable effect of the social stimulus is matched by an intensification of the opponent negative withdrawal state (now called B'). Thus, faced with disrupted social relationships, many people exert strong efforts to terminate the aversive opponent withdrawal state (B'), triggered when the social support is reduced, by reestablishing state A. This opponent-process view maintains that the loneliness experienced following the loss of a friend or loved one reflects the natural effects of a change in social relationships and that *social addiction* represents the dependent person's dysfunctional, overreactive method of coping with the pain of social withdrawal. The well-adjusted person will be able to terminate his or her loneliness by forming new, pleasurable social attachments.

Solomon (1977) suggested that environmental cues present during the opponent withdrawal state can become conditioned to produce "withdrawal symptoms." Thus, through classical conditioning the absence of the friend or loved one becomes associated with the aversive withdrawal state, thereby producing a conditioned withdrawal state. As a result of conditioning, even the potential loss of this social support can initiate unpleasant withdrawal symptoms, therefore intensifying the dependent person's social motives.

The development of competence, discussed in Chapter 8, will break the addictive cycle by enabling the dependent person to develop effective social skills. These new social skills will reduce or eliminate the aversive withdrawal state by allowing the establishment of new rewarding social relationships. Also, in competent people the absence of others can be associated with positive rewarding experiences rather than with the pain of social isolation. For the competent, being alone can provide the pleasures of privacy rather than the agony of loneliness.

The nature of our strong social motives has for the past 50 years aroused the interest of psychologists. Some theorists suggest that social needs are innate, though others propose that we construct our social motives from what we learn during our interactions with the environment (see Figure 9.1). Certain personality theorists believe that our social behaviors directly satisfy social needs; others hold that the function of social behaviors is to resolve other motives (e.g., hunger, sex, security). Opponent-process theory indicates why some people show excessive social motivation. We now direct our attention to the different ways in which the major personality theorists have envisioned the basis of our social motives. Our discussion will focus on the mechanisms which develop attachments and on the function of social behavior.

PERSONALITY THEORIES OF SOCIAL ATTACHMENT

Biological Approaches

Freud's view. Freud suggested that the function of social behavior is to satisfy innate biological needs. (See Chapter 1 for a discussion of Freud's theory of personality.) According to Freud, biological deficiencies create increases in psychic energy; the purpose of behavior is to reduce this tension. The behavior of the very young child is guided solely by instinctive drives (originating in the *id*) aimed at immediate reduction of tension. There are, however, some realistic situations in which such immediate gratification will be frustrated or behaviors based on id impulses could lead to problems. These situations cause the development of the *ego*, which serves to generate behavior that can reduce the level of tension while meeting the constraints of reality. Such ego-directed behavior thus can produce pleasure and avoid pain.

Social behavior represents one way in which the ego satisfies biological needs. Attachments develop when social behaviors are successful in meeting biological needs. The nature of satisfaction and the basis of social attachment vary during the different stages of psychosexual development. In the Freudian system, attachment to the mother develops during the *oral stage* because hunger is satisfied. The child responds socially to his or her mother because she provides nourishment. The male child's attachment to the

Figure 9.1
Processes which determine the level of motivation to be with other people.

father develops during the *phallic stage.* From about age 3 to 6 a boy experiences strong sexual desire for his mother, but fears retaliatory castration by his father. The child resolves this conflict, or *Oedipus complex,* through identification with his father. Thus the boy adopts his father's masculine sex-role behavior (see Chapter 6) in order to prevent castration. As the male child develops this attachment to his father, his erotic feelings for his mother change to those of tender affection. According to Freud, the young girl also transfers her original affection from her mother to her father during the phallic stage. This change in attachment develops because of the girl's envy of the male penis; she attributes her absence of a penis to her mother. The penis is a valuable object to the female in the Freudian system and represents a major problem *(Electra complex)* for the young girl. Partial resolution of this conflict occurs when the young girl identifies with her mother. This identification causes the female child to exhibit female sex-role behavior and results in the attachment of the young girl to her mother.

Freud's theory asserts that the child's early attachments are based on narcissistic individual gratification, whereas during adolescence and young adulthood *(the genital stage)*, the number of attachments normally expands. The bodily pleasure of the young child is replaced by external satisfaction. These attachments are frustrating as well as satisfying because they fail to reduce tension completely. The individual will be nervous and restless while he or she continues to seek complete reduction of tension through established attachments. Apparently, one cost of civilization is that individuals must rely on others for satisfaction of biological needs—a process that is only partially successful.

Jung's theory.   In contrast with the Freudian interpretation of experiental development of attachments, Jung (1938) proposed that our social relationships and motives not only reflect attachments based on past personal satisfactions, but also are based on hereditary predispositions to respond to other people *(archetypes)*. These predispositions, stored in the *collective unconscious,* are based on the experiences of past generations which historically aided in the survival of humans. Let's now examine several examples of inherited predispositions which, Jung proposed, influence our social behavior.

Young children show strong attachments to their mothers. According to Jung, this attachment to the mother is based on an inherited tendency to orient favorably toward the mother *(maternal archetype)*. This inherited response has strong survival value and represents a preset emotional response to a mother figure. Jung also proposed that every person is essentially bisexual, possessing the capacity to develop both masculine and feminine characteristics (see Chapter 6). Our bisexuality not only reflects behavioral characteristics, but also indicates a biological predisposition to respond to members of both sexes. According to Jung, the failure to develop both our masculine characteristics (animus) and our feminine characteristics (anima) can result in severe behavioral disorders. Our discussion indicates that in Jung's view our social motives are partly determined by instinctive emotional response systems.

Freud and Jung portrayed our social behavior as being driven in order to satisfy biological needs. In contrast, the writings of other psychological theorists like Adler and Fromm proposed that our social behavior is caused by the existence of actual innate social needs which are independent of biological needs.

Social Approaches

Adler's view. Adler (1927) moved away from the Freudian psychoanalytic tradition by minimizing the contribution of sexual instincts and proposing that we are primarily motivated by inborn social urges. The types of social relationships which a person develops are determined by the nature of society. Although the particular pattern of social behavior varies from culture to culture, each person's unique set of behaviors will be oriented to obtain social satisfaction and social approval.

Although we are born with feelings of inferiority and weakness, we can gain a sense of superiority through social interaction and effectiveness (Adler, 1927). We compensate for our inherent weaknesses by our social interests. When individuals learn to subordinate their private satisfaction to the good of society, a sense of dignity and worth is established.

Fromm's view. The social theory of Fromm (1941) expanded Adler's earlier views by suggesting that our social motives stem from five basic social needs. According to Fromm, we have a need for *relatedness, transcendence, rootedness, identity,* and *frame of orientation.* Our social behavior will be successful when it satisfies these five basic needs. We feel lonely and isolated when separated from nature and others. The development of what Fromm calls *productive love* enables a human being to reestablish his or her sense of *relatedness* to nature. Productive love is characterized by mutual caring, respect, and understanding. *Transcendence* refers to our need to rise above our animal background; this need causes the development of love and hate, which Fromm feels are uniquely human behaviors. In addition, we need to feel part of something; therefore, our social attachments permit us to satisfy our need for *rootedness.* Although all people need to have a sense of *identity,* this need is often frustrated; identification with and social attachment to another individual or group permits us to satisfy it. Finally, we need a *frame of reference* or stability. Our social attachments provide us with a consistent way of viewing the world. We will be satisfied only when these five social needs are met.

Fromm noted that young children's rebellion from their parents causes them to feel lonely. Similar loneliness can occur as each person attempts to attain independence from sources of authority. However, according to Fromm, we can obtain joy through social attachments. In his book *Escape from Freedom* (1941), Fromm argues that the satisfaction of social needs is fulfilled either by cooperating with others or by gaining security through submission to authority figures. Unfortunately, the appeal of totalitarian forms of government lies in their ability to satisfy our inherent social needs. Parents and educators should enable children to resist the temptation of conformity by developing cooperative forms of social behavior. Our social motives are innate, but the form social behavior takes is dependent upon society.

A Security Approach

Adler and Fromm described social needs as innate. Sullivan (1947), on the other hand, asserts that social motives are the result of interpersonal experience. Anxiety is created during interpersonal interaction when one's security is threatened. Social behavior develops in order to minimize or avoid anxiety and to obtain security. For example, the young child's attachment to his or to her mother is based on the transmission of security; the level of attachment depends upon the amount of security which the child experiences. As we grow older, our interpersonal experiences expand. If these encounters provide additional security, other attachments will form. However, a person who views social acquaintances as enemies will regress to infancy, experiencing only the security obtained from family. Sullivan labels this regression to infantile attachments a *malevolent transformation*. The main feature of Sullivan's theory as it relates to attachment is the idea that our behavior is motivated by the need for security. This sense of security can be satisfied through social behavior which leads to social attachments. Any society which interferes with the individual's security will precipitate severe anxiety and pathological behavior.

A Growth Approach

Maslow's humanistic theory (Maslow, 1968) differs radically from the psychoanalytic theories. Although Maslow acknowledges the presence of basic need, or *deficiency needs* (for example, hunger, affection, security, and self-esteem), the central aspect of Maslow's theory is the concept of growth or *meta needs* (refer to Figure 1.7). The deficiency needs are represented in previous theories, but the idea that humans possess a need to grow is a unique aspect of Maslow's theory. Once our basic needs are satisfied, we seek to satisfy our meta needs—justice, goodness, beauty, order, and unity, for example. According to Maslow, humans have an inherent potential to grow or become *self-actualized*—that is, to reach a state in which they are able to assess objectively and to accept without anxiety their own and others' strengths and weaknesses. They do not demand perfection of themselves or others but are capable of realistic attempts at improvement. This self-actualization process enables humans to satisfy their meta needs.

The social attachments of the self-actualized human are characterized by the development of profound intimate relationships with a few special people. Thus, as we attempt to reach our social potential, the large number of casual acquaintances demanded by the socially insecure are exchanged for several deep, meaningful social relationships. Although only a few individuals reach the self-actualized level, anyone whose social motives mature beyond satisfying the more primitive needs will attempt to develop more meaningful relationships.

Conditioning Approaches

A classical conditioning model. The stimulus-response theory of Neal Miller and John Dollard (Miller & Dollard, 1941; Dollard & Miller, 1950) asserts that social attachments are acquired as the result of classical conditioning experiences. In their view, the presence of intense internal arousal (drive) motivates behavior (previously described in Chapters 1 and 2). External stimuli associated with internal drive states acquire motivational properties through classical conditioning. In addition, environmental cues can also develop incentive motivation when associated with reduction of tension (reward). For example, we are motivated to drink because the presence of an attractive drink (for example, a martini) produces both conditioned thirst (drive) and pleasure (incentive).

According to the Miller-Dollard theory, our attachments to other people reflect the development of acquired motives. Your attachment to your mother, as reflected in the tendency to interact with her, is caused by your association of her with primary drives such as hunger, thirst, pain, and social needs, as well as with reduction of tension through her provision of food, milk, safety, or affection. Therefore, our relationships with other people are based on their capacity to motivate us (acquired drive) and by our attraction to them (acquired incentive motivation). Furthermore, positive feelings, developed in infancy and generated by the mother, can generalize to other people and cause us to respond favorably to them also. However, parents who permit intense unpleasant states to persist in their children may cause their children to associate them with these aversive states. Miller and Dollard suggest that the lack of attachment develops when parents motivate their children to avoid them.

An operant conditioning theory.   B. F. Skinner's explanation of the cause of attachment differs from other theoretical prospectives (Skinner, 1938, 1953; see Chapter 1). Skinner does not propose that reduction of tension is responsible for the formation of social attachments. In Skinner's system, reward is characterized only by its effect on behavior. An event is a reward (or reinforcement) if it increases the frequency of behavior that precedes it. Skinner felt no need to identify the internal representation of reward; it was sufficient to establish the effect of reinforcement on behavior. According to Skinner's operant conditioning theory, attachments to people develop from their association with reinforcement. Any event that is associated with reward will become a secondary reinforcer. Since people distribute reinforcement, they themselves will acquire reinforcing properties: we respond to other people because their presence is reinforcing.

In addition, other people are likely to have reinforced social behavior that maintains attachments. For example, when a child hugs his or her mother, the mother is likely to reinforce that behavior. That reinforcement will increase the frequency of hugging, thereby intensifying the child's response to the mother and the mother's response to the child. Generalization of affectional behaviors can lead to positive response to other people. Additional reinforcement would then act to strengthen social behavior and solidify attachments.

An Overview

Our discussion indicates that psychologists have proposed a number of different motivational mechanisms which are responsible for the establishment of social attachments. Although you might intuitively believe that some views are valid while others seem illogical, the evidence shows that each approach explains some aspect of attachment formation (refer to Figure 9.1). The research demonstrating the contribution of each approach to understanding affiliative motivation will be examined in the remainder of this chapter. Several examples are provided to illustrate that many factors are involved in our motivation to be with others. Harry Harlow's classic research with primates and Stanley Schachter's experimentation with humans points to the tension-reducing aspect of security; their observations that both animals and humans seek security when they are frightened and that the presence of others frequently reduces fear are consistent with Sullivan's psychoanalytic view. Harlow's additional data indicate that the satisfaction of biological needs influences the strength of affiliative motivation— confirming a prediction made by Freud in the early twentieth century. Recent primatology research demonstrates the existence of inherited social behavior patterns which produce attachment formation and assist the survival of a particular species. Similar social patterns, supporting Adler's view of innate social motives, have been seen in primitive human cultures. Moreover, social psychologists have demonstrated that our liking of people depends upon the nature of our experiences with them: pleasant experiences cause us to like certain people and to be motivated to be with them. In contrast, unpleasant experiences cause us to dislike some other people and avoid contact with them. Miller and Dollard proposed that the classical conditioning process influences social attachments; the social psychological literature clearly supports their view. Jones' ingratiation research demonstrates that others will be nice to us when they want us to provide them with social reward, nonsocial reward, or both. These observations clearly agree with Skinner's view of attachments as formed by operant conditioning. Finally, the social psychologists Berscheid and Walster (1978) showed that although sexual motivation plays an important role in establishing romantic relationships, we will be motivated to maintain these attachments only if they provide close, intimate, and caring experiences. The process of developing lasting attachments, called *companionate love* by Berscheid and Walster, suggests a maturational change in the motivational basis of social relationships; the need for shared intimacy and experience replaces the biological sexual need. The change from romantic to companionate love provides validation of the growth approach advocated by Maslow. These examples are only a sample of studies indicating that each of many motivational processes proposed by the personality theories influences the formation of social relationships. Let's examine more closely the determinants of affiliative motivation in the remaining two sections of the chapter. In the first of these sections, we will study the processes motivating different types of social relationships. The factors leading to our failure to establish attachments, as well as the negative consequences of a lack of social contact, will be addressed in the last section.

AFFECTIONAL SYSTEMS

Harry Harlow's primate studies focused on the factors important to the development of social attachments (see Harlow, 1958, 1965). Harlow defined *love* as an "affectional feeling for others" and identified five basic forms of love: *maternal love,* a mother's love for her child; *infant love,* a child's love for his or her mother; *peer* or *age-mate love,* the social bond between children or adults; *heterosexual love,* the passion of one sex for another; and *paternal love,* a father's affection for his offspring. Harlow's studies identified some variables which motivate each type of love, as well as those which lead to the failure to experience love. Although Harlow's experimentation used rhesus monkeys, factors identical to those of the rhesus monkey have been found in other primates and humans. Other psychologists have described additional processes which influence the establishment of social bonds. It is important to note that all primate species and many human cultures do not act exactly as Harlow's rhesus monkeys did. For example, the natural rejection of a child by his or her mother in baboons (DeVore, 1963b) or langur monkeys (Jay, 1963) is more severe than that which Harlow observed in his rhesus monkeys; and the separation process is more gradual, and in many instances is never completed, in chimpanzees (Goodall, 1968) and humans. However, these differences do not detract from the general pattern of affectional responses which Harlow described as being present in all primate species and humans. We are indebted to Harlow for his significant contribution to enhancing our understanding of the nature of the attachment process.

We will examine both primate and human research in this section. As you compare Harlow's primate studies with what you know about human development, note that comparable ages in humans are approximately four times the ages of rhesus monkeys

(Harlow, 1971). Harlow defines *babyhood* as birth to 3 months in primates and birth to 1 year in humans. *Infancy* in primates is the period between babyhood and 1 year; in humans, infancy extends from babyhood to 3 or 4 years. *Childhood* is the period between infancy and *adolescence;* in primates, it occurs at approximately 2 years, and in humans it occurs between 10 and 14 years.

Maternal Love

A mother's love for her child is extremely variable in humans. Some mothers exhibit strong maternal behavior toward their offspring by being very protective and caring. Other mothers display weak maternal attachment and seem unconcerned for their children's welfare. Let's look at the factors which act to motivate maternal behavior, as well as those which could produce maternal rejection.

Stages of maternal behavior. The function of maternal behavior is to care for the dependent child. The strongest maternal behavior of the mother toward her baby occurs during Harlow's stage of *care and comfort.* This care involves the provision of comfort, feeding, and protection while the child is an infant. Harlow found that an infant's presence elicits a strong positive emotional response from the primate mother and initiates maternal support. The maternal response involves cradling the infant, the closeness providing maximal body contact. This *contact comfort* experienced by both the mother and the infant is extremely pleasant and plays an important role in their attachment to each other. Maternal behavior also involves nursing the infant, thereby satisfying its biological needs. The close body contact, seen in Figure 9.2, aids in establishing the infant's feeding reflexes. Finally, maternal behavior serves an important protective function. Any threat of danger to the infant elicits maternal aggression (see Chapter 7), and the mother will retrieve her young when they wander too far away.

Immediately after a primate or human mother has given birth, her maternal behavior is indiscriminate; later the maternal response will be directed toward only her

Figure 9.2
Primate mother cuddling and caressing her infant.
(Courtesy of Harry F. Harlow, University of Wisconsin Primate Laboratory.)

own child. Harlow observed that while early removal of a primate's baby elicited signs of distress, any baby could calm the distraught mother. Approximately 1 week to 10 days after birth, only a mother's own baby is able to reduce this distress (Jensen, 1965). Similarly, human mothers report impersonal feelings for their babies until the child reaches 4 to 6 weeks of age (Robson & Moss, 1970). From then on the mother exhibits a restricted attachment, focused on only her own child. Robson and Moss noted that when a human infant of approximately 3 months of age is taken away from the mother, the mother regards the absence of her infant as an aversive event (even when she is aware of the temporary nature of the separation), and she experiences satisfaction when her infant returns. This intense maternal behavior is characteristic of the care and comfort stage but does not last forever.

The baby's clinging behavior serves to maintain maternal motivation. If a primate baby is removed for even a short time from its mother, the mother will reject it (Harlow, 1971). However, if the baby is immediately replaced by another object, the mother will try to accept this substitute object. For example, Harlow replaced a rhesus baby with a young kitten; the rhesus mother tried to "love" the kitten, but since the kitten could not cling, the mother soon stopped showing affection for it. In addition, the replacement of the rhesus baby with an autistic rhesus baby which violently rejected maternal affection produced a rapid decline in maternal behavior. On the other hand, a substitute blind rhesus baby which would cling reinstated the mother's maternal response.

Harlow observed that maternal behavior does wane in the typical primate mother. Its decline occurs in two stages—*maternal ambivalence* and *relative separation* (Harlow, Harlow, & Hansen, 1963). Although the protectiveness of the primate mother is strong during the first month after birth of an infant, it quickly declines during the next 4 months. The infant begins to stray farther from the mother before being retrieved; and a greater threat of danger must be present before maternal protective behavior will be initiated. As noted by Rheingold and Eckerman (1971), this increase in the distance an infant is allowed to travel before retrieval has parallels in human behavior. Rheingold and Eckerman found that in an unfamiliar area, the farthest distance traveled by human infants from the mother increased from 6.9 meters in 1-year-olds to 10.6 meters in 4-year-olds.

When maternal protectiveness declines as the child grows older, the mother shows an increased resistance to nursing and to close contact. The infant's attempts to elicit maternal care are met by negative maternal behavior—rejection, threats, and physical punishment. The incidence of maternal punishment increases drastically in the primate over the next 4- to 5-month period. In humans, the period of maximal maternal protectiveness occurs when the child is approximately 3 to 6 months old; protective behavior decreases and punishment increases over the next 2 to 3 years. Harlow notes that physical punishment is not always necessary in order to discourage feeding and clinging behavior. Chimpanzees will tickle or play with their offspring to distract them and thus prevent demands for maternal behavior. The human mother may take her child to nursery school to prevent dependency and to encourage independence. Thus, during the stage of maternal ambivalence, maternal behavior is characterized by a decrease in protective behavior and a corresponding increase in the rejection of nursing and contact behavior.

The "break" between mother and child is completed during the stage of relative separation. The incidence of punishment declines as the child reduces his or her attempts to nurse and cling. As you will see shortly, the child's increased independence is responsible for the reduction in maternal behavior. This phase of the separation process typically is slow: in Harlow's primates it lasted 10 to 15 months of age; in human children it lasts from 4 to 8 years. Although the separation process is far from complete during this age span, human children learn to do many things without the mother: go outdoors, entertain themselves, go to school, etc. In primates, separation can be hastened by the arrival of a new baby for which the mother must care; the mother's maternal behavior shifts to the new child, and the firstborn must now take care of itself. Fortunately, most human mothers are sufficiently able and loving to care for more than one child at a time, and the separation process is thus considerably longer for humans than for primates.

A number of factors appear to influence the separation process. The physical characteristics of the environment are one important factor (Hansen, 1966). Hansen found that for primates in a small living space, the mother-infant bond remained strong even after the young primate reached 2 years of age (adolescence). Harlow (1971) built a large living cage to house four nuclear primate families. In this living arrangement, the firstborn continued to attempt to receive maternal affection for months after the birth of a new sibling. When the mother rejected these attempts, the firstborn was content to play with peers during the day but still sought maternal comfort during the night. On the occasions when the mother rejected these overtures, the young primate would cling to the father. "Apparently, any body is better than nobody at all" (Harlow, 1971). There are also considerable differences among species in the degree of mother-infant separation. Kaufman and Rosenblum (1969) studied two species of macaque monkeys. In bonnet macaques, adolescent and mature primates typically interact socially with members of their group other than their own family; pigtail macaques respond primarily to the mother and close family members. Finally, there are substantial cultural differences. For example, in some groups of wild langur monkeys, adult interaction is as likely to occur with other group members as with the mother; in other langur groups, however, social interaction is almost entirely with the mother and family members. To summarize, then, the degree of maternal rejection depends upon spatial, cultural, and species differences.

The nature of maternal motivation. Is human maternal behavior instinctive or learned? This question is difficult to answer. You might think that since not all women are maternal, then maternal behavior must be learned. However, the absence of a behavior in some members of a species does not necessarily mean that the behavior is learned: it may simply be that the appropriate releasing stimuli for that behavior are absent (refer to Chapter 2 for a review of modern instinct theory). Nor does the similarity of a general pattern of maternal response within a particular species indicate that inherited factors determine a specific behavior. It may be that the similarity of response is due to a common experience conveyed by the social structure of that group. However, some evidence does indicate that both instinctive and learned processes, with their relative importance varying among individuals, may govern human maternal behavior. The significance of internal neural and hormonal factors and their external release argues for a role for instinctive processes in maternal motivation. In contrast, the influence of experience, both beneficial and detrimental, suggests that learning also plays a role. Let's briefly discuss this evidence.

Rosenblatt (1967) discovered that virgin female rats placed with young rats (or pups) become maternal after approximately 6 days. These results indicate that the neural systems capable of producing maternal behavior were present in these nonexperienced rats. Yet, why did it take these rats so long to release maternal behavior? According to Rosenblatt, the internal hormonal systems necessary for maternal behavior were not present when the pups were introduced. Maternal behavior would have occurred sooner if they had been present. To demonstrate this point, Terkel and Rosenblatt (1968) injected their female rats with blood from a nursing mother; onset of maternal behavior occurred within 48 hours. Similarly, Moltz, Lubin, Leon, and Numan (1970) observed that timed injections of estrogen, progesterone, and prolactin induced maternal behavior within several days in their female rats. However, why did a period of a few days elapse before maternal behavior appeared, even after an internal maternal hormonal state had been established? The reason for this delay is that birth serves an important role in eliciting maternal behavior—a process called the *termination effect*. Moltz, Robbins, and Park (1966) found that maternal behavior in rats did not occur until 2 days after caesarian delivery.

The decline in hormone levels influences infant-mother separation. Rosenblatt (1969) introduced young pups (5 to 10 days old) for 1 hour a day to a nursing mother whose own pups were older. Rosenblatt reported that this mother's maternal responsivity to the pups, even though they still needed maternal care, decreased as her maternal behavior toward her own offspring declined. In all likelihood, the natural reduction in the internal hormonal systems associated with motherhood was responsible for the loss of responsivity to the young pups.

The internal hormonal state alone is not sufficient to produce maternal care: the presence of an appropriate young animal is also necessary both to stimulate and maintain maternal behavior. Rosenblatt removed infant rats from their mothers after birth and found that maternal responding in most of the mothers was not present when he introduced 5- to 10-day-old test pups 1 week later. The pups needed care, but the lowered hormonal levels caused by the absence of nursing rendered these females unresponsive. In contrast, maternal behavior is extended when the young remain dependent. To show this process, Rosenblatt removed a mother's infants before they matured and replaced them with younger animals. He observed that maternal care remained longer than is usual.

Our discussion indicates that both internal hormonal systems and the presence of the infant influence the level of maternal behavior—an observation suggesting that instinctive factors have a role in maternal motivation. Let's look at the evidence suggesting that another factor, experience, also plays a substantial role in maternal behavior.

In both primates and humans, considerable differences exist in the quality and quantity of maternal care. Some mothers are extremely protective, while others ignore their infants; some mothers are extremely efficient in their maternal care, yet others seem totally disorganized. Though we may attribute these variations to the level of maternal instinct, experience clearly affects maternal care. The direct experience of motherhood is definitely an important factor in the level of maternal care. A first-time uncertain mother—*a primiparous mother*—becomes a confident, efficient, experienced *multiparous mother* if she bears more offspring. However, experience may not be the crucial learning factor in maternal behavior. Although the quality of care does improve with experience, most primiparous mothers typically respond effectively to their young and are sometimes more efficient than experienced mothers (see Goodall, 1968). Even the first-time mother has observed her own mother's behavior as well as the maternal action of others. Furthermore, she has probably been able to play with infants during her childhood. These experiences undoubtedly are crucial to the quality of maternal behavior.

Several psychological experiments support the idea that social experience influences maternal care. For example, Yerkes (1943) reported that captive primiparous chimpanzee mothers were frightened by their infants and refused to allow them to cling. In 1959, Van den Berghe observed that a primiparous gorilla mother bit off her infant's hand, then bit off a foot, and finally punctured its skull with her teeth. Other primiparous gorillas were less abusive, but some ignored their infants. In an experimental investigation of the nature of this disturbed maternal behavior, Harlow, Harlow, and Hansen (1963) found that socially deprived rhesus monkeys displayed similar abnormal maternal care; the deprived mothers either abused or ignored their infants. These observations indicate that social experience is a crucial factor in maternal motivation. Up to this point, we have seen that both innate and learned factors influence a mother's response to her infant. Let's now look at the processes which motivate a child's attachment to the mother.

Infant Love

Substantial differences exist in our society in the degree of attachment which children have for their mothers. Some young children demand constant attention from the mother and exhibit extreme discomfort when she is away even for a short period of time. Other young children seem uninterested in their mother's affection and show no concern when the mother leaves them. Harry Harlow's research demonstrates that the level of a mother's warmth, as well as the attractiveness of environmental events, determines the intensity and duration of the child's attachment. We begin our discussion of the infant's love for the mother by presenting Harlow's stages of infant attachment to and disattachment from the mother. Later in this section, we turn to the factors which motivate the child to love the mother, and the process which breaks this important bond.

Stages of infant attachment. Harlow (1971) identified five consecutive stages of infant love: (1) *organic affection,* (2) *comfort and attachment,* (3) *security and solace,* (4) *exploration and disattachment,* and (5) *relative independence.*

During the first stage (organic affection), the baby relies on the mother for satisfaction of organic or biological needs. The mobility of a human or primate baby is limited, although the baby does possess several instinctual reflexes which aid in nursing. For example, the sucking reflex provides nourishment from the mother's nipple; the rooting reflex causes the infant's head to move toward the mother's nipple, enabling the baby to bring its mouth to the mother's breast. Finally, the baby's strong upward-ventral climbing reflex allows the baby to move up the mother's body to the breast areas. Human mothers sometimes experience dismay when their children constantly move forward in their cribs until there is pressure on their heads. Yet, this behavior simply reflects a significant innate biological reflex.

The second stage (comfort and attachment) begins as soon as the baby can cling to its mother (and may overlap with the first stage). Clinging begins at birth in the primate but is nonexistent in human babies until they attain 2 months of age; this clinging behavior quickly increases during the next 6 months. Primates have been observed to cling up to 1 year of age, and it is not unusual to see a human child of 6 to 8 years clinging to his or her mother. The attachment of the child to the mother during this second stage is also determined by the child's primary object-following reflex (Bowlby, 1969). The child imitates the mother's actions; when the mother eats, so does her child. The purely reflexive nature of the bond to the mother during this stage is indicated by the child's lack of concern when the mother leaves; an infant's emotional bond does not develop until the third stage. In addition, the infant exhibits no fear during the second stage. Sackett (1966) observed no fear of a threatening situation in 3-month-old monkeys. Continued observation revealed that during stage 3 these same monkeys exhibited extreme fear to an identical danger. Schaffer and Emerson (1964) observed similar behavior in human children. Obviously, the extreme maternal protectiveness during stage 2 is adaptive for the "fearless" infant.

As the child develops fear of danger and the unknown during the third stage (security and solace), the mother's provision of security begins to become important and the love of the infant for the mother develops. (The third stage begins when a primate is approximately 3 months of age and when a human child is between 6 months and 1 year old.) During the third stage the infant often exhibits extreme terror when the mother

Figure 9.3
Rhesus infant exhibiting fear in a strange
environment in the absence of the mother.
(Courtesy of Harry F. Harlow, University of
Wisconsin Primate Laboratory.)

leaves (see Figure 9.3) and quickly runs to her when she returns. René Spitz reported in 1946 that 6- to 10-month-old human infants were distressed when their mother left them in a strange place. However, conditions do exist in which young primates or humans do not feel extreme terror during maternal separation. Later in the chapter we will discuss the circumstances which influence these separation disturbances as well as the consequences of *separation anxiety* on development.

During the third stage the infant begins to explore the environment; this process intensifies during the fourth stage (exploration and disattachment). The infant's increased exploration corresponds to the decline in maternal protection and attachment. As the child becomes attracted to the environment, the mother simultaneously allows the child to become more independent. The lure of attractive objects in the environment initiates the child's separation from the mother. Rheingold and Eckerman (1970) found that toys placed in a room away from a child increased exploration. Because the child begins to explore, maternal behavior wanes, and the mother punishes attempts to cling. Such punishment accelerates the disattachment process. Although a nonpunitive mother retards the process, most children are attracted to the environment and eventually break away from even the most nonpunitive mother.

The break becomes final during the fifth stage (relative independence). During times of stress the primate will continue to attempt to cling to the mother but eventually will seek security among other members of the group. In human cultures, this separation occurs when the young person goes to work or to college. Although separation often is traumatic, failure to separate interferes with the individual's abilities to form other meaningful relationships.

The nature of infant love.   There are two systems which determine the infant's bond to the mother: one process acts during the "fearless" stage of infancy; the second process causes the infant to love the mother when terror begins. We will first examine Harlow's research and then discover that processes which Harlow described are identical to processes operating in human infants.

Harlow developed two inanimate surrogate mothers to investigate the factors which influence the child's attachment to the mother (see Figure 9.4). Each mother had a bare body of welded wire; one mother retained only the wire body, but the second was covered with soft terry cloth. In the typical study, a primate was raised with both a wire and

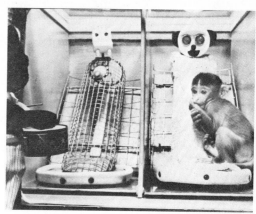

Figure 9.4
Cloth and wire surrogate mothers. (Courtesy of Harry F. Harlow, University of Wisconsin Primate Laboratory.)

a cloth-covered surrogate mother. The animal's preference is thought to indicate the factors responsible for maternal attachment. During the second stage of infancy the attachment to the mother was determined by her ability to impart pleasure and the young infant preferred a cloth mother to a wire one. The infant spent 15 to 20 hours a day clinging to a cloth mother; almost no time was spent on the wire surrogate mother. Even when only the wire mother provided nourishment, she was quite unpopular; however, the infant did spend enough time with the wire mother to satisfy his or her hunger.

The young monkey's liking for the cloth mother does not reflect an avoidance of the wire mother as such: the infant monkey also preferred a cloth mother over a rayon, vinyl, or sandpaper surrogate (Harlow & Suomi, 1970). Nor does it prove that nourishment has no impact on the mother-infant bond: Harlow and Zimmerman (1959) found that infant primates preferred a nursing to a nonnursing cloth mother. It is interesting to note, in addition, that the young primates spent more time clinging to a rocking surrogate mother than a stationary one, and preferred a warm mother (in terms of temperature) to a cold one. The child's clinging response acts to produce maternal behavior, and a mother who satisfies the child's organic needs will ensure that the "fearless" child remains protected.

Although young primates are physically attached to their mothers, the attachment is not an emotional one. The mother's absence evokes no distress, and an upset young infant obtains no comfort from the mother. As the infant begins to explore the environment, the fear system develops. The infant becomes terrified by a strange or novel object. At this time, the infant experiences a rapid reduction in fear when clinging to the mother. Primate infants are extremely frightened when introduced to a mechanical monster or plastic toy and will run to the mother—clinging to her apparently causes fear to dissipate. As fear declines, the infant begins to examine the strange object. Soon, the infant leaves the mother in order to explore the new object. The infant runs back and forth from object to mother until it finally interacts physically with the object. Apparently, the infant senses safety when the mother is present. A primate exploring a new toy in the presence of the mother can be seen in Figure 9.5.

Figure 9.5
Infant playing in a strange environment in the
presence of a cloth mother. (Courtesy of
Harry F. Harlow, University of Wisconsin
Primate Laboratory.)

Reduction of fear during clinging appears to be innate; the natural physical characteristics of the mother impart security to the child. However, an infant monkey also experiences reduction of fear when clinging to an inanimate cloth surrogate monkey. Obviously, the cloth mother could not exhibit any behavior that provided security. The tactile comfort provided by clinging to one's mother is the stimulus which initiates security; the infant continues to experience fear if its only solace is a wire surrogate mother. The mother's nursing is not responsible for the child's sense of security; a nursing wire mother is no more a haven of security than a nonnursing wire mother. Frightened infants are extremely motivated to reach their cloth mother; they will jump over a high plexiglas barrier in order to get to their cloth mother. Also, the young primate prefers to remain with the cloth mother in the presence of a dangerous object than to run away alone (Harlow & Zimmerman, 1959).

Mary Ainsworth and her associates (see Blehar, Lieberman, & Ainsworth, 1977) reported a similar importance of security in human infants. They initially observed the maternal behavior of white middle-class Americans feeding their infants from birth to 54 weeks of age and identified two categories of maternal care: one group of mothers showed responsivity and sensitivity to their children during feeding; the other mothers were indifferent to their infants' needs. During the second stage of their study, Blehar, Lieberman, and Ainsworth examined the behavior of these same infants at the age of 1 year in a strange environment. In the unfamiliar place, the interested mothers' children occasionally sought their mothers' attention and after having been left alone in a strange situation were highly motivated to remain with the mother when reunited. In addition, once these children felt secure in the new place, they explored and played with toys. The researchers called this type of mother-infant bond a *secure relationship*. The behavior of these secure children strikingly resembles the response of Harlow's rhesus monkeys to the cloth mother. In contrast to this secure relationship, children of indifferent mothers frequently cried and were apparently distressed. Their alarm was not reduced by the presence of the mother. Also, Blehar, Lieberman, and Ainsworth reported that these children avoided contact with their mothers, either because the mothers were uninterested or because the mothers actually rejected them. The researchers labeled this mother–infant interaction an *anxious relationship*. The failure of the mothers of these anxious children to induce security certainly parallels the infant primates' response to the wire surrogate mother.

How strong is an infant's attachment to his or her mother? To investigate this process, Harlow constructed four very abusive "monster mothers." One rocked violently from time to time; a second projected an air blast in the infant's face. Primate infants clung to these mothers even while being abused. The other two monster mothers were even more abusive: one of them tossed the infant off her, and the other shot brass spikes as the infant approached. Although the infants were unable to cling to these mothers continuously, they resumed clinging as soon as possible when the abuse stopped. Apparently, a child's love for the mother makes possible the forgiveness of even the strongest abuse. The fact that some frightened people, such as Kevin in the story that begins this chapter, continue to seek their mothers even into adolescence and adulthood is not surprising. Nonetheless, the attractiveness of peers coupled with the decline of maternal behavior typically causes the child to seek security away from the mother. We now turn our attention to our attachment to peers.

Peer Love

Two young children in my neighborhood, an 8-year-old boy and his 6-year-old sister, exhibit very different social behavior. The boy is quite social; he races outside to play as soon as he comes home from school. In contrast, the girl prefers to remain alone indoors with her books and toys. Their differences in social behavior probably stem from the abundance of boys and the absence of girls in their neighborhood. The attraction of his playmates initiated the boy's social bonds, while toys and mother were the only attractions for the girl. In our society, social behavior is extremely important; the development of peer bonds and the ability to form new social relationships represent a critical determinant of long-term personal adjustment.

The importance of play.   Harry Harlow's research stresses the importance of attractive playmates in maternal separation and in the establishment of strong peer bonds. Childhood *play* is one factor which Harlow believes determines the efficacy of social behavior. Play is defined as a nonserious activity in which individuals participate only for the pleasure it brings. The play of young children establishes the foundation of later social effectiveness. This section discusses the maturation of children's play and its function in social attachment. Later in the chapter, other variables determining the likelihood and strength of social bonds are explored.

The affectional system of age-mates or peers begins as the mother–infant bond weakens and as the young child begins to explore the physical environment (Harlow, 1971). During the establishment of the peer affectional system, children develop attachments to members of their group outside of their family. The social attachments typically are with children of the same age and sex. Harlow found that social bonds begin to develop at 4 to 6 months of age in primates (this corresponds to 2 years of age in humans), are strongest during the end of the second year (9 to 10 years of age in humans), and decline during the third year (the onset of adolescence in humans). The child plays or interacts with children of his or her own age because of their comparable physical and emotional development; biological, physical, and behavioral differences typically cause children of different sexes to avoid each other. It is not uncommon for 8- to 10-year-old boys and girls to dislike each other; the boys and girls in my neighborhood appear to take particular pleasure in taunting each other. This antagonism wanes during the onset of adolescence.

The influence of security.   The young primate is able to begin to interact with other primates as a result of the contact comfort and sense of security received from his or her mother. The mother's positive attributes generalize to other people and act to attract the young person to age-mates. The sense of security provided by peers serves to cement the peer bond. Harlow (1971) found that even the slightest terror inhibited a primate's solitary play. However, two primates playing together exhibited no fear when going places and doing things which they would not do alone. This sense of security is experienced with a peer and motivates the primate to behave in often unpredictable and sometimes dangerous ways. Harlow's research demonstrated that the presence of fear and stress acted to motivate his primates' social behavior, while social contact served to provide security and reduce tension.

A similar influence of the presence of others occurs in humans. Stanley Schachter has uncovered experimental evidence which indicates that during times of fear and uncertainty people need to affiliate with other people; moreover, the presence of these other people reduces fear and anxiety. The reduction in fear acts to stimulate social and nonsocial behaviors which a person would not otherwise exhibit when afraid. The following example illustrates this. I recently took my two sons (aged 8 and 10 years) and their two friends of similar ages to the local recreation center. Becoming bored, they actually decided to walk the several miles home. They displayed no evidence of experiencing fear during this escapade. Peer-induced security allowed them to do in a group what none would try alone although the danger was approximately the same. Let's now examine Schachter's research on the security provided by other people.

Motivational influence of fear. In 1959, Stanley Schachter conducted a classic experiment on affiliative motivation. College students participated in an experiment which they were led to believe involved a determination of the physiological effects of electric shock. Some subjects were told that their exposure to electric shock would be quite aversive, a procedure designed to initiate a high level of fear ("high fear" condition); others were informed that the shocks would not be painful ("low fear" condition). Evaluation of the arousal level of subjects in each condition showed a large difference in their subjective feelings of fear: subjects in the "high fear" condition were considerably more disturbed by the experiment than those in the "low fear" condition. Following assessment of their arousal level, the subjects were told that they were to wait in another room for 10 minutes while the equipment was prepared. The experimenter told the subjects that there were a number of rooms available—some small rooms with a single comfortable armchair, or a classroom with other people waiting to participate in the study. The subjects were asked to indicate their preference. The results of Schachter's study shown in Table 9.1 confirmed his expectations: the presence of high threat increased the subjects' need to be with other people, and the level of affiliative motivation was directly related to their level of fear. The greater the fear experienced, the stronger were their affiliative needs.

Fear-reducing effects. Harlow's research indicates that the presence of either the mother or age-mates produces a strong sense of security for the primate during fearful

Table 9.1
Influence of Fear on Affiliation

Condition	Percentage Choosing			Strength of Affliation*
	Together	Don't Care	Alone	
High fear	62.5	28.1	9.4	.88
Low fear	33.0	60.0	7.0	.35

*Figures are ratings on a scale from -2 to $+2$.

Adapted from: *The psychology of affiliation* by Stanley Schachter with the permission of the publishers, Stanford University Press. © 1959 by the Board of Trustees of the Leland Stanford Junior University.

situations. A number of experiments show that the same relationship is true for adult humans; during aversive situations we experience a reduction of fear when we are in the presence of others. The reinforcing effect of this certainly intensifies our attachments and our need for others in times of stress. Schachter (1959) conducted an additional study to test this interpretation of social interaction. In this study, subjects in the "high fear" condition were told that if they chose to wait with others, they could not talk about the experiment. As the experiment caused fear, Schachter predicted that subjects who could not talk about the experiment would be less motivated to wait with others than subjects who could talk about the study would be. Schachter found, in support of his hypothesis, that subjects told not to discuss the experiment exhibited less affiliative motivation than subjects who could talk about it. In addition, Schachter found that a person's tendency to affiliate when he or she is afraid decreases with birth order: firstborn children show stronger affiliative motives than second-born children, and second-born children than third-born children (see Figure 9.6). This relationship is true regardless of the number of children in a family. According to Schachter, the firstborn, when afraid, is more likely to receive contact comfort than later-born children are; thus, they develop stronger affiliative motives than their young siblings do.

Wrightsman (1960) also found support for Schachter's hypothesis. In a study similar to Schachter's, Wrightsman exposed his subjects to a "high threat" condition which was followed either by having the subjects wait with other people or by forcing them to wait alone. Wrightsman discovered that firstborn subjects who waited alone were more fearful after the waiting period than subjects who waited with other people, but later-born subjects were not influenced by the presence of others. However, if fear is to be reduced by the presence of other people, those other people must themselves be calm. Anxious people only serve to heighten our fears. Schmidenberg (1942) compared the influence

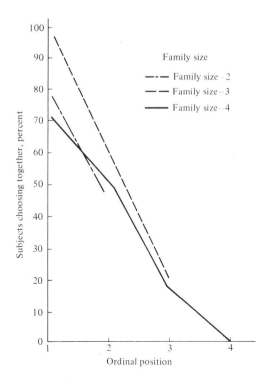

Figure 9.6
Influence of birth order on the tendency to affiliate when afraid. (Reprinted from The psychology of affiliation *by Stanley Schachter with the permission of the publishers, Stanford University Press. © 1959 by the Board of Trustees of the Leland Stanford Junior University.)*

which being with people had on severely frightened Londoners during the bombings of World War II. He found that frightened people were calmed by the presence of less-disturbed people, but their fears were intensified by more-frightened people. Apparently, the presence of other people reduces tension only when those people can impart a sense of security to us.

An avoidance of others.   At certain times when we are aroused, we may not want to discuss the source of our distress; at those times, therefore, we do not wish to be with other people. Sarnoff and Zimbardo (1961) discovered that their subjects exhibited less affiliative motivation under high levels of potential embarrassment than under low levels. Two conditions in their study were identical to those in Schachter's initial study: "high fear" or "low fear" (of pain). Two other groups were exposed to situations designed to arouse embarrassment. Subjects in these groups were told that they had to suck on a variety of objects. Those in "high embarrassment" condition were informed that they had to suck on oral or infantile objects such as a breast shield or rubber nipples; those in the "low embarrassment" condition were told that they must suck on acceptable items such as a whistle. All four groups were then asked to indicate whether they would like to remain alone or with other people before the study began. The results presented in Figure 9.7 indicate that the "high fear" condition increased affiliative motivation—a finding identical to Schachter's. The "high embarrassment" condition produced the opposite result: the need to be with others was decreased. Sarnoff and Zimbardo's results indicate that when our feelings embarrass us, we are motivated to avoid people who might ridicule us.

This raises the question of whether or not the presence of others would be desirable if the possibility of ridicule were reduced. To test this, Firestone, Kaplan, and Russell (1973) replicated Sarnoff and Zimbardo's experiment, but added another dimension. Half of their subjects stayed with other people participating in the same study (similar subjects), while the other subjects remained with people from another study (dissimilar subjects). The results of the "similar" condition were identical to Sarnoff and Zimbardo's; fear increased the need for affiliation needs, but embarrassment decreased it. However, exactly opposite results were found in the "dissimilar" condition: fear decreased affiliative motivation but embarrassment increased it. The most logical interpretation of these results is that the highly embarrassed subjects' arousal created their need to be with

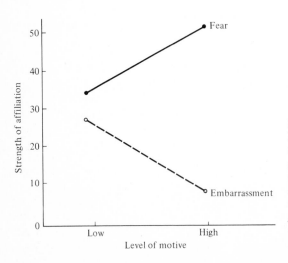

Figure 9.7
Relationship between type of emotion (embarrassment versus fear) and the strength of affiliative motivation. [Adapted from Sarnoff, I., & Zimbardo, P. G. Anxiety, fear, and social affiliation. Cited in J. L. Freeman, D. O. Sears, & J. M. Carlsmith, Social psychology (3rd ed.). Englewood Cliffs, N. J.: Prentice-Hall, 1978.]

others. They avoided people who might embarrass them, but they could receive comfort from the presence of nonthreatening dissimilar people. The type of people whom we seek when we are under stress depends upon the nature of our stress and the similarity of our social companions.

Interpersonal attraction. Most of us have a few close friends and a number of casual acquaintances, while there are also some people whom we may dislike or even hate. Our previous discussion indicated that we have needs to be with others, especially during stressful times. We now focus our attention on the process which determines whom we like or dislike.

The associative process. Ask yourself why you like a close friend or dislike a fellow student. You will probably respond that you like your friend because you enjoy his or her company and that you feel uneasy in the presence of the student whom you dislike. Contemporary views of attraction stress the importance of reinforcement and punishment in the development of friends and enemies (Byrne & Clore, 1970). Byrne and Clore proposed that if our contact with others is rewarding or pleasant, we begin to associate those people with reward; therefore, we like them. However, if our experiences with certain people are unpleasant or aversive, we develop a dislike for these people. This model assumes that friendship and enmity are based on traditional classical conditioning principles (see Chapter 1 and Miller and Dollard's view described earlier in the present chapter). According to this approach, positive emotional conditioned responses, motivating us to be with certain people, develop through association with reward; negative emotional conditioned responses, motivating us to avoid certain others, are acquired when we associate these other people with punishment.

The role of reward and punishment in forming attachments was explored in a study by Griffitt (1970). In this study, men and women became acquainted in either a comfortable environment or an unpleasant one, such as an overheated room. Griffitt observed that pleasant surroundings enhanced liking. In 1961, Lott and Lott also investigated the influence of reward on attachment. Three-member groups of children, drawn from the same class, participated in a game. In some groups, children were rewarded for participating; in other groups, the children received no reward. After the study, the experimenters asked the children which two class members they would like to take on a family outing. The rewarded children chose their own group members, while nonrewarded children selected children from outside their group. Obviously, the circumstances surrounding our interaction with people are important: pleasant experiences promote friendship and unpleasant ones promote dislike.

The negative impact of an aversive experience can be overcome through additional experience, as shown by Saegert, Swap, and Zajonc (1973). Each of their subjects looked at pictures of faces from one to four times while drinking a beverage. Some subjects had been given a pleasant-tasting beverage, the others an unpleasant one. Next, the experimenters asked the subjects not only to rate the extent to which they liked the beverage but also to disclose whether they thought they would like the person pictured. The psychologists observed that with only one exposure, context was important—the subjects liked the other person better when the picture was viewed under pleasant conditions. The effect of context was not evident after one exposure; instead, liking increased as familiarity increased. However, this effect of enhanced liking as familiarity increases is true only for stimulus objects (or people) which are inherently positive or neutral. When an object or person is perceived to be negative, increased exposure does not produce liking, according to Perlman and Oskamp (1971). Those researchers requested their subjects to view pictures of people who were dressed either "positively"

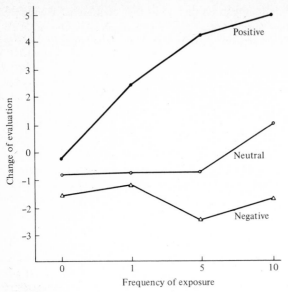

Figure 9.8
Effect of picture content (positive, neutral, or negative) and frequency of experience on interpersonal attraction. (From Perlman, D., & Oskamp, S. The effect of picture content and exposure frequency on evaluations of Negroes and whites. Journal of Experimental Social Psychology, *1971, 7, 503–514.)*

(e.g., clergyman), "neutrally" (e.g., man in suit), or "negatively" (e.g., janitor). Increased exposure to both positive and neutral pictures enhanced the subjects' liking; however, additional exposure to negative pictures increased disliking. In addition, "positive" photographs stimulated more liking than "neutral" ones. The results of their study are presented in Figure 9.8.

The reciprocity rule. Young children readily admit that they like their friends just because their friends "like them back," while they base their dislike for other children on a perceived notion that these children dislike them. According to the "reciprocity of liking" rule (Berscheid & Walster, 1978), we like people who like us and dislike those who do not. Since others typically do not tell us if they like or dislike us, praise is thought to be an indicator of liking. When others offer us praise, we assume that they like us, and, as a result, our liking for them increases. Criticism indicates dislike, activates discomfort, and causes us to avoid the criticism.

Aronson and Linder (1965) tested this reciprocity rule by having each of their subjects interact with a confederate (an assistant of the experimenter who the subject thought was another subject) on several occasions. Following each interaction, the subject overheard an interview between the confederate and the experimenter. In the first condition ("positive evaluation throughout") the confederate praised the subject in each interview and indicated a liking for the subject. In the second condition ("negative evaluation throughout"), subjects overheard the confederate criticize them in each interview and voice unsureness about liking them. In the third condition ("negative-positive evaluation") the confederate began with a negative response but became more positive in subsequent sessions. By the last session, the confederate's evaluation was as flattering as that in condition 1. In the fourth condition ("positive-negative evaluation") the confederate began with a positive response but became negative in subsequent

Table 9.2
Effect of Approval on Interpersonal Attraction

Condition	Liking*
Positive evaluation throughout	6.42
Negative evaluation throughout	2.52
Negative-positive evaluation	7.67
Positive-negative evaluation	0.87

*Figures are ratings on a scale from -10 to $+10$.

Adapted from: Aronson, E., and Linder, D. Gain and loss of esteem as determinants of interpersonal attractiveness. *Journal of Experimental Social Psychology*, 1965, 1, 156–171.

sessions. By the last session, the confederate's response to the subject was as negative as in condition 2. Upon completion of the study, the subjects were asked whether or not they liked their partner. The results of this study are presented in Table 9.2 and show that the subjects reciprocated the confederates' evaluations: subjects liked or disliked the confederates who liked or disliked them. However, the degree of liking did not depend entirely on this factor. If praise were the only determinant of liking, the degree of liking should have been equal in both "positive evaluation" conditions. However, Aronson and Linder found that confederates whose initial evaluations were negative were more liked than those who gave positive evaluations throughout. In addition, there was a tendency toward greater disliking of confederates whose initial evaluations were positive than those who were critical throughout. Apparently, the value which praise or criticism has on establishing social attachments is often determined by the contrast between praise and criticism.

A need for praise. The influence which praise has on liking also appears to depend on a person's need for praise. Deutsch and Solomon (1959) proposed that people with high self-esteem value praise, but those with low self-esteem may doubt the sincerity of praise. Deutsch and Solomon assumed that dislike would occur if the motivation for praise was questionable. In a group participation task, half of their women subjects were told that they had performed well ("high esteem" condition); the other half were told that they had performed poorly ("low esteem" condition). After completion of the task, all the subjects' teammates, who were in fact confederates, wrote the subjects a note either praising or criticizing their performance. When the subjects were then asked to indicate their feelings toward their teammates, Deutsch and Solomon found that in the "high esteem" condition confederates who gave favorable evaluations were liked more than those who gave unfavorable comments. In the "low esteem" condition confederates who praised and those who criticized were liked equally. According to the authors, the negative impact of perceived insincerity canceled the positive effect of praise and eliminated the typical result of praise (liking).

Dutton (1972) suggested that perhaps low esteem was not created in all the subjects in Deutsch and Solomon's study, but rather that uncertainty was induced in some. According to Dutton, a person uncertain of his or her ability values being praised, but a person convinced of his or her low ability devalues praise. To test this idea, Dutton had subjects participate in a game of logic. A comparison with the performance of others was used to institute either certainty or uncertainty regarding one's own ability. Some subjects were led to conclude that they were better performers than their teammates;

others were led to conclude that they were worse than their teammates. A third group of subjects did not receive sufficient information to allow them to evaluate their ability. Dutton found that persons who are certain of their abilities like people whose judgments are in agreement with their own: people with high self-esteem like others who praise them; people with low self-esteem like people who criticize them. In addition, Dutton observed that if we are not certain of our ability, we value praise and like people who praise us.

The ingratiation process. Earlier in the chapter we described Skinner's explanation of affiliative motivation. According to Skinner, our behavior is often directed toward winning the approval of others in order to obtain reinforcement. As an example of this view, consider the student who wants to obtain a professor's favorable recommendation to law school. One method which the student might use is to study hard and do well in the course. However, the student might not feel that good performance is sufficient, especially in a large class. Under these circumstances the student might offer assistance to the professor or make favorable comments concerning the quality of this professor's course. Although you probably know a more colloquial term for this process, social psychologists (see Jones, 1964) use the word *ingratiation* to describe favors or flattery as a method of obtaining reward. Evidence collected by Jones and other social psychologists indicates that (1) people will employ ingratiation when they are motivated to obtain reward from others, (2) ingratiation will typically gain the target person's acceptance if that person is not aware of being manipulated, and (3) ingratiation will cause the target person to provide the desired reinforcement. Apparently, ingratiation represents an effective and frequently employed instrumental behavior motivated to gain reward. Ingratiation also represents a strategy to influence the behavior of others. We will describe the ingratiation process in detail in Chapter 12.

Heterosexual Love

Young children develop friendships with their same-sex peers; adolescents and adults, however, exhibit romantic love or passion for members of the opposite sex. Our heterosexual attraction is physically, behaviorally, and culturally different from our childhood friendships. Heterosexual motivation begins at puberty, reaches maximum intensity during late adolescence, and continues to operate throughout our lifetime. Harlow (1971) proposed three separate subsystems which act to motivate heterosexual attraction: (1) *a sequence of postures which are elicited by external stimuli serve to initiate and maintain sexual intercourse;* (2) *a group of sex hormones either directly or indirectly facilitate sexual behavior;* (3) *emotional responsivity, developed during infancy and childhood, serves as the foundation of heterosexual attraction.* We will now examine each of these subsystems. Special emphasis, based on Harlow's contribution to our understanding of heterosexual love, will be placed on the process responsible for the development of each subsystem. (See Chapter 6 on sexual motivation for a detailed analysis of the physical and hormonal determinants of heterosexual love.)

Motivational systems. The *mechanical subsystem* consists of two classes of instinctual responses: discrete and complex reflexes. The three *discrete reflexes*—penile erection, clitoral erection, and male pelvic thrusting—are present in infancy. The three *complex reflexes*—ventrodorsal positioning, female support of the male, and male-female genital propinquity—develop during childhood. Harlow (1971), observing all of these reflexes in monkeys, speculated that childhood social play is responsible for the maturation of the more complex reflex systems. These mechanical subsystem responses serve as the foundation for the hormonal and romantic subsystems which bloom following puberty.

The *hormonal subsystem* affects the intensity and patterning of sexual motivation (Harlow, 1971). Although it is clear that in adult humans sexual motivation can exist in the absence of hormonal influence, the presence of sex hormones is likely to have one direct and one indirect effect on heterosexual attachment. The onset of sexual hormone production directly enhances the affective sexual response to erotic stimuli. The physical characteristics induced by sexual hormones (e.g., development of the breasts in females and growth of body hair in males) indirectly influence sexual motivation by increasing sexual attractiveness.

All primate species develop selective male-female pair bonding during mating. While primate bonds typically last for only several hours or days, some primates (e.g., gibbons) develop permanent monogamy. Early experience plays a critical role in development of the *romantic subsystem.* Attachment and the ability to trust developed during infancy and childhood are vital prerequisites to the cementing of adult heterosexual bonds. Participants are placed in a vulnerable situation during sexual intercourse, and the sense of security with others which was established early in childhood enables them to overcome their fears. The contact comfort experienced during infancy and childhood acts to motivate sexual behavior in adults and to reinforce heterosexual attachments.

Failure to develop age-mate affectional attachments prevents the mechanical and romantic subsystems from developing but has little impact on hormonal development (Harlow, Harlow, & Suomi, 1971). Even when cultural punishment and social isolation prevent the development of mechanical sexual efficacy or heterosexual romance, our hormones will continue to motivate sexual behavior. The tragedy of socially deprived people is that they still desire sex despite having neither the physical nor the social skills to develop meaningful sexual relationships. Harlow's work explains the etiology of such dysfunction. Recent clinical developments (Masters & Johnson, 1971) help rectify it. The effectiveness of Masters and Johnson's techniques for treating sexual inadequacy (see Chapter 6) undoubtedly lies in the development of mechanical and romantic skills to complement the existing motivational base.

Social psychologists have investigated the importance of physical attraction in heterosexual relationships. Their observations indicate that while physical processes determine the intensity of *romantic love,* psychological factors—intimacy and shared experiences—control the duration of a relationship. In a lasting relationship, other meaningful events must take the place of passion, which often diminishes with time. Let's examine the factors which motivate us to develop and maintain heterosexual relationships.

Romantic love. Dating couples often unrealistically describe their relationship and their partner as being perfect; flaws are overlooked and positive attributes are exaggerated. Each thinks that he or she cannot live without the other, and they derive great satisfaction by being together. Walster and Walster (1978) define this intense love of the members of a couple for each other as *passionate love,* or "a state of intense absorption in another."

Our intense passion for our partner often diminishes as time passes. The high divorce rate may indicate that without passionate love, and with nothing to fill the void, many partners are likely to separate. Other couples remain together after their romance wanes; their romantic love is replaced by a different kind of love, an intense liking based on affection and concern. Berscheid and Walster (1978) call the liking of established partners *companionate love,* or "the affection we feel for those with whom our lives are deeply intertwined." We will first discuss romantic love, followed by a description of companionate love.

   An attributional approach.   Imagine yourself dating an attractive person of the opposite sex for the first time. Although you know only a little about your date, you are anxiously anticipating the evening. Perhaps you are apprehensive; your palms are sweating, your heart is pounding, and when you finally meet your date, his or her sexual attractiveness produces an additional emotional arousal. How do you feel about your date? You might attribute your emotions to "being in love." Berscheid and Walster (1978) developed a theory of romantic love based on Schachter and Singer's two-component theory of emotion (see Chapter 2). They suggest that the apprehension of dating, as well as the sexual attractiveness of the person being dated, causes arousal. Unfortunately, you are unable to identify the source of your arousal. In our society, when a person is aroused by and feels attracted to another, the person identifies his or her emotion as passionate love. The nature of the emotion is misinterpreted; it is not recognized as anxiety or sexual arousal.
   A number of studies support Berscheid and Walster's two-component theory of passionate love. One well-known study was conducted by Stephan, Berscheid, and Walster (1971). These experimenters kept their male subjects in a waiting room before the beginning of a dating experiment. Before meeting a potential date, the subjects read either sexually arousing material or articles about sea gulls. Then the experimenter described the potential date; and after this description was given, the subjects were asked to indicate their impressions of her. Those subjects who had been sexually aroused by the reading material felt that their dates were more beautiful and sexually responsive than the other subjects did. In a similar study, Griffitt, May, and Veitch (1974) asked men and women subjects to rate either sexually explicit material or geometric figures. The subjects then were assigned an opposite-sex partner with whom they were to complete a questionnaire. Subjects who viewed the erotic stimuli and were aroused were more attracted to the opposite-sex partner than the other subjects were.

   The influence of aversive events.   Unpleasant experiences, as well as sexual arousal, have been reported to increase passion. Hoon, Wincze, and Hoon (1977) found that sexually oriented stimuli produced stronger arousal in subjects after an anxiety-inducing film than after a neutral film. In addition, Driscoll, Davis, and Lipitz (1972) reported that parental interference increased the intensity of a couple's romantic love. Apparently, parents' attempts to discourage their children's dating preferences merely act to intensify the children's romantic feelings.
   In an interesting test of the importance of fear in romantic love, Dutton and Aron (1974) asked their male subjects to cross a long, narrow, flexible suspension bridge which spans a gorge and river in a park in Vancouver, British Columbia. This experience was quite frightening; the wooden planks swayed while the subjects crossed above rocks and rapids 200 feet below. After crossing the bridge, the men met a very attractive woman experimenter who questioned them about their experiences. The woman approached the men either immediately after their participation when they were still aroused by their fearful experience or 10 minutes later when their arousal had diminished. After the interview, the woman gave the subjects her telephone number and indicated that they could call her to learn more about the study. Dutton and Aron predicted that if the men were attracted to the woman, they would call her. They found that 65 percent of the subjects in the arousal condition telephoned woman, but only 30 percent in the nonaroused condition did.
   Dutton and Aron also conducted a laboratory investigation of the influence of fear

on attraction. Male subjects in this study were told that they would receive electric shocks. Some subjects, who were told that the shocks would be painful, were highly aroused; other subjects, who were informed that their shocks were to be mild, were not very aroused. Each subject met an attractive female confederate who he believed would be his partner in the study. Before the study began, the subjects indicated their attraction to their partner. Dutton and Aron discovered that highly aroused subjects were more attracted to their partner than unaroused subjects. Dutton and Aron's experiments point that our physical attraction to the opposite sex may at least partially reflect a misattribution of fear or anxiety which is present when we meet a member of the opposite sex.

Companionate love. Once romantic passion begins to decline, other processes determine whether partners will continue their attachment or will sever their relationship. Altman and Taylor's *social penetration theory* (1973) proposed that the growth of *intimate relationships* is based on shared rewards and punishments. Intimate relationships are established not only between couples whose lives are intertwined but also between friends, siblings, and parent-child dyads. Shared experiences are vital components for the development of intimacy, and their absence prevents the establishment of long-term attachments. A willingness to share our feelings with others, a process called *self-disclosure,* plays an important role in the development of intimate relationships. Taylor (1968) observed the level of self-disclosure in college roommates who developed close attachments to each other. As the roommates increased their number of shared activities, their level of self-disclosure increased, although they increased the amount of trivial information they shared at a faster rate than they did intimate information.

Situation-appropriate self-disclosure frequently causes the other person to reciprocate at a matching level of intimacy. Chaikin and Derlega (1974a) found that reciprocated self-disclosure promotes liking and trust, which can result in the development of attachments. In their study, subjects were shown videotapes of how two females, who were meeting for a first time in a school cafeteria, responded to each other. Three conditions existed in the study. In condition 1, subjects were shown a tape in which both women revealed highly intimate information (e.g., sexual relationships and family behavioral problems); in condition 2, subjects saw a tape in which intimacy of shared information was low (e.g., problems in course work); in condition 3, the subjects saw a tape which displayed discrepant intimacy—one woman revealed intimate information, whereas the other shared little. The students were then asked to relate their feeling about each woman. Chaikin and Derlega found that liking was increased if each woman's self-disclosure was reciprocated. When one woman's shared information was not identical in depth to that of the other, the students thought that the woman who disclosed less was cold and the one who disclosed more was maladjusted. In addition, if too much information is revealed too soon, the development of social attachments is retarded or even prevented (Chaikin & Derlega, 1974b). Apparently, shared thoughts can lead to close interpersonal relationships, but only when both partners feel comfortable with the level of mutual self-disclosure.

The nature of sexual attraction. Several weeks ago, my 13-year-old daughter came home from school very excited. She had learned from one of her girl friends that a boy whom she likes also likes her. Although my daughter's relationship with this boy remains casual, many girls and boys in her junior high school are "going steady." The intense patterns of social relationships found in my daughter's school are not unusual; dating and the subsequent attachment process are typical of American adolescents. Most adults want to establish permanent heterosexual relationships, and marriage is a goal of the social behavior of many people in our culture. Failure to maintain intimate relationships permanently, exemplified by our high divorce rate, does not detract from our strong motivation to form them. A divorced person frequently remarries, indicating a need to reestablish a permanent attachment.

Why are we so motivated to develop monogamous relationships? One explanation of human sexual relationships is that we have learned that dating and marriage are expected of us. Thus, our behavior represents an attempt to obtain these social goals. However, contemporary evidence from primatology suggests that the process of sexual attachment reflects an innate social behavior pattern.

According to the ethological view described in Chapter 2, the goal of any species is to ensure its survival. In order to increase the likelihood of survival, paternal protection of the young is essential. Yet, how can a species make sure that the father will protect his offspring? According to Desmond Morris (1967), an inherited motivation to form male-female bonds produces the conditions essential for paternal protection. But the bond cannot be brief; it must be fostered until offspring are mature enough to protect themselves. Morris suggested that continuous sexual responsivity in human females maintains pair bonding and ensures paternal care. The availability of sexual satisfaction at any time during the female reproductive cycle, as well as the male's inability to be certain of paternity (owing to the lack of any obvious sign of ovulation), promotes the establishment of a relatively permanent social bond between the male and female of a species (see Hrdy, 1979).

Several types of evidence support the hypothesis that human heterosexual relationships reflect an innate social behavior pattern. *First, continuous receptivity has been noticed in primates as well as humans.* In 1965, Conaway and Koford observed that female rhesus macaques copulate throughout their entire reproductive cycle. A similar pattern has been seen in baboons (Smith & Credland, 1977) and in human females of both western and primitive hunting cultures (Adams, Gold, & Burt, 1978; Worthman, 1978). *Second, sexual responsivity increases in the first and second trimesters of pregnancy in humans* (Masters & Johnson, 1966) *and primates* (Hrdy, 1979). The most likely reason for this change is that sexual responsivity functions to increase the intensity of attachment and to conceal paternity. The behavior of marmosets, a group of New World monkeys, provides strong evidence for Morris's view (See Hearne, 1978). Hearne observed that marmosets are monogamous, provide extensive paternal care, copulate throughout the cycle, show no signs of ovulation, and do not menstruate. You should not conclude that any particular social pattern or the choice of partner is innate in humans; the variety of human heterosexual behavior patterns argues against such specific instinctive behaviors or at least against their resistance to social modification (see Chapter 6). However, there is certainly strong evidence of an innate motivational system which is not altered by our experience. The next section describes the evidence which supports the idea that the male is protective of his offspring.

Paternal Love

Unlike the female, who is typically responsive to her young, the male will be indifferent toward infants and children unless appropriate conditions foster a social attachment between a male and young members of his species. Mitchell's observations (1969) of primates established that proximity is one factor leading to the development of male-infant attachment. If the infant is near, the male will be attracted to it and will develop an attachment to it. Adams (1960) suggested that the cultural conditions which create strong mother-infant and male-female dyads (or pairs) act to initiate paternal behavior. This social dyad system undoubtedly causes the male to be in close contact with the infant. Harlow, Harlow, and Suomi (1971) observed the development of paternal bonds in their arrangement of nuclear primate families. In this social system, four male-female pairs of monkeys lived with their offspring in close but separate living quarters. Males and females had physical access to their young and each had close visual and auditory experiences of the other children. The psychologists observed that the adult males did not allow another member of their family or neighboring families to abuse or abandon any of the young. The adult males not only guarded the young against predators (who in this case were the experimenters) but also showed affection for the young. Males were more likely than females to engage in social play with their children. The common expression that every male is a "child at heart" may have some truth. Also, Harlow, Harlow, and Suomi (1971) found that fathers endured torment (e.g., pinching, biting) from their young which they would not tolerate from other adults. Although preadolescent males would not exert effort to play with young children, they did protect the young if danger arose.

A similar paternal attachment called *engrossment* has been noted in human father-child relationships. Greenberg and Morris (1974) interviewed new fathers and found most of them interested in their babies before the babies were 3 days old. Also, Pederson and Robson (1969) found that three-fourths of the 9-month-old babies they observed became excited when seeing their fathers. In addition, Kotelchuck (1973) noticed a protest response from many infants when their fathers left them. Apparently, the potential for paternal motivation exists in all primate and human males; it only needs to be established by the appropriate environmental conditions.

AN ABSENCE OF LOVE
We have just examined the factors which contribute to the formation of social relationships and described the importance of love in our psychological development. However, what are the effects of an absence of love? In the next section, you will discover that failure to receive love can be extremely detrimental. Two types of situations will be examined: (1) a temporary loss of love (separation) and (2) a permanent absence of loving relationships (deprivation). We will also study methods of altering the psychological consequences of separation or deprivation.

Maternal Separation

An emotional disturbance.   The young infant's or child's need for security is intense. Separation from the mother can precipitate extreme emotional distress in the young primate or human. The child, during periods of stress and uncertainty, expends considerable effort to reach his or her mother and is greatly relieved when they are reunited. René Spitz (1946) observed that when some human infants were separated for several days from their mothers, these infants' initial protest (for example, crying, screaming) was soon replaced with a withdrawal response. When reunited with the mother, some of these children directed hostility rather than affection toward her. As time passed, this hostility slowly diminished. Spitz termed emotional response to maternal separation "anaclitic depression." Bowlby (1969) found this response in children from 6 months to 6 years of age.

A similar emotional response caused by maternal separation has been reported in primates. When Seay and Harlow (1965) separated infant monkeys from their mothers for several weeks, they observed severe emotional reactions in the infants. At first, the infant monkeys protested their mothers' removal with increased vocalizations and activity. Over the course of the separation period, the infants' overt protest decreased, and they became withdrawn and inactive. These infants exhibited a number of bizarre behavioral patterns: many of them stared into space, a behavior characteristic of catatonic schizophrenia; others rocked back and forth, a behavior characteristic of childhood autism. These infants' behavioral abnormalities vanished when they were reunited with their mothers. Immediately after the reunion they spent more time with their mothers than before the separation; however, the infants quickly resumed play with peers.

A lack of concern. The extreme despair described above is not always observed in either humans (Robertson & Robertson, 1971) or primates (Young, Lewis, & McKinney, 1975). Young, Lewis, and McKinney (1975) raised monkeys under two different conditions: some were raised only with their mothers; others were raised not only with their mothers but also with other mother-infant pairs. The conditions of mother-infant separation also differed in their study: some infants, when separated from their mothers, were housed next to them, while others were boarded away from their mothers in separate rooms. The authors observed great variation in the emotional response to separation: some primates showed extreme protest and despair; others displayed more protest than despair or vice versa; some primates exhibited a less severe emotional response; and a few showed almost no response to separation.

Suomi and Harlow (1977) identified several factors which influence the intensity and duration of the emotional response to separation. First, the primate's age is an extremely important factor. Suomi, Collins, and Harlow (1973) found that the most severe response occurred at 3 months of age, the age when the young primate's fear begins to mature. The level of attachment to the mother is the second factor: the more attached the primate is to the mother, the more distressed it becomes when separated (Hinde & Spencer-Booth, 1970). The third factor which Suomi and Harlow found was that the presence of peers helped to diminish the severity of the emotional response to separation. Kaufman and Rosenblum (1969) noted that bonnet monkeys, when separated from their mothers, increased their attachment to other monkeys. A similar observation was made by Ainsworth (1976) in human children. The length of the separation is a fourth important factor: the longer the separation, the more severe the emotional response in primates (Suomi, 1976) and humans (Spitz, 1946). Finally, Seay, Hansen, and Harlow (1962) observed that the greatest distress occurred in primates who could see their mothers but could not reach them.

The circumstances surrounding separation also are important. For example, Ainsworth and Bell (1970) reported that many young children cried if they saw their mothers close the door when she left them. In contrast, many of the youngsters continued to play if their mothers did not close the door upon leaving (Corter, Rheingold, & Eckerman, 1972). Also, Rutter (1971) discovered that parental separation caused by family discord or divorce produced four times more antisocial behavior than separation caused by a vacation or hospitalization. In contrast to the varied influence of separation, maternal deprivation is more likely to have negative impact on development. Let's now examine the effect of maternal deprivation.

Maternal Deprivation

An infant who has never experienced a mother's love may never be able to love anyone. Harlow (1959) deprived infant monkeys of their mothers for 8 months. After the period of deprivation, these monkeys were allowed access to both wire and cloth surrogate mothers. Although they were initially fearful of the surrogate mothers, they soon behaved as normal monkeys do with their real mothers: they spent 8 to 10 hours a day clinging to their cloth mothers. However, unlike normal monkeys, the deprived monkeys did not develop any attachment to the surrogate mothers. While the normal monkeys experienced relief when placed in a novel environment with their mothers, the deprived monkeys remained frightened. This absence of security in the deprived monkey is similar to the behavior of a primate raised with only a wire surrogate mother. Figure 9.9 illustrates the emotional behavior of deprived and nondeprived infant monkeys in a new environment when the mother was either present or absent.

Spitz (1945) observed a devastating influence of maternal deprivation in human children. Children just under 1 year of age who were healthy upon being institutionalized (this institutionalizing is called *hospitalism*) were, after approximately 1 year of hospitalism, compared with home-reared 2-year-old children. Children in one institution, the "nursery," appeared to have developed normally, as did the home-reared children. In contrast, children in a second institution, the "foundling home," had not developed normally. Compared with children from the nursery and home-reared children, the children from the foundling home were shorter, weighed less, and were more susceptible to disease; also, many died during their stay in the home. What caused these dramatic differences? Spitz discovered quite different maternal behavior in the two institutions. In the nursery, the babies were well cared for by their mothers—delinquent girls, many who were retarded or disturbed—or substitute mothers. In contrast, the children in the foundling home received little care, and eight nurses watched 91 youngsters. These results clearly show that maternal deprivation can affect children negatively. Fortunately, Spitz's research has led to a shift from institutionalizing healthy infants to placing them in foster homes where, it is hoped, the ill effects of maternal deprivation will be lessened.

The presence of other infants can have a positive impact on maternally deprived primates (Harlow & Harlow, 1962). Harlow and Harlow raised four infants together (without their mothers) for 1 year. The monkeys were allowed to play for 20 minutes a day with one another in a specially constructed playpen. Initially, these motherless monkeys spent their time tightly clinging to each other. However, several months later they clung less and showed an increased interest in play. After these motherless monkeys had lived for a year with their peers, the psychologists found no behavioral deficits in

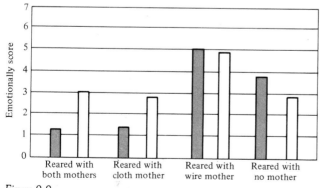

Figure 9.9
Emotional response to a strange environment when mother is present (black) or absent (white). Scores under 2 indicate absence of fear. (From Harlow, H. F. Love in infant monkeys. Scientific American, 1959, 200, 68–74. Copyright © 1959 by Scientific American, Inc. All rights reserved.)

their social development. These observations indicate that maternal support can be provided by peers for maternally deprived primates.

In contrast to the lack of despair in maternally deprived primates with social support, motherless monkeys separated from their peers developed severe emotional disturbances (Suomi, Harlow, & Domek, 1970). From the time these monkeys were 3 months old until they were 9 months old, they were separated 20 times from their peers for periods ranging from 1 to 4 days. The primates showed strong protest at the beginning of each separation; emotional withdrawal soon followed the protest. This pattern of behavior is identical to the behavioral pattern that results from maternal separation. These motherless monkeys became more disturbed with each separation. Their development was completely arrested at the end of the 6-month study: their emotional and social behaviors were identical to those displayed at the beginning of the study when they were 3 months old. Apparently, the youngster needs some form of maternal support to serve as a reliable source of security, or he or she will be unable to mature emotionally.

Social Separation

Our friends, especially during periods of stress, provide us with security and support. A young child or an adult who has lost a close friend experiences extreme emotional distress similar to that in maternal separation. Suomi and Harlow (1975) found that young primates, when isolated from their peers, exhibited protest and despair. A restricted environment during separation and strong preexisting bonds to peers produce an intense emotional response to separation. However, young primates normally are extremely resilient; the introduction of a new peer (friend) reinstates their social responsivity. The young child who moves away from close friends will be apathetic for a while but quickly cultivates new friends and exhibits no symptoms of the earlier disturbance.

The initial attempts to produce extreme despair in adult primates by separating them from their peers were unsuccessful (Suomi & Harlow, 1977). McKinney, Suomi, and Harlow (1972) for instance, raised infant monkeys with their mothers and peers for 2 years. For the next year the primates were housed alone and then, at 3 years of age, they were divided into two groups. All members of each group were allowed to mix freely with peers. After strong attachments were formed, the primates in one group were separated from their peers. Although these separated adult monkeys exhibited strong protest, little evidence of extreme despair was found. Erwin, Mobalbi, and Mitchell (1971) noted similar behavior in juvenile rhesus monkeys.

Recent studies, however, indicate that distress induced by separation can be produced in adult primates when a sense of isolation is created. These results support the idea that a loss of social reinforcement is one cause of human depression (see Chapter 8). Suomi (1973) reared monkeys with peers and later separated them from their peers by placing them alone in either an isolation chamber or their normal home cage. The emotional response of these adults was more intense for monkeys placed in the isolation chamber than for those in normal cages. The animals in the isolation chamber exhibited stronger protest, greater despair, and more difficulty in resuming normal social behaviors when they were rejoined with their peers. Suomi, Eisele, Grady, and Harlow (1975) raised monkeys in nuclear family units for 5 years. Then they separated their monkeys and placed them either with friends, with strangers, or in individual cages (with only visual interaction with strangers). The monkeys housed with either friends or strangers showed only mild protest, while animals housed alone exhibited strong despair. Their despair was similar to that of young animals separated either from their mothers or from peers. Furthermore, they responded passively even when reunited with their families. A sense of isolation caused by loss of social support apparently can induce symptoms of depression in adult primates.

A study by Young, Suomi, Harlow, and McKinney (1973) indicates that if children experience long-term separation from their group, this separation sensitizes them to loss of peers as adults. They raised monkeys initially with both their mothers and peers. Then half of those monkeys were isolated from others for 30 days sometime between the ages of 6 months and 1 year. The other monkeys were not separated from their group during childhood; this was the control condition. Next, all the monkeys were housed with their peers until they attained 2 years of age. Finally, each of the monkeys was separated from peers for 23 hours a day for a period of 23 days. The authors observed a more intense response to separation in monkeys who had the early history of separation than in the other monkeys. Early separation appears to predispose an animal to experience despair in later experiences of separation.

Social Deprivation

A young child who is deprived of maternal support can obtain security from peers, but a child who is deprived of social contact has no alternative source of security and will develop abnormal behavioral tendencies. Harlow and Harlow (1962) described the effects which complete social isolation has on behavioral development. They placed animals in an isolation chamber at birth for either 3, 6, or 12 months and then allowed them to interact with appropriate age-mates. Those monkeys which were isolated for the first 3 months of life and then exposed to a normal environment initially exhibited extreme emotional disturbances. However, those deprived animals rapidly recovered and quickly interacted with their peers. As you recall from our earlier discussion, primate infants develop fears of the outside world and attachment to the mother at 2 to 3 months of age. Failure to obtain maternal emotional support during the first 3 months of life does not appear to be a crucial factor necessary for the development of later social behavior.

However, the behavioral effects of 6 months of social deprivation are quite severe. Harlow and Harlow found that monkeys socially isolated from birth to 6 months exhibited autistic behavior (e.g., self-clasping, self-mouthing, and rocking) and did not effectively interact with their normal peers. These socially deprived primates behaved aggressively with primates of their own ages and attacked infant primates. They played with other isolates but never were able to play with normal primates. The effects of 1 year of social deprivation were even more extreme. Monkeys socially deprived for the first year of life showed little exploration of their environment and made no attempt at even simple play with their peers. For these primates, the effect of social deprivation was complete; their withdrawal into themselves had become permanent. Although these socially deprived monkeys cannot recover by themselves, the work of Harry Harlow has led to the development of a therapeutic approach which enables them to recover their social potential (Harlow, Harlow, & Soumi, 1971).

Rehabilitation

I recall from my adolescence a young boy of approximately 10 years of age whose social behavior resembled that of Harlow's socially deprived monkeys. This boy's age-mates, who often verbally abused him, resisted his attempts to play; otherwise, they typically avoided him. The extremely shy young boy isolated himself from his peers after his early social failures. When he did socialize, he played with 3- to 5-year-old children. These younger children readily accepted him, and they appeared to play well together.

Unfortunately, the younger children's parents could not accept a 10-year-old boy playing with their children and soon refused to permit it. I do not recall ever seeing him outside after he was no longer allowed to play with the younger children.

A recent observation by Harlow, Harlow, and Suomi (1971) showed that a socially deprived primate can be rehabilitated by interacting with younger primates. This observation indicates that the older child I knew would have benefited from playing with the younger children if only the young children's parents had allowed the friendship to continue. Experience with young primates enabled an older socially deprived monkey to overcome its fear and social deficiency. Harlow, Harlow, and Suomi (1971) chose three 4-month-old normal infant monkeys to serve as "therapists" for a 6-month-old socially deprived monkey. The young therapists, not yet aggressive, still possessed strong needs for contact and were just beginning to develop social play. The isolate and the therapist monkeys were placed in a special cage with removable panels which could either separate the monkeys or allow them to mingle. The monkeys were allowed a 2-hour period together in their cage and a 2-hour period together in the playroom; they spent the remainder of the day alone. As the experiment progressed, time spent together in the home cage decreased, while time spent in the playroom increased. On first encountering the playroom, the isolate retreated to a corner and displayed "rocking" behavior. However, the "therapists" persisted in clinging to the isolate. Soon the isolate was playing with the younger monkeys. At the end of the 6-month treatment period the authors noticed that the isolate's emotional and social behavior was normal. Remarkably, the use of younger "therapists" provided the isolate with a medium for effective social development. Without the problem of rejection or attack by peers, the isolate was able to develop social attachments. This rehabilitative technique perhaps could provide the conditions necessary to overcome the consequences of social deprivation if parents of potential "therapists" are understanding of the situation.

SUMMARY

We enter this world as helpless babies; our mothers' support and protection enable us to survive. During infancy, our environment arouses curiosity within us, but our lack of maturity makes us vulnerable. When our mother is there to lend security, we are motivated to explore our environment. As we mature, we begin to develop new relationships, and we become less dependent on our mother. When we play with other children, our mutual social interaction acts to establish childhood friendships. These new social relationships provide us with an opportunity to learn new social behavior, as well as supplying us with a new source of security. As we stray farther and farther from our mothers, our friends become our source of security and comfort. The attachments formed in infancy and childhood cause us to develop strong affiliative motivation. Our friends are especially important during times of stress. Stress increases our motivation to be with other people and to experience security in their presence. The ability of others to provide security helps us to establish adult social attachments.

Our initial social response to people, or our liking for them, depends upon the environmental circumstances surrounding our social interaction. We like people whom we meet during pleasurable circumstances; people we meet under adverse circumstances are disliked. In addition, we are attracted to people who can provide us with both the social and nonsocial reinforcements which we desire.

In heterosexual relationships, we may misinterpret our initial emotional response to an attractive member of the opposite sex and believe that we are "in love." However, passionate love typically diminishes as time passes. Unless we substitute affection for romance, our relationship most likely terminates when our passion diminishes. We can develop meaningful adult social relationships: sometimes we form these attachments with a spouse, but they can also exist between close friends or relatives. Liking may become loving when we share intimate social experiences without the threat of rejection or disapproval.

Early maternal and social deprivation hampers the deprived individual's ability to develop meaningful social attachments. Deprived people are motivated by their social needs, but are frightened of rejection. Moreover, their fears act to intensify their need for affiliation. Unfortunately, their deprivation prevents such people from developing effective social behaviors, and this deficiency in turn causes them to experience frequent rejection. The intense depression occurring in deprived people results from their failure to establish meaningful social relationships.

The loss of social attachments can also lead to feelings of isolation and loneliness. The positive, rewarding aspects of social relationships often diminish with time. As the reduction in the positive aspects of social relationships occurs, the opponent withdrawal process of separation intensifies. The development of social tolerance causes a person to make excessive demands for affection, to be extremely depressed when separated from his or her source of support, and even to be disturbed by the threat of separation. Considering the demands of such a dependent person, only the most supportive person is able to continue a relationship. Obviously, every attempt must be made to develop mutually rewarding and continually growing relationships that provide satisfaction and security.

$\mathcal{A}$CHIEVEMENT MOTIVATION

CHAPTER 10

The ladder of success

Mary usually plans her week's work on Mondays, during the 30-minute train ride to the office. However, last Friday she learned of her promotion to head the company's sales force, and only this one thought preoccupies her mind today. Although some of Mary's coworkers were offended—at age 33, she is younger than many of them and has not been with the company as long—Mary is not at all surprised by her promotion; in fact, she expects to be the company president someday.

Mary joined the company 12 years ago after graduating from college with honors. She had had a dozen offers to choose from. Mary's father, a top official with a major competitor of the firm which Mary chose, had wanted his daughter to work for his company. But Mary desired independence and did not want to be shown any favoritism.

One year after having finished her company's management training program, Mary was the top salesperson of the western regional sales division. From the beginning,

hard work has characterized Mary's days; she is usually the first person to arrive for work and the last to leave, and she often comes to the office on Saturday or Sunday. Challenges have always excited Mary, and as a salesperson she often accepted clients whom most of her associates rejected. Although she did not always persuade people to buy, most of the time her thoroughness, determination, and vibrant personality convinced her clients to consider the company she represented.

Five years ago Mary became the head of the company's western regional sales division, the first woman made a divisional sales director. Determined to be as successful in her new position as she was as a salesperson, she has continued to work long hours with the salespeople in her division. Mary's diligence, intelligence, and enthusiasm have paid off. Sales in her division were the company's second lowest when she began as director; but for the last 2 years they were the company's highest. Considering Mary's past successes, her expectations of future success seem reasonable.

We often refer to a person's level of *achievement motivation;* we assume that some people, like Mary, have an intense motivation to succeed, while others seem to be uninterested in achieving. Also, we often assume that many people fail because of their lack of achievement motivation and that if their need to achieve could be enhanced, they would not ,continue to fail. For nearly half a century, psychologists have been interested in the concept of achievement motivation. As a result of their efforts, we now understand better the factors influencing our level of achievement motivation and what can be done to alter our need to achieve. This chapter describes what these psychologists have learned about the achievement motivation process, beginning with the work of Henry Murray (1938). Murray considered achievement motivation an important motive and listed it as one of 27 acquired human motives. In his personality theory, Murray defined the concept of the need to achieve. He also developed a personality test later used by David McClelland and his associates in the 1950s to measure achievement motivation. The contribution of McClelland and other psychologists interested in achievement motivation will follow the description of Murray's view of achievement.

THE NEED TO ACHIEVE

Murray's theory of personality incorporates ideas from Freud's and McDougall's theories (see Chapter 1). Murray's concept of *need* resembles Freud's concept of *instinct.* According to Murray, a need is a physiochemical force which can be aroused either from within by internal visceral processes or from situational effects called *press* which are related to the need. An unsatisfying situation arouses the need, and the force motivates behavior aimed toward an environment which can satisfy the need. Unlike Freud but like McDougall, Murray assumed that each need produces a characteristic emotion, and this emotion is the force which motivates behavior. However, Murray's theory differs from Freud's and McDougall's views by assuming that needs can be both instinctive and learned. Murray's personality theory includes many basic needs—intake of essential substances such as food and water, output of noxious substances such as urine and feces, and avoidance of unpleasant events such as heat, cold, and pain. Some of the 27 secondary acquired needs are dominance, affiliation, nurturance, autonomy, sex, abasement, deference, aggression, exhibition, and achievement.

How did Murray define achievement motivation? According to Murray, the need to achieve, n Ach, is a desire to accomplish something difficult, such as the manipulation or organization of physical objects, ideas, or other people. A person striving to achieve usually works independently of others and as rapidly as possible. The need to achieve causes a person to overcome great obstacles not only to attain a high standard of excellence but also to surpass the success of others. The high achiever in Murray's view is an ambitious and competitive person determined to be successful. Mary's competitive behavior, described in the opening vignette, definitely reflects the influence of a high need to achieve.

Although Murray did not directly investigate the process of achievement motivation, he contributed in two important ways to research in the area. First, he developed the *Thematic Apperception Test* (*TAT*) to measure the internal needs of a person. The TAT consists of a series of ambiguous pictures like those illustrating stories in magazines; the person taking the test constructs a story about each picture, describing *(1) what is happening in the picture, (2) what led to the scene depicted, (3) what the people in the picture are thinking or feeling, and (4) what will happen at the end of the story.* Presumably, through this story, the person reveals important aspects of his or her personality. Thus, clinical psychologists often use the TAT as a diagnostic tool to indicate the presence of a particular behavior pathology. As you will discover shortly, McClelland and his associates (1953) employed the thematic apperception method to measure a person's need to achieve.

Second, these stories reflecting a person's needs can be affected by specific environmental circumstances. Measuring the level of fear reflected in children's stories before and after a "spooky game of murder with the lights out," Murray (1933) provided an initial test of his assertion that an environmental event can influence a person's level of need. Murray discovered that the stories reflected more fear after the game than before it, assuming that the game induced fear and that the TAT detected the increased level of fear. Sanford (1936, 1937) and McClelland and Atkinson (1948) showed that people's level of hunger could also be revealed in their stories. They found that as a person's hunger increased, the frequency of food-related themes in the story also increased. These observations indicate that a change in someone's needs which is induced by an altered environmental event will be revealed in the person's responses to the TAT. In the next section, you will learn that environmental events can affect our level of achievement motivation and that changes in our need to achieve can also be reflected in our response to ambiguous pictures.

Murray felt that the need to achieve is an important human motive. David McClelland and his associates demonstrated the influence that achievement motivation has on a person's behavior and the processes which influence a person's need to achieve. Let's next examine McClelland's contribution to our understanding of achievement motivation.

THE ACHIEVING PERSON

Measuring the Need to Achieve

David McClelland and his associates (see McClelland, 1958, 1961; McClelland, Atkinson, Clark, & Lowell, 1953; McClelland & Winter, 1969) used the thematic apperception technique to investigate achievement motivation. They presented subjects —typically in group settings—with four to six pictures similar to the one shown in Figure 10.1 and then asked them to answer the following four questions in the form of a story: *(1) What is happening? (2) What has led up to this situation? (3) What is being thought? (4) What will happen?* Subjects had 4 minutes to write a story answering these four questions. Each person received an "achievement motivation level" score for each story, and the sum of the scores for all the stories written by a subject indicated the level of that subject's need to achieve.

How is a person's achievement motive level rated from the stories? Scorers are trained to determine whether or not a person's story contains achievement-related imagery. Eleven areas of achievement—including unique accomplishments, long-term concerns, instrumental activities, and expectations of success or failure—are scored in each story. A story containing imagery related to a particular area of achievement receives a + 1 score, whereas it receives a 0 score if no imagery relates to that particular area (for example, goal expectations). A story having imagery about each area receives a +11 score, indicating a high level of achievement motivation. The score is directly related to the achievement imagery; that is, the lower a score, the less achievement imagery in the story.

Is the TAT a good technique for measuring achievement motivation? Before drawing a conclusion about its usefulness, several questions must be answered. First, is the test *reliable*; is it consistent? This question has to do with both internal consistency and test-retest reliability. Some researchers using the TAT (see Entwisle, 1972) have found its

Figure 10.1
*Example of a picture which is used in assessing achievement motivation level. [From McClelland, D. C.,
Atkinson, J. W., Clark, R. W., & Lowell, E. L. The achievement motive (2nd ed.). New York:
Irvington, 1976.]*

internal consistency very low; but removing those story cards which probe other motives
(for example, affiliative or power needs) produces high consistency (see McClelland,
Atkinson, Clark, & Lowell, 1953). A test must also be reliable—that is, produce
essentially the same results each time a person takes it. For the TAT, test-retest reliability
is quite low; this is not surprising, since environmental circumstances strongly influence
the level of achievement motivation. However, people classified as having either a high
or a low need to achieve typically will be placed in the same category each time they take
the TAT test (see McClelland, Atkinson, Clark, & Lowell, 1953). McClelland,
Atkinson, Clark, and Lowell conclude that the reliability of the TAT is sufficient to
investigate the process influencing achievement motivation although not to pinpoint a
person's exact level of achievement motivation. As you will soon see, the way people
behave in various settings is a better measure than the TAT of their need to achieve.

Second, is the TAT *valid?* That is, how well does the test measure what it intends to
measure? Two types of validity are relevant to the TAT—concurrent and predictive.
Concurrent validity refers to whether or not the test score relates to some other current
behavior; the TAT will have concurrent validity if people's scores relate to their
achievement behavior in other settings. *Predictive validity* is the relationship between the
test score and future behavior. If the TAT has predictive validity, a person's score will
relate to future achievement. The next sections will show that the TAT is a valid measure
of the need to achieve.

Arousal of the Need to Achieve

Recall our earlier description of Murray's personality theory. Murray assumed that all
needs, including the need to achieve, could be aroused by environmental circumstances

related to the specific need. In contrast, an environment unrelated to a given need will lower the level of that need.

To test the validity of Murray's view, McClelland, Atkinson, Clark, and Lowell (1953) exposed their subjects—male college students—to one of six conditions which differed in their relation to achievement motivation.

(1) The "relaxed" condition was structured to minimize arousal of the subjects' need to achieve. In this condition the experimenter dressed informally, introduced himself as a graduate student, and asked the subjects to work on a 30-minute series of tasks in the developmental stage. The experimenter also indicated that he was interested not in the performance of any particular subject but only in the characteristics of the task. McClelland and his associates predicted that in the "relaxed" condition the subjects' need to achieve would be suppressed. (2) The subjects in the "achievement-oriented" condition performed tasks identical to those in the "relaxed" condition but were told that these tasks were tests of important abilities. The experimenter dressed formally, indicated that each subject was to put his name on each task, and emphasized the importance of performing well. McClelland and his associates assumed that this situation would arouse the subjects' need to achieve. (3) Subjects in the "success" condition were treated exactly like those in the "achievement-oriented" condition, except that they were told that they had performed well compared with other students who had previously done the tasks. McClelland and his associates felt that the knowledge of success would lower the need to achieve which the achievement-oriented task has aroused. (4) Subjects in the "failure" condition encountered the same tasks, but extremely high norms were set, so that these subjects would feel that they had performed poorly in comparison with other students. McClelland and his associates predicted that failure would produce dissatisfaction, thereby increasing the level of arousal above that which the achievement-oriented situation had produced. (5) In the "success-failure" condition, subjects were initially successful in their tasks but failed near the end. Presumably, this condition would produce the highest arousal, since contrasting success with failure would heighten dissatisfaction. Having completed the tasks, all subjects were given four pictures and asked to write a story about each picture; the subjects' response to this TAT would indicate their level of achievement motivation following task exposure. (6) Subjects in the "neutral" condition were given the same TAT but without having done the tasks beforehand. The achievement motivation level of these subjects would represent a baseline for assessing the impact of specific environmental circumstances.

The results of this study confirmed the experimenters' predictions and thus support Murray's view that environmental events can alter the level of the need to achieve (see Table 10.1). They found that achievement imagery was lower if subjects had just previously been in a situation which minimized achievement (the "relaxed" condition) than if they had not. Exposure to an achievement-oriented environment, as the subjects' imagery revealed, aroused the need to achieve. Failure increased the level of achievement motivation beyond that which had been aroused by participating in a task situation; and success decreased the achievement motivation level. Subjects who had first succeeded and then failed showed the highest achievement imagery. These observations indicate that the intensity of the need to achieve can be influenced by the nature of the external environment. Situations which are ego-involving arouse achievement motivation; environmental circumstances which minimize achievement lower a person's need to achieve.

Many psychologists have demonstrated, through subjects' imaginative responses to the TAT, that achievement-oriented instructions arouse males' need to achieve. Both Martine (1956) and O'Connor (1960) found that male college students showed a

Table 10.1
The Achievement Motive Levels Revealed in
TAT Stories Following Exposure to Various
Experimental Treatments

Condition	N	Mean
Relaxed	39	1.95
Neutral	39	7.33
Achievement-oriented	39	8.77
Success	21	7.92
Failure	39	10.10
Success-failure	39	10.36

From: McClelland, D. C., Atkinson, J. W., Clark, R. W.,
and Lowell, E. L. *The achievement motive* (2nd ed.). New
York: Irvington, 1976.

heightened need to achieve following exposure to achievement-oriented tasks. Male high school students behaved in a similar manner (see Ricciuti, Clark, & Sadacca, 1954).

The influence of achievement-arousing conditions appears to differ in men and women. Veroff, Wilcox, and Atkinson (1953) reported that female high school and college students, unlike male students, did not show an increase in achievement-related imagery after exposure to an achievement-oriented situation, compared with women in a neutral condition. Apparently, achievement-oriented instructions do not arouse women's need to achieve—only men's. McClelland, Atkinson, Clark, and Lowell (1953) discovered that women's need to achieve was actually lower in the achievement-oriented condition than in a relaxed, or "nonachievement," condition.

The consequences of these observations are quite interesting. According to McClelland (1958), a test of motive strength is valid only if it reflects temporary arousal states caused by exposure to environmental circumstances. Since the achievement-oriented situation did not increase the need to achieve in women, McClelland concluded that the measure of achievement motivation in the TAT is invalid for females. As a result of McClelland's statement, achievement-motivation research was limited almost exclusively to males until 10 years later, when Matina Horner suggested why women in achievement-oriented circumstances may respond differently from men. Horner's research and the current views concerning women's achievement motivation will be described later in the chapter.

Individual Differences in Need to Achieve
Each of us can probably recall a high school classmate who showed an intense desire to be successful. This student studied long hours in the library to be sure of earning top grades. In this section we'll look at (1) *the behavioral characteristics typical of people with a high need to achieve,* (2) *the developmental process which causes persons to develop a high achievement motivation,* and (3) *what happens to most highly motivated persons.*

Differences in motive level. McClelland, Atkinson, Clark, and Lowell (1953) found that people revealed different levels of achievement-related imagery in their stories. Some people, *High n Ach* persons, showed a significantly higher need-to-achieve level than others, *Low n Ach* persons. These differences, which were revealed by the subjects' imagery, occurred in both achievement and nonachievement situations. McClelland, Atkinson, Clark, and Lowell presented their subjects with pictures varying in achievement content. Some pictures contained achievement-related cues (for example, two men working together in a wood shop); others had no such cues (for example, the heads of two men). McClelland, Atkinson, Clark, and Lowell noted that High n Ach persons used more achievement imagery than the other subjects in describing both kinds of pictures.

Other investigators (for example, French, 1955; Haber & Alpert, 1958) reported that High n Ach persons revealed a higher need to achieve on the TAT after receiving either a relaxed (nonachievement) treatment or an achievement-oriented treatment. These observations indicate that there are individual differences in achievement motivation independent of environmental circumstances. An achievement-oriented situation increases our need to achieve, but for each of us the level of achievement motivation depends upon both our internal level and the prevailing environmental conditions.

Behavioral differences. Are these individual differences important? Evidence clearly indicates that under some—but not all—conditions, High n Ach persons behave differently from Low n Ach persons. If knowing they are successful is the only reward for doing well in an achievement-oriented situation, High n Ach persons perform at a higher level than Low n Ach people. However, providing other rewards (for example, social approval) for success extinguished any behavioral differences in performance between High n Ach and Low n Ach people; this indicates that an intrinsic need to be successful motivates the High n Ach person, whereas Low n Ach persons are effective only if other motives are aroused. Let's examine several studies which show that when only achievement motivation is involved, High n Ach people perform better than Low n Ach people. Later in the chapter we will examine evidence that the presence of other motives can eliminate the behavioral differences between High and Low n Ach persons in achievement-oriented situations.

The impact of success. Lowell (1952) asked both High and Low n Ach subjects to complete an arithmetic task (addition problems) and a verbal task (unscrambling anagrams). He discovered that High n Ach subjects performed significantly better on both tasks than Low n Ach subjects. For both of these tasks, in which the only reward was an intrinsic knowledge of success, High n Ach people were motivated to do well; Low n Ach people were not. Other researchers (for example, Atkinson, 1953; Atkinson & Raphelson, 1956; French, 1955; Wendt, 1955) also observed that High n Ach persons performed better in achievement situations than Low n Ach persons.

Our discussion has indicated that High n Ach people have a more intense desire to be successful than Low n Ach people. Moreover, their higher achievement motive causes them to work harder than Low n Ach persons in achievement-oriented situations. The assumption that success is the motivating force in High n Ach people is supported by French's study (1958). While attempting to solve problems, one group of French's subjects were told whether or not they were progressing accurately; other subjects were not given such feedback. French observed that High n Ach subjects who received feedback worked more efficiently than High n Ach subjects who had not. Evidently, High n Ach people striving toward success are more successful when they receive feedback about their progress.

In many situations in which people are working for their group, the contributions of individuals are not readily apparent to others. How do High n Ach people act under these circumstances? Investigating this type of situation, French (1958) assigned two groups of subjects a task. In one condition, individual subjects were to submit their own solution to the problem; in the other condition, only a single group solution was to be given. French learned that High n Ach subjects worked just as hard for their group goal as for their individual goal. deCharms (1956) reported results identical to French's. However, High n Ach individuals will not work for the group if others in it tell them exactly what to do (see deCharms, Morrison, Reitman, & McClelland, 1955). Thus, our discussion suggests that though High n Ach persons need no recognition for their contribution to their group, they do need to feel that they have contributed to its success.

Risk preference and need to achieve. When success depends upon one's own effort, High n Ach and Low n Ach people required to participate in achievement situations show different preferences in the type of tasks they choose. High n Ach persons prefer tasks involving moderate risk rather than extreme risk; that is, they typically select tasks in which success is probable but failure is nevertheless possible. They participate only infrequently in situations in which success is assured (low risk) or not likely (high risk). Low n Ach persons are less likely than High n Ach persons to choose a task involving moderate risk and more apt to choose one involving extreme risk. Thus, the High n Ach person is more of a "moderate risk taker" and less of an "extreme risk taker" than the Low n Ach person. Let's continue with several studies demonstrating this.

McClelland (1958) gave 5- and 6-year-old children 10 throws in a ring-toss game, which requires throwing a ring onto a wooden peg. Each child could choose to stand anywhere between 10 and 64 inches from the peg. McClelland noted that High n Ach children most frequently stood at an intermediate distance (20 to 45 inches) (see Figure 10.2). This distance provided the children a good chance of success but did not ensure it. McClelland found that Low n Ach children more often stood either very close to the peg or very far from it.

Other experimenters have also reported that High n Ach persons typically are

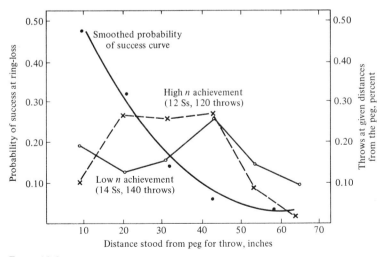

Figure 10.2
Percentage of throws made at each distance from the peg for High n Ach and Low n Ach boys. The smooth curve shows the probability of success at each distance. [From McClelland, D. C. Risk-taking in children with high and low need for achievement. In J. W. Atkinson (Ed.), Motives in fantasy, action, and society. Princeton, N. J.: Van Nostrand, 1958. © 1958 by D. Van Nostrand Company. Reprinted by permission of the publisher.]

moderate risk takers, whereas Low n Ach people are more apt to take extreme risks. Using college students as subjects, Atkinson and Litwin (1960) replicated McClelland's results with the ring-toss game. In addition, Atkinson, Bastian, Earl, and Litwin (1960) instructed High n Ach and Low n Ach college students to choose their preferred distance in a shuffleboard game; again, High n Ach people typically chose moderate distances, and Low n Ach people were more likely to select either a close or far distance. Finally, Litwin's subjects (1958) selected from holes of different sizes the one into which they would attempt to throw pennies. Again, High n Ach people typically selected a moderate risk, an intermediate-size hole; Low n Ach people were more likely to throw their pennies at either a large or a small hole than High n Ach people were.

What factors cause these differences in achievement motivation? McClelland (1951) suggested that childhood experiences are critical in establishing adult levels of the need to achieve. According to McClelland, children who associate achievement with positive affective changes (or reward) become adults who show an intense need to achieve. Various evidence supports McClelland's view, as we will see next.

The development of a need to achieve. In 1958, Winterbottom pointed to the importance of early independence training in establishing a high need to achieve. Having obtained achievement motivation scores for 8- to 10-year-old boys, she interviewed their mothers. Winterbottom reported that the mothers of High n Ach boys recalled that they had allowed their sons to be independent earlier than the mothers of Low n Ach boys. She also discovered that the mothers of the High n Ach boys encouraged and rewarded their independence, whereas mothers of Low n Ach boys restricted their independence. Winterbottom's results suggest that early training for independence leads to the development of a High n Ach person. However, in another experiment, Rosen and D'Andrade (1959) indicated that achievement training, as well as independence training, is necessary to establish a high need to achieve.

Rosen and D'Andrade directly observed how the parents of some High n Ach boys and Low n Ach boys behaved while watching their blindfolded sons attempt to build a tower of wooden blocks. Rosen and D'Andrade allowed the parents to talk to their sons but not physically help them build the tower. Three important behavioral differences appeared between the parents of High n Ach boys and Low n Ach boys. *First, the parents of the High n Ach boys had higher expectations about their sons' achievements than the parents of Low n Ach boys.* This suggests that if parents do not expect their sons to do well, the boys will not value success. *Second, the parents of High n Ach boys showed more positive affects (for example, pleasantness, happiness, laughing, joking) while their sons worked on their tasks and were more rewarding of their sons' successes (for example, their mothers hugged and kissed them) than the parents of Low n Ach boys.* These results support McClelland's view that a high need to achieve will develop if achievement is associated with positive affect. *Finally, the fathers of High n Ach boys showed less dominating involvement in their sons' activities than father of Low n Ach boys.* This observation indicates that if a father makes his son's decisions, thereby placing little pressure on the boy to achieve by himself, this child will develop low self-esteem and a low level of achievement motivation.

Many investigators have found that the childrearing practices (permissiveness or restrictiveness, parental expectation about children's competence, physical affection, and provision of rewards) which McClelland assumed would affect achievement motivation are related to the need to achieve; but other researchers have been unable to show this relationship (see Weiner, 1980). We should not be surprised that psychologists have not always observed a relationship between childrearing practices and achievement motivation. Children undoubtedly experience situations outside their home which influence their need to achieve. Schools, for example, may reward children's achievements and this in turn affects the development of achievement motivation.

You may wonder if the differences between people in achievement motivation have any significance other than how many arithmetic problems can be solved. In the next section, we will see that High n Ach and Low n Ach people differ also in their real-world behavior.

The contribution of High n Ach people. The level of our need to achieve definitely influences how we act in natural settings. Not surprisingly, Atkinson, Lens, and O'Malley (1976) reported that High n Ach people are more likely to attend college than Low n Ach people. Also, High n Ach college students earn better grades for courses in their major area of study than Low n Ach people (Raynor, 1970). Minor and Neel (1958) concluded that High n Ach persons choose jobs higher in status than Low n Ach people. Apparently, High n Ach people, compared with Low n Ach people, have higher expectations of future success and work harder to secure a career which will allow them to be successful.

Does our level of achievement motivation actually influence whether or not we will have a successful career? McClelland's research (see McClelland, 1961, 1965) suggests that success in a career depends upon the type of career chosen. Remember that High n Ach people typically choose high-status occupations. According to McClelland, a High n Ach son has two types of high-status positions from which to select: *entrepreneurial* and *nonentrepreneurial.* Entrepreneurial positions involve buying, selling, producing, or providing capital. Entrepreneurs must (1) *take moderate but decisive risks on the basis of skill,* (2) *be energetic and exhibit novel instrumental activity,* (3) *be individually responsible for their own actions,* (4) *have knowledge of the results of their decisions,* (5) *anticipate future events,* and (6) *have organizational skills.* A business manager is one example of an entrepreneur. Nonentrepreneurial occupations include teaching, medicine, law, ministry, and accounting. Such occupations sometimes involve entrepreneurial activity, but in general, the people choosing them do not have to exhibit entrepreneurial behavior. For example, using information which they have previously acquired, teachers or doctors typically solve problems, whereas managers frequently provide new, risky, or challenging solutions to problems.

McClelland's research indicates that High n Ach persons are not only best suited to the role of entrepreneur, but also more likely to be successful if they choose an entrepreneurial occupation. Several lines of evidence support McClelland's contention. First, the variables (moderate risk, challenge, feedback about success, feelings of responsibility) which, as we saw earlier, influence the task performance of High n Ach people are the same behaviors which are involved in entrepreneurial activity and lead to the success of entrepreneurial endeavors. Second, McClelland found that successful unit managers (entrepreneurs) at General Electric Company had higher need to achieve (measured by TAT scores) than staff specialists (professionals) with similar social and economic background. He also discovered that successful entrepreneurs in Italy and Poland had a higher achievement motivation than comparable professionals (physicians, lawyers, teachers, clergy) in those countries. These observations suggest that people need a higher level of achievement motivation to succeed as entrepreneurs than as professionals. Third, McClelland discovered that people's success in entrepreneurial activities depends upon their level of achievement motivation. Using the TAT, he compared the need to achieve of entrepreneurs who had achieved various degrees of success, as indicated by their salaries. McClelland found a significant positive correlation between achievement motivation and success; that is, the higher the level of achievement motivation, the greater the success (i.e., in this case, the higher the salary). Finally, McClelland measured the achievement motivation level of male college students in 1947 and then evaluated whether the students' scores predicted their success 14 years later. Comparing the n Ach scores of these people as students with their scores as workers with successful entrepreneurial (sales, management) and nonentrepreneurial (personnel, credit) positions, he found that most (83 percent) of the successful entrepreneurs had shown high achievement 14 years earlier. In contrast, only 21 percent of the men who were successful in nonentrepreneurial positions had been in the High n Ach category in college. These observations indicate that High n Ach people will probably be successful in entrepreneurial positions but not in nonentrepreneurial positions.

Our discussion points out that people's level of achievement motivation influences their success as entrepreneurs; High n Ach people are more likely to be successful entrepreneurs than Low n Ach people. The next section points out that a society's level of achievement motivation influences its economic success.

The Achieving Society

In 1904, the German sociologist Max Weber suggested a link between the Protestant Reformation and economic development in western Europe (see Figure 10.3). In his book, *The Protestant Ethic and the Spirit of Capitalism,* Weber assumed that the Protestant philosophy advocated by Calvin and Luther created a type of person who worked hard. God, according to the Protestant view, had already selected those who would enter heaven; however, by performing their "calling" people could become convinced that they had been selected. This involved doing their best in whatever station God had assigned them to. Strict observance of church ritual was not as important as self-control, frugality, and hard work. Persons living up to these ideals could reduce their "fear of damnation." Protestants believed that people should not enjoy their prosperity but rather reinvest their profits to expand their business. This fear of damnation, a strong drive, motivated the Protestants to work diligently. Their hard work created economic success in their countries.

Weber's view asserts that the Protestant ethic caused Protestant countries to be more prosperous than Catholic (non-Protestant) countries. McClelland evaluated this assumption by comparing numerous measures of economic development (for example, consumption of electricity in kilowatt hours per capita) in 12 Protestant and 13 Catholic countries. (McClelland used only developed countries located outside the tropical zone.)

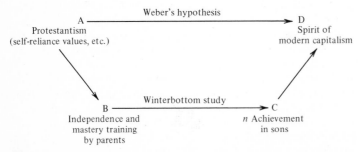

Figure 10.3
McClelland's proposed relationship between Protestantism, achievement motivation, and economic development. (From McClelland, D. C., The achieving society. Princeton, N.J.: Van Nostrand, 1961.)

He reported that the level of economic development was strongly related to religion; that is, Protestant countries were significantly more advanced than Catholic countries.

McClelland (1961) suggested that the independence and achievement training created by the Protestant ethic produced a high level of achievement motivation, which in turn produced the entrepreneurial activity necessary to enhance economic development (refer to Figure 10.3). McClelland presented several lines of evidence to support his view. First, McClelland, Rindlisbacher, and de Charms (1955) examined the childrearing practices of Protestant and Catholic parents in Connecticut who were matched for socioeconomic status. Interestingly, Protestant parents stressed earlier self-reliance than did Catholic parents. As McClelland predicted, the Protestant parents did provide earlier independence training than the Catholic parents. Second, McClelland, Sturr, Knapp, and Wendt (1958) compared the level of achievement motivation in German male university students from three different socioeconomic backgrounds. They found that Protestant students had a significantly higher need to achieve than comparable Catholic students. Finally, McClelland's hypothesis assumes that Protestants are more likely than Catholics to enter business activities because their need to achieve is higher than that of Catholics. McClelland reported that more Protestant university students in Germany were enrolled in technical schools or business schools than Catholics. Apparently, Protestants are more likely to become entrepreneurs than Catholics are, because the Protestants have greater achievement motivation.

McClelland's view links the Protestant value system, childrearing practices, high achievement motivation, and entrepreneurial activity. However, McClelland does not believe that a country's economic success is directly linked with its religious beliefs. According to McClelland, any society which stresses independence and mastery training will induce high levels of achievement motivation and entrepreneurial behavior. Japan, for example, has a high level of economic development but is not Protestant. It is this interest in business activity which brings economic prosperity.

You may have noticed a problem with these data. Is it possible that economic development produces a higher level of achievement motivation rather than the other way around? Let's look at how McClelland solved this problem.

Prosperity is a temporary phenomenon; in any society, it rises at some points and then declines at others. If McClelland's theory is accurate, an increase in the level of a society's achievement motivation must precede an improvement in economic development, and a decrease in its need to achieve must precede a decline in its prosperity. McClelland developed an ingenious way to assess a society's level of achievement motivation. He assumed that stories which parents read to their children transmit cultural values. Thus, the level of achievement imagery in children's stories should indicate the level of achievement motivation present in any given culture. Economic development, of course, can be measured in many ways; the production of electricity, in kilowatthours per capita, is one example. McClelland observed that changes in achievement motivation in many past cultures preceded increases and decreases in their economic prosperity. Let's look at some examples of this relationship.

McClelland sampled the levels of achievement imagery in children's readers printed in 1929 in 23 countries and compared these levels with the increase in electrical production between 1929 and 1950. McClelland controlled for possible confounding variables such as differences in natural resources and war damages. As McClelland predicted, he found a significant positive relationship ($r = +.53$) between level of achievement imagery in children's books in 1929 and the increase in electrical production in the ensuing 21 years. These results suggest that modern societies stressing achievement in children's stories have experienced the greatest improvement in economic prosperity.

McClelland also studied the expression of the need to achieve (for example, in drama, accounts of sea voyages, street ballads) and economic success (as reflected in changes in coal exports) in England between 1500 and 1800. He discovered that the need to achieve reflected in literature significantly declined between 1600 and 1650, and an economic decline followed 50 years later (see Figure 10.4). Achievement motivation expressed in literature increased between 1700 and 1750; economic improvement occurred 50 years later.

The rise and fall of Greek civilization between 900 and 100 B.C. provides another example of the relationship between need to achieve and economic development. Analyzing ancient Greek literature, McClelland assessed the level of achievement motivation. He then measured economic success in terms of the size of areas which traded with Greece: the larger the area, the higher the level of economic success. McClelland discovered that an increase in the level of achievement motivation preceded the expansion of Greek trade in 900 B.C. Also, a decline in achievement motivation occurred before the decline of the Greek economy in 400 B.C. In the next section our discussion of McClelland's approach ends by examining one procedure for changing a person's or a society's level of achievement motivation.

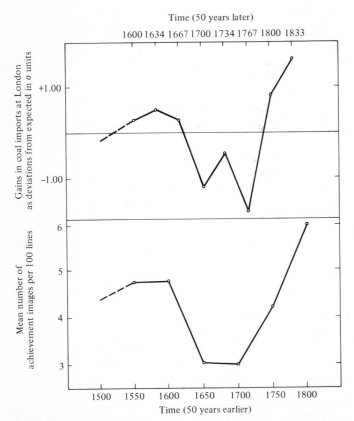

Figure 10.4
Changes in the levels of the need to achieve as reflected in English literature between 1550 and 1880 (bottom) and the gain in coal imports at London between 1600 and 1833 (top). (From McClelland, D. C. The achieving society. Princeton, N.J.: Van Nostrand, 1961.)

Achievement Motivation Training Program

McClelland and Winter (1969) developed 3- and 6-week training courses to create high achievement motivation in Low n Ach persons. This program entails two steps. *First, the participants are introduced to the concept of achievement motivation and its relationship to personal and societal successes.* They are given lectures about achievement motivation, demonstrations of achievement-oriented behavior, and case histories of successful entrepreneurs. *Second, the trainees are taught to think and act as High n Ach people.* They learn how to write stories emphasizing high achievement motivation. Participating in achievement-oriented situations teaches them to take only moderate risks and think of long-term goals. For example, the trainees play a simulated business game requiring them to estimate how many Tinker Toy objects (for example, an airplane) they can build in a given amount of time. The participants earn profit by building the objects but lose profit if their estimate is too high. The aim of this task and similar tasks is to instill realistic expectations and increase the level of motivated behavior. Later in the program, trainees apply their acquired knowledge to career planning. They are instructed to develop their career goals and describe means of attaining them. Individual and group counseling sessions round out the program. It is hoped that this aspect of the program will enable the trainees to establish new friendships and become part of a new reference group.

Numerous programs have successfully implemented McClelland and Winter's procedure, causing positive behavioral changes in underachievers (Heckhausen, 1975; Kolb, 1965). Positive results have also been obtained for schoolteachers (de Charms, 1972) and businessmen (Aronoff & Litwin, 1968; McClelland, 1965; McClelland & Winter, 1969). To illustrate their effectiveness, three of these programs are presented next.

Kolb (1965) evaluated the influence of such a program with underachieving boys who attended a summer camp. Although these boys had IQs above 120, their school performance was below average. Success was defined in terms of the boys' grade averages 6 months and 18 months after the study. Kolb also examined how effective the program was with boys of low and high socioeconomic status. He found that boys of both low and high socioeconomic status who participated in the program showed a significant improvement in grades 6 months after the program, compared with boys who did not participate. However, only the boys with high socioeconomic status maintained their improvement 18 months later. Kolb argued that the subculture of the boys with low socioeconomic status did not value achievement and that it was unreasonable to expect these boys to maintain a high need to achieve without external support. Kolb's results indicate that if such a program is to be effective, the environment must value and reward achievement.

Aronoff and Litwin (1968) conducted a study using middle-level American businessmen. Sixteen men participated in their 5-day program; a comparable control group received no achievement training. Success was defined in terms of promotions and raises during the 2 years following the program; on this basis, Aronoff and Litwin concluded that their treatment was successful. Compared with the men who had not participated in the program, their subjects achieved significantly more advancement. Aronoff and Litwin's results indicate that following an achievement-motivation course, middle-level businessmen act like High n Ach people; that is, they are more successful in entrepreneurial activities than others. We have seen that such a program can enhance a person's success; as we will see next, it can also increase a society's economic prosperity.

McClelland and Winter (1969) conducted an extensive achievement-training program among businessmen in two small Indian cities, Kakinada and Vellore. They reported that in the 2 years before the program only 18 percent of these businessmen had been classified as usually active in business; 2 years after the program, 51 percent were in that category. These results mean that the course in all likelihood caused these businessmen to work longer hours, initiate more new businesses, and make more capital investments. The economic benefits of their higher level of achievement behavior included the hiring of new workers and a significant increase in company profits. McClelland and Winter estimate that their program was responsible for creating 135 new jobs and 376,000 rupees of new capital investments in these two small cities. In a third Indian city, Rajahandry, which was demographically and industrially similar to the other two cities, there was no training program; this city showed no changes in business activity or economic prosperity. Apparently, an achievement-motivation course similar to McClelland and Winter's can increase a society's economic level as well as a person's success. Although McClelland and Winter's program has not been implemented on a wide scale, its successes demonstrate that it does represent a worthwhile approach to improving both individual and national prosperity.

The research of McClelland and his associates has taught us a great deal about achievement motivation. However, their approach did not address some important questions. Although we know that High n Ach people typically choose moderate risks while Low n Ach persons are more likely to choose extreme risks, their approach does not explain the motivational processes which cause these behavioral differences. John Atkinson directed his theory and research toward revealing the processes which determine the intensity of motivated behavior in various situations.

THE INFLUENCE OF SUCCESS OR FAILURE

Atkinson (1958, 1964) suggested that two separate motives operate in achievement situations. According to Atkinson, we are motivated by both a hope of success (T_S) and fear of failure (T_{AF}). He assumed that hope of success motivates us to engage in achievement tasks and fear of failure causes us to avoid them. Furthermore, Atkinson proposed that these two motives are conflicting; a person will work on an achievement task when the hope of success is stronger than the fear of failure but will avoid the achievement task when the fear of failure is stronger than the hope of success. The next sections will first describe the hope of success and then discuss the fear of failure. Later, we'll examine how the combined influence of these two motives governs achievement behavior.

The Hope of Success

Atkinson's view of achievement motivation (1958, 1964) reflects a combination of the drive and cognitive approaches outlined in Chapters 2 and 3. According to Atkinson, positive affective anticipation of success motivates a person to approach an achievement-oriented situation. The strength of this emotional response, or the tendency to approach success (T_S), is determined by the level of a person's internal desire to be successful (M_S), the perceived probability of success (P_S), and the incentive value of success (I_S). In mathematical terms, Atkinson assumes that $T_S = M_S \times P_S \times I_S$. Atkinson's M_S, P_S, and I_S are equivalent to the demand for a goal, the expectancy of obtaining a goal, and the value of a goal in Tolman's theory (see Chapter 3). The anticipation of success (T_S) and the behavior used to reach one's goal are similar to the concepts of anticipatory goal response (r_G) and habit in the Hull-Spence theory (see Chapter 2).

The motive to achieve.   In Atkinson's view, the M_S, the demand for a goal, is a person's stable personality disposition to seek success. This motive to achieve success, characterized as "a capacity to experience pride in accomplishment," remains stable from situation to situation. According to Atkinson, High n Ach people have a higher M_S value than Low n Ach people.

One index of this tendency to approach success is the relative length of time a person works on an achievement task. Atkinson and Litwin's study (1960) is an example. Atkinson and Litwin measured how long students worked on an examination before turning it in. Although the examination officially lasted 3 hours, very few students used the entire time. Atkinson and Litwin discovered that High n Ach students worked on the examination twice as long as Low n Ach students. It seems reasonable to conclude that the higher tendency to approach success produced the greater persistence showed by the High n Ach students.

The probability of success.   The P_S level reflects our expectation of succeeding at a particular task. We gain information about the probability of success in several ways. *First, our past history of reward in similar situations influences our perceived probability of success.* We have a higher expectation of succeeding at a task if we have succeeded at similar tasks in the past. *Second, the perceived difficulty of the task affects our expectation of success.* For example, McClelland (1961) discovered that in the ring-toss game, each subject's perceived probability of throwing a ring on the peg decreased as the distance from the peg increased. Similarly, you probably feel more apt to earn a high grade in an easy course than a difficult one. *Third, the degree of other people's success in a task you are considering influences your perception of succeeding in that task.* Knowing that many other people have succeeded gives you a high expectation of being successful; knowing that only a few others have succeeded leaves you with low expectations of success. *Finally, the likelihood of success often depends upon how many other people are competing for your desired reward.* You will have a higher expectation of being successful if you alone desire a reward than if many others are competing for it, too.

We have learned that several factors influence the perceived probability of success. But does the probability of success influence the level of achievement behavior? A study by Atkinson (1958) clearly indicated that participating in tasks involving moderate risk can produce the highest level of performance. He informed all the students in his study that they were competing against 19 other students on two 20-minute achievement tasks. Some students were told that only the person receiving the highest score would get a prize ("high risk"). Others were informed that either one-third or one-half of the subjects would receive a prize ("moderate risk"). Still other students were told that three-quarters of the subjects would get a prize ("low risk"). This procedure created varying expectations of success, or degrees of risk. Atkinson discovered that the highest level of performance was found in the "moderate risk" conditions and the lowest level in the "extreme risk" conditions. These observations indicate that the probability of success has an important influence on motivated behavior; that is, tasks involving moderate risk can produce the highest level of achievement behavior. It should be noted that this observation is true only for those persons whose hope of success is stronger than their fear of failure.

The value of success.   Atkinson assumed that the incentive value of success (I_S) is inversely related to the probability of success; that is, the more likely we are to perceive ourselves as obtaining success, the less value success will have when obtained. Consider the following example to illustrate this process. Suppose that you get an A in a course. How much satisfaction will you experience from that grade? If you earned it in a class in which few students received high marks, you probably will feel extreme satisfaction; however, if almost everyone received a good grade, your A probably will not give you much satisfaction.

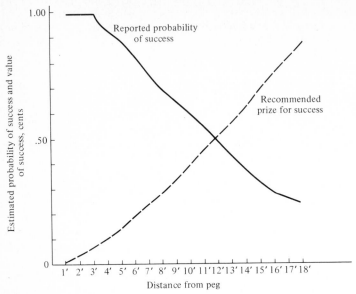

Figure 10.5
Average estimated probability of successfully throwing a ringer from various distances from the ring and average reported suitable monetary prize for success at each distance from the ring. (From Litwin, G. H. Motives and expectancies as determinants of preference for degrees of risk. Cited in J. W. Atkinson, An introduction to motivation. Princeton, N.J.: Van Nostrand, 1964. © 1964 by D. Van Nostrand Company. Reprinted by permission of the publisher.)

Litwin's study (1958) provides definitive evidence for Atkinson's view that the value of success is inversely related to the probability of success. Litwin asked one group of college students to estimate their performance in a ring-toss game by predicting how many times out of 10 turns (the probability of success) they thought they could, when standing from 1 to 18 feet from the peg, hook a ring on the peg. The results indicated that the reported probability of success decreased as the distance increased (see Figure 10.5). Having played the ring-toss game, another group of students were asked to suggest how much money (on a scale of 0 to $1) they should receive for a successful toss from each distance. The recommended prize increased with distance, demonstrating—as Atkinson predicted—that the value of success decreases as its probability increases. McClelland also noted that subjects who succeed from a close distance in the ring-toss game felt no satisfaction. As the distance increased, satisfaction experienced with success also increased.

The importance of any theory is its ability to predict how a person will behave in a particular situation. Let's see if Atkinson's formula $T_S = M_S \times P_S \times I_S$ predicts these two characteristic differences between High n Ach and Low n Ach people: risk preference and intensity of behavior.

A test of Atkinson's view. Table 10.2 presents the hypothetical probability of success (P_S) and the value of success (I_S) for six different tasks in a High n Ach person and a Low n Ach person. In Atkinson's view, increases in the T_S value yield more intense achievement behavior. As you can see from the table, the High n Ach person's T_S values are significantly greater for each task than those of the Low n Ach person. These different

Table 10.2
**The Tendency to Achieve Success (T_S) as a Function of the Motive
to Achieve Success (M_S), Expectancy of Success (P_S) and Incentive
Value of Success (I_S) for a Person with a High ($M_S = 8$) or a Low ($M_S = 1$) n Ach**

Task	P_S	I_S	$(T_S = M_S \times P_S \times I_S)$ When $M_S = 1$	When $M_S = 8$
A	.90	.10	.09	.72
B	.70	.30	.21	1.68
C	.50	.50	.25	2.00
D	.30	.70	.21	1.68
E	.10	.90	.09	.72

From: Atkinson, J. W. *An introduction to motivation.* Princeton, N.J.: Van Nostrand, 1964.
© 1964 by D. Van Nostrand Company. Reprinted by permission of the publisher.

T_S values correspond to the greater intensity of motivated behavior exhibited by High n Ach people, compared with Low n Ach people, in all achievement-oriented situations.

Suppose that the two persons depicted in Table 10.2 received several opportunities to choose between tasks A, C, and E. The High n Ach person will usually choose task C, the moderate-risk task, since its T_S value—and, therefore, its approach tendency—is clearly higher than that of tasks A or E, which involve extreme risks. On the other hand, the Low n Ach person will not have such an easy choice, since the T_S values differ only slightly. Thus, the Low n Ach person will sometimes choose the extreme tasks, A and E. The T_S values shown in Table 10.2, which represent High n Ach and Low n Ach people under tasks of various difficulty, do correspond to the differential risk-taking behavior of High n Ach and Low n Ach people. Evidently, Atkinson's mathematical formula does predict the behavioral differences between High n Ach and Low n Ach people in achievement situations.

However, you should not get the impression from this example that both High n Ach and Low n Ach people in the same or similar situation have identical expectations of success. A High n Ach person typically considers a particular task a lower risk than a Low n Ach person does. McClelland, Atkinson, Clark, and Lowell (1953) discovered that High n Ach people had higher expectations of success on their final examination than Low n Ach people. Similarly, Pottharst (1955) reported that High n Ach high school boys felt they would obtain a better score on a novel task than Low n Ach boys. These observations are not surprising; we saw earlier that the probability of success is partially based on past experience, and High n Ach persons typically are more successful than Low n Ach individuals. The difference in expectation of success between High n Ach and Low n Ach people will depend upon their degree of past experience with the same or similar tasks. In experimental situations, the differences in risk-taking behavior between High n Ach and Low n Ach people have been evaluated using tasks (such as the ring-toss game) in which past experience was probably minimal; therefore, P_S differences were not significantly greater for High n Ach than for Low n Ach persons.

The Fear of Failure
Atkinson also adopted the drive view and the cognitive view to explain people's motivation to avoid an achievement task. According to Atkinson, a negative affective

anticipation of failure motivates us to avoid achievement-oriented situations. In addition, when we are required to participate in an achievement task, this negative affective response impairs performance by antagonizing our need to achieve. The strength of this emotional response—the tendency to avoid failure (T_{AF})—is controlled by our level of internal desire to avoid failure (M_{AF}), the perceived likelihood of failure (P_F), and the negative incentive value of failure ($-I_F$). Atkinson's theory stated in mathematical terms assumes that $T_{AF} = M_{AF} \times P_F \times (-I_F)$. As is true of Atkinson's theory about the tendency to approach success, certain aspects of his view of the tendency to avoid failure contain elements from both cognitive and drive views. M_{AF} (motive to avoid failure), P_F (probability of failure), and $-I_F$ (negative incentive value of failure) represent cognitive concepts: the tendency to avoid failure (T_{AF}) and the behavior (habit) used to avoid failure reflect the operation of drive concepts. Let's now see the factors which determine the level of M_{AF}, P_F, and $(-I_F)$.

The motive to avoid failure. In Atkinson's theory, M_{AF} is a stable personality disposition to avoid failure. This motive to avoid failure represents "a capacity to experience shame and embarrassment when the outcome of performance is failure." Atkinson assumed that this disposition to avoid achievement-oriented tasks is aroused whenever we feel that our performance is being assessed and that failure is possible. Although our M_{AF} level remains constant in different situations, different people have different M_{AF} levels. According to Atkinson, the higher our M_{AF} level is, the stronger will be our motive to avoid an achievement situation.

How can the tendency to avoid failure be measured? Atkinson used the *Test Anxiety Questionnaire (TAQ)*, which Mandler and Sarason developed in 1952 to indicate M_{AF} level. The TAQ is a self-report questionnaire, consisting of items like these: *How do you feel beforehand? How often do you think of avoiding the test? How much do you worry while taking an intelligence test?* To evaluate whether or not a person's TAQ score is related to his or her behavior in an actual testing situation, Mandler and Sarason (1952) looked for overt signs of anxiety (perspiration, excessive movement, inappropriate laughter and exclamations, questioning of instructions, and hand movements) in subjects working on a complex task. They noted a good correspondence (phi = .59) between TAQ scores and overt anxiety. These observations indicate that people with high TAQ scores exhibit more behavioral signs of anxiety when engaging in achievement tasks than persons whose TAQ scores are low.

Atkinson's theory assumes that people with "high test anxiety," as revealed in the TAQ scores, are more likely to avoid achievement situations than people with "low test anxiety." The degree of a person's persistence on an examination is one measure of this tendency to avoid. How quickly a person leaves an examination reflects the desire to avoid achievement situations. Recall the description of Atkinson and Litwin's experiment (1960). Atkinson and Litwin found that High n Ach people worked twice as long on examinations as Low n Ach people. Atkinson and Litwin also measured the persistence of students with "high test anxiety" and "low test anxiety" and discovered that "high test anxiety" students left the examination twice as soon as "low test anxiety" students. This indicates that the higher the tendency to avoid failure, the lower the persistence in students with "high test anxiety" as compared with students with "low test anxiety."

"High test anxiety" people in achievement-oriented situations also perform more poorly than "low test anxiety" people. Atkinson and Litwin (1960) reported that their "high test anxiety" students scored significantly lower on their final examination than "low test anxiety" students. In addition, Spielberger (1959) noted that the grade-point averages of "high test anxiety" college students (except those having either very high or extremely low scholastic aptitude) were considerably lower than those of "low test anxiety" students of comparable ability. This observation that high levels of "test anxiety" impair performance is not surprising. Since "high test anxiety" people are motivated to avoid achievement situations, they will not focus their attention on the achievement task, and therefore they cannot do well.

The probability of failure. The P_F value represents our expectation of failure in a particular task. As with the expectation of success, we have several ways of gaining knowledge about the probability of failure. *First, our past experience with similar tasks affects our perceived probability of failure in any given task.* We have a higher expectation of failure if we have failed at similar tasks in the past. *Second, the expectation of failure increases as the difficulty of a task increases.* Thus, you are more apt to expect to fail a task perceived to be difficult than one perceived to be simple. *Third, the percentage of other people who have failed the task influences the expectation of failure.* Your expectation of failing is higher if most people have performed poorly than if most people have performed well. *Finally, the number of people competing for reward affects our expectation of failure.* Our expectation of failure increases if we think that many other people want the same reward we do.

The negative incentive value of failure. Suppose that you have failed a very difficult course. Although disappointed, you probably will not be ashamed of your performance or embarrassed by it. However, would you feel this way if you failed a very easy course? Under these circumstances, you probably would feel ashamed and embarrassed. Atkinson's view of the negative incentive value of failure ($-I_F$) corresponds to our description of our varied emotional responses to difficult or easy tasks. The negative value of failure ($-I_F$), according to Atkinson, is a negative affective response caused by the anticipation of not performing a task well. The intensity of this negative affective response is an inverse function of the difficulty of the task; that is, anticipated failure on tasks which are more difficult produces less negative emotional response. In mathematical terms, Atkinson states that $-I_F = -(1 - P_F)$.

Feather (1967), providing support for Atkinson's model of the negative incentive value of failure, asked subjects performing tasks of varying difficulty to rate the "repulsiveness" of failing. Feather reported that the aversive quality of failure diminished as difficulty increased. Apparently, anticipating failure on an easy task causes us more shame than expecting to fail a difficult task.

A test of Atkinson's view. Table 10.3 presents the hypothetical probability of failure (P_F) and the negative incentive value of failure ($-I_F$) for six different tasks performed by a person with "high test anxiety" and a person with a "low test anxiety." Atkinson assumes that a high tendency to avoid failure (T_{AF}) will produce an intense motivation to avoid achievement tasks. Also, the performance of people with "high test anxiety" will be poor on tasks they are required to perform. In contrast, a low tendency to avoid failure will make persons unmotivated to avoid achievement tasks; under these circumstances, other motives (for example, the need to achieve) will govern behavioral effectiveness. As Table 10.3 illustrates, in all achievement-oriented situations, T_{AF} values are higher for "high test anxiety" people than "low test anxiety" people.

Sarason, Mandler, and Craighill's study (1952) shows that "low test anxiety" people perform more efficiently on all achievement tasks than "high test anxiety" people. Their subjects worked on a digit-symbol substitution test. Before taking the test, one group, consisting of both "high test anxiety" and "low test anxiety" subjects, was told, "The test is designed so that it should be fairly easy for the average college student to complete it within the time limit." This created the expectation that the task was easy. A second

Table 10.3
The Tendency to Avoid Failure (T_{AF}) as a Function of the
Motive to Avoid Failure (M_{AF}), Expectancy of Failure (P_F),
and Negative Incentive Value of Failure (I_F) for a Person
with a High ($M_{AF} = 8$) or a Low ($M_{AF} = 1$) Test Anxiety

Task	P_F	$-I_F$	$(T_{AF} = M_{AF} \times P_F \times -I_F)$	
			$M_{AF} = 1$	$M_{AF} = 8$
A	.10	−.90	−.09	− .72
B	.30	−.70	−.21	−1.68
C	.50	−.50	−.25	−2.00
D	.70	−.30	−.21	−1.68
E	.90	−.10	−.09	− .72

From Atkinson, J. W. *An introduction to motivation.* Princeton, N.J.: Van
Nostrand, 1964. © 1964 by D. Van Nostrand Company. Reprinted by
permission of the publisher.

group of "high test anxiety" and "low test anxiety" subjects was led to believe the task was
extremely difficult; these subjects were told, "The test was constructed so that nobody
could finish within the time limit." Sarason, Mandler, and Craighill found that the
subjects with "high test anxiety" performed worse than those with "low test anxiety" in
both conditions. In addition, the scores of subjects with "high test anxiety" were equal in
both conditions. These results support Atkinson's view of the influence of a high
tendency to avoid failure (T_{AF}) on effectiveness in both easy tasks and difficult tasks.
Sarason, Mandler, and Craighill also reported that "low test anxiety" subjects performed
better on the difficult task than the easy task. Since very little "test anxiety" is being
produced in "low test anxiety" subjects, their motivation to avoid all achievement
situations is weak. In all likelihood, many of the subjects with "low test anxiety" had a
high achievement motive, viewed the difficult task as involving moderate risk, and were
more motivated to do well in this task than in an easy (low-risk) task. The predictions of
Atkinson's theory support this view.

Suppose that "high test anxiety" people and "low test anxiety" people had to choose
between tasks A, C, and E in Table 10.3. According to Atkinson, "high test anxiety"
people should take extreme risks; that is, they should select either A or E, since these
tasks have lower T_{AF} values than task C. Atkinson and Litwin (1960) allowed subjects
with "high test anxiety" to select the distance from which they would throw 10 rings at a
peg. These subjects chose either task A (low risk) or task E (high risk) more often than
task C (moderate risk). On the other hand, subjects with "low test anxiety," who should
have had little motive to avoid all the tasks, showed that their need to achieve controlled
which task they selected. If their need to achieve was high, they chose the moderate risk.
However, if their need to achieve was low, they chose the extreme risks and the moderate
risk equally.

We have seen in the last two sections that the tendency to approach success (T_S)
motivates us to work diligently on achievement tasks. In contrast, the tendency to avoid
failure (T_{AF}) either motivates us to avoid an achievement task or causes us to perform an
assigned achievement task poorly. According to Atkinson, these two motives are
antagonistic; the stronger tendency governs behavior, and the weaker tendency reduces
the impact of the other motive. For example, if T_S is the dominant motive, we will
approach achievement tasks, but the T_{AF} motive will reduce the intensity of achieve-

ment behavior. We have thus far examined the separate influence of these two motives. Although there are many people who have only one of these motives, there are others who have either a high or a low level of both. We have seen that High n Ach people have a high need to achieve but little "test anxiety." We have also seen that people with "high test anxiety" have no desire to be successful. The next section describes the behavioral characteristics of people who have either a high or a low level of both motives.

The Combined Influence of T_S and T_{AF}

We saw earlier in the chapter that people with a high need to achieve and "low test anxiety" show a strong tendency to approach achievement tasks and perform at a high level in all achievement situations but prefer tasks involving moderate risk. In contrast, persons with a low need to achieve but "high test anxiety" exhibit an intense avoidance of all achievement tasks and perform all required tasks poorly; however, they show a preference for extreme risks.

How do people with high or low levels of both motives act? According to Atkinson, these two motives antagonize each other, so that these people have a tendency neither to succeed nor to avoid failure. Miller's ideas about the approach-avoidance conflict (detailed in Chapter 2) influenced Atkinson. The antagonism of the tendencies to approach success and avoid failure described in Atkinson's theory reflects an application of the drive view of conflict to achievement situations.

Table 10.4 shows the canceling out of these opponent motives. Atkinson assumes

Table 10.4
Resultant Achievement Motivation (T_A) in Three Persons Who Differ in the Strength of the Motive to Achieve (M_S) and Motive to Avoid Failure (M_{AF})

Task	P_S	I_S	T_S	P_F	$-I_F$	T_{AF}	$T_S + T_{AF}$
			When $M_S = 3$ and $M_{AF} = 1$				
A	.90	.10	.27	.10	−.90	−.09	.18
B	.70	.30	.63	.30	−.70	−.21	.42
C	.50	.50	.75	.50	−.50	−.25	.50
D	.30	.70	.63	.70	−.30	−.21	.42
E	.10	.90	.27	.90	−.10	−.09	.18
			When $M_S = 3$ and $M_{AF} = 3$				
A	.90	.10	.27	.10	−.90	−.27	0
B	.70	.30	.63	.30	−.70	−.63	0
C	.50	.50	.75	.50	−.50	−.75	0
D	.30	.70	.63	.70	−.30	−.63	0
E	.10	.90	.27	.90	−.10	−.27	0
			When $M_S = 1$ and $M_{AF} = 3$				
A	.90	.10	.09	.10	−.90	−.27	−.18
B	.70	.30	.21	.30	−.70	−.63	−.42
C	.50	.50	.25	.50	−.50	−.75	−.50
D	.30	.70	.21	.70	−.30	−.63	−.42
E	.10	.90	.09	.90	−.10	−.27	−.18

From: Atkinson, J. W. An introduction to motivation. Princeton, N.J.: Van Nostrand, 1964. © 1964 by D. Van Nostrand Company. Reprinted by permission of the publisher.

that people with an equal desire to approach success and avoid failure ($M_S = M_{AF}$) would be ambivalent about achievement situations; that is, their tendency to approach an achievement task should equal their tendency to avoid it. Their ambivalence in situations in which the opposing motives are equal would cause them not to exert any effort to approach an achievement task; yet, if required to perform an achievement task, they would not be motivated to escape.

We can find evidence of this ambivalence in Atkinson and Litwin's study of persistence in examinations. We saw earlier in this chapter that a higher tendency to approach success increased persistence, whereas a higher tendency to avoid failure decreased persistence. In focusing on one motive at a time, we actually underestimated the effects of these opposing tendencies. Examining both motives together will give us a clearer picture of the strong approach tendency of "High n Ach–low test anxiety" people, the strong avoidance tendency of "Low n Ach–high test anxiety" people, and the indifference of both "High n Ach–high test anxiety" people and "Low n Ach–low test anxiety" people. Atkinson and Litwin found that "High n Ach–low test anxiety" students showed a great deal of persistence on the examinations; "Low n Ach–high test anxiety" students showed little persistence. Atkinson and Litwin noted that the "High n Ach–high test anxiety" students and the "low n Ach–low test anxiety" students were equally persistent. In level of persistence, they fell between the "High n Ach–low test anxiety" students and the "Low n Ach–high test anxiety" students. These results suggest that subjects for whom both motives are either high or low have neither an intense desire to perform an achievement test nor a strong motive to leave the testing situations. Furthermore, Atkinson was apparently correct in asserting that the tendencies to approach success and avoid failure are antagonistic motives, neither of which, when their values are equal, controls a person's actions.

The Influence of Extrinsic Motives

According to Atkinson (1964), the motive to approach success and the motive to avoid failure are not the only motives operating in an achievement task. Atkinson suggests that *extrinsic motives*, "any motive or incentive which can influence achievement behavior other than those intrinsically related to success or failure," also influence our achievement behavior. In mathematical terms, Atkinson assumes that achievement behavior (T_A) = achievement-related motivation ($T_S + T_{AF}$) + extrinsic motivation. We will briefly examine the influence of three of these extrinsic motives (affiliative motivation, aggression, and monetary incentive) on achievement behavior.

Affiliative motivation. Recall from Chapter 9 that people often have a strong need to form and maintain social relationships. A person may engage in achievement situations in order to satisfy this motivation. Such persons feel that to establish and maintain social relationships, they must do well in achievement settings. For example, students might think that they must earn good grades in order to maintain a positive relationship with their parents; athletes may assume that others won't like them if they don't perform skillfully. However, in some circumstances, affiliative motives can actually impair the level of achievement. For example, in some groups high levels of achievement are looked upon disapprovingly. Under these conditions, someone may deliberately perform poorly in order to win friends.

Several studies (for example, Atkinson & Raphelson, 1956; French, 1955) using college students as subjects have indicated that when an experimenter explicitly appeals for cooperation, the level of the students' need for social approval (or affiliation) is positively related to their task performance. Apparently, many High n Affiliation people learn that achievement produces social approval; thus, when an achievement situation arouses their affiliative motivation, High n Affiliation people work hard to obtain social acceptance.

Aggression. In Chapter 7, *aggression* was defined as behavior intended to harm someone else. The aggressive motive can either enhance or impair one's effectiveness in an achievement situation. A salesperson deliberately choosing a competitor's clientele reflects aggression as a stimulating influence; a blue-collar worker performing below his or her potential in order to make a superior appear incompetent illustrates aggression as a negative influence. An athlete deliberately playing a game poorly in order to hurt the team is another example of how aggression can lower achievement behavior.

Some people reveal their aggressiveness through thematic apperceptive stories; insulting these people in a testing situation causes their stories to reflect additional aggression (see Feshbach, 1956). In addition, psychologists (refer to McClintock & Van Vermaet, 1981) have discovered that some people will work hard when their achievement behavior adversely affects other persons. Evidently, there are people whose achievement behavior is motivated to prevent others from being successful.

Monetary incentive. Does the amount of money which we are paid influence our level of achievement behavior? Evidence indicates that as the monetary incentive provided for success increases, so does the level of achievement behavior. Atkinson (1958) told some of his subjects that they would receive $1.25 for successful performance in each of two 20-minute achievement tasks; other subjects were told they would receive $2.50 for the same tasks. Atkinson found that the higher-paid subjects performed at a significantly higher level. However, there is one exception to the rule that higher pay produces greater achievement performance. We will examine this exception next.

Suppose that you're promoted to a higher-paying job. After your promotion, you work harder and longer; however, 6 months later, you discover that your salary is less than that of a coworker with a comparable job. How would you respond when you learned this? Adams's *equity theory* (1963) suggests that the value we place on a particular monetary reward depends upon the reward which others receive for an identical performance. According to Adams, we have a feeling of equity when we think that we receive the same monetary incentive for the same level of work as another person. However, we feel a sense of inequity if we are undercompensated (receive less reward than others for similar performance) or overcompensated (receive more reward than others for similar performance). If an inequity exists, we are motivated to restore equity. Let's now see how you would respond to eliminate your feeling of inequity and restore your feeling of equity.

According to Adams, our behavioral changes occurring when inequity exists depend upon the way in which we are paid—that is, on whether we are paid on the basis of time (for example, hourly) or on the basis of actual performance (for example, for piecework). If we are paid by time, Adams asserts, feeling undercompensated will cause us to *decrease* our efforts. If we are paid for piecework, feeling undercompensated will cause us to *increase* our efforts. Adams attributes this difference to the fact that we can alter our pay in piecework situations but not hourly situations. Thus, undercompensated people work harder to increase their pay for piecework, but only by *decreasing* their effort will they feel accurately compensated for hourly work.

The behavioral change produced by overcompensation also depends upon the type of task. Adams proposed that people who feel overcompensated for piecework will *decrease* their effort. Thus, by reducing their pay, overcompensated people can feel that they are accurately paid. In contrast, overcompensated people who are paid on an hourly basis cannot reduce their pay. To restore equity, they will increase their effort. The experimental evidence indicates that we will change our level of achievement behavior after discovering an inequity between our compensation and that received by another, or others, for a level of performance which equals ours. Let's now examine two studies supporting Adams's equity theory.

Adams and Rosenbaum (1962) "hired" the subjects in their study to conduct interviews. The experimenters created a feeling of overcompensation in one group of subjects by telling them that although not qualified for their job, they were hired because no qualified people were available ("overcompensation" condition). Subjects in the other groups received no information about their qualifications. These subjects felt that their pay was correct—that no inequity existed ("equity" condition). Half of the subjects in the "overcompensation" condition and half in the "equity" condition were paid on an hourly basis; the remaining subjects in each condition were paid for piecework. Adams and Rosenbaum discovered that the level of performance corresponded to the predictions of equity theory: the subjects being "overcompensated" on an hourly basis worked harder than the equitably paid hourly workers. In contrast, the subjects "overcompensated" for piecework were less productive than subjects paid equitably for piecework.

Pritchard, Dunnette, and Jorgenson (1972) evaluated the equity theory using male subjects who felt either undercompensated or overcompensated for their performance. Theirs was a two-phase study. In the first phase, "hired" subjects performing temporary clerical jobs were paid either a fixed hourly rate or a modified sliding piecework rate. After 3 days of work, the second phase began and the subjects exchanged pay schedules. This procedure created feelings of overcompensation and undercompensation for subjects in each type of pay schedule. Subjects who had been highly productive on an hourly schedule earned more on a piecework schedule and, therefore, felt overcompensated. On the other hand, subjects who had been unproductive on the hourly schedule earned less when shifted to the sliding pay scale. This shift caused them to feel underpaid. The productive workers on the piecework schedule lost when shifted to the hourly schedule and thus felt undercompensated. Finally, unproductive subjects on the piecework schedule earned more on the hourly schedule; this shift caused them to feel overcompensated. Pitchard, Dunnette, and Jorgenson's results supported the predictions of the equity theory. Subjects who felt overcompensated decreased their performance on the piecework schedule and increased it on the hourly schedule. Subjects who felt undercompensated increased their performance on the piecework schedule but decreased it on the hourly schedule. These observations indicate that our response to perceived inequity depends upon the nature of the inequity (undercompensation or overcompensation) and the type of situation in which it occurs.

The Dynamics of Action

Atkinson's theory of achievement motivation, developed during the late 1950s and early 1960s, emphasized the individual and situational determinants of achievement behavior. Thus, according to Atkinson's view, the intensity of achievement behavior depends upon a person's motivational disposition and the characteristics of the achievement task. However, Atkinson and his colleague David Birch recognized in the late 1960s that achievement behavior does not reflect an isolated unit of behavior whose immediate consequences are the only determinant of its occurrence. Instead, Atkinson and Birch's *dynamics of action* theory (see Atkinson & Birch, 1970, 1978) assumes that the perceived consequences of achievement behavior on the attainment of future goals also significantly influence achievement behavior. According to Atkinson and Birch, achievement behavior will be more important to someone whose performance affects future success or failure than to someone whose behavior does not influence the attainment of distant goals. The precise impact of the instrumentality of a task on future success or failure depends upon the person's motivational disposition. The achievement behavior of "High n Ach–low test anxiety" persons is increased by situations in which they expect performance to lead to a future goal. In contrast, "Low n Ach–high test anxiety" persons are motivated to avoid any task which they expect to result in future failure. These observations also indicate that the greatest differences between "High n Ach–low test anxiety" and "Low n Ach–high test anxiety" people will occur in important achievement tasks. Numerous studies have shown the significant impact of future goals on achievement behavior; let's examine two of these studies.

Raynor (1970) first asked introductory psychology students to indicate the significance which their course grade had for their career goals. Students were classified as perceiving the course to be either very important ("high instrumentality") or not important ("low instrumentality"). The perceived instrumentality was then correlated with each student's grade. Raynor discovered that "High n Ach–low test anxiety" students who believed that the course was important had higher grades than "High n Ach–low test anxiety" students who perceived the course to be unimportant. In contrast, among "Low n Ach–high test anxiety" students, grades were higher for those who thought that the course was not instrumental to their career goals than for those who believed that their performance affected distant goals. As expected, the difference between "High n Ach–low test anxiety" and "Low n Ach–high test anxiety" students was greater in students who felt that the class was important. These results show the important influence which the relationship between current behavior and the attainment of future goals has on the level of achievement behavior.

In an experimental study, Raynor and Rubin (1971) told some subjects that their continuance in the experiment—and, therefore, the opportunity to be successful—depended upon how well they performed each task. Other subjects were told that the opportunity to continue was independent of their performance. The number of problems attempted by the "High n Ach–low test anxiety" subjects was higher when achievement performance influenced the opportunity to participate in future tasks than when it did not. "Low n Ach–high test anxiety" subjects attempted more problems if their performance on each task did *not* affect future events than if it did. Again, the greatest difference in performance between "High n Ach–low test anxiety" subjects and "Low n Ach–high test anxiety" subjects occurred in tasks where performance influenced the attainment of future goals.

ACHIEVEMENT MOTIVATION IN WOMEN

If you think that women do not want to do well in competitive achievement tasks, you have an incorrect impression. McClelland, Atkinson, Clark, and Lowell's study (1953) indicated that women tested under a "relaxed" (or "nonachievement") condition do reveal achievement needs on the thematic appreception measure. However, placing women in achievement-oriented conditions decreased their scores on need to achieve. Atkinson (1958) did recognize the importance of sex differences in achievement motivation, but he could not explain why women's desire to be successful decreased under the conditions which produce men's achievement behavior. In 1968, Matina Horner offered an explanation for this.

The Fear of Success

Horner (1968) suggested that women as well as men are motivated to be successful. However, in many women the tendency to approach competitive achievement tasks (T_S) is suppressed by an antagonistic motive similar to the motive to avoid failure (T_{AF}) which inhibits the achievement behavior of many males. According to Horner, many women regard success in competitive achievement tasks as a negative rather than a positive outcome. Horner called this inhibitory motive the *motive to avoid success* (T_{AS}).

Using a modification of the thematic apperception measure of the need to achieve, Horner measured the fear of being successful. Instead of pictures, Horner gave her subjects, 90 women and 88 men enrolled in introductory psychology sections at the University of Michigan in 1965, the first two sentences of stories and then asked them to complete the stories. One of her stories began: "After the first term finals, Ann (John) finds herself (himself) at the top of her (his) med school class." The subjects' response to these stories revealed the motive to avoid success.

Horner reported that 63 percent of the women and 9 percent of the men used imagery in their stories indicating a fear of success. Three main reasons emerged from the stories to explain why women feared success. *First, many women feared that social rejection would result from success.* According to Horner, these women had strong affiliative needs which they thought would be threatened by success in a competitive achievement situation. For example, numerous women's stories indicated that successful female medical doctors are not likely to date or marry. Many women even suggested that women in a competitive achievement situation are deliberately unsuccessful in order to retain friends or marry. *Second, many women feared that success would cause a loss of their femininity or normality.* Horner discovered that many women felt that successful women lose feminine traits and thus are not considered normal by others. *Third, many women denied that women could even be successful in a competitive achievement situation.* For example, some of the women's stories suggested that women could not possibly be medical students; others asserted that only luck could enable women in this situation to get top grades.

Perhaps you're wondering whether the fear of success which is revealed in a story reflects how a male or female will act in a competitive achievement situation. To test the influence of the fear of success on achievement behavior, Horner asked her subjects to participate in either a competitive game or a noncompetitive game 4 days after they had completed the stories. Horner reported that women (and men) who scored high in "fear of success" did better in a noncompetitive task than in a competitive one. In contrast, those women—and most men—who scored low in "fear of success" performed better in a competitive situation than a noncompetitive one. Furthermore, in a noncompetitive achievement task, there were no differences in performance between women with a high fear of success and those with a low fear of success.

The Fear of Failure

Horner assumed that avoidance of success and avoidance of failure were separate motives, both of which reduced the tendency to approach achievement-oriented situations. However, Jackaway and Teevan (1976) proposed that people do not, in fact, fear success. Instead, their apparent fear of success, reflected in their stories, is really a fear that being successful in achievement situations leads to failure in other aspects of their lives. That is, they fear the negative consequences of success, not success itself. Therefore, Jackaway and Teevan's approach assumes that avoidance of success and avoidance of failure are a single motive acting to prevent a person from failing. Let's examine the evidence supporting their view.

The negative consequences of success.   Why does a person fear failure? According to Jackaway and Teevan, there are three reasons. *First, a person's failure conveys information about an underlying personal characteristic.* For example, failing a test can reflect a lack of ability. *Second, failure can cause a loss of social status.* In our society, achievement is a means of attaining social status and approval. People who fail in school lose status or approval. *Finally, failure can lead directly to aversive events other than loss of self-esteem and social devaluation.* Someone who loses a job will also lose the income from that job.

According to Jackaway and Teevan, the stories written by women with high fear of success indicate that their real fear is that failure will follow success. A dominant theme portrayed in their stories is loss of femininity by successful women. Since society considers femininity to be a desired attribute, its loss would represent a negative consequence of success. A second major theme revealed in the stories is social rejection resulting from success. Social rejection reflects failure to attain desired social acceptance and approval, and it is thus an aversive event.

It is not difficult to understand why many women believe that achievement will produce a loss of femininity and social rejection. Our culture provides clear evidence of the conflict which exists between many women's need to achieve and society's expectations for them (see Feather & Raphelson, 1974). According to traditional sex-role stereotypes, if a woman attempts to have a career, this aspiration will interfere with her being able to marry and rear a family. In contrast, society assumes that males are able to have both a successful career and a family. One vivid illustration of this conflict between achievement motives and affilitative motives which occurs in women but not in men can be seen in the portrayal of successful men and women on television. Mances and Melynk (1974) discovered that television usually characterizes successful women as single, divorced, or widowed. The successful man, on the other hand, almost always has a wife and children. If a woman attempts to have a career, her conflict is likely to be intensified by other people's actions. For example, Winter, Steward, and McClelland (1977) reported that husbands sometimes oppose their spouse's attempt to pursue a career. Spence (1974) noted that many males express negative feelings toward successful women.

In addition to the conflict between marriage and career, sex-role stereotypes also make it difficult for successful career women to consider themselves feminine. The study by Williams, Bennett, and Best (1975) illustrates that most people view male behavior and female behavior differently. They asked male college students and female college students to select adjectives from a list of 300 words describing males and females. Interestingly, the results showed a 75 percent agreement among both males and females on 33 male characteristics and 30 female traits. The students described males as being more ambitious, assertive, confident, dominant, independent, logical, rational, and unemotional than females. In contrast, they thought females to be more affectionate, charming, emotional, fickle, frivolous, high-strung, nagging, sentimental, and talkative than males. These stereotypes, reflecting how both males and female *think* both sexes should act, also imply that any substantial variation from these stereotyped traits is likely to produce rejection from others. For example, potential clients are likely to avoid an aggressive female salesperson; but an aggressive male salesperson is frequently accepted and, therefore, successful.

Empirical support.   Several types of evidence support Jackaway and Teevan's view that fear of success is in reality a fear of the aversive consequences of success. The significant positive correlations between measures of the fear of success and the fear of failure which Jackaway and Teevan reported represent indirect support of their view. This result indicates that people who fear success are also likely to fear failure. We should note, however, that the correlation is not perfect ($r = .42$ for males and $r = .57$ for females); this is not surprising since "fear of success" imagery does not reflect the negative consequences of failure. Many people do expect to fail at achievement tasks; this expectation would be evident in their "fear of failure" stories but not in their "fear of success" stories. Nevertheless, the high correlations do indicate that the two measures are related. We now turn our attention to more direct support for the view that fear of success equals fear of failure.

If Jackaway and Teevan's analysis of the fear of success is accurate, then women with a high fear of success should exhibit the same characteristics as men with a high fear of failure. Evidence does point out that women with a high fear of success and men with a high fear of failure who expect to fail in achievement situations do in fact respond in similar ways.

We saw earlier in the chapter that men with a high fear of failure avoid achievement tasks because they expect to fail. Patty's study (1976) indicates that women with a high fear of success avoid those careers in which they feel that being successful would have negative consequences. He reported that such women were often career-oriented but chose traditional female occupations which do not lead to a perceived loss of femininity or social rejection. In contrast, women with a low fear of success aspired to nontraditional occupations.

Recall that men with a high need to achieve and a high fear of failure showed a strong ambivalence toward achievement tasks; this suggests a strong conflict between the motive to succeed and the motive to avoid failure. A similar conflict between achievement and social needs can be seen in women with a high fear of success. Patty (1976), reporting that these women felt ambivalent toward their professional goals and their interpersonal goals, demonstrated a perceived antagonism between those goals.

Although Horner's original study (1968) indicated that women with a high fear of success performed better at noncompetitive tasks than competitive tasks, Zuckerman and Wheeler (1975) found no consistent evidence in the literature to indicate that competition affects these women adversely. Argote, Fisher, McDonald, and O'Neal's study (1976) indicated that only when people expect their success on a competitive task to lead to rejection will fear of success lead to poor performance. In their study, male and female subjects competed with either a member of the same sex or a member of the opposite sex on an anagram task. Only one person in each competition was a "real" subject; the other was a confederate who deliberately won the competition with some subjects and deliberately lost with other subjects. Following completion of the task, the experimenter informed the subject and confederate that they would be interviewed separately to give their evaluation of each other. Then the real subjects, wearing earphones, heard the confederate's evaluation of them. In the "acceptance" condition, the subjects heard the confederate indicate a liking of them and a desire to work with them again. In the "rejection" condition, the confederate indicated a dislike of the subjects and no desire to work with them again.

Argote, Fisher, McDonald, and O'Neal found that the "rejection" condition coupled with success on the task or "acceptance" coupled with failure caused subjects to perform more poorly with a second confederate than they had performed with the first. These results indicate that when social acceptance seems to conflict with achievement, subjects reduce their level of achievement behavior in order to prevent future rejection. The experimenters also reported that achievement behavior with a second confederate was not affected when the "acceptance" condition was coupled with success on the first task or the "rejection" condition was coupled with failure. Failure should reduce the subjects' performance with the second confederate; but it is reasonable to assume that in this case fear of social rejection for having failed counteracted the effects of fear of failure. This interpretation suggests that people will continue to exhibit a high level of achievement behavior until the fear of failure outweighs the negative consequences (social rejection) of failure.

It should be noted that the percentage of women revealing a high fear of success in their stories has significantly declined since Horner's observations in 1965. Horner reported that 63 percent of the women in her study revealed a high fear of success. In studies conducted during the early 1970s (Zuckerman & Wheeler, 1975) the percentage was found to be between 20 and 40. These results suggest that the perceived negative consequences of success for females in "masculine" tasks has declined since 1965. In contrast, the percentage of males with a high fear of success has increased dramatically since 1965. Horner found that only 9 percent of her male subjects revealed a high fear of success in their stories; Zuckerman and Wheeler (1975) reported that the percentage of males with a high fear of success appears to be equivalent to the percentage of females. However, males' and females' stories differ slightly with regard to fear of success. Tresemer (1976) evaluated such stories and reported that men with a high fear of success are more likely to devalue success and achievement and to doubt the worth of their sacrifices for success. In contrast, women with a high fear of success more often revealed social rejection, loss of gender identity, and affiliative loss. Evidently, the negative consequences of success in competitive tasks are as evident now for males as for females; yet, the nature of the aversive consequences differs between the sexes.

Although most research exploring women's achievement motivation has focused on fear of success, evidence indicates that in noncompetitive tasks women reveal as much need to achieve as men (Macoby & Jacklin, 1974). In addition, Bar-Tal and Frieze (1977) discovered that women also have individual differences in the level of their motive to be successful; in their TAT stories, some women show a high need to achieve and others a low need. These observations indicate that many women are motivated to approach success in achievement situations.

It seems that there are also women who actually do fear failure at competitive achievement tasks. Recall that Jackaway and Teevan did not observe a perfect correspondence between women's scores on "fear of failure" and their scores on "fear of success." This suggests that factors other than fear of success contribute to women's fear of failure. One likely source of fear of failure, other than fear of success, is anxiety over perceived failure to reach a stated goal. Several observations support this view. You learned earlier that men with a high fear of failure have a low expectation of success in achievement situations. Numerous studies (see Crandall, 1969; Feather, 1969; House, 1974; Macoby & Jacklin, 1974) have pointed out that many females have low expectations of success in competitive achievement tasks with males. An expectation of failure causes males with a high fear of failure to perform achievement tasks poorly. Similarly, Morgan and Mauser (1973) discovered that many competent women placed in competition with a male performed at a lower level than the male, even when the male was less competent than the female and the woman's level of fear of success was unrelated to her level of task performance. Apparently, many women's expectation of failing in a competitive achievement situation causes them to perform poorly.

AN ATTRIBUTIONAL VIEW

Suppose that you did either well or poorly on the last examination in your motivation course. What determines your expectation of future success or failure on the next one? According to Weiner (1980), the perceived cause of the grade on the last examination determines your expectation of doing well or poorly on the next one. If this is so, you will probably want to know what process governed your perception of the cause of success or failure.

Two processes determine your perception: attributional style and situational factors. *First, people attribute their success or failure to different causes.* Two people with different attributional styles may believe that different causes lead to success or failure. If these two persons develop different attributions of success or failure in a task, their expectation of future success on that task or a similar task will also differ. *Second, there are situational determinants of causal attributions.* A person may perceive that different causes produced success or failure in two separate achievement tasks. If so, he or she will have different expectations about future success or failure on these two tasks (or similar tasks). The relative contribution of individual and situational determinants of causal attributions varies. Some people employ the same attributional style in all situations; others treat each type of achievement task separately. The next two sections will describe the individual and situational factors which determine causal attributions in achievement situations. Experimental evidence supporting the situational determinants of causal attributions was presented in Chapter 3. This section examines the role of situational attributions only briefly; the focus is on how individual causal attributions influence achievement behavior. Interested readers should consult Weiner (1980) for a review of the research supporting the influence of the situation in determining causal attributions of success and failure. You may find it helpful now to review the section on attribution theory in Chapter 3.

Situational Determinants of Causal Attributions

Weiner (1980) identified four factors—ability, effort, difficulty, and luck—to which a person can attribute past successes or failures on an achievement task. According to Weiner, high ability, intense effort, ease of the task, and good luck are thought to increase the likelihood of success; low ability, lack of effort, difficulty of the task, and bad luck can increase the perceived probability of failure.

As we saw in Chapter 3, whether or not a particular attribution of past success or failure leads to an expectation of future success or failure is a complex but predictable matter. Someone who has attributed past success in a *simple* task to either high ability or high effort will expect future success on the same (or a similar) achievement task. In contrast, only someone who believes that a lack of both ability and effort caused failure will expect to fail future simple achievement tasks. This observation is true because an intense effort can offset a low ability, and high ability can counteract a lack of effort.

The expectation of future success in *difficult* tasks depends upon the attribution of past success to both high ability and great effort. If a person attributes past failure in a difficult task to either low ability or lack of effort, this person will expect to fail the same type of future task. This conclusion is based on the assumption that both ability and effort are necessary to succeed in a difficult task; the absence of either high ability or intense effort will automatically lead to failure in a difficult task.

We must note that such attributions are independent of the influence of luck. A person attributing past success to good luck may expect to succeed on future achievement tasks even when ability or effort is absent. In contrast, people believing that they have bad luck may expect to fail even when ability or effort is present.

Our discussion thus far has been based on the idea that the factors which cause success or failure are stable. Persons who assume that perceived causes are unstable may change their future expectations after either success or failure. For example, students attributing failure on an examination to lack of effort may not expect future failure if they believe that they can increase their effort. Persons attributing past success to good luck may not expect future success if they think that their good luck will change.

How do we decide if ability or luck determined our success or failure in an achievement situation? Four decision rules were described on Chapter 3: distinctiveness, consistency, consensus, and type of setting. These are used, along with specific information about the environment, to determine what factor or factors actually lead to success or failure. Let's see how the first three of these decision rules influence the attribution process in an achievement situation. (The influence of the type of setting was detailed earlier in this section.)

We may attribute a *distinctive* (or unique) outcome to an external factor (difficulty of a task, luck) and a nondistinctive (or typical) outcome to an internal factor (ability, effort). Consider the following example to illustrate this decision rule. Suppose that you have always received high grades on your motivation examinations. If you get another good grade, you might attribute your success to ability, effort, or both. If you fail, you may think that the test was too difficult or that you were unlucky, or both.

The *consensus* of outcome also determines whether you will assume an internal or external factor to be responsible for success or failure in an achievement task. If most other people have done as well as you, or as poorly as you, on an achievement task, you are likely to attribute your own performance to an external rather than an internal factor.

The *consistency* of past experiences controls whether or not we attribute success or failure to a stable factor (ability, difficulty) or an unstable factor (effort, luck). A person who has consistently either passed or failed a subject is likely to attribute that outcome to a stable factor rather than an unstable factor.

We have focused on the ideal situational determinants of causal attributions of success and failure in achievement situations. However, sometimes the environmental information is not precise. For example, suppose that you and all your classmates did well on your last motivation examination and on all previous ones. You would then be receiving information low in distinctiveness but high in consensus. Would you base your attribution on distinctiveness or consensus? The low distinctiveness suggests an internal attribution, but the high consensus implies an external one. In this case, what you will perceive as the cause depends upon your attributional style. Some people would attribute success to an internal factor (high ability or effort); others to an external factor (ease of task, or luck).

Some people make the same attributions in all achievement situations. Other people use one attributional style for one type of achievement circumstances and another style for a different type of circumstances. For example, a student may attribute failure in mathematics to lack of ability and failure in English to lack of effort. Such an attribution will cause this student to stop trying to succeed in mathematics but to intensify his or her efforts in English. Let's turn our attention to the influence of attributional style in achievement situations.

Attributional Style and Achievement Behavior

In Chapter 8, we saw that our attributional style affects the likelihood of our becoming severely depressed. Weiner's attributional approach to achievement behavior assumes that "High n Ach–low test anxiety" and "Low n Ach–high test anxiety" people make different attributions for their successes and failures. Their different attributional styles cause them to develop different expectations of future success and failure on achievement tasks. These different expectations, according to Weiner, produce the achievement behavior characteristic of them. This section describes the attributional styles of these two types of people. The studies investigating attribution theory refer to "High n Ach–low test anxiety" people as *high-achievement-motivated* people and to "Low n Ach–high test anxiety" people as *low-achievement-motivated* people. This terminology is used in the following description of attribution theory.

Attributional style of high-achievement-motivated people. Why do high-achievement-motivated people approach achievement-related activities? According to the attributional view, they attribute past successes to high ability and effort and, thus, expect future success. This expectation motivates them to approach achievement tasks.

Also, high-achievement-motivated people assume that a high degree of effort, as well as ability, is necessary for them to be successful. The expectation that effort results in success causes the high level of achievement behavior characteristic of these people.

Suppose that a high-achievement-motivated person fails in an initial attempt to reach a goal. The person who attributes success to effort believes that a lack of effort causes failure. Thus, following failure, this person actually increases the intensity of achievement behavior. Heightened effort after failing is responsible for the high level of persistence displayed by high-achievement-motivated people.

Attributional style of low-achievement-motivated people. Low-achievement moti- vated people attribute past failures to a lack of ability and past successes to external factors. Furthermore, they believe that effort is not a causal agent in producing success; therefore, they do not feel that increased effort will produce success. Since success in achievement tasks requires ability, effort, or both, low-achievement-motivated persons expect to fail an achievement task. This expectation of failure motivates them to avoid achievement tasks. In contrast, they will approach any situation in which external factors, such as luck, lead to success.

Perhaps you have noticed that the attributions for failure (internal, stable, global) made by depressives and people susceptible to depression are similar to those made by low-achievement-motivated people. There is one difference: the depressive expects to fail in all situations, whereas the low-achievement-motivated person will probably expect to fail only in achievement situations.

The belief of the low-achievement-motivated person that level of effort does not affect outcome in achievement situations also determines the intensity of achievement behavior. Since low-achievement-motivated people assume that effort does not affect outcome, they feel no need to exert effort to obtain a desired goal. This expectation produces the low level of effort which these people exhibit when they do participate in an achievement task. Their lack of effort, again, resembles the apathetic behavior typical of depressives. However, the motivated behavior of depressed persons differs from that of low-achievement-motivated people: depressives typically exhibit a low level of motiva- tion in all situations; low-achievement-motivated people limit their lack of effort to achievement tasks.

From an attributional viewpoint, what causes the lack of persistence shown by low-achievement-motivated people who have failed? According to this theory, these people believe that lack of either ability or luck caused their failure. This attribution, plus the belief that success is impossible without ability or luck, will increase their expectation of future failure; and that expectation increases their motivation to escape from achievement tasks. The low persistence often shown by these people after failure reflects this increased motivation to leave the achievement situation. Once again, this lack of persistence resembles depressives' lack of effort. The difference between low-achievement-motivated people and clinically depressed people is the extent of their lack of persistence: low-achievement-motivated people limit low persistence to achievement tasks; clinically depressed people show it in all situations.

Empirical support. Weiner (1980) has noted that although some investigations show the predicted differences between high-achievement-motivated people and low-achievement-motivated people, others do not. In addition, some studies report attributional differences in the predicted direction which, though significant, are not as pronounced as one would expect after having read the achievement motivation literature. There is a logical reason for this lack of consistency. Instead of using only "very high" and "very low" achievement-motivated people, attribution studies have merely split the subject population above and below the mean. As a result of this procedure, people whose attributions depend upon the situation appear in both of these groups. It seems that limiting such studies to "very high" and "very low" subjects would provide more definitive results. In Chapter 8, we saw that attributional style can be used to predict susceptibility to depression. A similar technique could be used to validate the significance of attributional style and achievement behavior. However, there is sufficient evidence from direct research to allow the tentative conclusion that Weiner's attributional view of achievement behavior is accurate. In addition, Weiner's approach is consistent with all the literature on the behavioral differences between high-achievement-motivated people and low-achievement-motivated people.

Kulka (1972) investigated the attributions of success and failure on achievement tasks of high- and low-achievement-motivated male subjects. The subjects were asked to guess whether the next number in a series of digits would be 0 or 1. The subjects had been led to believe that the series of digits formed a pattern, but in fact the digits were presented at random. As a result, some subjects believed that they had succeeded and others that they had failed. After responding, the subjects were asked to indicate the reason for their success or failure. Kulka reported that the high-achievement-motivated subjects were more likely than the low-achievement-motivated subjects to attribute success to a high degree of ability and effort and failure to lack of effort. Low-achievement-motivated subjects were more likely than high-achievement-motivated subjects to attribute failure to lack of ability. These results support Weiner's view.

Kulka's data also show that high-achievement-motivated men believe that they have high ability on achievement tasks and that effort and outcome are related. High-achievement-motivated males who fail achievement tasks believe that lack of effort caused their failure and that trying harder would have enabled them to succeed. This indicates that high-achievement-motivated men think that they can control outcome (success or failure). In contrast, low-achievement-motivated males feel that they have low ability and that effort cannot compensate for this. Consequently, they do not feel that they can control achievement-oriented events.

Other studies have also evaluated the attributions of high- and low-achievement-motivated people. Let's examine two of them. The first shows results identical to Kulka's and the second shows results slightly different from Kulka's.

Frieze (1973) obtained identical results from an anagram task in which high- and low-achievement-motivated males participated. Using high- and low-achievement-motivated male and female subjects, Bar-Tal and Frieze (1977) replicated Frieze's anagram study. Bar-Tal and Frieze reported that high-achievement-motivated males and females were more apt to attribute success to high ability and effort than low-achievement-motivated males and females. In contrast, low-achievement-motivated men and women were more likely to believe that lack of ability caused their failure. These results, predicted by Weiner's attributional approach, are identical to Kulka's and Frieze's.

However, one observation from Bar-Tal and Frieze's study appears to contradict Weiner's attributional approach. Bar-Tal and Frieze did not find that high-achievement-motivated males and females attributed failure at an achievement task to lack of effort. There is an explanation for this: the high-achievement-motivated males and females considered the task easier than the low-achievement-motivated males and females. We saw in Chapter 3 that ability or effort alone is sufficient to produce success in an easy task. High-achievement-motivated people cannot attribute failure at an easy task to lack of effort, because they perceive that they have the ability to succeed at it despite lack of effort. Under these circumstances, they must attribute failure to bad luck. This apparently contradictory result indicates that environmental circumstances can alter the type of attributions which people typically make for success and failure. It also presents another likely reason why research investigating the attributional style of high-achievement-motivated people and low-achievement-motivated people does not always produce the same results.

A change in attributional style.   Can our attributional style in achievement tasks be altered? And if so, would this affect our achievement behavior? The answer to both questions appears to be positive, suggesting that one effective method of altering people's lack of achievement motivation is to change the way in which they account for past successes and failures. It also suggests one reason why the treatment developed by McClelland and Winter (described earlier in this chapter) effectively altered the behavior of low-achievement-motivated people.

Heckhausen (1972) selected 30 fourth-grade low-achievement-motivated subjects: these children had poor school records but average IQs. Ten of them underwent a 14-week motivation-training program. The program included the procedures outlined earlier in our discussion of McClelland and Winter's treatment as well as cognitive restructuring procedures designed to help the children plan goals, calculate their own output of effort, state causal attributions, and reward themselves for success. Before the program, these children—like other low-achievement-motivated subjects—attributed failure to low ability. After the program, they attributed failure less to lack of ability and more to lack of effort. In addition, they set their goals more realistically, rewarded themselves more for success, and punished themselves less for failure, and their academic achievement improved dramatically. Heckhausen employed two control conditions in his study. One control group merely worked on simple scholastic exercises and played games for a time period equivalent to that of the training program. The second control group received only the pretests and posttests for attributional style and achievement behavior. No changes in causal attributions of either success or failure—or any of the achievement behaviors—occurred in the two control groups. Apparently, a change in attributional style accompanies the increased achievement behaviors produced by motivation-change treatments. Although it cannot be determined whether the change of attribution caused the increased achievement behavior, that seems to be a reasonable conclusion if we consider our understanding of the influence of cognitive processes on motivated behavior. Additional research is necessary to indicate whether cognitive restructuring of attributional style represents a potentially effective way of improving the achievement behavior of low-achievement-motivated people.

SUMMARY

All of us differ in our response to achievement situations. Some of us show an intense desire to perform achievement tasks well, while others seem indifferent to achievement-oriented situations. Still others actively avoid engaging in achievement tasks.

McClelland's research focuses on the need to achieve, showing that High n Ach people are more motivated to perform in achievement situations, are more likely to choose tasks involving moderate risks, respond at a more efficient level, and persist longer following failure than Low n Ach people. In addition, McClelland reported that training for independence and mastery in early childhood seems to be responsible for the development of achievement motivation; and the need to achieve appears to make people suitable for a successful entrepreneurial career. Finally, McClelland also noted that a particular society's level of achievement motivation influences its economic level.

Atkinson identified another motive, the fear of failure, which antagonizes the hope of success. "High test anxiety" people are motivated to avoid achievement-oriented situations; if required to engage in achievement tasks, they are more likely than "low test anxiety" people to select tasks involving extreme risk. Also, high fear of failure lowers both the efficiency and the persistence of achievement behavior.

According to Atkinson, our achievement behavior (T_A) reflects the combined influence of the hope of success (T_S) and the fear of failure (T_{AF}). The tendency to approach success is equal to a person's internal motive to achieve success (M_S) × the perceived probability of success (P_S) × the incentive value of success (I_S). In contrast, the tendency to avoid failure is equal to each person's internal motive to avoid failure (M_{AF}) × the perceived expectancy of failure (P_F) × the negative incentive value of failure $(-I_F)$. The achievement behavior of High n Ach people, described by McClelland, occurs when $M_S > M_{AF}$. The achievement behavior of "high test anxiety" people, described by Atkinson, occurs when $M_S < M_{AF}$. If these two motives are equivalent $(M_S = M_{AF})$, a person exhibits ambivalence toward achievement situations. When required to participate in achievement tasks, "High n Ach–high test anxiety" and "Low n Ach–low test anxiety" people exhibit behavior that falls between that of high- and low-achievement-motivated people. Atkinson and Birch's "dynamics of action approach" indicates that both immediate and distant consequences determine the intensity of achievement behavior.

Early research on achievement motivation in women indicated that the arousal conditions which intensify achievement imagery in TAT stories actually reduced the level of achievement motivation which women's stories revealed. Horner suggested that for most women, achievement-oriented situations activate a fear of success. This fear of success inhibits their need to achieve, so that their achievement motivation is lowered. However, recent research indicates that women's fear of success actually reflects a fear of its aversive consequences: loss of femininity, social rejection, or both. Fear of these consequences motivates many women to avoid achievement tasks. Although women's level of fear of success has declined during the last decade, many males now appear to be afraid of the negative consequences of success. In the case of males, these consequences are perceived as the effort needed for success, loss of other environmental rewards, or both. Such perceptions motivate men with a high fear of success to avoid achievement tasks. Other research shows that many women, like many men, have either a strong need to achieve, an intense fear of failure, or both.

Weiner, investigating the attributional determinants of people's expectations of success or failure in achievement situations, discovered that there are both situational and personal factors involved. Many people use specific environmental information to evaluate whether ability, effort, difficulty of a task, and luck affect performance on achievement tasks. Other people make global attributions for their successes or failures. High-achievement-motivated people usually attribute success to high ability and effort, and failure to lack of effort. In contrast, low-achievement-motivated people seem to attribute success to external factors and failure to lack of ability.

However, there is hope for low-achievement-motivated people. McClelland and Winter developed a motivation-change program which significantly improved the performance of low-achievement-motivated people. This treatment also changed the subjects' attributional style: before treatment, they attributed failure to low ability; after treatment, they attributed it to lack of effort. This change may be responsible for the increased achievement produced by such programs.

CONSISTENCY MOTIVATION

CHAPTER 11

An act of mercy

*J*une's physical appearance shocked her brother Wesley. She had seemed to be in perfect health just 6 months ago when they had seen each other at home during Christmas vacation. They had even skied several times; Wesley still marveled over the fact that she was by far the better skier. During their walks from home to town, June talked enthusiastically of her plans to attend law school next year. She seemed to know what she wanted from life, and he was glad to see her happy.

Six months later, illness abruptly interrupted June's life. When Wesley learned of June's sickness, his first impulse was to be with her; however, his parents persuaded him to remain at medical school and finish the semester which would end in only a few weeks. Wesley managed to stay, but he flew home as soon as he had taken his last examination. Although his parents had told him of June's condition, he was unprepared for her frailty. He now wished that he had come home to be with her before she had become so weak.

June talked to Wesley alone, telling him of her intolerable pain and that, although the doctors tried to encourage her, she knew that death was inevitable. She thought that her illness has been an enormous burden to their parents, and she did not want them to suffer any longer. Wesley suspected the direction that his sister's conversation was taking, but before he could stop her, she had blurted it out: she wanted him to help her die. She did not want her family to remember her as an invalid, but as the vital person she had been before her illness.

Wesley was dumbfounded by June's request. He mulled the idea over and over again in his mind; however, he could not waver from his belief that mercy killing was wrong. If medical school had taught him anything, he felt that it should have taught him this. In fact, he remembered recently discussing the morality of euthanasia with several other medical students and asserting that he was against it. When he visited June in the hospital the next day, he told her of his decision.

But as the endless, agonizing days became endless agonizing weeks, Wesley was no longer certain that his decision was right. June continued to endure excruciating pain—and to make the same request each time he visited her. Finally, unable to tolerate the situation any more, Wesley told June that he would help her when she was ready. Three days later, she asked him for

the pills which would end her ordeal. He stayed with her while she took them, kissed her, and tearfully watched as she died. Although he would miss his sister dearly, he now felt that mercy killing was appropriate under certain circumstances. The thought of June dying a slow, painful death made his decision seem correct.

You might think that someone who feels that mercy killing is wrong would not have helped his sister and certainly would not feel afterwards that this action was justifiable. However, under some conditions, people like Wesley act in a manner that is inconsistent with their attitudes. In addition, doing something that is contrary to their attitudes often causes these persons to change their beliefs. Yet, in other circumstances, people do not change their attitudes, even though they behave inconsistently. This chapter discusses the conditions in which we will and will not change our attitudes. Chapter 12 will detail the processes which motivate us to act in a manner which is inconsistent with our attitudes.

THE NEED TO BE CONSISTENT

Cognitive Consistency

Leon Festinger (1957) suggested that we desire consistent information about ourselves and our environment. This knowledge, providing certainty and stability to our lives, also enables us to interact effectively with our environment in order to obtain desired rewards and to avoid adversity.

How do we establish this consistent information about ourselves and our environment? We form *attitudes* about objects, persons, or issues which provide us with a cognitive understanding of the environment and inform us how to respond to it. We are motivated to adhere to our attitudes in order to maintain our sense of consistency. Suppose that a classmate asks you to attend a party at his or her house this weekend. Will you go? Your decision depends upon whether you have a positive or a negative attitude toward the classmate or toward parties. In order to understand the basis for your decision, we must look at the concept of an attitude, how attitudes are formed, and their influence on motivated behavior.

What Is an Attitude?

Psychologists (see Berkowitz, 1980) have not always agreed on the definition of *attitude*. Early definitions were much more restrictive than the contemporary view. Louis Thurstone (1946) stated that an attitude is an evaluation of or a feeling toward an object, a person, or an issue. According to Thurstone's view, your positive or negative feeling about your classmate and parties is an example of an attitude. Gordon Allport's definition (1935) assumed that an attitude was not only an affective reaction, but also a readiness to respond in a specific manner toward an object, person, or issue. Thus, you not only like or dislike your classmate and parties but also will react in a particular way when this classmate asks you to a party. If you like your classmate or parties (or both), you probably will go; on the other hand, if you dislike this person or parties (or both), you undoubtedly will not attend.

These early approaches to defining an attitude reflect the drive view which dominated psychology during the 1930s through the 1950s. However, in addition to the affective behavioral components of an attitude, contemporary cognitively oriented psychologists see a third component, the cognitive aspect. This cognitive aspect reflects our understanding of the causes of the affective and behavioral components. To illustrate the cognitive aspect of an attitude, let's return to our example and consider why you like or dislike the classmate and parties. The cognitive approach suggests that the reason will be either favorable or unfavorable past experiences. Attending or not attending the party reflects an expectation of repeating positive experiences or avoiding negative ones.

The Establishment of an Attitude

Three processes appear to govern the formation of an attitude: *classical conditioning, instrumental conditioning,* and *imitation* (see Lamberth, 1980). The next three sections will present evidence which indicates that this is true.

Classical conditioning.   An attitude can be developed through the classical conditioning process. According to this view, we develop either a positive or a negative attitude to a conditioned stimulus—an object, a person, or an issue—by associating it with an unconditioned stimulus—either a pleasant or an unpleasant experience. Let's see how the classical conditioning process can explain your attitude toward your classmate and parties. If you have enjoyed yourself with your classmate and at parties, you probably will develop a positive attitude toward this person and parties. However, if your past experiences with your classmate and parties have been unenjoyable, you will have a negative attitude toward both of them.

Arthur Staats and his colleagues (see Staats, 1970; Staats & Staats, 1957, 1958; Staats, Staats, & Biggs, 1958; Staats, Higa, & Reid, 1970; Staats, Minke, Martin, & Higa, 1972) demonstrated that an attitude can be developed through the classical conditioning process. In their studies, subjects saw either a name, a neutral word, or a nonsense syllable paired with an emotionally laden word. For example, the name Bill (or a neutral word like *red* or the nonsense syllable YOF) was presented with a pleasant word such as *happy;* the name Tom (or the neutral word *yellow* or the nonsense syllable XEH) was paired with an unpleasant word such as *ugly.* After the names (or neutral words or nonsense syllables) and emotional words were presented, the subjects were asked to rate the names (or neutral words or nonsense syllables) on a "pleasant-unpleasant" dimension. Staats reported that the classical conditioning experience altered the emotional reaction to a name or a neutral word. Other researchers (for example, Berkowitz & Knurek, 1969; Blandford & Sampson, 1964; Das & Nauda, 1963) have also shown that the affective response to names or neutral words can be developed by pairing them with either a pleasant word or an unpleasant word.

Zanna, Kiesler, and Pilkonis's study (1970) indicated that an affective reaction to a word can be acquired by using positive or negative events rather than emotionally laden words. In the first phase of their study subjects were shocked. Before receiving the shock, some subjects heard the word *light;* before the shock was terminated, these subjects heard the word *dark.* Other subjects heard the word *dark* before the shock and *light* before its termination. In the second phase of the study, a second experimenter was introduced to the subjects, to give them the impression that they were now participating in a different study. In this phase of the study, the subjects completed a number of tasks, one of which included a semantic differential scale with the words *light* and *dark.* Such a scale gives an

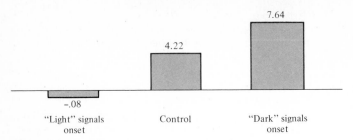

Figure 11.1
Affective reaction to the word light *when it preceded onset of shock, when it was not associated with shock, or when it preceded termination of shock. (From Zanna, M. P., Kiesler, C. A., & Pilkonis, P. Positive and negative attitudinal effect established by classical conditioning.* Journal of Personality and Social Psychology, *1970, 14, 321–328. Copyright 1970 by the American Psychological Association. Reprinted by permission.)*

indication of a subject's affective response to an object, a person, or an issue. Zanna, Kiesler, and Pilkonis found that their subjects exhibited a neutral attitude to the word (*light* or *dark*) associated with onset of shock and a slightly favorable reaction to control words (see Figure 11.1). In contrast, they showed a strong positive attitude to the word (*dark* or *light*) paired with termination of shock, a positive experience. These results again illustrate that both positive and negative attitudes are acquired as the result of experience with pleasant or unpleasant events.

You might think that there is a great difference between an affective reaction to a word and an emotional response to a person or a situation. However, recall from Chapter 9 that we like people whom we meet under pleasant conditions and dislike those whom we meet under unpleasant conditions.

Attitudes also can be acquired vicariously. Bandura (1965) assumed that we can develop attitudes by observing the experiences of other people. Thus, if you have never been to one of your classmate's parties, you can still develop a positive or a negative attitude toward the forthcoming party by listening to other people's experiences. Berger's study (1962) demonstrates the vicarious conditioning of an affective reaction to a neutral stimulus. His subjects listened to a neutral tone and then saw another person apparently receiving a painful electrical shock (this other person was actually a confederate who only pretended to be hurt). Subjects who repeatedly witnessed the scene preceded by the tone developed an emotional response to the tone.

Instrumental conditioning. We can develop attitudes through the instrumental conditioning process. Reward for expressing an opinion (or a belief) about an object, a person, or an issue creates a positive attitude; likewise, punishment for expressing an opinion (or a belief) about an object, a person, or an issue creates a negative attitude. (An opinion or a belief is the cognitive component of an attitude; a value reflects the affective aspect of the attitude.) As the result of this reward (or punishment), you develop a positive (or a negative) attitude toward the object, person, or issue.

Let's use our example of the party to illustrate the influence of instrumental conditioning on attitudes. Suppose that when another classmate asks you if you are going to the party, you reply, although you are unsure of whether or not to attend, that you think that you will go. The instrumental conditioning approach assumes that this classmate's reaction to your answer will affect your attitude toward the party. If the classmate indicates that you are making the correct decision, this social approval will cause you to develop a positive attitude toward the party. However, if the classmate says that your decision to attend is foolish, you will acquire a negative attitude about the party.

Numerous studies (see Lamberth, 1980) support the important role which instrumental conditioning plays in the development of an attitude. To illustrate this effect, let's consider Insko's study (1965). Insko's assistants telephoned students at the University of Hawaii, asking them 15 redundant questions concerning whether or not an "Aloha Week" festival should be established each fall. For half the subjects, the interviewer said "good" when they indicated support of the festival; for the other half, the interviewer said "good" when they gave a response which indicated opposition to the festival. A week after the interview, all the subjects received a questionnaire about various issues; one question concerned the proposed festival. Insko discovered that subjects who had received the verbal reinforcement for positive comments expressed a significantly more favorable attitude toward the festival than the subjects who had been given verbal reinforcements for statements opposed to the festival. These results demonstrated that reinforcement can lead to acquisition of an attitude.

We saw earlier that we can acquire attitudes vicariously by observing other people's pleasant or unpleasant experiences. It also seems that we can develop an attitude by watching other people being rewarded or punished for expressing their attitude. For example, suppose that you see someone being criticized for indicating that he or she is going to your classmate's party. As the result of your observation, you will probably develop a negative attitude toward the party.

Imitation. An attitude can also be established through imitation. In Chapter 3, we learned that when children's aggressive motivation is aroused, they will imitate aggressive behaviors which they have just seen adults exhibit. These children's aggressive imitative behavior illustrates Bandura's social-learning view that we can learn many behaviors through watching or listening to others. The reduced aversiveness of a phobic object which occurs through modeling (see Chapter 3) is another example of the imitative-learning process.

Does Our Attitude Affect How We Act?

Suppose that you like parties; that is, you have a positive affective reaction to parties, you expect to have a pleasant time at them, and you have a strong approach response to attend parties. Will this positive attitude motivate you to attend your classmate's party? You probably think that since you like parties, the answer is yes. However, the answer to this question, as well as to the more general one of whether attitudes predict behavior, involves more than just your attitude. We'll see next that personal characteristics and situational factors determine whether or not our attitudes result in overt behavior.

Investigations of the relationship between attitude and behavior have yielded quite disparate results. Some studies indicate that the correlation between how people feel and how they act is often quite low; other experiments demonstrate that people do act according to their attitudes. How can we reconcile these different observations? Berkowitz (1980) identified four conditions which govern the transformation of an attitude into behavior. *First, the situation must arouse our attitude. Second, we must be confident of the correctness of our attitude. Third, we must intend to carry out the required behavior. Fourth, we must know how to implement the appropriate response.* Unless each of these four conditions is satisfied, our behavior may not reflect our attitude.

Motive arousal.   We often behave automatically without thinking about the relationship between our behavior and our attitude. Sometimes we respond contrarily to our attitude. Only when a situation arouses our affective reaction and causes us to consider how we should act in a particular situation can our behavior always coincide with our attitude.

Consider the following example to illustrate motive arousal. Most of us feel that all people should receive equal pay for the same type of work. Suppose that you read that a particular company has discriminatory pay practices. Would this stop you from buying its products? In all likelihood, it would not, even though this behavior is contrary to your attitude. The reason for your probable failure to adhere to your attitude is that reading the story did not cause you to recall that you oppose this company's practices. Even remembering your negative attitude toward such discrimination might not cause you to recognize that it is inconsistent for you to continue buying from this company. However, if the story reminded you of your attitude by pointing out that purchasing this company's products implies an endorsement of discrimination, you might stop buying them. Snyder and Swann's study (1976) illustrates this kind of influence.

Snyder and Swann assessed the attitudes of male undergraduate students toward affirmative action for women. Several weeks later, the same subjects were asked to state their attitudes about a lawsuit involving affirmative action. Before replying, half of them were asked to organize their thoughts about affirmative action—a device to remind them of the attitude they had stated earlier. Several questions guided organization of their thoughts; for example, one question asked the subjects to think about whether or not they believed that men and women should have equal employment opportunity. The rest of the subjects were not given any treatment to remind them of attitudes they had stated earlier. Snyder and Swann reported that subjects who were reminded of the view they had expressed previously typically made a decision in accord with it. In contrast, the other subjects showed significantly less consistency between attitude and behavior. Apparently, our behavior may be inconsistent with our attitudes unless we think about the relationship between the two.

Why do situations influence whether or not we act in conformity with our attitude? Berkowitz (1980) suggests that we believe that our actions must be consistent with our beliefs. If we act without thinking, we do not notice any inconsistency, and therefore our behavior may not agree with our attitude. However, if we recall the relationship between our attitude and our behavior, we recognize inconsistency; thus, we are motivated to behave in accordance with out attitude to maintain our cognitive consistency.

The certainty of our attitudes.   How convinced are you of the correctness of your attitude that equal work deserves equal pay? Fazio and Zanna's research (1978a, 1978b) indicates that the more confident we are of our attitude, the more likely we are to behave in accordance with it.

One factor which influences the degree of confidence is how the attitude was formed. According to Fazio and Zanna, we feel more confident of an attitude that developed out of direct experience than one developed indirectly from other people's experiences. A study by Regan and Fazio (1977) supports this view. They assessed students' attitudes about how their university was handling a housing emergency and whether or not the students wanted to take direct action to end the crisis. Some of these students lived in temporary housing and, thus, were directly involved in the crisis; other students lived in permanent housing and were experiencing the crisis only indirectly. Regan and Fazio discovered that students who acquired their attitudes through direct experience were more likely to indicate a willingness to act than students whose experience was indirect. Fazio and Zanna (1978b) discovered that subjects who acquired their attitude directly rather than indirectly showed more consistency between attitude and action; further-more, their subjects were more confident of attitudes developed through direct experi-ence than attitudes acquired through indirect experience. However, you should not feel that the nature of our experiences is the only determinant of certainty. Fazio and Zanna (1978b) reported that some persons who acquire their attitudes indirectly were neverthe-less confident, and that their attitudes and behavior were as consistent as those of confident people whose attitudes were developed through direct experience.

In the last section, you learned that subjects who were reminded of their previously stated attitude behaved in accordance with it. Berkowitz (1980) feels that this motivation—cognitive consistency—is also influenced by the subjects' confidence in their attitude. According to Berkowitz, people who are confident of their attitude are more likely to recognize a disparity between it and any behavior that is inconsistent with it. Thus, confident persons are more motivated to maintain consistency between attitudes and actions.

The intention to carry out an attitude. We may recognize inconsistency between our attitude and behavior but continue to act inconsistently. According to Fishbein and Ajzen (1974, 1975), we must expect to be able to carry out the specific behavior which is congruent with our attitude. Fishbein and Ajzen noted three factors which determine whether or not we intend to respond in a manner consistent with out attitude. *First, we must assess the consequences of our actions.* If we believe that they are negative, we are less likely to behave in agreement with our attitude than if we believe that they are positive. *Second, we must determine how other people expect us to act.* The likelihood of behaving in a particular way is much greater if we believe that this is the way other people expect us to act than if we expect others to disapprove. *Third, we must decide whether we want to comply with the expectations of others.* We may decide to behave according to our attitude, disregarding the wishes of others; or we may choose to comply with the desires of others and, thus, behave in a manner contrary to our attitude. Next, evidence is presented which indicates that our expectations influence the consistency between our behavior and our attitude. Chapter 12 looks at social influences and examines those factors which motivate us either to comply or to resist complying with the wishes of others.

Let's use the example of equal pay to illustrate how our behavioral intentions influence the congruity between attitude and behavior. You might realize that continuing to buy a particular company's products indirectly supports its discriminatory policies and that your behavior is inconsistent with your attitude. Perhaps you continue purchasing its products because comparable goods are too expensive. Or perhaps the manager of the store which carries its products is your friend, and you feel that he or she will not approve of your buying a competitor's products elsewhere. Under both these circumstances, your behavior—continuing to buy this company's products even though you are aware of the inconsistency between your attitude and your behavior—is in accordance with the description of behavioral intentions given by Fishbein and Ajzen (1974).

Numerous researchers have supported Fishbein and Ajzen's analysis of the effect of behavioral intention on the consistency between attitude and behavior. For example, their model has been tested in marketing and consumer behavior (see Wilson, Mathews, & Harvey, 1975), family planning (Vinokur-Kaplan, 1978), and adolescent drinking (Schlegal, Crawford, & Sanborn, 1977). Let's examine Vinokur-Kaplan's study to illustrate the validity of Fishbein and Ajzen's view.

Vinokur-Kaplan interviewed 141 married couples with at least one child to ascertain if they intended to have another. These couples were also asked to give the factors which they believed to have influenced their decision and, specifically, whether other significant people in their lives thought that these couples should have another child.

Responses to these questions indicated the couples' perceived consequences of their behavior as well as the perceived expectations of other significant people. One year after this interview, the couples reported whether or not they did have another child.

Vinokur-Kaplan's experiment evaluated the two major predictions of Fishbein and Ajzen's model. *First, it evaluated whether the perceived consequences of having another child (attitude toward the behavior) and the expectations of other people (normative social pressure) correlated with behavioral intention.* As you can see from Table 11.1, these two measures are significantly related to behavioral intention; this indicates that our intention to act in a particular manner is influenced by both our attitude toward the act and our belief about the expectations of other people. We should note that in Vinokur-Kaplan's study other people's expectations were more important than the perceived consequences of the behavior. However, other experiments have shown that the attitude toward the behavior is more significant than the expectations of other people (see Wilson, Mathews, & Harvey, 1975). This observation indicates that the contribution of each factor in determining a person's behavioral intention varies from situation to situation. Thus, in order to predict our intention to execute a desired behavior, we must not only know the strength of each component of Fishbein and Ajzen's model but also be aware of the relative contribution of each component to each specific situation.

The second major prediction of Fishbein and Ajzen's model which Vinokur-Kaplan evaluated was whether behavioral intention related to actual behavior—or, in this case, whether a couple's intention to add a child to their family did, in fact, play a role in

Table 11.1
Vinokur-Kaplan's Family Planning Test of Fishbein and Ajzen's Behavioral Intentional Model

	Correlations*		
	Attitude toward Act	Normative Component	Multiple Correlation†
Relationships of measures with behavioral intentions			
Total sample ($N = 282$)	.65	.83	.85
One-child families ($N = 142$)	.55	.73	.76
Two-child families ($N = 140$)	.43	.61	.64
Relationships of measures with actual behavior‡			
Total sample ($N = 239$)	.29	.40	.42
One-child families ($N = 119$)	.21	.17	.23
Two-child families ($N = 120$)	.04 (ns)	.32	.34
Correlation between behavioral intentions and actual behavior‡			
total sample ($N = 239$)		.55	
One-child families ($N = 119$)		.49	
Two-child families ($N = 120$)		.38	

*All the above relationships except the one marked ns are statistically significant.

†The multiple correlation assesses the relationship between the criterion variable (either the intention or the actual behavior) and the combination of the attitude toward the act and the normative component.

‡Whether they did have another child or not 1 year later.

From: Vinokur-Kaplan, D. To have—or not to have—another child: Family planning attitudes, intentions, and behavior. *Journal of Applied Social Psychology,* 1978, 8, 29–46.

having another offspring. Vinokur-Kaplan reported that the couples' behavioral intention correlated significantly with their actual behavior. Evidently, we often behave in a manner which is consistent with our intentions. Our discussion indicates, just as Fishbein and Ajzen's model suggested, that Vinokur-Kaplan's results do support the important influence of behavioral intentions on overt behavior.

You might have noticed that Vinokur-Kaplan's data did not show a perfect correspondence either between intending to have a child and having one or between not intending to reproduce and not reproducing. There are several likely reasons for this. First, the data did not take disagreement between spouses into account. Certainly, if the husband's and wife's intentions are different, the wishes of both cannot be fulfilled. Second, people's intentions to have children are not always realized: some persons intending to have children do not; others not intending to reproduce do so. Although other researchers have reported a higher correspondence between intention and behavior than Vinokur-Kaplan did, the correlations are not perfect, because people do not always know how to carry out their intentions. Therefore, let's see how the environment helps provide us with information which is necessary to translate an attitude into behavior.

Behavioral instruction. We often need to know how, when, and where to exhibit a desired behavior. The environment must provide this information if we are to be able to translate our intentions into behavior. Recall the example of the company with discriminatory salary practices and your attitude toward it. Even though you may not want to buy this company's products, you may not know which products these are. Unless you can identify the products, you will not be able to boycott them.

Leventhal, Singer, and Jones's study (1965) illustrates the process of behavioral instruction. Some of their subjects were given frightening information about a student who suffered from tetanus; the rest of the subjects received less distressing information about the disease. Leventhal, Singer, and Jones told half of the subjects in both conditions how they could obtain a tetanus inoculation at the university health center and asked them to consider when they could be inoculated. The rest of the subjects in each condition did not receive this information. Although the frightening news did arouse the subjects' attitude concerning the positive value of a tetanus shot, this treatment was not sufficient to motivate them to acquire an inoculation at the health center. Only those students who were told specifically where to receive the shot and instructed to decide when to carry out the behavior went to the health center in appreciable numbers. Apparently, we often need to know how to execute a particular behavior before our attitudes can be translated into overt action.

Thus far, we have focused on the motivational influence which our attitudes have on our behavior. However, on many occasions, people try to alter our attitude or other circumstances require us to change our attitude. In both of these cases, if our attitude changes, we are likely to alter our actions to conform to our new attitude. You will see in the next section the conditions which motivate us to change our attitude and, thereby, our behavior.

CHANGING AN ATTITUDE

Many children, perhaps, most, have a negative attitude toward homework, viewing it as an aversive event keeping them from participating in exciting, interesting activities. This negative attitude causes them to avoid their homework until their parents force them to do it. Many parents struggle with the problem of instilling in their children the idea that they will benefit from homework. Such an idea would motivate children to complete their homework without being coerced by their parents.

Although you may think that changing a child's negative attitude toward homework to a positive one is an impossible task, social-psychological research indicates that there are many different ways to induce attitude change. These methods fall into one of two categories. *First, cognitive inconsistency may cause additional changes. Second, attitudes may be changed by persuasive communication.* These methods are not always effective, because many conditions enable us to maintain old attitudes despite the use of persuasion or perceived cognitive inconsistency. To illustrate this, we'll describe the way in which parents might change their children's negative attitude toward homework and also see the inherent dangers in their effort. We'll first look at the influence of cognitive inconsistency; after that, we'll examine the influence of persuasion on attitude change as well as the conditions under which we do not alter our attitudes.

Cognitive-Inconsistency Approaches

Suppose that a child who dislikes homework overhears a friend expressing a positive attitude toward homework. According to the cognitive-inconsistency view, this child will perceive an inconsistency between his or her cognitions and those of the friend. The child, viewing inconsistency as aversive, is motivated to restore perceived cognitive consistency. How does the child do this? Heider's balance theory offers an explanation.

Balance theory.   *Heider's original approach.*   Heider's balance theory (1946) focused on people's perceptions of their social relationships. These relationships involve a person (P) who is interacting with another person (O) and their views about an object, a third person, or an issue (X). According to Heider, a balanced relationship yields cognitive consistency. To illustrate this concept, consider one child's liking of another and their attitude toward homework. Figure 11.2 shows four possible balanced relationships between P, O, and X. In Heider's view, a + value indicates a positive, or liking, unit relationship and a − value reflects a negative, or disliking, relationship between two components of the P-O-X triad. A balanced state exists if multiplying the three signs yields a positive sum. For example, a balanced state is present either when the children, (P) and (O), like each other and dislike homework or when they like homework and like one another.

Some situations are not balanced. Heider asserts that an imbalanced state occurs if multiplying the three signs yields a negative sum. As you can see, Figure 11.2 also presents four imbalanced states. In our example, imbalance occurs if children (P) and (O) like each other but have a different attitude toward homework. One child disliking the other when they both like homework is another example of cognitive imbalance.

Imbalance, according to Heider, is an aversive state which motivates us to alter our cognitions in order to eliminate it—that is, to restore a balanced state. Heider suggests that we can restore balance in numerous ways. To illustrate his approach, let's consider our example of the child (P) who dislikes homework but whose friend enjoys it. The child could recreate balance either by no longer liking the friend or by liking homework instead of disliking it.

Empirical support.   Heider assumed that an imbalanced state is arousing and unpleasant. In 1958, Burdick and Burnes demonstrated that an imbalanced state was physiologically arousing, confirming Heider's belief. They measured their subjects' galvanic skin response (GRS), an index of arousal, when another person from whom the subjects had previously indicated a liking either agreed or disagreed with a subject's viewpoint. According to Heider's balance theory, disagreement would produce an

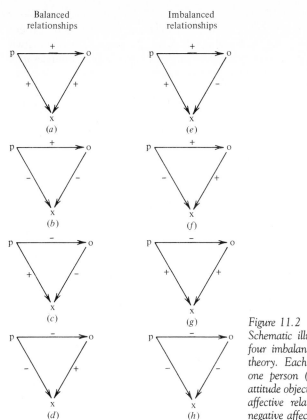

Balanced relationships

(a) (b) (c) (d)

Imbalanced relationships

(e) (f) (g) (h)

Figure 11.2
Schematic illustration of the four balanced and four imbalanced social relationships in Heider's theory. Each drawing shows the relationship of one person (P), another person (O), and an attitude object (X). A + value indicates a positive affective relationship; a − value represents a negative affective relationship.

imbalanced state, whereas agreement should reflect a balanced state. As predicted, the subjects were more aroused by disagreement than by agreement.

Additional research (see Heider, 1958) has indicated that people do seem to form balanced interpersonal relationships. In Kogan and Tagiuri's study (1958) illustrating this influence of balance, sailors who had been at sea for at least 2 months were asked to suggest the three crew members whom they would like to have join them on a 72-hour furlough. The crewmates were also asked to suggest their choices of three sailors. Kogan and Tagiuri's results demonstrated that balance operated in the formation of the sailors' interpersonal relationships: a sailor was not likely to choose two crew members who disliked each other.

However, other research has indicated two major weaknesses in Heider's balance theory. *First, not all balanced relationships are considered positive and not every imbalanced condition is considered aversive.* Newcomb's approach (1953, 1968) provided a solution to this problem. *Second, Heider's balance theory does not predict how a person will reduce the imbalanced condition.* Osgood and Tannenbaum's congruity theory (1955) addressed this weakness.

Newcomb's balance approach. Newcomb (1953) suggested that we are motivated to avoid people whom we dislike and do not care whether we agree or disagree with them about X. Under these conditions, balance is not preferred, and imbalance is not perceived as aversive. Using our homework example to illustrate Newcomb's view, let's assume that the child who dislikes homework sees someone whom he or she dislikes doing homework. This will not influence the attitude of the child who dislikes homework; however, if they were friends, the imbalance would motivate the child to reassess his or her attitude toward both the friend and homework.

In support of Newcomb's view, Jordan (1953) demonstrated that two people consider balance to be pleasant only when they have a positive relationship with each other (balanced relationships *a* and *b* in Figure 11.2). Jordan discovered that two people who dislike one another (relationships *c* and *d* in Figure 11.2) do not consider a balanced condition to be pleasant. Cartwright and Harary (1956) and Price, Harburg, and Newcomb (1966) also reported that balance with positive interpersonal relationships is pleasant, whereas balance with negative interpersonal relationships is unpleasant.

Crano and Cooper (1973) noted that subjects who had a negative relationship with each other interacted less than subjects with a positive relationship. In addition, Crockett (1974) discovered that the balance theory is applicable only when P-O relationships are positive.

Osgood and Tannenbaum's congruity theory.   Osgood and Tannenbaum suggested a method of predicting the direction of attitude change. Instead of asserting that interpersonal relationships are either positive or negative, Osgood and Tannenbaum assumed that attitudes are on a continuum from highly positive to highly negative. Also, instead of assuming that imbalance causes only one aspect of the P-O-X triad to change, Osgood and Tannenbaum think that all the components change until the differences are not great enough to be considered incongruent or imbalanced. For example, from Osgood and Tannenbaum's viewpoint, if two friends disagree about an important issue (such as politics), balance will be restored if the friends decrease the degree of their disagreement, their friendship, or both.

Many studies support Osgood and Tannenbaum's view; we'll examine Stachowiak and Moss's study (1965) as an example. Stachowiak and Moss asked their subjects to evaluate a number of concepts, which included the words *Negro* and *experimenter*. Then the subjects listened to the experimenter present a favorable 11-minute talk about Negroes. Again, the subjects rated the concepts which contained the words *experimenter* and *Negro*. Stachowiak and Moss reported that the subjects' ratings of the word *experimenter* had decreased, while their ratings of the word *Negro* had increased. They also discovered that although incongruity motivates attitude changes with regard to the objects involved in the incongruity, the value of the objects does not always change to the same degree: if one object is polarized, its value will change less than that of a nonpolarized object.

Balance theory focuses on the inconsistency which exists during interpersonal relationships; however, cognitive inconsistency does not always involve interpersonal situations. For example, cognitive inconsistency can occur if we act in ways which are inconsistent with our attitudes. Leon Festinger's cognitive-dissonance theory (1957) represents a broader approach.

Cognitive dissonance.   Festinger proposed that encountering inconsistent information or behaving in a manner incongruent with our cognitions causes us to experience a disturbing internal emotional state which he labeled *cognitive dissonance*. If cognitive dissonance occurs, according to Festinger, we are motivated to reduce it so as to reinstate our sense of cognitive consistency.

Dissonance-arousing conditions. Which circumstances elicit the unpleasant state of cognitive dissonance? Festinger suggests three types of situations in which cognitive dissonance is aroused. *First, exposure to new information which is antagonistic to an existing cognition arouses dissonance.* For example, suppose that you like chocolate ice cream but have recently learned that you are allergic to it. Your positive response to chocolate ice cream conflicts with the knowledge that this food makes you sick; this creates an aversive state, dissonance. *Second, dissonance is aroused when a choice has been made between two equally attractive or two equally unattractive alternatives.* Suppose that you like parties and basketball games but could attend only one or the other last Saturday night. Regardless of your choice, dissonance is aroused because you have rejected an attractive alternative. *Finally, acting contradictorily to our attitudes arouses dissonance.* Suppose we know that smoking can lead to cancer but continue to smoke, or suppose we realize that obesity is dangerous to our health but continue to eat rich foods. In these situations, we have acted in a manner contrary to our cognitions. Our inconsistent behavior, according to Festinger's view, arouses dissonance.

Our response to dissonance. How do we cope with cognitive dissonance? Festinger's approach suggests three ways to reduce our aversive cognitive dissonance. *First, we could add a new cognition.* For example, the child who experiences cognitive dissonance because he or she has played rather than studied for an impending test could reduce this dissonant state by convincing himself or herself of already being well-prepared for the examination. *Second, we could minimize the importance of the dissonant information.* People who eat food to which they are allergic can reduce their dissonance by arguing that the allergic reaction will not be severe. This is one example of reducing importance in order to reduce dissonance. *Finally, we could change our cognitions.* The smoker who decides that he or she does not like cigarettes and stops smoking, and the obese person who gives up rich foods by viewing them with disgust, are two examples.

Considerable research supports Festinger's view that cognitive inconsistency can produce changes in our cognitive structure. This research also shows the factors which determine how we reduce cognitive dissonance. Let's examine several types of studies which support dissonance theory.

FORCED-COMPLIANCE STUDIES. Festinger and Carlsmith's classic study (1959) tested the effects of acting, without justification, in a manner contrary to one's attitude. Festinger and Carlsmith required their subjects, one at a time, to turn pegs repeatedly in holes, an extremely boring task. Each subject was then asked to persuade the next subject (a confederate) to participate in the study by telling him or her that the experiment was very interesting and enjoyable. Subjects in one group were offered $20 apiece for describing the study; those in a second group were offered $1. After a subject had tried to persuade the confederate to participate, the subject was asked to indicate his or her feelings about how interesting the study was. A control group of subjects, instead of being required to describe the study, were requested only to rate its interest. Festinger and Carlsmith discovered that the control group and the subjects who had been offered $20 rated the study as boring; the subjects who had been offered $1 rated the study as mildly interesting (see Figure 11.3).

What factors account for these differences? According to Festinger and Carlsmith, the attitude of control subjects reflected the actual nature of the study; for the subjects who were asked to say that the study was interesting when, in fact, they thought it boring, a condition of dissonance was created. The subjects who were paid $20 had sufficient justification for their inconsistent behavior—that is, they were being paid enough to do something contrary to their beliefs—and this justification enabled them to

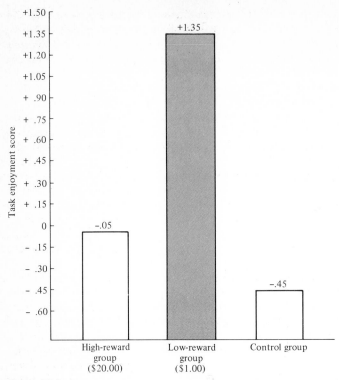

Figure 11.3
Subjects' enjoyment ratings of their participation in the three treatment groups in Festinger and Carlsmith's forced-compliance experiment. (From Festinger, L., & Carlsmith, J. M. Cognitive consequences of forced compliance. Journal of Abnormal and Social Psychology, 1959, 58, 203–210. Copyright 1959 by the American Psychological Association. Reprinted by permission.)

reduce their feelings of dissonance (see Figure 11.4). However, the subjects who were paid $1 could not use the payment to justify their actions; to reduce dissonance, these subjects could only change their cognitions, and so they indicated that they liked the study. Apparently, if we have insufficient justification for cognitive inconsistency, we must alter our cognitive structure in order to reestablish our sense of cognitive consistency.

Like Festinger and Carlsmith's experiment, Cohen's study (1962) rewarded subjects for exhibiting "counterattitudinal" behavior. Cohen asked Yale students to write an essay favorable to the actions of the police in handling a fight among students; in fact, it was widely alleged that the police had been unnecessarily aggressive. The subjects were offered 50 cents, $1, $5, or $10 for writing the essay. Subjects in a control condition did not write an essay. Cohen found that the less money the subjects were offered for writing the positive story, the more they supported the actions of the police. These results indicate that a strong change in attitude occurs if we behave in a manner contrary to our attitude and have no justification for doing so.

Aronson and Carlsmith (1963) also used forced compliance to investigate cognitive dissonance. Their subjects were children. These children were shown a group of five attractive toys but were forbidden to play with one of them. The prohibition was

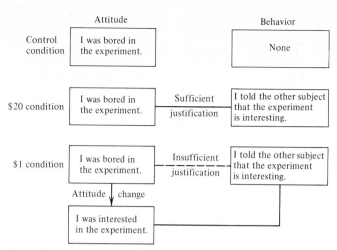

Attitude   Behavior

Control
condition | I was bored in
               the experiment.   None

$20 condition | I was bored in   Sufficient | I told the other subject
               the experiment.   justification   that the experiment
                                                           is interesting.

$1 condition | I was bored in   Insufficient | I told the other subject
               the experiment.   justification   that the experiment
                                                           is interesting.
               Attitude ↓ change

               I was interested
               in the experiment.

Figure 11.4
Hypothesized cognitions aroused during subjects' participation in Festinger and Carlsmith's forced-compliance study. (From Buck, R. S. Human motivation and emotion. New York: Wiley, 1976.)

accompanied by a "strong threat," a "mild threat," or "no threat." The children were then left alone with the toys and secretly observed to see if they played with the prohibited one. Aronson and Carlsmith asked the children to rate their liking of all the toys both before and 45 days after the children had played with them. They found that compared with "no threat," the "strong threat" did not influence the children's opinion about the attractiveness of the toys; however, the "mild threat" caused the children to devalue the forbidden toy. According to dissonance theory, the inconsistency between wanting to play with the desired toy and being forbidden to play with it created a dissonant state (see Figure 11.5). The children who received the "severe threat" were justified in not playing with the forbidden toy; but subjects in the "mild threat" condition had insufficient justification—if this toy was attractive to them, they should have ignored the threat and played with it. Under these circumstances, these children could reduce dissonance only by reducing the value of the forbidden toy.

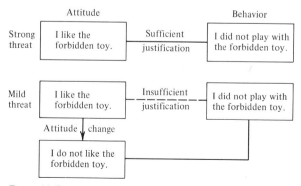

Attitude   Behavior

Strong | I like the   Sufficient | I did not play with
threat   forbidden toy.   justification   the forbidden toy.

Mild | I like the   Insufficient | I did not play with
threat   forbidden toy.   justification   the forbidden toy.
            Attitude ↓ change

            I do not like the
            forbidden toy.

Figure 11.5
Hypothesized cognitions aroused during subjects' participation in Aronson and Carlsmith's forced-compliance experiment. (From Buck, R. S. Human motivation and emotion. New York: Wiley, 1976.)

Freedman (1965) replicated Aronson and Carlsmith's study; but instead of having the children rate the toys, he wanted to see whether they would play with the forbidden toy if they were placed in a different situation, in which there was no danger of punishment. In this study, which was conducted 40 days after the initial experience, 78 percent of the children in the "strong threat" condition played with the toy, but only 33 percent of the children in the "mild threat" condition played with it. Apparently, the devaluation of the toy produced by the "mild threat" caused these children to choose not to play with it even when there was no danger of being punished.

FREE-CHOICE EXPERIMENTS.   Brehm (1956) evaluated the influence of having to choose between two equally attractive items on one's view of those items after the decision. In this study, female college students were asked to help a marketing firm by evaluating consumer items (for example, a toaster, an electric coffee pot, a silkscreen print). After rating the products, the subjects were allowed to choose one item to keep. In the "high dissonance" condition, subjects were allowed to choose between two items of close value. In the "low dissonance" condition, subjects could choose between two products which varied greatly in value. In the control condition, the experimenter gave the subjects one product. After the subjects in the "high dissonance" and "low dissonance" conditions had made their choice, they were asked to read a research report written by the manufacturer of each item and then to rerate all the items.

On this second rating, subjects in the "high dissonance" condition rated the attractiveness of their chosen item higher and that of the rejected item lower (see Table 11.2). On the other hand, subjects in the "low dissonance" condition rated the chosen item only slightly higher and did not change their rating of the rejected item. The subjects in the control condition did not change their rating at all. Brehm's results support the idea of cognitive dissonance. The "high dissonance" subjects, who were asked to choose between two equally attractive items, experienced a cognitive inconsistency. To reduce this dissonance, they changed their view of the items, creating two items which differed in attractiveness. Since the "low dissonance" subjects were not asked to choose between equally valued items, they did not experience dissonance and

Table 11.2
The Postdecisional Perceived Attractiveness of Chosen and Nonchosen Items

	Changes from 1st to 2nd Rating for		
Condition	Chosen Item	Nonchosen Item	Net Change
Low dissonance (items of disparate value)	+0.11	0.00	+0.11
High dissonance (items of close value)	+0.38	−0.41	+0.79
Gift—control	0.00		

Note: A positive sign indicates an increase in attractiveness; a negative sign indicates a decrease. The "net change" represents the degree of "spreading apart" of the alternatives following a choice.

From: Brehm, J. W. Post-decision changes in the desirability of alternatives. *Journal of Abnormal and Social Psychology*, 1956, 52, 384–389. Copyright 1956 by the American Psychological Association. Reprinted by permission.

therefore were not motivated to alter their view. The control subjects, as noted above, also showed no change in their valuation of the item which the experimenter gave them.

Brock (1963) conducted a free-choice study which was similar to Brehm's experiment with children. He asked his young subjects to rate the attractiveness of three kinds of toys (a ring-toss game, a spinning top, and a yo-yo) and three types of crackers (soda, graham, and cheese) both before and after choosing between two equally valued objects. Brock reported that after the children had rated the toys and the crackers, they showed an increased liking for the alternative which they had picked and a decreased liking for the alternative they had not chosen. This observation again indicates that we are motivated to change our attitude toward two items when we can choose only one of two equally preferred objects.

In 1975, Lawler, Kuleck, Rhode, and Sorenson conducted a study illustrating this same effect with alternative jobs. Their subjects were accounting students. The students were asked to rate the attractiveness of job alternatives in the fall of their senior year before they had chosen a job, in the spring of their senior year after they had chosen a job, and in the following spring. Initially, the experimenters found that some jobs were equally attractive to the students. However, once the students had made their decision, the chosen job seemed more attractive, while the rejected job lost its attractiveness and continued to lose attractiveness during these students' first year of employment. Apparently, we will alter our view after choosing between equally attractive alternatives in order to reduce the dissonance produced by our decision.

SELECTIVE-EXPOSURE STUDIES.   Earlier in this section, we learned that we can reduce dissonance by reducing the importance of inconsistent information and by increasing the importance of consistent information. We can accomplish this by ignoring incongruent information and attending only to information which supports our consistent information. The behavior of cigarette smokers illustrates how selective exposure reduces dissonance.

In a government study reported by Festinger (1957), smokers—light, medium, and heavy—and nonsmokers were asked to indicate whether they thought that the evidence linking smoking and cancer was conclusive or inconclusive. This study found that 45 percent of the nonsmokers, 32 percent of the light smokers, 25 percent of the medium smokers, and 14 percent of the heavy smokers believed that evidence that smoking causes cancer to be conclusive. As you can see, the cognitions regarding smoking and cancer in nonsmokers and heavy smokers are quite different. Undoubtedly, the heavy smokers' belief that the evidence was inconclusive represented one effective way of reducing their cognitive dissonance.

Brock and Balloun's study (1967) indicates that selective exposure is probably responsible for the different cognitions of smokers and nonsmokers: both attend to information that is congruent with their attitudes and avoid incongruent information. Brock and Balloun asked their subjects—male and female college students—to judge the persuasiveness of a number of talks prepared by high school students. These were presented to the subjects on six 5-minute tapes. Only two of these tapes were crucial to developing an opinion about the relationship between smoking and cancer. On one tape, it was argued that smoking leads to lung cancer; on the other, that no relationship exists between smoking and lung cancer. Before turning on a tape, the experimenter told each subject that considerable electrical interference would be heard during each talk and that pressing a button would remove some of the interfering static. The experimenters assumed that the number of times a subject pressed the button during a particular talk indicated the subject's desire to hear a particular message. Brock and Balloun discovered that smokers tried harder than nonsmokers to hear the segment of the tape which suggested that smoking does not lead to cancer. In contrast, nonsmokers were more interested than smokers in hearing the message that smoking leads to cancer. These results indicate that people are more willing to hear information which is consistent with their attitudes than information which is inconsistent with them.

You should not believe that the use of selective exposure to maintain cognitive consistency and reduce dissonance occurs only in cigarette smokers. Brock and Balloun (1967) also reported that frequent churchgoers were less willing than people who seldom went to church to hear a conversation asserting that Christianity is evil. Frey (1980) gave intelligence tests to West German teenagers and then gave these teenagers feedback which indicated that they had done worse than they had expected. He next gave them the opportunity to obtain (for a small fee) articles which either favored or criticized IQ tests. Frey reported that the teenagers were more interested in purchasing information which was consistent with their beliefs—information critical of IQ tests—than in purchasing information inconsistent with their beliefs.

Although we can undoubtedly ignore dissonant information sometimes, at other times we cannot escape it (see Wicklund & Brehm, 1976). Under these circumstances, we must use other means to reinstate cognitive consistency. Lowin (1967, 1969) reported that dissonant information would not disturb people who dismissed it as silly or inaccurate. Other means of reducing dissonance include altering our cognitions and adding new cognitions. For example, while many heavy smokers may not be convinced of the link between cancer and smoking, they cannot ignore all the dissonant information and, therefore, will have some doubt about the wisdom of smoking. Since tolerance eliminates the physiological effects of smoking for heavy smokers (see Chapter 4), the belief of many heavy smokers that smoking is pleasurable probably reflects an altered cognition designed to justify continued smoking. Some smokers may, however, accept the dissonant information and stop smoking as a result of having developed a negative attitude toward it.

We have seen in the preceding sections that perceived cognitive inconsistency produces cognitive dissonance, which in turn motivates cognitive changes in order to reduce dissonance. However, there are three factors—*control over attitude-discrepant behavior, commitment to attitude-discrepant behavior, and consequences of attitude-discrepant behavior*—which determine if dissonance will induce changes in attitudes (see Worchel & Cooper, 1979). We now turn our attention to these three factors.

Factors influencing dissonance-induced attitude change.   ONE'S FREEDOM TO CHOOSE. Although Festinger and Carlsmith's study and similar experiments were called *forced-compliance* studies earlier in this chapter, in fact the subjects were asked to participate and could have refused to exhibit "counterattitudinal" behavior. Several studies (see Davis & Jones, 1960; Linder, Cooper, & Jones, 1967) point out that if Festinger and Carlsmith's subjects had been forced to describe the study favorably, the subjects receiving only $1 for telling the next subject that the study was enjoyable would not have changed their attitude. The reason for this hypothetical result is that these subjects could have attributed their behavior to coercion.

How do you coerce subjects into exhibiting "counterattitudinal" behavior? Let's examine the study by Linder, Cooper, and Jones (1967) to illustrate the effects of free choice and coercion on attitude change. We should note that subjects' freedom of choice in an experiment is more of an illusion than a reality. Few subjects refuse to act as an experimenter requests; for example, subjects have reportedly undergone extreme physical effort (see Wicklund, Cooper, & Linder, 1967), shocked other students (see Brock & Buss, 1962), and eaten grasshoppers (see Zimbardo, Weisenberg, Firestone, & Levy, 1965). However, although the difference between choice and coercion typically is only an illusion, it is quite important.

Linder, Cooper, and Jones's subjects (1967) were induced to write an essay supporting a law which would forbid people to "take the Fifth Amendment"—that is, refuse to testify against themselves. Half of the subjects were *coerced*—i.e., required to write the essay ("no choice" condition). The rest were *asked* to write it ("choice" condition). The subjects who were required to write the essay were not promised a reward but received either 50 cents or $2.50 after they had written it; the subjects who had made their own decision about participating were promised either the high or the low reward. The attitude of all the subjects toward banning the Fifth Amendment was assessed both before they wrote the essay and after they had received their reward. Linder, Cooper, and Jones reported that the results obtained in the "choice" condition corresponded to those of previous dissonance studies; that is, subjects receiving the large reward showed little change in attitude, but subjects receiving the small reward changed their attitude significantly to correspond with their essays (see Table 11.3). In contrast, in the "no choice" condition subjects who received the small reward showed no change in attitude after their "counterattitudinal" behavior. These observations indicate that coercion can negate the typical tendency of low reward to change attitudes. Notice that in the "no choice" condition subjects receiving the large reward did show changes in attitude. Apparently, when we are forced to behave in a way that is contrary to our attitude, only a large reward will alter our attitude. Later in the chapter, we will see why high reinforcement effectively changes the attitude of subjects in a "no choice" condition.

COMMITMENT.   You learned from the last section that dissonance induces attitude change only when subjects believe that they have *chosen* to exhibit "counterattitudinal" behavior. This effect of dissonance can also be eliminated if subjects only *think* about an attitude-discrepant act rather than publicly *commit* themselves to a position contrary to their actual attitude (see Brehm & Cohen, 1962). According to Brehm and Cohen, *commitment* means that our behavior supporting a particular cause cannot be undone. Thus, someone who has made a public attitude-discrepant statement cannot deny it and, therefore, must justify it; but statements which we make to ourselves can be denied and need not be justified. Many studies (see Carlsmith, Collins, & Helmreich, 1966; Davis & Jones, 1960) indicate that commitment is an essential factor in dissonance-induced attitude change. Let's examine the study by Carlsmith, Collins, and Helmreich to illustrate the effect of commitment on attitude change.

Carlsmith, Collins, and Helmreich's subjects (1966) participated in the same dull task as Festinger and Carlsmith's subjects (1959)—turning a peg. Half of the subjects publicly tried to convince the next subject to participate in the study; this, too, was the

Table 11.3
The Amount of Attitude Change Following Counterattitudinal Behavior in Choice and No-Choice Conditions

Amount of Payment	No Choice	Choice
$ .50	1.7	3.0
$2.50	2.3	1.6

From: Linder, D. E., Cooper, J., & Jones, E. E. Decision freedom as a determinant of the role of incentive magnitude in attitude change. *Journal of Personality and Social Psychology*, 1967, 6, 245–254. Copyright 1967 by the American Psychological Association. Reprinted by permission.

procedure used by Festinger and Carlsmith. The other half of the subjects were asked to write an anonymous essay indicating that they believed the study to be valuable. Thus all the subjects had to exhibit "counterattitudinal" behavior, but some did so publicly and some privately. Next, all the subjects were requested to rate how enjoyable the task had been. Carlsmith, Collins, and Helmreich reported that the subjects who had publicly exhibited attitude-discrepant behavior changed their attitude to make it conform to their behavior, but the subjects whose attitude-discrepant behavior was private did not change their attitude.

THE CONSEQUENCES OF OUR ACTIONS.   Earlier, a child's negative attitude toward homework was described. Suppose that this child's mother asks him or her to try to convince a younger sibling of the value of homework. According to the dissonance theory, the older child's attitude toward homework should change as a result of this attitude-discrepant act. However, several studies (see Cooper & Worchel, 1970; Collins & Hoyt, 1972) have demonstrated that the consequences of the attitude-discrepant behavior determine whether or not cognitive inconsistency induces a change in attitude. These experiments show that only when attitude-discrepant behavior has unwanted or aversive consequences will we be motivated to change our attitude. According to this view, the child's attitude toward homework will change if he or she convinces the young sibling to enjoy homework; however, if the younger sibling ignores the information, the older sibling's attitude will not change. Let's consider the study by Cooper and Worchel (1970) to document the influence of the consequences of our actions on the likelihood of our altering our attitude.

All of Cooper and Worchel's subjects initially performed the boring task Festinger and Carsmith had used—turning a peg—and tried to convince the next subject, a confederate, that the task would be exciting. To some of the subjects, the confederate replied, "You are entitled to your opinions, but every experiment I have ever been in has been dull." This statement was intended to indicate to a subject that he or she had not convinced the next subject (the confederate) that the boring task was interesting. With other subjects, the confederate became excited and enthusiastic about the idea of being in the study; the purpose of this action was to convey the impression that the subject had convinced the next subject (confederate) of the value of the boring study. Next, all the subjects, including a control group who had not exhibited attitude-discrepant behavior, were asked to rate how enjoyable the study was. Cooper and Worchel discovered that the subjects who believed that they had convinced the next subject (the confederate) of the value of the study felt the study to be enjoyable. On the other hand, the control subjects and the subjects whose attempts at persuasion were apparently unconvincing considered the study unenjoyable. These observations indicate that following attitude-discrepant behavior, we will change our attitudes only when the consequences of our actions are unwanted or aversive.

Why are the consequences of our attitude-discrepant behavior important? It seems reasonable to conclude that if we cannot convince someone of an attitude, this attitude probably is inaccurate. We probably will then use the information provided by this other person to reduce our dissonance and, thereby, maintain our previous attitude.

Is cognitive inconsistency arousing?   Festinger (1957) assumed that the dissonance state energizes behavior and that reduction of dissonance is reinforcing. We must realize that Festinger's view reflects a combined drive and cognitive approach to attitude change—which, by the way, is the view advocated in this book. According to Festinger, perceived cognitive inconsistency activates dissonance, and cognitive processes are responsible for terminating the drive state.

Many studies (for example, Cooper, Zanna, & Taves, 1978; Kiesler & Pallak, 1976; Pallak, 1970; Pallak & Pittman, 1972; Zanna & Cooper, 1974, 1976) have shown that arousal is necessary if attitude change is to occur in cognitive dissonance studies. Let's look at two studies which explain why current thinking assumes that drive motivates such attitude change.

Zanna and Cooper's subjects (1974) volunteered to participate in a study investigating the effects of various drugs on memory. All subjects ingested a placebo pill which they believed would affect their memory and either (1) cause them to become aroused and tense within several minutes ("aroused" condition), (2) cause them to become relaxed within several minutes ("relaxed" condition), or (3) have no side effects ("no side effects" condition). After taking the pill, the subjects were either asked ("choice" condition) or required ("no choice" condition) to participate in another study until the "drug" became effective: they were to write an essay supporting a ban on a controversial speaker—a position that the subjects did not in fact advocate. Following this "counterattitudinal" behavior, the subjects were asked to state their attitude about banning controversial speakers.

Festinger's dissonance theory makes specific predictions about the results of Zanna and Cooper's study. According to dissonance theory, perceived cognitive inconsistency caused by attitude-discrepant behavior arouses dissonance, which is an aversive state. Subjects in the "aroused" condition could reduce dissonance by attributing it to the drug. In contrast, subjects in the "relaxed" and "no side effects" conditions could not attribute dissonance to the drug; they could reduce dissonance only by changing their attitude. In fact, the actual arousal of the subjects in the "relaxed" condition should seem most severe, since it would contrast sharply with the expected effect of the "drug"; therefore, subjects in this condition should show a greater change in attitude than those in the "no side effects" condition. However, these predictions refer only to the subjects who chose to write the essay ("choice" condition), because all the subjects in the "no choice" condition could attribute their actions to experimental coercion.

Zanna and Cooper's study provides clear support for Festinger's theory (see Figure 11.6). As in previous research, subjects who were forced to write the essay ("no choice" condition) did not change their attitudes; that is, despite their "counterattitudinal" behavior, they continued to disapprove of the ban. Subjects in the "choice–no side effects" condition substantially changed their attitude to correspond to their behavior. In contrast, subjects in the "choice–aroused" condition did not change their attitude. As predicted, subjects in the "choice–relaxed" condition showed the strongest change in attitude. Zanna and Cooper's results indicate that voluntary attitude-discrepant behavior produced internal arousal. When that internal arousal could be attributed to an external source (the "drug"), the subjects did not have to change their attitude to reduce dissonance. However, when the internal arousal could not be attributed to the "drug," the subjects had to change their attitude to reduce dissonance.

A later study by Zanna and Cooper (1976) contributed even stronger support for Festinger's view. In this study, all the subjects ingested a pill which they believed would have no side effects. However, in reality, one group of subjects had taken an amphetamine, a drug which produces arousal; the second group of subjects had received a tranquilizer, a drug which decreases arousal; and the third group of subjects—the control group—had received a placebo. After taking the pill, all the subjects agreed to write a "counterattitudinal" essay; and after they had written the essay, Zanna and Cooper assessed their attitude change. Subjects who had taken the tranquilizer showed no change in attitude; Zanna and Cooper attributed this effect to the fact that the tranquilizer reduced the aversive state of dissonance and thereby eliminated the need for these

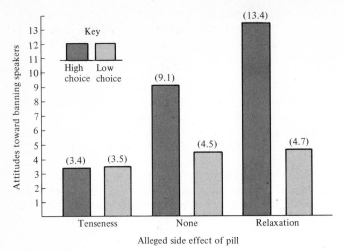

Figure 11.6
Subjects' attitude toward banning controversial speakers as a function of their perceived choice of writing a counterattitudinal essay and the pill's alleged side effects. (From Zanna, M. P., & Cooper, J. Dissonance and the pill: An attribution approach to studying the arousal properties of dissonance. Journal of Personality and Social Psychology, 1974, 29, 703–709. Copyright 1974 by the American Psychological Association. Reprinted by permission.)

subjects to change their attitudes. Subjects who had taken amphetamine showed more attitude change than subjects who had taken the placebo. According to dissonance theory, the amphetamine increased the arousal caused by dissonance and, thus, intensified these subjects' motivation to change their attitude.

Earlier in the chapter, we looked at the plight of parents who want their children to recognize the value of homework. What we've learned about the effects of cognitive inconsistency suggests several different ways of accomplishing this. For example, the child could observe a close friend who was seemingly enjoying doing homework; the parents could have the child choose between homework and an even less attractive endeavor, such as cleaning his or her room; the parents could ask the child to write an essay espousing the virtues of homework. In each of these situations, if the child recognizes the cognitive inconsistency, the aversive state of cognitive dissonance will be aroused. Under specific circumstances, this dissonance will motivate the child to change his or her attitude. However, the parent may not be able to create an inconsistency: the child may refuse to exhibit "counterattitudinal" behavior; or dissonance could be reduced without an alteration in attitude—for example, the child could attribute the inconsistency to external causes.

If cognitive inconsistency turns out to be an ineffective approach, another method can be employed. Earlier in the chapter we saw that people who are forced to exhibit attitude-discrepant behavior and then are highly rewarded for it will adopt the attitude that they had been forced to advocate. Carl Hovland and his associates (see Hovland, Janis, & Kelley, 1953) outlined a reinforcement theory to explain how people can be persuaded to accept a different attitude. Our next section examines their theory.

A Reinforcement Approach

Hovland, Janis, and Kelley (1953) asserted that people can be induced to change their attitude through *persuasive communication*, a process in which one person communicates with another, telling him or her of the value of an attitude. In order for persuasive communication to be effective, the person receiving the communication must attend to it (people are not likely to attend to an unfamiliar or uninteresting communication) and comprehend the new information. However, attention and comprehension do not ensure an attitude change. People must accept the value of a new attitude before they will adopt the attitude.

Why would we accept an attitude which is contrary to a previously established one? According to Hovland, Janis, and Kelley, people need an incentive before they will accept persuasive communication. Such an incentive, offered during the communication, motivates a person to adopt a new attitude. Receiving a reward for acceptance of a new attitude solidifies the person's adoption of that attitude.

Four factors influence the effectiveness of persuasive communication. (See Freedman, Sears, & Carlsmith, 1978). *First, the communicator's characteristics influence the acceptance of a new attitude.* We are likely to listen to and accept some people's opinions more than other people's. *Second, the content of the communication affects the adoption of a new attitude.* The communication must be presented in a specific way in order to be effective. *Third, desired incentives must be provided before the new attitude will be accepted.* The reward to be provided for adoption of the new attitude must be sufficient to motivate a person to change his or her attitude. *Finally, the person receiving a communication often possesses techniques for resisting persuasion.* These techniques reduce the likelihood that the persuasive communication will be effective. Thus, the communication must be strong enough to overcome any resistance to attitude change. The next four sections of this chapter will describe the factors which increase or decrease the effectiveness of a persuasive communication.

The communicator. Two main characteristics of the communicator influence the persuasiveness of his or her message. An effective communicator must be considered credible and trustworthy. Let's now examine evidence which indicates that these two characteristics influence the persuasiveness of the communicator.

Credibility. Credibility refers to the target's opinion of the communicator's expert ability; the higher the opinion, the more effective the message. For example, a political commentator is more likely to alter your preference for a particular candidate than a letter to your local newspaper. Numerous studies have documented the importance of credibility on the effectiveness of persuasive communication. The study by Hovland and Weiss (1952) will illustrate it.

Hovland and Weiss's subjects listened to separate communications about four different issues. The subjects believed that a source with a high credibility had presented some of the messages and that a source with a low credibility had presented others. For example, one communication concerned the practicality of building an atomic-powered submarine and was assumed to reflect the views of J. Robert Oppenheimer, a noted physicist (high credibility); another communication on the same subject was assumed to reflect the views of *Pravda*, a Russian newspaper (low credibility). Hovland and Weiss reported significantly more attitude change when the communicator possessed high credibility rather than low credibility.

Trustworthiness. For a communication to be effective, the target must believe that the communicator will not gain from his or her attitude change. Communicators whose intentions are not doubtful will produce more attitude change than those whose motives are questionable. For example, suppose that your faculty advisor tells you of the value of a certain class after you have decided on your schedule. If you believe that your advisor, who will teach this class, is worried that not enough students have enrolled in it and is recommending it for that reason, the message will have less impact than if you know that your advisor will not teach the class or that many students have already signed up for it.

To demonstrate the importance of trustworthiness, Walster and Festinger (1962) asked their subjects to listen to speakers discussing the link between cigarette smoking and cancer. These speakers advocated the position that there is not a conclusive link between cigarette smoking and cancer. In the "overheard" condition, subjects believed the speakers to be unaware of their presence. In the "regular" condition, subjects were told that the speakers were aware of their presence. Walster and Festinger assumed that the subjects in the "regular" condition would be more doubting of the trustworthiness of the message. Several days after this study, the subjects who had participated were among a group asked to respond to a health survey. One of the questions in the survey asked respondents about how certain they were that there is a link between smoking and cancer. Walster and Festinger reported that the subjects in the "overheard" condition expressed more doubt about the link than subjects in the "regular" condition. These results indicate that a communicator who is trusted produces more attitude change than one who is not.

The communication. The nature of the message also influences attitude change. Research indicates that two factors are critical: (1) the discrepancy between the attitude contained in the message and the target's attitude and (2) the level of fear induced by the message. Let's examine how these factors influence the persuasiveness of a communication.

The discrepancy between the communication and the target's attitudes. The relationship between the communication and the target's attitude and the level of attitude change induced by the message is an inverted U-shaped function; that is, the amount of discrepancy at first increases the level of attitude change, but further increases in discrepancy beyond the optimum level act to decrease the amount of attitude change. We should note that the degree of discrepancy which can induce attitude change, as well as the amount of attitude change, depends upon the source's credibility. Thus, a source with high credibility can advocate a great discrepancy and still produce a change in the target's attitude (see Figure 11.7). Many studies (see Bochner & Insko, 1966; Freedman, 1964; Rhine & Severance, 1970) have demonstrated the importance of both credibility and attitude discrepancy on the degree of attitude change; the study by Bochner and Insko (1966) will illustrate this influence.

Bochner and Insko (1966) presented their subjects with messages which described the average number of hours of sleep a person needs per night. The message received by each subject purported to be by a source with high credibility (a Nobel Prize winner) or one with low credibility (a YMCA instructor). In addition, each subject was told that a different number of hours, ranging from zero to 8, was best. Since the subjects felt that approximately 8 hours of sleep was needed, the discrepancy between the message and their attitude was zero if they received a message advocating 8 hours; the discrepancy was 1 hour when the message advocated 7 hours; the discrepancy was 2 hours when the message advocated 6 hours; and so on. Figure 11.7 shows that greater attitude change occurred with moderate discrepancy than with extreme discrepancy. However, the optimum level of discrepancy was greater with a "high credibility" source than a "low credibility" source. The results show that discrepancy has an important impact on the level of attitude change induced by the communicator.

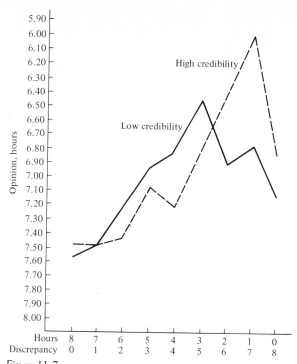

Figure 11.7

Subjects' attitude toward the amount of sleep needed each night following the reading of an essay on this topic as a function of the social credibility and the discrepancy between subject and communication attitude. (From Bochner, S., & Insko, C. A. Communicator discrepancy, source credibility, and opinion change. Journal of Personality and Social Psychology, 1966, 4, 614–621. Copyright 1966 by the American Psychological Association. Reprinted by permission.)

   The influence of fear.   Fear is often used to motivate people to change their attitudes. We are told that if we eat too much, we will become fat and unattractive; if we smoke, we will develop lung cancer; if we cheat, we will be expelled from school; if we drive too fast, we will get a summons; if we steal, we will go to jail. How effective are fear-arousing communications in inducing attitude change?

   In 1953, Janis and Feshbach conducted research in this area, and their results greatly influenced society's perception of how to structure a message which is designed to induce attitude change. Janis and Feshbach used different levels of fear to persuade people to brush their teeth more carefully and to improve other oral hygiene practices. Subjects in the "low fear" condition were vividly told about the painful consequences of diseased gums and teeth and shown techniques to improve dental hygiene. For subjects in the "moderate fear" condition, the aversiveness of diseased gums was made even more vivid, and the same methods of oral hygiene were described. Subjects in the "high fear" condition was exposed to a very aversive experience: they were told that gum infections can cause other diseases and were shown pictures of decayed teeth and the results of oral infections. One week after these messages had been presented, all the subjects were asked to report their oral hygiene practices. Any change in behavior would reflect an attitude change produced by the fear, which in turn had been aroused by the communication. Janis and Feshbach discovered that the "low fear" condition produced the greatest attitude change; the "high fear" condition did not induce any attitude change. These observations indicate that high levels of fear are not always an effective method of motivating changes in attitudes.

Janis and Feshbach's results have fostered the belief that intense fear should not be used to induce people to change their attitudes. However, most research (see Higbee, 1969) which has studied the influence of fear on attitude change has shown that high fear produces the greatest level of attitude change. For example, Dabbs and Leventhal (1966) varied the level of fear which was aroused by a message advising people to be inoculated against tetanus; they discovered that the higher the fear, the more likely the target was to get the shot. High fear has also been reported to motivate people to follow recommendations for driving safely (Leventhal & Niles, 1965) and to adopt improved dental hygiene practices (Evans, Rozelle, Lasater, Dembroski, & Allen, 1970).

Insko (1967) suggested that high fear will motivate attitude change unless it evokes defensive reactions. According to Insko, these defensive reactions motivate avoidance behavior rather than attitude change. Unfortunately, evidence validating this view is inconclusive. The most reasonable conclusion at this time is that under most conditions, high fear produces the greatest level of attitude change.

We have seen that the persuasiveness of a message depends upon the characteristics of both the communicator and the communication. However, no message will be persuasive unless the target expects and receives reinforcement for adopting the view advocated in the message. Next, we'll look at the evidence which shows that reward determines our acceptance of a persuasive communication.

The influence of reward. Hovland, Janis, and Kelley suggested that three major expectations motivate us to adopt the attitude advocated in a message. *First, we want to adopt the "right" rather than the "wrong" view.* We base our desire on past experiences in which we have been rewarded for being correct but punished (or not rewarded) for being incorrect. Suppose that an expert advocates a view contrary to ours. Unless we change our attitude to conform to the expert's view, the message will arouse our expectation of being wrong, since we perceive the expert to be more knowledgeable than we are. Thus we are likely to change our attitude to agree with the expert's view in order to perceive that we are right. In contrast, we are not motivated to adopt the view of someone who is not an expert; we believe that such a view is not any more likely to be correct than our own. We saw earlier that an expert's message produces more attitude change than a nonexpert's message. Hovland, Janis, and Kelley's analysis indicates the reason for this.

Second, we do not want to be manipulated by another person. This motive is based on the belief that people trying to influence our judgment for their own ends will undoubtedly cause us to suffer. Thus, we will not adopt views advocated by untrustworthy sources, because we assume that they are manipulative and will lead to nonreward or punishment. In contrast, we expect that we are not likely to suffer by adopting views advocated by trustworthy sources; this causes us to listen to their views. Earlier in this chapter, we saw that a trustworthy communicator produces greater attitude change than one who is not trustworthy. Hovland, Janis, and Kelley's reinforcement approach provides an explanation for this.

Finally, we want to obtain social approval. This motivation causes us to adopt attitudes which lead to social approval and avoid those which lead to social disapproval. According to Hovland, Janis, and Kelley, we will adopt the view advocated by a persuasive communicator because we expect that doing so will produce social approval and not doing so will produce social disapproval. Chapter 12 will show that social expectations play an important role in motivating behavior. These observations will support the reinforcement view that social expectations motivate attitude change.

Hovland, Janis, and Kelley's reinforcement view suggests that our expectation of reward motivates us to adopt the communicator's view. This expectation is assumed to be based on past experience; that is, when we altered an attitude in the past, we obtained reward. If this view is accurate, presentation of reward following "counterattitudinal" behavior should lead to attitude change. In addition, the reinforcement approach indicates that the level of attitude change depends upon the amount of reward received for a counterattitudinal behavior; that is, the larger the reward, the greater the change. Numerous studies (see Insko, 1967) have demonstrated that when we are rewarded for expressing a view contrary to our actual attitude, we change our attitude, and that the greater the reward, the greater the change in attitude. Let's examine several studies which document the role of reward in producing changes in attitude.

Scott (1957) administered questionnaires to 29 discussion sections of introductory psychology classes to assess students' attitudes on three controversial issues. Four students, two in favor of and two against one of these issues, were selected from each discussion section to present a debate for their classmates; however, they were required to advocate the view which they opposed. After the debate, the classmates rated each debater's performance, but Scott did not give the debaters the results of these ratings. Instead, he falsified the scores so that they would show that half of each group—the pro statement and the con statement—had won the debates (reinforcement, or reward) while the other half of the subjects received information that they had lost (nonreward). After the debaters had received their ratings, they again answered the questionnaire on attitude. Scott discovered that the debaters who were rewarded changed their attitude to conform to the view they had advocated in the debate. In contrast, no attitude change occurred in the absence of reward. Wallace (1966) observed a similar effect of reward which followed a debate on capital punishment. Apparently, people who are required to exhibit attitude-discrepant behavior will change their attitude if the behavior is rewarded but will not change it if there is no reward.

Recall the earlier description of Linder, Cooper, and Jones's study (1967). We saw that subjects required to write a "counterattitudinal" essay showed more attitude change if they were given a large reward than if they were given a small reward. Several other studies (Holmes & Strickland, 1970; Sherman, 1970a, 1970b) have demonstrated that when subjects have no choice about performing an attitude-discrepant behavior, a large reward produces more attitude change than a small one. These observations support Hovland, Janis, and Kelley's reinforcement theory.

The factors which enable a communication to persuade a person to change an attitude have been described. You might have the impression that the target passively responds to the level of pressure which the communicator applies. However, targets of persuasive communication play an active role in determining the effectiveness of the message. Targets, before any change in their attitude can occur, must attend to the message and comprehend it. Some people will resist all attempts to have their attitude altered, but most people will change their attitude when a concerted effort is exerted by the communicator to motivate the target. A brief discussion of the personal and situational factors responsible for people's resistance to attempts to have their attitude changed will end the description of attitude change.

Resistance to persuasive communication. This discussion of resistance to attitude change will address three key questions: (1) *Which techniques do people employ to counteract* *the effects of a persuasive communication?* (2) *Who are the people most likely to use these resistance techniques?* (3) *Which situations will most often activate people's resistance to changing their attitude?* Let's begin by considering how people resist attempts to have their attitudes altered.

Resistance techniques. We are often exposed to information on television and in magazines and newspapers advocating a position contrary to ours. How can we resist the effect of this persuasive communication? Freedman, Sears, and Carlsmith (1978) identified five methods which we can use to counter the persuasive influence of messages. *First, we can refute the arguments presented in the message by providing evidence to support our position or demonstrating the illogical or inconsistent aspects of the communication.* This method is often difficult to employ, for two reasons: (1) We must be sufficiently motivated to search for refuting evidence; (2) persuasive material is usually presented logically with strong supporting evidence by someone who is more knowledgeable than we are. Since this method typically requires great effort, most of us resist changing our attitudes by using procedures which are less logical but more easily implemented.

Second, we can derogate the source of the message. Earlier in the chapter, we saw that expertise and trustworthiness critically influence the effectiveness of persuasive communications. We can reduce the impact of messages by perceiving that the source of the communication is not proficient or not trustworthy. For example, some people who have read an article supporting birth control might claim that the message was communist-inspired. Attributing the article to a negative source would enable them to dismiss the message without dealing with any cognitive inconsistency presented in it.

Third, we can distort the content of the message. We can accomplish this distortion in several ways. We might either forget or reconstruct parts of the message and, thereby, assume that the evidence against our view is inconclusive. For example, smokers who have read an article claiming that smoking leads to cancer might alter their memory of the message, arguing that the source only suggested a possible causal link between smoking and cancer. Targets can also exaggerate the discrepancy between their attitude and the one advocated by the source. Recall that an optimal level of discrepancy produces attitude change. By increasing the discrepancy, targets no longer feel the need to alter their attitude. Consider the following example to illustrate this process. Suppose that a businessperson reads an environmentalist's pamphlet advocating pollution controls. By maintaining that the environmentalist is arguing against economic growth, this businessperson eliminates the motivation to change his or her attitude toward controlling pollution.

Fourth, we can employ rationalization and other defensive reactions. Chapter 1 detailed the Freudian defense mechanisms which people use to deal with conflict. Abelson (1959) suggested that we can employ these defense mechanisms to resist the influence of persuasive communications. For example, suppose that a landlord who refuses to rent apartments to minority group members is confronted by a couple who argue that their freedom is being denied. This landlord can avoid altering his or her attitude by denying that failure to rent this couple (or minorities) an apartment interferes with their freedom, or by asserting that renting to this couple (or to minorities) would deny the landlord's own freedom.

Finally, we can reject the message without providing a logical reason. Instead of trying to reduce the impact of the persuasive communication by refuting the arguments, derogating the source, altering the message, or using a defensive reaction, we can simply reject the argument without any apparent reason. Consider cigarette smokers who are presented with strong evidence that they should stop smoking but merely say that the evidence is insufficient. This observation indicates that we often respond in illogical, irrational ways in order to maintain our attitudes. It is no wonder that persuading people to change their attitudes is frequently difficult.

You might wonder about the effectiveness of these techniques in resisting the influence of persuasive communication. William McGuire (see McGuire, 1961, 1964) not only provided evidence of the effectiveness of these resistance techniques but also showed how these methods can be established.

To investigate the process of resistance, McGuire used *cultural truisms*—attitudes for which no defenses against persuasion have been developed. He asserts that our society has many cultural truisms, that is, attitudes universally assumed to be true by everyone in our society. For example, most people in the United States believe that when it is possible, we should brush our teeth after every meal. Since cultural truisms are generally accepted, we have not been exposed to evidence contrary to many of them. As a result, we have not developed any resistance to attempts to alter some of our attitudes. According to McGuire, this absence of means to resist attack renders these cultural truisms very susceptible to change by a persuasive argument. McGuire argues that to provide resistance, we should be inoculated against persuasive communication.

McGuire suggests that doing this is analogous to the way in which we strengthen our bodily resistance to disease: we can immunize ourselves to resist attempted persuasion. Vitamins, the right foods, and exercising, among other things, can strengthen our general resistance to diseases. Likewise, increasing the use of the resistance devices described above can increase our resistance to persuasive communication. In addition, building up antibodies can increase our resistance to a particular disease. Similarly, providing ourselves with arguments which refute the information provided in a particular persuasive communication increases our resistance to it. Many studies (see McGuire & Papageorgis, 1961; Macaulay, 1965; Tannenbaum & Norris, 1965) support McGuire's theory. Let's examine several of these studies.

McGuire and Papageorgis's subjects (1961) read essays which defended two of four cultural truisms (for example, "The effects of penicillin have been, almost without exception, of great benefit to humanity"; and "Mental illness is not contagious"). One essay contained information which supported a truism; the other essay contained information refuting the arguments against a second truism. Forty-eight hours later, the subjects read essays which attacked three of the four truisms—including the two which had been defended. Next, the subjects indicated their level of support for all four truisms. McGuire and Papageorgis reported that the subjects indicated strong support for the truism which had not been attacked. In contrast, the essays attacking the truisms produced a strong change in attitude toward those truisms which 2 days earlier had been either defended by supportive evidence or not defended at all. These observations indicate that the attack produced significant attitude changes and that merely knowing evidence to support our attitude does not provide resistance to persuasive communication. However, no change in attitude occurred when the subjects had read information which refuted the attack. Apparently, we can resist persuasive information if we possess knowledge which enables us to refute the arguments in a message designed to alter our attitude.

A study by Macaulay (1965) investigated the influence of two defense techniques, denial and refutation, on resistance to a persuasive communication. His results indicate that both denial and refutation reflect effective techniques for people to use to resist changing their attitudes. Also, Tannenbaum, Macaulay, and Norris (1966) discovered that attacking the source represents an effective method of resistance. In addition, Tannenbaum and Norris (1965) found that combining defense mechanisms provides more resistance than using a single resistance technique. Apparently, these resistance techniques can be used to prevent attitude change. In the next section, we will see what type of person is most likely to use these techniques.

A person's sensitivity to persuasion.   Are some people more persuadable than others? Hovland and Janis (1959) discovered that persons who are influenced by persuasion in one situation *tend* to be affected by persuasive communication in other situations. Although these observations suggest the existence of a persuadable personality, the persuasive communicator's effect is weak and, therefore, very dependent upon the prevailing environmental conditions.

Self-esteem seems to influence persuadability somewhat. Studies (see Cohen, 1959; Gollob & Dittes, 1965) have demonstrated that people with low self-esteem (feelings of inadequacy, social inhibitions, social inadequacy, social anxiety, test anxiety) tend to be more persuadable than people with high self-esseem. The reason for this is thought to be that people with high self-esteem make greater use of denial, or repression of information that is threatening to their attitudes, than people with low self-esteem do (Cohen, 1959; Silverman, 1964). Since people with low self-esteem do not think highly of their opinions, they will resist less than people with high self-esteem, who are convinced of the correctness of their view.

The higher degree of sensitivity to persuasive communication observed in people with low-self esteem (as compared with people with high self-esteem) depends upon the complexity of the situation (see McGuire, 1969). If the attack is relatively simple and the arguments against a particular view are easily understood, a person with low self-esteem will be less resistant to the persuasive influence of the message than a person with high self-esteem. However, if the message is complex and the arguments are difficult to understand, people with high self-esteem show more attitude change than people with low self-esteem. This effect is thought to reflect the fact that people with low self-esteem have greater difficulty in understanding complex communications. These observations indicate that the degree to which both people with high self-esteem and those with low self-esteem can be persuaded to change their attitude depends upon the nature of the communication.

We should note that the differences in persuadability between people with low self-esteem and those with high self-esteem merely reflect tendencies. Many people with low self-esteem are not susceptible to persuasion, while many people with high self-esteem are. Also, other factors (for example, intelligence, authoritarianism) have been suggested as influencing persuadability (see Freedman, Sears, & Carlsmith, 1978); however, since the evidence that these factors influence responsiveness to persuasion is very weak, it appears that personality characteristics do not have a strong influence on our resistance to persuasive communication. The effect of personality is weak because the source, the content of the message, and the situation can either activate our defenses or hinder our resistance to changing our attitudes. Earlier in the chapter, we saw how the source and content of a communication influence attitude change; let's end our examination of attitude change by looking at the influence of the *situation*.

Situational influences on resistance.   Two important situational variables have been identified which affect the resistance to persuasive communication: *forewarning* and *distraction*. Forewarning typically reduces the impact of a persuasive message; distraction usually enhances it.

Informing people in advance that their attitude is about to be threatened usually reduces the influence of the attack (see Freedman & Sears, 1965). Freedman and Sears told some teenagers 10 minutes beforehand that they were going to listen to a lecture on why teenagers should not drive. Other teenagers were not given the warning before they heard the lecture. Freedman and Sears reported that the forewarned subjects showed significantly less attitude change following the talk than the subjects who were not given the warning. Apsler and Sears (1968) and Dean, Austin, and Watts (1971) observed a similar effect.

However, forewarning counteracts the effects of a persuasive message only for people who are highly committed to their attitude. Forewarning does not decrease the influence of a persuasive communication for people who are uncommitted on an issue. In fact, forewarning can actually increase the level of attitude change if the subject is expecting to discuss the issue with the source of the message (Cialdini, Levy, Herman, & Evenbeck, 1973).

Freedman, Sears, and Carlsmith (1978) offered a reasonable explanation for the varied influence of forewarning. They asserted that forewarning will activate the resistance techniques of highly committed people (for example, counterarguments are generated), and this reduces the impact of the persuasive message. In contrast, since uncommitted people are not likely to resist having their attitude shaped by a persuasive communication, being forewarned will not be effective with these people. Furthermore, forewarned people with low commitment who expect to interact with the communicator are motivated to adopt the communicator's attitude in order to gain social approval.

Our discussion has revealed that committed people will actively resist attempts to alter their attitude. Active resistance requires the ability to focus attention on implementing resistance techniques. A number of studies (see Festinger & Maccoby, 1964; Zimbardo, Snyder, Thomas, Gold, & Gurwitz, 1970) have indicated that a distraction can increase the level of attitude change induced by a persuasive message, presumably by preventing people from using the techniques which are essential to resisting attitude change. In Festinger and Maccoby's study, subjects listened to a speech against fraternities while they viewed a film. In the "nondistraction" condition the film showed the speaker delivering the speech; in the "distraction" condition the film was *The Day of the Painter,* a funny, zany satire about modern art. Festinger and Maccoby assumed that the subjects who watched the satirical film would be distracted from listening to the persuasive message. As predicted, the speech produced greater attitude change for subjects in the "distraction" condition than for subjects in the "nondistraction" condition.

Zimbardo, Snyder, Thomas, Gold, and Gurwitz (1970) demonstrated that distraction typically influences people who are initially strongly opposed to the view advocated in the message and who are very familiar with the topic and attend to the distraction rather than to the message. Apparently, distracting highly committed persons from the persuasive comunication increased the effectiveness of the message. However, the distraction cannot be too effective, or the target will not attend to any of the message. These observations suggest that an attractive source can facilitate attitude change but should not be so attractive that the message is not noticed. For example, television commercials apply the distraction principle when they use attractive actors and actresses to persuade people to buy unwanted or unnecessary products.

SUMMARY

We have a strong motivation to develop a consistent understanding of the structure of our environment; this awareness enables us to obtain desired rewards and to avoid adversity. Our consistency motivation causes us to develop attitudes toward objects, people, and issues. An attitude consists of an affective and a behavioral reaction toward the attitude object as well as a cognition which indicates the basis of the affective and the behavioral components of our attitude.

Three processes are responsible for the development of an attitude: (1) association of a neutral stimulus with either pleasant or unpleasant experiences (classical conditioning), (2) reinforcement when we express a particular view (instrumental conditioning), or (3) our imitation of the attitudes of other people. We will act in accord with our attitudes if (1) the situation arouses our attitude, (2) we are confident of the correctness of our attitude, (3) we intend to express the attitude in actions, and (4) we know how to implement the appropriate behavior.

There are conditions which motivate attitude change. Perceived cognitive inconsistency is one potential cause of attitude change. Heider's balance theory assumes that we strive to maintain balanced P-O-X social relationships. Unbalanced P-O-X relationships are aversive and motivate us to reinstate balance by altering our attitudes. However, we will be motivated to eliminate imbalance only when our relationship with another person is positive: if we do not like someone, we do not concern ourselves with his or her views.

According to Festinger, cognitive inconsistency occurs when (1) we encounter new information which is antagonistic to an existing cognition, (2) we have chosen between two equally unattractive alternatives, or (3) our actions are contradictory to our attitudes. The perceived cognitive inconsistency arouses an aversive internal state, cognitive dissonance. Since dissonance is aversive, we are motivated to eliminate it. We can reduce cognitive dissonance and still maintain our attitude either by adding a new cognition to justify the inconsistency or by minimizing the importance of the dissonant information. However, when circumstances are such that we cannot reduce dissonance and still retain our attitude, we are forced to alter our attitude. Cognitive dissonance produced by "counterattitudinal" behavior leads to attitude change if we (1) choose to exhibit the attitude-discrepant behavior, (2) have publicly committed ourselves to the discrepant attitude, and (3) feel that the consequence of our action is unwanted or aversive.

Persuasive communication represents another potentially effective method of changing our attitudes. In order for a message to persuade us to alter our attitude, we must attend to, comprehend, and accept the view advocated in the communication. Several factors determine whether or not the message will change our attitude. We are more likely to accept messages from experts and trustworthy sources than from nonexperts and untrustworthy sources. The communication itself also influences its persuasiveness; we are most apt to be influenced by communications which reflect an optimum level of discrepancy between the source's attitude and ours, which arouse fear, or both. In addition, we may accept the source's attitude because we anticipate reward; the level of reward produced by our expression of acceptance determines the level of attitude change induced by the persuasive communication. However, we do not always passively accept changing our attitudes. Several resistance techniques (refuting the argument, attacking the source, distorting the content, using defense mechanisms, and simply rejecting the message) can counteract the effects of a persuasive communication. These methods are developed through experience and are most likely used by people with high self-esteem. Furthermore, the environment can be structured either to facilitate (by forewarning) or to hinder (by distraction) the use of these resistance techniques.

SOCIAL INFLUENCE

An act of defiance

*P*at and Ellen, friends since childhood, have worked for 10 years at the local furniture plant. Both women were content with their jobs; although their pay was low, they enjoyed their work and the atmosphere at the plant. This tranquility ended abruptly when the plant was unionized 3 months ago. The two women supported the establishment of the union and hoped that it would bring higher wages. This hope soon vanished: the company's offer was below the union's demands. After a month of negotiations, union officials decided that the workers must strike.

Ellen experienced turmoil in deciding whether to vote for the strike. Her husband was killed in an automobile crash two years ago, and she is responsible for providing for their 8-year-old child. Ellen felt that the union's demands were fair but knew that she could not survive without an income. Pat's thoughts about the strike did not coincide with Ellen's; her husband earns a good salary, and loss of her income would only mean sacrificing some luxuries. Pat told

Ellen that she would loan her money; but Ellen, who believes that self-sufficiency is important, did not want help. The union voted to strike, and the picket line was set up the following morning.

Ellen decided to strike with the union. She still had some of her husband's insurance money and hoped for a rapid resolution of the strike. The first few weeks passed smoothly; Ellen was able to spend more time with her child and Pat. However, as the strike continued and her savings dwindled, Ellen began to wonder if her decision had been right. Two weeks ago she returned to work. She is not happy with this choice; but she did not want either to apply for food stamps or to accept Pat's help. Pat understands Ellen's decision, but her other friends do not, and she has become the target of severe verbal abuse for crossing the picket line. She has also received threatening telephone calls, the tires of her car have been slashed, and her friends have snubbed her. This intense pressure was causing Ellen to consider rejoining the strike.

Last night Ellen learned that the plant has offered the union a new contract, to be voted upon soon. Ellen, of course, hopes that the union will accept the contract and | *thus end the strike. The end of the strike will provide relief from her conflict, although she realizes that her friends may never again accept her.*

Ellen's conflict between the social pressure from the union and its members and her own personal needs is not unusual. Each of us knows the feeling produced by a clash between the demands of society and our own values or desires. There are several ways to resolve this conflict; the easiest is to yield to the social pressure. Ellen responded by resisting the union; this is not a typical reaction, but it does occur. The rejection which follows such defiance is usually sufficient to ensure compliance. This chapter discusses the factors which motivate us to yield to social pressure and also examines the processes which motivate resistance to social influences.

SOCIETY'S NEEDS

Every group or organization establishes goals. For example, one goal of a university is to educate its students. All groups formulate rules specifying the behavior that their members exhibit in order to reach common objectives. A university indicates which courses students must take to receive a degree. However, no group can reach goals unless members behave appropriately; a group must motivate members to behave in those ways which will enable the group to attain goals. The appropriate behavior in a particular group is called a *norm*. Norms may differ from group to group or culture to culture, but all members of a particular group are expected to obey the norms established by it. For instance, cooperation between group members may be expected in one group but unacceptable in another.

Even though many of our behaviors do not directly help our group reach its goals, the group still specifies the appropriateness of our behaviors. On the one hand, our culture expects us to inhibit our negative emotions; on the other, it expects us to have a positive regard for the welfare of others. These and other social rules render life more predictable; we can anticipate and interpret the cause of the behavior of others. This predictability enables societies to function smoothly and increase the probability of reaching goals. Thus, every behavior either directly or indirectly allows a group to obtain objectives.

The establishment of norms is not sufficient to ensure that group members will obey them; the group must create conditions which motivate its members to exhibit the appropriate behaviors. The pressure in some situations is subtle: a member unsure of exactly how to behave watches the behavior of others and responds as they do. *Conformity* is the term which social psychologists use for a situation in which an individual adopts the group norms as a result of uncertainty. We accept our behavior without questioning the necessity of our actions when we conform to group pressure. We have no cause to doubt the "why" for many of our behaviors; we see no other alternative. Consider your clothes. You probably do not question why you wear them: you are merely behaving as others do. Yet, in another culture your clothes might appear unusual, and you might feel awkward. Thus, society determines the clothes you wear and the food you eat, but you are not aware of the social pressure motivating you to conform.

Informational Pressure

Why do we conform to the norms of our culture? Harold Kelley suggested in 1952 that groups link us with reality; we use their information to indicate how and when to behave.

According to Kelley, we conform to group norms because there is no other source of information. People near us supply information allowing us to interact more effectively with our environment. This reliance on others for information motivates us to behave in accordance with group standards, and this conformity in turn enables us to continue to receive this valuable information. Kelley termed the social pressure producing conformity *information pressure.*

Consider the following example to illustrate conformity. You are uncertain whether or not to enroll in a particular course. You could take the class and discover its value or lack of value yourself. In that case, you would gain knowledge about your environment from your own experiences. We might call this *personal reality.* However, it is less risky to rely on information provided by others. Therefore, you will probably ask several people who have taken the course about it. If they tell you that the course is good, you are likely to take it; if they react negatively, you probably will not enroll. When you behave in accordance with information provided by others, you are conforming to the information-al pressure supplied by their guidance. Your friends did not force you to enroll; in the absence of direct experience, your response is to use their experience or knowledge to guide you. Such *social information* gained from others furnishes a second type of reality—*social reality.* Our need for social reality causes us to conform to a group's norms.

There are various situations in which we doubt our group's wisdom. Under these conditions, our group will exert direct pressure on us to behave in accordance with its norms. This pressure may take the form of either a request or an order. Conflict exists in this type of situation because we must decide whether to behave as we want or as the group wants. Krech, Crutchfield, and Ballachey (1962) felt that without this pressure, we would not yield and behave in the manner specified by our group. Thus, *compliance* to social influence occurs when we change our intended or actual behavior as the result of overt group pressure.

Normative Pressure

In order to ensure compliance, the group specifies sanctions if a member does not comply. These sanctions frequently represent the loss of potential reward; if we do not behave according to the norms established by our group, we will be rejected by it, and therefore reward available to the group will not be available to us. For example, athletes who do not observe a curfew can be suspended from the team. Expecting to be rejected from a group when we do not adhere to its norms is known as responding to *normative social pressure* (Deutsch & Gerard, 1955). The compliance to normative pressure exerted by an authority is called *obedience.* This normative social pressure, according to Kiesler and Kiesler (1969), can be either real or imagined. However, people comply regardless of whether any actual sanctions occur: people comply with group pressure as long as they expect to be rejected or punished for not complying. Suppose that while you are studying, several of your friends ask you to go to a movie. You feel that you should study but agree to go. Why did you comply? One explanation is that you fear that rejecting their invitation might cause them to exclude you next time.

Rejection of deviates. Schachter's experiment (1951) demonstrates that groups do reject those who do not comply with their desires. Schachter placed three confederates in each of several groups of naive subjects. Each group was to discuss how to treat a juvenile deliquent named Johnny Rocco. In the discussion, one of the confederates (the *deviate*) consistently disagreed with the group's opinion; the second confederate (the *slider*) initially disagreed but quickly complied; and the third confederate (the *mode*) agreed with the group throughout. At first, each group would direct its attention to the deviate in an attempt to convince this person of the group's wisdom. However, the deviate's continued disagreement was met with silence from the group. After the discussion, group members were asked to indicate how much they liked or disliked the confederate. Schachter found that each group disliked the deviate but liked the slider and the mode, and that the slider and the mode were equally well liked. This suggests that a group will like a convert as much as a person who has always complied with group pressure. Schachter also asked group members to nominate, from among themselves, candidates for several future tasks. Some of the tasks appeared quite attractive, while others seemed unattractive. The groups did not choose deviates to participate in the attractive tasks; this indicates that rejection prevented the deviates from obtaining reward. However, groups did nominate the deviates for the unattractive tasks. This observation suggests that a group's sanctions involve aversive treatment of dissenters.

Punishment of deviates. The group may impose severe punishment—even death—on those who have failed to obey the rules. The behavior of workers at the Hawthorne plant of the Western Electric Company demonstrates punishment of deviates as pressure for compliance (see Homans, 1961). The employees at this plant had established their own standard level of acceptable performance; no one could work either above or below it without suffering consequences. Their standard provided good performance without too much hard work. Those who overstepped these boundaries by overworking were called "rate busters"; those who exerted too little effort were called "chiselers." These deviates received a sharp blow—called a "binge"—on the upper arm from any other worker who thought that they were not complying with the group code of behavior. Deviates could not retaliate but had to accept their punishment—and the rejection which it indicated.

Why does a group need to employ sanctions to prevent or modify the behavior of those who do not comply to its norms? These sanctions ensure that deviance from group rules does not become contagious. Solomon Asch's research (1956) demonstrates that compliance to a group decreases dramatically when even one person fails to comply. The attainment of a group's goals typically requires that its members obey the rules. Group goals will not be reached if deviance is allowed to persist. Therefore, sanctions are often necessary to ensure compliance with established norms. Consider the example of Ellen's returning to work during the strike. The union's goal was higher wages. If employees continue to work at current wages, the company would have no incentive to offer a better contract. Thus, the union's threats to Ellen were necessary to motivate her to rejoin the strike and thereby enhance everyone's chances of securing a better contract.

The reward for compliance. Not only do groups use fear of rejection or punishment to motivate compliance; they also reward those members who comply with group standards and withhold reward from members who do not comply. Parents who promise their children a new toy for completing homework are using reward to motivate compliance with their demands. An employee of a large firm who adheres to work standards in order to receive a salary is another example of a group's use of reward to motivate compliance. Parents can also withhold reinforcement to ensure that their children will comply; for example, the children may be forbidden to watch a favorite television show if their toys are not picked up. Soldiers can lose part of their salaries if they fail to behave in accordance with standards for performance.

A person's only motive for compliance with a group's norms may be acceptance by the group. Thibaut and Strickland's study (1956) provides evidence that the need to belong to a specific group motivates compliance (see Figure 12.1). Thibaut and Strickland structured their experiment to create interest in social relationships for half of their subjects and concern for ability to solve problems in the other half. The subjects

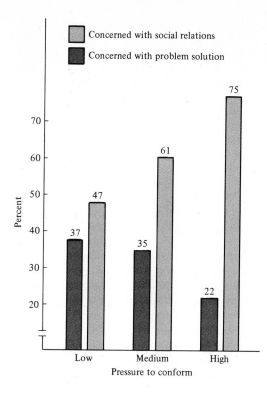

Figure 12.1
Percentage of subjects complying as a function of social pressure and the subjects' interest. [From Thibaut, J. W., & Strickland, L. H. Psychological set and social conformity. Journal of Personality, 1956, 25, 115–129. Reprinted by permission of the publisher. Copyright 1956, Duke University Press (Durham, N.C.)]

were placed in small groups and given a task involving complex perceptual judgments. Initially, each subject made a private judgment and was informed that this judgment would have to be defended later. Next, each subject was informed that the other subjects in the group unanimously opposed this initial judgment. After receiving this information, all subjects received a written message from one of their partners which urged compliance with the group's judgment. The letters applied either a low, a moderate, or a high degree of pressure. Thibaut and Strickland reported that increased social pressure produced greater compliance in subjects interested in social acceptance. These results imply that people will comply with a group norm to ensure social reinforcement. In contrast, social pressure created the opposite effect in subjects who were concerned with solving problems; the greater the pressure, the less the compliance. Why did group pressure actually reduce compliance for subjects interested in problem solving? These subjects, once committed to their judgment, probably viewed the opinions of other group members as hampering attainment of the goal. According to Jack Brehm (1966), when we believe that external forces reduce our ability to reach our goals, we act to regain control. Brehm called this process of responding to reinstate control *reactance*. Reactance, therefore, decreases compliance when group pressure threatens our self-control.

Public Behavior or Private Acceptance
The distinction between conformity and compliance is important. Social psychologists (for example, Allen, 1975) assume that when we comply because of fear of rejection or punishment or the desire to obtain reward, our public behavior does not indicate our private beliefs. We will behave in accord with our private beliefs only if social pressure is

removed. Consider prisoners of war who make negative statements about their country but repudiate them after being released. This observation suggests that the prisoners did not actually believe the statements but gave them in response to pressure from their captors. However, our social behavior may also reflect our private beliefs. It does so if we conform in response to informational pressure rather than to normative social pressure. There is evidence that such private acceptance of one's own behavior does not change after a person leaves the group.

Newcomb's studies (1943, 1963) of the attitudes of women attending Bennington College during the late 1930s demonstrate private acceptance. Newcomb discovered that the women's attitudes became more liberal the longer they remained at Bennington. By the time they were seniors, their attitudes were identical to the prevailing liberal sentiments at the college. These attitudes reflect the process of conformity: Newcomb noted that 25 years after these women had graduated from Bennington, their attitudes remained liberal; these same women were significantly more liberal in 1960 than a comparable group of women who had not attended Bennington. Sufficient informational pressure at Bennington changed these women's behavior. In contrast to the women whose attitudes did change, the small number of women who maintained their conservative attitude while at Bennington were less popular and influential with their classmates. Some of these women were unaware of the prevailing liberalism at Bennington because they maintained close friendships only with a few women who shared their conservatism. Others who did not conform were aware of the liberal attitude, but strong ties to conservative families prevented them from conforming.

Social psychologists have investigated the processes of conformity and compliance; the next two sections will describe the process which influence our motivation to conform or comply with social pressure. Not all people respond to their group's influence. The factors which cause them to defy group norms, as well as the implications of this dissent, also will be explored in these sections. The process of conformity begins our discussion.

CONFORMITY

In many situations, we are unsure how to act, think, or feel. Under these circumstances, we look at the behavior of those around us to determine our actions or feelings. We conform to the informational pressure provided by their behavior and respond as they do. Our tendency to conform leads us to accept these actions or feelings as appropriate, and we will continue to behave in this manner even when those who originally motivated us are no longer nearby.

Muzafer Sherif's research showed that the behavior of others governs our actions when we are confronted with a perceptually uncertain event. Other psychologists have demonstrated that (1) *once we yield to informational pressure, this conforming behavior will continue even in the absence of those who motivated it,* and (2) *the certainty of our judgments determines our sensitivity to social information—the more certain we are of the correctness of our behavior, the less likely we are to conform to informational pressure.* Let's now look at the evidence indicating that uncertainty motivates us to act like those around us.

The Need to Conform

Muzafer Sherif's classic study (1935) investigated the influence of group norms in an ambiguous situation (see Figure 12.2). Sherif showed his subjects a single pinpoint of light in a dark room and asked them to estimate the distance which the spot moved. In such a situation, although the light is stationary, it appears to move: this is called the

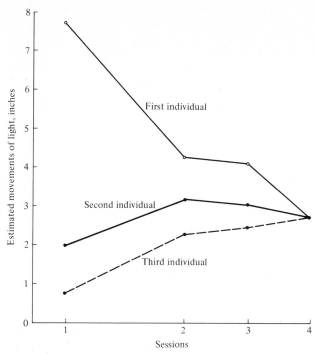

Figure 12.2
Establishment of a standard judgment of light movement for Sherif's study. In session 1, each subject made individual judgments. In sessions 2 and 3, three subjects in each group made their judgments together. In session 4, the subjects gave individual judgments again. [Page 103 (fig. 6) in The psychology of social norms by Muzafer Sherif. Copyright 1936 by Harper & Row, Publishers, Inc., renewed 1964 by Muzafer Sherif. Reprinted by permission of the publisher.]

autokinetic effect. Different subjects perceive different amounts of apparent movement. After Sherif's subjects made their initial judgments, they were placed in groups of three and asked to continue their estimates of the movement. Sherif reported that although the initial judgments of the subjects in each group differed, their estimates converged after several sessions until the judgments coincided. Apparently, a standard judgment (norm) was established and all members of each group "saw" approximately the same amount of movement. The norm for each group differed, but all members within a particular group responded in accordance with its established norm. Sherif demonstrated in this ambiguous situation that the behavior of the other group members influenced the judgment of each subject.

The behavior of Sherif's subjects reflected both private acceptance of and public response to a group's norms: these subjects continued to give the group's estimate after being removed from the group and tested alone—that is, after the direct influence of the group had been removed. The information needed to provide reality in this ambiguous situation was obtained by observing the behavior of others; this informational pressure acted to motivate conformity among group members.

Jacobs and Campbell (1961) demonstrated that a group norm could be established for the autokinetic effect which was very different from that of the normal judgment of any subject in the group. These researchers created the artificial norm by placing three confederates with one subject. The confederates estimated that the light had moved about 15 to 16 inches—a value highly different from the initial judgments of the actual subjects. Jacobs and Campbell found that the subjects reported seeing the extreme movement after having heard the confederates' estimates. Apparently, the three confederates established an unnatural standard judgment of movement which governed the actual behavior of subjects. This standard continued to control the subjects' behavior even after the confederates were removed from the experiment. Jacobs and Campbell replaced the confederates one by one with naive subjects. These subjects continued to use the group standard even though the confederates responsible for having established the norm were no longer present. These results indicate the importance of group judgment in ambiguous situations.

Second-Generation Conformity

Norms established by previous generations govern many of our behaviors; we act in accordance with these norms even though we did not create them. Jacobs and Campbell (1961) observed continuance of group standards in subjects who had not been present when the group created the standards. But although the new subjects conformed to the established standard group estimates of the autokinetic effect, the norms slowly changed over a period of several generations toward natural judgments. According to MacNeil and Sherif (1976), the group norms disintegrated because the standard was simply too unnatural and could not be maintained after the confederates had left the study. MacNeil and Sherif instructed their confederates to make estimates either very different or only slightly different from natural judgments. In either case, a standard judgment could be established and conformity could be maintained, but the slightly discrepant standard was more enduring. McNeil and Sherif observed that if confederates had made very unnatural estimates, the norms returned to the natural level within several generations after naive subjects had replaced the confederates. In contrast, the slightly arbitrary norm passed through many future generations with no apparent change.

Our discussion has indicated that when we need information to judge appropriate behavior, the accepted standard will motivate conformity. This norm will continue to elicit the conformity in future generations if it is not obviously at variance with the environmental sensory information. However, we do not all act, think, or feel alike. One reason for the diversity of human behavior is that we do not always enter into a new situation unsure of how to behave. Our past experiences can guide us: they can assure us that our particular mode of response is correct and eliminate our need to respond in the same manner as those around us. Thus, unless others exert overt pressure on us to comply, our certainty that our behavior is appropriate keeps us from conforming. We will now turn our attention to evidence that certainty influences the level of conformity.

Self-Confidence Studies

The importance of informational pressure in motivating conformity is best illustrated by studies evaluating how confidence in one's judgment influences the level of conformity. These experiments (for example, Coleman, Blake, & Mouton, 1958; Krech, Crutchfield, & Ballachey, 1962; Rosenberg, 1961; Snyder, Mischel, & Lott, 1960) show that subjects who are confident of their initial judgments will subsequently conform less in group situations—they are not likely to turn to their group for information regarding their actions. Let's briefly examine several of these studies.

Coleman, Blake, and Mouton (1958) presented their subjects with a series of factual questions. They varied the difficulty of the items—and, therefore, the certainty which subjects would feel about their own judgments—and observed that greater conformity to the group's judgment occurred with the harder items. Rosenberg (1961) had his subjects estimate the length of lines and then gave them feedback on their performance—half were told that they had done well, the other half that they had done poorly. On later tasks, Rosenberg found that those subjects who felt confident of their abilities conformed less than those who were uncertain.

The study by Krech, Crutchfield, and Ballachey (1962) assessed the influence of self-confidence on conformity more directly than the two studies just described. They asked their subjects to indicate the certainty of their judgments and reported that the surer the subjects were of their estimates, the less they conformed (see Figure 12.3). Interestingly, the majority of their subjects, even when uncertain, did not conform. There are two likely reasons for this. First, we must not only be uncertain of our own judgments but also confident of the correctness of the actions or feelings of others before we will conform. Many of Krech, Crutchfield, and Ballachey's subjects may have not been certain of the other subjects' judgment. Second, many subjects may have been skeptical about the purpose of psychological experiments and may therefore have viewed the other subjects as attempting to influence their judgments. As you will learn in the next section, many people do resist perceived pressure to comply. Thus, the absence of conformity may have been caused by defiance of perceived normative pressure. The circumstances leading people to resist social influence will be described in the next section.

Our discussion has indicated that we are more apt to conform when uncertain of our judgments than when sure of them. The study of Snyder, Mischel, and Lott (1960) shows

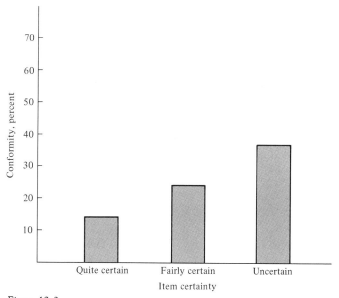

Figure 12.3
Percentage of subjects conforming to social influence as a function of the subjects' level of certainty. [From Krech, D., Crutchfield, R. S., & Ballachey, E. Cited in J. L. Freedman, D. O. Sears, & J. M. Carlsmith. Social psychology (3rd ed.). Englewood Cliffs, N.J.: Prentice-Hall, 1978.]

that our past experience can increase the certainty of our judgments and, thereby, reduce the impact of the actions of those around us. The following example will illustrate how our past experiences govern our level of conformity.

Suppose that you cannot decide whether to vote for the Republican or the Democratic candidate in the next presidential election. After discussing the political scene with your friends, you realize that most will vote Democratic. Our previous discussion has implied that your uncertainty probably will cause you to conform and vote as your friends will. However, would you still be likely to conform if you had recently read an article which had convinced you that the Republican candidate's views matched your own? The results of Snyder, Mischel, and Lott's study demonstrate that you would be less likely to agree with your friends if you had first read the article. Half of Snyder, Mischel, and Lott's subjects listened to a lecture about art before making artistic judgments; the other half did not hear the lecture. The researchers discovered that subjects who had received the artistic information conformed significantly less than did subjects who had not. These results suggest that people will exhibit less conformity when they have sufficient information other than that of group norms on which to base their judgments. Thus, conformity is more likely to occur when the group is our only source of information.

Our judgments do not always coincide with those of our group; nonetheless, we often act in agreement with its norms. In such instances, groups, having decided that it is important for our behavior not to deviate from their standards, exert overt or normative pressure in order to ensure our compliance with their norms. We now focus on compliance.

COMPLIANCE

Consider the following example to illustrate an important difference between conformity and compliance. Your friends enroll in a particular course which you are considering. Although you are uncertain of this course's value, your friends have told you that the instructor is an excellent teacher. If the information from your friends convinces you to enroll, you have conformed. However, if you believe that the instructor is not a good teacher and that you will not benefit from the course, yet enroll because your friends want you to, you have complied. Why would you comply and enroll in the course when you were uncertain of its value? Fear of your friends' disfavor probably causes you to enroll in the course—and comply.

It was pointed out in the introduction to this chapter that compliance occurs in response to normative pressure: we comply either to prevent rejection or punishment or to attain reinforcement, even though we do not believe that adherence to the group's norms is the correct response. We will now study the research which investigated the compliance process.

Asch's Studies of Compliance

During the 1950s, Solomon Asch (1951, 1952, 1956, 1958) conducted a series of experiments to investigate compliance. In a typical experiment, each subject's task was to match a line of standard length with one of three standard comparison lines (see Figure 12.4). This is a relatively simple task, and a subject's correctness is readily apparent. Each subject participated in a room with six other subjects. Sitting at a large table, they were instructed that the purpose of the experiment was to evaluate the accuracy of visual

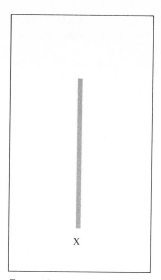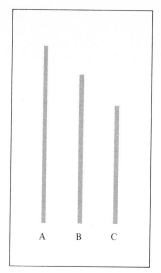

Figure 12.4
Stimuli similar to those used in Asch's study. The subjects' task was to indicate which of the three comparison lines (A, B, or C) matched the standard line (X).

perception. In each case, only one of these people was a true subject; the others were confederates instructed to give incorrect judgments at various times during the study. The true subject always responded fifth; thus the true subject's judgment was given after four of the confederates had answered. On the first few trials, the confederates gave the obviously correct answer. However, the confederates then conspired to give an incorrect response. For example, the standard might be 3 inches and the choices 3¾, 4¼, and 3 inches. Although the obvious reply is the last alternative, all the confederates would choose the second answer. The confederates gave incorrect choices on 12 of 18 trials. Asch found that one-third of the actual subjects responded incorrectly on each trial, even though they were aware that their choice was incorrect. Most subjects complied on some of the trials; but one-quarter never complied. Asch also reported that subjects felt conflict between agreeing with the group and responding correctly, indicating that they perceived pressure to comply. Some of the factors which operate to give rise to this perceived pressure are discussed in the following sections.

Asch's procedure does have a major drawback: an experimenter can test only one subject at a time and needs to use six confederates with each subject. Thus this procedure requires considerable experimental effort—and considerable cost—to complete a single study. To decrease the cost, Richard Crutchfield (1955) developed an automated procedure which enables an experimenter to test five subjects simultaneously without the need for confederates. Crutchfield placed each of his subjects in a small enclosed booth with a panel which enabled the subject both to respond and to obtain other subjects' responses. He told all subjects that they were subject number 5 and could not respond until they were presented with the responses of the first four subjects. It was in fact Crutchfield who provided the responses of the "first four subjects." Crutchfield's technique has been used for many different tasks, such as perceptual, informational, and attitude judgments. Although compliance with responses of the "imaginary" subjects does occur in Crutchfield's procedure, several studies (for example, Argyle, 1957) have demonstrated that there is less compliance than with Asch's method. Apparently, the physical presence of other people influences our level of compliance.

Our discussion has indicated that some people respond to group pressure and behave in agreement with their group's standards. However, other people do not comply. Many factors interact to determine compliance; some of them increase the chances of compliance, others decrease it. To predict if a person will comply, the characteristics of a specific situation must be known; let's first look at the personality factors influencing compliance and follow with a description of the situational determinants of compliance.

Personality Determinants of Compliance

Social psychological research has shown that some people are more likely to respond to group pressure than others (see Crutchfield, 1955). Crutchfield evaluated compliance levels among businessmen and military men and discovered that those who complied were less intelligent, showed less leadership ability, exhibited greater feelings of inferiority, and were more authoritarian than those who did not yield to group pressure.

Why are compliers more responsive to social influence than noncompliers? Adorno, Frenkel-Brunswick, Levinson, and Sanford's research (1950) on the *authoritarian personality* suggests that early experience with the consequences of noncompliance determines the effectiveness of social pressure to comply. Adorno, Frenkel-Brunswick, Levinson, and Sanford discovered that authoritarians have the following traits: (1) *a high level of compliance,* (2) *dependence on authority,* (3) *overcontrol of feelings and impulses,* and (4) *rigidity of thinking.* Very strict parental control plays an important role in the development of the authoritarian personality: severe punishment by parents teaches children to inhibit anger and resentment and to develop the attitude that yielding to authority permits survival. As adults, these people continue to believe that obedience to authority is appropriate and to displace their anger on those not belonging to their group.

Some psychologists have criticized research on the authoritarian personality (see Rokeach, 1960). But for several reasons their criticism—however valid—does not detract from the idea that early experience determines susceptibility to social pressure. First, the main objections involve the proposed link between the authoritarian personality and right-wing prejudice toward minority groups. Current thinking (refer to Billig, 1976) suggests that being authoritarian does not create prejudice; rather, the social structure establishes an acceptance of prejudice, and authoritarians' sensitivity to social pressure motivates them to accept their group's hatred of other groups. Thus authoritarians do not have a specific set of beliefs: it is their willingness to comply with group norms which leads to prejudice. Second, the type of experiences (for example, punishment for noncompliance) leading to the development of an authoritarian personality have been found to motivate compliance. Finally, research (for example, Crutchfield, 1955) has discovered that authoritarian people are more compliant in experimental settings than nonauthoritarian people. Apparently, early experience plays a significant role in determining our sensitivity to social influence.

Stanley Milgram's research (1961, 1977) demonstrates that a group's acceptance of noncompliance also influences the responsivity of individuals in that group to social pressure. Milgram studied compliance in Norwegian and French subjects and found Norwegian subjects more responsive to social influence. Milgram suggested that differences in cultural background caused these results. Norwegians, who are believed to possess intense feelings of group identity, have established strong social institutions for the protection and care of others. In contrast, the French have shown less consensus in their social and political attitudes. These observations point to the importance of the socialization process in our response to group pressure.

Although our personality traits clearly influence compliance, behavioral characteristics determine only our tendency to yield to social pressure. The strongest determinant of compliance is the situation; we may comply in one instance but not in another. Stricker, Messick, and Jackson's study (1970) shows that a person's compliance to group opinion does not occur in all occasions. They measured the degree of compliance in four different situations and evaluated the possibility that a subject who had complied in one situation would also comply in another. In one case, the experimenters found no transference of compliance from one task to another; subjects who had complied in one situation were no more likely to comply in the second situation than those who had not complied. In another comparison, there was a moderate tendency for subjects who had complied in one situation to comply in the other. However, most of Stricker, Messick, and Jackson's comparisons displayed only a weak tendency for subjects to respond identically in two different situations. This suggests that the environment has a critical role in determining compliance; situational characteristics can alter our behavioral tendencies.

One possible reason for the significance of environmental influence is that different situations place different pressure on us to comply. Another explanation is that we consider the pressure appropriate and comply in some cases, while at other times we consider the pressure inappropriate and do not comply. We will now examine the situational factors which determine whether or not we comply.

Situational Determinants of Compliance

People sometimes respond to group pressure and behave in agreement with their group's standards. At other times, people ignore group pressure and do not comply. Social psychological research indicates that some situational circumstances increase compliance, while others decrease it. Let's now examine those situational factors.

Group unanimity. The level of agreement within a group strongly influences the level of compliance; the presence of dissent significantly reduces compliance (Asch, 1956). In one of his experiments, Asch instructed one confederate, who responded before the actual subject, to disagree with the other confederates. The presence of a single dissenter produced an 8 percent level of compliance, which contrasts sharply with the 35 percent compliance rate if no dissenter, or confederate, was used.

The dissenter's characteristics did not seem important. Malof and Lott (1962) observed that a black dissenter among white subjects reduced compliance as much as a white dissenter. In addition, Morris and Miller (1975) discovered that the decrease in compliance was equivalent when the dissenter was a high-prestige expert or a low-prestige nonexpert. Finally, the deviant does not even have to answer correctly; Allen and Levine (1969) observed decreased compliance in both a perceptual and an information task when a dissenter provided either a correct or an incorrect response. Although Allen and Levine's results showed only a tendency toward less compliance when a dissenter gave an unpopular opinion, Wilder and Allen (1978) demonstrated reduced compliance in an opinion situation even if the dissenter's opinion was unpopular. In Wilder and Allen's study, the opinions of the majority were at one end of the scale, the dissenters' opinions at the other end, and the actual subjects' opinions in between. The experimenters reported less compliance when there was dissent than when there was unanimity. Apparently, dissent is sufficient to reduce compliance.

Why does dissent dramatically decrease compliance? It is clear that information conveyed by the dissent does not reduce compliance; subjects who participated in compliance studies believed that their answers were correct even without having known of the dissenter's response. Compliance is reduced, in all probability, because dissent indicates to us that our opinion is permissible and will not lead to rejection or punishment. Thus, if someone sees that a dissenter is neither rejected nor punished, others will follow this pattern and soon there will be no compliance. This observation suggests that a group which believes that compliance is necessary to accomplish goals must punish deviance. The brutal public executions of deviants in some cultures illustrate both the importance of preventing the reduction in compliance produced by deviance and the extreme measures which some take to ensure compliance.

Group size. The size of a group strongly influences the likelihood that members will comply with its pressure: the more people in our group, the greater the level of our compliance. However, the effect of size on compliance is limited. Asch (1951) made comparisons of compliance when each of his subjects was with either 1, 2, 3, 4, 8, or 15 confederates. His results revealed that subjects' compliance was greatest when 4 or more confederates participated. Employing Crutchfield's technique, Rosenberg (1961) found a similar effect: compliance was greatest when 4 confederates were used. However, other studies have indicated that greater compliance occurs in groups which are larger than 4. For example, Gerard, Wilhelmy, and Connolley (1968) demonstrated that compliance increased up to a group size of 8.

A particular situation may affect how many in a group are necessary for maximum compliance to occur. In some circumstances, only a small number of group members may be needed to produce compliance; in other situations, a large group may be necessary. Since a relatively large number of factors influence compliance, the observation that the effect of group size differs from situation to situation is not surprising. The number of people needed to motivate someone to comply will depend upon the relative influence of the other factors which are present when group pressure is applied.

Social status.   It is unlikely that all members of a group will be involved in pressuring an individual to conform. In most instances, only a few individuals from a large group attempt to produce compliance. Norma Feshbach's research (1967) points out that the status of group members influences the amount of compliance showed by a person who wants to belong to the group. Feshbach used four members of a college fraternity—two popular (high status) and two unpopular (low status). Their task was to estimate which card had the most dots. A correct response produced a monetary reward; an incorrect response cost the fraternity money. Feshbach observed that the low-status subjects agreed with the high-status subjects even if they believed that the high-status subjects were responding incorrectly. In contrast, high-status subjects were more likely to deviate from the views of low-status subjects.

Why should people's status determine the level of compliance which they can induce in others? We have previously related that a group will reject or punish those who deviate from the group norms. Threat of rejection or punishment is one reason why we comply when pressured. Since high-status people typically control the process of rejection or punishment, low-status persons comply with those above them in order to reduce the likelihood of rejection or punishment. Because high-status people feel secure in their position within the group, they experience less threat if they do not comply.

Compliance also results from efforts to obtain the rewards available to group members. Since low-status people typically want to be accepted, they can gain acceptance—reward—by acting like the high-status group members. On the other hand, high-status people are already receiving acceptance (reward) and so feel less pressure to comply. Supporting the view that acceptance plays an important role in motivating compliance, Dittes and Kelley (1956) noted that those who did not feel secure about their acceptance by a group exhibited the highest level of compliance.

Reactance. In our description of reactance we learned that when people believe that their self-control is threatened, an intense internal reactance state is created motivating them to act in a way which reinstates control. Thus, if strong social pressure to comply creates reactance, a person might resist complying in order to reinstate control. Brehm and Sensenig's study (1966) is one example demonstrating the importance of reactance in producing resistance. They gave their subjects a choice of working on two problems. Subjects were erroneously told that some would perform better on task A and others would perform better on task B. Before choosing one task, each subject received a note from his or her partner—a confederate—stating the confederate's preferences and exerting pressure to comply. In the "low pressure" condition, the note said, "I choose problem A"; in the "high pressure" condition, the note read, "I think that we should both do problem A." Brehm and Sensenig found that whereas 70 percent of the subjects in the "low pressure" condition complied, only 40 percent of those in the "high pressure" condition chose the task that their partner picked. Evidently, intense pressure to comply produces the opposite effect; people resist social pressure when their freedom is threatened.

The reactance process appears to represent an example of the drive system detailed in Chapter 2: the perceived loss of control creates an internal arousal which motivates a person to reduce it by regaining control. In the case of compliance, this person's behavior will also have negative anticipated consequences; group rejection or physical punishment is likely to occur following the resistance. This expectation of the negative consequences of failing to yield to social pressure should prevent resistance. Reactance arousal obviously is often a more intense motivator than the expectation of social rejection or punishment. Yet cognitive processes do play an important role in producing resistance. People will resist social pressure if they do not expect disapproval to follow their resistance. A situation where there is an expectation of safe resistance is described in the next section.

Deindividuation. We have discussed the idea that fear of deviance undoubtedly represents an important motive which produces compliance. If this idea is valid, it follows that we will resist social influence when we do not fear the consequences of noncompliance. One way to evaluate this statement is to create a situation in which a person feels anonymous and thus feels that he or she is not likely to be noticed for noncompliance. Fortunately, Philip Zimbardo's research (see Zimbardo, 1970) describes a process called *deindividuation* in which people lose their sense of identity. Deindividuation happens when members of a group have no distinctive characteristics. Zimbardo found that people with power become more aggressive when their unique identity is lost, while those without power not only become the target of this aggression but are also passively willing to accept the aggression directed at them.

Deindividuation also decreases the probability that we will comply (Singer, Brush, & Lublin, 1965). One group of Singer, Brush, and Lublin's subjects wore white laboratory coats in order to reduce their distinctiveness; subjects in a second group wore dresses or suits and name tags to increase their distinctiveness. The experimenters reported significantly less compliance in the first group. Absence of a unique identity makes it difficult for individual group members to be singled out and punished. Therefore, if persons believe that their deviance is not likely to be punished, they probably will not comply with group pressure.

The Conversion of the Majority

What if merely resisting established group norms did not satisfy you? Suppose that you want to convince your peer group of the wisdom of your judgment, in order to change the group standards. You might feel, too, that unless you modify your peers' views, they will not allow you to continue your resistance and remain in the group. A member of a minority group can use two approaches to produce compliance in the majority group. *First, you can confront your peers with the logic of your view. Second, you can use a more subtle approach: you can win your peers' approval by using flattery or favors and then request their compliance with your values.* Edward Jones (1964) called the second method *ingratiation.* Evidence indicates that under appropriate conditions both the direct and the indirect approach represent an effective method for motivating compliance by the majority. We will now examine this evidence.

A direct approach.   Consider this example: How could you motivate your peers to adopt your standards of fashion? You can change prevailing group norms, according to Moscovici and Faucheux (1972), by forcefully presenting your beliefs in a consistent and coherent manner. Your determination will raise doubts in the majority and provide them with new information which eventually will change their views. However, you must not present your view rigidly. It must be clear to the majority that you feel their beliefs are reasonable—only less valid than yours. For instance, you might suggest that although the standard fashion is attractive, yours is more fashionable. In support of this view, Mugny (1975) found that the majority accepted a minority view argued in a reasonable and firm way more than one presented dogmatically. A direct presentation of a minority view, though not the approach for the timid, can alter the majority's standards. Eventual acceptance of antiwar sentiments during the Vietnamese war is one example of the effectiveness of a determined effort by a minority to motivate conformity by the majority.

Moscovici and Faucheux suggest that a minority group member must be perceived as self-confident before dissent can be successful; this self-assurance often causes a majority to doubt the wisdom of its beliefs. However, one dissenter is not likely to cause the majority to feel that the minority view is correct, although one dissenter's self-confidence may cause the majority to question its standards (Nemeth, Wachtler, & Endicott, 1977). Moreover, the majority will not alter its beliefs unless it perceives that the minority view is correct.

Nemeth, Wachtler, and Endicott investigated the importance of size of a minority on both the perceived correctness of the minority view and the degree of conformity by the majority. They placed either 1, 2, 3, or 4 confederates (the minority) with a group of six naive subjects (the majority). The subjects were shown colors and asked to judge them. The confederates' responses were obviously incorrect. But Nemeth, Wachtler, and Endicott noticed that conformity of the majority to those incorrect responses was greater as the size of the minority increased. This was also correlated with the subjects' perception that the minority view was correct: subjects believed the minority opinion to be more valid when the minority was larger. Table 12.1 presents the results of their study. These results suggest that to change majority standards a dissenter must enlist others' support. Therefore, some of your peers must adopt your taste in clothing before you can change your group's standards of fashion. Assuming that you do influence several peers,

Table 12.1
Influence of Minority Size on the Perceived Competence of the
Minority and Majority Compliance

| | Minority Size | | | |
	1	2	3	4
Number of times minority judgment was adopted	1.35	1.31	2.25*	1.88
Perceived competence of the minority†	3.78	4.28	4.42	4.52

Note: Subjects in a control condition never gave the minority view expressed by the confederate. The higher the value, the greater the compliance with, and perceived competence of, the minority view.

*This value is significantly greater than the number in the one-confederate condition.

†There was a significant increase in the perceived competence as minority size increased.

Adapted from: Nemeth, C., Wachtler, J., & Endicott, J. Increasing the size of the minority: Some gains and some losses. *European Journal of Social Psychology,* 1977, *7,* 15–27. Copyright 1977 by John Wiley & Sons, Ltd. Reprinted by permission of John Wiley & Sons, Ltd.

and that your group is unable to modify your dissent, the group will then probably adopt your view.

This direct approach is not without peril: the majority will exert great pressure to "break" a dissenter. Minorities often use a more subtle approach, ingratiation. How ingratiation works is our next topic.

Ingratiation: A subtle approach.   Before acceptance of a minority view by the majority can develop, the individual holding the minority view must win the approval of one member of the majority—the *target*. Ingratiation can be used for this purpose. Jones (1964) suggested that the ingratiator has four methods for doing this. First, the ingratiator can flatter the target to gain the target's liking. Second, the ingratiator can present himself or herself in a positive way to impress the target. A misrepresentation of the ingratiator is sometimes needed to gain approval and acceptance from the target. Third, the ingratiator can give a target favors in the expectation that the target will reciprocate the favors later. Finally, the ingratiator might even comply with some of the target's views in order to gain the liking necessary for subsequent compliance.

The evidence collected by Edward Jones and other researchers indicates that ingratiation does motivate conformity in the majority. We will briefly describe evidence that (1) *ingratiation does occur when people are motivated to influence majority group members,* (2) *these tactics do produce a target's acceptance and approval of an ingratiator,* and (3) *a target does comply with a minority person's views.* Let's look at an ingratiator's actions.

The need to be an ingratiator.   We have suggested that the purpose of ingratiation is to gain approval. Supporting this view, Zanna and Pack's study (1975) illustrates that ingratiation takes place only when someone seeks acceptance; it does not occur when approval is not desired. Zanna and Pack asked each of their subjects—female undergraduate college students—to describe herself to an unseen male partner. The women were given one of two descriptions of their partner: (1) "Physically unattractive; involved in a close relationship with a woman; not interested in meeting other women." With this description, the subjects gave honest descriptions of themselves which indicated that they had no desire to win their male partner's approval. (2) "Physically attractive; unattached; intelligent; interested in meeting women." With this description, the female subjects not only described themselves favorably, but also gave presentations specifically designed to impress their partner. When told that the man had conservative values, they asserted that they cherished traditional relationships. On the other hand, when informed that the man believed that women should be career-minded, independent, and ambitious, the subjects presented themselves as liberated. These results indicate that ingratiation occurs only when approval is desired and the ingratiator's self-presentation is structured to win the acceptance of a specific target. You will next see the results of an ingratiator's efforts to gain acceptance and approval and to induce compliance by a majority.

The success of ingratiation.   Effective ingratiation causes a member of the majority to like a member of the minority. Chapter 9 described factors producing attraction; praise and reward are important determinants of liking. The ingratiator's tactics provide the praise and reward necessary to induce liking. Thus, the ingratiator's actions establish the conditions necessary for the establishment of social relationships. However, the ingratiator must be extremely careful not to communicate his or her actual intent to the target. A too flattering or self-serving ingratiator may cause the target to suspect an ulterior motive. Under these circumstances, the probability that the ingratiator will induce liking is reduced. Furthermore, dislike may result if the target believes that the ingratiator is attempting to control him or her.

Past research indicates that ingratiation produces liking if the target does not suspect manipulation. Dickoff's study (1961) illustrates the effectiveness of ingratiation in interpersonal attraction. Dickoff's women subjects listened to an evaluation of themselves by a graduate student who previously had viewed each subject from behind a one-way mirror while the subjects (who were aware that they were being observed) answered questions concerning their backgrounds, values, and opinions. The graduate student gave each subject one of three evaluations: (1) an unrealistic, extremely positive evaluation, (2) a realistic evaluation corresponding to the subject's previously established measure of self-esteem, and (3) a neutral evaluation. The experimenters gave the subjects different explanations of why the graduate student was participating in the study. Half of the subjects in each evaluation condition thought that the graduate student was giving an honest and objective appraisal; these subjects had been told that the graduate student was using them to test a special clinical training procedure aimed at preventing feelings from affecting judgment. Dickoff found that under this condition, subjects who were uncritically praised developed a strong liking for the graduate student. The other half of the subjects suspected that the graduate student had an ulterior motive; these subjects had been told that the graduate student had agreed to substitute for another assistant (who was ill), in the hope that the same subjects would later agree to participate in a study of her own. These subjects reported greater liking for the graduate student if she evaluated them realistically than if she gave uncritical praise. Dickoff's results demonstrate that praise by an ingratiator produces liking only if the target does not suspect an ulterior motive. If an ulterior motive is suspected, the ingratiator will be more effective by using an honest appraisal.

An ingratiator's actions can not only produce liking but also motivate compliance (see Jones, Gergen, & Jones, 1963). In the study by Jones, Gergen, and Jones, some subjects were motivated to act as ingratiators: each of these subjects—low-status naval ROTC students (freshmen)—was told that in order to measure his potential leadership

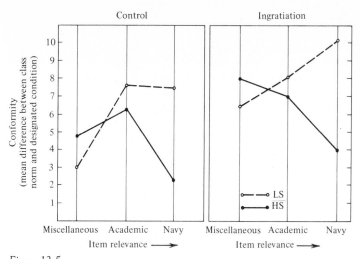

Figure 12.5
Level of compliance ("conformity") in high- and low-status subjects as a function of treatment and item relevance. [From Jones, E. E., Gergen, K. J., & Jones, R. G. Tactics of ingratiation among leaders and subordinates in a status hierarchy. Psychological Monographs, 1963, 77 (3, whole no. 566). Copyright 1963 by the American Psychological Association. Reprinted by permission.]

ability, he must get his partner—a high-status upperclassman—to like him. The pairs were separated and instructed to communicate with each other about topics related to the Navy, academic concerns, and other activities. Control subjects were similarly paired and separated but were instructed to make their discussions as accurate as possible. In this study, half of the high-status subjects were also motivated to be ingratiators; but our main concern is whether the low-status subjects did behave in an ingratiating manner and, if so, whether this affected the target (high-status) persons. The experimenters intercepted the messages and altered them to provide a standard input to all subjects. Jones, Gergen, and Jones observed that low-status subjects in the "ingratiation" condition complied more often than low-status control subjects on issues relating to the Navy. High-status subjects considered these Navy-related topics extremely important; the low-status subjects undoubtedly complied on these topics in order to increase their acceptance and approval. One indication of this liking was compliance by the high-status subjects to the opinions of the low-status ingratiators on issues unrelated to the Navy. The experimenters reported that low-status subjects in the "ingratiation" condition conformed more than low-status control subjects on topics related to the Navy. In contrast, high-status "ingratiation" subjects agreed with their low-status partners' views unrelated to the Navy more than high-status control subjects did. These results, shown in Figure 12.5, demonstrate that ingratiation produced compliance in a target majority person.

An Attributional Role in Compliance

Suppose that you are watching your favorite television show when several friends ask you to go out with them for a pizza. You tell them that you do not want to go, but they insist. You are faced with two questions: (1) Why are my friends asking me? and (2) Why am I resisting their request? The first question concerns the motives for your friends' behavior; the second involves the attribution of your motives. Your decision to comply or not comply with their request depends upon the comparison you make between your motives and theirs. If you feel that everyone will gain from your yielding, you are likely to comply; however, if you believe that their gain will outweigh yours, you probably will not go. For example, you might believe your car is the only reason for their asking you, and you know that if you go out you will not see your show. Thus, only they would benefit from your compliance. Under these circumstances, you will probably resist yielding to group pressure.

Ross, Bierbraver, and Hoffman (1976) investigated the influence of causal attributions on compliance in a task involving perceptual judgment. Compliance was reduced if subjects attributed the confederates' incorrect responses to a desire to obtain a larger payoff. In contrast, subjects complied when they felt that both they themselves and the confederates would benefit equally from having responded incorrectly. Apparently, our causal attributions of why people behave differently from ourselves do play an important role in determining whether we will change our behavior and respond as others do.

Applications of the Social Influence Process

Two techniques employed to produce compliance are *low-balling* and *foot-in-the-door*. Each involves having people respond acceptably; their actions are then used to motivate them to behave in a manner inconsistent with their attitudes or values. However, these two methods differ slightly. In low-balling, a person is committed to an acceptable action, and then the situation is altered. Participation in the new situation would be unacceptable if the prior commitment had not been made—but once committed, the person now feels forced to accept the altered circumstance. In contrast, in the foot-in-the-door technique a small acceptable request is followed by a more substantial one. A person's compliance with the small request makes him or her more likely to yield to the second, large request.

Low-balling a customer.   Consider an automobile salesperson using low-balling to coerce a customer into accepting a "bad deal." The customer is initially offered a new car at an attractive price and agrees to a deal. However, the salesperson then informs the customer that these terms have been discussed with the manager, and a mistake has been made—too much money was offered for the customer's old car, and this would leave the company unable to make a profit. The customer can still purchase the car, but it will cost several hundred dollars more. The customer ordinarily would not buy this car at the higher price but, having been once committed, will now comply and pay the new price. Although a reprehensible practice, low-balling is both a widespread and, typically, an effective technique for motivating compliance (*Consumer Reports*, May 1974).

Cialdini, Cacioppo, Bassett, and Miller (1978) investigated low-balling in real-world and laboratory settings; their research demonstrates its effectiveness in producing compliance. Let's consider one of their studies. These experimenters asked 63 college students to participate in a psychology experiment. There were two conditions: (1) Subjects in the "low-balling" condition first agreed to participate and were then told that the experiment would begin at 7 A.M. (2) Control subjects were informed of the time before they agreed to participate. Cialdini, Cacioppo, Bassett, and Miller found that 56 percent of the subjects in the "low-balling" condition agreed to participate, as compared with only 31 percent of the control subjects. Additionally, 53 percent of the "low-balling" subjects, but only 24 percent of the control subjects, actually arrived at 7 A.M. Since most college students feel that 7 A.M. is suitable only for sleeping, the greater participation by the subjects who had committed themselves beforehand shows the effectiveness of low-balling. Cialdini, Cacioppo, Bassett, and Miller suggested that once we have decided to act, we become *personally committed* to the action. Even if the situation is altered, failure to carry out our commitment would lower our self-image.

The foot-in-the-door technique. The foot-in-the-door technique is also frequently employed by salespeople to motivate compliance on the part of customers. A salesperson using this method initially makes a small, reasonable request of a potential customer and then, after the customer has complied, makes a more substantial request. If the foot-in-the-door technique is effective, customers will comply with the second request—a request which they probably would not have agreed to if they had not agreed to the initial one.

To illustrate the foot-in-the-door method, consider Freedman and Fraser's experiment (1966). The subjects were women who lived in houses with front lawns. Subjects in one group were asked if a small sign urging motorists to drive safely could be installed on their lawns. Several weeks after these women had agreed to this small request, each was asked to place a huge sign with the same message on her lawn. Seventy-five percent complied with this large request, as compared with only 20 percent of the control subjects (who had not received a prior request). Freedman and Fraser showed that the two requests need not be related in order for the technique to be effective. Another group of subjects were first asked to sign a petition on a different matter—increased beautification; 50 percent of these subjects later agreed to put the ugly signs on their lawns. These results indicate that likelihood of compliance with a substantial request can be increased by first having people agree to a small request.

Why is this foot-in-the-door technique effective? According to Freedman and Fraser, we create a positive self-image when we agree to do a small favor for someone. Then, if someone asks us to comply with a larger request, our positive self-image motivates our compliance. Several studies support this perceptual model of compliance: (1) Snyder and Cunningham (1975) observed that different organizations can make the first and second request; (2) Seligman, Bush, and Kirsch (1976) showed that the initial request cannot be too easy. Apparently, the initial compliance must be sufficient to cause us to believe that we did something important. Once we have created this positive self-concept, we will try to live up to our self-image, and therefore will be susceptible to complying to a larger request—even one from another organization.

We have pointed out that people comply when they are experiencing social pressure. Are there any behaviors that people will not exhibit in response to pressure from others? As we have seen, subjects working on a task involving perceptual judgment will report that a short line is long. When they are exposed to social pressure, will these same people respond in a manner which is antagonistic to their morality? The research of Stanley Milgram (see Milgram, 1974) shows dramatically that most psychologically sound people will inflict severe harm on another person in response to the demands of a legitimate authority.

OBEDIENCE

The Inhumanity within Us

The atrocities committed by the Nazis during World War II shocked the world: approximately 12 million men, women, and children—Jews and others—were murdered; and the enormity and brutality of these acts continue to disturb humanity. Unfortunately, the Nazis were not unique: mass murders of minority groups have occurred all too often. The Spanish Inquisition was responsible for killing many heretics, and the communists executed millions of noncommunists after the Russian Revolution—these are only two of the more striking examples of human brutality. What processes could motivate people to commit such atrocities?

The German generals' justification of their war crimes suggests the mechanism which caused their brutality (see Arendt, 1963). They did not think that their behavior was inappropriate: they were merely following their superiors' orders and could not be responsible for the thousands of citizens whom their soldiers shot. These generals' behavior is an example of *obedience*. Berkowitz (1980) defines obedience as an automatic, relatively unthinking response to an authority figure within a group. Adherence to group values occurs in both obedience and compliance. When we *comply*, we respond to pressure from peers. When we *obey*, we respond to a superior's command. However, there is an important difference between obedience and compliance. Obedience is more likely to cause you to act contrary to your morality (Milgram, 1974). The German generals' justification for their actions illustrates the three components of obedience: (1) *acceptance of the rightfulness of the behavior*, (2) *belief that the action occurred in response to the command of a legitimate authority*, and (3) *belief that the responsibility for the consequences of this behavior rests with the authorities who initiated the order*.

Was the obedience of the German generals to their superiors' orders an isolated incident which is not likely to happen again? Unfortunately, the evidence suggests that this level of inhumanity can and probably will occur again. The smaller-scale murder of innocent civilians at My Lai by Charlie Company during the Vietnamese war provides another reminder that human beings have great potential for brutality (see *Time*, December 5, 1969). Expecting to encounter strong enemy resistance, Charlie Company entered the village of My Lai to find only old men, women, and children. The soldiers herded 45 civilians into the center of the village and then searched for weapons. The massacre began when Lieutenant William Calley ordered his soldiers to kill the Vietnamese. During the rest of the day, between 450 and 550 civilians were killed; they were either placed in huts which were then set afire or herded into ditches and shot. Some of the soldiers reported that they did not want to kill the civilians but did so to keep from being court-martialed. Others felt that they were only obeying their officers' legitimate orders. Still others indicated that they had acted only after having seen their friends shooting civilians. However, not all the soldiers of C Company were involved in the massacre; several refused to shoot, and one sholdier shot himself in the foot so that he would not have to kill anyone. Perhaps the most disturbing aspect of this incident was that the soldiers who committed these crimes were otherwise apparently normal. They were not experienced soldiers, having been in Vietnam for only 1 month, but they were a very close-knit group. They seemed unlikely candidates for the horrors which they committed. These observations suggest that each of us, under some circumstances, might participate in a similar crime. Shortly, we will examine more compelling evidence for this statement.

Why did these soldiers massacre civilians at My Lai? The answer lies in the nature of the obedience process. Hannah Arendt (1978) suggests that we follow orders because we accept the idea that our superiors have the right to tell us what to do. This compliance results from our past experience with authority figures. We know that a judge will fine us if we drive above the speed limit. As children, we learned that our parents would punish us if we failed to take care of our belongings and that our teacher would fail us for not completing assigned projects. Thus, authority figures possess power and can punish our failure to obey.

This authority must be accepted in order for obedience to occur. French and Raven (1959) observed that people are more likely to adopt the views of an elected official than the views of one who has seized command. Blau (1964) suggested that group members' collective approval transfers authority to a particular person or persons. This process has made their authority legal, and the group members will subsequently yield to the authorities' commands. Thus, once legitimate, an authority can under certain conditions motivate subordinates to commit brutal acts against others. Stanley Milgram's research demonstrates how easy it is for authority figures to motivate obedience. Milgram's work depicts both the power of an authority figure and the factors which determine the level of obedience.

Milgram's Research on Obedience

Original study. Stanley Milgram's laboratory research evaluated the conditions influencing obedience. In considering his research, we focus first on the conditions producing the highest level of obedience and then on the factors causing this level of obedience, as well as factors which decrease obedience.

Milgram (1963) placed advertisements in newspapers to recruit male subjects; thus, he had a wider diversity of subjects—blue-collar workers, salesmen, businessmen, and professionals between the ages of 20 and 50—than a typical psychology experiment does. Upon entering the laboratory, each subject individually met the experimenter, who wore a white laboratory coat, and another "subject" who was actually a confederate. The experimenter told each subject that he was participating in a "learning experiment" aimed at investigating the influence of punishment on learning. The actual subjects served as "teachers"; the confederate served as the "learner." The "teacher" was to administer an electrical shock whenever the "learner" made an error; this was done by pressing a switch displayed on a panel in front of the "teacher" (see Figure 12.6). The panel contained 30 switches with voltage designations between 15 and 450 volts in increments of 15 volts. Also, the 30 switches were divided into 8 voltage ranges with accompanying labels explaining the severity of shock for each range. The experimenter instructed each "teacher" to administer the lowest shock for the "learner's" first mistake and to increase the intensity by 15 volts for each subsequent error. The experimenter then led the "teacher" and the "learner" to an adjacent room in which the "learner" would receive the shocks. The experimenter gave the "teacher" a 45-volt sample shock to increase the authenticity of the study, and then the "teacher" watched as the experimenter attached the electrodes which would present the shocks to the "learner."

Next, the "teacher" returned to the control panel in the adjoining room, and the "learning experiment" began. During it, the "learner"—that is, the confederate—made 30 mistakes at predetermined times. For each mistake, as has been noted, the "teacher"—that is, the actual subject—was to administer shock. In reality, the confederate did not receive any shocks, but the actual subject did not know this. A "teacher" who presented all 30 shocks to the "learner" would believe that all the shocks were unpleasant and that the last shocks were sufficient to harm the "learner."

Before he began this experiment, Milgram had asked his students and colleagues to predict how his subjects would behave. They predicted that only extremely disturbed persons would administer shocks which they believed harmful. Milgram's students and colleagues were wrong: Milgram found that many of his subjects severely punished the confederate. These results are particularly alarming because the subjects could see that the confederate was middle-aged and had been told that he had a heart condition (see Figure 12.6).

The experiment progressed smoothly until each "teacher" reached switch 20 (300 volts). At this point, the "learner" would pound on the wall and refuse to answer the "teacher's" question. If the "teacher," reluctant to proceed, asked the experimenter for

(a)

(b)

(c)

Figure 12.6
(a) Shock generator used in Milgram's study. (b) Learner-confederate being strapped into the chair and electrodes being attached to his wrists. (c) Subject receiving the sample shock. (Copyright 1965 by Stanley Milgram. From the film Obedience, distributed by the New York University Film Library.)

instructions, the experimenter would tell him to wait 5 seconds and then punish the "learner" if he did not respond. If a "teacher" was still reluctant to continue, the experimenter would give a stricter order. The first command was, "Please continue." If this prod was not effective, a sequence of three more commands was employed: (1) "The experiment requires that you continue"; (2) "It is absolutely essential that you continue"; and (3) "You have no choice but to go on." If none of these instructions produced obedience, the experiment was discontinued. In many cases, the "teachers" requested information concerning their responsibility for any injury to the "learner"; they were told that the experimenter was responsible. When the "learner" was to receive shock from switch 21, he pounded on the wall again; thereafter, he was silent.

Milgram discovered that only 22 percent of the actual subjects—the "teachers"—stopped giving shocks at switch 20 or 21. A few more stopped administering shock between switches 22 and 29; but 65 percent continued the shocks through the final switch, which was labeled *dangerous*. Table 12.2 presents Milgram's results.

Although Milgram's original study used male subjects, other experiments (for example, Milgram, 1974; Sheridan & King, 1972) have obtained similar results with women. Evidently each of us is susceptible to the influence of an authority figure. Shanab and Vahya (1977) observed the same response in children. Their subjects were Jordanian children; they found that most of these children administered what purported to be an extremely dangerous electrical shock to a 15-year-old child of the same sex when ordered to do so by a female experimenter. Shanab and Vahya demonstrated an equal level of obedience in three age groups—6–8, 10–12, and 14–16 years. Motivation to yield to an authority figure is apparently present early in our development.

You should not think that Milgram's subjects were not influenced by their actions; most experienced an extreme emotional response during the study. Yet they continued to follow the experimenter's orders and administered what they believed were extremely dangerous shocks to the confederate. These subjects' responses are comparable to the German generals' justification of their war crimes: they were participating in an important study and following the orders of a legitimate authority who was responsible for the conduct of the experiment. Milgram concluded that if an experimenter in a white laboratory coat can cause seemingly normal subjects to hurt another person, it is not surprising that atrocities occur in response to pressure exerted by a stronger authority figure.

Milgram's research may provide the most dramatic example of obedience, but obedience to authority has also been demonstrated in other situations. One is a study by Hofling, Brotzman, Dalrymple, Graves, and Pierce (1963). In this study, a physician (the confederate) telephoned 22 nurses on hospital duty and instructed them to give one of

Table 12.2
The Number and Percentage of Subjects Who Stopped
Administering Shocks at Various Levels of Intensity

Voltage Indication	Number of Subjects	Percentage of Subjects
Slight shock	0	0
Moderate shock	0	0
Strong shock	0	0
Very strong shock	0	0
Intense shock	5	12.5
Extreme-intensity shock	8	20.0
Danger: severe shock	1	2.5
Switch 30, the final shock	26	65.0

Note: All subjects administering the highest intensity shock continued until the experiment ended; the number and percentage in each voltage group represents a combined value for the specific voltage levels within that voltage category.

Adapted from: Milgram, S. Behavioral study of obedience. *Journal of Abnormal and Social Psychology*, 1963, 67, 376. Copyright 1963 by the American Psychological Asssociation. Reprinted by permission.

their patients a drug. The nurses did not know this physician, and the dose which he ordered was two times the maximum dosage indicated on the bottle. Yet 21 of the 22 nurses obeyed. These results illustrate the power of authority to produce obedience.

Factors influencing obedience level.   Milgram's study (1963) maximized the conditions which produce obedience: (1) *an experimenter instructed each subject to punish the confederate,* (2) *the experimenter was present when each subject responded,* and (3) *the confederate occupied a room adjacent to that of the subject, who could only hear the confederate pounding on the wall to indicate the level of suffering produced by the "shock."* We will briefly address the role which these factors have on obedience level.

   Proximity of confederate.   In 1965, Milgram varied the proximity of each subject and confederate by using the following four conditions: (1) *"Remote"* condition. This was identical to the original procedure, described in the preceding section. (2) *"Voice feedback"* condition. In this condition, each subject could hear the confederate's voice, because the door connecting the subject's room and the confederate's room was left open. (3) *"Proximity"* condition. In this condition, the subject and the confederate shared the same room, maintaining a distance of 1½ feet from each other. (4) *"Touch proximity"* condition. In this condition, the subject had to place the confederate's hand on a shock plate if he resisted (see Figure 12.7). Milgram found that a subject's obedience decreased when the subject and confederate were physically closer. Nevertheless, an almost incredible proportion of the subjects—30 percent—continued to obey the experimenter and administered the maximal shock even when they had to hold the reluctant confederate's hand down on the shock plate. Figure 12.8 presents the results of Milgram's study. This provides additional evidence of the power of authority.

Figure 12.7
In this scene, the experimenter has ordered the subject to hold the victim's hand on the shock panel. (Copyright 1965 by Stanley Milgram. From the film Obedience, *distributed by the New York University Film Library.)*

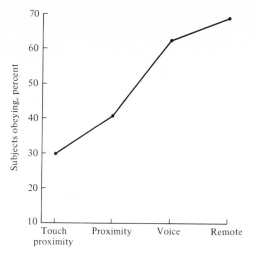

Figure 12.8
Percentage of subjects obeying as a function of the proximity of the teacher to the learner. (From Milgram, S. Some conditions of obedience and disobedience to authority. Human Relations, *1965, 18, 57–76.)*

Proximity of authority figure. The physical presence of an authority figure is also a vital determinant of obedience. Milgram (1965a) employed three conditions to investigate this factor. In the first condition, the experimenter and subject occupied the same room. In the second condition, the experimenter was present initially to give instructions but then left the room and thereafter telephoned the orders. In the third condition, subjects received instructions only from a tape recorder. Milgram found that obedience increased as the proximity between the experimenter and subject increased; this indicates that the physical presence of an authority increases obedience.

Personal responsibility. Some studies have evaluated how much responsibility people accept for their level of compliance. Results of these studies established that people who feel personally responsible for the effect of their behavior on others will be less likely to follow a superior's directions. Mantrell (1971) conducted an obedience study in West Germany which was similar to Milgram's original study. In Mantrell's experiment, one group of subjects were told by the experimenter to administer electric shocks to the confederate; this created a lack of responsibility for these subjects. Mantrell reported that 85 percent of these subjects administered the maximum shock level. Another group of subjects had the responsibility of deciding whether to punish and how much punishment a confederate should receive after having made an error. Of these subjects who personally had to decide the fate of others, only 7 percent gave the highest shock. Tilker (1970) observed an analogous influence of personal responsibility in his study, conducted in the United States. Obviously, the fact that most people do not blame themselves for the consequences of their actions significantly increases their responsivity to an authority's dictates.

You may be surprised by the absence of personal responsibility in people who have responded to their superior's orders to commit awful crimes. Considering the enormity of their actions, the lack of remorse displayed by the Nazis after World War II is amazing. Milgram's subjects (1977) showed a similar lack of remorse after his experiment. Although they believed that they had harmed the confederate, when they were questioned after in the study, 84 percent said that they were glad to have participated in it; only 1 percent wished they had not taken part. Although neither the German generals nor Milgram's subjects felt responsible for their actions, how do you view their behavior? You probably condemn them for their inability to resist authority and act normally. This would suggest that obedient people do not feel responsible for their crimes, yet observers of their actions assume that they are. The sentences passed on many Nazi officials after the war indicate that the Allies held them responsible for their brutality.

Recall from Chapter 3 our discussion of the differences between causal attributions of an actor and those of an observer. These differences can explain why obedient people do not feel responsible while others assume that they are. Jones and Nisbett (1972) demonstrated that people acting in a particular way are often apt to attribute their behavior to external or situational causes, though observers feel that personal factors caused the behavior. Thus, obedient people attribute their responses to external forces and observers attribute obedience to the inherent brutality of these people. In support of this, West, Gunn, and Chernicky (1975) investigated the causal attributions of actors and observers in a simulated Watergate-type obedience study. They found that actors were more likely to attribute their criminal act to environmental forces than to personal forces. In contrast, observers exhibited the opposite pattern: they more often attributed the actors' criminality to their personal dispositions.

However, observers do not always attribute criminal actions to personal factors; many in the United States did not blame Lieutenant Calley for his actions at My Lai and disapproved of his conviction. Kelman and Lawrence (1972) identified two classes of observers: *approvers* and *disapprovers*. Approvers felt that Calley's conviction was justified, as he was responsible for his behavior; disapprovers believed that higher authorities forced Calley's actions and that his conviction was therefore not justifiable. Kelman and Lawrence's results suggest that whether or not an observer blames someone for criminal action depends on how much control the observer believes the person had over the situation.

An observer will not blame an actor for a crime if the observer feels that a superior forced the actor to behave. Hamilton (1978) investigated attribution of responsibility in a simulated jury trial resembling that of Lieutenant Calley. The defendant, a corporal accused of killing unarmed prisoners, argued that he had merely followed his superior's orders. Hamilton manipulated the corporal's ability to disobey orders by varying the superior's rank, and predicted that the defendant would be considered less able to resist a captain's order than a sergeant's. The jurors indicated both the defendant's guilt and what they perceived as the cause of his behavior. Hamilton reported that more jurors found the defendant guilty and therefore responsible for his crime when the superior was a sergeant rather than a captain. Interestingly, the superior was held responsible regardless of rank. These results point out that our attributions of someone's guilt depend upon how able we believe this person is to resist an authority figure's order.

Personality characteristics of obedient people. Are some people more likely to be obedient? Evidence suggests that authoritarian persons are more obedient than nonauthoritarian ones (Elms & Milgram, 1966). Elms and Milgram administered the Minnesota Multiphasic Personality Inventory (MMPI) and the California F (authoritarian) Scale to 20 "compliers" and 20 "resisters" who had participated in Milgram's original obedience study. The "compliers" and the "resisters" displayed no differences on the MMPI test; this indicates that personality characteristics associated with abnormality probably do not influence obedience. This observation confirms that under certain conditions psychologically normal people will harm others. In contrast, there were significant differences on the F Scale: the "compliers" were more authoritarian than the "resisters." Apparently, the developmental experiences which create authoritarian personalities make them more apt to respond to a superior's commands to hurt another person or persons.

Influence of peers. Milgram's research has addressed two questions central to our discussion of obedience. First: Will a person harm someone in response to pressure from peers? Milgram (1965b) evaluated this question by having two confederates act as "teachers" who urged the actual subjects to shock "learners" (also confederates). In contrast to 65 percent of the subjects who were obedient to the experimenter, Milgram found that only 18 percent of the subjects responded to peer pressure by giving the "learner" the maximum shock intensity. These results indicate that an authority figure is more likely than a peer to motivate us to act contrary to our wishes.

The second question centering on the influence of peers on obedience is: Will others' dissent influence our level of obedience? Milgram (1965b) instructed confederates acting as "teachers" to refuse to obey the experimenter's commands. Under this condition, actual subjects' obedience decreased to 10 percent when they were asked to administer the most intense shock, as compared with 65 percent who obeyed when the confederates did not dissent. Thus, dissent produced the same reduction in obedience which we observed for conformity and compliance.

An Overview

Milgram's research has received much critical analysis during the past 15 years. One fault frequently mentioned is that Milgram conducted his original studies at Yale University: Orne and Holland (1968) suggested that the prestige of Yale was responsible for the experimenter's authority and that parallel results would not be observed under other conditions. To counter this argument, Milgram (1974) conducted several studies in a run-down office building in Bridgeport, Connecticut. There was no connection with Yale in these studies; the Research Associates of Bridgeport conducted them. This time the experimenter did not wear a white laboratory coat. Nevertheless, 48 percent of the subjects administered the severe shock. These results strengthen the argument that many people are responsive to the demands of an authority figure.

Milgram never expected to find that his subjects would obediently follow orders to harm the confederate. Nonetheless, many did. Milgram's research vividly reminds us of human beings' potential brutality. Yet, not all of Miligram's subjects yielded to the pressure; their resistance indicates that brutality is not inevitable.

SUMMARY

Each group of people—large or small—establishes goals. To reach these goals, a group specifies which behaviors, called *norms*, are appropriate or inappropriate. Some group norms help a group attain goals. Other norms are not directly involved in obtaining goals, but serve to produce group stability and behavioral predictability. An unstable group or one whose members cannot predict the behaviors of other group members cannot focus its attention on striving to reach its goals.

Effective group norms require that each group member adhere to them. People often conform to group standards because no other alternatives are obvious. When someone conforms to a group, the informational pressure of its collective knowledge ensures adherence to the norms. However, there are some occasions when a group member doubts the group's judgment. Under these conditions, the group must exert normative pressure to produce compliance with its norms. This normative pressure can take one or more forms: (1) group acceptance and approval is given only to members who yield to social influence; (2) the rewards available to group members are withheld from people who defy the group's standards; (3) physical or psychological punishment is directed toward members who do not adhere to the group norms. Normative pressure is typically effective: most people do comply with their group's standards.

Compliance occurs when someone yields to social pressure by peers. In contrast, obedience occurs when someone obeys the group's norms as a result of an order from an authority within the group. An authority figure has impressive power to motivate obedience. The most striking example of this power is the obedience of many people to an authority who has ordered them to harm or kill others.

Yet, not all people yield to social pressure; some are deviant and do not adhere to group norms. There is resistance to group standards when: (1) reactance is aroused by perceived lack of control, (2) a person feels anonymous and therefore not likely to be rejected or punished, and (3) others successfully resist, which leads to an expectation that it is safe not to yield to group pressure. Sometimes a resister attempts to modify the group's standards. Such a minority person might present his or her view confidently, in hopes of gaining support and eventually altering the attitude of the majority. Although this direct approach can be successful, the dissenter typically receives extreme pressure from the majority to yield to group norms. Ingratiation is a subtle method through which a minority member can produce compliance in a target member of the majority. An ingratiator uses flattery, favors, positive self-presentation, or even compliance to some issues in order to gain acceptance and approval from a target person. The establishment of this social relationship motivates the target to comply with the resister's views.

Our environment surrounds us with other people. To coexist with our peers, we must obey the standards established by our group. Most of the time, this social influence is a positive agent enhancing the quality of our lives. However, at times, social processes motivate behavior which is detrimental to us and others.

PROSOCIAL BEHAVIOR

BEHAVIOR

CHAPTER 13

An act of heroism

Aaron, a lawyer, has always loved to run. Since moving from the city to a small town, he has really cultivated his hobby and now runs 10 to 12 miles each day. On this lovely fall morning, as the leaves are beginning to turn vibrant hues of yellow, red, and orange, he is anxious to start out.

After running for several miles, he notices two unfamiliar boys playing near a lake in which four children have drowned during the past year. Aaron slackens his pace as thoughts of warning the youngsters whir through his mind. Then he suddenly remembers that he has an appointment—with an important client whom he should not keep waiting—and resumes his pace.

Aaron's route is usually circular; he does not ordinarily return home by the lake road, as the uphill grade is brutal. But today he decides to endure the hill in order to check on the boys. He has been running for about 8 miles and is beginning to tire as he approaches the lake. At first he does not see the boys and assumes that they have gone

home. However, he soon notices that one boy is in the middle of the lake and in obvious danger. The other boy is swimming toward shore and calling for someone to help his friend.

Although Aaron is not an expert swimmer, he runs to the lake, jumps in, and begins swimming as quickly as he can to the drowning boy. Upon reaching the boy, he encounters extreme difficulty: the fear-stricken child drags him under water several times before Aaron can control him. After a struggle, Aaron finally tows him to shore—the entire episode takes nearly 15 minutes. Fortunately, the boy does not seem to have suffered any real harm from the incident. Instructing him and his friend never to swim in the lake again, Aaron sends them home.

Although now near exhaustion, Aaron remembers his appointment—or what would be remaining of it—and hurries directly home. Since neither the rescued boy nor his parents had met Aaron before the incident, they cannot reward or even thank him.

Social psychologists would label Aaron's heroic action as *altruistic behavior*. This voluntary behavior, unmotivated by an overt social pressure, occurs when persons place themselves in a dangerous position in order to rescue someone. It often occurs in the presence of bystanders who do not help and in the absence of any expected gain. The heroic acts frequently are not verbally acknowledged by the victim; the youngsters Aaron helped forgot to thank him. Altruistic persons may even lose their own lives while saving others. For example, the soldier who thrusts himself on a grenade in the hope of saving comrades dramatically demonstrates the danger inherent in many instances of altruistic behavior.

Altruism is one example of *prosocial behavior*—behavior which serves the function of enhancing the welfare of another person or persons. There are two major forms of prosocial behavior—cooperative behavior and helping behavior. *Cooperation* exists when two or more persons work together for their mutual benefit. When people cooperate, the likelihood increases that both, or all, will be rewarded. In contrast, *competition* causes one person to receive more reward than the other person or persons. *Helping behavior*, the other form of prosocial behavior, occurs when one's social behavior benefits another person rather than oneself. It is categorized into three types—a *favor*, a *donation*, and *altruism*. Although a favor often requires little sacrifice of time and effort, it does benefit another person. We are typically willing to offer such help if it is requested, and a favor often serves to reciprocate help we ourselves have received previously. In contrast to a favor, a donation is more of an individual sacrifice and has less reciprocity; however, both favors and donations are often performed in order to obtain social approval. There are other situations in which we volunteer our help to someone else at extreme personal cost and without thought of social approval. The altruistic behavior of Aaron represents an example of such unselfish helping behavior. Later on, this chapter describes factors which motivate these types of helping behaviors. We will now begin discussing the influence which cooperation and competition have on social effectiveness.

THE DIVISIVE IMPACT OF COMPETITION

The Creation of Hostility

Many Americans believe that competition builds character and that young children should compete with their peers in order to mature. In contrast with this view, the classic research of Muzafer Sherif and his associates (Sherif, Harvey, White, Hood, & Sherif, 1954; Sherif & Sherif, 1956) demonstrated that competition often has an extremely negative impact on social behavior; antisocial behavior which would not be tolerated in other situations often emerges from competition. On the other hand, cooperation has a beneficial influence on interpersonal relationships. Our cooperative responses allow us to share rewarding experiences with others, thus increasing our emotional attachment to them (see Chapter 9). To study the effects of competition and cooperation on behavior, Sherif established summer camps in Connecticut, New York, and Oklahoma in which 11- to 12-year-old boys from white, middle-class, Protestant homes served as subjects. He divided the boys in each camp into two groups which competed in various activities, giving each group a distinctive name (for example, Bull Dogs, Red Devils, Pythons, Eagles). In each case, competition led to the formation of antagonism between groups, although the expression of the boys' hostilities differed slightly in each camp. The pattern of behaviors produced by competition between the Bull Dogs and Red Devils is typical of the effect of competition on social behavior. During the early stages of competition, positive feelings existed between the groups (for instance, the winners cheered the losers and vice versa), even though only the winning team received reward (for example, points). However, the mutual respect existing between group members soon changed to feelings of hostility. The winning team often was accused of cheating and became the target of much verbal abuse.

In an attempt to examine the depth of the antagonism between the two groups, Sherif and his associates arranged a "reconciliation party." They placed party refreshments on a long table; half of the table displayed delicious foods, while crushed and unappealing foods were on the other half. The authors arranged for the Red Devils to arrive first, and these boys proceeded to eat the best-tasting foods. Although the Bull Dogs consumed the remaining food, they were obviously unhappy: they insulted the Red Devils, calling them "pigs," "jerks," and other more objectionable names. Although the boys were told that the purpose of the party was to change their negative feelings toward members of the other group, the effect of the party was to intensify hostility. During breakfast the following morning, the Red Devils incited the Bull Dogs; the Red Devils then began smearing their tables with cocoa, sugar, and syrup. Each group then hung threatening, derogatory posters in the dining hall. At lunch, the members of each group gathered on opposite sides of the cafeteria taunting each other; several fights even erupted between members of opposite groups. The behavior of the Bull Dogs and the Red Devils serves as a good example of how competition can elicit objectionable forms of social behavior.

Sherif and his associates then decided to modify the boys' antisocial hostility. They first created several pleasant situations (for example, watching a movie) which were intended to provide rewarding social contact. But these shared experiences only served to increase animosity between groups, possibly because the presence of members of the other group created an unpleasant environment or because the boys found aggressive acts to be rewarding (see Chapter 7). Next, Sherif and his colleagues attempted to diminish hostility by merging the two groups into one: they formed a camp softball team which competed against a team from a nearby town. This strategy did accomplish its objective; the authors found that the hostility between the camp groups decreased. Instead, hostility was directed toward the other team—the new enemy. Sherif also discovered that hostility could be reduced by encouraging cooperation. The experimenters deliberately sabotaged the boys' water-supply system; only cooperation between the two groups could restore the camp's water. The boys did cooperate to repair the system, and their hostility diminished further. The experimenters also noticed that campers cooperated to obtain money to pay for a movie and to move a supply truck that had broken down on its way to the camp. Evidence of the effect of cooperation was apparent: enmity between groups decreased and friendship increased.

A few psychologists have replicated Sherif's original study; the most frightening one is Lefty Diab's experiment (1970) with Lebanese boys, again in a camp setting. In this study, the intense hostility created by competition led to a level of conflict which Diab could not control. Several boys were knifed during the study, and finally the police were needed to evacuate the camp. The negative consequences of competition which Sherif and others have observed in camp settings has also been documented in other settings. Let's now examine one of these situations.

Blake and Mouton (1961) noticed the negative effects of competition in an industrial setting. Groups of managers competed on several different tasks. Although the competition created greater solidarity within groups, the managers demanded increased loyalty and obedience within their groups and would not tolerate deviant ideas. The authors reported that hostility developed between the groups during the competition. As communication between groups declined, negative stereotypes of members of the other groups emerged. Blake and Mouton's observations again point to the detrimental aspects of competition.

A Direct Comparison of Competition and Cooperation

The preceding section described studies in which hostility did not occur when groups cooperated to achieve a common goal. However, a direct comparison of competition and cooperation was not conducted in these studies. The decline in hostility when the cooperative goals were introduced represented the only evidence of the different effects of each procedure. A number of researchers have compared the effects of competition and cooperation. Their results do not contradict the studies described in the previous section, but rather present a slightly different picture of the effects of competition and cooperation. Hostility is typically created when other people or groups are viewed as representing a barrier to obtaining desired goals. The nature of competitive situations— one person wins more often than others do—typically establishes the conflict situation which is necessary to block goals and induce hostility. In contrast, in cooperative situations, everyone can obtain reward by cooperating. When people cooperate and their combined efforts produce the desired goal, hostility will not occur. However, if their cooperative effort fails, interpersonal conflict does occur, usually when the participants see their partner's behavior as being responsible for failure.

The contrasting effects of competition and cooperation can be clearly observed in academic settings. Deutsch's classic study (1949) is one example of the negative impact of competition in a classroom environment. Deutsch formed two types of five-member groups of students which met for 3 hours each week, to fill the requirements of his introductory psychology course. The "cooperative" groups (type 1) were told that their grades depended upon the quality of their combined group effort. The "competitive" groups (type 2) were informed that grades would be awarded on the basis of each student's relative contribution to the group's success. Deutsch found that the cooperative groups were more productive: they solved simple problems more readily and provided more realistic solutions to complex problems. In addition, Deutsch reported that students in the cooperative groups communicated more with each other than students in the competitive groups did and had more positive and less negative feelings toward other members of their group. Perhaps our educational system should recognize the value of Deutsch's and other psychologists' research, which has indicated that students who cooperate rather than compete will perform better and feel more positively toward their classmates.

Jacob Rabbie and his associates (see Rabbie, 1981) have observed a similar disruptive effect of competition in intergroup relationships. They found that the expectation of competition did not create intergroup hostility; before conflict, we do not typically expect to lose. Yet Rabbie reported that hostility between groups was produced when the competitive behavior of another group interfered with the attainment of reward.

The amount of hostility exhibited during competition depends upon the level of interaction with the other group: the more direct contact with an opponent, the stronger the intergroup hostility. For example, Rabbie and Van Oostrum (1977) compared intergroup antagonism in two kinds of groups: (1) groups whose representatives either had to consult with their constituents before interacting with the opponent; (2) groups whose representatives could act without conferring with the members of their group. The researchers observed more hostility in groups of type 1 than in groups of type 2. They interpreted their results as indicating that in groups of type 1, the greater direct involvement of each member with the conflict was responsible for the more intense hostility.

You have learned that competition produces hostility and that cooperation creates positive feelings toward others. However, cooperation can induce hostility when a person feels that the absence or loss of reward was caused by another person or group (for example, Rabbie, Visser, & Vernooij, 1976). Thus, the negative aspects of competition are absent with cooperative behavior only when the cooperation produces reward for all the individuals involved. (It should be noted that Rabbie, Visser, and Vernooij found greater hostility toward outsiders in competitive groups than in cooperative ones.)

Our discussion has pointed out that both cooperative and competitive behaviors are motivated to obtain reward and that hostility is induced when either cooperation or competition fails to produce the desired goal. What is the goal of people who have participated in the competitive and cooperative situations described in this chapter? Many of the subjects who competed may not have wanted to do better than their opponent but merely desired to obtain the most rewards possible for themselves. Similarly, some people in the cooperative tasks may not have cared if their partners obtained rewards but may simply have viewed cooperation as the only method available to attain their own goals. Thus, these subjects' behavior may reflect the operation of *individualistic motives* rather than social motives. We cannot be certain of people's motives when they have been instructed to behave in a particular way. We learned from Chapter 12 that people typically comply and behave according to instructions. The subjects in these studies might not have cooperated or competed if they had had to choose between their own motives and the motives of others. For instance, they might have chosen to maximize their own reward and to be unconcerned with the effects of their actions on other people. Or they might have chosen to lose reward so that others would win as much as they did (cooperation) or less than they did (competition). In the next section, you will learn that different people behave differently when they are faced with the choice of satisfying either their own needs or the needs of others. Some people are typically concerned only with their own welfare: others are concerned not only with their own interests but also with those of others. We will see that the specific choices which people make reflect their own motivational or value system. These different motives and the factors responsible for their establishment will also be examined. Finally, we will discuss how an environment can be structured to motivate cooperative behavior in people who would not ordinarily cooperate with others.

COOPERATIVE BEHAVIOR

Consider the following example to illustrate the differences between competitive, individualistic, and cooperative motives. Suppose that you are a real estate agent taking a client to view houses. If you are concerned only with maximizing your gain (an individualistic motive), you might show your client only those houses on which you would receive a large commission. Or you might bypass a suitable house listed by a coworker if you did not want this coworker to gain from your sale. Thus, if your behavior is competitively motivated, you might sacrifice some money (reward) to ensure that an opponent will not gain. Yet, what if you wanted to sell a house which is listed by a coworker? Under these circumstances, you and your coworker would both profit from your cooperative motivation. The specific behavior which occurs depends both on your motivation and on the environmental circumstances. For example, an individualistic person may cooperate to ensure obtaining the maximum reward. Or a cooperative person may compete if he or she views the other person as attempting to block the desired reward. Social psychologists have developed a number of games to investigate the ways in which people respond in social situations. Two of these games are the "trucking game" and "prisoner's dilemma."

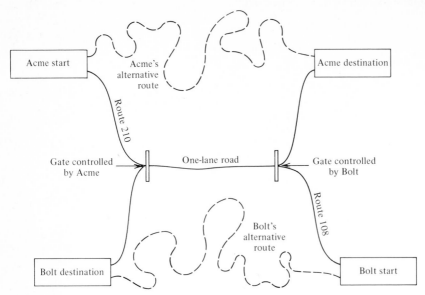

Figure 13.1
Road map in Deutsch and Krauss's trucking game. (From Deutsch, M., & Krauss, R. M. The effect of threat on interpersonal bargaining. Journal of Abnormal and Social Psychology, 1960, 61, 183. *Copyright 1960 by the American Psychological Association. Reprinted by permission.)*

The "Trucking Game"

Procedure. Deutsch and Krauss (1960) developed a simulated trucking game to investigate competition and cooperation among college students. They instructed pairs of students to imagine that they were the presidents of two trucking companies—Acme and Bolt. The objective of the game was to accumulate points by traveling from a home base to a destination as quickly as possible. Each company was assigned a different base and destination, yet both companies shared the most rapid route. Each subject could use a longer alternative route which would result in the loss of points (see Figure 13.1). In one condition—"bilateral threat"—each player had a gate (a roadblock) to prevent the opponent's use of the shared roadway. In a second condition—"no threat"—neither player had access to a gate.

The player's response. Deutsch and Krauss found that subjects in the "no threat" pairs cooperated and gained a profit; subjects in the "bilateral threat" pairs always finished the game as losers. The optimal strategy was cooperation; yet only the "no threat" subjects cooperated enough to earn a profit. In this study, the presence of threat produced conflict and motivated competition rather than cooperation. This observation suggests that one method of increasing cooperation is to reduce conflict. Later in this section, we will discuss several ways to decrease hostility and motivate cooperative behavior.

"Prisoner's Dilemma"

Procedure. In 1957, Luce and Raiffa demonstrated that a social-psychological game, "prisoner's dilemma," based on problems frequently encountered by actual prisoners who

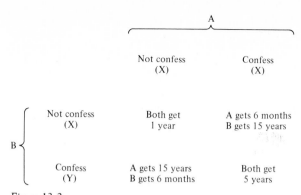

Figure 13.2

Prototype of "prisoner's dilemma" game. In this situation, two players choose between confessing and not confessing. Cooperative behavior (not confessing) depends upon trusting that the partner will not confess and results in inmates going to prison for a short time. In contrast, competitive behavior (confessing) produces a mild sentence only when the other person cooperates (does not confess).

are suspected of jointly committing a crime, is another situation in which many subjects choose to compete even though cooperation is more adaptive. In a real-life situation, the suspects are isolated and the district attorney attempts to obtain a confession from one or both of them. Each prisoner's dilemma is whether or not to confess. If neither confesses, both suspects receive a light sentence for a minor crime, since without a confession, there probably is not enough evidence to convict either of them of a major crime. However, if one confesses because of the promise of a short sentence, the other receives a long sentence. A moderate sentence is imposed if both prisoners confess. The situation is diagrammed in Figure 13.2.

Subjects in a simulated "prisoner's dilemma" game play for either points or money rather than for jail sentences. Each subject has two choices, X and Y, and must pick one. If the players cooperate and choose X, both gain moderately. A player can compete and obtain a large reward by choosing Y only if the opponent cooperates and chooses X. If the players compete and both choose Y, they both lose.

The player's response.   How do subjects respond in "prisoner's dilemma"? Consider the reward structure of Kelley and Stahelski's study (1970b). Their matrix is typical of those used by social psychologists (see Figure 13.3). Kelley and Stahelski found that almost half of their subjects usually competed, even though cooperation was the safest strategy. Other researchers (for example, Rapoport and Chammah, 1965) who have used reward matrixes similar to the one employed by Kelley and Stahelski have reported a strong competitive motive in many subjects.

The player's motive.   In Kelley and Stahelski's study a successful competitive response by one subject would deprive the other subject of reward. But did these "competitive" subjects want to do better than their partners? Although the term *competitive response* implies a motive to obtain more reward than that which another person or persons receives, competitive behavior does not have to reflect the operation of a competitive motive. The research of several psychologists (for example, Guyer & Rapoport, 1972; MacCrimmon & Messick, 1976; Tyska & Grzelak, 1976) indicates that although some subjects do, in fact, have competitive motives, most subjects' competitive behavior in the reward structure used by Kelley and Stahelski reflects the operation of individualistic

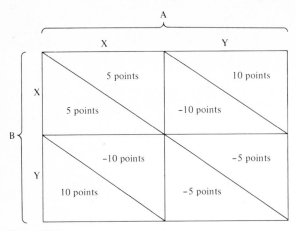

Figure 13.3
Reward matrix employed in Kelley and Stahelski's study. The matrix favors cooperative behavior; moderate gain is produced when both subjects choose X. Competition produces maximum gain only if the other subject does not choose to compete; if both compete, they both lose. (From Kelley, H. H., & Stahelski, A. J. The influence of intentions from moves in the prisoner's dilemma game. Journal of Experimental Social Psychology, *1970, 6, 401–419.)*

motives. In Kelley and Stahelski's study, both individualistic subjects (those desiring to maximize their own gain) and competitive subjects (those wanting to do better than their opponent) felt that the competitive choice represented the best way of attaining their goals.

Whereas the competitive behavior in Kelley and Stahelski's experiment could reflect both individualistic and competitive motives, only a cooperative person would choose to cooperate. A competitive subject would recognize the equality represented by cooperation; an individualistic subject would recognize that maximum gain could not be obtained by cooperation. Therefore, cooperative behavior would not satisfy the motives of either the individualistic or the competitive person.

There are some reward structures in which cooperative behavior can satisfy the motives of both individualistic and competitive subjects. For example, if subjects are aware that maximum gain will be produced by cooperation, individualistic subjects will choose to cooperate. In addition, if a cooperative response produces a reward for both subjects but still allows the competitive person to do slightly better than the other person, the competitive person will cooperate. Later in the chapter we will discuss evidence that use of certain reward structures can motivate cooperative behavior in noncooperative people.

The type of questions which a subject asks concerning the reward structure to be used in a study is another indication of a subject's motivation. To establish his subjects' motivational style, Janusz Grzelak (1980) presented them with 16 choices of game outcomes in which their gain and their partner's gain varied. He instructed the subjects to rank the 16 choices; the choices indicated their motivation. After assessing the subjects' motivational style, he described an ambiguous game situation and allowed the subjects to ask questions about potential rewards for themselves and their partner. Grzelak found that subjects who exhibited an individualistic response tendency asked more questions about their rewards than other subjects did. In contrast, nonindividualistic subjects were more interested in how their choices affected their partners than individualistic people were. Grzelak's results suggest that people usually seek only that information which they need to translate their motives into goal-seeking behavior.

Our discussion has revealed that one of three motives— individualistic, competitive, or cooperative—influences behavior in situations in which two or more people (or groups) interact to obtain a goal. Individualistic people are unconcerned with the gains or losses of other people and are interested only in maximizing their individual profits. Competitive people are motivated to do better than others. Cooperative people want themselves and others both to do well. However, the specific behavior employed by each type of person will vary from situation to situation; the environmental context determines which response satisfies a person's needs.

What factors influence the behavior of people in social situations? The next section focuses on two factors: (1) past experiences in obtaining reward and (2) expectations about the behavior of other people and how it will influence one's own ability to reach a goal.

Determinants of a Person's Motivational Style

Past history.   The players' perception of the best strategy to be used in social-psychological games undoubtedly stems from their past experience. Madsen (1967) investigated the role of experience in cooperation and competition with children. He developed a game (see Figure 13.4) to compare the social behavior of children from various cultures. Four children, each sitting in a different corner, hold a string with which they can pull a pen to their corners and thus gain points. Although the game appears competitive, the only effective strategy is cooperation: if each child pulls independently, none of them will obtain a reward. Madsen discovered that middle-class Mexican children competed and thus earned little reward. Poorer Mexican children cooperated and received more reward than their richer counterparts. One logical interpretation of these results suggests that in order to survive, poor children learn to cooperate with their peers; on the other hand, in middle-class cultures, competitive behavior typically leads to success. Although no one has attempted to distinguish between the past experiences of competitive and individualistic people, it seems reasonable to conclude from Madsen's

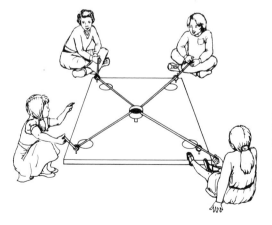

Figure 13.4
Game developed by Madsen to study cooperation and competition. (Reprinted with permission of author and publisher from: Madsen, M. C. Cooperation and competition motivation of children in three Mexican subcultures. Psychological Reports, 1967, 20, 1307–1320, fig. 1.)

study that individualistic people learn that they can obtain reward only by looking out for their own interests, while competitive people probably develop the expectation that they have to do better than other people in order to attain reward.

The player's view of the intention of others.   Recall the example of the real estate agent earlier in the chapter. What might motivate an agent to compete with a coworker and not attempt to sell the coworker's listing? Or why would a salesperson cooperate with a coworker and concentrate on selling houses that provide gain for both of them? Kelley and Stahelski's research (1970a, 1970b) answers these two questions. Kelley and Stahelski discovered that competitive people expected others also to be competitive. Thus, according to their view, the competitive real estate agent expects that a similar motive exists in the coworker and that competition represents the only method of attaining reward. Although no distinction was made between competitive and individualistic people in their study, many of their subjects who chose the competitive response were, in fact, individualistic. Therefore, it seems safe to assume that individualistic people, as well as competitive people, are concerned only about their own interests and expect others to act like them. From this viewpoint, our individualistic real estate agent would feel that other agents are looking out for themselves and that the only way to survive is to sell as much property as possible.

Kelley and Stahelski discovered that this narrow view of others exhibited by competitive—and individualistic—people was not a characteristic of cooperative people. They discovered that cooperative subjects expected some people to compete and some to cooperate. Thus, the agent who cooperates with his or her coworker and attempts to sell the coworker's house does not always expect a similar response from the coworker.

What are the agent's feelings if the coworker does not cooperate? Kelley and Stahelski (1970a) examined how people responded to competitive and cooperative behavior of others. Competitive and cooperative subjects were paired with either similar or dissimilar partners in the "prisoner's dilemma" game. Kelley and Stahelski found that competitive people competed 70 percent of the time, regardless of the behavior of others. Yet, whereas cooperative people cooperated 90 percent of the time with a cooperative partner, they cooperated only 65 percent of the time with a competitive partner. These results indicate that a cooperative salesperson is less likely to cooperate with a competitive coworker.

We have learned that past experiences and expectations about the actions of others influence the way people behave in interpersonal goal-seeking activities. Some people prefer to cooperate; others want to compete; a concern for only oneself is characteristic of others. However, cooperative people do not always cooperate, and uncooperative people do occasionally exhibit cooperative behavior. Several techniques are available which motivate cooperative behavior in both cooperative and noncooperative people. Let's see how these methods work.

Motivating Cooperative Behavior

Four approaches may be used to increase the level of cooperation. *First, people can be instructed to cooperate.* In Chapter 12, we saw that normative social pressure motivates obedience. This pressure, created by the instructions, also represents an effective way of motivating cooperative behavior. *Second, cooperative behavior is increased when participants are allowed to communicate.* At the beginning of an experiment, a subject may be uncertain how his or her partner is going to act. Communication, by increasing the accuracy of a person's perception of his or her partner's intentions, will motivate cooperation when cooperative behavior will lead to reward. *Third, people are more apt to cooperate if they trust their partner to cooperate.* Players want to obtain reward, and therefore, are not likely to cooperate if they expect that their own failure to reach their goal could be caused by their partner's failure to cooperate. Earlier in this chapter we saw that conflict decreases cooperative behavior and that, in all likelihood, trust and communication also motivate cooperation by decreasing conflict. *Finally, changes in the reward structure can motivate cooperative behavior.* Individualistic and competitive people will cooperate when cooperative behavior satisfies their needs.

There is a danger in motivating noncooperative people to cooperate. If this cooperative effort ends in failure, increased hostility toward their partners develops. A study by Worchel, Andreoli, and Folger (1977) demonstrated that the effect of cooperation is not always positive. These experimenters established two groups of subjects—a "cooperative" group and a "competitive" group. During the first phase of the study the two groups worked independently on a number of projects. The experimenters told the subjects in the "competitive" group that they were competing against another group and that the team which exhibited the highest level of performance would win a prize. They informed the subjects in the "cooperative" group that a prize would be awarded to.both teams if both performed well. The results of the first phase of this study confirmed previous observations: people in the "cooperative" group felt positively toward members of the other group; people in the "competitive" group showed intergroup hostility. In the second phase of the study, the "cooperative" group and the "competitive" group were each divided in half. All four of the subgroups thus formed were told that they could win a prize if they cooperated with another group. However, only one "cooperation" subgroup and one "competition" subgroup were actually rewarded; the other two subgroups were not. The authors observed that at the end of phase 2 both subgroups formed from the initial "cooperation" group claimed to like the members of the other group with which they were supposed to work, regardless of whether or not they were rewarded with a prize. For the subgroups drawn from the initial "competitive" group, however, responses depended upon whether or not the cooperative effort was rewarded. If cooperation led to a prize, the previously established intergroup hostility was reduced. If the prize was withheld, however, the "competitive" subgroup blamed its failure on the members of the group with which it was supposed to cooperate, and its hostility towards that group increased. It seems that when people with a history of competing cooperate on a task but their cooperation fails, the normally facilitative social effect of cooperation does not materialize. Assuming that cooperative behavior is likely to succeed, let's discuss the evidence indicating that the four techniques described at the beginning of this section can motivate cooperative behavior.

Instructions. One method which can be used to overcome the inherent negative influence of competition is the explicit instruction to cooperate with others to obtain reward. In a classic study, Deutsch (1960) gave three types of instructions to subjects before their participation in the "prisoner's dilemma" game. One group of subjects were directed to cooperate, and the importance of the other players' welfare was stressed ("cooperative" condition). A second group of subjects were told to earn as many points as possible and were informed that their performance would not be affected by that of other players ("individualistic" condition). The third group of subjects were told that their objective was to "beat" their opponent ("competitive" condition). The results of this study are presented in Table 13.1. The type of instructions clearly influenced the level of cooperative behavior. Subjects instructed to cooperate made the greatest number (93 percent) of cooperative choices, whereas the use of competitive instructions acted to

Table 13.1
The Effects of Motivation Instructions and Communication on Cooperation and
Competition

Motivation Instructions	Percentage of Cooperative Choices		
	No Communication	Communication	Average
Cooperative	89.1	96.9	93.0
Individualistic	35.0	70.6	52.8
Competitive	12.5	29.2	20.9

From: Deutsch, M. The effect of motivational orientation upon trust and suspicion. *Human Relations*,
1960, *13*, 122–139.

minimize cooperative responses (21 percent). Subjects who were instructed that their
reward depended only on their own performance cooperated during approximately 50
percent of the trials.

Instructions to cooperate not only increase the amount of cooperative behavior, but
also enhance performance and create a pleasant working environment. In their
introductory psychology courses, Haines and McKeachie (1967) divided discussion
sections into two categories in order to investigate the influence of instructions on
classroom behavior. For half of their subjects, performance would be evaluated on an
individual basis ("competitive" condition); for the other half, performance would be
determined by group action ("cooperative" condition). Subjects in the "competitive"
condition were anxious and tense; students in the "cooperative" condition reported that
they enjoyed their classes. In addition, the experimenters rated the quality of discussion
higher in the "cooperative" sections than in the "competitive" ones.

Another example of the positive influence of cooperation is dramatically illustrated
in a study by Blau (1954). He established a "cooperation" section and a "competition"
section in an employment agency. Blau instructed interviewers in the "competition"
section that their own job security depended on the number of job placements they made;
this was not important for interviewers in the "cooperation" section, who were told that
their reward would be based upon the section's performance. He found that people in the
"competition" section concealed information by not talking to each other. On the other
hand, the interviewers in the "cooperation" section enjoyed their work and helped each
other in the placement of clients. The important observation of this study is that the
"cooperation" section placed more applicants than the "competition" section. It is clear
that people who are instructed to cooperate are better performers and enjoy their work
more than people whose reward depends on competition.

Communication.   How can we be aware of the intentions of the people with whom we
will interact? Will they cooperate and allow us and them to benefit, or will they merely
attempt to maximize their own gain? Only by communicating can we develop an
expectation of our partners' intentions and how their anticipated acts will affect us.
Deutsch (1960) investigated the influence of communication on cooperative behavior
(refer to Table 13.1). He allowed some subjects who were participating in a "prisoner's
dilemma" game to talk with their partner ("communication" condition); other subjects
could not ("noncommunication" condition). Pairs of subjects in both conditions were
then given either "competition," "cooperation," or "individualistic" instructions.
Deutsch reported that for subjects given "individualistic" instructions, cooperative

behavior doubled if the subjects communicated. Apparently, people who simply sought to maximize their own rewards realized by talking to their partner that they would gain only through cooperation. However, for subjects given "cooperation" and "competition" instructions, communication resulted in only a slight increase in cooperative behavior. One explanation of these results is that since "cooperative" instructions produced cooperative behavior, .the impact of communication was reduced. Furthermore, subjects given "competition" instructions perceived competition as the optimal strategy, and communication did not appreciably modify their view. Thus, it seems that the major result of communication is to increase cooperative behavior of persons who are uncertain how their partner's behavior will influence the ability to obtain reward. Deutsch and Krauss (1960) observed a similar increase in cooperative behavior by combining "individualistic" instructions and the "communication" condition in their trucking game. However, Smith and Anderson (1975) discovered that communication actually decreased cooperative behavior if both subjects could threaten each other with a competitive response. Communication increased cooperative behavior only if neither player could threaten the other—a "nonthreat" condition. Evidently, threatened persons communicate a competitive rather than a cooperative intention.

Trust. People must believe that another person will cooperate, or they will not be motivated to cooperate. Rotter (1971) defined trust as "a general expectancy that the word, promise, or verbal [i.e., oral] or written statement of another can be relied upon." People who do not trust their partner to cooperate are not likely to cooperate themselves. In all likelihood, only one betrayal is needed to establish distrust (Worschel, 1979), thus creating a vicious circle—distrust leads to the perception that another person is a threat, which results in greater distrust.

Reciprocal concessions appear to represent a method of reducing hostility and distrust, thereby increasing cooperative behavior (Esser & Komorita, 1975). Esser and Komorita designed a study in which one subject—actually a confederate—made a small concession to another subject. The results indicated that this small concession increased cooperative behavior. In contrast, if the confederate made too large a concession, the other subject increased competitive behavior because he or she viewed the confederate as being weak. Obviously, a concession instills trust and facilitates cooperative behavior only if the concession is viewed as an active cooperative gesture rather than an indication of weakness.

Reward structure. How can a social organization motivate cooperative behavior in typically noncooperative people? One approach is to arrange the reward structure so that noncooperative people realize that it is clearly advantageous to reach their goals through cooperation rather than competition. Some experimenters have attempted to motivate cooperative behavior by increasing the reward for cooperation. However, these studies have produced inconsistent results. For example, Gallo (1966) found more cooperation in a trucking game if subjects played for money rather than for points; however, Oskamp and Kleinke (1970) discovered that the greater the potential reward (up to $9), the lower the level of cooperative behavior. On the other hand, Friedland, Arnold, and Thibaut (1974) observed that higher stakes produced increased cooperation.

One possible explanation for this discrepancy is that although the absolute reward increased for cooperation, it still may have been more profitable to compete. And since individualistic people want to maximize their gain, they will continue to choose competition until the value of cooperation is greater than the reward obtained by competing. Therefore, our discussion points to the importance of the relationship between competitive and cooperative choices and not necessarily to the relevance of the absolute value of cooperation or competition. A recent series of experiments by Tyszka and Grzelak (1976) evaluated how relative levels of reward which were earned through cooperation and competition affected the level of cooperative behavior. To accomplish their objective, they had subjects participate in several different "prisoner's dilemma" games. The relationship between gain obtained by cooperation and that obtained by competition differed for each game: the reward structure favored cooperation in some games and competition in others. The authors reported that as it became more profitable to cooperate than to compete, competitive players shifted their behavior to cooperation. In addition, the absolute amount of gain received from either choice was not important; rather, the relationship between cooperative and competitive choices determined the competitive players' behavior. Interestingly, once the players had chosen to cooperate, they would continue to cooperate even if competition provided the maximum reward. Evidently, once people are motivated to cooperate, they will continue, at least for a while, to view cooperation as beneficial to them.

Although changing the reward structure to favor cooperation did increase cooperative behavior, many subjects in Tyska and Grzelak's study continued to compete. The most reasonable interpretation of these results is that many subjects considered the intrinsic reinforcement of winning greater than any extrinsic reward gained by cooperation. According to this view, competitive people will cooperate if they do not know how well their partner is performing. In this situation, competitive behavior cannot provide reward, since subjects are not aware of their partner's gain, and cooperation represents the only method of obtaining reward. McClintock and McNeel (1966) conducted an investigation to see, first, whether subjects' cooperative behavior was influenced by their awareness of their opponent's gain and, second, whether the level of reward would increase cooperation. In their study, subjects could earn either a small reward (up to 66 cents) or a large reward (up to $13.20) for cooperative behavior. Half of the subjects in both the "small reward" condition and the "large reward" condition were given information concerning only their own performance; the other half of the subjects in both conditions were informed about their own and an opponent's progress. High reward increased cooperative behavior only when the opponent's performance was unknown; the magnitide of the reward did not influence cooperative behavior when subjects knew about their opponent's performance. These results indicate that competitive people can be motivated to cooperate—but only if their competitive motives do not interfere with cooperative behavior.

Implications

A society that rewards competitive behavior can expect hostility to exist between its members. The fact that many adults in our society are unable to develop meaningful social relationships is not surprising. Our parents and teachers stressed the importance of success—which frequently meant performing better than another person—when we were children. In fact, children's games typically are competitive, are controlled by parents, and stress winning as the most important objective. I have often heard parents comment that they are "happy" if their child is a member of a "winning" team, even though their child plays infrequently. My son's 8-year-old friend became quite upset and confused upon overhearing his coach say that the younger children on his football team would rather "sit on the bench" than participate and chance losing the game. Most adults seem to think that being a "winner" is more important than developing effective behaviors; parents frequently are hostile toward the coach who is not "winning." The fact that their children are profiting from playing—learning the rules of the game, socializing with other children, and becoming coordinated—is often not appreciated. Most children in school must compete with their peers in order to obtain reward and satisfaction; as early as elementary school, youngsters compete for positions in student government and on athletic and debating teams. Teachers often institute "spelling bees" in which one child wins and the remainder of the class loses. High school students compete for entry into college; among college students, competition is fierce for admission into medical, veterinary, law, or graduate school. Two people frequently compete for the affection of a member of the opposite sex. The fact that competitive motivation is rewarded causes people to treat all situations as if they involve competition; therefore, the participating persons do not recognize that cooperative behavior benefits them.

Our social systems must be structured to motivate cooperative behavior; if they are not, people will not think that they will gain through cooperation with others. If we fail to institute cooperative reward systems, our competitive motivations will continue to dominate our behavior, increasing our existing hostility and further reducing our ability to interact pleasantly with others. The following rules should help parents and teachers to increase children's cooperative behavior, which should in turn enhance their satisfaction and performance.

1. *A cooperative reward system should be established and then communicated to each person.* A person must understand that cooperation yields reward.
2. *People should be encouraged to communicate.* Only through communication can we learn how others will react to us.
3. *A sufficient level of incentive must be established in order for each person to value participating in a cooperative situation.* Otherwise, a person's strong individualistic or competitive motives will prevent cooperative behavior.
4. *People must be willing to make small concessions to others in order to motivate cooperative behavior.* When a person learns that "giving in" at times is not a sign of weakness, he or she will have available a mechanism which can be used to develop trust and effective interpersonal action.

HELPING BEHAVIOR

Your roommate asks you to help change the tire on his or her automobile or to obtain a library book. Perhaps a stranger needs 20 cents for a telephone call. Although you probably believe that you would help in each of these situations, social-psychological research indicates that people do not always respond to a request for help. In the following sections, we will discuss the many factors which determine whether or not people are motivated to help others, as well as how to enhance one person's tendency to help another.

Altruism—Instinct or Learned Behavior?

Two Navy pilots died in 1977 when their jet aircraft crashed in a field approximately 3 miles from my home. Their airplane began to have engine problems upon approaching the main airway at Oceana Naval Air Station in Virginia Beach. A study of the crash indicated that the pilots were aware of the improbability of reaching the runway and could have easily ejected to save their lives. But they remained in the airplane in order to ensure that it would not crash into the residential areas surrounding the air station. Their heroic act undoubtedly saved the lives of several dozen defenseless people. Figure 13.5 provides a newspaper description of this incident.

What factors motivate people to risk their own lives for the protection of others? Occasionally we hear of people who lose their lives to save others—the firefighter who

2 Killed in Crash of F14 at Beach

**By PETER GALUSZKA
and GEORGE BRYANT**
Virginian Pilot Staff Writers

VIRGINIA BEACH — Two Navy fliers were killed Friday morning when their flaming, wobbling F14 Tomcat fighter narrowly missed a row of houses, crashed in an open field, and exploded.

Witnesses said that the plane's crewmen apparently sacrificed their lives to avoid crashing in densely-populated residential areas west of London Bridge Road near Shipps Corner Road.

Dead are the fighter's pilot, Lt. William R. Johnson, 29, and the flight officer, Lt. Stephen V. Miller, 30, both of Virginia Beach. They were attached to fighter squadron VF-101 based at Oceana Naval Air Station.

They had taken off to the northeast on a routine training mission from Oceana's Runway 5 when an air-traffic controller spotted flames in the aircraft's midsection and radioed. "You're torching," Navy spokesmen said.

Johnson and Miller circled, and as they cleared the Magic Hollow section heading for the field they crashed into open land several hundred feet from an empty warehouse owned by First Development, Inc.

Witnesses said the plane ex-ploded on impact, shooting flames and debris 200 feet into the air.

The Navy could not say if the crewmen tried to eject from the plane. One body was found next to an open orange parachute near the wreckage. Both bodies were tossed clear of the wreckage.

Louis Green, a carpenter working on a construction site in the 1200 block of New Land Drive, said he saw the fighter overhead.

"She had a big, bright fireball in the back section of the plane. One half was on fire. The pilot tried to keep above the houses. The plane went on a little bit and dropped.

"There was a big explosion, like a bomb. Big black smoke and flames were everywhere," Green said.

Another construction worker, Steve Twine, said the $16-million fighter was "twirling" when it passed overhead. "When it came over me flames were coming out," he said.

After the plane crashed and exploded, Twine and Larry Woods, a co-worker, ran to the plane and found one of the victims. "There was no sign of life," Woods said.

Friday's crash is the third in

three months in the Virginia Beach area.

Aug. 17, Lt. Robert F. Spencer, pilot of an A4 Skyhawk, died when his plane plummeted into the ocean about a mile off Rudee Inlet. A flight officer, Ens. David L. Kaufman parachuted and survived.

Navy investigators said that Spencer may have sacrificed himself to avoid hitting tourist-filled beaches.

Aug. 15, an A6 Intruder crashed short of an Oceana runway, killing the radio intercept operator, Lt. Cmdr. Wayne A. Stevens. The attack bomber's pilot, Lt. (j.g.) Michael Clark, ejected safely.

A crash similar to Friday's happened in 1972 when an F4 Phantom based at Oceana crashed in a wooded area near the Laurel Cove subdivision off Great Neck Road. The plane missed houses by about 100 yards. Both crewmen were killed.

The Navy's newest operational fighter, F14s have been grounded four times in the last two years for mechanical problems. However, the Navy has said that the plane's safety record is better than that of its predecessor, the F4 Phantom.

Figure 13.5
An example of altruism. (From Norfolk Virginian-Pilot, November 5, 1977.)

rushes into a burning building to help a trapped victim, the soldier who throws himself on a grenade to protect comrades, police officers who risk their own lives to free hostages, a bystander who jumps into the water to save a drowning swimmer. Our initial reaction is to think that altruism reflects a learned response to emergencies. We are instructed during childhood to help others; a heroic act is an extension of this behavior. Although altruism may indeed be learned, the biologist E. O. Wilson (1975) suggested that our altruistic behavior is genetically determined. Wilson hypothesized that altruism reflects a natural part of human nature, a part which played an important role in the survival of our species. He described numerous examples of altruistic behavior in other animal species. For example, an intruder attacking a termite hive must contend with the "soldier" termites defending it. These "soldiers" are exposed to great danger: they place themselves in front of the intruder. Fire ants also protect their nest against an intruder. If any of the ants are injured—and are thus less useful to the group—the injured ants become quite aggressive in their defense against the intruder. Another example of altruistic behavior is seen in baboon groups exposed to danger. The adult male members of the group remain to protect the group, while adult females and younger baboons flee from the danger. In Chapter 7 we discussed another motivated behavior in humans—aggression—which some psychologists propose as having an instinctive base. To consider that there may exist a positive aspect of human behavior contrasting with the negative aspects of aggression is a reassuring hypothesis.

Is there a genetic mechanism responsible for the transmission of altruism from one generation to the next? The process is clearly different from that which exists for other inherited behaviors. If mating were the mechanism responsible for inheritance of altruistic behavior, the gene for altruism would have perished long ago: many altruistic animals and humans are killed defending their species. However, the sociobiological view suggests that each member of a specific group has a gene for altruism and that altruistic behavior saves the lives of these group members. If altruism increases the likelihood that a group will survive, the gene is more apt to be transmitted to future generations than the gene for nonaltruism. Although there is evidence that humans are more likely to help people who are like themselves, additional evidence is needed to validate this evolutionary view of altruism. However, social psychologists have uncovered several processes which motivate helping when the cost of helping is less dangerous than that in our previous examples. Let's now study the factors motivating helping behavior.

Bystander Intervention

The Kitty Genovese incident. Few events have aroused as much indignation and despair as an incident which occurred on Austin Street in Queens, New York, during the early morning hours of March 13, 1964. Upon returning from work, Kitty Genovese parked her car in the lot of a train station two blocks from her home. Unaware that someone had been following her car for several blocks, she began walking to her apartment. The stranger followed her for one block on foot before attacking her. After being stabbed several times, Kitty escaped from her assailant and screamed, "He stabbed me. Please help me." One of Kitty's neighbors heard her screams and shouted to Kitty's assailant, a man named Winston Mosley. Alarmed by the bystander's shouts, the attacker returned to his car. Expecting the police to appear, for several minutes he circled the block. To his surprise, no police officers arrived; he then parked in the station lot and again attacked Kitty, this time in the lobby of her apartment building. To no avail, she pleaded to her neighbors—or to anyone—for help. When the police arrived, Kitty Genovese was dead, and her murderer had escaped. Reporters for the *New York Times* were startled to discover that at least 38 residents of Austin Street had heard Kitty's screams and that no one had come to her aid or summoned help until a neighbor in Kitty's apartment house telephoned the police almost an hour after the attack began—too late to save her life. Unfortunately, we cannot dismiss this as an isolated incident: too often our newspapers report the failure of people to respond during emergencies. We now examine a few of these events.

Other cases of bystander indifference. On a cold January day in 1973, a man raped a 20-year-old woman on a bridge in Trenton, New Jersey. The attack was witnessed by at least 25 employees of a local roofing company; but no bystander responded until after the crime was committed. Consider also the murder, by stabbing, of Sandra Zander on

Woman badly beaten in parking lot as witnesses look on and do nothing

By BUZZY BISSINGER
Ledger-Star Staff Writer

VIRGINIA BEACH — As witnesses looked on and did nothing, a 23-year-old woman was savagely beaten in a shopping center parking lot Saturday night when she attempted to report to police a minor accident involving her car.

Mrs. Carol Anne Holden, of the 1000 block of Old Dam Neck Road, suffered a broken nose and needed at least 20 stitches for cuts on her face. In addition, her right eye swelled completely shut and her left eye was severely blackened.

Detective Frank Drew called the assault "the most senseless beating" he has ever seen during his 10 years as a police officer. Drew also said at least four people witnessed the beating of the 5-foot-4, 105-pound woman, but made no effort to stop it.

Drew said the incident occurred about 6:30 p.m. Saturday in the Hilltop West Shopping Center parking lot.

Arrested Sunday were Richard M. Overton and Donald J. Flatt, the two occupants of the vehicle that police say struck the car Mrs. Holden was using.

Overton, 23, of Virginia Beach, was charged with malicious assault, hit-and-run and driving with a revoked license. Flatt, 22, was charged with malicious assault, hit-and-run and possession of marijuana.

According to Drew, it was Overton who assaulted Mrs. Holden when she told him she was going to report the accident to police.

Her car was parked at the time, said Drew, and the other vehicle, backing out of a parking space, accidentally struck her fender.

Drew said Mrs. Holden told Overton she had to make the report to police because the car was a new Lincoln Continental and was owned by the company she works for, Stohl Realty.

Overton told the woman she was not going to make a police report, according to Drew.

The detective and Overton then pulled her back and struck her numerous times in the face. Drew said the woman turned and tried to run but was unable to.

Mrs. Holden was taken to the General Hospital of Virginia Beach, where she was treated and released.

Immediately after the beating, police were supplied with a description of the car that had hit Mrs. Holden's vehicle.

Early Sunday morning, Patrolman Phil Flannagan spotted a car fitting that description at a Virginia Beach model.

Flatt was arrested at 4 a.m. Sunday, and Overton was arrested at 9 p.m.

Interviewed Sunday night by Drew, Overton told the detective he didn't want Mrs. Holden to file a report about the accident because he was driving on a revoked driver's license, and didn't want the police to be called.

Figure 13.6
An example of the failure of a bystander to help a victim. (From Norfolk Ledger-Star, *October 31, 1977.)*

Christmas morning of 1974. This attack occurred 10 years after Kitty Genovese's death, on the same street—Austin Street. Unfortunately, Sandra's screams did not have any more impact than Kitty Genovese's. Each of us has read of similar incidents—incidents in which a person is attacked while others watch or listen but do not respond. Figure 13.6 describes an incident recently reported in my local newspaper. Two assailants attacked a young woman in the parking lot of a shopping center. A group of people watched the incident, but no one helped. Fortunately, the woman was not killed, and her assailants were apprehended a short distance from the scene of the attack. The failure of people to help the victims in such incidents is in stark contrast to the behavior of the two Navy pilots who sacrificed their lives to save those of several dozen strangers.

Empirical support.   If you still think that most people will always help another person confronted with an emergency, consider the research of Bibb Latane and John Darley (Darley & Latane, 1968; Latane & Darley, 1968). They conducted extensive research on helping behavior and reported that whether or not an observer helps depends on the conditions surrounding the emergency; circumstances do exist in which none of us would help a distressed person. The likelihood that people will help—that, to use Latane and Darley's term, *bystander intervention* will occur—depends upon their first perceiving that an emergency exists and then deciding that they should intervene. We begin our discussion by examining several of Latane and Darley's original studies of bystander intervention. Later in the chapter, we will examine the conditions that determine whether or not people will be motivated to help another person.

In their original study (1968), Latane and Darley used male college students. Each subject was instructed to complete a questionnaire, either alone in a room, or in a room with two other naive subjects, or in a room with two purported subjects who were in fact confederates. After several minutes had elapsed, pungent smoke poured through a ventilator into the room, and the subjects' reaction times—that is, the time they took to obtain help—were recorded. The confederates did not respond to the smoke. The authors reported that subjects who were alone responded quickly; within 6 minutes, 75 percent of them reported the smoke. A longer period of time elapsed before the subjects who were with two other naive subjects responded; only 30 percent of the subjects in this condition responded within 6 minutes. The slowest to respond were those who were with two unresponsive confederates; only 10 percent of these subjects responded within 6 minutes. Latane and Darley concluded that the likelihood of helping behavior decreases when our potential helpers are available, and that the behavior of those nearby us also influences our helping behavior.

We will now examine two additional studies which illustrate the effect of the presence of other people on our tendency to help another person. In one experiment (Latane & Rodin, 1969), male subjects participated either alone or with another person who was either a friend, a stranger, or a passive confederate. After the experimenter—a woman—had given the subjects a questionnaire to be filled in, she told them that she would be working in a room adjacent to theirs. The subjects soon heard the sound of the woman falling, screaming in agony, and crying that she had hurt her ankle. When alone or with a friend, 70 percent of the subjects helped the woman; when with a stranger, 40 percent helped. Remarkably, only 7 percent of the subjects helped if they were with a confederate who had been instructed not to help. Again, the presence of other bystanders reduced the motivation to help.

In a second study (Darley & Latane, 1968), some students at New York University participated in a discussion of their adjustment to college life. The subjects were told that in order to prevent possible embarrassment, they would be placed in separate booths from which they could hear each other. Each subject was told that either one, two, or five other people were participating in the study. In fact, there was only one subject at a time; what this subject actually heard while in the booth was a tape recording of a voice or voices purporting to be the other subject or subjects. The first voice heard was the "victim." This person spoke of adjustment difficulties—and even frequent seizures. For some subjects there were supposed to be one or four "other subjects" in addition to the "victim" and the true subject; for these subjects, the taped voices of these "others" would be heard next. When only the "victim" and the true subject were supposed to be taking part in the experiment, no other voices were heard. The real subject spoke last. The "victim" then told the real subject something which suggested that the "victim" was having a seizure. The results of this study are similar to those found in other "bystander intervention" studies; see Table 13.2. As the number of individuals in the group increased, the likelihood decreased that a member of the group (the true subject) would demonstrate helping behavior.

Numerous real-world observational studies have reported the influence which the size of a group has on bystander intervention. Latane and Darley's study (1970) is one

Table 13.2
The Influence of Group Size on Helping Behavior in Simulated Seizure Situation

Group Size	Number of Subjects	Percentage of Subjects Responding by End of Seizure	Mean Time to Respond, Seconds
2 (subject and victim)	13	85%	52
3 (subject, victim, and 1 other)	26	62%	93
6 (subject, victim, and 4 others)	13	31%	166

From: Darley, J. M., & Latane, B. Bystander intervention in emergencies: Diffusion of responsibility. *Journal of Personality and Social Psychology*, 1968, 8, 377–383. Copyright 1968 by the American Psychological Association. Reprinted by permission.

example. They created a stiuation in which several cases of beer were "stolen" from a grocery store in New York City. The authors observed that a lone witness was more likely to report the crime to the store's owners than a person who was with one or more other people.

The results of such experiments indicate that the presence of others usually does inhibit one's motivation to help another. It is also clear that other variables play an equally important role. Although several studies report 100 percent helping if an individual is alone (for example, Clark & Word, 1974), the typical study indicates that only 70 to 80 percent of the subjects help even if alone with the victim. Obviously, other characteristics of either the subject or the situation (or both) prevented helping when a single subject was with the victim. In addition, although the number of people motivated to help is typically low with others present, some people do help. Research has established that a number of situational and individual factors determine the likelihood of helping behavior. We will now investigate the factors which determine whether one person will be motivated to help another.

The Aversive Quality of an Emergency

Jane Piliavin and her associates (see Piliavin, Dovidio, Gaertner, & Clark, 1981) have developed a motivational approach to explain when helping behavior will or will not occur. They suggest that witnessing an emergency situation is arousing: the more severe the emergency, the greater the bystander's arousal level. Since arousal is also aversive, an aroused bystander is motivated to reduce this unpleasant state. You might imagine that helping will automatically occur once the bystander senses his or her arousal. However, two factors determine whether the arousal will motivate helping behavior. First, the bystander must attribute the arousal to the victim's plight: a bystander who attributes the arousal to the emergency will be motivated to help. However, if a bystander feels that other events (for example, not feeling well) produced the arousal, he or she will not help. After having attributed arousal to the emergency, the bystander then compares the cost of helping the victim with the cost of failing to intervene. When the cost of intervening is greater than the perceived cost of not intervening, the bystander will reduce arousal by avoiding the victim. Arousal motivates helping behavior only when the perceived result of not helping is more aversive than the perceived cost (to the bystander) of helping. Piliavin's analysis of helping behavior is consistent with the motivational framework of this text; motivation reflects a combined influence of drive and cognitive processes. Let's examine the evidence supporting Piliavin's view of helping.

An arousing experience. According to Piliavin, an emergency situation creates the arousal states which motivate our helping behavior. Numerous studies (for example, Geer & Jarmecky, 1973; Lazarus, 1974) have reported that arousal of bystanders increases with the severity of the emergency. Arousal also increases directly with the length of time during which the bystander views the emergency (Gaertner & Dovidio, 1977). These findings clearly show that an emergency situation creates arousal in onlookers. But does this arousal motivate helping behavior? Two lines of evidence support the view that helping behavior is motivated by this state of arousal. First, people who help in an emergency are more aroused than those who fail to intervene (Krebs, 1975). Also, Piliavin, Piliavin, and Trudell (1974) found that the greater the arousal, the faster their subjects would intervene in an emergency. Second, people who witness an emergency alone are more aroused than those who are with others (Gaertner & Dovidio, 1977). Recall our discussion earlier in the chapter of Latane and Darley's studies of bystander intervention. We saw that people who are by themselves are more likely to help than those who are with others. One probable reason why people often fail to intervene when others are present is that they are not sufficiently aroused in order to be motivated to act in an emergency.

Why are we aroused? Piliavin assumes that we must attribute our arousal to the emergency if we are to intervene and help the victim. Gaertner and Dovidio (1977) created a situation in which their subjects attributed their arousal to the side effects of a placebo rather than to the plight of a victim. They reported that these people were less likely to help than subjects who attributed their arousal to the emergency. In contrast, Sterling (1977) observed that the incidence of helping increased if subjects had misattributed their arousal: a prior, unrelated event had caused the subjects' arousal, but the subjects helped since they believed that the emergency had triggered their arousal. These observations support Piliavin's view that helping will occur only when the arousal is attributed to the emergency situation.

The cost of helping. Unfortunately, attributing our arousal to a victim's plight does not always motivate us to help. After we have attributed our arousal to the emergency, then we evaluate the "costs" of helping. If we view these costs as reasonable, we are more apt to help than if we view them as prohibitive. Even if we want to help, the danger or unpleasantness of the situation may motivate us to flee rather than to stay and help the victim. Piliavin maintains that the emotional "defense reaction" produced by high-cost situations motivates a bystander to avoid helping (see Figure 13.7). In contrast, the emotional responses of "empathic arousal," "feelings of moral obligation," and "promotive tension" cause a bystander to help. The following section examines evidence upholding the idea that people typically avoid helping when the cost is high. We will then discuss those emotional responses which motivate helping.

A study by Piliavin, Piliavin, and Rodin (1975) provides a test of this "cost analysis" of helping behavior. They created a simulated emergency on subway cars in New York City. A confederate who acted as a victim would moan and then faint. The experimenters increased the discomfort of some bystanders by having the victim expose an ugly birthmark just before fainting. The victim did not expose the unpleasant

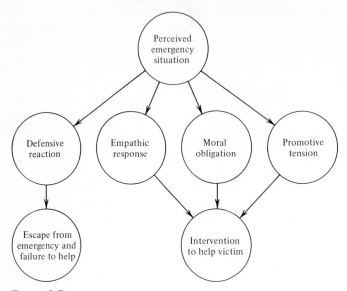

Figure 13.7
Schematic drawing of Piliavin's model of helping: the four psychological changes produced when an emergency is perceived. One emotion, a defensive reaction, motivates a bystander to fail to help the victim. The other three changes motivate helping.

birthmark to other bystanders. Their results indicate that the bystanders who saw the ugly birthmark helped the victim less than those who did not. As the cost of helping increases—in this case, the cost would include having to endure the sight of an ugly birthmark—the likelihood of helping behavior decreases.

Suedfeld, Bochner, and Wnek (1972) manipulated the cost of helping in a slightly different manner. A young woman (a confederate) would ask male participants in a peace demonstration (this was during the Vietnamese war) to help her sick male friend. In a "low cost" condition (for example, being asked to move the victim away from a large crowd of people), 98 percent of the bystanders helped. However, in a "high cost" condition (for example, being asked to carry the victim to a first aid station), only 66 percent helped. In a "very high cost" condition (being asked to help the man to his home, 7 miles away), only 19 percent helped. Once again, we have results to support the idea that bystanders are less motivated to help as their cost of helping becomes severe.

Pancer, McMullen, Kabatoff, Johnson, and Pond (1979) demonstrated that persons confronted with "high cost" circumstances do actively avoid helping. The authors placed a table between the library and the arts building at the University of Saskatchewan. There were three conditions: (1) In condition 1, a sign was placed on the table requesting a charitable donation. (2) In condition 2, no sign appeared. (3) In condition 3, there was not only a sign but also a person seated at the table. The experimenters measured the distances people maintained from the table when walking past it. In condition 1, not only did very few people donate to the advertised charity, but the subjects also maintained greater distances from the table than in condition 2. Furthermore, people maintained a still greater distance from the table when the person and the sign were there (condition 3). Apparently, the presence of a person requesting a donation increased the aversiveness of the situation, thus motivating people to avoid helping.

To fail to intervene, bystanders do not even have to avoid the victim; they can alter their earlier perception—that is, their belief that an emergency exists—and deny that the situation is really an emergency. Intense arousal may motivate bystanders to do just that. In support of this view, Piliavin, Piliavin, and Trudell (1974) discovered that their subjects were more likely to question the reality of an emergency in a "high cost" situation (a theft) than in a "low cost" situation (a woman injured in an accident).

Our discussion up to this point has indicated that the unpleasant arousal produced by a "high cost" emergency motivates us not to help in order that our arousal will be reduced. If this is true, why does anyone ever help during an emergency? According to Piliavin, there are several possible causes of our intense internal arousal. In addition to the alarm created by the danger to us in the emergency, we can also attribute our arousal to an empathic concern for the victim's welfare or to a moral obligation to help the victim. Also, we may experience internal tension—called *promotive tension* by Hornstein (1976)—when people close to us fail to obtain reward. Each of these three factors—empathy, moral concern, and promotive tension—can motivate helping behavior. We will aid those who need our help if our cost of helping is not greater than the combined influence of empathy, moral obligation, and promotive tension. Evidence that these factors motivate helping is presented next.

The Motivation to Help

A concern for the victim.   Batson, Darley, and Coke (1978) suggested that if bystanders attribute their arousal to the victim's distress, the bystanders are then motivated to help the victim in order to reduce their own intense emotional state (refer to Figure 13.7). However, bystanders who attribute their distress to other factors will avoid helping.

A study by Coke and Batson (1977) evaluated the validity of this hypothesis. All their subjects listened to a taped radio newscast describing the plight of a victim. Subjects in the "empathy" condition were asked to imagine the feelings of the victim. Subjects in the "nonempathy" condition were asked to observe the technical aspects of the broadcast. All subjects were given a placebo before hearing the newscast. Half of the subjects in the "empathy" condition and half in the "nonempathy" condition were told that the placebo was a drug that acted as a relaxant. These subjects were expected to attribute any subsequent arousal to the victim's need. The other half of the subjects in each condition were told that the placebo was a drug that would produce arousal. These subjects were expected to attribute subsequent arousal to the drug. Coke and Batson predicted that attribution of arousal to the drug would reduce the probability of helping behavior. In order to minimize the cost of helping, the authors told the subjects that anyone who offered help to the victim would remain anonymous. Coke and Batson reported that 70 percent of the subjects in the "empathy" condition who thought that they had taken a relaxing drug offered to help, while only 30 percent of the other subjects did so. These results indicate that we are more motivated to help a victim when we attribute our arousal to the victim's plight than when we attribute it to other factors.

A moral obligation to help.   Shalom Schwartz (1981) proposed that internalized moral norms which are activated when people encounter an emergency motivate helping behavior (see Figure 13.7). In Schwartz's view, two classes of moral norms—personal and social—are acquired through experience. *Personal norms* reflect our value system, and *social norms* present our expectation of how we should behave in certain situations. You will discover that some people have personality traits which motivate them to help and that others do not. However, even prosocial persons do not always help in situations in which the cost of helping is great. On the other hand, there are settings in which most people not only help but are expected to help. Social pressure in these instances activates the internalized social norms and motivates helping. Let's now study the evidence supporting the idea that internalized personal and social norms influence the level of helping behavior.

The search for the good Samaritan.   Recent evidence collected by Staub (1978) validates the idea that there are prosocial people who are motivated by their desire to help others. These prosocial people all possess three essential characteristics: a positive orientation toward others, a value for the welfare of others, and feelings of personal responsibility for them. Staub (1978) reported studies in which persons' prosocial personality characteristics predicted the likelihood of their helping behavior. However, these results indicated that high scorers on Staub's prosocial personality tests showed only a tendency to be more helpful than low scorers. Thus, it appears that the environment still plays an important role in determining helping behavior, and certain conditions may counteract the beneficial aspects of a prosocial personality.

The following three studies illustrate the importance of both internal personality factors and environmental events on the motivation to help others. In the first study (Feinberg, 1978), two female students—one actual subject and one confederate—worked together on a task. During the study, the confederate described the "loss" of her boyfriend. In the "high need" condition, the confederate stated that this loss had occurred the day before and that to be reminded of it was quite painful. In the "low need" condition, the confederate told the subject that the loss had occurred a year before and said that although it was very distressful at the time, she now no longer was disturbed by it. In the "high need" condition, Feinberg found that highly prosocial students helped more during the task and were more responsive to the needs of the confederate than subjects who were not very prosocial. No differences in helping behavior were observed in the "low need" condition. If persons are in need of help, highly prosocial people apparently are motivated to help them.

The second study (Grodman, 1978) showed that prosocial people help only if they consider that the "cost" of helping is not extreme. Like Feinberg, Grodman identified both "high" and "low" prosocial subjects and varied the confederates' apparent need for assistance. But Grodman's study was unlike Feinberg's in one way: for half of Grodman's subjects, the cost of helping was high. The experimenters created the "high cost" condition by informing the subjects that their performance in the experiment could provide them with valuable feedback about their personality; therefore, a subject was less likely to receive important information about herself if she helped the confederate than if she did not. In the "low cost" condition, the experimenter did not give the subject any information about feedback. Grodman discovered that in the "low cost" condition, highly prosocial people were more helpful than low-prosocial people if their help was needed (for example, they were more responsive to the confederate during the task and more willing to talk with the confederate after the session). In addition, the confederates, who did not know whether or not the subjects were "high" or "low" prosocial personalities, rated the highly prosocial people as more likable, responsive, and sympathetic than the low-prosocial people. However, highly prosocial people helped less when they considered the cost of helping to be high. In fact, no difference existed between highly prosocial and low-prosocial people in the "high cost" condition. In all probability, prosocial people are most likely to help when conflicting motivations do not interfere with helping.

The best example of the importance of situational determinants of helping, even in highly altruistic people, is seen in a study by Darley and Batson (1973). There are certain people whom we intuitively believe should help those in distress. For example, we might predict that a priest certainly is one type of person who would be motivated to help. Surprisingly, Darley and Batson (1973) noted that many factors interact to determine helping behavior and that even the most altruistic person may not be motivated to help others in certain conditions. The authors asked seminary students to volunteer to present a speech. They instructed half of the volunteers to speak on the ethical, moral, and social aspects of the parable of the good Samaritan (Luke 10:29–37). (In this story, the Samaritan aided a man wounded by thieves. His behavior was noteworthy because— unlike the priest who passed by the victim—the Samaritan voluntarily helped the man by carrying him to an inn, caring for his wounds, and paying for his expenses while he recovered. The Samaritan was not of the same religious group as the victim, felt no responsibility for helping him, and neither asked for nor received a reward. The Samaritan's response to the victim was definitely a noble act.) The authors requested the remaining volunteers to talk about employment opportunities for seminarians. Next, they told the students that their speeches were to be tape-recorded with equipment located in an adjoining building and that they should go there. Immediately before the seminary students left, Darley and Batson led some of them to believe that they were late for their speech and others to think that they were in plenty of time. During their walk between buildings, each student encountered a man in distress. The man, seen in Figure 13.8, sat in the doorway of the adjoining building with his head bowed and his eyes closed, and he coughed and groaned as each student passed. The results of the study

Figure 13.8
Victim in need to help in Darley and Batson's good Samaritan study. (Courtesy of John M. Darley.)

indicated that those seminary students who were not in a hurry stopped to help him. However, seminary students who thought they were late for their appointment—even an appointment to present a talk on the good Samaritan—were less likely to help than were those who did not assume that they were late. In fact several "late" students, on their way to talk about altruism, actually stepped over the victim. Many of these students later reported that they had not seen the man in distress. Thus, we can apparently conclude that occasions do exist in which even the most altruistic person will not be motivated to help another person. Yet there are some situations in which most of us feel that we must help. We will now discuss those social settings which create sufficient pressure to motivate helping. The social conditions in which we do not believe that helping is necessary will also be explored.

Responsibility. Many experimental results indicate that the likelihood of helping behavior decreases if a person is with others. Latane and Darley (1970) assume that if two or more bystanders are present during an emergency, the responsibility for helping the victim is diffused. Thus, each individual experiences less motivation to respond if others are present. However, responsibility can be instilled in an individual even when others are there; a person in the presence of others can perceive that the responsibility to help is his or her own. One way to create this feeling is through direct communication of responsibility to the bystander. To test this idea, Moriarty (1975) conducted a field study at Jones Beach in New York City. Young men—the confederates—placed their blankets next to those of sunbathers who were the subjects. Some confederates turned on a radio and then asked the subjects to watch their belongings while they were away. All the subjects agreed to this request. Other confederates did not request assistance. After each confederate left, a second male confederate stole the first's belongings. Moriarty observed that 95 percent of the subjects who were requested to watch the belongings attempted to stop the thief. Some of these subjects shouted to him, others chased him, and still others physically restrained him. In contrast, only 20 percent of the subjects who had not been asked to watch the confederate's belongings tried to stop the robber. Shaffer, Rogel, and Hendrick (1975) observed a similar effect of a direct request on helping behavior in a public library. Apparently, as noted in these studies, a direct request for help increases helping behavior through the creation of the bystander's sense of responsibility for the victim.

Bystanders feel more responsibility toward a victim when they are certain that the others near the victim either cannot help or are not in a position to help. Bickman (1971) placed his subjects in an emergency situation either (1) alone, (2) in a booth with another subject occupying an adjoining booth, or (3) in a booth in which communication was possible with another subject in a separate building. For subjects in conditions 1 and 2, the results conform with those of previous "bystander intervention" studies: subjects who were not alone showed less helping behavior in an emergency situation than those who were alone. However, in condition 3—in which the other observers were in separate buildings and thus could not help the victim—the subjects responded as rapidly as they did when alone. Apparently, if others are not in a position to help, we feel more responsibility for victims and thus usually help them.

Furthermore, we are more motivated to help another if those nearby cannot help. For example, if a child is injured while playing ball with other children, and only one adult is present, the adult will help the injured child. The children cannot provide help for their playmate; therefore, the adult is responsible for the victim. Ross (1971) evaluated the influence of either children or adults as bystanders on the likelihood of a subject's helping. When an accident occurred near his subjects, 92 percent of those who were alone helped, as compared with only 16 percent who helped when two other adults were present. Ross found that the presence of two children rather than two adults increased helping: 50 percent of the adult subjects helped the victim when two children were present.

By contrast, it has been found that we actually help *less* if we think that others are more capable of aiding an emergency victim than we are. Schwartz and Clausen (1970) conducted an experiment in which one confederate—a woman—fell and hurt herself. The subject (a student) and the "victim" were in the presence of a second confederate. Some subjects had been led to believe that the second confederate was a student like themselves; others, that the confederate was a premedical student. The authors reported that subjects helped less if they thought that the bystander was a premedical student. Evidently, we assume that we are less responsible for a victim than are others at the emergency who have greater abilities than ours.

Finally, in an emergency situation we are less motivated to help people who we feel are responsible for their own plight. Piliavin, Rodin, and Piliavin's study (1969) demonstrated this phenomenon. Their subjects were presented with a simulated emergency during a 7-minute ride on a New York subway. In the first condition, a male confederate appeared to be taken ill: he staggered forward, fell to the floor, and then lay still, staring at the ceiling. In the second condition, the confederate appeared to be drunk: he behaved the same way, but smelled of alcohol. The authors found that while the victim who seemed ill received assistance within seconds, several minutes elapsed before the victim who appeared drunk was helped. Figure 13.9 presents a real-world example of the results of this study.

Man In Path of Train Jeered by Bystanders

CHICAGO (AP)—Some of the dozens of bystanders laughed and jeered as the man with one arm in a sling frantically tried to climb out of the way of a subway train roaring into the station, police said.

But no one went to the aid of Stanley Simmons, 32, of Evanston, an unemployed cement mason and father of two children. He was crushed between the boarding platform and the third car of a four-car train in an underground State Street station in downtown Chicago on Tuesday.

While subway traffic was tied up for 25 minutes, firemen freed Simmons with a hydraulic jack that tilted the train away from the platform where he was wedged.

Simmons died three hours later during surgery at Northwestern Memorial Hospital.

Fire Lt. John Victor was told at the scene that the crowd was "laughing and jeering" as Simmons tried to climb back to the platform, but was hindered by an injured arm he had in a sling.

"People don't like to get involved with people who seem down and out," Victor said. He added that some of the bystanders apparently thought they would be electrocuted if they touched the man while he was on the tracks.

But Victor said the electrified third rail is the farthest from the platform and people "can't possibly be electrocuted helping someone onto a platform."

Officer Ray Sloma said Simmons, who was divorced, apparently was intoxicated and that he was carrying a bottle.

Connie Ray, 22, a college student, was among the bystanders.

"About 60 or 70 people" watching him grabbing for the platform without helping, he said.

"When he heard the train, he tried to get up, but he couldn't," Ray said. "His arm was in a sling. Everybody saw him. They didn't help. He didn't ask for any. But they should have anyway, I guess. I was a little scared of him myself. I don't know what he was doing down there (on the tracks)."

Figure 13.9
An example of the failure of bystanders to help a victim who appeared responsible for his plight. (From Norfolk Virginian-Pilot, *October 9, 1980.)*

The influence of others.   We have learned that helping behavior typically decreases as the number of bystanders increases. Yet, notice how many people often help the victims of a highway accident. I have sometimes observed several drivers veer to the side of the highway and then intervene following an accident. Under these conditions, the presence of some helpers serves to motivate others to help. Also, the behavior of a bystander witnessing an emergency is often influenced by past experiences similar to the current situation; the likelihood of our helping increases if we have seen other people help in the past. It is likely that seeing others help creates an expectation that we must help.

Evidence clearly indicates that modeling has an important impact on helping behavior. Bryan and Text (1967) evaluated the probability that drivers would stop to assist a woman changing a tire on her car if they had just observed a man helping a different woman change a tire. They set up such a condition and a control condition (in which motorists had not recently seen helping behavior), and found that the influence of modeling did increase helping behavior: motorists were more helpful if they had just witnessed another person helping than if they had not. Also, Macaulay (1970) discovered that people were more likely to donate money to a representative of the Salavation Army standing outside a department store if they had just seen a middle-aged woman (the model) make a contribution. Evidently, we are more motivated to help people after we have just observed others helping them.

However, when people present at an apparent emergency convey to us the impression that the victim is not in danger, we are less likely to help. Latane and Rodin (1969) set up apparent emergencies (for example, a woman would cry for help after falling from a chair) at which confederates were present; these confederates did not respond to the victim's request for help. The authors observed that if such a passive confederate was present, helping behavior by a bystander (the subject) decreased to 7 percent as compared with 40 percent when another naive subject was present. One interpretation of these results is that the passive model communicated a sense of "nonemergency" to the subject, thus decreasing the subject's motivation to intervene. In a similar study, Bickman (1971) instructed his confederates to tell the subjects that the situation was either an emergency, a possible emergency, or not an emergency. The confederates' information influenced the subjects: the probability of helping behavior decreased when the confederate conveyed the impression that no emergency existed.

Reciprocity.   Another variable influencing the probability of helping behavior is whether or not the victim has helped us; we are motivated to help in order to _reciprocate_ previous helping. In a typical experiment, Regan (1978) discovered that subjects were more willing to help another person—a confederate—who had previously helped them. Regan's experiment tested pairs of people—each pair consisting of a confederate and a real subject—who were asked to rate their liking of photographs of various people. During the first rest break the confederate would ask the experimenter to be allowed to leave the room. In one condition the confederate would return with two soft drinks and hand one to the subject, saying, "I asked him [the experimenter] if I could get myself a drink and he said it was OK, so I brought one for you." In the second condition, the confederate did not do this. The experimenter would then give each pair a second series of pictures to rate. During a second work break, the confederate would write a note asking the subject to buy one or more raffle tickets, priced at 25 cents apiece, for the construction of a new gymnasium at the confederate's high school; the prize was a new sports car. The confederate told the subject that the person who sold the most tickets would win $50; the confederate also indicated a pressing personal need for this money. Regan observed that subjects who had previously received a soft drink from the confederate bought more raffle tickets than those who had not. We apparently are more motivated to help a victim who has previously helped us.

Other studies identify two additional factors—the size of the favor which we must perform and the reason that someone performed a favor for us—as contributing to our tendency to reciprocate help. Greenberg and Frisch (1972) found greater help from subjects who were reciprocating large favors than from subjects reciprocating small favors. Also, subjects who can ascribe a victim's earlier help to either accident or environmental pressure feel less obliged to the victim. Thus, subjects felt less obligation to reciprocate a favor which was not done intentionally. Worchel and Andreoli (1974) observed that if a subject attributed the cause of a confederate's favor to the environment (for example, if the subject believed that the confederate was forced to bring the subject a drink), reciprocal helping behavior declined.

Guilt. During a playful wrestling match, a young boy injures his friend. Later the same day the boy helps this friend to deliver newspapers—a behavior which is quite atypical of him. It is very likely that the boy felt guilty after having harmed his friend. This guilt, producing strong negative feelings, motivated the boy to help his friend, which in turn served to relieve his own guilt, made him feel better, and solidified their attachment (see Chapter 9).

Laboratory studies have well documented the theory that guilt increases helping behavior. The study by Carlsmith and Gross (1969) is typical. They informed their subjects that the experiment in which they were participating had to do with learning; then they paired the subjects and assigned one member of each pair to the role of "learner" and the other to that of "teacher." Actually, the "learner" was always a confederate—a setup similar to that used by Milgram (see Chapter 12). The experimenter instructed the "teacher" (the real subject) to press a button when the "learner" (the confederate) made a mistake. In the "high guilt" condition, the experimenter told the "teacher" that the "learner" received a mild electric shock when the button was pressed. In the "no guilt" condition, the experimenter told the "teacher" that "learner" received a signal, indicating an incorrect response, when the button was pressed. At the conclusion of trials, the experimenter requested each pair to answer a short questionnaire. During this period, the confederate would ask the subject to perform a favor—to make several telephone calls in a campaign to save the California redwood trees. The confederates asked the subjects to indicate if they would help and how many calls they would make. Carlsmith and Gross found that although 75 percent of the subjects helped the confederate in the "high guilt" condition, only 25 percent helped in the "no guilt" condition. These results indicate that the subjects who believed they had administered shock felt guilty because they had hurt the confederates; therefore, their guilt motivated them to help the confederates.

Guilt frequently motivates us to help people other than those we injured. We can apparently reduce our guilty feelings by performing a good deed for someone other than the person whom we injured. Carlsmith and Gross (1969) noticed that subjects in their "high guilt" condition were more willing than subjects in the "no guilt" condition to help a third person. In fact, it appears that under some conditions, "transgressors" prefer to help another person and to avoid the person whom they actually injured. Guilty persons who help others without having close contact with their victims exemplify the maximum influence of guilt; subjects exhibit less willingness to help those they are responsible for injuring but with whom they must associate. This situation resembles the approach-avoidance conflict described in Chapter 2. Guilt motivates people to approach their victims in order to help them, yet the potential of retaliation probably creates arousal in these guilty people. Their arousal then motivates them to avoid the injured persons. This conflict can be resolved by the presence of a needy bystander. Avoiding the victim by helping another person reduces the arousal. Obviously, if another person is not available, guilty persons may be forced to help their victims in order to relieve their guilt.

There are some situations in which guilty persons cannot help their victims. Berscheid and Walster (1967) observed that some people who were unable to help their victims reported that these victims were not good people and deserved harm. Other people minimized their guilt by reducing the perceived harm which the victim suffered; they felt that the victim's injury was not serious. In addition, Berscheid and Walster noticed that some other subjects justified their actions by indicating that although they had hurt the victim, they did it for a good reason (for example, for science) or had been ordered to do it by the experimenter. Each of these methods serves to reduce subjects' guilt and thereby enables them to avoid helping their victims.

Guilty persons can use one final method in order to avoid helping—they can reduce their guilt by confessing it, so that they are no longer motivated to help the victim. Carlsmith, Ellsworth, and Whiteside (1978) designed a study to instill guilt in two-thirds of their subjects: confederates gave these subjects information which led them to believe that their participation had ruined the study. This was the "guilt" condition. The experimenter allowed half of the subjects in the "guilt" condition to confess that they had spoiled the study; the other half could not confess. A control group of subjects received no information that their participation had ruined the study; this was the "no guilt" condition. At the end of the experiment, all of the subjects could volunteer a certain amount of time for a future study; volunteering supposedly indicated willingness to help the experimenter. The authors noted that guilt served to increase helping behavior; this is consistent with other studies. But it was also noted that subjects in the "guilt" condition who had been allowed to confess indicated much less willingness to help the experimenter than subjects in the "guilt" condition who had not confessed. Apparently, when we confess our transgressions, we are less motivated to help the people we have hurt. Children who readily admit their guilt to their parents reduce not only their own guilt but also their obligation to be helpful to their parents.

Our discussion has pointed out that people are more motivated to help under some conditions than others. We learned that people who believe that they are responsible for the welfare of others, who have seen others help in past similar situations, who feel obligated to reciprocate prior helping, or who believe that they caused a victim's plight typically will help. These situations share a common characteristic: they induce a moral commitment to help and an expectation that one will be criticized for not helping. According to Schwartz's view, internalized social norms—activated by the settings—motivate helping behavior.

However, normative social pressure can be too intense and, therefore, can actually decrease the likelihood of helping. We may feel so morally obligated to help that we sense that our option not to help is being threatened. We learned in Chapter 12 that the potential loss of control—a process called *reactance*—motivates us to resist social pressure. We will next discover that when we are in a state of reactance, we can regain control and reduce our intense negative feelings by not helping the victim. Thus, our perceived loss of control, induced when we feel committed to help, will act to decrease our helping behavior. Let's now examine the evidence which supports the theory that reactance decreases helping behavior.

Reactance.   Brehm and Cole (1966) conducted a test to measure the influence of reactance on helping behavior. Their subjects were male college students. Each actual subject was paired with a confederate. Before the experiment began, the confederate would ask the experimenter to be allowed to leave the room for a short period of time.

Table 13.3
The Influence of Prior Favor and Bystander
Cost on Helping Behavior

	Low Importance	High Importance
Favor	93%	13%
No favor	60%	47%

Note: Entries are percentages of subjects helping the confederate stack papers.

From: Brehm, J. W., & Cole, A. Effect of a favor which reduces freedom. *Journal of Personality and Social Psychology*, 1966, 3, 420–426. Copyright 1966 by the American Psychological Association. Reprinted by permission.

While the confederate was absent, the experimenter asked the subject to rate the confederate on the basis of first impressions. In the "important" condition, the experimenter told the subject that accuracy was vital, as the results would be used in applying for a research grant. In the "unimportant" condition, the experimenter told the subject that the rating would be used only in a student's class project. For half of the subjects in both the "important" and the "unimportant" condition, the confederate would then return with a soft drink for the subject, thus creating a feeling of obligation. The other half of the subjects in both conditions did not receive a soft drink. Next, after the subject had completed his rating, the experimenter placed a stack of rating forms in front of the confederate and asked him to sort the forms into 10 piles of 5 forms each. This provided an opportunity for the actual subject to help the confederate. The authors predicted that subjects in the "important" condition would experience reactance because they would feel it was imperative to help. These subjects could regain their control by not reciprocating the confederate's earlier favor—bringing the soft drink. On the other hand, the subjects in the "unimportant" condition would feel no restriction upon their freedom and would reciprocate the favor. The results of this experiment are presented in Table 13.3. Brehm and Cole found that although half of the subjects in the "important" condition who had *not* received a favor helped the confederates, only 13 percent of the subjects in the "important" condition *reciprocated* helping behavior. In contrast, in the "unimportant" condition, where there was no reason to avoid helping the confederates, 14 of the 15 subjects reciprocated helping behavior. The authors suggested that in the "important" condition, the obligation to reciprocate was sufficiently strong to limit the subjects' freedom and thereby reduce helping.

Those we help.   We have learned that empathic arousal and feelings of moral obligation motivate "bystander intervention." Harvey Hornstein (1976) suggested that another form of emotional response, *promotive tension*, causes people to help others (refer to Figure 13.7). According to Hornstein, promotive tension occurs when we become aware that people we are close to are unable to obtain a goal which we value, and this tension motivates us to help. Hornstein suggests that our level of tension is related to our relationship to the other person: the closer the relationship, the stronger our tension, and thus the more likely we are to help. Also, we experience greater promotive tension if we are attracted to the people who need our help. We are, according to Hornstein's theory, more apt to help a friend or relative than a stranger because of the high level of promotive tension induced when people close to us need our help. Recall our discussion of the nature of altruism earlier in this chapter. If we interpret altruism in terms of instinct, we would predict that persons similar to altruistic people will benefit more than dissimilar persons. Promotive tension does favor helping similar people and provides support for the sociobiological view of altruism.

Consider the following example of promotive tension. Walking to class, you see someone trying to pick up scattered books. Promotive tension is induced, since this person is attempting to collect the books in order to get to class; you both share this goal of attending class. You have plenty of time before your next class, and so this is not a high-cost situation for you. If you then notice that this person is a friend, sufficient promotive tension is produced, and you stop to help. However, if the person is a stranger, a weak promotive response occurs, and you walk away. Let's now see why we will help some people but not others.

Benson, Karabenick, and Lerner (1976) discovered that we are more motivated to help attractive people than unattractive ones. A confederate left some material—an application to graduate school, a photograph, and a stamped envelope—in a public telephone booth. It was clear to anyone using the telephone that the material should be mailed. The experimenters varied the attractiveness of the person in the photograph: for some subjects, the photograph showed an attractive person; for others, an unattractive one. It was assumed that the number of applications mailed would indicate the influence of attractiveness on helping behavior, and the results bore this out: people were more motivated to help an attractive victim than an unattractive one.

The following study supports the idea that we are more likely to help an individual whom we perceive as closely resembling ourselves. Emswiller, Deaux, and Willits (1971) instructed their confederates—both males and females, dressed either in jeans or sports clothing—to ask a bystander to give them a dime in order to place a telephone call. The results indicated that bystanders were more apt to give a dime to those dressed in attire similar to their own than to those dressed differently from them.

Overview

Our discussion of "bystander intervention" has indicated that four different emotional responses are created when we perceive that other people need our help. The defense reaction, produced when a high cost is attached to helping, motivates us to avoid the person or persons needing our help. The other three emotional responses—empathy, feelings of moral obligation, and promotive tension—motivate us to help others. According to Piliavin's analysis, the defense reaction is stronger than the other emotions and, therefore, is responsible for the avoidance of a victim which is usually seen in situations involving high cost. Low-cost situations induce one or more of the other three emotions, which then initiate helping behavior.

However, some people do help even in situations involving extremely high cost. The story of the two Navy pilots who sacrificed their lives to save innocent people, described earlier in this chapter, is one example of helping at great risk. Another example is firefighters who place their safety in jeopardy to rescue people trapped in fires. What processes motivate people to risk their lives to help someone they do not know? Unfortunately, there has been no evaluation of these people's perceptions during extremely high-cost situations. Do they not sense the danger inherent in the emergency, or is their empathy or moral commitment to the victim so intense as to inhibit their fears? Although the answer to this question awaits future investigation, we can only be grateful that some people do possess the altruistic motivation that enables them to help those in great danger.

SUMMARY

As social beings, we engage in a wide range of interpersonal situations. Sometimes we interact with others in order to obtain reward and avoid punishment; at other times, other people request our aid so that they can obtain reward and avoid punishment. In each of these situations, we can respond in a positive, prosocial manner; our behavior not only produces individual gain for us but also reflects a concern for the welfare of others. On the other hand, we may choose to behave in a negative, egocentric manner by concerning ourselves only with our personal gain and ignoring what happens to others.

Many of us choose competitive behavior to satisfy our needs. Some of us feel that competition provides maximum gain; others think that by being competitive we can "beat" an opponent. A competitive response often results in the production of feelings of hostility toward those with whom we compete. Our hostility causes us not only to distrust these other people but also to become isolated as we become more competitive. Although social situations exist in which cooperation can produce reward for all participants, many ignore the benefits of cooperation and choose to compete. A number of techniques are effective in motivating cooperative behavior: people cooperate more when (1) they are instructed to cooperate, (2) they are allowed to communicate with others, (3) they are adequately rewarded for their cooperation, and (4) the behaviors of others instill a sense of trust. The benefits of cooperation are decreased hostility, greater accomplishment, and stronger interpersonal attachment. Cooperative behavior has a positive effect on both individuals and their society: It is imperative that our social system institute techniques to increase cooperative motives in a society plagued with distrust and loneliness.

There are times when we encounter people who need our help; unfortunately, we too often ignore their needs. It is easy for us to assume that victims do not need our help, that they brought their misfortune on themselves, that they can help themselves, or that others nearby them are responsible. Too frequently we pass a person whose car is disabled or ignore a cry of distress. Yet there are times when we do help: each of us has done a favor for a friend, donated money to a charity, or taken a neighbor to the doctor. Some people will even risk or sometimes lose their own lives to help someone in danger.

Social psychologists have discovered several processes which serve either to motivate or to suppress helping behavior. We will help if (1) our perception of the victim's plight creates an empathic reaction, (2) we are morally committed to help because of personal norms or social expectations, or (3) we sense that people for whom we have strong feelings cannot obtain rewards which we value. We are unlikely to help if the defense reaction induced by the perceived cost of helping motivates us to avoid a victim. The likelihood that any or all of these four emotions will be produced depends upon both the individual and the situation. It seems that there are some people who have prosocial personalities; they are generally responsive to the needs of others. Yet, even prosocial people may not help during conditions in which they perceive the cost of helping to be extreme. In contrast, there are some conditions—those in which cost is low—where most people will help. Although there probably will always be instances in which a victim will not receive help, developmental experiences could be instituted to increase our social awareness. The environment could easily be structured to increase our motivation to help others. Prosocial behavior has a positive influence on society; in order for society to improve, each of us must decide to encourage and reward prosocial responses.

A SMALL DOSE OF ANATOMY AND PHYSIOLOGY

APPENDIX

In the text, there are frequent references to the influences of particular neural systems in motivation. Some knowledge of how the nervous system carries out its functions and the locations of specific neural structures will enhance your appreciation of the biological control of your motivated behavior. This appendix provides only an overview of neural physiology and anatomy, focusing on those systems involved in motivation. (Refer to an introductory physiology and anatomy textbook for a more complete and detailed description of neural physiology and anatomy.) It begins by discussing the nature of neural functioning and follows with a view of the location of important neural structures. Finally, ways in which physiological psychologists can investigate the influence of a particular neural system on motivated behavior are described.

NEURAL PHYSIOLOGY

Structural Components

There are two major components of the nervous system: *neurons* and *glial cells* (refer to Figure A.1). Neurons are cells which carry out the information-processing and communication function of the nervous system. Neurons also activate muscles, thereby enabling us to interact with the environment. Glial cells provide a physical support for neurons by protecting them and holding them in place. Some glial cells also transport nutrients to neurons and waste products out of these neurons. Other glial cells insulate the neurons so that neural communications are not inadvertently transmitted to neighboring neurons not involved in processing a given message. Still other glial cells regulate the chemistry of the environment surrounding the neurons.

484

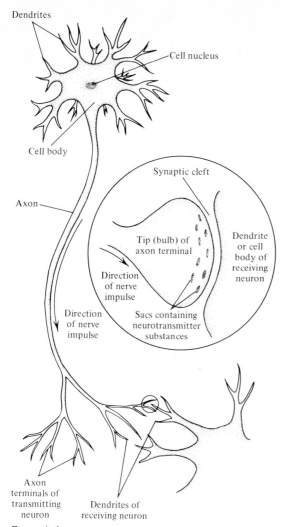

Figure A.1
A neuron and its component parts. This enlarged insert illustrates the synapse. [From Morgan, C. T., King, R. A., & Robinson, N. M. Introduction to psychology (6th ed.). New York: McGraw-Hill, 1979.]

Neurons share many characteristics with other cells. They have (1) a *nucleus* containing genetic material, (2) a cell body or *soma* containing cytoplasm or cellular fluid, and (3) an outer semipermeable membrane which allows certain materials into the cell and keeps others out. Also, neurons conduct the metabolic processes which enable them to operate efficiently. However, neurons have several unique structural aspects; these structures enable neurons to perform information-processing and communication functions.

Neural Transmission

Information detection.　Neurons receive information from other neurons as well as from the external and internal environment. The site of this reception is the *dendrite projections* of the cell body (see Figure A.1). Not all information received is transmitted to other neurons; the importance of a message is determined at the dendrite projections.

Impluse transmission.　Once dendrite projections have deemed a piece of information important, the neuron is obligated to communicate this information to other neurons. However, since neurons are physically separated, information is transmitted by the elongated *axon projections* of each cell body; this type of communication is analogous to the transmission of a telephone call, although the transmission between neurons is in just one direction from the cell body.

Interneuron communication.　At the end of the axon are numerous small bulbs called *terminal buttons* (refer to Figure A.1). Inside the buttons are many sacs, or *vesicles*, containing a chemical substance. Since there is no physical connection between neurons (or between neurons and muscles), the chemical substance provides the means of communication. The small gap between neurons is a *synapse;* the space between a neuron and a muscle is the *neuromuscular junction.*

The chemical substance contained in the vesicles is released when the neural information reaches the terminal buttons. A diffusion process then allows the chemical substance to be carried across the synapse. You might recall from high school chemistry that substances move from points of higher concentration to regions of lower concentration. There is no chemical substance near the next neuron or muscle, and so the chemical diffuses across the synapse. These chemicals are labeled *neurotransmitter substances* because they provide the means of communication between neurons or between neurons and muscles.

This neural communiction is very brief. The effect of the neurotransmitter is terminated by either enzyme deactivation at the postsynaptic membrane or transmitter reuptake by the presynaptic neuron. In addition, other chemicals can influence the effectiveness of a particular transmitter substance. Several neurotransmitters play a significant role in motivating behavior; let's briefly examine them.

Cholinergic transmission.　One important neurotransmitter is *acetylcholine* (ACh). When ACh is the neurotransmitter substance, the transmission is *cholinergic.* The combination of acetyl coenzyme A and choline produces acetylcholine. The synthesis of ACh occurs only in the presence of the enzyme *choline acetylase.* Released ACh, having reached the synapse of the next neuron, is quickly deactivated by the enzyme *acetylcholinesterase* or AChE. AChE splits ACh into acetate and choline. After deactivation, most of the choline is taken up by the terminal button, where it can be reused to synthesize new ACh.

Many drugs influence cholinergic transmission: some enhance cholinergic action; others interfere with it (see Table A.1). Drugs can enhance cholinergic transmission by either imitating the action of ACh or antagonizing the deactivation function of AChE. Those drugs (for example, nicotine) which mimic ACh can directly activate cholinergic neurons, whereas chemicals (for example, physostigmine) which are anti-AChE drugs act only to increase the effectiveness of released ACh. Some chemicals can also block the effect of ACh. These *anticholinergic drugs* interfere with cholinergic transmission by preventing synaptic depolarization.

Table A.1
Substances That Affect Cholinergic Transmission

Drug	Mode of Action
Cholinergic Drugs	
Carbachol	Imitate the action of ACh at
Muscarine	certain cholinergic synapses—cause
Nicotine	depolarization (synaptic transmission)
Anticholinesterase Drugs	
Physostigmine	
Neostigmine	Cause ACh to accumulate in the
Organophosphates (includes the insecticide	cholinergic synapse by blocking
parathion, the nerve gases	AChE—cause depolarization
sarin, soman, tabun, DFP)	(synaptic transmission)
Anticholinergic Drugs	
Curare	Block the depolarizing effect of ACh
Atropine	at certain cholinergic synapses—inhibit
Scopalamine	depolarization (synaptic transmission)

From: Buck, R.S. *Human motivation and emotion.* New York: Wiley, 1976, p. 420.

Adrenergic transmission. Two additional neurotransmitters central to motivation are the catecholamine substances *norepinephrine* (noradrenaline) and *dopamine.* (When dopamine is the transmitter substance, the transmission is sometimes referred to as *dopaminergic.*) Both norepinephrine (NE) and dopamine (DA) are produced from the amino acid tyrosine. Figure A.2 shows the synthesis of NE and DA. Although both norepinephrine and dopamine are catecholamines, in a particular neuron only one serves as the transmitter substance. Unlike ACh, which is deactivated by AChE, adrenergic transmission stops with the reuptake of either NE or DA by the terminal buttons.

There are chemicals which enhance or impair adrenergic transmission. Some of these drugs influence both norepinephrine and dopamine, while others act selectively on either NE or DA. The effectiveness of all adrenergic neurons is diminished by (1) the prevention of NE and DA synthesis by *methyl-para-tyrosine* (AMPT), (2) the prevention of NE and DA storage by *reserpine,* or (3) the breakdown of either NE or DA by *monamine oxidase* (MAO) or *catechol-o-methyltransferase* (COMT). Other drugs increase the action of all adrenergic neurons in one of the following ways: (1) a MAO inhibitor—such as *pargyline*—prevents MAO from breaking down NE or DA, or (2) an *amphetamine* stimulates the release of NE or DA.

Some drugs act selectively on neurons which have either norepinephrine or dopamine as the transmitter substance. Either *phentolamine* or *propranolol* blocks norepinephrine transmission at the postsynaptic dopamine membrane, while *chlorpromazine* can suppress postsynaptic transmission. The drug *isoproterenol* can stimulate norepinephrine neurons, and *apomorphine* can activate dopamine neurons. Our discussion indicates that there are several ways in which a drug can either activate or suppress the influence of adrenergic neurons.

In addition to cholinergic and adrenergic chemical transmission, several other

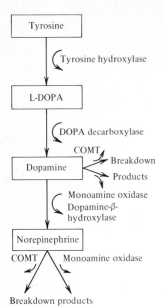

Figure A.2
Synthesis of norepinephrine and dopamine from amino acid tyrosine. (From Carlson, N. R. Physiology of behavior. Boston: Allyn and Bacon, 1977.)

chemicals have some influence on motivated behavior. These other transmitter substances which affect behavior include *serotonin* (5-H5), *glutamic acid,* and *gamma-amino butyric acid* (GABA).

Why are there so many different chemical transmitter substances? In many instances, especially in the brain, neurons serving different functions are in close physical proximity. The use of varied neurotransmitters for different functions prevents undesired communication between neurons. Evidently, the evolution of many chemical transmitters has a valuable adaptive significance.

Mechanism of Neural Transmission
How do our sensory neurons detect environmental information? Or how does one neuron detect the information conveyed by a neurotransmitter substance? Although there are some differences between how a neuron detects environmental stimuli and how a neuron detects information from another neuron, the basic process is the same for both types of detection. Let's see how neurons detect the influence of both important environmental events and other neurons.

Resting membrane potential.   Neurons are electrically *polarized,* or charged, like a battery. The inside of the cell is negatively charged, and the outside of the cell is positively charged. The difference between the interior and exterior charge is the *membrane potential.* When the neuron is not being influenced by outside forces, this difference is referred to as the *resting membrane potential.*

The detection process.   Although the entire cell membrane is polarized, the detection process takes place at the dendrite portion of the neuron. When a neuron is stimulated by either an environmental event or another neuron, a decreased electrical charge results. This reduction in charge is called *depolarization*.

Neurons do not detect the presence of all events—only important ones. How, then, does the neuron decide what is an important event? A crucial point, the *threshold*, is where the decision is made. If the stimulus produces sufficient depolarization to reach the threshold, the neuron decides that the event is important and then transmits that decision to the next neuron in the information-processing chain. However, a stimulus which does not produce sufficient depolarization to reach the threshold is never detected. Thus, once the stimulation is removed, the resting membrane potential is restored and no evidence of the event exists.

However, when threshold is reached, the cell membrane undergoes a radical change in polarization: the inside of the cell becomes positive while the outside of the cell becomes negative. This change in charge, referred to as an *action potential*, causes the transmission of the neural information. Once the neuron has "fired," the information is propagated along the length of the axon to the terminal buttons.

A period of insensitivity.   The dendrite membrane potential rapidly returns to the resting potential, although there is a short time, an *absolute refractory period*, when the cell is insensitive to further stimulation. Following the absolute refractory period, a second or *relative refractory* period occurs when the neuron can be stimulated only by a more intense event than that which normally activates the neuron. As soon as the resting membrane potential is restored, the cell can process new information normally. Figure A.3 shows the change in the charge which takes place when a neuron is stimulated and an action potential is produced.

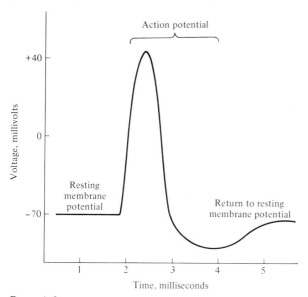

Figure A.3
Voltage changes which occur during the action potential. (From Groves, Philip, and Schlesinger, Kurt. Introduction to biological psychology. © 1979, Wm. C. Brown Company, Publishers, Dubuque, Iowa. Reprinted by permission.)

The all-or-none law. A neuron automatically transmits a message when an action potential is generated. The fact that the neuron propagates the impluse once a decision is reached is known as the *all-or-none law*. Let's examine how the message is carried along the axon. To illustrate this process, Carlson (1977) suggests that you imagine that the axon consists of a series of segments, each stimulating the next segment and thus creating a flow of depolarization along the length of the neuron. Once a particular segment arouses the next segment, that segment's potential returns to the resting potential. (The axon is not actually segmented and propagation is a smooth and continuous process; however, the concept of segments conveys that one area of the axon stimulates the next area, thus causing depolarization to move down the axon from the soma to the terminal buttons.) When depolarization reaches the terminal buttons, the neurotransmitter substance is released and the information passed to the next neuron (see Figure A.1). Most neurons contain a *myelin sheath* covering the axon. These myelin coverings, produced by glial cells, have some spaces of naked axon, called *nodes of Ranvier*, between myelinated segments. Rather than the continuous transmission typical of nonmyelinated neurons, the depolarization of myelinated neurons jumps from node to node, creating a more rapid transmission of information. Obviously, increasing the speed at which information is handled enables us to process more information.

The Inhibition Process

We have seen how a neuron is stimulated by either an environmental event or another neuron. However, neurons can also prevent other neurons from detecting information or transmitting that information to another neuron. *Inhibition* refers to this process of prevention. Let's first see why inhibition is considered important and then examine the nature of the process.

Suppose that you want to study but can find no quiet place to concentrate. Although you might decide not to study, your brain does possess the capacity to inhibit environmental sounds from being transmitted. Therefore, you could study by preventing your auditory system from picking up any distracting noises. This process, called *selective attention*, occurs because of neural inhibition. Perhaps another example will help stress the importance of the inhibition process. Having just eaten two servings of your favorite food, you are tempted to take yet a third serving. Fortunately, your nervous system can inhibit your motivation to eat the third serving. The significance of the inhibition process is frequently encountered throughout the text.

How does the nervous system prevent detection of information? In addition to producing depolarization, a chemical transmitter substance can increase or *hyperpolarize* the membrane potential. Hyperpolarizing the postsynaptic dendrite membrane increases the difference between the resting membrane potential and threshold. Thus, stronger excitation is required to activate an inhibited neuron than an uninhibited one. Therefore, inhibition can prevent, or at least impair, detection by decreasing the neuron's sensitivity to information.

You should not think that neural inhibition means that behavior is being suppressed. Behavioral inhibition can be quite different from neural inhibition. For example, neural inhibition can lead to motivated behavior if the system being inhibited normally suppresses behavior. In contrast, excitation of an area that suppresses behavior can lead to the inhibition of behavior. In addition, behavioral inhibition can also occur owing to excessive arousal of many brain systems. Thus, we can be so aroused that we cannot respond. Only by identifying the influence of a particular area can the influence of either neural excitation or neural inhibition on motivated behavior be determined.

The Combined Influence of Excitation and Inhibition

Neurons often receive input from many other neurons. Some of this input is excitatory; other input is inhibitory. The combined influence of excitation and inhibition determines whether or not information is detected or transmitted. Neural processing of information can be an extremely complex process. However, this complexity provides the nervous system with the flexibility to interact effectively in many different environmental settings.

Hormonal Influence

Most often, a neuron transmits important information to one or several other neurons. However, there are times when the communication must be more diffuse. Under these conditions, neurons in the *endocrine glands* release another type of chemical transmitter into the bloodstream, which carries it to targeted areas. Such transmitters are *hormones*. Although hormones are slower means of communication, they provide transmission of information to a larger number of neurons.

Hormones activate specific neurons or muscles to produce their desired effects. Table A.2 shows most of the hormones discussed in the text. For example, activation of the adrenal glands causes the release of *epinephrine* (E or *adrenaline*) into the bloodstream. Stimulation of neurons and muscles in the sympathetic nervous system, sensitive to epinephrine, produces intense internal arousal. Hormones stimulate not only neurons but also body organs. The hormone insulin causes storage of blood sugar (glucose) in the liver. Hormones often have an important influence on motivated behavior.

NEURAL ANATOMY

Anatomical Directions

Just as we need geographical directions (for example, north or south) to locate places we wish to go, anatomists have a system for locating structures in our bodies (see Figure A.4). The front end of an object is the *anterior section*; the back end is the *posterior section*. The top part of a structure is the *dorsal surface*; the bottom is the *ventral surface*. The outer surface of a structure is the *lateral surface*; the *medial surface* is the middle surface of a structure. The text often refers to a particular section of the brain or a brain structure. From the name of the structure, you often can tell where the structure is located.

Sensory Receptors

Our sensory receptors detect a variety of environmental events. For example, visual receptors detect light waves, and auditory receptors react to sound waves. Receptors are sensitive not only to external stimuli but also to internal events. The brain receptors which detect the level of *osmotic pressure* in the blood are but one example of an internal receptor. When this pressure is high, our fluid level is low; this indicates that we need water. Detecting the high pressure produces thirst which then motivates our search for water.

Peripheral Nervous System

Information concerning environmental events is received at the body's periphery. The *peripheral nervous system* carries this sensory information to the *central nervous system*

Table A.2
Some Important Mammalian Hormones

Source	Hormone	Principal Effects
Adrenal medulla	Adrenaline (epinephrine)	Stimulates syndrome of reactions commonly termed "fight or flight"
	Noradrenaline (norepinephrine)	Stimulates reactions similar to those produced by adrenaline, but causes more vasoconstriction and is less effective in conversion of glycogen into glucose
Adrenal cortex	Glucocorticoids (corticosterone, cortisone, hydrocortisone, etc.)	Stimulate formation (largely from noncarbohydrate sources) and storage of glycogen; help maintain normal blood-sugar level
	Mineralocorticoids (aldosterone, deoxycorticosterone, etc.)	Regulate sodium-potassium metabolism
	Cortical sex hormones (adrenosterone, etc.)	Stimulate secondary sexual characteristics, particularly those of the male
Anterior pituitary	Growth hormone	Stimulates growth
	Thyrotrophic hormone	Stimulates the thyroid gland
	Adrenocorticotrophic hormone (ACTH)	Stimulates the adrenal cortex
	Follicle-stimulating hormone (FSH)	Stimulates growth of ovarian follicles and of seminiferous tubules of the testes
	Luteinizing hormone (LH)	Stimulates conversion of follicles into corpora lutea; stimulates secretion of sex hormones by ovaries and testes
	Prolactin	Stimulates milk secretion by mammary glands
Intermediate lobe of pituitary	Melanocyte-stimulating hormone	Controls cutaneous pigmentation
Posterior pituitary	Oxytocin	Stimulates contraction of uterine muscles; stimulates release of milk by mammary glands
	Vasopressin	Stimulates increased water reabsorption by kidneys; stimulates constriction of blood vessels (and other smooth muscle)
Testes	Testosterone	Stimulates development and maintenance of male secondary sexual characteristics and behavior
Ovaries	Estrogens	Stimulate development and maintenance of female secondary sexual characteristics and behavior
	Progesterone	Stimulates female secondary sexual characteristics and behavior and maintains pregnancy

Reprinted from *Biological science* by William T. Keeton. Illustrated by Paula DiSanto Bensadoun. By permission of W.W. Norton & Company. © 1967 by W.W. Norton & Company.

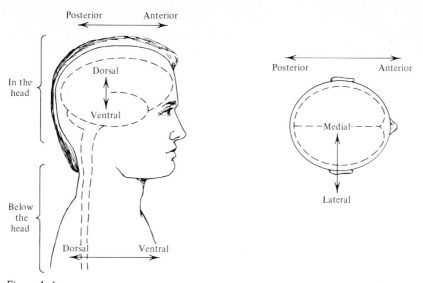

Figure A.4
Anatomical directions used to locate an organ and show its relationship to other structures. (From Buck, R. Human motivation and emotion. *New York: Wiley, 1976.*)

(CNS). Although most information processing occurs in the central nervous system, some does take place in the peripheral nervous system. For example, information from visual events is integrated as the millions of retinal cells converge into the optic nerve. The optic nerve, actually a bundle of nerve fibers, conveys the detected visual information to the central nervous system. However, most information processing occurs in the central nervous system.

The peripheral nervous system also conveys signals from the central nervous system to peripheral organs and muscles. *Afferent neurons* carry sensory information to the CNS; *efferent neurons* convey directives from the CNS.

The peripheral nervous system is divided into two subsystems, the *somatic nervous system* and the *autonomic nervous system.* The somatic nervous system contains afferent neurons which travel from the sensory receptors to the CNS and efferent neurons which run to the striped muscles from the CNS. Efferent neurons of the autonomic nervous system activate the glands and smooth muscles.

The autonomic nervous system contains two segments, the *sympathetic nervous system* and the *parasympathetic nervous system* (see Figure A.5). The action of these two systems is typically antagonistic. For example, the sympathetic nervous system increases heart rate and the parasympathetic nervous system decreases heart rate. There is also some cooperative functioning between the two systems. When a man sees an attractive woman, the activity of his sympathetic system may increase his heart rate and respiration rate; the parasympathetic system may cause penile erection.

The sympathetic and parasympathetic nervous systems have quite different structures. The *presynaptic sympathetic neurons* (the neurons entering the ganglia) which leave the spinal cord are short and synapse with the *postsynaptic sympathetic neurons* (the neurons exiting the ganglia) in the *sympathetic ganglia* (see Figure A.5). On the other hand, the postsynaptic sympathetic neurons are long and synapse on the target organ (for example, the heart). In contrast, the *presynaptic parasympathetic neurons* are long and

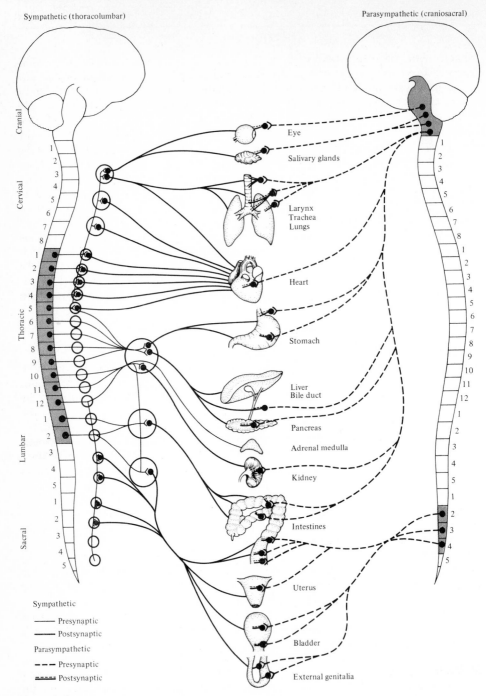

Sympathetic (thoracolumbar)

Parasympathetic (craniosacral)

Figure A.5

Schematic drawing of the autonomic nervous system. The solid lines present the sympathetic projections; the broken lines represent the parasympathetic projections. (Reproduced from Biological science by William T. Keeton, illustrated by Paula DiSanto Bensadoun. By permission of W. W. Norton & Company, Inc. Copyright 1967 by W. W. Norton & Company.)

synapse with the *postsynaptic parasympathetic neurons* close to the target organ. The *postsynaptic parasympathetic neurons* are short and synapse with the target organ. The presynaptic sympathetic neurons enter the ganglia either at the level where they left or one or two levels above or below. In addition, one presynaptic sympathetic neuron can activate up to 20 or 30 postsynaptic neurons; this allows it to stimulate several different target organs. In contrast, the activation of a parasympathetic neuron produces a more specific effect. Since the *presynaptic parasympathetic neurons* are long and synapse near the target organ, stimulation of a parasympathetic neuron activates only a single target organ.

Acetylcholine is the chemical transmitter substance in the parasympathetic nervous system and the presynaptic sympathetic neurons. The chemical transmitter substance in the postsynaptic sympathetic neurons is typically norepinephrine. The one exception is the sympathetic sweat glands which have acetylcholine as the transmitter substance.

Chemical differences between cholinergic and adrenergic transmission also provide for more intense sympathetic action. Whereas acetylcholine is rapidly deactivated, norepinephrine is only slowly reabsorbed by the presynaptic neuron. The slower reuptake allows norepinephrine to diffuse widely and activate many other neurons. In addition, the adrenal medulla, a sympathetic target organ, releases epinephrine which then activates many additional sympathetic neurons.

Central Nervous System

The central nervous system consists of the *brain* and *spinal cord*. The spinal cord, a thick tube with a hollow center, carries our sensory and motor input to and from the brain. Although our brain controls most of our behavior, some reflexes occur without the intervention of the brain. In these *spinal reflexes,* an afferent sensory input enters the spinal cord and leaves at the appropriate efferent motor neuron.

The brain, representing the bulk of the central nervous system, is where most information processing takes place. Figure A.6 illustrates two views of its key structures. We'll now look at the role which some key structures serve in the neural processing of information.

Cerebrum.   The *cerebrum,* or *cerebral cortex,* controls our perception of events and our motor responses to them. In addition, the cerebrum is the center of control for intelligence, memory, consciousness, and language. The cerebrum is divided into two hemispheres: left and right. It is also divided into four lobes: frontal, parietal, temporal, and occipital (see Figure A.6). Although motor neurons and sensory neurons are scattered throughout the cerebrum, several cerebral areas appear to have specialized function. The motor cortex (refer to Figure A.6) controls the movement of voluntary muscles, and the sensory area receives information from the sense receptors. There even seem to be other regions associated with higher functioning. For example, the Broca's area in the frontal lobe is involved with speech.

Midbrain.   The midbrain has two parts, the *tectum* and *tegmentum.* The tectum contains neurons which transmit visual and auditory information and control simple reflexes such as blinking and sound volume. The tegmentum contains two main structures, the *substantia nigra* and the *recticular formation.* Damage to the substantia nigra, part of the motor system, causes Parkinson's disease, which is characterized by muscular tremors and difficulty initiating motor movements. The chemical transmitter substance for the substantia nigra system is dopamine. Scientists have found *L-DOPA,* a substance which can be converted to dopamine, effective in treating Parkinson's disease. The other major structure in the tegmentum, the reticular formation or reticular activating system (RAS),

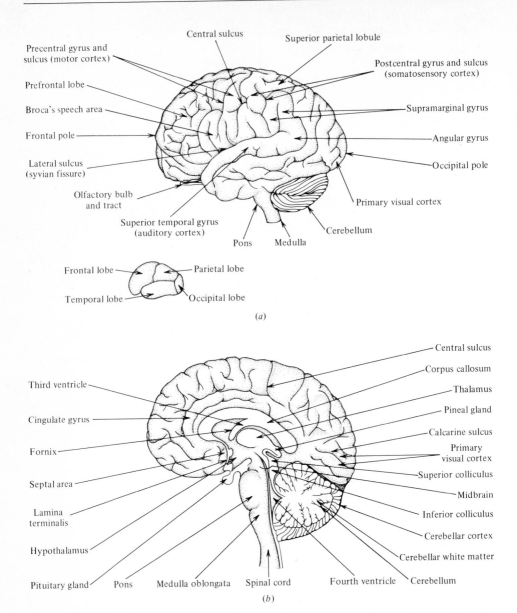

Figure A.6
Schematic drawings showing two views of the brain. (a) Surface view. (b) Midsagittal section which divides the brain into a right and a left half. (Adapted from Noback, C. R., & Demarest, J. R. The human nervous system: Basic principles of neurobiology. New York: McGraw-Hill, 1975.*)*

is a diffuse, interconnected network of neurons. Its function is to maintain consciousness and to play an important role in arousal and sleep.

Forebrain. The forebrain contains two central structures: the *hypothalamus* and *thalamus*. The thalamus is the main relay station for sensory inputs. Thalamic neurons

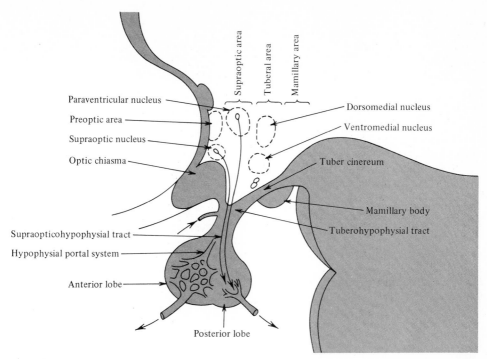

Figure A.7
Hypothalamus and pituitary gland. In this diagram the lateral hypothalamus is not shown, but it would be found behind the ventromedial hypothalamus. (Adapted from Noback, C. R., & Demarest, J. R. The nervous system: Introduction and review. New York: McGraw-Hill, 1972.)

transmit particular bits of sensory information to appropriate neurons in the cerebrum. The hypothalamus is the control center for detecting motivational states (refer to Figure A.7). Stimulating appropriate segments of the hypothalamus produces the motivation necessary for a specific behavior. For example, stimulating the lateral hypothalamus motivates eating.

The hypothalamus, connecting with the pituitary gland via the pituitary stalk at the base of the hypothalamus, controls the release of the pituitary hormones. These pituitary hormones include growth hormone, GH; thyroid-stimulating hormone, TSH; prolactin, which stimulates milk secretion; adrenocorticotrophic-stimulating hormone, ACTH, which stimulates glucocorticoid hormone production; gonadotrophic hormones, which stimulate the reproductive system; and antidiuretic hormone, ADH, which stimulates water reabsorption.

Limbic system.   The limbic system contains several structures (medial forebrain bundle, periventricular tract, amygdala, spectum, and hippocampus) which play an important role in motivation. The *medial forebrain bundle* appears to be the reward center of the brain; the punishment center is to be located in the *periventricular tract;* the *septum* and *amygdala* seem to influence aggression. The *hippocampus* appears to affect memory processing.

Psychologists use several major methods to study the functioning of a particular neuron or group of neurons. Our general description of physiology and anatomy ends with a brief discussion of these methods.

TECHNIQUES OF DISCOVERING BEHAVIORAL FUNCTION

Ablation of Neural Tissue

One technique of identifying the behavioral function of a particular area of the brain is to destroy the neurons in that area. An animal is first anesthetized and then placed in a special surgical instrument, a *stereotaxic apparatus* (refer to Figure A.8), in order to ablate or lesion a particular region of the brain. There are two methods of producing a brain lesion: (1) The brain's outer cover (or dura matter) is cut away, and the underlying cortical tissue is removed. (2) Subcortical lesions are produced by guiding a small stainless steel or platinum wire, insulated except for the tip, to the desired area and passing an electric current through the tip of the wire. The current carries enough intensity to destroy the appropriate neurons. The amount of brain tissue destroyed depends upon the intensity and duration of the electrical current.

A stereotaxic atlas can identify the area to be lesioned. Using the *bregma*—the junction of the sagittal and coronal sutures of the skull—as a guide, the atlas indicates where and how deep the electrode should be placed. A psychologist can identify the

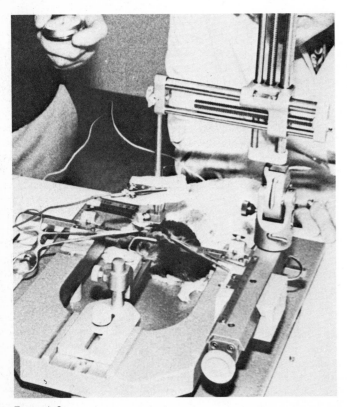

Figure A.8
Stereotaxic apparatus which is used to perform brain surgery on rats. (Courtesy of R. D. Hodnett.)

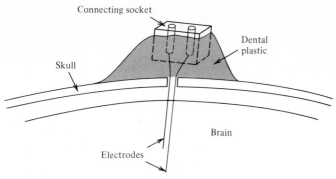

Figure A.9
How an electrode can be permanently implanted in an animal's brain. (From Carlson, N. R. Physiology of behavior. Boston: Allyn and Bacon, 1977.)

influence of a particular area of the brain by observing the behavioral changes which occur after lesioning.

Electrical Recording

Another method of detecting the function of a particular region of the brain is to record the electrical activity of that area while the animal or human is behaving. The potential changes which occur during neural transmission can be recorded in several ways: (1) Electrodes can be placed on the scalp and cortical activity recorded. The electroencephalogram (EEG) is a recording of this cortical activity. (2) A small metal or glass tube which detects single-cell activity, or a small stainless steel or platinum wire which records the activity of many neurons, is guided to a subcortical area. This procedure is employed where the surface electrodes cannot detect activity. The tube or wire, insulated except at the tip, records neural activity occurring at this tip. After the electrode is in place, an electric socket, attached to the electrode, is cemented to the animal's skull with dental plastic. After surgery, the psychologist can "plug" the animal into the recording system and detect the occurrence of electrical activity (see Figure A.9). An oscillograph, or polygraph, amplifies the electrical activity and permanently records the changes in electrical potential.

Brain Stimulation

Rather than destroying a particular area of the brain or recording its activity, experimenters can assess its function by stimulating the neurons in that area. An area can be stimulated by a weak electric current passed through a small wire implanted in the area. The behavior produced by stimulation provides information concerning the influence of that area on behavior.

Psychologists are also interested in identifying the neurotransmitters in a particular area. This identification process requires several stages: (1) Using sacrificed animals, dead tissue is stained to ascertain which chemicals are located in the area. (2) Using living subjects, those chemicals are then injected into a small metal tube, a cannula, located in the brain area being studied, and subsequent behavioral changes are noted (see Figure A.10). (3) Chemicals which inhibit the identified neurotransmitter are also injected; their effects are then observed. Various drugs influence behavior by either stimulating or

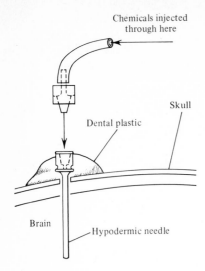

Chemicals injected
through here

Skull

Dental plastic

Brain

Hypodermic needle

Figure A. 10
Permanent cannula implant. The chemicals can be placed
into the brain with this technique. (From Carlson, N. R.
Physiology of behavior. Boston: Allyn and Bacon,
1977.)

inhibiting the functioning of a particular area; using this technique provides information
concerning whether a drug activates or inhibits neural activity.

Overview

Why are different methods needed to study brain functioning? Because of the complexity
of information processing, the results of these techniques do not always coincide. For
example, an area may not be crucial to motivating a particular behavior. Thus, a lesion
may not influence a certain behavior, yet stimulation of that area will activate that
specific behavior. Or an area may be active when a specific behavior occurs, but
stimulation will not be sufficient by itself to produce that specific behavior. Only the
combination of these techniques can indicate the precise role that an area has in
motivating behavior.

References

ABBOTT, P. A., BLAKE, C., & VINCZE, C. Treatment of mentally retarded with thioidazine. *Diseases of the Nervous System*, 1965, 26, 583–585.

ABELSON, R. Modes of resolution of belief dilemmas. *Journal of Conflict Resolution*, 1959, 3, 343–352.

ABRAMSON. L. Y. *Universal versus personal helplessness: An experimental test of the reformulated theory of learned helplessness and depression*. Unpublished doctoral dissertation, University of Pennsylvania, 1977.

ABRAMSON, L. Y., & SACKEIM, H. A. A paradox in depression: Uncontrollability and self-blame. *Psychological Bulletin*, 1977, 84, 838–851.

ABRAMSON, L. Y., SELIGMAN, M. E. P., & TEASDALE, J. D. Learned helplessness in humans: Critique and reformulation. *Journal of Abnormal Psychology*, 1978, 87, 49–74.

ADAMS, D. B. Defense and territorial behavior dissociated by hypothalamic lesions in the rat. *Nature*, 1971, 232, 573–574.

ADAMS, D. B. Brain mechanisms for offense, defense, and submission. *Behavioral and Brain Sciences*, 1979, 2, 201–241.

ADAMS, D. B., GOLD, A. R., & BURT, A. D. Rise in female-initiated sexual acitvity at ovulation and its suppression by oral contraceptives. *New England Journal of Medicine*, 1978, 229, 1145–1150.

ADAMS, J. A., & CREAMER, L. R. Proprioception variables as determinents of anticipatory timing behavior. *Human Factors*, 1962, 15, 218–222.

ADAMS, J. S. Toward an understanding of inequity. *Journal of Abnormal and Social Psychology*, 1963, 64, 422–436.

ADAMS, J. S., & ROSENBAUM, W. B. The relationship of worker productivity to cognitive dissonance about wage inequities. *Journal of Applied Psychology*, 1962, 46, 161–164.

ADAMS, R. N. An inquiry into the nature of the family. In G. E. Dole & R. L. Carneiro (Eds.), *Essays in the science of culture in honor of Leslie A. White*. New York: Crowell, 1960.

ADELMAN, H. M., & MAATSCH, J. L. Resistance to extinction as a function of the type of response elicited by frustration. *Journal of Experimental Psychology*, 1955, 50, 61–65.

ADLER, A. *The practice and theory of individual psychology*. New York: Harcourt, Brace & World, 1927.

501

ADOLPH, E. E., BARKER, J. P., & HOY, P. A. Multiple factors in thirst. *American Journal of Physiology*, 1954, *178*, 538–562.

ADORNO, T. W., FRENKEL-BRUNSWICK, E., LEVINSON, D. J., & SANFORD, R. N. *The authoritarian personality*. New York: Harper & Row, 1950.

AGNEW, H. W., JR., WEBB, W. B., & WILLIAMS, R. L. Comparison of stage 4 and 1 REM sleep deprivation. *Perceptual and Motor Skills*, 1967, *24*, 851–858.

AINSWORTH, M. D. S. Discussion of Suomi and Bowlby by chapters. In G. Serban & A. King (Eds.), *Animal models in human psychobiology*. New York: Plenum Press, 1976.

AINSWORTH, M. D. S., & BELL, S. M. Attachment, exploration and separation: Illustrated by the behavior of one-year-olds in a strange situation. *Child Development*, 1970, *41*, 49–67.

ALDERTON, H. & HODDINOTT, B. A. A controlled study of the use of thioridazine in the treatment of hyperactive and aggressive children in a children's psychiatric hospital. *Canadian Psychiatric Association Journal*, 1964, *9*, 239–274.

ALEXANDER, M., & PERACHIO, A. A. The influence of target sex and dominance on evoked attack in rhesus monkeys. *American Journal of Physical Anthropology*, 1973, *38*, 543–547.

ALLEN, V. L. Social support for nonconformity. In L. Berkowitz (Ed.), *Advances in experimental social psychology* (Vol. 8). New York: Academic Press, 1975.

ALLEN, V. L., & LEVINE, J. M. Consensus and conformity. *Journal of Experimental Psychology*, 1969, *5*, 389–399.

ALLPORT, G. Attitudes. In C. Murchison (Ed.), *A handbook of social psychology*. Worcester, Mass.: Clark University Press, 1935.

ALTMAN, I. *The environment and social behavior*. Monterey, Calif. Brooks/Cole, 1975.

ALTMAN, I., & TAYLOR, D. A. *Social penetration: The development of interpersonal relationships*. New York: Holt, Rinehart & Winston, 1973.

ALTMAN, M. Naturalistic studies of maternal care in the moose and elk. In H. L. Rheingold (Ed.), *Maternal behavior in mammals*, New York: Wiley, 1963.

AMIR, M. *Patterns of forcible rape*. Chicago: University of Chicago Press, 1971.

AMOROSO, D. M., BROWN, M., PRUESSE, M., WARE, E. E., & PILKEY, D. W. An investigation of behaviorial, psychological, and physiological reactions to pornographic stimuli. In *Technical report of the commission on obscenity and pornography* (Vol. VIII). Washington, D. C.: U.S. Government Printing Office, 1971.

AMSEL, A. The role of frustrative nonreward in noncontinuous reward situations. *Psychological Bulletin*, 1958, *55*, 102–119.

AMSEL, A., & COLE, K. F. Generalization of fear motivated interference with water intake. *Journal of Experimental Psychology*, 1953, *46*, 243–247.

AMSEL, A., & MALTZMAN, I. The effect upon generalized drive strength of emotionality as inferred from the level of consummatory response. *Journal of Experimental Psychology*, 1950, *40*, 563–569.

AMSEL, A., & ROUSSEL, J. Motivational properties of frustration: I. Effect on a running response of the addition of frustration to the motivational complex. *Journal of Experimental Psychology*, 1952, *43*, 363–368.

ANAND, B. K., & BROBECK, J. R. Hypothalamic control of food intake in rats and cats. *Yale Journal of Biology and Medicine*, 1951, *24*, 123–140.

ANAND, B. K., CHHINA, G. S., & SINGH, B. Effect of glucose on the activity of hypothalamic "feeding centers." *Science*, 1962, *138*, 597–598.

ANAND, B. K., & DUA, S. Electrical stimulation of the limbic system of the brain ("visceral brain") in the waking animal. *Indian Journal of Medicinal Research*, 1956, *44*, 107–119.

ANDEN, N. E., & STOCK, G. Effects of clozapine on the turnover of dopamine in the corpus striatum and the limbic system. *Journal of Pharmacy and Pharmacology*, 1973, *25*, 346–348.

ANDERSSON, B. The effect of injections of hypertonic NaCl solutions in different parts of the hypothalamus of goats. *Acta Physiologica Scandinavica*, 1953, *28*, 188–201.

ANDERSSON, B., & MCCANN, S. M. A further study of polydipsia evoked by hypothalamic stimulation in the goat. *Acta Physiologica Scandinavia*, 1955, *33*, 333–346.

ANDERSSON, B., & MCCANN, S. M. The effect of hypothalamic lesions on the water intake of the dog. *Acta Physiologica Scandinavica*, 1956, *35*, 312–320.

ANDERSSON, B., & WYRWICKA, W. The elicitation of a drinking motor conditioned reaction by electrical stimulation of the "drinking area" of the goat. *Acta Physiologica Scandinavica*, 1957, *41*, 194–198.

ANNAU, Z., & KAMIN, L. J. The conditioned emotional response as a function of intensity of the US. *Journal of Comparative and Physiological Psychology*, 1961, *54*, 428–432.

ANTELMAN, S. M., ROWLAND, N. E., & FISHER, A. E. Stimulation bound ingestive behavior: A view from the tail. *Physiology and Behavior*, 1976, *17*, 743–748.

ANTELMAN, S. M., SZECHTMAN, H., CHIN, P., & FISHER, A. E. Tail pinch-induced eating, gnawing, and licking behavior in rats: Dependence on the nigrostriatal dopamine system. *Brain Research*, 1975, *99*, 319–337.

ANTON, A. H., SCHWARTZ, R. P., & KRAMER, S. Catecholamines and behavior in isolated and grouped mice. *Journal of Psychiatric Research*, 1968, *6*, 211–220.

APSLER, R., & SEARS, D. O. Warning, personal involvement, and attitude change. *Journal of Personality and Social Psychology*, 1968, *9*, 162–166.

ARCHEA, I. The place of architectural factors in behavioral theories of privacy. *The Journal of Social Issues*, 1977, *33*, 66–84.

ARCHER, J. The effect of strange male odor on aggressive behavior in male mice. *Journal of Mammalogy*, 1968, *49*, 572–575.

ARCHER, J. Effect of population density on behaviour in rodents. In J. H. Cook (Ed.), *Social behaviour in birds and mammals*. London: Academic Press, 1970.

ARDREY, R. *The territorial imperative*. New York: Atheneum, 1966.

ARENDT, H. *Eichmann in Jerusalem*. New York: Viking, 1963.

ARENDT, H. *The Jew as pariah*. New York: Grove Press, 1978.

ARGOTE, L. M., FISHER, J. E., MCDONALD, P. J., & O'NEAL, E. C. Competitiveness in males and females: Situational determinants of fear of success behavior. *Sex Roles*, *1976*, 295–304.

ARGYLE, M. Social pressures in public and private situations. *Journal of Abnormal and Social Psychology*, 1957, *54*, 172–175.

ARONOFF, J., & LITWIN, G. Achievement motivation training and executive advancement. *Journal of Applied Behavioral Science*, 1971, *7*, 215–229.

ARONSON, E., & CARLSMITH, J. M. The effect of the severity of threat on the devaluation of forbidden behavior. *Journal of Abnormal and Social Psychology*, 1963, *66*, 584–588.

ARONSON, E., & LINDER, D. Gain and loss of esteem as determinants of interpersonal attractiveness. *Journal of Experimental Social Psychology*, 1965, *1*, 156–171.

ASCH, S. E. Effects of group pressure upon the modification and distortion of judgments. In H. Guetzkow (Ed.), *Groups, leadership, and men*. Pittsburgh, Pa.: Carnegie Press, 1951.

ASCH, S. E. *Social psychology*. Englewood Cliffs, N.J.: Prentice-Hall, 1952.

ASCH, S. E. Studies of independence and conformity: I. A minority of one against a unanimous majority. *Psychological Monographs*, 1956, *70* (Whole No. 9).

ASCH, S. E. Effects of group pressure upon modification and distortion of judgments. In E. E. Maccoby, T. M. Newcomb, & E. L. Hartley (Eds.), *Readings in Social Psychology* (Vol. 3). New York: Holt, 1958.

ASHCROFT, G., CRAWFORD, T., & ECCLESTON, E. 5-Hydroxyindole compounds in the cerebrospinal fluid of patients with psychiatric or neurological disease. *Lancet*, 1966, *2*, 1049–1052.

ATKINSON, J. W. The achievement motive and recall of interrupted and completed tasks. *Journal of Experimental Psychology*, 1953, *46*, 381–390.

ATKINSON, J. W. *Motives in fantasy, action, and society*. Princeton, N. J.: Van Nostrand, 1958.

ATKINSON, J. W. *An introduction to motivation*. Princeton, N. J.: Van Nostrand, 1964.

ATKINSON, J. W., BASTIAN, J. R., EARL, R. W., & LITWIN, G. H. The achievement motive, goal setting, and probability preferences. *Journal of Abnormal and Social Psychology*, 1960, *60*, 27–36.

ATKINSON, J. W., & BIRCH, D. *The dynamics of action*. New York: Wiley, 1970.

ATKINSON, J. W., & BIRCH, D. *An introduction to motivation* (2nd ed.). New York: Van Nostrand, 1978.

ATKINSON, J. W., LENS, W., & O'MALLEY, P. M. Motivation and ability: Interactive psychological determinants of intellectual performance, educational achievement, and each other. In W.

H. Sewell, R. H. Hanser, & D. L. Featherman (Eds.), *Schooling and achievement in American society* New York: Academic Press, 1976.

ATKINSON, J. W., & LITWIN, G. H. Achievement motive and test anxiety conceived as motive to approach success and motive to avoid failure. *Journal of Abnormal and Social Psychology*, 1960, 60, 52–63.

ATKINSON, J. W., & RAPHELSON, A. C. Individual differences in motivation and behavior in particular situations. *Journal of Personality*, 1956, 24, 349–363.

AUERBACH, S. M., KENDALL, P. C., CUTTLER, H. F., & LEVITT, N. R. Anxiety, locus of control, type of preparatory information, and adjustment to dental surgery. *Journal of Consulting and Clinical Psychology*, 1976, 44, 809–818.

AX, A. F. The physiological differentiation between fear and anger in humans. *Psychosomatic Medicine*, 1953, 15, 433–443.

AZRIN, N. H. Aggression. Paper presented at the American Psychological Association Meeting, Los Angeles, September 1964.

AZRIN, N. H., HUTCHINSON, R. R., & HAKE, D. F. Extinction induced aggression. *Journal of Experimental Analysis of Behavior*, 1966, 9, 191–204.

AZRIN, N. H., HUTCHINSON, R. R., & McLAUGHLIN, R. The opportunity for aggression as an operant reinforcer during aversive stimulation. *Journal of the Experimental Analysis of Behavior*, 1965, 8, 171–180.

AZRIN, N. H., HUTCHINSON, R. R., & SALLERY, R. D. Pain aggression toward inanimate objects. *Journal of the Experimental Analysis of Behavior*, 1964, 7, 223–228.

BAERENDS, G. P., BROUWER, R., & WATERBOLK, H. Tj. Ethological studies on *Lebistes reticulatus* (Peters): I. An analysis of the male courtship pattern. *Behaviour*, 1955, 8, 249–334.

BAHRICK, H. P., FITTS, P. M., & RANKIN, R. E. Effect of incentives upon reactions to peripheral stimuli. *Journal of Experimental Psychology*, 1952, 44, 400–406.

BAILEY, C. J., & MILLER, N. E. The effect of sodium amytal on an approach-avoidance conflict in cats. *Journal of Comparative and Physiological Psychology*, 1952, 45, 205–208.

BAKER, J. W. II, & SCHAIE, K. W. Effect of aggressing "alone" or "with another" on physiological and psychological arousal. *Journal of Personality and Social Psychology*, 1969, 12, 80–96.

BALL, J. The female sex cycle as a factor in learning in the rat. *American Journal of Physiology*, 1926, 78, 533–536.

BANDLER, R. J. Direct chemical stimulation of the thalamus: Effects on aggressive behavior in the rat. *Brain Research*, 1971, 26, 81–93. (a)

BANDLER, R. J. Chemical stimulation of the rat midbrain and aggressive behavior. *Nature*, 1971, 229, 222–223. (b)

BANDLER, R. J., CHI, C. C., & FLYNN, J. P. Biting attack elicited by stimulation of the ventral midbrain tegmentum of cats. *Science*, 1972, 177, 364–366.

BANDURA, A. Influence of models' reinforcement contingencies on the acquisition of imitative responses. *Journal of Personality and Social Psychology*, 1965, 1, 589–595.

BANDURA, A. Vicarious processes: A case of no-trial learning. In L. Berkowitz (Ed.), *Advances in experimental social psychology* (Vol. II). New York: Academic Press, 1965.

BANDURA, A. *Social learning theory*. Morristown, N.*J.: General Learning Press, 1971.

BANDURA, A. *Aggression: A social learning analysis*. Englewood Cliffs, N. J.: Prentice-Hall, 1973.

BANDURA, A. Self-efficacy: Toward a unifying theory of behavior change. *Psychological Review*. 1977, 84, 191–215.

BANDURA, A., & ADAMS, N. E. Analysis of self-efficacy theory of behavioral change. *Journal of Personality and Social Psychology*, 1977, 35, 125–139.

BANDURA, A., ADAMS, N. E., & BEYER, J. Cognitive processes mediating behavioral change. *Journal of Personality and Social Psychology*, 1977, 35, 125–129.

BANDURA, A., BLANCHARD, E. B., & RITTER, R. The relative efficacy of desensitization and modeling approaches for inducing behavioral, affective, and attitudinal changes. *Journal of Personality and Social Psychology*, 1969, 13, 173–199.

BANDURA, A., GRUSEC, J. E., & MENLOVE, F. L. Vicarious extinction of avoidance behavior. *Journal of Personality and Social Psychology*, 1967, 5, 16–23.

BANDURA, A., JEFFREY, R. W., & GAJDOS, F. Generalizing change through participant modeling with self-directed mastery. *Behavior Research and Therapy*, 1975, 13, 141–152.

BANDURA, A., & MENLOVE, F. L. Factors determining vicarious extinction of avoidance behavior through symbolic modeling. *Journal of Personality and Social Psychology*, 1968, 8, 99–108.

BANDURA, A., & PERLOFF, B. Relative efficacy of self-monitored and externally imposed reinforcement systems. *Journal of Personality and Social Psychology*, 1967, 7, 111–116.

BANDURA, A., ROSS, D., & ROSS, S. A. Transmission of aggression through imitation of aggressive models. *Journal of Abnormal and Social Psychology*, 1961, 63, 575–582.

BANDURA, A., ROSS, D., & ROSS, S. A. Imitation of film-mediated aggressive models. *Journal of Abnormal and Social Psychology*, 1963, 66, 3–11.

BANERJEE, V. Influence of some hormones and drugs on isolation induced aggression in male mice. *Communications in Behavioral Biology*, 1971, 6, 163–170.

BARCLAY, A. M. Linking of sexual and aggressive motives: Contributions of "irrelevant" arousals. *Journal of Personality*, 1971, 39, 481–492.

BARFIELD, R. J., BUSCH, D. E., & WALLEN, K. Gonadal influence on agonistic behavior in the male domestic rat. *Hormones and Behavior*, 1972, 3, 247–259.

BARKER, R., DEMBO, T., & LEWIN, K. Frustration and regression: An experiment with young children. *University of Iowa Studies in Child Welfare*, 1941, 18 (Whole No. 386).

BARNETT, S. A. *A study of behavior*. London: Methuen, 1963.

BARNETT, S. A. The biology of aggression. *Lancet*, 1964, 8, 803–807.

BARNETT, S. A. Attack and defense in animal societies. In C. D. Clemente & D. B. Lindsley (Eds.), *Aggression and defense: Neural mechanisms and social patterns (Vol. V), Brain Function*. Los Angeles: University of California, 1967.

BARNETT, S. A. *The rat: A study of behavior*. Chicago: Chicago University Press, 1975.

BARON, R. A. *Human aggression*. New York: Plenum Press, 1977.

BARON, R. A. & RANSBERGER, V. M. Ambient temperature and the occurrence of collective violence: The "long, hot summer" revisted. *Journal of Personality and Social Psychology*, 1978, 36, 351–360.

BARRETT, A. M., CAIRNCROSS, K. D., & KING, M. G. Parameters of novelty, shock predictability, and response contingency in corticosterone release in the rat. *Physiology and Behavior*, 1973, 10, 901–907.

BARSA, J., & SAUNDERS, J. C. Comparative study of chlordiazepoxide and diazepam. *Diseases of the Nervous System*, 1964, 25, 244–246.

BAR-TAL, D., & FRIEZE, I. H. Achievement motivation for males and females as a determinant of attributions for success and failure. *Sex Roles*, 1977, 3, 301–313.

BATSON, C. D., DARLEY, J. M., & COKE, J. S. Altruism and human kindness: Internal and external determinants of helping behavior. In L. A. Pervin, & M. Lewis (Eds.), *Perspectives in International Psychology*. New York: Plenum Press, 1978.

BAUER, D. Endocrine and other clinical manifestations of hypothalamic disease. *Journal of Clinical Endocrinology*, 1954, 14, 13–20.

BAUM, M. Extinction of avoidance responding through response prevention (flooding). *Psychological Bulletin*, 1970, 74, 276–284.

BAYRAKAL, S. The significance of electroencephalographic abnormality in behavior-problem children. *Canadian Psychiatric Association Journal*, 1965, 10, 387–392.

BEACH, F. A. Effect of injury to the cerebral cortex upon sexually receptive behavior in the female rat. *Psychosomatic Medicine*, 1944, 6, 40–55.

BEACH, F. A. Bisexual mating behavior in the male rat: Effects of castration and hormone administration. *Physiological Zoology*, 1945, 18, 195–221.

BEACH, F. A. A review of physiological and psychological studies of sexual behavior in mammals. *Psychological Review*, 1947, 27, 240–307.

BEACH, F. A. The descent of instinct. *Psychological Review*, 1955, 62, 401–410.

BEACH, F. A. Normal sexual behavior in male rats isolated at fourteen days of age. *Journal of Comparative and Physiological Psychology*, 1958, 51, 37–38.

BEACH, F. A. It's all in your mind. *Psychology Today*, 1969, 3, 33–35.

BEACH, F. A., & FOWLER, H. Individual differences in the response of male rats to androgen. *Journal of Comparative and Physiological Psychology*, 1959, 52, 50–52.

BEACH, F. A., & HOLTZ-TUCKER, M. Effects of different concentrations of androgen upon sexual behavior in castrated male rats. *Journal of Comparative Psychology*, 1949, XLII, 443–453.

BEACH, F. A., & JORDAN, L. Sexual exhaustion and recovery in the male rat. *Quarterly Journal of Experimental Psychology*, 1956, 8, 121–133.

BEACH, F. A., ZITRIN, A., & JAYNES, J. Neural mediation of mating in male cats: II. Contribution of the frontal cortex. *Journal of Experimental Zoology*, 1955, *130*, 381–401.

BECHTEREV, V. M. *La psychologie objective*. Paris: Alcan, 1913.

BECK, A. T. *Depression: Clinical, experimental and theoretical aspects*. New York: Harper & Row, 1967.

BECK, A. T. *Cognitive therapy and the emotional disorders*. New York: International Universities Press, 1976.

BECKER, E. E., & KISSILEFF, H. R. Inhibitory controls of feeding by the ventromedial hypothalamus. *American Journal of Physiology*, 1974, *226*, 383–396.

BEEMAN, E. A. The effect of male hormone on aggressive behavior in mice. *Physiological Zoology*, 1947, *20*, 373–405.

BELLOWS, R. T. Time factors in water drinking in dogs. *American Journal of Physiology*, 1939, *125*, 87–97.

BENSON, H. *Relaxation response*. New York: Morrow, 1975.

BENSON, P. L., KARABENICK, S. A., & LERNER, R. M. Pretty pleases: The effect of physical attraction, race, and sex on receiving help. *Journal of Experimental Social Psychology*, 1976, *12*, 409–415.

BERGER, S. M. Conditioning through vicarious instigation. *Psychological Review*, 1962, *69*, 450–466.

BERGHE, VAN DEN. Naissance d'un gorille de montagne à la station de zoologie experimentale de Tshibati. *Folia Scientifica Africae Centralis*, 1959, *4*, 81.

BERKOWITZ, L. *Aggression: A social psychological analysis*. New York: McGraw-Hill, 1962.

BERKOWITZ, L. Aggressive cues in aggressive behavior and hostility catharsis. *Psychological Review*, 1964, *71*, 104–122.

BERKOWITZ, L. Some aspects of observed aggression. *Journal of Personality and Social Psychology*, 1965, *2*, 359–369.

BERKOWITZ, L. *Roots of aggression*. New York: Atherton Press, 1969.

BERKOWITZ, L. The contagion of violence: An S-R mediational analysis of some effects of observed aggression. In M. Page (Ed.), *Nebraska Symposium on Motivation, 1970*. Lincoln: University of Nebraska Press, 1971.

BERKOWITZ, L. Some determinants of impulsive aggression: Role of mediated associations with reinforcement for aggression. *Psychological Review*, 1974, *81*, 165–176.

BERKOWITZ, L. Do we have to believe we are angry with someone in order to display "angry" aggression toward that person? In L. Berkowitz (Ed.), *Cognitive theories in social psychology: Papers reprinted from the Advances in Experimental Social Psychology*. New York: Academic Press, 1978.

BERKOWITZ, L. *A survey of social psychology* (2nd ed.). New York: Holt, Rinehart & Winston, 1980.

BERKOWITZ, L., COCHRAN, S., & EMBREE, M. Influence of aversive experience and the consequences of one's aggression on aggressive behavior. Cited in L. Berkowitz, *Survey of social psychology*. New York: Holt, Rinehart, and Winston, 1980.

BERKOWITZ, L., & GEEN, R. G. Film violence and the cue properties of available targets. *Journal of Personality and Social Psychology*, 1966, *3*, 525–530.

BERKOWITZ, L., & LE PAGE, A. Weapons as aggression-eliciting stimuli. *Journal of Personality and Social Psychology*, 1967, *7*, 202–207.

BERKOWITZ, L., & KNUREK, D. A. A label-mediated hostility generalization. *Journal of Personality and Social Psychology*, 1969, *13*, 200–206.

BERKUN, M. M., KESSEN, M. L., & MILLER, N. E. Hunger-reducing effects of food by stomach fistula versus food by mouth measured by a consummatory response. *Journal of Comparative and Physiological Psychology*, 1952, *45*, 550–554.

BERLYNE, D. E. *Conflict, arousal, and curosity*. New York: McGraw-Hill, 1960.

BERLYNE, D. E. Curiosity and exploration. *Science*, 1966, 25–33.

BERLYNE, D. E. *Aesthetics and psychobiology*. New York: Appleton-Century-Crofts, 1971.

BERMANT, G. Response latencies of female rats during sexual intercourse. *Science*, 1961, *133*, 1771–1773. (a)

BERMANT, G. Regulation of sexual contact by female rats. Unpublished doctoral dissertation, Harvard University, 1961. (b)

BERMANT, G., & DAVIDSON, J. M. *Biological bases of sexual behavior.* New York: Harper & Row, 1974.

BERNARD, L. L. *Instinct: A study in social psychology.* New York: Henry Holt, 1924.

BERNSTEIN, I. L. Learned taste aversions in children receiving chemotherapy. *Science,* 1978, *200,* 1302–1303.

BERNSTON, G. G. Blockade and release of hypothalamically and naturally elicited aggressive behavior in cats following midbrain lesions. *Journal of Comparative and Physiological Psychology,* 1972, *81,* 541–554.

BERSCHEID, E., & WALSTER, E. U. When does a harm-doer compensate a victim? *Journal of Personality and Social Psychology,* 1967, *6,* 435–441.

BERSCHEID, E., & WALSTER, E. U. *Interpersonal attraction.* Reading, Mass.: Addison-Wesley, 1978.

BEST, P. J., BEST, M. R., & MICKLEY, G. A. Conditioned aversion to distinct environmental stimuli resulting from gastrointestinal distress. *Journal of Comparative and Physiological Psychology,* 1973, *85,* 250–257.

BEXTON, W. H., HERON, W., & SCOTT, T. H. Effects of decreased variation in the sensory environment. *Canadian Journal of Psychology,* 1954, *8,* 70–76.

BICKMAN, L. The effect of another bystander's ability to help on bystander intervention in an emergency. *Journal of Experimental Social Psychology,* 1971, *7,* 367–379.

BIEBER, I., et al. *Homosexuality—a psychoanalytic study.* New York: Basic Books, 1962.

BILLIG, M. *Social psychology and intergroup relations.* New York: Academic Press, 1976.

BINDRA, D. A motivational view of learning, performance, and behavior modification. *Psychological Review,* 1974, *81,* 199–213.

BINGHAM, H. C. Sex development in apes. *Comparative Psychology Monograph,* 1928, *5,* 1–165.

BIRCH, D., BURNSTEIN, E., & CLARK, R. A. Response strength as a function of hours of food deprivation under a controlled maintenance schedule. *Journal of Comparative and Physiological Psychology,* 1958, *51,* 350–354.

BIRK, L., HUDDLESTON, W., MILLERS, E., & COHLER, B. Avoidance conditioning for homosexuality. *Archives of General Psychiatry,* 1971, *25,* 314–323.

BLACKWOOD, B. *Both sides of Buka Passage.* Oxford: Clarendon Press, 1935.

BLAKE, R. R., & MOUTON, J. S. Reactions to intergroup competition under win-lose conditions. *Management Science,* 1961, *7,* 420–435.

BLANCHARD, D. C., & BLANCHARD, R. J. Innate and conditioned reactions to threat in rats with amygdaloid lesions. *Journal of Comparative and Physiological Psychology,* 1972, *81,* 281–290.

BLANDFORD, D., & SAMPSON, E. Induction of prestige suggestion through classical conditioning. *Journal of Abnormal and Social Psychology,* 1964, *69,* 332–337.

BLASS, E. M., & EPSTEIN, A. N. A lateral preoptic osmosensitive zone for thirst in the rat. *Journal of Comparative and Physiological Psychology,* 1971, *76,* 378–394.

BLAU, D. M. *Exchange and power in social life.* New York: Wiley, 1964.

BLAU, P. Cooperation and competition in a bureaucracy. *American Journal of Sociology,* 1954, *59,* 530–535.

BLEHAR, M. C., LIEBERMAN, A. F., & AINSWORTH, M. D. S. Early face-to-face interaction and its relation to later infant-mother attachment. *Child Development,* 1977, *48,* 182–194.

BLODGETT, H. C., & McCUTCHAN, K. Place versus response-learning in a simple T-maze. *Journal of Experimental Psychology,* 1947, *37,* 412–422.

BLODGETT, H. C., & McCUTCHAN, K. The relative strength of place and response learning in the T-maze. *Journal of Comparative and Physiological Psychology,* 1948, *41,* 17–24.

BLUM, R. H. Drugs and violence. In D. J. Mulvihill, M. M. Tumin, & L. A. Curtis (Eds.), *Crimes of violence: A staff report to the National Commission on the Causes and Prevention of Violence (Vol. 13),* Washington, D.C.: U.S. Government Printing Office, 1969.

BLUMENTHAL, J. A., WILLIAMS, R., KING, Y., SCHANBERG, S. M., & THOMPSON, L. W. Type A behavior and angiographically documented coronary disease. *Circulation,* 1978, *58,* 634–639.

BLUMER, D., & MIGEON, C. Treatment of impulsive behavior disorders in males with medroxyprogesterone acetate. Paper presented at the annual meeting of the American Psychiatric Association, May 1973.

BLUMSTEIN, P. W., & SCHWARTZ, P. Lesbanism and bisexuality. In E. Goode (Ed.), *Sexual deviance and sexual deviants*. New York: Morrow Press, 1974.

BLUMSTEIN, P. W., & SCHWARTZ, P. Bisexual women. In J. P. Wiseman (Ed.), *The social psychology of sex*. New York: Harper & Row, 1976.

BLURTON, N. G. An ethological study of some aspects of social behavior of children in nursery school. In D. Morris (Ed.), *Primate ethology*. London: Doubleday, 1969.

BOCHNER, S., & INSKO, C. A. Communicator discrepancy, source credibility, and opinion change. *Journal of Personality and Social Psychology*, 1966, 4, 614–621.

BOLLES, R. C. The readiness to eat and drink: The effect of deprivation conditions. *Journal of Comparative Psychology*, 1962, 55, 230–234.

BOLLES, R. C. Readiness to eat: Effects of age, sex, and weight loss. *Journal of Comparative Physiological Psychology*, 1965, 60, 88–92.

BOLLES, R. C. Avoidance and escape learning: Simultaneous acquisition of different responses. *Journal of Comparative and Physiological Psychology*, 1969, 68, 355–358.

BOLLES, R. C. Species-specific defense reactions and avoidance learning. *Psychological Review*, 1970, 77, 32–48.

BOLLES, R. C. Reinforcement, expectancy, and learning. *Psychological Review*, 1972, 79, 394–409.

BOLLES, R. C. *Theory of motivation* (2nd ed.). New York: Harper & Row, 1975.

BOLLES, R. C. *Learning theory* (2nd ed.). New York: Holt, Rinehart & Winston, 1979.

BOLLES, R. C., & COLLIER, A. C. The effect of predictive cues on freezing in rats. *Animal Learning and Behavior*, 1976, 4, 6–8.

BOLLES, R. C., GROSSEN, N. E., HARGRAVE, G. E., & DUNCAN, P. M. Effects of conditioned appetitive stimuli on the acquisition and extinction of a runway response. *Journal of Experimental Psychology*, 1970, 85, 138–140.

BOLLES, R. C., UHL, C. N., WOLFE, M., & CHASE, P. B. Stimulus learning versus response learning in a discriminated punishment situation. *Learning and Motivation*, 1975, 6, 439–447.

BONKALO, A. Electrocephalography in criminology. *Canadian Psychiatric Association Journal*, 1967, 12, 281–286.

BOOTH, D. A. Conditioned satiety in the rat. *Journal of Comparative and Physiological Psychology*, 1972, 81, 457–471.

BOOTH, D. A. Satiety and appetite are conditioned reactions. *Psychosomatic Medicine*, 1977, 39, 76–81.

BOOTH, D. A., COONS, E. E., & MILLER, N. E. Blood glucose responses to electrical stimulation of the hypothalmic feeding area. *Physiology and Behavior*, 1969, 4, 991–1001.

BOOTH, D. A., LEE, M., & MCALEAVEY, C. Acquired sensory control of satiation in man. *British Journal of Psychology*, 1976, 67, 137–147.

BOOTH, D. A., & MILLER, N. E. Lateral hypothalamus mediated effects of a food signal on blood glucose concentration. *Physiology and Behavior*, 1969, 4, 1003–1009.

BOOTH, N. P. An opponent process theory of motivation for jogging. Cited in R. L. Solomon, the opponent-process theory of motivation. *American Psychologist*, 1980, 35, 691–712.

BOWLBY, J. *Attachment and loss* (Vol. I), *Attachment*. New York: Basic Books, 1969.

BRADLEY, P. G. Effects of atropine and related drugs on EEG and behavior. *Progress in Brain Research*, 1968, 28.

BRADY, J. V. Motivational-emotional factors and intracranial self-stimulation. In D. E. Sheer (Ed.), *Electrical stimulation of the brain*. Austin: University of Texas Press, 1961.

BRADY, J. V. & NAUTA, W. J. H. Subcortical mechanisms in emotional behavior: The duration of affective changes following septal forebrain lesions in the albino rat. *Journal of Comparative and Physiological Psychology*, 1955, 48, 412–420.

BRAIN, P. F., NOWELL, N. W., & WOUTERS, A. Some relationships between adrenal function and effectiveness of a period of isolation in inducing intermale aggression in albino mice. *Physiology and Behavior*, 1971, 6, 27–29.

BRAMEL, D., TAUB, B., & BLUM, B. An observer's reaction to the suffering of his enemy. *Journal of Personality and Social Psychology*, 1968, 8, 384–392.

BRAUD, W., WEPMAN, B., & RUSSO, D. Task and species generality of the "helplessness" phenomenon. *Psychonomic Science*, 1969, 16, 154–155.

BRAY, G. A., & GALLAGHER, T. F., JR. Manifestations of hypothalamic obesity in man: A comprehensive investigation of eight patients and a review of the literature. *Medicine*, 1975, *54*, 301–330.

BREHM, J. W. Post-decision changes in the desirability of alternatives. *Journal of Abnormal and Social Psychology*, 1956, *52*, 384–389.

BREHM, J. W. *A theory of psychological reactance.* New York: Academic Press, 1966.

BREHM, J. W., & COHEN, A. *Explorations in cognitive dissonance.* New York: Wiley, 1962.

BREHM, J. W., & COLE, A. Effect of a favor which reduces freedom. *Journal of Personality and Social Psychology*, 1966, *3*, 420–426.

BREHM, J. W., & SENSENIG, J. Social influence as a function of attempted and implied usurpation of a choice. *Journal of Personality and Social Psychology*, 1966, *4*, 703–707.

BREIT, S. Arousal of achievement motivation with causal attributions. *Psychological Reports*, 1969, *25*, 539–542.

BRELAND, K., & BRELAND, M. The misbehavior of organisms. *American Psychologist*, 1961, *16*, 681–684.

BREMER, J. *Asexualization.* New York: Macmillan, 1959.

BRIDDELL, D. W., & WILSON, G. T. The effects of alcohol and expectancy set on male sexual arousal. *Journal of Abnormal Psychology*, 1976, *85*, 225–234.

BRIDDELL, D. W., RIMM, D. C., CADDY, G. R., KRAWITZ, G., SHOLIS, D., & WUNDERLIN, R. J. Effects of alcohol and cognitive set on sexual arousal to deviant stimuli. *Journal of Abnormal Psychology*, 1978, *87*, 418–430.

BRILL, H. Drugs and aggression. *Medical Counterpart*, 1969, *1*, 33–38.

BRISCOE, C. W., & SMITH, J. B. Depression in bereavement and divorce: Relationships to primary depressive illness: A study of 128 subjects. *Archives of General Psychiatry*, 1975, *32*, 439–443.

BROADHURST, P. L. Emotionality and the Yerkes-Dodson law. *Journal of Experimental Psychology*, 1957, *54*, 345–352.

BROBECK, J. R., TEPPERMAN, J., & LONG, C. N. H. Effects of experimental obesity upon carbohydrate metabolism. *Yale Journal of Biology and Medicine*, 1943, *15*, 893–904.

BROCK, T. C. Effect of prior dishonesty on post decision dissonance. *Journal of Abnormal and Social Psychology*, 1963, *66*, 325–331.

BROCK, T. C., & BALLOUN, J. L. Behavioral receptivity to dissonant information. *Journal of Personality and Social Psychology*, 1967, *6*, 413–428.

BROCK, T. C., & BUSS, A. H. Dissonance, aggression, and evaluation of pain. *Journal of Abnormal and Social Psychology*, 1962, *65*, 192–202.

BROOKHART, J. M., DEY, F. L. C., & RANSON, S. W. Failure of ovarian hormones to cause mating reactions in spayed guinea pigs with hypothalamic lesions. *Proceedings of Society for Experimental Biology*, 1941, *44*, 61–64.

BROWN, I., JR., & INOUYE, D. K. Learned helplessness through modeling: The role of perceived similarity in competence. *Journal of Personality and Social Psychology*, 1978, *36*, 900–908.

BROWN, J. S. Gradients of approach and avoidance responses and their relation to level of motivation. *Journal of Comparative and Physiological Psychology*, 1948, *41*, 450–465.

BROWN, J. S., & FARBER, I. E. Emotions conceptualized as intervening variables—with suggestions toward a theory of frustration. *Psychological Bulletin*, 1951, *48*, 465–495.

BROWN, J. S., & JACOBS, A. Role of fear in motivation and acquisition of response. *Journal of Experimental Psychology*, 1949, *39*, 747–759.

BROWN, P. L., & JENKINS, H. M. Autoshaping of the pigeon's key peck. *Journal of Experimental Analysis of Behavior.* 1968, *11*, 1–8.

BRUCH, H. *Eating disorders.* New York: Basic Books, 1973.

BRÜCKE, E. *Lectures on physiology.* Vienna: University of Vienna, 1874.

BRUNER, J. S., MATTER, J., PAPANEK, M. Breadth of learning as function of drive level and mechanization. *Psychological Review*, 1955, *62*, 1–10.

BRYAN, J. H., & TEXT, N. Models and helping: Naturalistic studies in aiding behavior. *Journal of Personality and Social Psychology*, 1967, *6*, 400–407.

BUCK, R. S. *Human motivation and emotion.* New York: Wiley, 1976.

BUECHNER, H. K. Territorial behavior in the Uganda kob. *Science*, 1961, *133*, 698–699.

BUNNEY, W. E., GOODWIN, F. K., & MURPHY, D. L. The "switch process" in manic-depressive illness. *Archives of General Psychiatry*, 1972, *27*, 312–217.

BURDICK, H., & BURNES, A. A test of "strain toward symmetry" theories. *Journal of Abnormal and Social Psychology,* 1958, *57,* 367–370.

BURGESS, E. P. The modification of depressive behaviors. In R. D. Rubin & C. M. Franks (Eds.), *Advances in behavior therapy.* New York: Academic Press, 1968.

BURT, W. H. Territoriality and home range concepts as applied to mammals. *Journal of Mammalogy,* 1943, *24,* 346–354.

BURTON, M. J., MORA, F., & ROLLS, E. T. Visual and taste neurons in the lateral hypothalamus and substantia innominata: Modulation of responsiveness by hunger. *Journal of Physiology,* 1975, *252,* 50–51.

BUSS, A. *The psychology of aggression.* New York: Wiley, 1961.

BUSS, A., BOOKER, A., & BUSS, E. Firing a weapon and aggression. *Journal of Personality and Social Psychology,* 1972, *22,* 296–350.

BUTLER, J. M., and RICE, L. N. Adience, self-actualization, and drive theory. In J. M. Wepman and R. W. Heine (Eds.), *Concepts of Personality.* Chicago: Aldine, 1963.

BUTLER, R. A., & HARLOW, H. F. Persistence of visual exploration in monkeys. *Journal of Comparative and Physiological Psychology,* 1954, *47,* 258–263.

BYRNE, D., & CLORE, G. L. A reinforcement model of evaluative responses. *Personality: An International Journal,* 1970, *1,* 103–128.

CAGGIULA, A. R., & SZECHTMAN, H. Hypothalamic stimulation: A biphasic influence on the copulation of the male rat. *Behavioral Biology,* 1972, *7,* 591–598.

CAHNAN, W. J. The stigma of obesity, *Sociology Quarterly,* 1968, *9,* 283–299.

CALDWELL, W. E., & JONES, H. B. Some positive results on a modified Tolman and Honzik insight maze. *Journal of Comparative and Physiological Psychology,* 1954, *47,* 416–418.

CALHOUN, J. B. Population density and social pathology. *Scientific American,* 1962, *206,* 139–187.

CALVIN, J. S., BICKNELL, E., & SPERLING, D. S. Establishment of a conditioned drive based upon the hunger drive. *Journal of Comparative and Physiological Psychology,* 1953, *46,* 173–175.

CAMPBELL, M. B. Allergy and behavior: Neurologic and psychic syndromes. In F. Speer (Ed.), *Allergy of the nervous system.* Springfield, Ill.: Thomas, 1970.

CANNON, W. B. *Bodily changes in pain, hunger, fear, and rage: An account of recent researches into the function of emotional excitement.* New York: Appleton-Century-Crofts, 1915.

CANNON, W. B. *Bodily changes in pain, hunger, fear, and rage* (2nd ed.). New York: Appleton, 1929.

CANNON, W. B. Hunger and thirst. In Murchison, E. (Ed.), *A handbook of general experimental psychology.* Worcester, Mass.: Clark University Press, 1934.

CANNON, W. B., & WASHBURN, A. L. An explanation of hunger. *American Journal of Physiology,* 1912, *29,* 441–454.

CARLSMITH, J. M., & GROSS, A. E. Some effects of guilt on compliance. *Journal of Personality and Social Psychology,* 1969, *11,* 232–239.

CARLSMITH, J. M., COLLINS, B. E., & HELMREICH, R. L. Studies of forced compliance: I. The effect of pressure for compliance on attitude change produced by face-to-face role playing and anonymous essay writing. *Journal of Personality and Social Psychology,* 1966, *4,* 1–13.

CARLSMITH, J. M., ELLSWORTH, P., & WHITESIDE, J. Guilt, confession, and compliance. Cited in J. L. Freeman, D. O. Sears, & J. M. Carlsmith, *Social Psychology* (3rd ed.). Englewood Cliffs, N. J.: Prentice-Hall, 1978.

CARLSON, N. R. *Physiology of behavior.* Boston: Allyn and Bacon, 1977.

CARLTON, P. L. Brain-acetylcholine and inhibition. In J. T. Tapp (Ed.), *Reinforcement and behavior.* New York: Academic Press, 1969.

CARPENTER, C. R. A field study in Siam of the behavior and social relations of the gibbon. *Comparative Psychology Monographs,* 1940, *16,* 1–212.

CARPENTER, C. R. Sexual behavior of free ranging Rhesus monkeys *(Macaca mulatta). Journal of Comparative Psychology,* 1942, *33,* 113–142.

CARPENTER, C. R. Territoriality: A review of concepts and problems. In A. Roe & G. G. Simpson (Eds.), *Behavior and evolution.* New Haven: Yale University Press, 1958.

CARPENTER, C. R. *Naturalistic behavior of nonhuman primates.* University Park: Pennsylvania State University Press, 1964.

CARTWRIGHT, D. & HARARY, F. Structural balance: A generalization of Heider's theory. *Psychological Review,* 1956, *63,* 277–293.

CATTELL, R. B., KAWASH, G. F., & DE YOUNG, G. E. Validation of objective measures of ergic tension: Response of the sex urge to visual stimulation. *Journal of Experimental Research in Personality*, 1972, 6, 76–83.

CAUTELA, J. R. The treatment of over-eating by covert conditioning. *Psychotherapy: Theory, Research, and Practice*, 1972, 9, 211–216.

CHAIKIN, A. L., & DERLEGA, V. J. Liking for the horn-breaker in self-disclosure. *Journal of Personality*, 1974, 42, 112–129. (a)

CHAIKIN, A. L., & DERLEGA, V. J. Variables affecting the appropriateness of self-disclosure. *Journal of Consulting and Clinical Psychology*, 1974, 42, 588–593. (b)

CHANCE, M., & JOLLY, C. *Social groups of monkeys, apes and men.* New York: Dutton, 1970.

CHEIN, I., GERARD, D., LEE, R., & ROSENFELD, E. *Narcotics, delinquency, and social policy.* London: Tavistock, 1964.

CHI, C. C., & FLYNN, J. P. Neural pathways associated with hypothalamically elicited attack in cats. *Science*, 1971, 171, 703–705.

CHRISTIE, M. H., & BARFIELD, R. J. Restoration of social aggression by androgen implanted into brain of castrated male rats. *American Zoologist*, 1973, 13, 1267.

CIALDINI, R. B., CACIOPPO, J. T., BASSETT, R., & MILLER, J. A. Low-ball procedure for producing compliance: Commitment then cost. *Journal of Personality and Social Psychology*, 1978, 36, 463–476.

CIALDINI, R. B., LEVY, A., HERMAN, P., & EVENBECK, S. Attitudinal politics: The strategy of moderation. *Journal of Personality and Social Psychology*, 1973, 25, 100–108.

CLARK, R. A. The effects of sexual motivation on fantasy. *Journal of Experimental Psychology*, 1953, 44, 391–399.

CLARK, R. A., & SENSIBER, M. R. The relationship between symbolic and manifest projections of sexuality with some incidental correlates. *Journal of Abnormal and Social Psychology*, 1955, 50, 327–334.

CLARK, R. D. III, & WORD, L. E. Where is the apathetic bystander? Situational characteristics of the emergency. *Journal of Personality and Social Psychology*, 1974, 29, 279–287.

CLEMENS, L. G., WALLEN, K., & GORSKI, R. Mating behavior: Facilitation in the female rat after cortical application of potassium chloride. *Science*, 1967, 157, 1208–1209.

COHEN, A. R. Some implications of self-esteem for social influence. In C. I. Hovland & I. L. Janis (Eds.), *Personality and persuasibility.* New Haven, Conn.: Yale University Press, 1959.

COHEN, A. R. An experiment on small rewards for discrepant compliance and attitude change. In J. W. Brehm & A. R. Cohen (Eds.), *Explorations in cognitive dissonance.* New York: Wiley, 1962.

COHEN, M. L., GAROFALO, R., BOUCHER, R., & SEGHORN, T. The psychology of rapists. *Seminars in psychiatry.* 1971, 3, 307–327.

COHEN, S. Abuse of centrally stimulating agents among juveniles in California. In F. Sjoquist & M. Tuttle (Ed.), *Abuse of central stimulants.* New York: Raven Press, 1969.

COKE, J. S., & BATSON, C. D. Empathy as a mediator of helping behavior: A dose of kindness. Paper presented at the annual convention of the American Psychological Association, San Francisco, Calif., August 1977.

COLE, J. O., GOLDBERG, S. C., & DAVIS, J. M. Drugs in the treatment of psychosis: Controlled studies. In P. Solomon (Ed.), *Psychiatric drugs.* New York: Grune & Stratton, 1966.

COLEMAN, J. F., BLAKE, R. R., & MOUTON, J. S. Task difficulty and conformity pressures. *Journal of Abnormal and Social Psychology*, 1958, 57, 120–122.

COLLIER, G., & MYERS, L. The loci of reinforcement. *Journal of Experimental Psychology*, 1961, 61, 57–66.

COLLINS, B. E., & HOYT, M. G. Personal responsibility for consequences. An integration and extension of the "forced compliance" literature. *Journal of Experimental Social Psychology*, 1972, 8, 558–593.

CONAWAY, C. H., & KOFORD, C. B. Estrous cycles and mating behavior in a free-ranging band of rhesus monkeys. *Journal of Mammalogy*, 1965, 45, 577–588.

CONGER, J. J. Effect of alcohol on conflict behavior in the albino rat. *Quarterly Journal of Studies of Alcohol*, 1951, 12, 1–29.

CONNOR, J. Olfactory control of aggressive and sexual behavior in the mouse (*Mus musculus* L). *Psychonomic Science*, 1972, 27, 1–3.

COONS, E. E., & CRUCE, J. A. F. Lateral hypothalamus: Food and current intensity in maintaining self-stimulation of hunger. *Science*, 1968, *159*, 1117–1119.

COOPER, A. J. A case of fetishism and impotence treated by behavior therapy. *British Journal of Psychiatry*, 1964, *109*, 649–652.

COOPER, D. R., COTT, J. A., & BREESE, G. R. Effects of acetylamine-depleting drugs and amphetamine on self-stimulation of the brain following various 6-hydroxy-dopamine treatments. *Psychopharmacologia*, 1974, *37*, 235–248.

COOPER, J., & WORCHEL, S. Role of undesired consequences in arousing cognitive dissonance. *Journal of Personality and Social Psychology*, 1970, *16*, 199–206.

COOPER, J., ZANNA, M. P., & TAVES, P. A. Arousal as a necessary condition for attitude change following induced compliance. *Journal of Personality and Social Psychology*, 1978, *36*, 1101–1106.

COPPEN, A., & KESSEL, N. Menstruation and personality. *British Journal of Psychiatry*, 1963, *109*, 711–721.

CORTER, C. M., RHEINGOLD, H. L., & ECKERMAN, C. O. Toys delay the infant's following of his mother. *Developmental Psychology*, 1972, *6*, 138–145.

COULTER, X., RICCIO, D. C., & PAGE, H. A. Effects of blocking an instrumental avoidance response: Facilitated extinction but persistance of "fear." *Journal of Comparative and Physiological Psychology*, 1969, *68*, 377–381.

CRAIG, R. L., & SEIGEL, P. S. Does negative affect beget positive effect? A test of opponent-process theory. *Bulletin of Psychonomic Society*, 1980, *14*, 404–406.

CRANDALL, V. C. Sex differences in expectancy of intellectual and academic reinforcement. In C. P. Smith (Ed.), *Achievement-related motives in children*. New York: Russell Sage, 1969.

CRANO, W. D., & COOPER, R. E. Examination of Newcomb's extension of structural balance theory. *Journal of Personality and Social Psychology*, 1973, *27*, 344–353.

CRAVENS, R. W., & RENNER, K. E. Conditioned appetitive drive states: Empirical evidence and theoretical status. *Psychological Bulletin*, 1970, *73*, 212–220.

CRESPI, L. P. Quantitative variations of incentive and performance in the white rat. *American Journal of Psychology*, 1942, *55*, 467–517.

CRESSEY, D. R. Crime. In R. K. Merton & R. A. Nisbet (Eds.), *Contemporary social problems*. New York: Harcourt, Brace & Jovanovich, 1961.

CROCKETT, W. H. Balance, agreement, and subjective evaluations of P-O-X triads. *Journal of Personality and Social Psychology*, 1974, *29*, 102–110.

CROOK, J. H. The nature and function of territorial aggression. In M.F.A. Montagu (Ed.), *Man and agression*. London: Oxford University Press, 1968.

CRUSER, L. G. Polydipsia's contribution to the temporal discrimination of rats. Unpublished master's thesis. Norfolk, Va.: Old Dominion University, 1980.

CRUTCHFIELD, R. A. Conformity and character. *American Psychologist*, 1955, *10*, 191–198.

CUNNINGHAM, J. D., & KELLEY, H. H. Causal attributions for interpersonal events of varying magnitudes. *Journal of Personality*, 1975, *43*, 74–93.

CUTLER, N. R., & COHEN, H. B. The effect of one night's sleep loss on mood and memory in normal subjects. *Comprehensive Psychiatry*, 1979, *20*, 61–66.

DABBS, J. M., & LEVENTHAL, H. Effect of varying the recommendations in a fear arousing communication. *Journal of Personality and Social Psychology*, 1966, *4*, 525–531.

DaFONSECA, A. F. Analise heredo-clinica des perturbacoes affectivas. Unpublished doctoral dissertation, Universide de Porto, Portugal, 1959.

DALTON, K. Menstruation and crime. *British Medical Journal*, 1961, *3*, 1752–1753.

DALTON, K. *The premenstrual syndrome*. Springfield, Ill.: Thomas, 1964.

DALY, H. B. Learning of a hurdle-jump response to escape cues paired with reduced reward or frustrative nonreward. *Journal of Experimental Psychology*, 1969, *79*, 146–157.

D'AMATO, M. R. *Experimental psychology: Methodology, psychophysics and learning*. New York: McGraw-Hill, 1970.

D'AMATO, M. R., FAZZARO, J., & ETKIN, M. Anticipatory responding and avoidance discrimination as factors in avoidance conditioning. *Journal of Experimental Psychology*, 1968, *77*, 41–47.

D'AMATO, M. B., & SCHIFF, D. Long-term discriminated avoidance performance in the rat. *Journal of Comparative and Physiological Psychology*, 1964, *57*, 123–126.

DANELLI, J. F., & BROWN, R. *Symposia of the Society for Experimental Biology* (No. 4), *Physiological mechanisms in animal behavior.* New York: Academic Press, 1950.

DARLEY, J. M., & BATSON, C. D. "From Jerusalem to Jericho": A study of situational and dispositional variables in helping behavior. *Journal of Abnormal and Social Psychology,* 1973, 27, 100–108.

DARLEY, J. M., & LATANE, B. Bystander intervention in emergencies: Diffusion of responsibility. *Journal of Personality and Social Psychology,* 1968, 8, 377–383.

DARLEY, J. M., & LATANE, B. Bystander intervention in emergencies: Diffusion of responsibility. *Journal of Personality and Social Psychology,* 1972, 2, 24–33.

DARWIN, C. *Origin of species* (1936 ed.) New York: Modern Library, 1859.

DAS, J., & NAUDA, P. Mediated transfer of attitudes. *Journal of Abnormal and Social Psychology,* 1963, 66, 12–16.

DAVIDOFF, L. L. *Introduction to Psychology* (2nd ed.). New York: McGraw-Hill, 1980.

DAVIDSON, J. M. Activation of male rats' sexual behavior by intracerebral implantation of androgen. *Endocrinology,* 1966, 79, 783–794. (a)

DAVIDSON, J. M. Characteristics of sex behavior in male rats following castration. *Animal Behavior,* 1966, 14, 266–272. (b)

DAVIS, D. E., & READ, C. P. Effect of behavior on development of resistance in Trichinosis. *Proceedings for the Society of Experimental Biology and Medicine,* 1958, 99, 269–272.

DAVIS, F. C. The measurement of aggressive behavior in laboratory rats. *Journal of Genetic Psychology,* 1933. 43, 213–217.

DAVIS, J. M. A two factor-theory of schizophrenia. *Journal of Psychiatric Research,* 1974, 11, 25–30.

DAVIS, J. M., KLERMAN, G., & SCHILDKRAUT, J. Drugs used in the treatment of depression. In L. Efron, J. O. Cole, D. Levine, & J. R. Wittenborn, *Psychopharmacology, A review of progress.* Washington, D. C.: U.S. Clearinghouse of Mental Health Information, 1967.

DAVIS, K., & JONES, E. E. Changes in interpersonal perception as a means of reducing cognitive dissonance. *Journal of Abnormal and Social Psychology,* 1960, 61, 402–410.

DAVISON, G. C. Systematic desensitization as a counterconditioning process. *Journal of Abnormal Psychology,* 1968, 73, 91–99.

DAVISON, G. C., & NEALE, J. M. *Abnormal psychology: An experimental clinical approach* (2nd ed.). New York: Wiley, 1978.

DEAN, R. B., & RICHARDSON, H. Analysis of MMPI profiles of forty college-educated overt male homosexuals. *Journal of Consulting Psychology,* 1964, 28, 483.

DEAN, R. B., AUSTIN, J. A., & WATTS, W. A. Forewarning effects in persuasion: Field and classroom experiments. *Journal of Personality and Social Psychology,* 1971, 18, 210–221.

DE CHARMS, R. The effects of individual motivation on cooperative and competitive behavior in small groups. Unpublished doctoral dissertation, University of North Carolina, 1956.

DE CHARMS, R. Personal causation training in schools. *Journal of Applied Social Psychology,* 1972, 2, 95–113.

DE CHARMS, R., MORRISON, H. W., REITMAN, W., & McCLELLAND, D. C. Behavioral correlates of directly and indirectly measured achievement motivation. In D. C. McClelland (Ed.), *Studies in motivation.* New York: Appleton-Century-Crofts, 1955.

DECI, L., VARSZEGI, M. K., & MEHES, J. Direct stimulation of various subcortical brain areas in unrestrained cats. In K. Lissak (Ed.), *Recent developments of neurobiology in Hungary (Vol. II), Results in neurophysiology, neuropharmacology and behavior.* Budapest: Akademiai Kiado, 1969.

DECKE, E. Effects of taste on the eating behavior of obese and normal persons. Cited in S. Schachter, *Emotion, obesity, and crime.* New York: Academic Press, 1971.

DELGADO, J. M. R., & ANAND, B. K. Increase in food intake by electrical stimulation of the lateral hypothalamus. *American Journal of Physiology,* 1953, 172, 162–168.

DELGADO, J. M. R., ROBERTS, W. W., & MILLER, N. E. Learning motivated by electric stimulation of the brain. *American Journal of Physiology,* 1954, 179, 587–593.

DELTAAS, A. M. Epilepsy and criminality. *British Journal of Criminology,* 1963, 3, 248–257.

DEMBROSKI, T. M., MacDOUGALL, J. M., & SHIELDS, J. L. Physiologic reactions to social challenge in persons evidencing the Type A coronary-prone behavior pattern. *Journal of Human Stress,* 1977, 3, 2–10.

DEMENT, W. C. Recent studies on the biological role of REM sleep. *American Journal of Psychiatry,* 1965, 122, 404–408.

DEMENT, W. C. The biological Role of REM sleep (ca. 1968). In A. Kales (Ed.), *Sleep: Physiology and pathology*. Philadelphia: Lippincott, 1969.

DEMENT, W. C., & KLEITMAN, N. Cyclic variations in EEG during sleep and their relation to eye movement, bodily motility and dreaming. *Electroencephalography and Clinical Neurophysiology*, 1957, 9, 673–690.

DENGERINK, H. A., SCHNEDLER, R. W. & COVEY, M. V. The role of avoidance in aggressive responses to attack and no attack. *Journal of Personality and Social Psychology*, 1978, 36, 1044–1053.

DENNISTON, R. H. Quantification and comparison of sex drives under various conditions in terms of learned response. *Journal of Comparative and Physiological Psychology*, 1954, 47, 437–440.

DENNY, M. R. Relaxation theory and experiments. In F. R. Brush (Ed.), *Aversive conditioning and learning*. New York: Academic Press, 1971.

DENNY, M. R., KOONS, P. B., & MASON, J. E. Extinction of avoidance as a function of the escape situation. *Journal of Comparative and Physiological Psychology*, 1959, 52, 212–214.

DENNY, M. R., & WEISMAN, R. G. Avoidance behavior as a function of the length of shock confinement. *Journal of Comparative and Physiological Psychology*, 1964, 58, 252–257.

DEPUE, R. A. & EVANS, R. *The psychobiology of the depressive disorders: Implications for the effects of stress.* New York: Academic Press, 1976.

DEPUE, R. A., & MONROE, S. M. Learned helplessness in the perspective of the depressive disorders: Conceptual and definitional issues. *Journal of Abnormal Psychology*, 1978, 87, 3–20.

DESISTO, J. M. Hypothalamic mechanisms of killing behavior in the laboratory rat. Unpublished doctoral dissertation, Tufts University, 1970.

DESISTO, J. M., & HUSTON, J. P. Facilitation of interspecific aggression by subreinforcing electrical stimulation in the posterior lateral hypothalamus. Paper presented at the Eastern Psychological Association Meeting, Atlantic City, 1970.

DESISTO, J. M., & ZWEIG, M. Differentiation of hypothalamic feeding and killing. *Physiological Psychology*, 1974, 2, 67–70.

DEUTSCH, M. An experimental study of the effects of cooperation and competition upon group processes. *Human Relations*, 1949, 2, 81–95.

DEUTSCH, M. The effect of motivational orientation upon trust and suspicion. *Human Relations*, 1960, 13, 122–139.

DEUTSCH, M., & GERARD, H. B. A study of normative and informational social influences upon individual judgment. *Journal of Abnormal and Social Psychology*, 1955, 51, 629–636.

DEUTSCH, M., & KRAUSS, R. M. The effect of threat on interpersonal bargaining. *Journal of Abnormal and Social Psychology*, 1960, 61, 181–189.

DEUTSCH, M., & SOLOMON, L. Reactions to evaluations by others as influenced by self-evaluations. *Sociometry*, 1959, 22, 93–112.

DEVORE, I. Comparative ecology and behavior of monkeys and apes. In S.L. Washburn (Ed.), *Classification and human evolution*. New York: Wenner-Gren Foundation, 1963. (a)

DEVORE, I. Mother-infant relations in free-ranging baboons. In H. L. Rheingold (Ed.), *Maternal behavior in mammals*. New York: Wiley, 1963. (b)

DEVORE, I. *Primate behavior: Field studies of monkeys and apes.* New York: Holt, 1965.

DEWEY, J. *Psychology*, New York: Harper & Row, 1886.

DIAB, L. N. A study of intragroup and intergroup relations among experimentally produced small groups. *Genetic Psychology Monographs*, 1970, 82, 49–82.

DIAMENT, C., & WILSON, G. T. An experimental investigation of the effects of covert sensitization in an analogue eating situation. *Behavior Therapy*, 1975, 6, 499–509.

DICKOFF, H. Reactions to evaluations by another person as function of self-evaluation and the interaction context. Unpublished doctoral dissertation, Duke University, 1961.

DIENER, C. I., & DWECK, C. S. An analysis of learned helplessness: Continuous changes in performance, strategy, and achievement cognitions following failure. *Journal of Personality and Social Personality*, 1978, 36, 451–462.

DIENSTBIER, R. A., & MUNTER, P. O. Cheating as a function of the labeling of natural arousal. *Journal of Personality and Social Psychology*, 1971, 17, 208–213.

DIGUSTO, E. L., CAIRNCROSS, K., & KING, M. G. Hormonal influences on fear-motivated responses. *Psychological Bulletin*, 1971, 75, 432–444.

Dinsmoor, J. A. Pulse duration and food deprivation in escape-from-shock training. *Psychological Reports,* 1958, *4,* 531–534.

Dittes, J. E., & Kelley, H. H. Effects of different conditions of acceptance upon conformity to group norms. *Journal of Abnormal and Social Psychology,* 1956, *53,* 100–107.

Dixon, A. K., & Mackintosh, J. H. Effects of female urine upon the social behavior of adult male mice. *Animal Behaviour,* 1971, *19,* 138–140.

Dollard, J., Doob, L. W., Miller, N. E., Mowrer, O. H., & Sears, R. R. *Frustration and aggression.* New Haven, Conn: Yale University Press, 1939.

Dollard, J., & Miller, N. E. *Personality and psychotherapy: An analysis in terms of learning, thinking, and culture.* New York: McGraw-Hill, 1950.

Donnerstein, E., & Wilson, D. W. Effects of noise and perceived control on ongoing and subsequent aggressive behavior. *Journal of Personality and Social Psychology,* 1976, *34,* 774–781.

Dorfman, D. D. Esthetic preference as a function of pattern information. *Psychonomic Science,* 1965, *3,* 85–86.

Doty, R. Neural organization of deglutition. In C. F. Code (Ed.), *Handbook of physiology* (Sec. 6, Vol. 4). Washington, D. C.: American Physiological Society, 1967.

Driscoll, R., Davis, K. E., & Lipitz, M. E. Parental interference and romantic love: The Romeo and Juliet effect. *Journal of Personality and Social Psychology,* 1972, *24,* 1–10.

Dryer, P. L., & Church, R. M. Reinforcement of shock-induced fighting. *Psychonomic Science,* 1970, *18,* 147–148.

Duffy, E. *Activation and behavior.* New York: Wiley, 1962.

Dunner, D. L., Stallone, F., & Fieve, R. F. Lithium carbonate and affective disorders: A double-blind study of prophylaxis of depression in bipolar illness. *Archives of General Psychiatry,* 1976, *33,* 117–120.

Dunstone, J. J., Cannon, J. T., Chickson, J. T., & Burns, W. K. Persistence and vigor of shock-induced aggression in gerbils (*Meriones unguiculatus*). *Psychonomic Science,* 1972, *28,* 272–274.

Dutton, D. G. Effect of feedback parameters on congruency versus positivity effects in reactions to personal evaluations. *Journal of Personality and Social Psychology,* 1972, *24,* 366–371.

Dutton, D. G., & Aron, A. P. Some evidence for heightened sexual attraction under conditions of high anxiety. *Journal of Personality and Social Psychology,* 1974, *30,* 510–517.

Dweck, C. S. The role of expectations and attributions in the alleviation of learned helplessness. *Journal of Personality and Social Psychology,* 1975, *31,* 674–685.

Dyck, R., & Rule, B. G. The effect of causal attributions concerning attack on retaliation. *Journal of Personality and Social Psychology,* 1978, *36,* 521–529.

Easterbrook, J. A. The effect of emotion on cue utilization and the organization of behavior. *Psychological Review,* 1959, *66,* 183–201.

Egbert, L., Battit, G., Welsh, C., & Bartlett, M. Reduction of postoperative pain by encouragement and instruction of patients. *New England Journal of Medicine,* 1964, *270,* 825–827.

Eibl-Eibesfeldt, I. Beitrage zur Biologie der Haus-und der Ahrenmaus nebst einigen Beohachtungen an andere Nagern. *Zietschrift fur Tierphychologie,* 1950, *7,* 558–587.

Eibl-Eibesfeldt, I. The fighting behavior of animals. *Scientific American,* 1961, *205,* 112–122.

Eibl-Eibesfeldt, I. *Ethology: The biology of behavior.* New York: Holt, 1970.

Eisenberg, B. C. Etiology: Inhalants. In F. Speer (Ed.), *Allergy of the nervous system.* Springfield, Ill.: Thomas, 1970.

Eisenberg, J. F., & Leyhausen, P. The phylogenesis of predatory behavior in mammals. *Zeitchrift fur Tierphychologie,* 1972, *30,* 59–93.

Eliot, R. S. *Stress and the major cardiovascular disorders.* Mount Kisco, N. Y.: Futura, 1979.

Elliott, M. H. The effect of change of reward on the maze performance of rats. *University of California Publications in Psychology,* 1928, *4,* 19–30.

Ellis, D. P., & Austin, P. Menstruation and aggressive behavior in a correctional center for women. *Journal of Criminology and Police Science,* 1971, *62,* 388–395.

Ellis, V. Reinforcing effects of paired sucrose solutions as function of food deprivation. Unpublished master's thesis, Wake Forest University, 1968.

ELMADJIAN, F. J., HOPE, J., & LAMSON, E. T. Excretion of epinephrine and norepinephrine in various emotional states. *Journal of Clinical Endocrinology,* 1957, *17,* 608–620.

ELMS, A. C., & MILGRAM, S. Personality characteristics associated with obedience and defiance toward authoritative command. *Journal of Experimental Research in Personality,* 1966, *2,* 282–289.

EMMELKAMP, P. M. G., & WESSELS, H. Flooding in imagination vs flooding in vivo: A comparison with agoraphobics. *Behavior Research and Therapy,* 1975, *13,* 7–15.

EMSWILLER, R., DEAUX, K., & WILLITS, J. Similarity, sex, and requests for small favors. *Journal of Applied Social Psychology,* 1971, *1,* 284–291.

ENGBERG, L. A., HANSEN, G., WELKER, R. L., & THOMAS, D. R. Acquisition of key-pecking via autoshaping as a function of prior experience: "Learned laziness?" *Science,* 1973, *178,* 1002–1004.

ENGEL, B. T., & BLECKER, E. R. Application of operant conditioning techniques to the control of the cardiac arrhythmias. In P. A. Obrist, A. H. Black, J. Brener, & L. V. Di Cara (Eds.) *Cardiovascular psychophysiology.* Chicago: Aldine, 1974.

ENTWISLE, D. R. To dispel fantasies about fantasy-based measures of achievement motivation. *Psychological Bulletin,* 1972, *77,* 377–391.

EPSTEIN, A. N. Reciprocal changes in feeding behavior produced by intrahypothalamic chemical injections. *American Journal of Physiology,* 1960, *199,* 969–974.

EPSTEIN, A. N., & TEITELBAUM, P. Regulation of food intake in the absence of taste, smell, and other oropharyngeal sensation. *Journal of Comparative and Physiological Psychology,* 1962, *55,* 753–759.

EPSTEIN, A. N., FITZSIMMONS, J. T., & ROLLS, B. J. Drinking induced by injection of angiotensin into the brain of the rat. *Journal of Physiology,* 1970, *210,* 457–474.

EPSTEIN, A. N., KISSILEFF, H. R., & STELLAR, E. *The neuropsychology of thirst: New findings and advances in concepts.* Washington, D. C.: Winston, 1973.

EPSTEIN, D. M. Toward a unified theory of anxiety. In B. A. Maher (Ed.), *Progress in experimental personality research* (Vol. 4). New York: Academic Press, 1967.

ERVIN, F. R., MARK, V. H., & STEVENS, J. R. Behavioral and affective responses to brain stimulation in man. In J. Zubin and C. Shagass (Eds.), *Neurological aspects of psychopathology.* New York: Grune & Stratton, 1969.

ERWIN, J., & MAPLE, T. Ambisexual behavior with male-male anal penetration in male rhesus monkeys. *Archives of Sexual Behavior,* 1976, *5,* 9–14.

ERWIN, J., MOBALDI, J., & MITCHELL, G. Separation of rhesus monkey juveniles of the same sex. *Journal of Abnormal Psychology,* 1971, *78,* 134–139.

ESSER, J. K., & KOMORITA, S. S. Reciprocity and concession making in bargaining. *Journal of Personality and Social Psychology,* 1975, *31,* 864–872.

ESTES, R. D. Territorial behavior in the wildebeest (*Connochactes taurinus Burchell,* 1823). *Zietschrift fur Tierpsychologie,* 1969, *26,* 284–370.

ESTES, W. K., & SKINNER, B. F. Some qualitative properties of anxiety. *Journal of Experimental Psychology,* 1941, *29,* 390–400.

ETKIN, W. Reproductive behavior. In W. Etkin (Ed.), *Social behavior and organization among vertebrates.* Chicago: University of Chicago Press, 1964.

EVANS, R. I., ROZELLE, R. M., LASATER, T. M., DEMBROSKI, T. M., & ALLEN, B. P. Fear arousal, persuasion, and actual versus implied behavioral change: New perspectives utilizing a real-life dental hygiene program. *Journal of Personality and Social Psychology,* 1970, *16,* 220–227.

EVERITT, B. J., & HERBERT, J. Adrenal glands and sexual receptivity in Rhesus female monkeys. *Nature,* 1969, *222,* 1065–1066.

EYSENCK, H. J., & RACHMAN, S. *The causes and cures of neurosis.* London: Routledge, 1965.

FALK, J. L. Control of schedule-induced polydipsia: Type, size, and spacing of meals. *Journal of Experimental Analysis of Behavior,* 1967, *10,* 199–206.

FALK, J. L. Conditions producing psychogenic polydipsia in animals. *Annals of the New York Academy of Sciences,* 1969, *157,* 569–593.

FARMER, R. G. Behavior therapy and psychosexual disorders. Paper presented at the Australian and

New Zealand Association for the Advancement of Science (ANZAAS), Adelaide, August, 1969.

FAZIO, R. H., & ZANNA, M. P. Attitudinal qualities relating to the strength of the attitude-behavior relationship. *Journal of Experimental Social Psychology*, 1978, *14*, 398–408. (a)

FAZIO, R. H., & ZANNA, M. P. On the predictive validity of attitudes: The roles of direct experience and confidence. *Journal of Personality*, 1978, *46*, 228–243. (b)

FEATHER, N. T. Valence of outcome and expectation of success in relationship to task difficulty and perceived locus of control. *Journal of Personality and Social Psychology*, 1967, *7*, 372–386.

FEATHER, N. T. Attribution of responsibility and valence of success and failures in relation to initial confidence and task performance. *Journal of Personality and Social Psychology*, 1969, *13*, 129–144.

FEATHER, N. T., & RAPHELSON, A. C. Fear of success in Australian and American student groups: Motive or sex-role stereotype? *Journal of Personality*, 1974, *42*, 190–201.

FEDERAL BUREAU OF INVESTIGATION, *Uniform crime reports, Washington, D. C.: U.S. Government Printing Office*, 1975.

FEINBERG, H. K. Anatomy of a helping situation: Some determinants of helping in a conflict situation involving another's psychological distress. Cited in E. Staub. Predicting prosocial behavior: A model for specifying the nature of personality-situation interaction. In L. A. Pervin & M. Lewis (Eds.), *Perspectives in Interactional Psychology*, New York: Plenum Press, 1978.

FEINBERG, I. Effects of age on human sleep patterns. In A. Kales (Ed.), *Sleep: Physiology and pathology*. Philadelphia: Lippincott, 1969.

FELDMAN, M. D., & MacCULLOCH, M. J. *Homosexual behavior: Therapy and assessment.* Oxford: Permagon, 1971.

FELDMAN, S. M., & WALLER, H. J. Dissociation of electrocortical activation and behavioral arousal. *Nature*, 1962, 1320–1322.

FENWICK, S., MIKULKA, P. J., & KLEIN, S. B. The effect of different levels of pre-exposure to sucrose on the acquisition of a conditioned aversion. *Behavioral Biology*, 1975, *14*, 231–235.

FESHBACH, N. D. Nonconformity to experimentally induced group norms of high-status versus low-status members. *Journal of Personality and Social Psychology*, 1967, *6*, 55–63.

FESHBACH, S. The drive-reducing function of fantasy behavior. *Journal of Abnormal and Social Psychology*, 1956, *50*, 3–11.

FESHBACH, S. Dynamics of morality of violence and aggression: Some psychological considerations. *American Psychologist*, 1971, *26*, 281–291.

FESTINGER, L. *A theory of cognitive dissonance.* Stanford, Calif.: Stanford University Press, 1957.

FESTINGER, L., & CARLSMITH, J. M. Cognitive consequences of forced compliance. *Journal of Abnormal and Social Psychology*, 1959, *58*, 203–210.

FESTINGER, L., & MACCOBY, N. On resistance to persuasive communications. *Journal of Abnormal and Social Psychology*, 1964, *68*, 359–366.

FIRESTONE, I. J., KAPLAN, K. J., & RUSSELL, J. C. Anxiety, need, and affiliation with similar-state versus dissimilar-state others: Misery sometimes loves nonmiserable company. *Journal of Personality and Social Psychology*, 1973, *26*, 409–414.

FISHBEIN, M., & AJZEN, I. Attitudes towards objects as predictors of single and multiple behavioral criteria. *Psychological Review*, 1974, *81*, 59–74.

FISHBEIN, M., & AJZEN, I. *Belief, attitude, intention, and behavior: An introduction to theory and research.* Reading, Mass.: Addison-Wesley, 1975.

FITZSIMMONS, J. T., & LeMAGNEN, J. Eating as a regulatory control of drinking in the rat. *Journal of Comparative and Physiological Psychology*, 1969, *67*, 273–283.

FLANDERA, V., & NOVAKOVA, V. The development of interspecies aggression of rats towards mice during lactation. *Physiology and Behavior*, 1971, *6*, 161–164.

FLORY, R. K. Attack behavior as a function of minimum inter-food interval. *Journal of the Experimental Analysis of Behavior*, 1969, *12*, 825–828.

FLYNN, J. P. The neural basis of aggression in cats. In D. Glass (Ed.), *Neurophysiology and emotion*. New York: Rockefeller University, 1967.

FLYNN, J. P. Patterning mechanisms, patterned reflexes, and attack behavior in cats. In J. K. Cole

& D. D. Jensen (Eds.), *Nebraska Symposium on Motivation 1972.* Lincoln: University of Nebraska Press, 1972.

FLYNN, J. P., VANEGAS, H., FOOTE, W., & EDWARDS, S. B. Neural mechanisms involved in a cat's attack on a rat. In R. Whalen, R. F. Thompson, M. Verzeano, & N. Weinberger (Eds.), *The neural control of behavior.* New York: Academic Press, 1970.

FOLKINS, C. H., LAWSON, K. K., OPTON, E. M., JR., & LAZARUS, R. S. Desensitization and the experimental reduction of threat. *Journal of Abnormal Psychology,* 1968, *73,* 100–113.

FONBERG, E. Effect of partial destruction of the amygdaloid complex on the emotional-defensive behavior of dogs. *Bulletin de l'Academic Polanaise des Sciences. Cl. II.* 1965, *13,* 429–431.

FONBERG, E. The role of the amygdaloid nucleus in animal behaviour. *Progress in Brain Research,* 1968, *22,* 273–281.

FONBERG, E. Physiological mechanisms of emotional and instrumental aggression. In S. Feshbach & A. Fraczek (Eds.), *Aggression and behavior change.* New York: Praeger, 1979.

FORD, C., & BEACH, F. *Patterns of sexual behavior.* New York: Harper & Row, 1951.

FOSCO, F., & GEER, J. H. Effects of gaining control over aversive stimuli after differing amounts of no control. *Psychological Reports,* 1971, *29,* 1153–1154.

FOSS, G. The influence of androgens on sexuality in women. *Lancet,* 1951, *260,* 667–669.

FOX, M. W. Ontogeny of prey-killing behavior in canidae. *Behaviour,* 1969, *35,* 259–272.

FOX, M. W., & APELBAUM, J. Ontogeny of the orienting-jump response in the rabbit. *Behaviour,* 1969, *35,* 77–83.

FRANCHINA, J. J. Combined sources of motivation and escape responding. *Psychonomic Science,* 1966, *6,* 221–222.

FRANK, J. D. *Sanity and survival.* New York: Random House, 1967.

FRANKS, C. M., & WILSON, G. T. *Annual review of behavior therapy: Theory and practice* (Vol. II). New York: Brunner/Mazel, 1974.

FRANZEN, E. A. & MYERS, R. E. Neural control of social behavior: Prefrontal and anterior temporal cortex. *Neuropsychologia,* 1973, *11,* 141–157.

FRAZER, A. & WINOKUR, A. Therapeutic and pharmacological aspects of psychotropic drugs. In A. Frazer & A. Winokur (Eds.), *Biological bases of psychiatric disorders.* New York: Spectrum, 1977.

FREDERICSON, E. Response latency and habit strength in the relationship to spontaneous fighting in C57 black mice. *Anatomical Record,* 1949, *105,* 29.

FREDERICSON, E. The effect of food deprivation upon competitive and spontaneous combat in C57 black mice. *Journal of Psychology,* 1950, *29,* 89–100.

FREDERICSON, E. Time and aggression. *Psychological Review,* 1951, *58,* 41–51.

FREEDMAN, J. L. Involvement, discrepancy, and change. *Journal of Abnormal and Social Psychology,* 1964, *69,* 290–295.

FREEDMAN, J. L. Preference for dissonant information. *Journal of Personality and Social Psychology,* 1965, *2,* 287–289.

FREEDMAN, J. L., & FRASER, S. C. Compliance without pressure: The foot-in-the-door technique. *Journal of Personality and Social Psychology,* 1966, *4,* 195–202.

FREEDMAN, J. L., KLEVANSKY, S., & ENRLICH, P. I. The effect of crowding on human task performance. *Journal of Applied Social Psychology,* 1971, *1,* 7–25.

FREEDMAN, J. L., & SEARS, D. O. Warning, distraction, and resistance to influence. *Journal of Personality and Social Psychology,* 1965, *1,* 262–265.

FREEDMAN, J. L., SEARS, D. O., & CARLSMITH, J. M. *Social psychology* (3rd ed.). Englewood Cliffs, N. J.: Prentice-Hall, 1978.

FRENCH, E. G. Some characteristics of achievement motivation. *Journal of Experimental Psychology,* 1955, *50,* 232–236.

FRENCH, E. G. Effects of the interaction of motivation and feedback on task performance. In J. W. Atkinson (Ed.), *Motives in fantasy, action, and society.* Princeton, N. J.: Van Nostrand, 1958.

FRENCH, J. R. P., JR., & RAVEN, B. The basis of social power. In D. Cartwright (Ed.), *Studies in social power.* Ann Arbor, Mich.: Institute of Social Research, 1959.

FREUD, S. Three essays on the theory of sexuality. In J. Riviere (trans.), *Collected papers of Sigmund Freud* (Vol. IV). London: Hogarth Press, 1949 (1st German Ed., 1905).

FREUD, S. The unconscious. In J. Riviere (trans.), *Collected papers of Sigmund Freud*, Vol. IV. London: Hogath Press, 1949 (1st German Ed., 1915). (a)

FREUD, S. Instincts and their vicissitudes. In J. Riviere (trans.), *Collected papers of Sigmund Freud* (Vol. IV). London: Hogath Press, 1949 (1st German Ed., 1915). (b)

FREUD, S. Mourning and melancholia. In J. Strachey (Ed. and trans.), *Standard edition of the complete psychological works of Sigmund Freud* (Vol. 14). London: Hogarth Press, 1957 (1st German Ed., 1917).

FREUD, S. *Civilization and its discontent.* In J. Strachey (Ed. and trans.), Standard edition of the complete psychological works of Sigmund Freud (Vol. 21). New York: W. W. Norton & Co, 1961 (1st German Ed., 1930).

FREY, D. Cited in L. Berkowitz, *A survey of social psychology* (2nd Ed.), New York: Holt, 1980.

FRIAR, L. R. & BEALTLY, J. Migraine: Management by trained control of vasoconstriction. *Journal of Consulting and Clinical Psychology*, 1976, 83, 409–431.

FRIEDLAND, N., ARNOLD, S. E., & THIBAUT, J. Motivational bases in mixed-motive interactions: The effects of comparison levels. *Journal of Experimental Social Psychology*, 1974, 10, 188–199.

FRIEDMAN, D. The treatment of impotence by brietal relaxation therapy. *Behaviour Research and Therapy*, 1968, 6, 257–261.

FRIEDMAN, M., & ROSENMAN, R. H. *Type A behavior and your heart.* New York: Knopf, 1974.

FRIEDMAN, M., BYERS, S. O., DIAMANT, J., & ROSENMAN, R. H. Plasma catecholamine response of coronary-prone subjects (Type A) to a specific challenge. *Metabolism*, 1975, 4, 205–210.

FRIEDMAN, M. I., & STRICKER, E. M. The physiological psychology of hunger: A physiological perceptive. *Psychological Review*, 1976, 83, 409–431.

FRIEDMAN, S. B., ADER, R., & GLASGOW, L. A. Effects of psychological stress in adult mice inoculated with Coxsachie B viruses. *Psychosomatic Medicine*, 1965, 27, 361–368.

FRIEZE, I. H. Studies of information processing and the attributional process. Unpublished doctoral dissertation, University of California, Los Angeles, 1973.

FRIEZE, I. H. Causal attributions and information seeking to explain success and failure. *Journal of Research in Personality*, 1976, 10, 293–305.

FROHMAN, L. A., GOLDMAN, J. K., & BERNARDIS, L. L. Metabolism of intravenously injected ^{14}C-glucose in weanling rats with hypothalamic obesity. *Metabolism*, 1972, 21, 799–805.

FROMM, E. *Escape from freedom.* New York: Holt, 1941.

FROMM, E. *The sane society.* New York: Rinehart, 1955.

FRUMKIN, K., & BROOKSHIRE, K. H. Conditioned fear training and later avoidance learning in goldfish. *Psychonomic Science*, 1969, 16, 159–160.

FULLER, J. L., & JACOBY, G. A. Central and sensory control of food intake in genetically obese mice. *American Journal of Physiology*, 1955, 183, 279–283.

FUNKENSTEIN, D. H. The physiology of fear and anger. *Scientific American*, 1955, 192, 74–80.

GAERTNER, S. L., & DOVIDIO, J. F. The subtlety of white racism, arousal, and helping. *Journal of Personality and Social Psychology*, 1977, 35, 691–707.

GAGNON, J. H., & SIMON, W. *Sexual conduct: The social origins of human sexuality.* Chicago: Aldine, 1973.

GALEF, B. G. Aggression and timidity: Responses to novelty in feral Norway rats. *Journal of Comparative and Physiological Psychology*, 1970, 70, 370–381. (a)

GALEF, B. G. Target novelty elicits and directs shock-associated aggression in wild rats. *Journal of Comparative and Physiological Psychology*, 1970, 71, 87–91. (b)

GALLO, P. S. Effects of increased incentives upon the use of threat in bargaining. *Journal of Personality and Social Psychology*, 1966, 4, 14–20.

GALLUP, G. JR. Aggression in rats as a function of frustrative nonreward in a straight alley. *Psychonomic Science*, 1965, 3, 99–100.

GAMBARO, S., & RABIN, A. I. Diastolic blood pressure responses following direct and displaced aggression after anger arousal in high and low-guilt subjects. *Journal of Personality and Social Psychology*, 1969, 12, 87–94.

GANDELMAN, R. Mice: Postpartum aggression elicited by the presence of an intruder. *Hormones and Behavior*, 1972, 3, 23–28.

GARCIA, J., CLARK, J. C., & HANKINS, W. G. Natural responses to scheduled rewards. In P. P. G. Bateson & P. H. Klopfer (Eds.), *Perspectives in Ethology.* New York: Plenum Press, 1973.

GARCIA, J., ERVIN, F. R., YORKE, C. H., & KOELLING, R. A. Conditioning with delayed vitamin injections. *Science,* 1967, *155,* 716–718.

GARCIA, J., HANKINS, W. G., & RUSINIAK, K. W. Behavioral regulation of the milieu interne in man and rat. *Science,* 1974, *185,* 824–831.

GARCIA, J., KIMELDORF, D. J., & HUNT, E. L. The use of ionizing radiation as a motivating stimulus, *Psychological Review,* 1957, *68,* 383–395.

GARCIA, J., KIMELDORF, D. J., & KOELLING, R. A. Conditioned aversion to saccharin resulting from exposure to gamma radiation. *Science,* 1955, *122,* 157–158.

GARCIA, J., & KOELLING, R. A. Relation of cue to consequence in avoidance learning. *Psychonomic Science,* 1966, *4,* 123–124.

GARCIA, J., RUSINIAK, K. W., & BRETT, L. P. Conditioning food-illness aversions in wild animals: *Caveant canonici.* In H. Davis & H. M. B. Hurwitz (Eds.), *Operant-Pavlovian interactions.* Hillsdale, N. J. Erlbaum, 1977.

GARFINKEL, P. E., KLINE, S. A., & STANCER, H. C. Treatment of anorexia nervosa using operant conditioning techniques. *Journal of Nervous and Mental Disease,* 1973, *157,* 428–433.

GATCHEL, R. J., & PROCTOR, J. D. Physiological correlates of learned helplessness in man. *Journal of Abnormal Psychology,* 1976, *85,* 27–34.

GATTOZZI, A. A. Lithium in the treatment of mood disorders. (U.S. Department of Health, Education and Welfare). Washington, D.C.: U.S. Government Printing Office, 1970.

GEEN, R. G., & BERKOWITZ, L. Some conditions facilitating the occurrence of aggression after the observation of violence. *Journal of Personality,* 1967, *35,* 666–676.

GEEN, R. G., & O'NEAL, E. L. Activation of cue-elicited aggression by general arousal. *Journal of Personality and Social Psychology,* 1969, *11,* 289–292.

GEEN, R. G., RAKOSKY, J. J., & PIGG, R. Awareness of arousal and its relation to aggression. *British Journal of Social and Clinical Psychology,* 1972, *11,* 115–121.

GEER, J. H., & JARMECKY, L. The effect of being responsible for reducing another's pain on subject's response and arousal. *Journal of Personality and Social Psychology,* 1973, *26,* 232–237.

GEER, J. H., DAVISON, G. C., & GATCHEL, R. I. Reduction of stress in humans through nonveridical perceived control of aversive stimulation. *Journal of Personality and Social Psychology,* 1970, *16,* 731–738.

GEER, J. H., MOROKOGG, P., & GREENWOOD, P. Sexual arousal in women: The development of a measurement device for vaginal blood volume. *Archives of Sexual Behavior,* 1974, *3,* 559–564.

GENTRY, W. D. Fixed-ratio schedule-induced aggression. *Journal of the Experimental Analysis of Behavior,* 1968, *11,* 813–817.

GERARD, H. B., WILHELMY, R. A., & CONNOLLEY, E. S. Conformity and group size. *Journal of Personality and Social Psychology,* 1968, *8,* 79–82.

GIAMBRA, L. M., & MARTIN, C. E. Sexual daydreams and quantitative aspects of sexual activity: Some relations for males across adulthood. *Archives of Sexual Behavior,* 1977, *6,* 497–505.

GINSBERG, H. J. & BRAUD, W. G. A laboratory investigation of aggression behavior in the Mongolian gerbil *(Meriones unguiculatus). Psychonomic Science,* 1971, *22,* 54–55.

GINSBURG, B., & ALLEE, W. C. Some effects of conditioning on social dominance and subordination in inbred strains of mice. *Physiological Zoology,* 1942, *15,* 485–596.

GIRODO, M. Yoga meditation and flooding in the treatment of anxiety neurosis. *Journal of Behavior Therapy and Experimental Psychiatry,* 1974, *5,* 157–160.

GLADFELTER, W. E., & BROBECK, J. R. Decreased spontaneous locomotor activity in the rat inducted by hypothalamic lesions. *American Journal of Physiology,* 1962, *203,* 811–817.

GLASS, D. C. *Behavior patterns, stress, and coronary disease.* Hillsdale, N. J.: Lawrence Erlbaum, 1977.

GLASS, D. C., & SINGER, J. E. *Urban stress: Experiments on noise and social stressors.* New York: Academic Press, 1972.

GLESER, G. C., GOTTESCHALK, L. A., FOX, R., & LIPPERT, W. Immediate changes in affect with chlordiazepoxide. *Archives of General Psychiatry,* 1965, *13,* 291–295.

GLUCKSMAN, M. L., & HIRSCH, J. The response of obese patients to weight reduction: A clinical evaluation of behavior. *Psychosomatic Medicine,* 1968, *30,* 1–11.

GODDARD, G. V. Functions of the amygdala. *Psychological Bulletin,* 1964, *62,* 89–109.

GOETZL, U., GREEN, R., WHYBROW, P., & JACKSON, R. X-linkage revisited. *Archives of General Psychiatry*, 1974, *31*, 665–671.

GOLDMAN, R., JAFFA, M., & SCHACHTER, S. Yom Kippur, Air France, dormitory food, and the eating behavior of obese and normal persons. *Journal of Personality and Social Psychology*, 1968, *10*, 117–123.

GOLDSTEIN, A. Opioid peptides (endorphins) in the pituitary and brain. Studies on opiate receptors have led to identification of endogenous peptides with morphine-like actions. *Science*, 1976, *193*, 1081–1086.

GOLDSTEIN, J. H., DAVIS, R. W. & HERMAN, D. Escalation of aggression: Experimental studies. *Journal of Personality and Social Psychology*, 1975, *31*, 162–170.

GOLLOB, H., & DITTES, J. Different effects of manipulated self-esteem on persuasibility depending on the threat and complexity of the communication. *Journal of Personality and Social Psychology*, 1965, *2*, 195–201.

GOODALL, J. A. The behavior of free-living chimpanzees in the Gombe Stream Reserve. *Animal Behavior Monographs*, 1968, *1*, 1–311.

GOODMAN, I. J., & BROWN, J. L. Stimulation of positively and negatively reinforcing sites in the avian brain. *Life Sciences*, 1966, *5*, 693–704.

GORANSON, R., & KING, D. Rioting and daily temperature: Analysis of the U.S. riots in 1967. Cited in L. Berkowitz, *A survey of social psychology*. New York: Holt, 1980.

GORER, G. *Himalayan Village*. London: Michael Joseph, 1938.

GOTTIEB, P. M. Neuroallergic reactions to drugs. In F. Speer (Ed.), *Allergy of the nervous system*. Springfield, Ill.: Thomas, 1970.

GOVE, W. R., HUGHES, M., & GALLE, O. R. Overcrowding in the home. *American Sociological Review*, 1979, *44*, 59–80.

GOY, R. W. Organizing effects of androgen on the behavior of Rhesus monkeys. In R. P. Michael (Ed.), *Endocrinology and human behavior*. London: Oxford University Press, 1968.

GOY, R. W., & PHOENIX, C. Hypothalamic regulation of female sexual behavior: Establishment of behavioral oestrus in sprayed guinea pigs following hypothalamic lesions. *Journal of Reproduction and Fertility*, 1963, *5*, 23–40.

GRANT, E. C. G., & MEYERS, E. Mental effects of oral contraceptives. *Lancet*, 1967, *2*, 945–946.

GRAY, J. A. *The psychology of fear and stress*. New York: McGraw-Hill, 1971.

GRAY, J. A. The psychophysiological nature of introversion-extroversion: A modification of Eysenek's theory. In V. D. Nebylitsyn & J. A. Gray (Eds.), *Biological basis of individual behavior*. New York: Academic Press, 1972.

GREEN, L. Temporal and stimulus factors in self-monitoring by obese persons. *Behavior Therapy*, 1978, *9*, 328–341.

GREENBERG, M., & MORRIS, N. Engrossment: The newborn's impact upon the father. *American Journal of Orthopsychiatry*, 1974, *44*, 520–531.

GREENBERG, M. S., & FRISCH, D. M. Effects of intentionality on willingness to reciprocate a favor. *Journal of Personality and Social Psychology*, 1972, *8*, 99–111.

GREENWELL, J., & DENGERINK, H. A. The role of perceived versus actual attack in human physical aggression. *Journal of Personality and Social Psychology*, 1973, *26*, 66–71.

GRIFFITT, W. Environmental effect of interpersonal affective behavior: Ambient effective temperature and attraction. *Journal of Personality and Social Psychology*, 1970, *15*, 240–244.

GRIFFITT, W., MAY, J., & VEITCH, R. Sexual stimulation and interpersonal behavior: Heterosexual evaluative responses, visual behavior, and physical proximity. *Journal of Personality and Social Psychology*, 1974, *30*, 367–377.

GRODMAN, S. M. The role of personality and situation variables in responding to and helping an individual in psychological distress. Cited in E. Staub. Predicting prosocial behavior: A model for specifying the nature of personality-situation interaction. In L. A. Pervin & M. Lewis (Eds.), *Perspectives in interactional psychology*. New York: Plenum Press, 1978.

GROSSBERG, J. M., & WILSON, H. K. Physiological changes accompanying the visualization of fearful and neutral situations. *Journal of Personality and Social Psychology*, 1968, *10*, 124–133.

GROSSEN, N. E., KOSTANSEK, D. J., & BOLLES, R. C. Effects of appetitive discriminative stimuli on avoidance behavior. *Journal of Experimental Psychology*, 1969, *81*, 340–343.

GROSSMAN, S. P. The ventromedial hypothalamus and aggressive behaviors. *Physiology and Behavior,* 1972, 9, 721–725.

GROTE, F. W., & BROWN, R. T. Deprivation level affects extinction of a conditioned taste aversion. *Learning and Motivation,* 1973, 4, 314–319.

GROVES, P. M., & SCHLESINGER, K. *Biological psychology.* Dubuque, Iowa: Brown, 1979.

GRUNT, J. A., & YOUNG, W. C. Differential reactivity of individuals and the response of the male guinea pig to testosterone proprionate. *Endocrinology,* 1952, 51, 237–248.

GRZELAK, J. L. Social interdependence: Do you know what we want to know? Unpublished manuscript, University of Warsaw, Poland, 1980.

GUSTAFSON, J. E., & WINOKUR, G. The effect of sexual satiation and female hormone upon aggressivity in an inbred mice strain. *Journal of Neuropsychiatry,* 1960, 1, 182–184.

GUYER, M. J., & RAPOPORT, A. 2 X 2 games played once. *Journal of Conflict Resolution,* 1972, 16, 409–431.

HABER, R. N. Discrepancy from adaptation level as a source of affect. *Journal of Experimental Psychology,* 1958, 56, 370–375.

HABER, R. N., & ALPERT, R. The role of situation and picture cues in projective measurement of the achievement motive. In J. W. Atkinson (Ed.), *Motives in fantasy, action, and society.* Princeton, N. J.: Van Nostrand, 1958.

HACKMANN, A., & MCLEAN, C. A. A comparison of flooding and thought stopping in the treatment of obsessional neurosis. *Behavior Research and Therapy,* 1975, 13, 263–269.

HAFT, J. I. Cardiovascular injury induced by sympathetic catecholamines. *Progress in Cardiovascular Diseases,* 1974, 17, 73–86.

HAINES, D. B., & MCKEACHIE, W. J. Cooperative versus competitive discussion methods in teaching introductory psychology. *Journal of Educational Psychology,* 1967, 58, 386–390.

HALL, C. S., & KLEIN, S. J. Individual differences in aggressiveness in rats. *Journal of Comparative and Physiological Psychology,* 1942, 33, 371–383.

HAMBURG, D. A. Recent research on hormonal factors relevant to human aggressiveness. *International Social Science Journal,* 1971, 23, 36–47.

HAMBURG, D. A., MOOS, R. H., & YALOM, I. D. Studies of distress in the menstrual cycle and postpartum period. In R.P. Michael (Ed.), *Endocrinology and human behavior.* London: Oxford University Press, 1968.

HAMILTON, G. V. A study of sexual tendencies in monkeys and baboons. *Journal of Animal Behavior,* 1914, 4, 295–318.

HAMILTON, V. L. Obedience and responsibility: A jury simulation. *Journal of Personality and Social Psychology,* 1978, 36, 126–146.

HAMMEN, C. L., & KRANTZ, S. Effect of success and failure on depressive cognitions. *Journal of Abnormal Psychology,* 1976, 85, 577–586.

HAMMOND, L. J. Increased responding to CS in differential CER. *Psychonomic Science,* 1966, 5, 337–338.

HAN, P. W., & LIU, A. C. Obesity and impaired growth of rats force fed 40 days after hypothalamic lesions. *American Journal of Physiology,* 1966, 211, 229–231.

HANER, C. F., & BROWN, J. S. Clarification of the instigation to action concept in the frustration-aggression hypothesis. *Journal of Abnormal and Social Psychology,* 1955, 51, 204–206.

HANSEN, E. W. The development of maternal and infant behavior in the rhesus monkey. *Behaviour,* 1966, 27, 107–149.

HARDING, C. F., & LESHNER, A. The effect of adrenalectomy on the aggressiveness of differently housed mice. *Physiology and Behavior,* 1972, 8, 437–440.

HARITON, E. B., & SINGER, J. L. Women's fantasies during sexual intercourse: Normative and theoretical implications. *Journal of Consulting and Clinical Psychology,* 1974, 42, 313–322.

HARLOW, H. F. The nature of love. *American Psychologist,* 1958, 13, 673–685.

HARLOW, H. F. Love in infant monkeys. *Scientific American,* 1959, 200, 48–74.

HARLOW, H. F. Sexual behavior in the rhesus monkey. In F.A. Beach (Ed.), *Sex and behavior,* New York: Wiley, 1965.

HARLOW, H. F. *Learning to love.* San Francisco: Albion, 1971.

HARLOW, H. F., & HARLOW, M. K. Social deprivation in monkeys. *Scientific American*, 1962, *207*, 137–146.

HARLOW, H. F., HARLOW, M. K., & HANSON, E. W. The maternal affectional system of rhesus monkeys. In H. L. Rheingold (Ed.), *Maternal behavior in mammals*. New York: Wiley, 1963.

HARLOW, H. F., HARLOW, M. K., & SUOMI, J. J. From thought to therapy: Lessons from a primate laboratory. *American Scientist*, 1971, *59*, 538–549.

HARLOW, H. F., & SUOMI, S. J. Nature of love—Simplified. *American Psychologist*, 1970, *25*, 161–168.

HARLOW, H. F., & SUOMI, S. J. Production of depressive behaviors in young monkeys. *Journal of Autism and Childhood Schizophrenia*, 1971, *1*, 246–255.

HARLOW, H. F., & ZIMMERMAN, R. R. Affectional responses in the infant monkey. *Science*, 1959, *130*, 721–732.

HARLOW, M. K., & HARLOW, H. F. Affection in primates. *Discovery*, 1966, *27*, 11–17.

HARRELL, W. A. Effects of extinction on magnitude of aggression in humans. *Psychonomic Science*, 1972, *29*, 213–215.

HARRIS, G. W. *Neural control of the pituitary gland*. London: Edward Arnold, 1955. (a)

HARRIS, G. W. The function of the pituitary stalk. *Bulletin of John Hopkins Hospital*, 1955, *17*, 358–375. (b)

HARRIS, M. B., & HUANG, L. C. Aggression and the attribution process. *Journal of Social Psychology*, 1974, *92*, 209–216.

HARRIS, W. C., & HEISTAD, G. T. Food-reinforced responding in rats during estrus. *Journal of Comparative and Physiological Psychology*, 1970, *70*, 206–212.

HART, B. Role of prior experience on the effects of castration on sexual behavior of male dogs. *Journal of Comparative and Physiological Psychology*, 1968, *66*, 719–725.

HARTMANN, E. L. *The function of sleep*. New Haven, Conn.: Yale University Press, 1973.

HARTMANN, E. L., BRIDWELL, T. J., & SCHILDKRAUT, J. J. Alpha-methylparatyrosine and sleep in the rat. *Psychopharmacologia*, 1971, *21*, 157–164.

HARTMANN, H. *Ego psychology and the problem of adaptation*. New York: International Universities Press, 1958.

HARVAID, B., & HAUGE, M. Hereditary factors elucidated by twin studies. In J. V. Neel, M. W. Shaw, & W. J. Schull (Eds.), *Genetics and the epidemiology of chronic diseases*. Washington, D. C.: U.S. Department of Health, Education and Welfare, 1965.

HASHIM, S., & VAN ITALLIE, T. Studies in normal and obese subjects with a monitored food-dispensing devise. *Annals of the New York Academy of Science*, 1965, *131*, 654–661.

HATCH, J. Collective territories in Galapagos mockingbirds with notes on other behavior. *Wilson Bulletin*, 1966, *78*, 198–207.

HAWK, G., & RICCIO, D. C. The effect of a conditioned fear inhibitor (CS-) during response prevention upon extinction of an avoidance response. *Behaviour Research and Therapy*, 1977, *15*, 97–102.

HAWKE, C. C. Castration and sex crimes. *American Journal of Mental Deficiency*, 1950, *55*, 220–226.

HAWKINS, J., PHILLIPS, N., MOORE, J. D., DUNBAR, S., & HICKS, R. A. Emotionality and REMD: A rat swimming model. *Physiology and Behavior*, 1980, *25*, 167–171.

HAYS, P. Etiological factors in manic-depressive psychoses. *Archives of General Psychiatry*, 1976, *33*, 1187–1188.

HEARNE, J. P. The endocrinology of reproduction in the common marmoset *Callithrix jacchus*. In D. Kleiman (Ed.), *The biology and conservation of the callithricidae*. Washington, D. C.: Smithsonian Institution, 1978.

HEATH, R. G. Correlations between levels of psychological awareness and physiological activity in the central nervous system. *Psychosomatic Medicine*, 1955, *17*, 383–395.

HEATH, R. G. Pleasure response of human subjects to direct stimulation of the brain: Physiologic and psychodynamic considerations. In R. G. Heath (Ed.), *The role of pleasure in behavior*. New York: Harper & Row, 1964.

HEATH, R. G., & MICKLE, W. A. Evaluation of seven years experience with depth electrodes studies in human patients. In E. R. Ramey & P. S. O'Doherty (Eds.), *Electrical studies on the unanesthetized brain.* New York: Harper & Row, 1960.

HEBB, D. O. Drives and the CNS (conceptual nervous system). *Psychological Review*, 1955, *62*, 232–254.

HECKHAUSEN, H. Die Interaktion der Sozialisation svariablen in der Genese des Leistungsmotivs. In C. F. Grauman (Ed.), *Handbuch der Psychologie, Social psychologie* [Vol. 7 (2)]. Gottingen: Hogrefe, 1972.

HECKHAUSEN, H. Fear of failure as a self-reinforcing motive system. In I. G. Sarason & C. D. Spielberger (Eds.), *Stress and anxiety* (Vol. 2). Washington, D. C.: Hemisphere, 1975.

HEIDER, F. Attitudes and cognitive organization. *Journal of Personality*, 1946, *21*, 107–112.

HEIDER, F. *The psychology of interpersonal relations.* New York: Wiley, 1958.

HEIDER, F., & SIMMEL, M. An experimental study of apparent behavior. *American Journal of Psychology*, 1944, *57*, 243–259.

HEIMAN, J. R. The psychology of erotica: Women's sexual arousal. *Psychology Today*, 1975, *8*, 90–94.

HEIMAN, J. R. A psychophysiological exploration of sexual arousal patterns in females and males. *Psychophysiology*, 1977, *14*, 266–274.

HEIMBURGER, R. F., WHITLOCK, C. C., & KALSBECK, J. E. Stereotaxic amygdalotomy for epilepsy with aggressive behavior. *Journal of the American Medical Association*, 1966, *198*, 165–169.

HEIMER, L., & LARSSON, K. Impairment of mating behavior in male rats following lesions in the preoptic-anterior hypothalamic continuum. *Brain Research*, 1966/1967, *3*, 248–263.

HELLER, H. C. Altitudinal zonation of chipmunks *(Eutamias)*: Intraspecific aggression. *Ecology*, 1971, *52*, 312–319.

HENNESSEY, J. W., & LEVINE, S. Stress, arousal, and the pituitary-adrenal system: A psychoendocrine hypothesis. In J. M. Sprague & A. N. Epstein. *Progress in Psychobiology and Physiological Psychology* (Vol. 8). New York: Academic Press, 1979.

HENNESSEY, J. W., KING, M. G., McCLURE, T. A., & LEVINE, S. Uncertainty as defined by the contingency between environmental events, and the adrenocortical response of the rat to electric shock. *Journal of Comparative and Physiological Psychology*, 1977, *91*, 1447–1460.

HERMAN, C. P., & POLIVY, J. Anxiety, restraint, and eating behavior. Unpublished manuscript, Northwestern University, 1974.

HERRERO, S. Human injury inflicted by grizzly bears. *Science*, 1970, *170*, 593–598.

HERSHER, L. RICHMOND, J. B., & MOORE, A. U. Maternal behavior in sheep and goats. In H. L. Rheingold (Ed.), *Maternal behavior in mammals.* New York: Wiley, 1963.

HESS, E. H. Space perception in the chick. *Scientific American*, 1956, *195*, 71–80.

HESS, E. H. Ethology: An approach toward the complete analysis of behavior. In R. Brown, E. Galanter, E. H. Hess, & G. Mandler (Eds.), *New directions in psychology.* New York: Holt, 1962.

HESS, W. R. *The functional organization of the diencephalon.* New York: Grune & Stratton, 1957.

HESSELLUND, H. Masturbation and sexual fantasies in married couples. *Archives of Sexual Behavior*, 1976, *5*, 133–147.

HESTON, L., & SHIELDS, J. Homosexuality in twins: A family study and a registry study. *Archives of General Psychiatry*, 1968, *18*, 149–160.

HETHERINGTON, A. W., & RANSON, S. W. Hypothalamic lesions and adiposity in the rat. *Anatomical Record*, 1940, *78*, 149–172.

HETHERINGTON, A. W., & RANSON, S. W. Effect of early hypophysectomy on hypothalamic obesity. *Endocrinology*, 1942, *31*, 30–34.

HICKS, R. A., MOORE, J. D., HAYES, C., PHILLIPS, N., & HAWKINS, J. REM sleep deprivation increases aggressiveness in male rats. *Physiology and Behavior*, 1979, *22*, 1097–1100.

HICKS, R. A., & SAWREY, J. M. REM sleep deprivation and stress susceptibility in rats. *Psychological Record*, 1978, *28*, 187–191.

HIGBEE, K. L. Fifteen years of arousal: Research on threat appeals 1953–1968. *Psychological Bulletin*, 1969, *72*, 426–444.

HINDE, R. A., & SPENCER-BOOTH, Y. Individual differences in the responses of rhesus monkeys to a period of separation from their mothers. *Journal of Child Psychology and Psychiatry*, 1970, *11*, 159–176.

HIROTO, D. S. Locus of control and learned helplessness. *Journal of Experimental Psychology*, 1974, *102*, 187–193.

HIROTO, D. S., & SELIGMAN, M. E. P. Generality of learned helplessness in man. *Journal of Personality and Social Psychology*, 1975, *31*, 311–327.

HITCHCOCK, E. Amygdalotomy for aggression. In M. Sandler (Ed.), *Psychopharmacology of aggression*. New York: Raven Press, 1979.

HITCHCOCK, E., LAITINEN, L., & VAERNET, K. *Psychosurgery*. Springfield, Ill.: Thomas, 1972.

HOEBEL, B. G. Feeding and self-stimulation. *Neural regulation of food and water intake. Annals of the New York Academy of Sciences*, 1969, *157*, 758–778.

HOEBEL, B. G. & TEITELBAUM, P. Weight regulation in normal and hypothalamic hyperphagic rats. *Journal of Comparative and Physiological Psychology*, 1966, *61*, 189–193.

HOFLING, C. K., BROTZMAN, E., DALRYMPLE, S., GRAVES, N., & PIERCE, C. M. An experimental study in nurse-physician relationships. *The Journal of Nervous and Mental Disease*, 1963, *67*, 214–218.

HOKANSON, J. E. Psychophysiological evaluation of the catharsis hypothesis. In E. I. Megargee & J. E. Hokanson (Eds.), *The dynamics of aggression*. New York: Harper & Row, 1970.

HOKANSON, J. E., & BURGESS, M. The effects of three types of aggression on vascular processes. *Journal of Abnormal and Social Psychology*, 1962, *64*, 446–449. (a)

HOKANSON, J. E., & BURGESS, M. The effects of status, type of frustration, and aggression on vascular processes. *Journal of Abnormal and Social Psychology*, 1962, *65*, 232–237. (b)

HOKANSON, J. E., BURGESS, M., & COHEN, M. F. Effects of displaced aggression on systolic blood pressure. *Journal of Abnormal and Social Psychology*, 1963, *67*, 214–218.

HOKANSON, J. E., & EDELMAN, R. Effects of three social responses on vascular processes. *Journal of Abnormal and Social Psychology*, 1966, *3*, 442–447.

HOKANSON, J. E., & SHETLER, S. The effect of overt aggression on level of physiological arousal. *Journal of Abnormal and Social Psychology*, 1961, *63*, 446–448.

HOKANSON, J. E., WILLERS, K. R., & KOROPSAK, E. The modification of autonomic responses during aggressive interchange. *Journal of Personality*, 1968, *36*, 386–404.

HOLMAN, R. B., ELLIOT, G. R., & BARCHAS, J. D. Neuroregulators and sleep mechanisms. *Annual Reviews of Medicine*, 1975, *26*, 499–520.

HOLMES, D. S. Effects of overt aggression on level of physiological arousal. *Journal of Personality and Social Psychology*, 1966, *4*, 189–194.

HOLMES, J. G., & STRICKLAND, L. H. Choice freedom and confirmation of incentive expectancy as determinants of attitude change. *Journal of Personality and Social Psychology*, 1970, *14*, 39–45.

HOLMES, T. H., & RAHE, R. H. The social readjustment rating scale. *Journal of Psychosomatic Research*, 1967, *11*, 213–218.

HOMANS, G. C. *Social behavior: Its elementary forms*. New York: Harcourt, 1961.

HOOKER, E. The adjustment of the male overt homosexual. *Journal of Projective Techniques*, 1957, *21*, 18–31.

HOON, P. W., WINCZE, J. P., & HOON, E. F. A test of reciprocal inhibition: Are anxiety and sexual arousal in women mutually inhibitory? *Journal of Abnormal Psychology*, 1977, *86*, 65–74.

HORNE, A. M., & MATSON, J. L. A comparison of modeling, desensitization, flooding, study skills, and control groups for reducing test anxiety. *Behavior Therapy*, 1977, *8*, 1–8.

HORNER, M. S. Sex differences in achievement motivation and performance in competitive and noncompetitive situations. Unpublished doctoral dissertation, University of Michigan, 1968.

HORNSTEIN, H. A. *Cruelty and kindness: A new look at aggression and altruism*. Englewood Cliffs, N. J.: Prentice-Hall, 1976.

HOUSE, W. C. Actual and perceived differences in male and female expectancies and minimal goal levels as a function of competition. *Journal of Personality*, 1974, *42*, 493–509.

HOUSTON, J. P., BEE, H., HATFIELD, E., & RIMM, D. C. *Invitation to psychology*. New York: Academic Press, 1979.

HOVLAND, C. I., & JANIS, I. L. *Personality and persuasibility*. New Haven, Conn.: Yale University Press, 1959.

HOVLAND, C. I., JANIS, I. L., & KELLEY, H. H. *Communication and persuasion*. New Haven, Conn.: Yale University Press, 1953.

HOVLAND, C. I., & WEISS, W. The influence of source credibility on communication effectiveness. *The Public Opinion Quarterly*, 1952, *15*, 635–650.

HOWARD, J. L., REIFLER, C. B., & LIPTZIN, M. B. Effects of exposure to pornography. In *Technical report of the Commission on Obscenity and Pornography* (Vol. VIII). Washington, D. C.: U.S. Government Printing Office, 1971.

HRDY, S. B. Infanticide among animals: A review, classification, and examination of the implications for the reproductive strategies of females. *Ethology and Sociobiology*, 1979, *1*, 13–40.

HULL, C. L. Goal attraction and directing ideas conceived as habit phenomena. *Psychological Review*, 1931, *38*, 487–506.

HULL, C. L. *Principles of behavior*. New York: Appleton, 1943.

HULL, C. L. *A behavior system*. New Haven, Conn.: Yale University Press, 1952.

HUNT, M. *Sexual behavior in the 1970s*. Chicago: Playboy Press, 1974.

HUNT, W. A., & MATARAZZO, J. P. Three years later: Recent developments in the experimental modification of smoking behavior. *Journal of Abnormal Psychology*, 1973, *81*, 107–114.

HUNZIKER, J. C. The use of participant modeling in the treatment of water phobias. Unpublished master's thesis, Arizona State University, 1972.

HUSSAIN, M. Z. Desensitization and flooding (implosion) in treatment of phobias. *American Journal of Psychiatry*, 1971, *127*, 85–89.

HUSTON, J. D., DeSISTO, M. J., & MEYER, E. D. Frog-killing by rats as influenced by territorial variables. Paper presented at Eastern Psychological Association Meeting, Philadelphia, April 1969.

HUTCHINSON, R. R., AZRIN, N. H., & HUNT, G. M. Attack produced by intermittent reinforcement of a concurrent operant response. *Journal of the Experimental Analysis of Behavior*, 1968, *11*, 489–495.

HUTCHINSON, R. R., & RENFREW, J. W. Stalking attack and eating behavior elicited from the same sites in the hypothalamus. *Journal of Comparative and Physiological Psychology*, 1966, *61*, 360–367.

HUTT, C., & McGREW, W. C. Effects of group density upon social behavior in humans. Paper presented at association for the Study of Animal Behavior, Symposium on changes in Behavior with Population Density, Oxford, England, July 1967.

HUTT, C., & VAIZEY, J. J. Differential effects of group density on social behavior. *Nature*, 1966, *209*, 1371–1372.

HYDE, J. S. *Understanding human sexuality*. New York: McGraw-Hill, 1979.

INCE, I. P. Behavior modification of sexual disorders. *American Journal of Psychotherapy*, 1973, *17*, 446–451.

INSKO, C. A. Verbal reinforcement of attitude. *Journal of Personality and Social Psychology*, 1965, *2*, 621–623.

INSKO, C. A. *Theories of attitude change*. New York: Appleton-Century-Crofts, 1967.

ISON, J. R., & ROSEN, A. J. The effects of amobarbital sodium on differential instrumental conditioning and subsequent extinction. *Psychopharmacologia*, 1967, *10*, 417–425.

JACKAWAY, R., & TEEVAN, R. Fear of failure and fear of success: Two dimensions of the·same motive. *Sex Roles*, 1976, *2*, 283–293.

JACOBS, R. C., & CAMPBELL, D. T. The perpetuation of an arbitrary tradition through several generations of a laboratory microculture. *Journal of Abnormal and Social Psychology*, 1961, *62*, 649–658.

JACOBSON, E. *Progressive relaxation*. Chicago: University of Chicago Press, 1938.

JACOBSON, E. *Depression: Comparative studies of normal, neurotic, and psychotic conditions*. New York: International Universities Press, 1971.

JAMES, W. A. *The principles of psychology* (Vols. I and II). New York: Holt, 1890.

JANDA, L. H., & KLENKE-HAMEL, K. E. *Human sexuality*. New York: Van Nostrand, 1980.

JANDA, L. H., & RIMM, D. C. Covert sensitization in the treatment of obesity. *Journal of Abnormal Psychology*, 1972, *80*, 37–42.

JANIS, I. L., & FESHBACH, S. Effects of fear-arousing communications. *Journal of Abnormal and Social Psychology*, 1953, *48*, 78–92.

JANOWITZ, H. D., & GROSSMAN, M. I. Some factors affecting the food intake of normal dogs and dogs with esophagostomy and gastric fistula. *American Journal of Physiology*, 1949, *159*, 143–148.

JANOWITZ, H. D., & HOLLANDER, F. Effect of prolonged intragastric feeding on oral ingestion. *Federation Proceedings*, 1953, *12*, 72.

JANOWSKY, D. S., EL-YOUSEF, M. K., DAVIS, J. M., HUBBARD, B., & SEKERKE, H. J. Cholinergic reversal of manic symptoms. *Lancet*, 1972, *1*, 1236–1237.

JAY, P. Mother-infant relations in langurs. In H. L. Rheingold (Ed.), *Maternal behavior in mammals*. New York: Wiley, 1963.

JENKINS, C. D. Recent evidence supporting psychologic and social risk factors for coronary disease. *New England Journal of Medicine*, April 29 and May 6, 1976, *294*, 987–994 and 1033–1038.

JENSEN, G. D. Mother-infant relationship in the monkey *Macaca menestrina:* Development of specificity of maternal response to own infant. *Journal of Comparative and Physiological Psychology*, 1965, *59*, 305–308.

JEWELL, P. A., & LOIZOS, C. *Play, exploration and territory in mammals.* London: Academic Press, 1966.

JOHNSON, E. E. The role of motivational strength in latent learning. *Journal of Comparative and Physiological Psychology*, 1952, *45*, 526–530.

JOHNSON, L. C., & NAITOH, P. The operational consequences of sleep deprivation and sleep deficit. *North Atlantic Treaty Organization Advisory Group for Aerospace Research and Development*, 1974, *193*, 1–43.

JOHNSON, R. N. *Aggression in man and animals.* Philadelphia: Saunders, 1972.

JOHNSON, W. G. The effect of prior-taste and food visibility on the food-directed instrumental performance of obese individuals. Unpublished doctoral dissertation, Catholic University of America, 1970.

JONES, E. E. *Ingratiation.* New York: Appleton-Century-Crofts, 1964.

JONES, E. E., GERGEN, K. J., & JONES, R. G. Tactics of ingratiation among leaders and subordinates in a status hierarchy. *Psychological Monographs*, 1963, *77* (Whole No. 566).

JONES, E. E., & NISBETT, R. E. The actor and the observer: Divergent perceptions of the causes of behavior. In E. E. Jones, D. E. Kanouse, H. H. Kelley, R. E. Nisbett, S. Valins, & B. Weiner (Eds.), *Attribution: Perceiving the causes of behavior.* Morristown, N. J.: General Learning Press, 1972.

JONES, H., & JONES, H. *Sensual drugs.* New York: Cambridge University Press, 1977.

JONES, J. W., & DURBIN, M. J. The effects of secondary cigarette smoke on aggressive behavior of non-smokers. Presented at summer meetings of the Illinois Alliance of Nonsmokers, Chicago, 1978.

JONES, M. C. The elimination of children's fears. *Journal of Experimental Psychology*, 1924, *7*, 383–390.

JONES, R. B., & NOWELL, N. W. The effect of familiar visual and olfactory cues on the aggresive behaviour of mice. *Physiology and Behavior*, 1973, *10*, 221–223.

JORDON, N. Behavioral forces that are a function of attitudes and of cognitive organization. *Human Relations*, 1953, *6*, 273–287.

JOUVET, M. Neurophysiology of the states of sleep. *Physiological Review*, 1967, *47*, 117–177.

JOUVET, M. Neurophysiological and biochemical mechanisms of sleep. In A. Kales (Ed.), *Sleep: Physiology and pathology.* Philadelphia: Lippincott, 1969.

JUNG, C. G. *Psychology and religion.* New Haven, Conn: Yale University Press, 1938.

JUNG, C. G. The archetypes and the collective unconscious. In *Collected works* (Vol. 9, Part I). Princeton, N. J.: Princeton University Press, 1959.

KAADA, B. R. Stimulation and regional ablation of the amygdaloid complex with reference to function representations. In B. E. Eleftheriou (Ed.), *The neurobiology of the amygdala.* New York: Plenum, 1972.

KAHN, I. S. Pollen toxemia in children. *Journal of the American Medical Association*, 1927, *88*, 241–242.

KAHN, M. W. The effect of severe defeat at various age levels on the aggressive behavior of mice. *Journal of Genetic Psychology*, 1951, *79*, 117–130.

KALANT, O. J. *The amphetamines: Toxicity and addiction.* Springfield, Ill.: Thomas, 1966.

KALAT, J. W. Taste salience depends on novelty, not concentration in taste aversion learning in the rat. *Journal of Comparative and Physiological Psychology,* 1974, 86, 49–50.

KALAT, J. W. & ROZIN, P. "Learned safety" as a mechanism in long-delay learning in rats. *Journal of Comparative and Physiological Psychology,* 1973, 83, 198–207.

KALINA, R. K. Diazepam: Its role in a prison setting. *Diseases of the Nervous System,* 1964, 25, 101–107.

KALLMAN, F. J. A comparative twin study on the genetic aspects of male homosexuality. *Journal of Nervous and Mental Diseases,* 1952, 115, 283.

KALLMAN, F. J. Genetic principles in manic-depressives psychoses: Depression. *Proceedings of the 42nd Meeting of the American Psychopathological Association,* 1952.

KAMIN, L. J. The effects of termination of the CS and avoidance of the US on avoidance learning. *Journal of Comparative and Physiological Psychology,* 1956, 49, 420–424.

KAMIN, L. J. "Attention-like" processes in classical conditioning. In M. R. Jones (Ed.), *Miami Symposium of the prediction of behavior, 1967: Aversive stimulation.* Coral Gables, Fla.: University of Miami Press, 1968.

KAMIN, L. J. Predictability, surprise, attention, and conditioning. In B. A. Campbell & R. M. Church (Eds.), *Punishment and aversive behavior.* New York: Appleton, 1969.

KAMIN, L. J., BRIMER, C. J., & BLACK, A. H. Conditioned suppression as a monitor of fear of the CS in the course of avoidance training. *Journal of Comparative and Physiological Psychology,* 1963, 56, 497–501.

KAMM, I., & MANDEL, A. Thioridazine in the treatment of behavior disorders in epileptics. *Diseases of the Nervous System,* 1967, 28, 46–48.

KAPLAN, H. S. *The new sex therapy.* New York: Brunner/Mazel, 1974.

KARLI, P. The Norway rat's killing response to the white mouse. *Behavior,* 1956, 10, 81–103.

KARLI, P., & VERGNES, M. Nouvelles données sur les bases neurophysiologigues du comportement d'aggression interspecifique rat-souris. *Journal de Physiologie,* 1964, 56, 384.

KARLI, P., VERGNES, M., & DIDIERGEORGES, F. Rat-mouse interspecific aggressive behavior and its manipulation by brain ablation and by brain stimulation. In S. Garattini & E. B. Sigg (Eds.) *Aggressive behaviour.* New York: Wiley, 1969.

KATCHER, A. H., SOLOMON, R. L., TURNER, L. H., LoLORDO, V. M., OVERMEIR, J. B., & RESCORLA, R. A. Heart-rate and blood pressure responses to signaled and unsignaled shocks: Effects of cardiac sympathetomy. *Journal of Comparative and Physiological Psychology,* 1969, 68, 163–174.

KAUFMAN, E. L., & MILLER, N. E. Effect of number of reinforcements on strength of approach in an approach-avoidance conflict. *Journal of Comparative and Physiological Psychology,* 1949, 42, 65–74.

KAUFMAN, H. *Aggression and altruism.* New York: Holt, 1970.

KAUFMAN, I. C., & ROSENBLUM, L. A. The waning of the mother-infant bond in two species of macaque. In B. M. Foss (Ed.), *Determinants of infant behavior* (Vol. IV). London: Methuen, 1969.

KAZDIN, A. E. Covert modeling, modeling similarity, and reduction of avoidance behavior. *Behavior Therapy,* 1974, 5, 325–340. (a)

KAZDIN, A. E. Covert modeling, model similarity, and reduction of avoidance behavior. *Behavior Therapy.* 1974, 5, 325–340. (b)

KEESEY, R. E., & POWLEY, T. L. Hypothalamic regulation of body weight. *American Scientist,* 1975, 63, 558–565.

KEETON, W. T. *Biological science.* New York: Norton, 1967.

KELLER, J. F., & SCHOENFELD, W. N. *Principles of behavior.* New York: Appleton-Century-Crofts, 1950.

KELLER, F. S., & HILL, L. M. Another "insight" experiment. *Journal of Genetic Psychology,* 1936, 48, 484–489.

KELLEY, H. H. Two functions of reference groups. In G. E. Swanson, T. M. Newcomb, & E. L. Hartley (Eds.), *Readings in social psychology.* New York: Holt, 1952.

KELLEY, H. H. Attribution theory in social psychology. In D. Levine (Ed.), *Nebraska symposium on motivation.* Lincoln: University of Nebraska Press, 1967.

KELLEY, H. H., & STAHELSKI, A. J. Errors in perception of intentions in a mixed-motive game. *Journal of Experimental Social Psychology,* 1970, *6,* 379–400. (a)

KELLEY, H. H., & STAHELSKI, A. J. The inference of intentions from moves in prisoner's dilemma game. *Journal of Experimental Psychology,* 1970, *6,* 401–419. (b)

KELLY, J. F., & HAKE, D. F. An extinction-induced increase in an aggressive response with humans. *Journal of the Experimental Analysis of Behavior,* 1970, *14,* 153–164.

KELMAN, H. C., & LAWRENCE, L. H. Assignment of responsibility in the case of Lt. Calley: Preliminary report of a national survey. *Journal of Social Issues,* 1972, *28,* 177–212.

KEMPF, E. J. The social and sexual behavior of infrahuman primates with some comparable facts in human behavior. *Psychoanalytic Review,* 1917, *4,* 127–154.

KENDALL, R. E. The classification of depressions: A review of contemporary confusion. *British Journal of Psychiatry,* 1972, *121,* 183–196.

KENDLER, H. H., & GASSER, W. P. Variables in spatial learning: I. Number of reinforcements during training. *Journal of Comparative and Physiological Psychology,* 1948, *41,* 178–187.

KENNEDY, G. C. The role of depot fat in the hypothalamic control of food intake in the rat. *Proceedings of the Royal Society* (Series B), London, 1953, *140,* 578–592.

KESNER, R. P., & KEISER, G. Effects of midbrain reticular lesions upon aggression in the rat. *Journal of Comparative and Physiological Psychology,* 1973, *84,* 194–206.

KESSEN, W., KIMBLE, G. A., & HILLMAN, B. M. Effects of deprivation and scheduling on water intake in the white rat. *Science,* 1960, *131,* 1735–1736.

KIESLER, C. A., & KIESLER, S. B. *Conformity.* Reading, Mass.: Addison-Wesley, 1969.

KIESLER, C. A., & PALLAK, M. S. Arousal properties of dissonance manipulations. *Psychological Bulletin,* 1976, *83,* 1014–1025.

KIMBLE, C. E., FITZ, D., & ONORAD, J. The effectiveness of counteraggression strategies in reducing interactive aggression by males. *Journal of Personality and Social Psychology,* 1977, *35,* 272–278.

KIMBLE, G. A. Behavior strength as a function of the intensity of the hunger drive. *Journal of Experimental Psychology,* 1951, *41,* 341–348.

KIMBLE, G. H. *Hilgard and Marquis' conditioning and learning* (2nd ed.). New York: Appleton-Century, 1961.

KING, F. A., & MEYER, P. M. Effects of amygdaloid lesions upon septal hyperemotionality in the rat. *Science,* 1958, *128,* 655–656.

KING, J. A. Maternal behavior in *Peromyscus.* In H. L. Rheingold (Ed.), *Maternal behavior in animals.* New York: Wiley, 1963.

KING, M. B., & HOEBEL, B. G. Killing elicited by brain stimulation in rat. *Communications in Behavioral Biology,* 1968, *2,* 173–177.

KINSEY, A., POMEROY, W. B., & MARTIN, C. E. *Sexual behavior in the human male.* Philadelphia: Saunders, 1948.

KINSEY, A., POMEROY, W. B., MARTIN, C. E., & GEBHARD, P. H. *Sexual behavior in the human female.* Philadelphia: Saunders, 1953.

KINTSCH, W. S. Runway performance as a function of drive and magnitude of reinforcement. *Journal of Comparative and Physiological Psychology,* 1962, *55,* 882–887.

KINTSCH, W. S., & WITTE, R. S. Concurrent conditioning of bar-press and salivation responses. *Journal of Comparative and Physiological Psychology,* 1962, *55,* 963–968.

KISSILEFF, H. R. Unpublished data cited by J. Le Magnen, Advances in studies on the physiological control and regulation of food intake. In E. Stellar and J. M. Sprague, *Progress in Physiological Psychology* (Vol. 4). New York: Academic Press, 1971.

KLEIN, D. C., & SELIGMAN, M. E. P. Reversal of performance deficits and perceptual deficits in learned helplessness and depression. *Journal of Abnormal Psychology,* 1976, *85,* 11–26.

KLEITMAN, N. *Sleep and Wakefulness* (2nd ed.). Chicago: University of Chicago Press, 1963.

KLERMAN, G. L., & PAYKEL, E. S. Depressive pattern, social background, and hospitalization. *Journal of Nervous and Mental Disease,* 1970, *150,* 466–478.

KLING, A. Effects of amygdalectomy and testosterone on sexual behavior of male juvenile macaques. *Journal of Comparative and Physiological Psychology,* 1968, *65,* 466–471.

KLING, A., DICKS, D., & GURWITZ, E. M. Amygdalectomy and social behavior in a caged-group of vervets (C. *aethiops*). *Proceedings of the 2nd International Congress of Primateology*, Atlanta, Ga., 1968.

KLUVER, H., & BUCY, P. C. "Psychic blindness" and other symptoms following bilateral temporal labectomy in rhesus monkeys. *American Journal of Psychology*, 1937, *119*, 352–353.

KLUVER, H., & BUCY, P. Preliminary analysis of functions of the temporal lobe in rhesus monkeys. *Archives of Neurology and Psychiatry*, 1939, *42*, 979–1000.

KNOTT, J. R. Electroencephalograms in psychopathic personality and murders. In W. Wilson (Ed.), *Applications of electroencephalography in psychiatry*. Durham, N. C.: Duke University Press, 1965.

KOGAN, N., & TAGIURI, R. Interpersonal preference and cognitive organization. *Journal of Abnormal and Social Psychology*, 1958, *56*, 113–116.

KOHLER, W. *The mentality of apes*. London: Routledge & Kegan Paul, 1925.

KOLARSKY, A., FREUND, K., MACHEK, J., & POLAK, O. Male sexual deviation: Association with early temporal damage. *Archives of General Psychiatry*, 1967, *17*, 735–743.

KOLB, D. Achievement motivation training for underachieving high school boys. *Journal of Personality and Social Psychology*, 1965,2, 783–792.

KOSTOWSKI, W., REWERSKI, W., & PIECHOCKI, T. Effects of some steroids on aggressive behaviour in mice and rats. *Neuroendoerinology*, 1970, *6*, 311–318.

KOTELCHUCK, M. The nature of the infant's tie to his father. Paper presented at the meeting of the Society for Research in Child Development, Philadelphia, March 1973.

KRAFT, T., & AL-ISSA, I. Behavior therapy and the treatment of frigidity. *American Journal of Psychotherapy*, 1967, *21*, 116–120.

KRANE, R. V., & WAGNER, A. R. Taste aversion learning with a delayed shock US: Implications for the "generality of the laws of learning." *Journal of Comparative and Physiological Psychology*, 1975, *88*, 882–889.

KRAPFT, J. E. Differential ordering of stimulus presentation and semiautomated versus live treatment in the systematic desensitization of snake phobia. Unpublished doctoral dissertation, University of Missouri, 1967.

KREBS, D. Empathy and altruism. *Journal of Personality and Social Psychology*, 1975, *32*, 1134–1146.

KRECH, D., CRUTCHFIELD, R. S., & BALLACHEY, E. L. *Individual in society*. New York: McGraw-Hill, 1962.

KRECH, D., CRUTCHFIELD, R. S., & BALLACHEY, E. L. Cited in J. L. Freeman, D. O. Sears, & J. M. Carlsmith. *Social psychology* (3rd ed.). Englewood Cliffs, N. J.: Prentice-Hall, 1978.

KREISKOTT, H. Some comments on the killing response behavior of the rat. In S. Garattini & E. B. Sigg (Eds.), *Aggressive behaviour*. New York: Wiley, 1969.

KRUUK, H. Surplus killing by carnivores. *Journal of Zoology*, London, 1972, *166*, 233–244.

KULKA, A. Attributional determinants of achievement-related behavior. *Journal of Personality and Social Psychology*, 1972, *21*, 166–174.

KUMMER, H. *Social organization of Hamadryas baboons: A field study*. Chicago: University of Chicago Press, 1968.

KUPFER, J. REM latency: A psychobiologic marker for primary depressive disease. *Biological Psychiatry*, 1976, *11*, 159–174.

KURLANDER, H., MILLER, W., & SELIGMAN, M. E. P. Learned helplessness, depression, and prisoner's dilemma. Cited in M. E. P. Seligman, *Helplessness*. San Francisco: Freeman, 1975.

KUSHNER, M. The reduction of a long standing fetish by means of aversive conditioning. In L. P. Ullman & L. Krasner (Eds.), *Case studies in behavior modification*. New York: Holt, 1965.

LACK, D. *The life of the robin*. London: Cambridge University Press, 1943.

LAGERSPETZ, K. Studies on the aggressive behavior of mice. *Annales Academiae Scientiarum Fennicae*, 1964, Series B, *131*, 1–131.

LAGERSPETZ, K., & NURMI, R. An experiment on the frustration-aggression hypothesis. *Reports from the Institute of Psychology, University Turku*, 1964, No. 10, 1–8.

LAGERSPETZ, K., & TALO, S. Maturation of aggressive behaviour in young mice. *Reports from the Institute of Psychology, University Turku*, 1967, No. 28, 1–9.

LAMBERTH, J. H. *Social psychology*. New York: Macmillan, 1980.

LANG, A. R., GOECKNER, D. J., ADESSO, V. J., & MARLATT, G. A. Effects of alcohol on aggression in male social drinkers. *Journal of Abnormal Psychology*, 1975, 84, 508–518.

LANGER, E. J., & ROTH, J. Heads I win, tails it's chance: The illusion of control as a function of the sequence of outcomes in a purely chance task. *Journal of Personality and Social Psychology*, 1975, 32, 951–955.

LA POINTE, K. A., & RIMM, D. C. Cognitive, assertive, and insight oriented group therapies in the treatment of reactive depression in women. Cited in D. C. Rimm & J. C. Masters, *Behavior therapy: Techniques and empirical findings*. New York: Academic Press, 1979.

LAPOLLA, A., & JONES, H. Placebo-control evaluation of desipramine in depression. *American Journal of Psychiatry*, 1970, 127, 335–338.

LATANE, B., & DARLEY, J. M. Group inhibition of bystander intervention in emergencies. *Journal of Personality and Social Psychology*, 1968, 10, 215–221.

LATANE, B., & DARLEY, J. M. *The unresponsive bystander: Why doesn't he help?* Englewood Cliffs, N. J., Prentice-Hall, 1970.

LATANE, B., & RODIN, J. A lady in distress: Inhibiting effects of friends and strangers in bystander intervention. *Journal of Experimental Social Psychology*, 1969, 5, 189–202.

LAW, D. T., & MEAGHER, W. Hypothalamic lesions and sexual behavior in the female rat. *Science*, 1958, 128, 1626–1627.

LAWLER, E. E., KULECK, W. J., RHODE, J. S., & SORENSON, S. E. Job choice and post decision dissonances. *Organizational Behavior and Human Performance*, 1975, 13, 133–145.

LAZARUS, A. A. Group therapy in phobic disorders by systematic desensitization. *Journal of Abnormal and Social Psychology*, 1961, 63, 504–510.

LAZARUS, A. A. The treatment of chronic frigidity by systematic desensitization. *Journal of Nervous and Mental Disease*, 1963, 136, 272–278.

LAZARUS, A. A. *Behavior therapy and beyond*. New York: McGraw-Hill, 1971.

LAZARUS, A. A. Multimodal behavioral treatment of depression. *Behavior Therapy*, 1974, 5, 549–554.

LAZARUS, R. S. *Psychological stress and the coping process*. New York: McGraw-Hill, 1974.

LAZARUS, R. S. *Patterns of Adjustment*. New York: McGraw-Hill, 1976.

LAZARUS, R. S., & ALFERT, E. Short-circuiting of threat by experimentally altering cognitive appraisal. *Journal of Abnormal and Social Psychology*, 1964, 69, 195–205.

LAZARUS, R. S., OPTON, R. M., JR., NUMIKOS, M. S., & RANKIN, N. O. The principle of short-circuiting of threat: Further evidence. *Journal of Personality*, 1965, 33, 622–635.

LAZARUS, R. S., SPEISMAN, J. C., MORDKOFF, A. M., & DAVIDSON, L. A. A laboratory study of psychological stress produced by a motion picture film. *Psychological Monographs: General and Applied*, 1962, 76 (34, Whole No. 554).

LEANDER, J. D. Effects of food deprivation on free-operant avoidance behavior. *Journal of Experimental Analysis of Behavior*, 1973, 19, 17–24.

LEFCOURT, H. M. Internal versus external control of reinforcement revisted: Recent developments. Research Report No. 27, University of Waterloo, Ontario, Canada, 1971.

LEFF, M., ROATCH, J., & BUNNEY, W. E. Environmental factors preceding the onset of severe depressions. *Psychiatry*, 1970, 33, 293–311.

LEFRANCOIS, G. L. *Psychology*. Belmont, Calif.: Wadsworth, 1980.

LE MAGNEN, J. Advances in studies in the physiological control and regulation of food intake. In E. Stellar & J. M. Sprague (Eds.), *Progress in physiological psychology* (Vol. 4), New York: Academic Press, 1971.

LE MAGNEN, J., & TALLON, S. La pariodicité spontancé de la prisé d'aliments ad libitum du rat blanc. *Journal of Physiology*, (Paris), 1966, 58, 323–349.

LEMIEUX, G., DAVIGNON, A., & GENEST, J. Depressive states during rauwolfia therapy for arterial hypertension. *Canadian Medical Association Journal*, 1956, 74, 522–526.

LEONARD, C. V. Depression and suicidality. *Journal of Consulting and Clinical Psychology*, 1974, 42, 98–104.

LESHNER, A. I., WALKER, W. A., JOHNSON, A. E., KELLING, J. S., KREISLER, S. J. & SVARE, B. B. Pituitary adrenocortical activity and intermale aggressiveness in isolated mice. *Physiology and Behavior*, 1973, 11, 705–711.

LEVENTHAL, H., & NILES, P. Persistence of influence for varying duration of threat stimuli. *Psychological Reports*, 1965, 16, 223–233.

LEVENTHAL, H., SINGER, R., & JONES, S. The effect of fear and specificity of recommendation upon attitudes and behavior. *Journal of Pesonality and Social Psychology*, 1965, *2*, 20–29.

LEVIS, D. J., SMITH, J. E., & EPSTEIN, W. Is fear present to the CS following short-latency avoidance responding? Paper presented at the nineteenth annual meeting of the Psychonomic Society, San Antonio, Texas, 1978.

LEVISON, P. K., & FLYNN, J. P. The objects attached by cats during stimulation of the hypothalamus. *Animal Behaviour*, 1965, *13*, 217–220.

LEWINSOHN, P. H. A behavioral approach to depression. In R. J. Friedman & M. M. Katz (Eds.), *The psychology of depression: Contemporary theory and research*. Washington, D. C.: Winston-Wiley, 1974.

LEWINSOHN, P. M., & ATWOOD, G. E. Depression: A clinical-research approach. *Psychotherapy: Theory, research, and practice*, 1969, *6*, 166–171.

LEWINSOHN, P. M., & LIBET, J. M. Pleasant events, activity schedules and depressions. *Journal of Abnormal Psychology*, 1972, *79*, 291–295.

LEWINSOHN, P. M., LOBITZ, W. C., & WILSON, S. "Sensitivity" of depressed individuals to aversive stimuli. *Journal of Abnormal Psychology*, 1973, *81*, 259–263.

LEWINSOHN, P. M., & SHAFFER, M. The use of home observations as an integral part of the treatment of depression: Preliminary report and case studies. *Journal of Consulting and Clinical Psychology*, 1971, *37*, 87–94.

LEWINSOHN, P. M., & SHAW, D. A. Feedback about interpersonal behavior as an agent of behavior change: A case study in the treatment of depression. *Psychotherapy and Psychosomatics*, 1969, *17*, 82–88.

LEWINSOHN, P. M., WEINSTEIN, M. S., & ALPER, T. A behaviorally oriented approach to the group treatment of depressed persons: A methodological contribution. *Journal of Clinical Psychology*, 1970, *4*, 525–532.

LEWIS, D. J. A control for the direct manipulation of the fractional anticipatory goal response. *Psychological Reports*, 1959, *5*, 753–756.

LEYENS, J. P., CAMINO, L., PARKE, R. D., & BERKOWITZ, L. The effects of movie violence on aggression in a field setting as a function of group dominance and cohension. *Journal of Personality and Social Psychology*, 1975, *32*, 346–360.

LEYHAUSEN, P. The communal organization of solitary mammals. *Symposium of the Zoological Society of London*, 1965, *14*, 249–263.

LIBERMAN, R. P., & RASKIN, D. E. Depression: A behavioral formulation. *Archives of General Psychiatry*, 1971, *24*, 515–523.

LIBET, J. M., & LEWINSOHN, P. M. The concept of social skill with special reference to the behavior of depressed persons. *Journal of Consulting and Clinical Psychology*, 1973, *40*, 304–312.

LICK, J., & BOOTZIN, R. Expectancy factors in the treatment of fear: Methological and theoretical issues. *Psychological Bulletin*, 1975, *82*, 917–931.

LIEBMAN, J. M., & BUTCHER, L. I. Comparative involvement of dopamine and noradrenaline in rate-free self-stimulation in the substantia nigra, lateral hypothalamus and mesencephalic central gray. *Naunyn-Schmiedeberg's Archives of Pharmacology*, 1974, *284*, 167–194.

LINDER, D. E., COOPER, J., & JONES, E. E. Decision freedom as a determinant of the role of incentive magnitude in attitude change. *Journal of Personality and Social Psychology*, 1967, *6*, 245–254.

LINDSLEY, D. B. Emotion. In S. S. Stevens (Ed.), *Handbook of experimental psychology*. New York: Wiley, 1951.

LISK, R. D. Diencephalic placement of estradiol and sexual activity in the female rat. *American Journal of Physiology*, 1962, *203*, 493–496.

LISK, R. D. Increased sexual behavior in the male rat following lesions in the mammillary region. *Journal of Experimental Zoology*, 1966, *161*, 129–136.

LISK, R. D. Neural localization for androgen activation of copulatory behavior in the rat. *Endocrinology*, 1967, *80*, 754–761.

LITTLE, L. M., & CURRAN, J. P. Covert sensitization: A clinical procedure in need of some explanations. *Psychological Bulletin*, 1978, *85*, 513–531.

LITWIN, G. H. Motives and expectancies as determinants of preference for degrees of risk. Unpublished honors thesis, University of Michigan, 1958.

LLOYD, C. W. Problems associated with the menstrual cycle. In C. W. Lloyd (Ed.), *Human reproduction and sexual behavior.* Philadelphia: Lea & Febiger, 1964.

LOCKIE, J. D. Territory in small carnivores. In P. A. Jewell & C. Loizos, *Play, exploration and territory in mammals.* London: Academic Press, 1966.

LOGUE, A. W. Taste aversion and the generality of the laws of learning. *Psychological Bulletin,* 1979, 86, 276–296.

LORAINE, J. A., ADAMPOPOULOUS, D. A., KIRKHAN, K. E., ISMAIL, A. A., & DOVE, G. A. Patterns of hormone excretion in male and female homosexuals. *Nature,* 1971, 234, 552–554.

LORENZ, K. The comparative method of studying innate behavior patterns. In Society for Experimental Biology, Symposium No. 4, *Physiological Mechanisms in animal behaviour.* New York: Academic Press, 1950.

LORENZ, K. The past twelve years in the comparative study of behavior. In C. H. Schiller (Ed.), *Instinctive behavior.* New York: International Universities Press, 1952.

LORENZ, K. *On aggression.* New York: Harcourt Brace Jovanovich, 1966.

LORENZ, K. Innate bases of learning. In K. H. Pibram (Ed.), *On the biology of learning.* New York: Harcourt, Brace, & World, 1969.

LORENZ, K., & TINBERGEN, N. Taxis und Instinkthandlung in der Eirollbewegung der Graigrans. *Zeitschrift für Tierpsychologie,* 1938, 2, 1–29.

LOTT, A. J., & LOTT, B. E. Group cohesiveness, communication level, and conformity. *Journal of Abnormal and Social Psychology,* 1961, 62, 408–412.

LOWELL, E. L. The effect of need for achievement on learning and speed of performance. *Journal of Psychology,* 1952, 33, 31–40.

LOWIN, A. Approach and avoidance: Alternate modes of selective exposure to information. *Journal of Personality and Social Psychology,* 1967, 6, 1–9.

LOWIN, A. Further evidence for an approach-avoidance interpretation of selective exposure. *Journal of Experimental Social Psychology,* 1969, 5, 265–271.

LUCE, R. D., & RAIFFA, H. *Games and decisions.* New York: Wiley, 1957.

LUTTGE, W. G., & HALL, N. R. Androgen-induced agonistic behavior in castrate male Swiss-Webster mice: Comparison of four naturally occurring androgens. *Behavioral Biology,* 1973, 8, 725–732.

LUXENBURGER, H. Psychiatrisch-neurologische Zwillingspathologie. *Z. Ges. Neurol. Psychiat,* 1930, 56, 145–180.

MAAS, J. W., DEKIRMENJIAN, H., & FAWETT, J. Catecholamine metabolism, depression and stress. *Nature,* 1971, 230, 330–331.

MACAULAY, J. A study of independent and additive models of producing resistance to persuasion derived from congruity and inoculation models. Unpublished doctoral dissertation, University of Wisconsin, 1965.

MACAULEY, J. A skill for charity. I. J. Macaulay & L. Berkowitz (Eds.), *Altrusim and helping behavior: Social psychological studies of some antecedents and consequences.* New York: Academic Press, 1970.

MACCORQUODALE, K., & MEEHL, P. E. Edward C. Tolman. In W. K. Estes et al. (Eds.), *Modern learning theory.* New York: Appleton, 1954.

MACCRIMMON, K., & MESSICK, D. Framework of social motives. *Behavioral Science,* 1976, 21, 86–100.

MACCULLOCH, M. J., & FELDMAN, M. D. Aversion therapy in the management of 43 homosexuals. *British Medical Journal,* 1967, 2, 594–597.

MACDONNELL, M. F., & FLYNN, J. P. Attack elicited by stimulation of the thalamus of cats. *Science,* 1964, 144, 1249–1250.

MACDONNELL, M. F., & FLYNN, J. P. Sensory control of hypothalamic attack. *Animal Behaviour,* 1966, 14, 399–405.

MACDONNELL, M. F., & FLYNN, J. P. Attack elicited by stimulation of the thalamus and adjacent structures of cats. *Behaviour,* 1968, 31, 185–202.

MACFARLANE, D. A. The role of kinesthesis in maze learning. *University of California Publications in Psychology,* 1930, 4, 277–305.

MACKAY, E. M., CALLAWAY, J. W., & BARNES, R. H. Hyperalimentation in normal animals produced by protamine insulin. *Journal of Nutrition,* 1940, 20, 59–66.

MacKintosh, J. H., & Grant, E. C. The effect of olfactory stimuli on agonistic behavior of laboratory mice. *Zeitschrift fur Tierpsychologie,* 1966, *23,* 584–587.

MacLean, P. D., & Delgado, J. M. R. Electrical and chemical stimulation of frontotemporal portion of limbic system in the waking animal. *Electroencephalography and Clinical Neurophysiology,* 1953, *5,* 91–100.

MacLennon, R. R., & Bailey, E. D. Seasonal changes in aggression, hunger, and curiosity in ranch mink. *Canadian Journal of Zoology,* 1969, *47,* 1395–1404.

MacNeil, M. K., & Sherif, M. Norm change over subject generations as a function of arbitrariness of prescribed norms. *Journal of Personality and Social Psychology,* 1976, *34,* 762–773.

Macoby, E., & Jacklin, C. *The psychology of sex differences.* Stanford: Stanford University Press, 1974.

MacPhillamy, D. J., & Lewinsohn, P. M. Depression as a function of levels of desired and obtained pleasure. *Journal of Abnormal Psychology,* 1974, *83,* 651–657.

Madsen, M. C. Cooperative and competitive motivation of children in three Mexican subcultures. *Psychological Reports,* 1967, *20,* 1307–1320.

Magoun, H. W. *Brain mechanisms of consciousness.* Oxford, England: Blackwell, 1954.

Mahl, G. F. Anxiety, HCL secretion and peptic ulcer etiology. *Psychosomatic Medicine,* 1949, *11,* 30–44.

Mahoney, M. J. *Cognition and behavior modification.* Cambridge, Mass.: Ballinger, 1974.

Maier, S. F., & Seligman, M. E. P. Learned helplessness: Theory and evidence. *Journal of Experimental Psychology: General,* 1976, *105,* 3–46.

Maier, S. F., & Testa, T. J. Failure to learn to escape by rats previously exposed to inescapable shock is partly produced by associative interference. *Journal of Comparative and Physiological Psychology,* 1975, *88,* 554–564.

Malamud, N. Psychiatric disorders with intracranial tumors of the limbic system. *Archives of Neurology,* 1967, *17,* 113–123.

Malleson, N. Panic and phobia. *Lancet,* 1959, *1,* 225–227.

Malmo, R. B. Finger sweat prints in differentiation of low and high incentive. *Psychophysiology,* 1965, *1,* 231–240.

Malof, M., & Lott, A. J. Ethnocentrism and the acceptance of Negro support in a group pressure situation. *Journal of Abnormal and Social Psychology,* 1962, *65,* 254–258.

Mances, A. L., & Melynk, P. Televised models of female achievement. *Journal of Applied Social Psychology,* 1974, *4,* 365–373.

Mandler, G., & Sarason, S. B. A study of anxiety and learning. *Journal of Abnormal and Social Psychology,* 1952, *47,* 166–173.

Mann, J., Berkowitz, L., Sidman, J., Starr, S., & West, S. Satiation of the transient stimulating affect of erotic films. *Journal of Personality and Social Psychology,* 1974, *30,* 729–735.

Mans, J., & Senes, M. Isocarboxazid, RO 5-0690 or chlordiazepoxide and RO 4-0403 a thioxanthene derivative. Study on their individual effects and their possibilities of combination. *Journal de Medicine de Bordeaux,* 1964, *141,* 1909–1918.

Mantrell, D. M. The potential for violence in Germany. *Journal of Social Issues,* 1971, *27,* 101–112.

Margules, D. L. Noradrenergic rather than serotonergic basis of reward in dorsal tegmentum. *Journal of Comparative and Physiological Psychology,* 1969, *67,* 32–25.

Margules, D. L., & Olds, J. Identical "feeding" and "rewarding" systems in the lateral hypothalamus of rats. *Science,* 1962, *135,* 374–375.

Margules, D. L., & Stein, L. Neuroleptics versus tranquilizers: Evidence from animal behavior studies of mode and site of action. In H. Brill et al. (Eds.), *Neuropsychopharmacology.* Amsterdam: Elsevier, 1967.

Margules, D. L., & Stein, L. Cholinergic synapses of a periventricular punishment system in the medial hypothalamus. *American Journal of Physiology,* 1969, *217,* 475–480.

Mark, V. H., & Ervin, F. R. *Violence and the brain.* New York: Harper & Row, 1970.

Marks, I. M., & Gelder, M. G. Transvestism and fetishism: Clinical and psychological changes during faradic aversion. *British Journal of Psychiatry,* 1967, *113,* 711–729.

MARKS, I. M., GELDER, M. G., & BANCROFT, J. Sexual deviants two years after electric aversion. *British Journal of Psychiatry*, 1970, *117*, 173–185.

MARMORE, J. Impotence and ejaculatory disturbances. In B. Sadock et al. (Eds.), *The sexual experience*. Baltimore: Williams & Wilkins, 1976.

MARTIN, L. K., & RIESS, D. Effects of US intensity during previous discrete delay conditioning on conditioned acceleration during avoidance extinction. *Journal of Comparative and Physiological Psychology*, 1969, *69*, 196–200.

MARTINE, J. G. Relationships between the self concept and differences in the strength and generality of achievement motivation. *Journal of Personality*, 1956, *24*, 364–375.

MASLOW, A. H. *Toward a psychology of being* (2nd ed.). Princeton, N. J.: Van Nostrand, 1968.

MASLOW, A. H. *Motivation and personality*. New York: Harper & Row, 1970.

MASSERMAN, J. H. *Behavior and neurosis*. Chicago: University of Chicago Press, 1943.

MASTERS, W., & JOHNSON, V. *Human sexual response*. Boston: Little, Brown, 1966.

MASTERS, W., & JOHNSON, V. *Human sexual inadequacy*. Boston: Little, Brown, 1970.

MATHEW, R. J., LARGEN, J., & CLAGHORN, J. L. Biological symptoms of depression. *Psychosomatic Medicine*, 1979, *41*, 439–443.

MAYER, J. Genetic, traumatic, and environmental factors in the etiology of obesity. *Psychological Review*, 1953, *33*, 472–508.

MAYER, J. Regulation of energy intake and body weight: The glucostatic theory and the lipostatic hypothesis. *Annuls of the New York Academy of Science*, 1955, *63*, 15–43.

MAYER, J. *Overweight: Causes, cost and control*. Englewood Cliffs, N. J.: Prentice-Hall, 1978.

McADAM, D. W., & KAEBLER, W. W. Differential impairment of avoidance in cats with ventromedial hypothalamic lesions. *Experimental Neurology*, 1966, *15*, 293–298.

McARTHUR, L. A. The how of what and why: Some determinants and consequences·of causal attributions. *Journal of Personality and Social Psychology*, 1972, *22*, 171–193.

McARTHUR, L. A., & POST, D. L. Figural emphasis and perception. *Journal of Experimental Social Psychology*, 1977, *13*, 520–535.

McCARRON, L. T. Psychophysiological discriminants of reactive depression. *Psychophysiology*, 1973, *10*, 223–230.

McCLELLAND, D. C. Measuring motivation in fantasy: The achievement motive. In H. Guertzkow (Ed.), *Groups, leadership, and men*. Pittsburgh: Carnegie Press, 1951.

McCLELLAND, D. C. Risk taking in children with high and low need for achievement. In J. W. Atkinson (Ed.), *Motives in fantasy, action, and society*. Princeton, N. J.: Van Nostrand, 1958.

McCLELLAND, D. C. *The achieving society*. Princeton, N. J.: Van Nostrand, 1961.

McCLELLAND, D. C. Achievement and entrepreneurship: A longitudinal study. *Journal of Personality and Social Psychology*, 1965, *1*, 389–392.

McCLELLAND, D. C., & ATKINSON, J. W. The projective expression of needs. I. The effects of different intensities of the hunger drive on perception. *Journal of Psychology*, 1948, *25*, 205–222.

McCLELLAND, D. C., ATKINSON, J. W., CLARK, R. W., & LOWELL, E. L. *The achievement motive*. New York: Appleton-Century-Crofts, 1953.

McCLELLAND, D. C., ATKINSON, J. W., CLARK, R. W., & LOWELL, E. L. *The achievement motive* (2nd ed.). New York: Irvington Publishers, 1976.

McCLELLAND, D. C., RINDLISBACHER, A., & DE CHARMS, R. C. Religions and other sources of parental attitudes toward independence training. In D. C. McClelland (Ed.), *Studies in motivation*. New York: Appleton-Century-Crofts, 1955.

McCLELLAND, D. C., STURR, J. F., KNAPP, R. H., & WENDT, H. W. Obligations to self and society in the United States and Germany. *Journal of Abnormal and Social Psychology*, 1958, *56*, 245–255.

McCLELLAND, D. C., & WINTER, D. G. *Motivating economic achievement*. New York: The Free Press, 1969.

McCLINTOCK, C. G., & McNEEL, S. P. Reward level and game playing behavior. *Journal of Conflict Resolution*, 1966, *10*, 98–102.

McCLINTOCK, C. G., & VAN AVERMAET, E. V. Social values and rules of fairness: A theoretical perspective. In J. Grzelak & V. Derlega (Eds.), *Living with other people: Theory and research on cooperation and helping.* New York: Academic Press, 1981.

McDougall, W. *An introduction to social psychology,* London: Methuen, 1908.

McGuire, R. J., Carlisle, J. M., & Young, B. G. Sexual deviations as conditioned behaviour: A hypothesis. *Behavior Research and Therapy,* 1965, *2,* 185–190.

McGuire, W. J. Resistance to persuasion confirmed by active and passive prior refutation of the same and alternative counterarguments. *Journal of Abnormal and Social Psychology,* 1961, *63,* 326–332.

McGuire, W. J. Inducing resistance to persuasion: Some contemporary approaches. In L. Berkowitz (Ed.), *Advances in experimental social psychology* (Vol. 1). New York: Academic Press, 1964.

McGuire, W. J. The nature of attitudes and attitude change. In G. Lindzey & E. Aronson (Eds.), *Handbook of social psychology* (2nd ed.), Reading, Mass.: Addison-Wesley, 1969.

McGuire, W. J., & Papageorgis, D. The relative efficacy of various types of prior belief-defense in producing immunity against persuasion. *Journal of Abnormal and Social Psychology,* 1961, *62,* 317–337.

McIntyre, A. Sex differences in children's aggression. *Proceedings of the Annual Convention of the American Psychological Association,* 1972, *7,* 93–94.

McKenna, R. J. Some effects of anxiety level and food cues on the eating behavior of obese and normal subjects. *Journal of Personality and Social Psychology,* 1972, *22,* 311–319.

McKinney, W. T., Suomi, S. J., & Harlow, H. F. Repetitive peer-separation of juvenile-age rhesus monkeys. *Archives of General Psychiatry,* 1972, *27,* 200–203.

McLean, D. D., & Hakstian, A. R. Clinical depression: Comparative efficacy of outpatient treatments. Unpublished manuscript, University of British Columbia, Vancouver, Canada, 1979.

McNamara, H. J., Long, J. B., & Wike, E. L. Learning without response under two conditions of external cues. *Journal of Comparative and Physiological Psychology,* 1956, *49,* 477–480.

Meichenbaum, D. H. Examination of model characteristics in reducing avoidance behavior. *Journal of Behavior Therapy and Experimental Psychiatry,* 1972, *3,* 225–227.

Mellgren, R. L. Positive and negative contrast effects using delayed reinforcement. *Learning and Motivation,* 1972, *3,* 185–193.

Mello, N. K., & Mendelson, J. H. Alcohol and human behavior. In L. L. Iversen, S. D. Iversen, & S. H. Snyder (Eds.), *Handbook of Psychopharmacology* (Vol. 12). New York: Plenum Press, 1978.

Mendels, J. *Concepts of depression.* New York: Wiley, 1970.

Mendels, J., & Cochrane, C. The nosology of depression: The endogenous-reactive concept. *American Journal of Psychiatry,* 1968, *124* (May Supplement), 1–11.

Mendelson, J. The role of hunger in T-maze learning for food by rats. *Journal of Comparative and Physiological Psychology,* 1966, *62,* 341–353.

Mendelson, J. Lateral hypothalamic stimulation in satiated rats: The rewarding effects of self-induced drinking. *Science,* 1967, *157,* 1077–1979.

Mendelson, J., & Chorover, S. L. Lateral hypothalamic stimulation in satiated rats: T-maze learning for food. *Science,* 1965, *149,* 559–561.

Meyer, V., Robertson, J., & Tatlow, A. Home treatment of an obsessive-compulsive disorder by response prevention. *Journal of Behavior Therapy and Experimental Psychiatry,* 1975, *6,* 37–38.

Meyer, W. U. Selbstverantwortlichkeit und Leitungs motivation. Unpublished doctoral dissertation, Ruhr Universität, Bochum, Germany, 1970.

Meyer-Bahlburg, H. F. L. Sex hormones and male homosexuality in comparative perspective. *Archives of Sexual Behavior,* 1977, *6,* 297–325.

Michael, R. P. Estrogen-sensitive neurons and sexual behavior in female cats. *Science,* 1962, *136,* 322–323.

Michael, R. P. Effects of gonadal hormones on displaced and direct aggression in pairs of rhesus monkeys of opposite sex. In S. Garattini & E. B. Sigg (Eds.), *Aggressive behaviour,* New York: Wiley, 1969.

Michotte, A. *La perception de la causalité.* Louvain, Ed. de l'Institut Superieur (Etudes de Psychologie), VIII, 1946.

MICHOTTE, A. *The perception of causality*. New York: Basic Books, 1963.

MICZEK, K. A., BRYKCZYNSKI, T., & GROSSMAN, S. P. Differential effects of lesions on the amygdala, periamygdaloid cortex, or stria terminalis on aggressive behavior in rats. *Journal of Comparative and Physiological Psychology*, 1974, 87, 760–771.

MILGRAM, S. Nationality and conformity. *Scientific American*, 1961, 205, 45–51.

MILGRAM, S. Behavioral study of obedience. *Journal of Abnormal and Social Psychology*, 1963, 67, 371–378.

MILGRAM, S. Some conditions of obedience and disobedience to authority. *Human Relations*, 1965, 18, 57–76. (a)

MILGRAM, S. Liberating effects of group pressure. *Journal of Personality and Social Psychology*, 1965, 1, 127–134. (b)

MILGRAM, S. Liberating effects of group pressure. *Harper's Magazine*, 1973, 247, 62–77.

MILGRAM, S. *Obedience to authority: An experimental view*. New York: Harper & Row, 1974.

MILGRAM, S. Subject reaction: The neglected factor in the ethics of experimentation. Hasting Center Report, October 1977, 19–23.

MILLER, A., BYRNE, D., & DeNINNO, J. The relationship between arousal response to erotic cues and marital adjustment. Cited in A. Baron, D. Byrne, & B. Kantowitz, *Psychology: Understanding Behavior* (2nd ed.). New York: Holt, 1980.

MILLER, H. R., & NOWAS, M. M. Control of aversive stimulus in systematic desensitization. *Behavior Research and Therapy*, 1970, 8, 57–61.

MILLER, N. E. The frustration-aggression hypothesis. *Psychological Review*, 1941, 48, 337–342.

MILLER, N. E. Studies of fear as an acquirable drive: I. Fear as motivation and fear reduction as reinforcement in the learning of new responses. *Journal of Experimental Psychology*, 1948, 38, 89–101.

MILLER, N. E. Learnable drives and rewards. In S. S. Stevens (Ed.), *Handbook of Experimental Psychology*, New York: Wiley, 1951.

MILLER, N. E. Experiments on motivation. *Science*, 1957, 126, 1271–1278.

MILLER, N. E. Liberalization of basic S-R concepts: Extensions of conflict behavior, motivation, and social learning. In S. Koch (Ed.), *Psychology: A study of a science* (Vol. II). New York: McGraw-Hill, 1959.

MILLER, N. E. Chemical coding of behavior in the brain. *Science*, 1965, 148, 328–338.

MILLER, N. E., BAILEY, C. J., & STEVENSON, J. A. F. Decreased "hunger" but increased food intake resulting from hypothalamic lesions. *Science*, 1950, 112, 256–259.

MILLER, N. E., AND DOLLARD, J. *Social learning and imitation*. New Haven, Conn.: Yale University Press, 1941.

MILLER, W. R., & SELIGMAN, M. E. P. Depression and the perception of reinforcement. *Journal of Abnormal Psychology*, 1973, 82, 62–73.

MILLER, W. R., & SELIGMAN, M. E. P. Depression and learned helplessness in man. *Journal of Abnormal Psychology*, 1975, 84, 228–238.

MILVY, P. (Ed.). *The marathon: Physiological, medical, epidemiological, and psychological studies* (Annals, Vol. 301). New York: New York Academy of Sciences, 1977.

MINEKA, S. The role of fear in theories of avoidance learning, flooding, and extinction. *Psychological Bulletin*, 1979, 86, 985–1010.

MINEKA, S., & GINO, A. Dissociative effects of different types and amounts of non-reinforced CS exposure on avoidance extinction and the CER. *Learning and Motivation*, 1979, 10, 141–160.

MINKOFF, K., BERGMAN, E., BECK, A. T., & BECK, R. Hopelessness, depression and attempted suicide. *American Journal of Psychiatry*, 1973, 130, 455–459.

MINOR, C. A., & NEEL, R. G. The relationship between achievement motive and occupational preference. *Journal of Counseling Psychology*, 1958, 5, 39–43.

MIRSKY, A. F. The influence of sex hormones on social behavior in monkeys. *Journal of Comparative and Physiological Psychology*, 1955, 48, 327–335.

MISCHEL, W. Toward a cognitive social learning reconceptualization of personality. *Psychological Review*, 1973, 80, 252–283.

MITCHELL, G. D. Paternalistic behavior in primates. *Psychological Bulletin*, 1969, 71, 399–417.

MOLOF, M. J. Differences between assaultive and non-assaultive juvenile offenders in the

California Youth Authority. Research Report N. 51, State of California, Department of Youth Authority, February 1967.

MOLTZ, H., LUBIN, M., LEON, M., & NUMAN, M. Hormonal induction of maternal behavior in the ovariectomized nulliparous rat. *Physiology and Behavior*, 1970, 5, 1373–1377.

MOLTZ, H., ROBBINS, D., & PARK, M. Caesarian delivery and the maternal behavior of primiparous and multiparous rats. *Journal of Comparative and Physiological Psychology*, 1966, 61, 455–460.

MONEY, J. Components of eroticism in man: The hormones in relation to sexual morphology and sexual drive. *Journal of Nervous and Mental Diseases*, 1961, 132, 239–248.

MONEY, J. Use of an androgen-depleting hormone in the treatment of male sex offenders. *The Journal of Sex Research*, 1970, 6, 165–172.

MONEY, J., & EHRHARDT, A. *Man and woman, boy and girl.* Baltimore: John Hopkins University Press, 1972.

MONROE, R. R. *Episodic behavioral disorders: A psychodynamic and neurophysiologic analysis.* Cambridge, Mass.: Harvard University Press, 1970.

MONSON, T. C., & SNYDER, M. Actors, observers, and the attribution process: Toward a reconceptualization. *Journal of Experimental Social Psychology*, 1977, 13, 89–111.

MONTAGU, M. F. A. *On being human.* New York: Hawthorn Books, 1966.

MONTI, P. M., & SMITH, N. F. Residual fear of the conditioned stimulus as a function of response prevention after avoidance or classical defensive conditioning in the rat. *Journal of Experimental Psychology: General*, 1976, 105, 148–162.

MOORE, H. T., & GILLILAND, A. R. The measurement of aggression. *Journal of Applied Psychology*, 1921, 5, 97–118.

MOOS, R. The development of a menstrual distress questionnaire. *Psychosomatic Medicine*, 1958, 30, 853–867.

MORDEN, B., MULLINS, R., LEVINE, S., COHEN, H., & DEMENT, W. Effect of REMS deprivation on the mating behavior of male rats. *Psychophysiology*, 1968, 5, 241–242.

MORGAN, C. T., KING, R. A., & ROBINSON, N. M. *Introduction to psychology* (6th ed.), New York: McGraw-Hill, 1979.

MORGAN, S. W., & MAUSER, B. Behavioral and fantasied indications of avoidance of success in men and women. *Journal of Personality*, 1973, 41, 457–470.

MORGANE, J. P. Alterations in feeding and drinking of rats with lesions in the globi pallidi. *American Journal of Physiology*, 1961, 201, 420–428.

MORIARTY, T. Crime, committment, and the responsive bystander: Two field experiments. *Journal of Personality and Social Psychology*, 1975, 31, 370–376.

MORRIS, D. *The naked ape.* London: Constable, 1967.

MORRIS, W. N., & MILLER, R. S. The effects of consensus-breaking and consensus-preempting partners on reduction of conformity. *Journal of Experimental Social Psychology*, 1975, 11, 215–223.

MORRISON, S. D. Control of food intake in cancer cachexia: A challenge and a tool. *Physiology and Behavior*, 1976, 17, 705–714.

MORUZZI, G. & MAGOUN, H. Brainstem reticular formation and activation of the EEG. *Electroencephalography and Clinical Neurophysiology*, 1949, 1, 455–473.

MOSCOVICI, S., & FAUCHEUX, C. Social influence, conformity bias, and the study of active minorities. In L. Berkowitz (Ed.), *Advances in experimental social psychology*, (Vol. 6). New York: Academic Press, 1972.

MOSHER, D. L., & KATZ, H. Pornographic films, male verbal aggression against women and guilt. Unpublished manuscript, summarized in Commission on Obscenity and Pornography. Washington, D. C.: U. S. Government Printing Office, 1970.

MOSS, R. L. Changes in bar-press duration accompanying the estrous cycle. *Journal of Comparative and Physiological Psychology*, 1968, 66, 460–466.

MOWRER, O. H. Two-factor learning theory reconsidered, with special reference to secondary reinforcement and the concept of habit. *Psychological Review*, 1956, 63, 114–128.

MOWRER, O. H., & LAMOREAUX, R. R. Avoidance conditioning and signal duration—a study of secondary motivation and reward. *Psychological Monograph*, 1942, 54 (Whole No. 247).

MOYER, K. E. Kinds of aggression and their physiological basis. *Communications in Behavioral Biology*, 1968, 2, 65–87.

MOYER, K. E. *The physiology of hostility.* Chicago: Markham, 1971.

MOYER, K. E. A physiological model of aggression: Does it have different implications. Presented at the Houston Neurological Symposium on neural basis of violence and aggression, March 1972.

MOYER, K. E. *The psychobiology of aggression.* New York: Harper & Row, 1976.

MUELLER, D., & DONNERSTEIN, D. The effects of humor-induced arousal upon aggressive behavior. *Journal of Research in Personality,* 1977, *11,* 73–82.

MUGNY, G. Negotiations, image of the other and the process of minority influence. *European Journal of Social Psychology,* 1975, *5,* 209–228.

MURPHY, M. R., & SCHNEIDER, G. E. Olfactory bulb removal eliminates mating behavior in the male golden hamster. *Science,* 1970, *167,* 302–304.

MURRAY, H. A. The effect of fear upon estimates of the maliciousness of other personalities. *Journal of Social Psychology,* 1933, *4,* 310–329.

MURRAY, H. A. *Explorations in personality.* New York: Oxford University Press, 1938.

MUSANTE, G. J. The dietary rehabilitation clinic: Evaluative report of a behavioral and dietary treatment of obesity. *Behavior Therapy,* 1976, *7,* 198–204.

MYER, J. S., & WHITE, R. T. Aggressive motivation in the rat. *Animal Behaviour,* 1965, *13,* 430–433.

MYERS, R. E. Role of prefrontal and anterior temporal cortex in social behavior and affect in monkeys. *Acta Neurobiological Experimentalis,* 1972, *32,* 567–579.

MYKYTOWYCZ, R. Territorial markings by rabbits. *Scientific American,* 1968, *218,* 116–126.

NARABAYASKI, H. Stereotaxic amygdalotomy. In B. Eleftheriou (Ed.), *The neurobiology of the amygdala.* New York: Plenum, 1972.

NAUTA, W. J. H. Hypothalamic regulation of sleep in rats: An experimental study. *Journal of Neurophysiology,* 1946, *9,* 285–316.

NEISSER, U. *Cognitive psychology.* New York: Appleton-Century-Crofts, 1966.

NEMETH, C., WACHTLER, J., & ENDICOTT, J. Increasing the size of the minority: Some gains and some loses. *European Journal of Social Psychology,* 1977, *7,* 15–27.

NEWCOMB, T. M. *Personality and social change.* New York: Holt, 1943.

NEWCOMB, T. M. An approach to the study of communicative acts. *Psychological Review,* 1953, *60,* 393–404.

NEWCOMB, T. M. Persistence and repression of changed attitudes: Long-range studies. *Journal of Social Issues,* 1963, *19,* 3–14.

NEWCOMB, T. M. Interpersonal balance. In Abelson, R. P. (Ed.), *Theories of cognitive consistency: A sourcebook.* Chicago: Rand McNally, 1968.

NEWMAN, J. R. Stimulus generalization of an instrumental response under high and low levels of drive. *American Psychologist,* 1955, *10,* 459–461.

NICE, M. M. The role of territory in bird life. *American Midland Naturalist,* 1941, *26,* 441–487.

NISBETT, R. E. Determinants of food intake in human obesity. *Science,* 1968, *159,* 1254–1255.

NISBETT, R. E., CAPUTO, C., LEGANT, P., & MARACEK, J. Behavior as seen by the actor and by the observer. *Journal of Personality and Social Psychology,* 1973, *27,* 154–164.

NISBETT, R. E., & GURWITZ, S. B. Weight, sex, and the eating behavior of human newborns. *Journal of Comparative and Physiological Psychology,* 1970, *73,* 245–253.

NOBACK, C. R., & DEMAREST, J. R. *The human nervous system: Basic principles of neurobiology.* New York: McGraw-Hill, 1975.

NOBACK, C. R., & DEMAREST, J. R. *The nervous system: Introduction and review.* New York: McGraw-Hill, 1972.

NORGREN, R. Gustatory responses in the hypothalamus. *Brain Research,* 1970, *21,* 63–77.

NOVIN, D., & MILLER, N. E. Failure to condition thirst induced by feeding dry food to hungry rats. *Journal of Comparative and Physiological Psychology,* 1962, *55,* 373–374.

OAKLEY, K., & TOATES, F. M. The passage of food through the gut of rats and its uptake of fluid. *Psychonomic Science,* 1969, *16,* 225–226.

O'CONNER, J., & STERN, L. Results of treatment in functional sexual disorders. *New York State Journal of Medicine,* 1972, *72,* 1927.

O'CONNOR, P. The representation of the motive to avoid failure in thematic apperception. Unpublished doctoral dissertation, University of Michigan, 1960.

OLDS, J. Self-stimulation experiments and differentiated reward systems. In H. H. Jasper, L. D. Proctor, R. S. Knighton, W. C. Noshav, & R. T. Costello (Eds.), *Reticular formation of the brain.* Boston: Little, Brown, 1958.

OLDS, J. Hypothalamic substrates of reward. *Physiological Review,* 1962, 42, 554–604.

OLDS, J., & MILNER, P. Positive reinforcement produced by electrical stimulation of the septal area and other regions of the rat brain. *Journal of Comparative and Physiological Psychology,* 1954, 47, 419–427.

OLDS, J., TRAVIS, R. D., & SCHWING, R. C. Topographic organization of hypothalamic self-stimulation functions. *Journal of Comparative and Physiological Psychology,* 1960, 53, 23–32.

OLDS, M. E. Comparative effects of amphetamine, scopolamine, chloriazepoxide and diphenylhydantoin on operant and extinction behavior with brain stimulation and food reward. *Neuropharmacology,* 1970, 9, 519–532.

OLDS, M. E. Effects of intraventricular 6-hydroxydopamine and replacement therapy with norepinephrine, dopamine and serotonin on self-stimulation in the diencephalic and mesencephalic regions in the rat brain. *Brain Research,* 1975, 98, 327–342.

OOMURA, Y., ONO, T., OOGAMA, H., & WAGNER, M. J. Glucose and osmosensitive neurons of the rat hypothalamus. *Nature,* 1969, 222, 282–284.

ORNE, M. T., & HOLLAND, C. C. On the ecological validity of laboratory deceptions. *International Journal of Psychiatry,* 1968, 6, 282–293.

ORNE, M. T., & SCHEIBE, K. E. The contribution of nondeprivation factors in the production of sensory deprivation effects: The psychology of the panic button. *Journal of Abnormal and Social Psychology,* 1964, 68, 3–12.

ORVIS, B. R., CUNNINGHAM, J. D., & KELLEY, H. H. A closer examination of causal inference: The role of consensus, distinctiveness, and consistency information. *Journal of Personality and Social Psychology,* 1975, 32, 605–616.

OSGOOD, C., & TANNENBAUM, P. The principle of congruity in the prediction of attitude change. *Psychological Review,* 1955, 62, 42–55.

OSKAMP, S., & KLEINKE, C. Amount of reward as a variable in the prisoner's dilemma game. *Journal of Personality and Social Psychology,* 1970, 16, 133–140.

OVERMIER, J. B., & SELIGMAN, M. E. P. Effects of inescapable shock upon subsequent escape and avoidance learning. *Journal of Comparative and Physiological Psychology,* 1967, 63, 28–33.

PADILLA, A. M. Effects of prior and interpolated shock exposures on subsequent avoidance learning by goldfish. *Psychological Reports,* 1973, 32, 451–456.

PAGE, M. M., & SCHEIDT, R. J. The elusive weapons effect: Demand awareness, evaluation apprehension, and slightly sophisticated subjects. *Journal of Personality and Social Psychology,* 1971, 20, 304–318.

PALLAK, M. S. The effects of expected shock and relevant or irrelevant dissonance on incidental retention. *Journal of Personality and Social Psychology,* 1970, 14, 271.

PALLAK, M. S., & PITTMAN, T. S. General motivational effects of dissonance arousal. *Journal of Personality and Social Psychology,* 1972, 21, 349–358.

PANCER, S. M., McMULLEN, L. M., KABATOFF, R. A., JOHNSON, K. G., & POND, C. A. Conflict and avoidance in the helping situation. *Journal of Personality and Social Psychology,* 1979, 37, 1406–1411.

PANKSEPP, J. The neural basis of aggression. Unpublished doctoral dissertation, University of Massachusetts, Amherst, 1969.

PANKSEPP, J. Effects of hypothalamic lesions on mouse-killing and shock-induced fighting in rats. *Physiology and Behavior,* 1971, 6, 311–316.

PANKSEPP, J., & TROWILL, J. Electrically induced affective attack from the hypothalamus of the albino rat. *Psychonomic Science,* 1969, 16, 118–119.

PAPAGEORGIS, D., & McGUIRE, W. J. The generality of immunity of persuasion produced by preexposure to weakened counterarguments. *Journal of Abnormal and Social Psychology,* 1961, 62, 481–495.

PARKE, R. D., BERKOWITZ, L., LEYENS, J. P, WEST, S. G., & SEBASTIAN, R. J. Some effects of violent and nonviolent movies on the behavior of juvenile delinquents. In L. Berkowitz (Ed.), *Advances in experimental social psychology* (Vol. 10). New York: Academic Press, 1977.

PATTERSON, G. R. Treatment of children with conduct problems: A review of outcome studies. In S. Feshbach & A. Fraczek (Eds.), *Aggression and behavior changes.* New York: Praeger, 1979.

PATTERSON, G. R., & FLEISCHMAN, M. J. Maintenance of treatment effects: Some considerations concerning family systems and follow-up data. *Behavior Therapy*, 1979, *10*, 168–185.

PATTERSON, G. R., LITTMAN, R. A., & BRICKER, W. Assertive behavior in children: A step toward a theory of aggression. *Monographs of Society for Research in Child Development*, 1967, *32*, 1–43.

PATTY, R. A. Motive to avoid success and instructional set. *Sex Roles*, 1976, *2*, 81–83.

PAUL, G. L. Outcome of systematic desensitization. II. Controlled investigations of individual treatment, technique variations, and current status. In C. M. Franks (Ed.), *Behavior therapy: Appraisal and status.* New York: McGraw-Hill, 1969.

PAVLOV, I. P. *Conditioned reflexes.* G. V. Annep (trans.). London: Oxford University Press, 1927.

PAXINOS, G., & BINDRA, D. Hypothalamic knife cuts: Effects on eating, drinking, irritability, aggression, and copulation in the male rat. *Journal of Comparative and Physiological Psychology*, 1972, *79*, 219–229.

PAYKEL, E. S. Classification of depressed patients: A cluster analysis derived grouping. *British Journal of Psychiatry*, 1971, *118*, 275–288.

PAYNE, R. W. Cognitive abnormalities. In H. J. Eysenck (Ed.), *Handbook of abnormal psychology*, New York: Basic Books. 1961.

PECK, J. W., & NOVIN, D. Evidence that osmoreceptors mediating drinking in rabbits are in the lateral preoptic region. *Journal of Comparative and Physiological Psychology*, 1971, *74*, 134–147.

PEDERSON, F. A., & ROBSON, K. S. Father participation in infancy. *American Journal of Orthopsychiatry*, 1969, *39*, 466–472.

PERIN, C. T. Behavior potentiality as a joint function of amount of training and the degree of hunger at the time of extinction. *Journal of Experimental Psychology*, 1942, *30*, 93–113.

PERLMAN, D., & OSKAMP, S. The effect of picture content and exposure frequency on evaluations of negroes and whites. *Journal of Experimental Social Psychology*, 1971, *7*, 503–514.

PERRIS, L. The separation of bipolar (manic-depressive) from unipolar recurrent depressive psychoses. *Behavioral Neuropsychiatry*, 1969, *1*, 17–25.

PFAFF, D. W., & PFAFFMANN, C. Olfactory and hormonal influences on the basal forebrain on the male rat. *Brain Research*, 1969, *15*, 137–156.

PHARES, E. J. Expectancy changes in skill and chance situations. *Journal of Abnormal and Social Psychology*, 1957, *54*, 339–342.

PHARES, E. J. Internal-external control as a determinant of amount of social influence exerted. *Journal of Personality and Social Psychology*, 1965, *2*, 642–647.

PHOENIX, C. H., SLOB, A. K., & GOY, R. W. Effects of castration and replacement therapy on the sexual behavior of adult male rhesuses. *Journal of Comparative and Physiological Psychology*, 1973, *84*, 472–481.

PILIAVIN, I. M., PILIAVIN, J. A., & RODIN, J. Costs, diffusion, and the stigmatized victim. *Journal of Personality and Social Psychology*, 1975, *32*, 429–438.

PILIAVIN, I. M., RODIN, J., & PILIAVIN, J. A. Good samariatanism: An underground phenomenon? *Journal of Personality and Social Psychology*, 1969, *13*, 289–299.

PILIAVIN, J. A., DOVIDIO, J. F., GAERTNER, S. L., & CLARK, R. D., III. Responsive bystanders: The process of intervention. In J. Grzelak & V. Derlega (Eds.), *Living with other people: Theory and research on cooperation and helping.* New York: Academic Press, 1981.

PILIAVIN, J. A., PILIAVIN, I. M., & TRUDELL, B. Incidental arousal, helping, and diffusion of responsibility. Unpublished manuscript, University of Wisconsin, 1974.

PLOTNICK, R., MIR. D., & DELGADO, J. M. R. Aggression noxiousness and brain stimulation in unrestrained rhesus monkeys. In B. E. Eleftheriou & J. P. Scott (Eds.). *The physiology of aggression and defeat.* New York: Plenum Press, 1971.

PLUTCHIK, R., & AX, A. F. A critique of "Determinants of emotional state" by Schachter and Singer (1962). *Psychophysiology*, 1967, *4*, 79–82.

POTTHARST, B. C. The achievement motive and level of aspiration after experimentally induced success and failure. Unpublished doctoral dissertation, University of Michigan, 1955.

POWLEY, T. L. The ventromedial hypothalamic syndrome, satiety, and a cephalic phase hypothesis. *Psychological Review*, 1977, *84*, 89–126.

Powley, T. L., & Keesey, R. E. Relationship of body weight to the lateral hypothalamic feeding syndrome. *Journal of Comparative and Physiological Psychology*, 1970, 70, 25–36.

Prescott, R. G. W. Estrous cycle in the rat: Effects on self-stimulation behavior. *Science*, 1966, 152, 796–797.

Price, R., Harburg, E., & Newcomb, T. Psychological balance in situations of negative interpersonal attitudes. *Journal of Personality and Social Psychology*, 1966, 3, 265–270.

Prien, R. F., Caffey, E. M., Jr., & Klett, C. J. Prophylactic efficacy of lithium carbonate in manic-depressive illness. *Archives of General Psychiatry*, 1973, 28, 337–341.

Pritchard, R. D., Dunnette, M. D., & Jorgenson, D. O. Effects of perception of equity and inequity on worker performance and satisfaction. *Journal of Applied Psychology*, 1972, 56, 75–94.

Rabbie, J. M. The effects of intergroup competition and cooperation on intra- and intergroup relationships. In J. Grzelak & V. Derlega (Eds.), *Living with other people: Theory and research on cooperation and helping*. New York: Academic Press, 1981.

Rabbie, J. M., & VanOostrum, J. The effects of influence structures upon intra- and intergroup relations. Paper presented to the International Conference on Socialization and Social Influence, Warsaw, Poland, 1977.

Rabbie, J. M., Visser, L., & Vernooij, G. Onzekerheid van omgeving, differentiatie en invloedsverdeling in universitaire instituten. *Nederlands Tijdschrift voor de Psychologie*, 1976, 31, 285–303.

Rachman, S. Sexual fetishism: An experimental analogue. *Psychological Record*, 1966, 16, 293–296.

Rachman, S. & Hodgson, R. Experimentally induced "sexual fetishism": Replication and development. *Psychological Record*, 1968, 18, 25–27.

Rahe, R. H., McKean, J. D., & Arthur, R. J. A. Longitudinal study of life change and illness patterns. *Journal of Psychosomatic Research*, 1967, 10, 355–366.

Rapoport, A., & Chammah, A. *Prisoner's dilemma.* Ann Arbor: University of Michigan Press, 1965.

Raymond, M. J. Case of fetishism treated by aversion therapy. *British Medical Journal*, 1956, 2, 854–857.

Raymond, M. J., & O'Keefee, K. A case of pin-up fetishism treated by aversion conditioning. *British Journal of Psychiatry*, 1965, 111, 579–581.

Raynor, J. O. Relationships between achievement-related motives, future orientation, and academic performance. *Journal of Personality and Social Psychology*, 1970, 15, 28–33.

Raynor, J. O., & Rubin, I. S. Effects of achievement motivation and future orientation on level of performance. *Journal of Personality and Social Psychology*, 1971, 17, 36–41.

Razani, J. Ejaculatory incompetence treated by deconditioning anxiety. *Journal of Behavior Therapy and Experimental Psychiatry*, 1972, 3, 65–67.

Regan, D. T., & Fazio, R. H. On the consistency between attitudes and behavior: Look to the method of attitude formation. *Journal of Experimental Social Psychology*, 1977, 13, 28–45.

Regan, J. W. Cited in J. L. Freeman, D. O. Sears, & J. M. Carlsmith, *Social psychology* (3rd ed.). Englewood Cliffs, N. J.: Prentice-Hall, 1978.

Renner, K. E. Delay of reinforcement: A historical review. *Psychological Bulletin*, 1964, 61, 341–361.

Rescorla, R. A. Probability of shock in the presence and absence of CS in fear conditioning. *Journal of Comparative and Physiological Psychology*, 1968, 66, 1–5.

Rescorla, R. A., & LoLordo, V. M. Inhibition of avoidance behavior. *Journal of Comparative and Physiological Psychology*, 1965, 59, 406–412.

Rescorla, R. A., & Solomon, R. L. Two-process learning theory: Relationships between Pavlovian conditioning and instrumental learning. *Psychological Review*, 1967, 74, 151–182.

Resnick, O. The psychoactive properties of diphenyhydantoin: Experiences with prisoners and juvenile delinquents. *International Journal of Neuropsychiatry*, 1967, Suppl. 2, S20–S47.

Revlis, R., & Moyer, K. E. Maternal aggression: A failure to replicate. *Psychonomic Science*, 1969, 16, 135–136.

Revusky, S. H. & Bedarf, E. W. Association of illness with prior ingestion of novel foods. *Science*, 1967, 155, 219–220.

Revusky, S. H., & Parker, L. A. Aversions to drinking out of a cup and to unflavored water produced by delayed sickness. *Journal of Experimental Psychology: Animal Behavior Processes*, 1976, *2*, 342–353.

Reynolds, W. F., & Pavlik, W. B. Running speed as a function of drive, reward, and habit strength. *American Journal of Psychology*, 1960, *73*, 448–453.

Rheingold, H. L., & Eckerman, C. O. The infant separates himself from his mother. *Science*, 1970, 78–83.

Rheingold, H., & Eckerman, C. O. Departures from the mother. In H. R. Schaffer (Ed.), *The origins of human social relations*. New York: Academic Press, 1971.

Rhine, R. J., & Severance, L. J. Ego-involvement, discrepancy, source credibility, and attitude change. *Journal of Personality and Social Psychology*, 1970, *16*, 175–190.

Ricciuti, H. R., Clark, R. A., & Sadacca, R. *A comparison of need-achievement stories written by experimentally "relaxed" and "achievement-oriented" subjects: Effects obtained with new pictures and revised scoring categories*. Princeton, N. J.: Educational Testing Service, 1954.

Richardson, D., & Scudder, C. L. Effect of olfactory bulbectomy and enucleation on behavior of the mouse. *Psychonomic Science*, 1970, *19*, 277–279.

Richter, C. P. Increased salt appetite in adrenalectomized rats. *American Journal of Psychology*, 1936, *115*, 155–161.

Rimm, D. C., & Masters, J. C. *Behavior therapy: Techniques and empirical findings* (2nd ed.). New York: Academic Press, 1979.

Ritter, B. The use of contact desensitization, demonstration-plus-participation, and demonstration alone in the treatment of acrophobia. *Behavior Research and Therapy*, 1969, *7*, 157–164.

Rizley, R. Depression and distortion in the attribution of causality. *Journal of Abnormal Psychology*, 1978, *87*, 32–48.

Roberts, W. W., & Kiess, H. O. Motivational properties of hypothalamic aggression in cats. *Journal of Comparative and Physiological Psychology*, 1964, *58*, 187–193.

Roberts, W. W., Steinberg, M. I., & Means, L. W. Hypothalamic mechanisms for sexual, aggressive, and other motivational behavior in the opossum, *Didelphus virginiana*. *Journal of Comparative and Physiological Psychology*, 1967, *64*, 1–15.

Robinson, B. W., Alexander, M., & Bowne, G. Dominance reversal resulting from aggressive responses evoked by brain telestimulation. *Physiology and Behavior*, 1969, *4*, 749–752.

Robinson, B. W., & Mishkin, M. Alimentary responses to forebrain stimulation in monkeys. *Experimental Brain Research*, 1968, *4*, 330–336.

Robinson, C. H. The effects of observational learning on sexual behaviors and attitudes in orgasmic dysfunctional women. Unpublished doctoral dissertation, University of Hawaii, 1974.

Robertson, J., & Robertson, J. Young children in brief separation: A fresh look. *Psychoanalytic Study of the Child*, 1971, *26*, 264–315.

Robson, K. S., & Moss, H. A. Patterns and determinants of maternal attachment. *Journal of Pediatrics*, 1970, *77*, 976–985.

Rodgers, W., & Rozin, P. Novel food preferences in thiamine-deficient rats. *Journal of Comparative and Physiological Psychology*, 1966, *61*, 1–4.

Rodin, J. Effects of distraction on the performance of obese and normal subjects. *Journal of Comparative and Physiological Psychology*, 1973, *83*, 68–78.

Rodin, J. The relationship between external responsiveness and the development and maintenance of obesity. In D. Novin, W. Wyrwicka, & G. A. Bray (Eds.), *Hunger: Basic mechanisms and clinical implications*. New York: Raven Press, 1976.

Rodin, J. Density, perceived choice, and response to controllable and uncontrollable outcomes. *Journal of Experimental Social Psychology*, 1976, *12*, 564–587.

Rodin, J. Bidirectional influences of emotionality, stimulus responsivity, and metabolic events in obesity. In J. D. Maser and M. E. P. Seligman (Eds.), *Psychopathology: Experimental models*. San Francisco: Freeman, 1977.

Rodin, J., Elman, D., & Schachter, S. *Obese humans and rats*. Washington, D. C.: Erlbaum/Wiley, 1974.

Rodin, J., & Slochower, J. Externality in nonobese: Effects of environmental responsiveness on weight. *Journal of Personality and Social Psychology*, 1976, *33*, 338–344.

Roeder, F., & Mueller, D. The stereotaxic treatment of pedophilic homosexuality. *German Medical Monthly* (English Language Monthly), 1969, *14*, 265–271.

Roffwarg, H. P., Muzio, J. N., & Dement, W. C. Ontogenetic development of the human sleep-dream cycle. In W. B. Webb (Ed.), *Sleep: An experimental approach.* New York: Macmillan, 1968.

Rogers, C. R. A theory of therapy, personality, and interpersonal relationships. In S. Koch (Ed.), *Psychology: A Study of a Science* (Vol. 3). New York: McGraw-Hill, 1959.

Rokeach, M. *The open and closed mind.* New York: Basic Books, 1960.

Ropartz, P. Mise en evidence du role de l'olfaction dans l'addressivite de la souris. *Rev. Comp. Anim.*, 1967, *2*, 97–102.

Ropartz, P. The relation between olfactory stimulation and aggressive behavior in mice. *Animal Behaviour*, 1968, *16*, 97–100.

Rosanoff, A. J., Handy, L. M., Plesset, I. R., & Brush, S. The etiology of so-called schizophrenic psychoses. *American Journal of Psychiatry*, 1934–1935, *91*, 247–286.

Rose, R. M. Testosterone, aggression, and homosexuality: A review of the literature and implications for future research. In E. J. Sachar (Ed.), *Topics in psychoendocrinology.* New York: Grune & Stratton, 1975.

Rose, R. M., Holaday, J. W., & Bernstein, I. S. Plasma testosterone, dominance rank and aggressive behavior in male rhesus monkeys. *Nature*, 1971, *231*, 366–368.

Rosellini, R., & Seligman, M. E. P. Learned helplessness and escape from frustration. *Journal of Experimental Psychology: Animal Behavior Processes*, 1975, *1*, 149–158.

Rosen, B. & D'Andrade, R. C. The psychosocial origins of achievement motivation. *Sociometry*, 1959, *22*, 185–218.

Rosen, D. H. *Lesbianism: A study of female homosexuality.* Springfield, Ill.: Thomas, 1974.

Rosenbaum, R. M. *A dimensional analysis of the perceived causes of success and failure.* Unpublished doctoral dissertation, University of California, Los Angeles, 1972.

Rosenberg, M. Group size, prior experience, and conformity. *Journal of Abnormal and Social Psychology*, 1961, *63*, 436–437.

Rosenberg, P. H. Management of disturbed adolescents. *Diseases of the Nervous System*, 1966, *27*, 60–61.

Rosenblatt, J. S. Effect of experience on sexual behavior in cats. In F. Beach (Ed.), *Sex and Behavior*, New York: Wiley, 1965.

Rosenblatt, J. S. Nonhormonal basis of maternal behavior in the rat. *Science*, 1967, *156*, 1512–1514.

Rosenblatt, J. S. The development of maternal responsiveness in the rat. *American Journal of Orthopsychiatry*, 1969, *39*, 36–56.

Rosenman, R. H., Brand, R. J., Jenkins, C. D., Friedman, M., Straus, R., & Wurm, M. Coronary heart disease in the Western Collaborative Group Study: Final follow-up experience of 8½ years. *Journal of the American Medical Association*, 1975, *223*, 872–877.

Rosenthal, D. *Genetic theory and abnormal behavior.* New York: McGraw-Hill, 1970.

Ross, A. S. Effect of increased responsibility on bystander intervention: The presence of children. *Journal of Personality and Social Psychology*, 1971, *19*, 306–310.

Ross, L. Cue- and cognition-controlled eating among obese and normal subjects. Unpublished doctoral dissertation, Columbia University, New York, 1969.

Ross, L. The intuitive psychologist and his short-comings: Distortions in the attribution process. In L. Berkowitz (Ed.), *Advances in experimental psychology* (Vol. 10). New York: Academic Press, 1977.

Ross, L., Bierbraver, G., & Hoffman, S. The role of attribution process in conformity and dissent: Resisting the Asch situation. *American Psychologist*, 1976, *31*, 148–156.

Ross, L., Rodin, J., & Zimbardo, P. G. Toward an attribution therapy: The reduction of fear through induced cognitive-emotional misattribution. *Journal of Personality and Social Psychology*, 1969, *12*, 279–288.

Ross, S., Swain, P. B., Zarrow, M. X., & Dennenberg, V. H. Maternal behavior in the rabbit. In H. L. Rheingold (Ed.), *Maternal behavior in mammals.* New York: Wiley, 1963.

ROSVOLD, H. S., MIRSKY, A. F., & PRIBAM, K. H. Influences of amygdalectomy on social behavior in monkeys. *Journal of Comparative and Physiological Psychology*, 1954, *47*, 173–178.

ROTTER, J. B. *Social learning and clinical psychology*. Englewood Cliffs, N. J.: Prentice-Hall, 1954.

ROTH, S., & KUBAL, L. The effects of noncontingent reinforcement on tasks of differing importance: Facilitation and learned helplessness effects. *Journal of Personality and Social Psychology*, 1975, *32*, 680–691.

ROTTER, J. B. Generalized expectancies for internal versus external control of reinforcement. *Psychological Monographs*, 1966, *80* (*1*, Whole No. 609).

ROTTER, J. B. External and internal control. *Psychology Today*, 1971, *5*, 37–42, 58–59.

ROTTON, J., BARRY, T., FREY, J., & SOLER, E. Air pollution and interpersonal attraction. *Journal of Applied Social Psychology*, 1978, *8*, 57–71.

ROUTTENBERG, A. The two-arousal hypothesis: Reticular formation and limbic system. *Psychological Review*, 1968, *75*, 51–80.

ROUTTENBERG, A., & LINDY, J. Effects of the availability of rewarding septal and hypothalamic stimulation on bar-pressing for food under conditions of deprivation. *Journal of Comparative and Physiological Psychology*, 1965, *60*, 158–161.

ROWLAND, N. E., & ANTELMAN, S. M. Stress-induced hyperphagia and obesity in rats: A possible model for understanding human obesity. *Science*, 1976, *191*, 310–312.

ROZIN, P., & KALAT, J. W. Specific hungers and poison avoidance as adaptive specializations of learning. *Psychological Review*, 1971, *78*, 459–486.

ROZKOWSKA, E., & FONBERG, E. Salivary reactions after ventromedial hypothalamic lesions in dogs. *Acta Neurobiologica Experimentalis*, 1973, *33*, 553–562.

RUSH, A. J., BECK, A. T., KOVACS, M., & HOLLON, S. Comparative efficacy of cognitive therapy and pharmacotherapy in the treatment of depressed outpatients. *Cognitive Therapy and Research*, 1977, *1*, 17–37.

RUSSEK, M. Hepatic receptors and the neurophysiological mechanisms controlling feeding behavior. In S. Ehrenpreis (Ed.), *Neurosciences Research* (Vol. 4). New York: Academic Press, 1971.

RUSSELL, R. K., & SIPICH, J. F. Cue-controlled relaxation in the treatment of test anxiety. *Journal of Behavior Therapy and Experimental Psychiatry*, 1973, *4*, 47–49.

RUTTER, M. Parent-child separation: Psychological effects on the children. *Journal of Child Psychology and Psychiatry*, 1971, *12*, 233–260.

RYCKMAN, R. N., & SHERMAN, M. F. Locus of control and student reaction to watergate break-in. *The Journal of Social Psychology*, 1976, *99*, 305–306.

RYSZKOWSKI, L. The space organization of nutria (*Myocastor Coypus*). P. A. Jewell & C. Loizos (Eds.), *Play, exploration, and territory in mammals*. London: Academic Press, 1966.

RYTAND, D. A. Hereditary obesity of yellow mice: A method for the study of obesity. *Proceedings of the Society for Experimental Biology and Medicine*, 1943, *54*, 340–341.

SACKETT, G. D. Monkeys reared in visual isolation with pictures as visual inputs: Evidence for an innate releasing mechanism. *Science*, 1966, *154*, 1468–1472.

SAEGERT, S., SWAP, W. C., & ZAJONC, R. B. Exposure, context, and interpersonal attraction. *Journal of Personality and Social Psychology*, 1973, *25*, 234–242.

SALLOWS, G. Responsiveness of deviant and normal children to naturally occurring parental consequences. Paper presented at Midwestern Psychological Association Convention, Chicago, 1973.

SANFORD, R. N. The effects of abstinence from food upon imaginal processes: A preliminary experiment. *Journal of Psychology*, 1936, *2*, 129–136.

SANFORD, R. N. The effects of abstinence from food upon imaginal processes: A further experiment. *Journal of Psychology*, 1937, *3*, 145–159.

SARASON, S. B., MANDLER, G., & CRAIGHILL, P. G. The effect of differential instructions on anxiety and learning. *Journal of Abnormal and Social Psychology*, 1952, *47*, 561–565.

SARNOFF, I., & ZIMBARDO, P. G. Anxiety, fear, and social affiliation. *Journal of Abnormal and Social Psychology*, 1961, *62*, 356–363.

SASSENRATH, E. N., ROWELL, T. E., & HENDRICKS, A. G. Perimenstrual aggression in groups of female rhesus monkeys. *Journal of Reproduction and Fertility*, 1973, *34*, 411–509.

SAWYER, C. H. Reproductive behavior. In J. Field (Ed.), *Handbook of Physiology. Section 1.: Neurophysiology* (Vol. II). Washington, D. C.: The American Physiological Society, 1960.

SAWYER, C. H., & ROBINSON, B. Separate hypothalamic areas controlling pituitary gonadotrophic function of mating behavior in female cats and rabbits. *Journal of Clinical Endocrinology*, 1956, 16, 914–920.

SAWREY, W. L., CONGER, J. J., & TURRELL, E. S. An experimental investigation of the role of psychological factors in the production of gastric ulcers in rats. *Journal of Comparative and Physiological Psychology*, 1956, 49, 457–461.

SAYLER, A. Effect of antiandrogens on aggressive behavior in gerbil. *Physiology and Behavior*, 1970, 5, 667–671.

SCALAFANI, A. Neural pathways involved in the ventromedial hypothalamic lesion syndrome in the rat. *Journal of Comparative and Physiological Psychology*, 1971, 77, 70–96.

SCALAFANI, A., ARAVICH, P. F., & SCHWARTZ, J. Hypothalamic hyperphagic rats overeat bitter sucrose octa acetate diets but not quinine diets. *Physiology and Behavior*, 1979, 22, 759–766.

SCALAFANI, A., & KLUGE, L. Food motivation and body weight levels in hypothalamic hyperphagic rats: A dual lipostat model of hunger and appetite. *Journal of Comparative and Physiological Psychology*, 1974, 86, 28–46.

SCARBOROUGH, B. B., & GOODSON, F. E. Properties of stimuli associated with strong and weak hunger drive in the rat. *Journal of Genetic Psychology*, 1957, 91, 257–261.

SCARUMELLA, T. J., & BROWN, W. A. Serum testosterone and aggressiveness in hockey players. *Psychosomatic Medicine*, 1978, 40, 262–265.

SCHACHTER, S. Deviation, rejection, and communication. *Journal of Abnormal and Social Psychology*, 1951, 46, 190–208.

SCHACHTER, S. *The psychology of affiliation.* Stanford, Calif. Stanford University Press, 1959.

SCHACHTER, S. Some extraordinary facts about obese humans and rats. *American Psychologist*, 1971, 26, 129–144. (a)

SCHACHTER, S. *Emotion, obesity, and crime.* New York: Academic Press, 1971. (b)

SCHACHTER, S. The interaction of cognitive and physiological determinants of emotional state. In L. Berkowitz (Ed.), *Advances in experimental social psychology* (Vol. I). New York: Academic Press, 1964.

SCHACHTER, S., GOLDMAN, R., & GORDON, A. Effects of fear, food deprivation, and obesity on eating. *Journal of Personality and Social Psychology*, 1968, 10, 91–97.

SCHACHTER, S., & RODIN, J. (Eds.). *Obese humans and rats.* Washington, D. C.: Erlbaum/Wiley, 1974.

SCHACHTER, S., & SINGER, J. E. Cognitive, social and physiological determinants of emotional state. *Psychological Review*, 1962, 69, 379–399.

SCHAFFER, H. R., & EMERSON, P. E. The development of social attachments in infancy. *Monographs Social Research in Child Development*, 1964, 29, 1–77.

SCHALLER, G. B. *The mountain gorilla: Ecology and behavior.* Chicago: University of Chicago Press, 1963.

SCHALLER, G. B. Life with the king of beasts. *National Geographic*, 1969, 135, 499–519.

SCHENKEL, R. Play, exploration, and territoriality in the wild lion. In P.A. Jewell & C. Loizos (Eds.), *Play, exploration, and territory in mammals.* London: Academic Press, 1966.

SCHENKEL, R., & SCHENKEL-HILLIGER, I. *Ecology and behavior of the black rhinoceros.* Hamburg: Parey, 1969.

SCHILL, T. R. Aggression and blood pressure responses of high- and low-guilt subjects following frustration. *Journal of Counseling and Clinical Psychology*, 1972, 38, 461.

SCHLEGAL, R. P., CRAWFORD, C. A., & SANBORN, M. D. Correspondence and mediational properties of the Fishbein model: An application to adolescent alcohol use. *Journal of Experimental Social Psychology*, 1977, 13, 421–430.

SCHMIDENBERG, M. Some observations on individual reactions to air raids. *International Journal of Psychoanalysis*, 1942, 23, 146–176.

SCHMITT, M. Influences of hepatic portal receptors on hypothalamic feeding and satiety centers. *American Journal of Physiology*, 1973, 225, 1089–1095.

SCHNEIRLA, T. C., ROSENBLATT, J. S., & TOBACH, E. *Maternal behavior in mammals.* New York: Wiley, 1963.

SCHNURR, R. Localization of septal rage syndrome in Long Evans rats. *Journal of Comparative and Physiological Psychology,* 1972, *81,* 291–296.

SCHREINER, L., & KLING, A. Behavioral changes following rhinencephalic injury in the cat. *Journal of Neurophysiology,* 1953, *16,* 643–658. (a)

SCHREINER, L., & KLING, A. Rhinencephalon and behavior. *American Journal of Physiology,* 1953, *16,* 643–658. (b)

SCHREINER, L., & KLING, A. Rhinencephalon and behavior. *American Journal of Physiology,* 1956, *184,* 486–490.

SCHUBOT, E. D. The influence of hypnotic and muscular relaxation in systematic desensitization. Unpublished doctoral dissertation, Stanford University, California, 1966.

SCHWARTZ, B., & WILLIAMS, D. R. Two different kinds of key peck in the pigeon: Some properties of responses maintained by negative and positive response-reinforcer contingencies. *Journal of the Experimental Analysis of Behavior,* 1972, *18,* 201–216.

SCHWARTZ, G. Biofeedback as therapy. *American Psychologist,* 1973, *28,* 666–673.

SCHWARTZ, M. Instrumental and consummatory measures of sexual capacity in the male rat. *Journal of Comparative and Physiological Psychology,* 1956, *49,* 328–333.

SCHWARTZ, M., & BEACH, F. A. Effect of adrenalectomy upon mating behavior in male dogs. *American Psychology,* 1954, *9,* 467–468.

SCHWARTZ, S. H. A self-based motivational model of helping. In J. Grzelak & V. Derlega (Eds.), *Living with other people: Theory and research on cooperation and helping.* New York: Academic Press, 1981.

SCHWARTZ, S. H., & CLAUSEN, G. T. Responsibility, norms, and helping in an emergency. *Journal of Personality and Social Psychology,* 1970, *16,* 299–310.

SCOTT, J. P. *Aggression.* Chicago: University of Chicago Press, 1958.

SCOTT, W. Attitude change through reward of verbal behavior. *Journal of Abnormal and Social Psychology,* 1957, *55,* 72–75.

SEARS, R. R. Development of gender role. In F. A. Beach (Ed.), *Sex and behavior.* New York: Wiley, 1965.

SEAY, B. M., HANSEN, E. W., & HARLOW, H. F. Mother-infant separation in monkeys. *Journal of Child Psychology and Psychiatry,* 1962, *3,* 123–132.

SEAY, B. M., & HARLOW, H. F. Maternal separation in the rhesus monkey. *Journal of Nervous and Mental Disease,* 1965, *140,* 434–441.

SEEMAN, M., & EVANS, J. W. Alienation and learning in a hospital setting. *America Sociological Review,* 1962, *27,* 772–783.

SELIGMAN, C., BUSH, M., & KIRSCH, K. Relationship between compliance in the foot-in-the-door paradiam and size of the first request. *Journal of Personality and Social Psychology,* 1976, *33,* 517–520.

SELIGMAN, M. E. P. On the generality of the laws of learning. *Psychological Review,* 1970, *77,* 406–418.

SELIGMAN, M. E. P. *Helplessness: On depression, development, and death.* San Francisco: Freeman, 1975.

SELIGMAN, M. E. P., & GROVES, D. Non-transient learned helplessness. *Psychonomic Science,* 1970, *19,* 191–192.

SELIGMAN, M. E. P., & MAIER, S. F. Failure to escape traumatic shock. *Journal of Experimental Psychology,* 1967, *74,* 1–9.

SELIGMAN, M. E. P., ROSELLINI, R. A., & KOZAK, M. Learned helplessness in the rat: Reversibility, time course, and immunization. *Journal of Comparative and Physiological Psychology,* 1975, *88,* 542–547.

SELYE, H. *The stress of life.* New York: McGraw-Hill, 1956.

SEM-JACOBSON, C. W. *Depth-electrographic stimulation of the human brain and behavior: From fourteen years of studies and treatment of Parkinson's disease and mental disorders with implanted electrodes.* Springfield, Ill.: Thomas, 1968.

SEMMEL, A., PETERSON, C., ABRAMSON, L., METALSKY, G., & SELIGMAN, M. E. P. Predicting depressive symptoms from attributional style and failure. Unpublished manuscript, University of Pennsylvania, 1981.

SEWARD, J. P. Aggressive behavior in the rat: I. General characteristics; age and sex differences. *Journal of Comparative Psychology*, 1945, 38, 175–197.

SEWARD, J. P., & HUMPHREY, G. L. Avoidance learning as a function of pretraining in the cat. *Journal of Comparative and Physiological Psychology*, 1967, 63, 338–341.

SHAFFER, D. R., ROGEL, M., & HENDRICK, C. Intervention in the library: The effect of increased responsibility on bystanders' willingness to prevent a theft. *Journal of Applied Psychology*, 1975, 5, 303–319.

SHANAB, M. E., & VAHYA, K. A. A behavioral study of obedience in children. *Journal of Personality and Social Psychology*, 1977, 35, 530–536.

SHARMA, K. N., ANAND, B. K., DUA, S., & SINGH, D. Role of stomach in regulation of activities of hypothalamic feeding centers. *American Journal of Physiology*, 1961, 201, 593–598.

SHEALY, C. & PEALE, J. Studies on amygdaloid nucleus of cat. *Journal of Neurophysiology*, 1957, 20, 125–139.

SHEARD, M. H. Behavioral effects of *p*-chlorophenylalanine in rats: Inhibition by lithium. *Communications in Behavioral Biology*, 1970, 5, 71–73. (a)

SHEARD, M. H. The effect of lithium on foot shock aggression in rats. *Nature*, 1970, 228, 284–285. (b)

SHEARD, M. H. Effect of lithium on human aggression. *Nature*, 1971, 230, 113–114.

SHEARD, M. H. Testosterone and aggression. In M. Sandler (Ed.), *Psychopharmacology of aggression.* New York: Raven Press, 1979.

SHEFFIELD, F. D. New evidence on the drive-induction theory of reinforcement. In R. N. Haber (Ed.), *Current research in motivation.* New York: Holt, 1966.

SHEFFIELD, F. D., & ROBY, T. B. Reward value of a non-nutritive sweet taste. *Journal of Comparative and Physiological Psychology*, 1950, 43, 471–481.

SHERIDAN, C. L., & KING, R. G. Obedience to authority with an authentic victim. *Proceedings, Eighth Annual Convention, American Psychological Association*, Honolulu, 1972. Washington, D. C.: American Psychological Association, 1972.

SHERIF, M. A study of some factors in perception. *Archives of Psychology*, 1935, No. 187.

SHERIF, M. *The psychology of social norms.* New York: Harper & Row, 1936.

SHERIF, M., HARVEY, O. J., WHITE, B. J., HOOD, W. R., & SHERIF, C. W. Experimental study of positive and negative intergroup attitudes between experimentally produced groups. Robber's Cove Study, Norman, Okla.: University of Oklahoma, 1954.

SHERIF, M., & SHERIF, C. W. *An outline of social psychology* (Rev. ed.), New York: Harper, 1956.

SHERMAN, S. J. Effects of choice and incentive on attitude change in a discrepant behavior situation. *Journal of Personality and Social Psychology*, 1970, 15, 245–252. (a)

SHERMAN, S. J. Attitudinal effects of unforseen consequences. *Journal of Personality and Social Psychology*, 1970, 16, 510–520. (b)

SHERRINGTON, C. S. *Integrative action of the nervous system.* New Haven, Conn.: Yale University Press, 1906.

SHERROD, D. R. Crowding, perceived control, and behavioral aftereffects. *Journal of Applied Social Psychology*, 1974, 2, 171–186.

SHUNTICH, R. J., & TAYLOR, S. P. The effects of alcohol on human physical aggression. *Journal of Experimental Research in Personality*, 1972, 6, 34–38.

SIEGEL, S. Evidence from rats that morphine tolerance is a learned response. *Journal of Comparative and Physiological Psychology*, 1975, 89, 498–506.

SIEGEL, S. Morphine tolerance acquisition as an associative process. *Journal of Experimental Psychology: Animal Behavior Processes*, 1977, 3, 1–13.

SIGG, E. B. Relationship of aggressive behaviour to adrenal and gonadal function in male mice. In S. Garattini & E. B. Sigg (Eds.), *Aggressive behavior,* New York: Wiley, 1969.

SILVERMAN, I. Self-esteem and differential responsiveness to success and failure. *Journal of Applied Social Psychology*, 1964, 69, 115–119.

SIMONS, L. S., FINN, M. R., LAYTON, J. F., & TURNER, C. W. Cited in C. W. Turner, L. S.

Simons, L. Berkowitz, & A. Frodi. The stimulating and inhibiting effects of weapons on aggressive behavior. *Aggressive Behavior*, 1977, *3*, 355–378.

SINGER, J. Hypothalamic control of male and female sexual behavior in female rats. *Journal of Comparative and Physiological Psychology*, 1968, 66, 738–742.

SINGER, J. E., BRUSH, C., & LUBLIN, S. D. Some aspects of deindividuation: Identification and conformity. *Journal of Experimental Social Psychology*, 1965, *1*, 356–378.

SINGH, D. Effects of preoperative training on food motivated behavior of hypothalamic hyperphagic rats. *Journal of Comparative and Physiological Psychology*, 1973, 84, 47–52.

SINGH, D., & SIKES, S. Role of past experience on food motivated behavior of obese humans. *Journal of Comparative and Physiological Psychology*, 1974, 86, 503–508.

SKINNER, B. F. *The behavior of organisms.* New York: Appleton, 1938.

SKINNER, B. F. Superstition in the pigeon. *Journal of Experimental Psychology*, 1948, 38, 168–172.

SKINNER, B. F. *Science and human behavior.* New York: Macmillan, 1953.

SLATER, E. *Psychotic and neurotic illness in twins.* London: Her Majesty's Stationary Office, 1953.

SMITH, G. P., & EPSTEIN, A. N. Increased feeding in response to decreased glucose utilization in the rat and monkey. *American Journal of Physiology*, 1969, *217*, 1083–1087.

SMITH, R. K. Effects of two target strategies upon aggressive responding in children. Unpublished Master's thesis, University of Illinois, Chicago Circle, 1977.

SMITH, R. R., & CREDLAND, P. F. Menstrual and copulatory cycles in the gelada baboon. *Theropithecus gelada.* In J. S. Olney (Ed.), *International Zoological Yearbook*, London: Zoological Society, 1977.

SMITH, W., & ANDERSON, A. Threats, communication, and bargaining. *Journal of Personality and Social Psychology*, 1975, *32*, 76–82.

SMOTHERMAN, W. P., HENNESSEY, J. W., & LEVINE, S. Plasma corticosterone levels as an index of the strength of illness-induced taste aversion. *Physiology and Behavior*, 1976, *17*, 903–908.

SNOWDEN, C. T. Motivation, regulation and the control of meal parameters with oral and intragastric feeding. *Journal of Comparative and Physiological Psychology*, 1969, 69, 91–100.

SNYDER, A., MISCHEL, W., & LOTT, B. Value, information, and conformity behavior. *Journal of Personality*, 1960, *28*, 333–342.

SNYDER, M., & CUNNINGHAM, M. R. To comply or not comply: Testing the self-perception explanation of the "foot-in-the door" phenomenon. *Journal of Personality and Social Psychology*, 1975, *31*, 64–67.

SNYDER, M., & SWANN, W. B., JR. Behavioral confirmation in social interaction: From social perception to social reality. *Journal of Experimental Social Psychology*, 1976, *14*, 148–162.

SNYDER, S. H. Catecholamines as mediators of drug effects in schizophrenia. In F. D. Schmitt & F. G. Worden (Eds.), *The neurosciences: Third study program.* Cambridge, Mass.: M. I. T. Press, 1974.

SNYDER, S. H., & SIMANTOV, R. The opiate receptor and ipioid peptides. *Journal of Neurochemistry*, 1977, *28*, 13–20.

SOLOMON, R. L. An opponent-process theory of motivation: IV. The affective dynamics of addiction. In J. D. Moser & M. E. P. Seligman (Eds.), *Psychopathology: Experimental models.* San Francisco: Freeman, 1977.

SOLOMON, R. L. The opponent-process theory of acquired motivation: The costs of pleasure and the benefits of pain. *American Psychologist*, 1980, *35*, 691–712.

SOLOMON, R. L., & CORBIT, J. D. An opponent process theory of motivation: Temporal dynamics of affect. *Psychological Review*, 1974, *81*, 119–145.

SOLOMON, R. L., KAMIN, L. J., & WYNNE, L. C. Traumatic avoidance learning: The outcomes of several extinction procedures with dogs. *Journal of Abnormal and Social Psychology*, 1953, 48, 291–302.

SOLOMON, R. L., & WYNNE, L. C. Traumatic avoidance learning: The principles of anxiety conservation and partial irreversibility. *Psychological Review*, 1954, 62, 353–385.

SOLOMON, S. S., ENSINCK, J. W., & WILLIAMS, R. H. Effect of starvation on plasma immunoreactive insulin and nonsuppressible insulin-like activity in normal and obese humans. *Metabolism*, 1968, *17*, 528.

SORENSEN, R. C. *Adolescent sexuality in contemporary America.* New York: World, 1973.

SPEER, F. The allergic tension-fatigue syndrome. *Pediatric Clinic of North America,* 1954, *1,* 1029–1037.

SPEER, F. The allergic tension-fatigue syndrome. In F. Speer (Ed.), *Allergy of the nervous system.* Springfield, Ill.: Thomas, 1970.

SPEISMAN, J. C., LAZARUS, R. S., MORDKOFF, A. M., & DAVIDSON, L. A. Experimental reduction of stress based on ego-defense theory. *Journal of Abnormal and Social Psychology,* 1964, *68,* 367–380.

SPENCE, J. T. The TAT and attitudes toward achievement in women: A new look at the motive to avoid success and a new method of measurement. *Journal of Consulting and Clinical Psychology,* 1974, *42,* 427–437.

SPENCE, K. W. *Behavior theory and conditioning.* New Haven, Conn.: Yale University Press, 1956.

SPENCE, K. W., & TAYLOR, J. A. Anxiety and strength of the US as a determinant of eyelid conditioning. *Journal of Experimental Psychology,* 1951, *42,* 183–188.

SPIELBERGER, C. D., & KATZENMEYER, W. C. Manifest anxiety, intelligence, and college grades. *Journal of Consulting Psychology,* 1959, *23,* 278.

SPITZ, R. A. Hospitalism: An inquiry into the genesis of psychiatric conditioning in early childhood. In D. Fenschel et al. (Eds.), *Psychoanalytic studies of the child* (Vol. I). New York: International Universities Press, 1945.

SPITZ, R. A. Anaclitic depression. In D. Fenschel et al. (Eds.), *The psychoanalytic study of the child* (Vol. III). New York: International Universities Press, 1946.

STAATS, A. W. A learning-behavior theory: A basis for unity in behavioral-social science. In A. R. Gilgen (Ed.), *Contemporary scientific psychology.* New York: Academic Press, 1970.

STAATS, A. W., HIGA, W. A., & REID, I. E. *Names as reinforcers: The social value of verbal stimuli* (Technical Report No. 9 under office of Naval Research). Honolulu: University of Hawaii, 1970.

STAATS, A. W., MINKE, K. A., MARTIN, C. H., & HIGA, W. R. Deprivation-satiation and strength of attitude conditioning: A test of attitude-reinforcer-discriminative theory. *Journal of Personality and Social Psychology,* 1972, *24,* 178–185.

STAATS, A. W., & STAATS, C. K. Attitudes established by classical conditioning. *Journal of Abnormal and Social Psychology,* 1958, *57,* 37–40.

STAATS, A. W., STAATS, C. K., & BIGGS, D. Meaning of verbal stimuli changed by conditioning. *American Journal of Psychology,* 1958, *71,* 429–431.

STAATS, C. K., & STAATS, A. W. Meaning established by classical conditioning. *Journal of Experimental Psychology,* 1957, *54,* 74–80.

STACHNIK, T. J., ULRICH, R. E., & MABRY, J. H. Reinforcement of intra- and interspecies aggression with intracranial stimulation. *American Zoologist,* 1966, *6,* 663–668. (a)

STACHNIK, T. J., ULRICH, R. E., & MABRY, J. H. Reinforcement of aggression through intracranial stimulation. *Psychonomic Science,* 1966, *5,* 101–102. (b)

STACHOWIAK, J., & MOSS, C. Hypnotic alterations of social attitudes. *Journal of Personality and Social Psychology,* 1965, *2,* 77–83.

STADDON, J. E. R., & AYRES, S. L. Sequential and temporal properties of behavior induced by a schedule of periodic food delivery. *Behaviour,* 1975, *54,* 26–49.

STADDON, J. E. R. & SIMMELHAG, V. L. The "superstition" experiment: A reexamination of its implications for the principles of adaptive behavior. *Psychological Review,* 1971, *78,* 3–43.

STARK, P., & BOYD, E. S. Effects of cholinergic drugs on hypothalamic self-stimulation response rates of dogs. *American Journal of Physiology,* 1963, *205,* 745–748.

STARR, M. D. An opponent process theory of motivation: VI. Time and intensity variables in the development of separation-induced distress calling in ducklings. *Journal of Experimental Psychology: Animal Behavior Processes,* 1978, *4,* 338–355.

STAUB, E. Predicting prosocial behavior: A model for specifying the nature of personality-situation interaction. In L. A. Pervin & M. Lewis (Eds.), *Perspectives in Interactional Psychology.* New York: Plenum Press, 1978.

STEA, D. Space, territory, and human movements. *Landscape,* 1965, *15,* 13–16.

STEIN, L. Chemistry of purposive behavior. In J. T. Tapp (Ed.), *Reinforcement and Behavior.* New York: Academic Press, 1969.

STEIN, L., & WISE, C. D. Release of norepinephrine from the hypothalamus and amygdala by rewarding medial forebrain bundle stimulation and amphetamine. *Journal of Comparative and Physiological Psychology,* 1969, 67, 189–198.

STEIN, L., & WISE, C. D. Possible etiology of schizophrenia: Progressive damage to the noradrenergic reward system of 6-hydroxydopamine. *Science,* 1971, 1032–1036.

STEIN, L. & WISE, C. D. Amphetamine and noradrenergic reward pathways. In E. Usdin & S. H. Snyder (Eds.), Frontiers in catechoamine research. New York: Pergamon Press, 1973.

STEIN, L. & WISE, C. D. Serotonin and behavioral inhibition. In E. Costa & P. Greengard (Eds.), *Advances in biochemical psychopharmacology.* New York: Raven Press, 1974.

STEPHAN, W., BERSCHEID, E. D., & WALSTER, E. Sexual arousal and heterosexual perception. *Journal of Personality and Social Psychology,* 1971, 20, 93–101.

STEPHENS, J. H., & SHAFFER, J. W. A controlled study of the effects of diphenylhydantoin on anxiety, irritabilitym, and anger in neurotic outpatients. *Psychopharmacologia,* 1970, 17, 169–181.

STERLING, B. The effect of anger, ambiguity, and arousal on helping behavior. Unpublished doctoral dissertation, University of Delaware, 1977.

STOLUROW, L. M. Rodent behavior in the presence of barriers: II. The metabolic maintenance method; a technique for caloric drive control and manipulation. *Journal of Genetic Psychology,* 1951, 79, 289–335.

STOYVA, J. Self-regulation and the stress-related disorders: A perspective on biofeedback. In D. Mostofsky (Ed.) *Behavior control and modification of physiological activity.* Englewood Cliffs, N. J.: Prentice-Hall, 1976.

STRICKER, E. M., ROWLAND, N., SALLER, C. F., & FRIEDMAN, M. I. Homeostasis during hypoglycemia: Central control of adrenal secretion and peripheral control of feeding. *Science,* 1977, 196, 79–81.

STRICKER, L. G., MESSICK, S., & JACKSON, D. N. Conformity, anticonformity, and independence: Their dimensionality and generality. *Journal of Personality and Social Psychology,* 1970, 16, 494–507.

STRONGMAN, K., & CHAMPNESS, B. G. Dominance hierarchies and conflict in eye contact. *Acta Psychologica,* 1968, 28, 376–386.

STRUBBE, J. H., & STEFFENS, A. B. Rapid insulin release after ingestion of a meal in the unanesthestized rat. *American Journal of Physiology,* 1975, 229, 1019–1022.

STUART, R. B. Behavior control of eating. *Behaviour Research and Therapy,* 1967, 5, 357–365.

STUNKARD, A. J., VAN ITALLIE, T. B., & REIS, B. B. The mechanism of satiety: Effect of glucagon on gastric hunger contractions in man. *Proceedings for Society of Experimental Biology and Medicine,* 1955, 89, 258–261.

STÜRÜP, G. K. Correctional treatment and the criminal sexual offender. *Canadian Journal of Correction,* 1961, 3, 250–265.

STÜRÜP, G. K. Castration: The total treatment on sexual behaviors. In H. L. P. Resnick & M. E. Wolfgang (Eds.) *Treatment of the sex offender.* Boston: Little, Brown, 1972.

SUCHOWSKY, G. K., PEGRESSI, L., & BONSIGUORI, A. The effect of steroids on aggressive behavior in isolated male mice. In S. Garattini & E. B. Sigg (Eds.), *Aggressive behavior.* New York: Wiley, 1969.

SUCHOWSKY, G. K., PEGRESSI, L., & BONSIGNORI, A. Steroids and aggressive behavior in isolated male and female mice. *Psychopharmacologia,* 1971, 21, 32–38.

SUEDFELD, P., BOCHNER, S., & WNEK, D. Helper-sufferer similarity and a specific request for help: Bystander intervention during a peace demonstration. *Journal of Applied Social Psychology,* 1972, 2, 17–23.

SULLIVAN, H. S. *Conceptions of modern psychiatry.* Washington, D. C.: William Alanson White Psychiatric Foundation, 1947.

SULLIVAN, H. S. *The interpersonal theory of psychiatry.* New York: Norton, 1953.

SUNDSTROM, E. A study of crowding: Effects of intrusion, goal blocking, and density on self-reported stress, self-disclosure, and nonverbal behavior. Unpublished doctoral dissertation, University of Utah, 1973.

SUOMI, S. J. Repititive peer separation of young monkeys: Effects of vertical chamber confinement during separation. *Journal of Abnormal Psychology*, 1973, 83, 1–10.

SUOMI, S. J. Factors affecting responses to social separation in rhesus monkeys. In G. Serban & A. Kling (Eds.), *Animal models of human psychobiology*. New York: Plenum Press, 1976.

SUOMI, S. J., COLLINS, M. L., & HARLOW, H. F. Effects of permanent separation from mother on infant monkeys. *Developmental Psychology*, 1973, 9, 376–384.

SUOMI, S. J., EISELE, C. J., GRADY, S. A., & HARLOW, H. F. Social preferences of monkeys reared in an enriched laboratory environment. *Journal of Abnormal Psychology*, 1975, 84, 576–578.

SUOMI, S. J., & HARLOW, H. F. Effects of differential removal from group on social development of rhesus monkeys. *Journal of Child Psychology and Psychiatry*, 1975, 16, 149–158.

SUOMI, S. J., & HARLOW, H. F. Production and alleviation of depressive behaviors in monkeys. In J. D. Maser & M. E. P. Seligman (Eds.), *Psychopathology: Experimental Models*. San Francisco: Freeman, 1977.

SUOMI, S. J., HARLOW, H. F., & DOMEK, C. J. Effects of repetitive infant-infant separation of young monkeys. *Journal of Abnormal Psychology*, 1970, 76, 161–172.

SVARE, B. B., & GANDELMAN, R. Postpartum aggression in mice: Experiental and environmental factors. *Hormones and Behavior*, 1973, 4, 323–334.

SVARE, B. B., & LESHNER, A. I. The adrenals and testis: Two separate systems affecting aggression. Paper presented at Eastern Psychological Association Meeting, Boston, 1972.

SWEET, W. H., ERVIN, F., & MARK, V. H. The relationship of violent behavior to focal cerebral disease. In S. Garattini & E. B. Sigg (Eds.), *Aggressive Behavior*. New York: Wiley, 1969.

SWENSON, L. C. *Theories of learning*. Belmont, Calif.: Wadsworth, 1980.

TANNENBAUM, G. A., PAXINOS, G., & BINDRA, D. Metabolic and endocrine aspects of the ventromedial hypothalamic syndrome in the rat. *Journal of Comparative and Physiological Psychology*, 1974, 86, 404–413.

TANNENBAUM, P., MACAULEY, J., & NORRIS, E. Principle of congruity and reduction of persuasion. *Journal of Personality and Social Psychology*, 1966, 3, 233–238.

TANNENBAUM, P., & NORRIS, E. Effects of combining congruity and reduction of persuasion. *Sociometry*, 1965, 28, 145–157.

TARPY, R. M. *Basic principles of learning*. Glenview, Ill.: Scott, Foresman, 1975.

TAULBEE, F. S., & WRIGHT, W. H. A psycho social-behavioral model for therapeutic intervention. In C. D. Spielberger (Ed.), *Current topics in clinical and community psychology* (Vol. III). New York: Academic Press, 1971

TAYLOR, D. A. The development of interpersonal relationships: Social penetration processes. *Journal of Social Psychology*, 1968, 75, 79–90.

TAYLOR, F. G., & MARSHALL, W. L. Experimental analysis of a cognitive behavioral therapy for depression. *Cognitive Therapy and Research*, 1977, 1, 59–72.

TAYLOR, J. A. Drive theory and manifest anxiety. *Psychological Bulletin*, 1956, 53, 303–320.

TAYLOR, J. C. Home range and agonistic behavior in the grey squirrel. In P. A. Jewell & C. Loizos (Eds.), *Play, exploration, and territory in mammals*. New York: Academic Press, 1966.

TAYLOR, S. P., & GAMMON, C. B. The effect of type and dose of alcohol on human physical aggression. *Journal of Personality and Social Psychology*, 1975, 32, 169–175.

TAYLOR, S. P., GAMMON, C. B., & CAPASSO, D. R. Aggression as a function of the interaction of alcohol and threat. *Journal of Personality and Social Psychology*, 1976, 34, 938–941.

TEEL, K. S. Habit strength as a function of motivation during learning. *Journal of Comparative and Physiological Psychology*, 1952, 45, 188–191.

TEITELBAUM, P. Sensory control of hypothalamic hyperphagia. *Journal of Comparative and Physiological Psychology*, 1955, 48, 156–163.

TEITELBAUM, P., CHENG, M. F., & ROZIN, P. Stages of recovery and development of lateral hypothalamic control of food and water intake. *Annals of the New York Academy of Sciences*, 1969, 157, 848–860.

TEITELBAUM, P. & EPSTEIN, A. N. The lateral hypothalamic syndrome: Recovery of feeding and drinking after lateral hypothalamic lesions. *Psychological Review*, 1962, 69, 74–90.

TENNEN, H., & ELLER, S. J. Attributional components of learned helplessness and facilitation. *Journal of Personality and Social Psychology*, 1977, 35, 265–271.

TERKEL, J., & ROSENBLATT, J. S. Maternal behavior induced by maternal blood plasma injected into virgin rats. *Journal of Comparative and Physiological Psychology*, 1968, 65, 479–482.

TERZIAN, H. & DALLEORE, G. D. Syndrome of Kluver and Bucy reproduced in man by bilateral removal of the temporal lobes. *Neurology*, 1955, 5, 378–380.

THIBAUT, J. W., & STRICKLAND, L. H. Psychological set and social conformity. *Journal of Personality*, 1965, 25, 115–129.

THOMAS, E., & BALTER, A. L. Learned helplessness: Amelioration of symptoms by cholinergic blockage of the septum. Cited in M. E. P. Seligman, *Helplessness*. San Francisco: Freeman, 1975.

THOMAS, E., & DEWALD, L. Experimental neurosis: Neuropsychological analysis. In J. D. Maser & M. E. P. Seligman (Eds.), *Psychopathology: Experimental models*. San Francisco: Freeman, 1977.

THOMKA, M. L., & ROSELLINI, R. A. Frustration and the production of schedule-induced polydipsia. *Animal Learning and Behavior*, 1975, 3, 380–384.

THOMPSON, T., & BLOOM, W. Aggressive behavior and extinction induced response rate increase. *Psychonomic Science*, 1966, 5, 335–336.

THORNDIKE, E. L. Animal intelligence: An experimental study of the associative processes in animals. *Psychological Review Monograph Supplement*, 1898, 2, 1–109.

THORNDIKE, E. L. *The fundamentals of learning*. New York: Teachers College, Columbia University Press, 1932.

THURSTONE, L. L. Comment. *American Journal of Sociology*, 1946, 52, 39–40.

TILKER, H. A. Social responsible behavior as a function of observer responsibility and victim feedback. *Journal of Personality and Social Psychology*, 1970, 14, 95–100.

TINBERGEN, N. Social releasers and the experimental method required for their study. *Wilson Bulletin*, 1948, 60, 6–52.

TINBERGEN, N. *The study of instinct*. Oxford: Oxford University Press, 1951.

TINBERGEN, N. *Tiere untereinander*. Berlin: Parey, 1955.

TINBERGEN, N., & VAN IERSEL, J. J. A. Displacement reactions in the three-spined stickleback. *Behaviour*, 1947, 1, 56–63.

TINKLENBERG, J. R., & STILLMAN, R. C. Drug use and violence. In D. N. Daniels, M. F. Gilula, & F. M. Ochberg (Eds.), *Violence and the struggle for existence*. Boston: Little, Brown, 1970.

TINKLEPAUGH, O. L. An experimental study of representative factors in monkeys. *Journal of Comparative Psychology*, 1928, 8, 197–236.

TINKLEPAUGH, O. L. Fur-picking in monkeys as an act of adornment. *Journal of Mammalogy*, 1931, 12, 430–431.

TOLMAN, E. C. *Purposive behavior in animals and men*. New York: Century, 1932.

TOLMAN, E. C. Principles of purposive behavior. In S. Koch (Ed.), *Psychology: A study of science* (Vol. II). New York: McGraw-Hill, 1959.

TOLMAN, E. C., & HONZIK, C. H. "Insight" in rats. *University of California Publications in Psychology*, 1930, 4, 215–232. (a)

TOLMAN, E. C., & HONZIK, C. H. Degrees of hunger; reward and nonreward; and maze learning in rats. *University of California Publications in Psychology*, 1930, 4, 241–256. (b)

TOLMAN, E. C., RITCHIE, B. F., & KALISH, D. Studies of spatial learning: II. Place learning versus response learning. *Journal of Experimental Psychology*, 1946, 36, 221–229.

TRAPOLD, M. A., CARLSON, J. G., & MYERS, W. A. The effects of noncontingent fixed- and variable-interval reinforcement on subsequent acquisition of the fixed-interval scallop. *Psychonomic Science*, 1965, 2, 261–262.

TRAPOLD, M. A., & WINOKUR, S. Transfer from classical conditioning and extinction to acquisition, extinction, and stimulus generalization of a positively reinforced instrumental response. *Journal of Experimental Psychology*, 1967, 73, 517–525.

TREISMAN, M. Temporal discrimination and the indifference interval. *Psychological Monograph*, 1963, *77*, 576.

TRESEMER, D. The cumulative record of research on "Fear of Success." *Sex Roles*, 1976, *2*, 217–236.

TROLAND, L. T. *The fundamentals of human motivation*. New York: Van Nostrand, 1928.

TSANG, Y. C. Hunger motivation in gastrectomized rats. *Journal of Comparative Psychology*, 1938, *26*, 1–17.

TURNER, C. W., & SIMONS, L. S. Effects of subject sophistication and evaluation apprehension on aggressive responses to weapons. *Journal of Personality and Social Psychology*, 1974, *30*, 341–348.

TURNER, L. H., & SOLOMON, R. L. Human traumatic avoidance learning: Theory and experiments on the operant-respondent distinction and failures to learn. *Psychological Monographs*, 1962, *76* (40, Whole No. 559).

TURPIN, J. P., & CLANON, T. L. Lithium and aggression control. Cited in K. E. Moyer, *The psychology of aggression*. New York: Harper & Row, 1976.

TYLER, V. O., JR., & BROWN, D. G. The use of swift, brief isolation as a group control device for institutionalized delinquents. *Behaviour Research and Therapy*, 1967, *5*, 1–9.

TYSZKA, T., & GRZELAK, J. L. Criteria and mechanisms of choice behavior in n-person games. *Journal of Conflict Resolution*, 1976, *20*, 352–376.

UDRY, J. R., & MORRIS, N. M. Distribution of coitus in the menstrual cycle. *Nature*, 1968, *220*, 593–596.

ULRICH, R. E. Pain as a cause of aggression. *American Zoologist*, 1966, *6*, 643–662.

ULRICH, R. E., WOLFF, P. C., & AZRIN, N. H. Shock as an elicitor of intra- and interspecies fighting behavior. *Animal Behaviour*, 1964, *12*, 14–15.

URSIN, A. Limbic control of emotional behavior. In E. Hitchcock, L. Laitinen, & K. Vaernet (Eds.), *Psychosurgery*. Springfield, Ill.: Thomas, 1972.

URSIN, H., & KAADA, B. R. Functional localization within the amygdaloid complex in the cat. *Electroencephalography and Clinical Neurophysiology*, 1960, *12*, 1–20.

VALENSTEIN, E. S. *Brain control*. New York: Wiley, 1973.

VALENSTEIN, E. S., & BEER, B. Continuous opportunities for reinforcing brain stimulation. *Journal of Experimental Analysis of Behavior*, 1964, *7*, 183–184.

VALENSTEIN, E. S., COX, V. C., & KAKOLESKI, J. W. Polydipsia elicited by the synergistic action of a saccharin and glucose solution. *Science*, 1967, *157*, 552–554.

VALENSTEIN, E. S., COX, V. C., & KAKOLEWSKI, J. W. The hypothalamus and motivated behavior. In J. T. Tapp (Ed.), *Reinforcement and behavior*. New York: Academic Press, 1969.

VANCE, E. B., & WAGNER, N. N. Written descriptions of organism: A study of sex differences. *Archives of Sexual Behavior*, 1976, *5*, 87–98.

VANDENBERG, J. G. Effects of gonadal hormones on aggressive behavior of adult golden hamsters (*Mesocricetus auratus*). *Animal Behaviour*, 1971, *19*, 589–594.

VAN DIS, H., & LARSSON, K. Induction of sexual arousal in the castrated male rat by intracranial stimulation. *Physiological Behavior*, 1971, *6*, 85–86.

VAN HEMEL, P. E. Aggression as a reinforcer: Operant behavior in the mouse-killing rat. *Journal of the Experimental Analysis of Behavior*, 1972, *17*, 237–245.

VANTRESS, F. E., & WILLIAMS, C. B. The effect of the presence of the provocator and the opportunity to counteraggress on systolic blood pressure. *Journal of General Psychology*, 1972, *86*, 63–68.

VERGNES, M., & KARLI, P. Effets de la stimulation de l'hypothalamus de l'amygdale et de l'hippocampe sur le comportement d'aggression interspecifique ratsouris. *Physiology and Behavior*, 1972, *9*, 889–892.

VERNEY, E. B. The antidiuretic hormone and the factors which determine its release. *Proceedings of Royal Society*, 1947, *135*, 25–106.

VEROFF, J., WILCOX, S., & ATKINSON, J. W. The achievement motive in high school and college age women. *Journal of Abnormal and Social Psychology*, 1953, *48*, 108–119.

VERPLANCK, W. S., & HAYES, J. R. Eating and drinking as a function of maintenance schedule. *Journal of Comparative and Physiology Psychology*, 1953, *46*, 327–333.

VINOKUR-KAPLAN, D. To have—or not to have—another child: Family planning attitudes, intentions, and behavior. *Journal of Applied Social Psychology*, 1978, 8, 29–46.

VITZ, P. C. Affect as a function of stimulus variation. *Journal of Experimental Psychology*, 1966, 71, 74–79.

VOGEL, G. W. A motivational function of REM sleep. In R. Drucker-Colin, M. Shkurovich, & M. B. Sterman (Eds.), *The function of sleep*. New York: Academic Press, 1979.

VOLPE, E. P. *Man, nature, and society*. Dubuque, Iowa: Brown, 1975.

VONDERAHE, A. R. The anatomic substratum of emotion. *The New Scholasticism*, 1944, 18, 76–95.

VON HOLST, E., & VON ST. PAUL, U. Electrically controlled behavior. *Scientific American*, 1962, 206, 50–59.

WAGNER, A. R. Conditioned frustration as a learned drive. *Journal of Experimental Psychology*, 1963, 66, 142–148.

WAGNER, A. R. Sodium amytal and partially reinforced runway performance. *Journal of Experimental Psychology*, 1963, 66, 474–477.

WAGNER, A. R. Stimulus selection and a "modified continuity theory." In G. H. Bower & J. T. Spence (Eds.), *The psychology of learning and motivation* (Vol. 3). New York: Academic Press, 1969.

WAGNER, A. R., RUDY, J. W., & WHITLOW, J. W. Rehearsal in animal learning. *Journal of Experimental Psychology*, 1973, 97, 407–426.

WALLACE, A. F. C. *Tornado in Worcester: An exploratory study of individual and community behavior in an extreme situation*. Washington: National Academy of Sciences—National Research Council (Publication 392, Disaster Study No. 3.), 1956.

WALLACE, J. Role of reward and dissonance reduction. *Journal of Personality and Social Psychology*, 1966, 3, 305–312.

WALLGREN, H., & BARRY, H. *Actions of alcohol* (Vol. 1). Amsterdam: Elsevier, 1970.

WALSTER, E. U., & FESTINGER, L. The effectiveness of "overheard" persuasive communications. *Journal of Abnormal and Social Psychology*, 1962, 65, 395–404.

WALSTER, E. U., & WALSTER, G. W. *A new look at love*. Reading, Mass.: Addison-Wesley, 1978.

WASHBURN, S. L., & DEVORE, I. Social behavior of baboons and early man. In S. L. Washburn (Ed.), *Social life of early man*. Chicago: Aldene, 1961.

WASMAN, M., & FLYNN, J. P. Directed attack elicited from hypothalamus. *Archives of Neurology*, 1962, 6, 220–227.

WATSON, J. B. The place of the conditioned reflex in psychology, *Psychological Review*, 1916, 23, 89–116.

WATSON, J. B. *Behaviorism*. New York: Norton, 1925.

WATSON, J. B., & MORGAN, J. J. B. Emotional reactions and psychological experimentation. *American Journal of Psychology*, 1917, 28, 163–174.

WATSON, J. B., & RAYNOR, R. Conditional emotional reactions. *Journal of Experimental Psychology*, 1920, 3, 1–14.

WAUGUIER, A., & NIEMEGEERS, C. J. E. The effects of dexetimide on pimozide-halopendol- and pipamperone-induced inhibition of brain stimulation in rats. *Archives Internationales de Pharmacodynamie et de Therapie*, 1975, 217, 280–292.

WEBB, W. B. Antecedents of sleep. *Journal of Experimental Psychology*, 1957, 53, 162–166.

WEBER, M. In T. Parsons (trans.), *The protestant ethic and the spirit of capitalism*. New York: Scribner, 1930 (original German publication, 1904).

WEHR, T. A., MUSCETTOLA, G., & GOODWIN, F. K. Urinary 3-methoxy-Y-hydroxyphenylglycol circadian rhythm: Early timing (phase-advance) in manic-depressives compared with normal subjects. *Archives of General Psychology*, 1980, 37, 257–263.

WEHR, T. A. WIRZ-JUSTICE, A., GOODWIN, F. K., DUNCAN, W., & GILLIN, J. C. Phase advance of the circadian sleep-wake cycle as an antidepressant. *Science*, 1979, 206, 710–713.

WEINER, B. *Human motivation*. New York: Holt, 1980.

WEINER, B., NIERENBERG, R., & GOLDSTEIN, M. Social learning (locus of control) versus attributional (causal stability) interpretations of expectancy of success. *Journal of Personality*, 1976, 44, 52–68.

WEINGARTEN, H., & POWLEY, T. L. Cited in T. L. Powley. The ventromedial hypothalamic syndrome, satiety, and a cephalic phase hypothesis. *Psychological Review*, 1977, 84, 89–126.

WEISS, J. M. Effects of coping on stress. *Journal of Comparative and Physiological Psychology*, 1968, 65, 251–260.

WEISS, J. M. Psychological factors in stress and disease. *Scientific American*, 1972, 226, 104–113.

WEISS, J. M., STONE, E. A., & HARRELL, N. Coping behavior and brain norepinephrine in rats. *Journal of Comparative and Physiological Psychology*, 1970, 72, 153–160.

WEISS, R. F. Deprivation and reward magnitude effects on speed throughout the goal gradient. *Journal of Experimental Psychology*, 1960, 78, 384–390.

WEISSMAN, A. Elicitation by a discriminative stimulus of water reinforced behavior and drinking in water-satiated rats. *Psychonomic Science*, 1972, 28, 155–156.

WEITZMAN, E. D., KRIPKE, D. F., GOLDMACHER, D., McGREGOR, T. & NOGEIRE, C. Acute reversal of the sleep-waking cycle in man. *Archives of Neurology*, 1970, 22, 483–489.

WELLS, M. J. *Brain and behavior in cephalopods.* London: Heinemann, 1962.

WENDT, H. W. Motivation, effort, and performance. In D. C. McClelland (Ed.), *Studies in motivation.* New York: Appleton-Century-Crofts, 1955.

WEST, S. G., GUNN, S. D., & CHERNICKY, P. Ubiquitous Watergate: An attributional analysis. *Journal of Personality and Social Psychology*, 1975, 32, 55–65.

WHALEN, R. Brain mechanisms controlling sexual behavior. In F. Beach (Ed.), *Human sexuality in four perspectives.* Baltimore: John Hopkins University Press, 1977.

WHEATLEY, M. D. The hypothalamus and affective behavior in cats. *Archives of Neurology and Psychiatry*, 1944, 52, 296–316.

WHITE, R. W. Motivation reconsidered: The concept of competence. *Psychological Review*, 1959, 66, 297–333.

WHITNEY, E., & HAMILTON, E. M. *Understanding Nutrition.* St. Paul, Minn.: West Publishing, 1977.

WICKLUND, R. A., & BREHM, J. W. *Perspectives on cognitive dissonance.* Hillsdale, N. J.: Lawrence Erlbaum, 1976.

WICKLUND, R. A., COOPER, J., & LINDER, D. E. Effects of expected effort on attitude change prior to exposure. *Journal of Experimental Social Psychology*, 1967, 3, 416–428.

WIKLER, A. *Opiate addiction.* Springfield, Ill.: Thomas, 1953.

WIKLER, A. & PESCOR, F. T. Classical conditioning of a morphine abstinence phenomenon, reinforcement of opoid-drinking behavior and "relapse" in morphine-addicted rats. *Psychopharmacologia*, 1967, 10, 255–284.

WILDER, D. A., & ALLEN, V. L. Veridical dissent, erroneous dissent, and conformity. Cited in J. L. Freedman, D. O. Sears, & J. M. Carlsmith, *Social psychology.* Englewood Cliffs, N.J.: Prentice-Hall, 1978.

WILLIAMS, D. Temporal lobe syndrome. In P. J. Vinken & G. W. Bruyn (Eds.), *Handbook of Clinical Neurology* (Vol. II). New York: Wiley, 1969.

WILLIAMS, D. R., & WILLIAMS, H. Auto-maintenance in the pigeon: Sustained pecking despite contingent non-reinforcement. *Journal of Experimental Analysis of Behavior*, 1969, 12, 511–520.

WILLIAMS, J. E., BENNETT, S. M., & BEST, D. L. Awareness and expression of sex stereotypes in young children. *Developmental Psychology*, 1975, 11, 635–642.

WILSON, A. Social behavior of free-ranging rhesus monkeys with an emphasis on aggression. Unpublished doctoral dissertation, University of California, Berkeley, 1968.

WILSON, D. T., MATHEWS, H. L., & HARVEY, J. W. An empirical test of the Fishbein behavioral intention model. *Journal of Consumer Research*, 1975, 1, 39–48.

WILSON, E. O. *Sociobiology, the new synthesis.* Cambridge, Mass.: Belknap Press of Harvard University Press, 1975.

WILSON, G. T. Alcohol and human sexual behavior. *Behaviour Research and Therapy*, 1977, 15, 239–252.

WILSON, G. T., & LAWSON, D. M. Expectancies, alcohol, and sexual arousal in male social drinkers. *Journal of Abnormal Psychology*, 1976, 85, 587–594. (a)

WILSON, G. T., & LAWSON, D. M. The effects of alcohol on sexual arousal in women. *Journal of Abnormal Psychology*, 1976, *85*, 489–497. (b)

WINKOUR, G., & CLAYTON, P. Family history studies: I. Two types of affective disorders separated according to genetic and clinical factors. In J. Wortis (Ed.), *Recent advances in biological psychiatry* (Vol. 9) New York: Plenum Press, 1967.

WINKOUR, G., CLAYTON, P. J., & REICH, T. *Manic-depressive illness*. St. Louis: Mosby, 1969.

WINTER, D. B., STEWART, A. J., & McCLELLAND, D. C. Husband's motives and wife's career level. *Journal of Personality and Social Psychology*, 1977, *35*, 159–166.

WINTERBOTTOM, M. R. The relation of need for achievement to learning experiences in independence and mastery. In J. W. Atkinson (Ed.), *Motives in fantasy, action, and society*. Princeton, N.J.: Van Nostrand, 1958.

WISEMAN, W. Four years' experience with ovulation inhibitors in clinical trial and routine use. In *Recent Advances in Ovarian and Synthetic Steroids and the Control of Ovarian Function* (proceedings of a symposium). Sydney, Australia: Globe Commercial Party, 1965.

WITT, D. M., KELLER, A. D., BATSEL, H. I., & LYNCH, J. R. Absence of thirst and resultant syndrome associated with anterior hypothalamectomy in the dog. *American Journal of Physiology*, 1952, *171*, 780.

WOLFF, C. *Love between women*. New York: Harper & Row, 1971.

WOLFF, C. T., FRIEDMAN, S. B., HOFER, M. A., & MASON, J. W. Relationship between psychological defenses and mean urinary 17-hydroxycorticosteroid excretion rates: I. A predictive study of parents of fatally ill children. *Psychosomatic Medicine*, 1964, *26*, 576–591.

WOLFGANG, M. E. *Patterns of criminal homocide*. New York: Wiley, 1958.

WOLPE, J. *Psychotherapy by reciprocal inhibition*. Stanford, Calif: Stanford University Press, 1958.

WOLPE, J. *The practice of behavior therapy*. Oxford: Pergamon, 1969.

WOLPE, J. *The practice of behavior therapy* (2nd ed.). Oxford: Pergamon, 1973.

WOLPIN, M., & KIRSCH, I. Visual imagery, various muscle states, and desensitization procedures. *Perceptual and Motor Skills*, 1974, *39*, 1143–1149.

WOLPOWITZ, E. The use of thioridazine (Melleril) in cases of epileptic psychosis. *South African Medical Journal*, 1966, *40*, 143–144.

WOOD, C. D. Behavioral changes following discrete lesions of temporal lobe structures. *Neurology*, 1958, *8*, 215–220.

WOODRUFF, R. A., GOODWIN, D. W., & GUZE, S. B. *Psychiatric Diagnosis*. New York: Oxford University Press, 1974.

WOODS, N. F. *Human sexuality in health and illness*. St. Louis: Mosby, 1975.

WOODWORTH, R. S. *Dynamic psychology*. New York: Columbia University Press, 1918.

WORCHEL, P. Trust and distrust. In W. Austin & S. Worchel, *The social psychology of intergroup relations*. Monterey, Calif.: Brooks/Cole, 1979.

WORCHEL, S., & ANDREOLI, V. Attribution of causality as a means of restoring behavioral freedom. *Journal of Personality and Social Psychology*, 1974, *9*, 237–245.

WORSCHEL, S., ANDREOLI, V. A., & FOLGER, R. Intergroup cooperation and intergroup attraction: The effect of previous interaction and outcome of combined effect. *Journal of Experimental Social Psychology*, 1977, *13*, 131–140.

WORCHEL, S., & COOPER, J. *Understanding social psychology*. Homewood, Ill.: Dorsey Press, 1979.

WORTHMAN, C. Psychoendocrine study of human behavior: Some interactions of steroid hormones with affect and behavior in the King San. Unpublished doctoral dissertation, Harvard University, 1978.

WRIGHTMAN, L. S. Effects of waiting with others on changes in level of felt anxiety. *Journal of Abnormal and Social Psychology*, 1960, *61*, 216–222.

WYLER, A. R., MASUDA, M., & HOLMES, T. H. Magnitude of life events and seriousness of illness. *Psychosomatic Medicine*, 1971, *33*, 115–122.

WYNNE-EDWARDS, V. C. *Animal dispersion in relation to social behavior*. New York: Harner, 1962.

YERKES, R. M. Sexual behavior in the chimpanzee. *Human Biology*, 1939, *2*, 78–110.

YERKES, R. M. *Chimpanzees*. New Haven, Conn.: Yale University Press, 1943.

YERKES, R. M., & DODSON, J. D. The relation of strength of stimulus to rapidity of habit formation. *Journal of Comparative Neurology and Psychology*, 1908, *18*, 459–482.

YERKES, R. M., & ELDER, J. H. Oestrus, receptivity, and mating in the chimpanzee. *Comparative Psychological Monographs*, 1936, *13*, 1–39.

YERKES, R. M., & MARGULIS, S. The method of Pavlov in animal psychology. *Psychological Bulletin*, 1909, *6*, 257–273.

YOSHII, N., ISHIWARA, T., & TANI, K. Juvenile delinquents and their abnormal EEGs 14 and 6 per second positive spikes pattern. *Medical Journal of Oska Univeristy*, 1963, *14*, 61–66.

YOUNG, L. D., LEWIS, J. K., & MCKINNEY, W. T. Response to maternal separation: A reconsideration. Paper presented at the meeting of the American Psychiatric Association, Anaheim, Calif. May 1975.

YOUNG, L.D., SUOMI, S. J., HARLOW, H. F., & MCKINNEY, W. T. Early stress and later response to separation. *American Journal of Psychiatry*, 1973, *130*, 400–405.

YOUNG, P. T. Hedonic organization and regulation of behavior. *Psychological Review*, 1966, *73*, 59–86.

YOUNG, P. T., & CHAPLIN, J. P. Studies of food preference, appetite, and dietary habit. III. Palatability and appetite in relation to bodily need. *Comparative Psychology Monographs*, 1945, *18* (3, Whole No. 95).

YOUNG, W. C. The hormones and mating behavior. In W. C. Young (Ed.), *Sex and Internal Secretions* (Vol. II). Baltimore: Williams & Wilkins, 1961.

YOUNG, W. C., & ORBISON, W. D. Changes in selected features of behavior in pairs of oppositely sex chimpanzees during the sexual cycle and after ovariectomy. *Journal of Comparative Psychology*, 1943, *37*, 107–143.

YULE, W., SACKS, B., & HERSOV, L. Successful flooding treatment of a noise phobia in an eleven-year-old. *Journal of Behavior Therapy and Experimental Psychiatry*, 1974, *5*, 209–211.

ZANNA, M. P., & COOPER, J. Dissonance and the pill: An attribution approach to studying the arousal properties of dissonance. *Journal of Personality and Social Psychology*, 1974, *29*, 703–709.

ZANNA, M. P., & COOPER, J. Dissonance and the attribution process. In J. H. Harvey, W. J. Iokes, & R. F. Kidd (Eds.), *New directions in attribution research* (Vol. 1). Hillsdale, N. J.: Lawrence Erlbaum, 1976.

ZANNA, M. P., KIESLER, C. A., & PILKONIS, P. Positive and negative attitudinal effect established by classical conditioning. *Journal of Personality and Social Psychology*, 1970, *14*, 321–328.

ZANNA, M. P., & PACK, S. J. On the self-fulfilling nature of apparent sex differences in behavior. *Journal of Experimental Social Psychology*, 1975, *11*, 583–591.

ZILBERGELD, B., & EVANS, M. The inadequacy of Masters and Johnson. *Psychology Today*, 1980, *14*, 29–43.

ZILLMAN, D. Excitation transfer in communication-mediated aggressive behavior. *Journal of Experimental Social Psychology*, 1971, *7*, 419–434.

ZILLMAN, D., & BRYANT, J. Effect of residual excitation on the emotional response to provocation and delayed aggressive behavior. *Journal of Personality and Social Psychology*, 1974, *30*, 782–791.

ZILLMAN, D., JOHNSON, R. C., & DAY, K. D. Attribution of apparent arousal and proficiency of recovery from sympathetic activation affecting excitation transfer to aggressive behavior. *Journal of Experimental Social Psychology*, 1974, *10*, 503–515.

ZILLMAN, D., KATCHER, A. H., & MILAVSKY, B. Excitation transfer from physical exercise to subsequent aggressive behavior. *Journal of Experimental Social Psychology*, 1972, *8*, 247–259.

ZIMBARDO, P. G. The human choice: Individuation, reason, and order versus deindividuation, impulse, and chaos. In W. J. Arnold & D. Levine (Eds.), *Nebraska Symposium on Motivation* (Vol. 17), Lincoln: University of Nebraska Press, 1970.

ZIMBARDO, P. G. SNYDER, M., THOMAS, J., GOLD, A., & GURWITZ, S. Modifying the impact of persuasive communications with external distractions. *Journal of Personality and Social Psychology*, 1970, *16*, 669–680.

ZIMBARDO, P. G., WEISENBERG, M., FIRESTONE, I., & LEVY, B. Communicator effectiveness in producing public conformity and private attitude change. *Journal of Personality*, 1965, *33*, 233–255.

ZUCKERMAN, S. *The social life of monkeys and apes.* London: Kegan Paul, Trench, Trubner, 1932.

ZUCKERMAN, M., & WHEELER, L. To dispel fantasies about the fantasy-based measure of fear of success. *Psychological Bulletin*, 1975, *82*, 932–946.

$\mathcal{I}$NDEXES

NAME INDEX

SUBJECT INDEX